SCHLEIERMACHER IN CONTEXT

*Papers from the 1988 International Symposium
on Schleiermacher
at Herrnhut, the German Democratic Republic*

Friedrich Daniel Ernst Schleiermacher

(1768 - 1834)

SCHLEIERMACHER IN CONTEXT

*Papers from the 1988 International Symposium
on Schleiermacher
at Herrnhut, the German Democratic Republic*

Edited by
Ruth Drucilla Richardson

Schleiermacher: Studies-and-Translations
Volume 6

The Edwin Mellen Press
Lewiston/Queenston/Lampeter

BX
4827
.S3
I58
1988

Library of Congress Cataloging-in-Publication Data

International Symposium on Schleiermacher (1988 : Herrnhut, Germany)
    Schleiermacher in context : papers from the 1988 International
Symposium on Schleiermacher at Herrnhut, the German Democratic
Republic / edited by Ruth Drucilla Richardson.
        p. cm. -- (Schleiermacher: studies-and-translations ; v. 6)
    English and German.
    Includes bibliographical references.
    ISBN 0-7734-9793-5
    1. Schleiermacher, Friedrich, 1768-1834--Congresses.
I. Richardson, Ruth, 1957- . II. Title. III. Series.
BX4827.S3I58 1988
230'.044'092--dc20.   91-3611
                                                                         CIP

This is volume 6 in the continuing series
Schleiermacher: Studies-and-Translations
Volume 6 ISBN 0-7734-9793-5
SST Series ISBN 0-88946-362-X

A CIP catalog record for this book
is available from the British Library.

The Edwin Mellen Press   The Edwin Mellen Press
        Box 450   Box 67
   Lewiston, New York   Queenston, Ontario
      USA 14092   CANADA, L0S 1L0

            The Edwin Mellen Press, Ltd.
             Lampeter, Dyfed, Wales
           UNITED KINGDOM SA48 7DY

      Printed in the United States of America

For Robert F. Streetman (1932-1989)
our beloved friend and colleague
who has too early fallen asleep

TABLE OF CONTENTS

SECTION THREE: SCHLEIERMACHER AND THE CHURCH

SECTION FOUR: SCHLEIERMACHER IN CONTEXT

EDITOR'S GENERAL INTRODUCTION

On June 21, 1988, a group of Schleiermacher scholars from the Federal Republic of Germany, the United States, Canada, Austria, and Italy gathered in Frankfurt am Main to begin a two-week "Schleiermacher-Reise" to visit important sites relating to Schleiermacher's life and works. We began our tour by driving to Weimar, where we met with a group of scholars from the German Democratic Republic. During the next two weeks we visited Jena, Halle, Herrnhut, Niesky, Potsdam, and Berlin and attempted to understand Schleiermacher's life and thought as it related to each of these places.[1]

The highlight of the Schleiermacher-Reise was a four-day symposium, from June 24 to June 27, at Herrnhut, center of the Moravian movement, which influenced Schleiermacher profoundly. Twenty-eight scholars from seven countries gathered for the academic exchange of ideas both during periods of *freie Geselligkeit* and during the following five academic sessions: (I) Der frühe Schleiermacher/The Early Schleiermacher; (II) Schleiermacher und die Philosophie/Schleiermacher and Philosophy; (III) Schleiermachers Philosophie/Schleiermacher's Philosophy; (IV) Schleiermacher und die Kultur/Schleiermacher and Culture; and (V) Schleiermacher und die Kirche/ Schleiermacher and the Church.

It is hoped that this book will bear witness to the great interest in Schleiermacher today, to the research being done on Schleiermacher across a number of disciplines, and to the international nature of Schleiermacher scholarship. This volume contains the papers presented at this symposium as well as two papers submitted later by Michael Eckert and Wichmann von Meding. The papers were regrouped into four major areas of research: (I) The Early Schleiermacher; (II) The Mature Schleiermacher; (III) Schleiermacher and the Church; and (IV) Schleiermacher in Context. Some

---

1. A description of the "Schleiermacher-Reise" can be found in Michael D. Ryan with Ruth Drucilla Richardson and Andreas Reich, "The Magnificant Prairie and City Culture of the German Democratic Republic: The Schleiermacher Tour to Weimar, Jena, Halle, Herrnhut, Niesky, Berlin, June 21 - July 2, 1988," in *New Athenaeum/Neues Athenaeum* 2 (1990); Peter Weiß, "Schleiermacher-Reise," *Standpunkt. Evangelische Monatsschrift* 7/2 (February 1989): 46-48.

of the papers represent major research papers. Others were written to be read aloud at the symposium. Consequently, the papers in this volume vary in length. Further, there are differences in the use of annotation and punctuation among scholars in various countries. No attempt was made to standardize style, but the usage employed by each scholar was respected.

The "Schleiermacher-Reise" and "Herrnhut-Symposium" were sponsored by the Edwin Mellen Press, which has been hosting yearly Schleiermacher Research Seminars since the year 1986. Many individuals also generously gave of their time and effort. Our Reise and Symposium would not have been possible were it not for the following: Terrence N. Tice and Horst J. Eduard Beintker, who were the original impetus behind the Reise; Christel Keller-Wentorf and Karl-Fr. Wiggermann, who saw to the overall functioning of the two-week trip; Günter Gerstmann, who planned our day in Jena and the program at the *Romantikerhaus*; Kurt Nowak, who arranged for our tours of Halle and Niesky; Edwina Lawler, who moderated the session programs at Herrnhut; Peter Weiß and Hans-Jürgen Gabriel, who assisted with numerous details; Wolfgang Virmond, who helped with the West Berlin portion of our trip; and Heinrich Fink and the Humboldt University, who arranged for our tour of East Berlin. Finally, I would like to thank Kurt-Victor Selge, director of the Schleiermacherforschungsstelle in Berlin, who was a generous host during my Fulbright year in West Berlin when I coordinated the "Schleiermacher-Reise."

Ruth Drucilla Richardson
Raymondville, Texas
January 1990

SECTION ONE

THE EARLY SCHLEIERMACHER

I

PERSPECTIVES ON
JOHANN GOTTLIEB ADOLPH SCHLEYERMACHER

Robert F. Streetman

Twenty years ago this summer, I was reading in two areas of study in preparation for the coming academic year. In the mornings I was reading *Aus Schleiermachers Leben in Briefen*[1] and encountering for the first time the corpus of letters to and from Friedrich Daniel Ernst Schleiermacher (1768-1834). In the afternoons I was preparing for a course in "Depth Psychology and Religion" by reading the autobiography of C. G. Jung (1875-1961).[2]

After getting well into both projects, I was struck by the confluence of two themes. For one thing, Jung wrote that deep within each person a principle of the opposite gender is at work. Thus, a part of the deep inner reality of each man is an *anima*, a feminine principle, while within each woman is a corresponding *animus*, or masculine power. To males, who Jung believed were the more sceptical of the two genders, he simply replied that they should never forget that they have breasts. It was axiomatic to Jung, the student of Asian religions, that psychic balance depended upon a healthy correlation, in *yang/yin* fashion, of both sides of one's nature.

At about the same time as I was struggling with Jung, I was learning of Schleiermacher's thoughts about women and how much he believed men needed to learn from them, while cultivating an inwardness reminiscent of Jung's *anima*. I was especially impressed that Schleiermacher regularly discussed many of his most important ideas with some remarkable women in Berlin, who were among the most rigorous and creative thinkers of his day. This first confluence of Jung and Schleiermacher is still a productive one to explore, but since I am completing a volume about Schleiermacher and women's issues, I shall pass this opportunity by and turn to another area of confluence of the thought of Jung and Schleiermacher – their relations to their fathers, both of whom were Reformed pastors who had severe crises of faith. And here, after relatively brief discussion of Jung's situation, I shall focus on Johann Gottlieb Adolph Schleyermacher (1727-1794), Schleiermacher's father, who remains, in my view, one of the most interesting and challenging pieces of the Schleiermacher puzzle. An additional feature of this study will be that I shall quote, wherever it is relevant, from translations by members of our travel seminar and team of translators. It will be interesting to discover how accessible they have made our subject to English readers.

Jung and His Father

Johann Paul Achilles Jung (d. 1896) had been a theological student specializing in Oriental languages and writing his dissertation on the Arabic translation of the Song of Songs. But, according to his son, his intellectual curiosity did not survive the seminary: "His days of glory had ended with his final examination. Thereafter, he forgot his lingustic talent."[3] The relation of the father and son was never a very happy one. As time went on, and the father grew more irritable, Jung tells us, "I suspected that it had to do with his faith. From a number of hints he let fall I was convinced that he suffered from religious doubts." Jung came to believe that his father had never had "the necessary experience" upon which genuine religious conviction is founded. Thus, lacking a firm foundation, the father could only give pat, "lifeless theological answers" to the probing questions of his son. Since Jung did claim to have an experiential foundation for his own faith, he felt much freer to explore religious issues and to reflect on the deteriorating situation of his father:

> I saw that my critical questions made him sad, but I
> nevertheless hoped for a constructive talk, since it appeared
> almost inconceivable to me that he should not have had
> experience of God, the most evident of all experiences. I knew
> enough about epistemology to realize that knowledge of this

sort could not be proved, but it was equally clear to me that it stood in no more need of proof than the beauty of a sunset or the terrors of the night.[4]

With no hope of meaningful guidance from his father, Jung sought support from two other persons. One particularly strategic figure was his mother, who reinforced his seeking and questioning side by encouraging him to read *Faust* and similar literature. In later years, this reading was to provide Jung, now a budding psychiatrist, with a fulcrum for turning aside the growing hostility of his father toward the entire enterprise of psychology. The basis of these latest outbursts, in Jung's view, was the father's "impression that psychiatrists had discovered something in the brain which proved that in the place where mind should have been there was only matter, and nothing 'spiritual'." For the father, blind faith was the answer:

> The arch sin of faith, it seemed to me [Jung], was that it forestalled experience. How did the theologians know that God had deliberately arranged certain things and "permitted" others, and how did the psychiatrists know that matter was endowed with the qualities of the human mind? I was in no danger of succumbing to materialism, but my father certainly was.[5]

Another portion of the void of meaningful theological dialogue was filled by conversations between Jung and a former vicar from his father's earlier days. The security of this man's faith made it possible for him to deal responsibly with Jung's probings and to assure Jung that theology need not be blind.

Upon a first reading of the situation of Jung and Schleiermacher with their fathers, it appeared that a much more detailed comparison of the two situations ought to be drawn. But deeper readings of both persons has failed to confirm that impression. Since *both* Schleiermachers now seem to me to be more complex than their Jungian counterparts, I believe that I can conclude this section in these words: I now believe that it can be said that Jung experienced a steadily deteriorating relation with his pastor father, who seemed progressively less able to cope either with his son's challenging questions or his own inability to be the paragon of faith which his office of pastoral role model required (thus far the parallel with Schleiermacher's situation holds). Moreover, this plight of Jung's father, when mixed with other stresses and strains, ended in a psychological breakdown. Well before the breakdown, it was clear that Jung no longer expected to hear anything of value from his father. Thus, there is nothing more of value that I can see in exploring his parental situation any further.

Schleiermacher and His Father

A great deal more about the father/son relation can be learned from Schleiermacher's situation. Since I have not yet had access to the primary source materials of the scandal involving Daniel Schleyermacher (1697-1765), Friedrich's grandfather, who was charged with witchcraft, I can only extrapolate from the gleanings of Redeker and Dilthey. These accounts convey the impression that this scandal hovered over Gottlieb like a great black cloud for his entire lifetime.[6] But even without some more specific details, it seems possible to form some clear impressions of what the situation must have been for a bright and deeply spiritual young person who must have loved his pastor father dearly and, although compelled to testify against him, was probably convinced during his entire lifetime of the latter's innocence. As I indicated, there is nothing more to say about the situation of the grandfather, until primary sources can be consulted, except that my impression is that he was eventually exonerated, if too late to allow him to resume his ministry.

I believe that an experience with a pastoral counselee has helped me to understand a part of the problem of Gottlieb in coming to terms with the terrible scandal, which functioned almost as a family curse. As a child, this counselee, this precocious and highly moral person, had seen his pastor father arrested and carried off to jail. Although it was fifteeen years later, as a seminarian, that he came to me for spiritual counsel, he spoke of the event as if it had only happened yesterday. I believe that the memory of Daniel Schleyermacher's shame remained equally vivid throughout Gottlieb's life, and that it influenced his entire perception of the growth to maturity of his own precocious son, who very early became involved in controversy.

Because this study has been an occasion of growth for me, I wish to begin this section by revealing where my thinking was at the threshold of this project. In my last essay, I described the situation as follows:

The paternal grandfather . . . had exhibited pietistic tendencies so intense that they swirled him into an extreme sectarian movement, and eventually caused him to be accused of dabbling in witchcraft and magical practices. In 1749 he fled to Holland to escape prison. His son Gottlieb was a case study in tension "between the thought of the Enlightenment and orthodox preaching [which] gave his personality some contradictory traits."[7] Over his entire lifetime, as a gifted intellectual, he devoured with relish the most crucial theological literature of the day. Letters to his son Friedrich continually recommended the works of Kant and other demanding thinkers to the young man. But, because of the problems of excess in the pietism of his father, Gottlieb suppressed the deep pietistic strains within himself, until, late in life, he encountered the Moravians. Although he held fast to his Reformed pastoral affiliation, he entrusted his children to the keeping of Moravian boarding-schools and one of their seminaries, all of which proved to be nearly perfect environments for developing and strengthening their pious feelings.[8]

There is nothing of importance in that initial impression which further study would make me wish to retract. But now it is clear that there is a great deal more to say on many topics – far more than it will be possible to deal with in the space of this essay.

While Jung had grown up in a parsonage with both parents at least present, Schleiermacher's relation to his father, who as a military chaplain was only very infrequently home, was almost entirely through the medium of correspondence. Although Elisabeth Maria Katharina (1736-1783), his mother, was a loving and supporting force in his life, he and the other two children were sent away to a Moravian boarding-school when quite young, and she died when he was only fifteen. After the father remarried, the stepmother gave the appearance of caring for the children, yet the parental influence remained confined to letters. From age seventeen, Friedrich found support in his uncle Samuel Ernst Timotheus Stubenrauch (1738-1807), his mother's brother and a professor at the University of Halle, who then filled the role of a substitute father. From his uncle, who opened his home to him and helped in his attempt to gain entrance to Halle, he received a great deal of good advice, some intellectual stimulation and some of the personal warmth and familial love that it was difficult to gain from letters.

From at least eleven, Friedrich experienced doubts and religious turmoil, as he later testified. Some years later, he wrote in his *Selbstbiographie*:

> I had already sustained manifold internal religious conflicts. The doctrine of eternal punishment and reward had already exercised a disturbing power over my childish imagination, and in my eleventh year I spent several sleepless nights in consequence of not being able to come to a satisfactory conclusion concerning the mutual relation between the sufferings of Christ and the punishment for which these sufferings were a substitute.[9]

The classic statement of his doubts, in a letter to his father, will be considered below. Later than the above words was his statement that during this time of spiritual upheaval it was "piety" which provided the anchor. Terrence Tice has rendered these words as follows:

> As I began to sift out the faith of my fathers and to clear the rubbish of former ages from my thoughts and feelings piety supported me. As the childhood images of God and immortality vanished before my doubting eyes piety remained. It led me headlong, without design, into an active adult life.[10]

Upon this foundation, let us build as much understanding as we can of the father's response to Friedrich's situation of spiritual turmoil.

The Great Earthquake

The spiritual upheaval and its deteriorating effect on the relation of the father and the son suggests Søren Kierkegaard's image of the "great earthquake," after his similar experience. The earliest letters of Gottlieb to his wife and to his son express the father's joy and great hopes for his son. But when his first extant letter to Friedrich was written (November 21, 1781), Gottlieb did not realize that his son had been experiencing the turmoil noted above for at least two years.[11] After several letters dealing with problems of money, clothing and other necessities, recommending various readings to his son, while suggesting that he leave theology to the theologians, the father received a letter from his son which rattled the very foundations of his being.

So important is this letter that I shall quote translations of the crucial passage by two members of the Schleiermacher: Studies-and-Translations team, after the original:

SCHLEIERMACHER

Ich kann nicht glauben, daß der wahrer ewiger Gott war, der sich selbst nur den Menschensohn nannte; ich kann nicht glauben, daß sein Tod eine stellvertretende Versöhnung war, weil er es selbst nie ausdrücklich gesagt hat, und weil ich nicht glauben kann, daß sie nöthig gewesen, denn Gott könne die Menschen, die Er offenbar nicht zur Vollkommenheit, sondern nur zum Streben nach derselben geschaffen hat, unmöglich darum ewig strafen wollen, weil sie nicht vollkommen geworden sind.[12]

MICHAEL RYAN

I cannot believe that it was the eternal, true God, who only called himself Son of Man; I cannot believe that his death was a substitutionary reconciliation, because he never expressly said that, and because I cannot believe that it was necessary; for it is impossible that God who apparently did not create human beings for perfection, but only for striving after it,

should therefore want to punish them eternally, because they
have not become perfect.[13]

ALBERT BLACKWELL

I cannot believe that he who named himself only the Son of
Man was the eternal and true God; I cannot believe that his
death was a substitutionary atonement, because he never
expressly said so himself, and because I cannot believe it was
necessary. God, who has evidently created humankind not for
perfection but only for the striving after perfection, cannot
possibly wish to punish persons eternally because they have not
become perfect.[14]

The eighteen-year-old Schleiermacher has just made three earth-
shaking denials of the tenets of the Evangelical orthodox faith of his day.
First, he cannot believe that the Redeemer, "who only called himself Son of
Man," was "the eternal and true God." For him, then, the presence of an
eternal divine principle in Jesus the Christ is impossible to accept. This, of
course, is the foundation stone of Evangelical orthodoxy and would be more
than sufficient to read him out of the faith. Yet he adds insult to injury.
Second, young Friedrich cannot believe that Christ's death affected a
substitutionary atonement for the sins of the world, because Christ himself
"never expressly said so." Nor, in the third place, could he believe that such
an atonement would have been necessary, since in his view God did not
intend eternal punishment for sinners. In the spirit of Lessing and other
seekers, Friedrich believed that God had created humankind for the quest,
for the pursuit of perfection, rather than the achievement of it.

It was this supercharged letter that produced the Great Earthquake.
The fuse that set the dislodgment in motion was doubt itself. The detonator
was doubt of the eternal divinity of the Redeemer, which as we saw is the
foundation stone on which his father's act of religious identification with
Evangelical orthodoxy (discussed below) rested. The blasting away of this
foundation stone produced the Great Earthquake. Careful readers will see
that Friedrich never substantially altered his position on any of these three
points, but only sharpened his thinking.[15]

The reply of Gottlieb has often been cited and discussed, and it has been rendered into English many times, beginning with the version of Frederica Rowan, which opens with these words: "O thou insensate son! who has deluded thee, that thou no longer obeyest the truth, thou, before whose eyes Christ was pictured, and who now crucifiest him?"[16] This may appear to be a fairly accurate English rendition of what the father is saying. But the translation of Blackwell below, which I first read without a copy of the original at hand, drove me hack to the German text, and indeed even beyond that to the New Testament, where I discovered the stylistic model for Gottlieb's opening words. The *KGA* confirms this reference.

BLACKWELL

O you foolish son, who has bewitched you, that you do not obey the truth? . . . Turn back! O my son, turn back! Human vitrue is not perfection, but to turn back from the way of error. O Lord Jesus, thou Shepherd of Humankind, lead back thyself thy strayed lamb! Do it for the glory of thy name! Amen! (p. 8).

GALATIANS 3:1-3 (RSV)

O Foolish Galatians! Who has bewitched you, before whose eyes Jesus Christ was publicly portrayed as crucified? Let me ask you only this: Did you receive the Spirit by works of the law, or by hearing with faith? Are you so foolish? Having begun with the Spirit are you now ending with the flesh?

GOTTLIEB

O! Du unverständiger Sohn! wer
hat Dich bezaubert, daß Du der
Wahrheit   nicht   gehorchest?
welchem Christus Jesus vor die
Augen gemahlet war, und nun von
Dir gecreutzigt wird. Du liefest
fein; wer hat Dich aufgehalten, der
Wahrheit nicht zu gehorchen?
Solch Ueberreden ist nicht von
dem, der Dich berufen hat. Aber
ein wenig Sauerteig versäuert den
ganzen Teig.   Das nemliche
Verderben   Deines   Herzens,
welches vor 4 Jahren Dir bange
machte, daß Du mit demselben in
der Welt werdest ganz verloren
gehen, und Dich damals zur
Gemeine hintrieb, ach! davon hast
Du leider noch immer etwas bei
Dir geheget. Das hat nun Dein
ganzes Wesen durchsäuert, und
treibt Dich wieder aus der
Gemeine. Ach, mein Sohn, mein
Sohn! wie tief beugest Du mich!
welche Seufzer pressest Du aus
meiner   Seele!   und   wenn
Abgeschiedene einige Notiz von
uns nehmen, o! welch grausamer
Störer der Ruhe Deiner se*ligen*
Mutter bist du dann jezt, da selbst
Deine Dir fremde Stiefmutter mit
mir Dich beweinet.[17]

GALATER 3:1-3; 5:7-9

O ihr unverständigen Galater, wer
hat euch bezaubert, daß ihr der
Wahrheit nicht gehorchet, welchen
Christus Jesus vor die Augen
gemalt war, als wäre er unter euch
gekreutzigt?   Das will ich allein
von euch lernen: Habt ihr den
Geist empfangen durch des
Gesetzes Werke oder durch die
Predigt vom Glauben? Seid ihr so
unverständig? Im Geist habt ihr
angefangen, wollt ihr's denn nun
im Fleisch vollenden? . . . Wer hat
euch aufgehalten, der Wahrheit
nicht zu gehorchen?   Solch
Ueberreden ist nicht von dem, der
euch berufen hat.   Ein wenig
Sauerteig versäuert den ganzen
Teig.

In this letter, Friedrich is not only "foolish" and "bewitched" but is a "strayed lamb." But very shortly, as the father struggles with this upheaval, his son becomes the "mangy sheep" (Blackwell) who may contaminate the entire flock.

Gottlieb's "Act of Religious Identification"

Michael D. Ryan's category of the "act of religious identification" will help us to come to terms with some of the issues that now demand treatment. Let us recall that the person who concerns us has been portrayed as highly intelligent and continuing to pursue a reading program containing some of the most challenging thinkers of his day; as possessing a deep pietistic strain which his father's sad experience caused him to suppress; and as trying to shelter his children within the warm circle of the Moravian community. He then tried to shelter his son Friedrich from the kind of intellectual curiosity which apparently had never left him (as contrasted with Jung's father). He was living under the tension which was earlier described as between "the thought of the Enlightenment and orthodox preaching." Living under the family cloud, for which he had in no way been responsible, he was forced as a very young man to seek a point of security in such a precarious world. This he could only find in an act of religious identification. As Dr. Ryan would explain it, Gottlieb must stand up and be counted; he must now make a public declaration, from this time forth and forever more, of exactly *which* community of the Christian faith is to be his dwelling place, and the source of his self-understanding. From Daniel's misfortune, Gottlieb has learned that, to paraphrase George Orwell's famous words, "some Christian communites are more equal than others." The one with seemingly the greatest equality appears to be the tradition of Evangelical preaching and orthodoxy. In conversation at Herrnhut, Dr. Ryan summed it up this way: "He had found a community to grow old with, and he did not want to upset the applecart." With this tradition he will stand.

In what follows, I shall paraphrase the material of the letters and draw some conclusions about the father/son relation as elucidated by Gottlieb's act of identification.

What, then, is so threatening about the doubts and spiritual turmoil of his son? In the light of Gottlieb's *public* identification with the orthodox preaching tradition (while reading controversial theological works in secret), I believe that we can see our way ahead. A person who so avidly read and thought so hard about modern theological issues could hardly be threatened by the pristine searchings of his teenage son. What, then, did he fear?

First, he feared that the pietistic depth that he had discerned in his son, who after all was a namesake of Daniel, might sweep him into the same maelstrom as the grandfather. Thus, he uses the Galater imagery of bewitchment advisedly. But we have to look at a second area – the act of identification – to see his deepest fear. Friedrich is, after all, appealing to his father for understanding in a painful childhood crisis. Who ought to be able to understand the turmoil of a son better than a father who himself had experienced spiritual and psychological pain in his youth, and very likely of a deeper sort? Why is his son no longer a lost lamb, for whom the Good Shepherd would leave the ninety and nine, but rather a mangy sheep, who should be shunned instead of helped? Where is the Moravian tradition of the salvific effect of meditation upon the healing wounds of Christ, in comparison to which a case of mange seems trivial?

The situation of his son, if taken seriously, would threaten to undermine the act of identification of Gottlieb with the orthodox/ Evangelical community, which bears the appearance of a tenuous defensive move rather than a genuine affirmation of faith. For him to give a sheltering wing to Friedrich would place Gottlieb in a mediatorial position between the son and the community. A blow by the community would strike him first, before hitting his son. His immediate response is to disown his son, not at all because he is hearing doubts and thoughts which are unfamilar to him, but rather because to face his son's situation seriously would test the authenticity of his act of identification. The son's crisis of faith is threatening to undermine the father's resolution of his own crisis.

The response of Friedrich in the next few letters is remarkable. Why, he asks, do you fail to see that I appealed to you precisely because I was aware of the pain you went through, and even more because I respected you for the resolution you made of a situation that no young person should ever have to go through? Since your situation must have been worse than mine, I was very hopeful that you would be able to steer me through this situation. In effect, Friedrich is suggesting, you are much better equipped to deal with my crisis than most fathers. Why, then, do you seem to have so little confidence in yourself that you would reject me? Why do I have greater faith in you than you have in yourself?

It soon becomes clear that Friedrich's faith in his father's resilience is well-founded. Within the span of only seven months, Gottlieb did begin to understand and to sympathize with the situation of his son.[18] In future years, with the healing of time, the mediatorial work of Stubenrauch and the progress of the son in the university, the relation of the father and the son reached a happier resolution. Perhaps Gottlieb finally realized that in calling his act of identification into question, Friedrich had been acting as the instrument of God. Thus we recall the words of Kierkegaard somewhere that "the greatest thing which one person can do for another is to inspire him with concern and unrest."

Notes

1. F. D. E. Schleiermacher, *Aus Schleiermachers Leben in Briefen*, vier Bände. Herausgegeben von Wilhelm Dilthey. (Berlin: Georg Reimer, 1860-1863).

2. C. G. Jung, *Memories, Dreams, Reflections,* recorded and edited by Aniela Jaffé, Tr. Richard and Clara Winston (New York: A Vintage Book, 1961, 1962, 1963).

3. Jung, *op. cit.,* p. 91.

4. Ibid., p. 92.

5. Ibid., p. 94.

6. Wilhelm Dilthey, *Leben Schleiermachers*, I. Band, zweite Auflage (Berlin: Walter de Gruyter, 1922); Martin Redeker, *Schleiermacher: Life and Thought,* tr. John Wallhausser (Philadelphia: Fortress Press, 1973).

7. Redeker, op. cit., p. 8.

8. Robert F. Streetman, "Romanticism and the *Sensus Numinis* in Schleiermacher," in *The Interpretation of Belief: Coleridge, Schleiermacher and Romanticism*, ed. David Jasper (London: Macmillan, 1986), p. 106.

9. F. D. E. Schleiermacher, "Autobiography," in *The Life of Schleiermacher, as Unfolded in His Autobiography and Letters*, Vol. I, tr. Frederica Rowan (2 vols.; London: Smith, Elder and Co., 1860), p. 6. Cited as "*Life of Schleiermacher.*"

10. F. D. E. Schleiermacher, *On Religion: Addresses in Response to Its Cultured Critics*, tr. Terrence N. Tice (Richmond: John Knox Press, 1969), p. 48; notes on variant readings omitted.

11. F. D. E. Schleiermacher, *Briefwechsel und biographische Dokumente, Briefwechsel 1774-1796*, edited by Andreas Arndt und Wolfgang Virmond, *Kritische Gesamtausgabe* V/1, ed. Hans-Joachim Birkner et al. (Berlin/New York: Walter de Gruyter, 1985), #2, p.1. Series cited as "*KGA.*"

12. Schleiermacher, *KGA*, V. 1, #53, lines 27-33, p. 50.

13. Michael D. Ryan, "Young Friedrich Schleiermacher's Act of Religious Identification: His Phenomenology of Finite Spirit," in *New Athenaeum/Neues Athenaeum*, Vol I, 1989, p.164.

14. Albert L. Blackwell, *Schleiermacher's Early Philosophy of Life: Determinism, Freedom and Fantasy* (Chico: Scholar's Press, 1982), p. 7.

15. It is a pleasure to acknowledge invaluable help from Dr. Durwood Foster in a conversation at Herrnhut in clarifying this point. First, there is Friedrich's use of the "Son of Man" imagery instead of that of eternal divinity. For both Gottlieb and Friedrich, this term continued to be understood as the parallel to "Son of God" as indicating a genuine human nature. It remained for Hans Lietzmann and others of more recent times to emphasize the apocalyptic character of the Son of Man. Even in the second edition of the *Glaubenslehre* (1831/32), published only two years before his death, Friedrich still understands "Son of God" in New Testament usage as "nur von dem Subjekt dieser Vereinigung und nicht von dem Göttlichen darin vor derselben" (while discounting John 1:18 and 17:5 as telling against his point) [*Der Christliche Glaube nach den Grundsätzen der evangelischen Kirche im zusammenhange dargestellt*, Band II, hg.v. Martin Redeker, Zwei Bände (Berlin: Walter de Gruyter, 1960), §96.1, S. 51.] In his Christology, he was able to affirm the divinity of Christ in a way that was suited to his system: "§94. Der Erlöser ist sonach allen Menschen gleich, vermöge der Selbigkeit der menschlichen Natur, von allen aber unterschieden durch die stetige Kräftigkeit seines Gottesbewußtseins, *welche ein eigentliches Sein Gottes in ihm war*" (italics added). But he still remained wary of the *eternal* element. For extensive discussion of his attempt to remove *eternal* divine distinctions both from trinitarian discussion and from dogmatics see Robert F. Streetman, "Friedrich Schleiermacher's Doctrine of the Trinity and Its Significance for Theology Today," an unpublished Ph.D. dissertation (Madison, New Jersey: Drew University, 1975), especially chapter iv. Second, Friedrich later demythologizes the substitutionary atonement, stressing the redemptive efficacy of the sufferings of Christ (§§ 101.3, 104.4-6). Third, there is no evidence that he ever changed his mind to accept eternal punishment (§84).

16. *Life of Schleiermacher*, p. 50.

17. *KGA*, V/1, §54, lines 1-14, p. 53.

18. The kind suggestions of three persons at the Herrnhut seminar have helped me to see that understanding Gottlieb is an even more complex task than I had envisioned. First, Dr. Kurt Nowak believes that Gottlieb's participation in Freemasonry needs to be accounted for. Second, Dr. Wolfgang Virmond of the Schleiermacher Forschungsstelle in Berlin [West] promptly provided bibliographical information about three primary sources by Gottlieb on Freemasonry, which I then ordered from the Akademie der Wissenschaften. This material has not arrived in time to be included in this volume. Thus, I shall have to deal with it in a future essay. Third, Dr. Kurt-Victor Selge, Director of the Schleiermacher Forschungsstelle in Berlin, [West] called my attention to the very important letter #79 (*KGA*, V/1, pp. 87-91) of Gottlieb to Friedrich, which encourages him to read Kant's first *Kritik* and *Prolegomena* as well

as *Theobald oder die Schwärmer*, a book against the enthusiasts by Stilling (Johann Heinrich Jung) and offers other encouragement. I agree with Dr. Selge that, for all his confidence in his father's spiritual strength, Friedrich probably did not fully understand the situation of his father at the time that he broke his sad news. While obviously Friedrich had a point in insisting on his right to come to a valid resolution of his own crisis, his teenage self-assurance about the clarity of his own perception of his evolving views may have clouded the reading which he made of his father. I see these suggestions as strengthening my initial thesis that Gottlieb was a much more interesting and complex character than has previously been recognized.

II

SCHLEIERMACHER'S "HIGHEST INTUITION" IN LANDSBERG (1794-1796)[1]

Terrence N. Tice

The Claim: Schleiermacher's Ethical Vision

Some great thinkers, usually early not late, reach an apex of awareness in some key area of their reflections, and this becomes a guiding image or organizing principle for large expanses of their subsequent thought. In the years after his apprenticeship with Socrates, for example, Plato (427-347 B.C.) had his vision of the Forms. For him, these were the transcendent, nonsensible, incorporeal, eternal, fixed ideas, real to the highest degree, forms in which all appearances whatsoever participate, and he loved them more than any person. Moreover, even though he developed penetrating critiques of the theory in later years he seems never to have given up the vision completely, a vision that had come to dominate his entire outlook on reality and on human life.[2] One day, when he was twenty-three, René Descartes (1596-1650) gained a deep conviction of the coherent rationality of method for knowing; moreover, his thoughts about how to achieve this method, mostly on that day and then in succeeding months, established a pattern of inquiry and a sense of personal identity from which he did not waver the rest of his life. Nearly all the remainder was elaboration; and he is often deemed the father of modern philosophy for his achievement.[3] In his mid-twenties Karl Marx (1818-1883) gained a twofold insight: that in all respects the quality of human life is highly dependent on the socio-economic system, even to the point of profound alienation in certain assignable conditions, and that society is to be viewed as a system of forces and relations of production. This way of looking at human beings and the deterministic framework that accompanied it drove all his subsequent study of economic relations, early and late.[4]

As with Plato, the highest organizing perspective does not always occur at such a young age or seemingly all at once. In his late thirties and early forties, for example, Sigmund Freud discovered basic, determinative patterns of unconscious mental functioning, particularly through analysis of his own dreams, and thus created psychoanalysis as a clinically oriented method of science and as a body of distinct knowledge about human behavior that is garnered mostly from the inside out.[5] Yet, it is fascinating to see how very often this sort of life-forming perspective does emerge within young persons of genius. As a young Reformed pastor, Karl Barth (1886-1968), in sharp reaction to the self-styled Schleiermacherians of that time, came to affirm the sovereign free grace of God, drawing from the springs of his tradition but adding a prophetic voice and, eventually, a long systematic account, unparalleled in his era. Moreover, despite counterevidence, he never gave up his dialectical critique of Schleiermacher, placing him solidly in the camp of Barth's opponents, despite some softening in the later years of his life and profound questioning toward the end.[6]

Also as a young man, it dawned on Schleiermacher that ethically, taken in the broadest sense, each individual is to represent humanity not so much according to a set of laws as in one's own unique fashion. Schleiermacher actually experienced a long series of breakthroughs. In his 1800 *Soliloquies*, a sometimes rhapsodic but argued set of ethical reflections, he speaks of a certain "highest intuition" *(höchste Anschauung)*[7] regarding human individuality that he had reached earlier. Now aged thirty-one, his famous 1799 addresses *On Religion* were already behind him, along with intense engagement with Romantic concerns in aesthetic culture, interpretive work expressed most strikingly in three volumes of translated sermons, and a significant body of mostly unpublished philosophical writings. Because much of his understanding of individual life evokes Romantic themes, it has routinely been supposed that the intuition of which he speaks emerged through his contact with Romantic culture after he had arrived in Berlin in September 1796. The preceding two-year period in Landsberg an der Warthe is passed over virtually in silence, except for occasional comment about the supposedly more "ethical" content of his sermons in this his first pastorate. In contrast, my claim is that the "highest intuition" occurred in Landsberg, within crucial circumstances of life, thus before he ever stepped foot within the Romantic circle.

During the period from October 1790 through the spring of 1793, Schleiermacher had served as tutor in the von Dohna family in Schlobitten. There, as he reports in the 1800 *Soliloquies*, his sense "for the beauty of existence in community" was first awakened. In his written reflections from the Schlobitten years he expressed having come to see that true freedom requires cultivation of the commonalities of human existence and having begun to look beyond appearances in order to recognize the same rich underlying human reality whatever its garb. He gained the deep conviction, too, that human life at its best is shared and that of all the manifold gifts of life the most beautiful of all is that one can be "at home."[8]

Schleiermacher further indicates in the *Soliloquies* that it did not satisfy him to have this feeling of freedom that he had discovered in Schlobitten, with the accompanying awareness of humanity in oneself as the inner and necessary tie between vision and action. As he viewed it, this vision of freedom in and of humanity was in itself a momentous achievement, unshakeable and permanent, leading to a quiet, simple, unbroken "consciousness of humanity as a whole within myself."[9] It was a powerful thing to find this insight embodied in reason and in the uniformity both of human existence and of right action, action the same for everyone and varied only with respect to the variability of circumstance. It gave a firm and sure sense of rootedness as a self, a quelling of shame, a deepgoing equanimity. Yet, significant doubt remained. The insight left the perception of humanity too rough and unshaped. It had not accounted for his own personality or his own transient stream of consciousness. Did these features in himself point to a still higher level of moral existence, he wondered?

The answer became yes as it became clear to him "that each person is to represent humanity in one's own way, combining its elements uniquely so that it may reveal itself in every mode." The higher moral task, then, is to continue the "initial free act" which focused on one's own unique, independent existence, to attend to "the further cultivation of one's nature and to every expression thereof." This difficult task, attended by many setbacks and never fully achieved, will yield a sure sense of what area of humanity is one's own and of where the overall basis of both one's limitations and one's potential is to be sought, to assess the whole content of one's being and to know one's boundaries at all points, hence by "free choice" "to act in keeping with one's own spirit and sensibility." Thus one comes gradually to "separate" one's unique being "from what one possesses in concert with humanity in general," to move toward "a full consciousness of one's distinctiveness," to "a continual, unbroken interconnectedness of clear self-consciousness." This, as discussed in the *Soliloquies*,[10] was the "highest intuition" that dawned on him in Landsberg.

Here Schleiermacher was speaking in a broadly ethical context, which did not directly include theology or even other philosophical concerns. That context was for him of major importance nonetheless, such that it was determinative in all other areas of reflection and interpretation. He was on his way to conceiving ethics as the science of the principles of history, as the fundamental approach to the human side of science. So we are to take his proffered "highest intuition" very seriously.[11]

When and under what circumstances did this vision arise for Schleiermacher? There is no evidence of it in the Schlobitten period, from which a significant body of writings and correspondence are extant, or during the year he spent in Berlin after the Spring of 1793, joining in a seminar for teachers, doing a couple of odd jobs teaching there, and taking exams to qualify him for a preaching position. Rather his search then was for maxims and for change through and as a means of overcoming skepticism; it was also a search for what he was to be, especially "for others," as he says in the 1792-93 essay on "The Value of Life" – this in the context of finding "what life can be for a human being" and is supposed to be.[12] So far, self-knowledge essentially meant knowledge of human nature; freedom meant being attuned to human nature. On the other hand, there is evidence of this new thought at or just before the point at which he returned to Berlin in September, 1796;[13] and he makes regular use of it thereafter, as a basic feature of his ethics, hermeneutics, dialectic and religious outlook. On May 3, 1802, on a hilltop over Gnadenfrei, where he had experienced his first marked religious awakening nearly twenty years before, and during a visit to his sister Charlotte there, Schleiermacher wrote of the sudden onrush of worshipful and loving feelings at sunset and added this thought: "the history of the world had made a place for the history of my soul."[14] This testimony can only be fully understood as a representation of his "highest intuition." No expression of that vision had yet appeared in his writings of 1793, nor was there as yet any room for it, but evidence of the vision does begin to appear in 1796. Thus, one must look for evidence, pro or con, between 1794 and 1796.

Typically, accounts of Schleiermacher's early development have not sought to place this fascinating moment of intuition within his life story, or they have assumed that it reflects a Romantic phase in Berlin, from late 1796 on. As a consequence, in my view an essential step in his development as both thinker and person is either missed or misplaced. Examination of the evidence has led me to this firm claim: that the decisive vision occurred during Schleiermacher's first pastorate, in Landsberg an der Warthe sometime between 1794 and 1796, at ages twenty-five to twenty-seven and in part, I believe, through the mediation of a close romantic, though sexually unconsummated relationship with his first cousin, Frau Beneke, a local official's wife whom he had met in 1789 and with whom he was experiencing the first sustained, shared romantic attachment to a woman since he left his mother's house at age fourteen, never to see her again.

Increasingly students of Schleiermacher's hermeneutics are coming to see that from early on he presented interpretation as ideally rooted in dialogue, in the interpersonal, if only implicitly. He offers his own ideas as emerging out of dialogue, out of intense listening to, engagement with and appropriation from other people. What means most to him, moreover, is conversation that mediates sharing at the deepest levels of feeling and consciousness. It should be no surprise, then, to discover that many of his own finest insights have arisen or found nurture within closely personal relationships.

Having stated the claim, in the remainder I shall first examine the nature of the evidence, exploring further what Schleiermacher's "highest intuition" can be taken to have meant at the time, and finally point out some implications for understanding his subsequent life and thought.

The Evidence: Schleiermacher's Life in Landsberg

Almost all the evidence so far available must be used indirectly and inferentially. There is largely a correspondence blackout for this one period in his life; even his letters to his sister were accidentally destroyed in a fire. No letters from or to Frau Beneke are extant, though they regularly corresponded from 1789 to 1809. We do have the lack of evidence before 1794 and some indication of the new insight by September 1796, just noted, and the order in which he presented ideas in the *Soliloquies*. In the Berlin Archives there are 134 sermon outlines – twenty-seven from 1794, sixty-two from 1795 and forty-five from 1796; and there are fourteen written sermons from Landsberg in volume II.7 of the collected works and some in volume II.1, though these were all subject to revision before later publication. Several of the outlines have been published by Johannes Bauer and Friedrich Zimmer.[15]

Schleiermacher spent a year at his Uncle Stubenrauch's house in Drossen in 1789-90. In the summer of 1789 he visited some relatives of his uncle in nearby Landsberg. There he had found Frau Beneke, the beautiful, intelligent wife of a civil servant (later to become Bürgermeister). Her father was Pastor Schumann, whom he was to assist there four years later. Schumann's wife was Stubenrauch's sister, thus Schleiermacher's own aunt on his mother's side. His mother's name was Katharina-Maria Stubenrauch (b. July 27, 1736, d. Nov, 17, 1783). This makes Schleiermacher and Frau Beneke first cousins, thus he sometimes referred to her as his "cousin" in letters to others. On August 8, 1789, he rapturously described her to his friend Gustav von Brinkmann:[16]

> My cousin is a young wife of such great merits that I cannot refrain from saying a few words about her. At first sight she is more imposing than attractive, but when one has an opportunity to engage her in conversation one instantly discovers such a store of good sense and of that same sort of

amiable wit at which Wieland has given us to marvel in his
Musarion that one cannot tear oneself away. She says a great
deal, and all that she says is intelligent (*Verstand*); she
combines being well-read with a very fine sense of taste. If the
situation demands it, she can shift with ease from the most
interesting dialogues to the most mundane affairs. She
instructs without knowing it, and she is unfailingly kind without
any apparent intention; she is the soul of every company, and
everyone notices this except herself. She is merry but not to
excess, open without being unduly naive. She seems to prefer
sociability and social pleasures over everything else; yet she
told me: "I gladly associate with people, but they must not be
puppets – they must reveal themselves, otherwise I would
rather have my hermitage and a good book." She is rather
contemptuous of the French but heartily loves everything
English. It must be the profound sensibility and freedom that
she marvels at in them, for Switzerland is likewise the object of
her adoration (NB not Lavater).

The external picture fits this internal one splendidly.
Imagine a tall blond woman, grown to be quite beautiful, with
a charming face. In front her hair extends to her eyebrows,
behind falls naturally over her back and shoulders. Her
clothing is likewise pure and simple. Ordinarily I see her in a
long, white dress with a wide, skyblue scarf tied over the hips
or a very short girdle of lilac or pale green. I have rambled on
more than I should, or would like to. At best my description is
sufficiently poor not to have given you the high account that
she deserves. I have had so much fortune as well as knack in
getting to know her that I believe that she would fit into the
circle of your ladies as she deserves to. It appears that in order
to be happy she neither needs to be dominated like Auguste
nor to dominate like Elise. To be sure, with her husband she
does what she wants, and that is nothing special, but with her

men and women friends she seems to move on an even keel –
she is neither all too obliging nor all too single-minded.

The essay on "Schaamhaftigkeit" enclosed with Schleiermacher's 1800
Letters on Schlegel's Lucinde, though probably written in 1799, may well have
derived in part from their conversations during his stay in Drossen and
subsequently. "On the Naive" (written in the Fall of 1789) and especially "To
Cecilie" (written in the Summer of 1790) very likely had her directly in
mind.[17]

The next known visit to Landsberg was an equally fateful one, in the
late summer of 1793; trips there following his 1794-96 stay occurred in 1797,
1798 and 1801. On August 11, 1801, having recently returned from a two-
week visit to Landsberg to see her, he wrote at length to his new confidant,
Ehrenfried von Willich, of circumstances in a relationship with a married
woman eight years earlier (i.e., 1783). Although she was not mentioned by
name, Heinrich Meisner correctly identified her as Frau Beneke; indeed, the
descriptions could not conceivably refer to anyone else. In a letter to his
sister Charlotte dated November 10, 1801, Schleiermacher mentioned of this
same visit, the first in three years, that they had quickly resumed their
accustomed "intimacy" (*Vertraulichkeit*); the Beneke's marriage was still not
very impressive. On September 3, 1798, during his previous visit in
Landsberg, he reported to his close friend Henriette Herz that he had
preached in his old pulpit, "to the great joy" of his cousin, that he had read his
essay on "Openness" to her, plus the "Catechism of Reason for Noble
Women" (*Athenaeum* I.2) and other short writings. He also noted that she
was "sulky" (*Schmollen*), according to her nature, though not without "fervor"
(*Heftigkeit*).

Now back to 1793. In a September 21, 1793, letter to his father,
Schleiermacher reported on a visit with "my good friends," Pastor
Schumann's daughter and her husband in Landsberg, this on his way back to
Berlin from Schlobitten, staying with Pastor Schumann. While there, he
noted, Schumann told him of his desire to have him appointed to an adjunct
position next year, to which Schleiermacher added: "One can make a living
with the position, it is a very agreeable place, a glorious environs, and I have
a household there to which I am greatly attached and where I am also much

loved." Indeed he was. His lengthy 1801 reminiscence to von Willich shows that he was still fascinated with her. She, a mature woman terribly unhappy in marriage and having unfulfilled needs, was more than drawn to him. Whether the ensuing events that he recalls took place during that 1793 visit or a year later, when he was daily in this charming woman's home, tutoring her small daughter Emilie and, as he thought, bearing some positive influence on her three-year-old son as well, is not certain. It is clear, however, that he had found himself running into trouble. Realizing what was happening, he talked the whole matter out with her, and she, standing on the brink of divorce, wonderingly listened to his sober, patient advice. Frau Beneke had him to thank for saving her marriage. During his year as assistant and the additional year after Schumann had died, he was often in the Beneke home, even daily at times, an endeared friend of the entire family. Because the incident is so little known and is yet very important, it makes sense to quote his account in full:[18]

> Nearly eight years ago I came into a close household union with a woman who is closely related to me and whom I had already got to know some years earlier, though only superficially. Besides an agreeable and very captivating form, she had so much world and culture in her as she could have given herself in the so-called good society of a small town, but many rough edges (*Roheit*) within. Her moral being could not have thrived in the uncivilized, strict, negligent, early motherless education she had, in the most profligate little city that I know, or in a marriage which none should be since it was morally nonexistent and could not be one physically. Under these circumstances she had readily found occasion and excuse for having other relationships; thus, twice she had unhappily fallen into company with men whom she dazzled by her beauty, drew to herself by her special qualities, and enchanted through the appearance of a good heart (this was the unique quality in her well-known moral eminence). I found the second of these unions already dissolved internally; but she lacked the courage to break it off externally and to separate herself from a wretch

whom she had already long scorned but who she feared would
be vengeful. I was able to be helpful to her with this and to
contribute something to her being freed from her tyrant. I
happened to be the first man she had got to know who was in
the higher sense cultured and moral, and I was delighted to see
that this new phenomenon made a great impression on her.
She was in that respect my neighbor, and it was my
responsibility to influence her; therefore, it was with joy that I
saw her esteem and friendship increase, but I also let sensuality
get mixed in, so that her friendship turned into the fondest
attachment, soon into a strong passion. This is what I accuse
myself of and what I should have warded off. Given the
unevenness in moral standing, I could not return her love in
this sense, and a total union, a sharing of life and soul, was not
to be thought of. I justified my actions to myself with the
notion that even without this means of connection my influence
on her would soon be felt and that with such a passionate spirit
every repulse would necessarily have a stronger effect than
anything that impelled her to love and respect me.
Nevertheless, I well know that this was not my only reason and
that I would probably have found a middle course were it not
for the presence of vanity and self-interest, which refuses to us
the real love that is so rarely granted or offered. Thus, for the
first reason I was not so candid as you, so as to make her aware
point-blank of the dissimilarity of our sentiments for each
other and of the impossibility of a sustained inner union. I felt
that this would destroy my purpose, that in this circumstance a
harshness would appear in me, a useless harshness. For this
failure to act there were several reasons, which lie precisely in
the difference between this relationship and yours. She must
not think at all of a divorce from her husband, to whom she
owed much gratitude and whom she had gradually learned to
honor in many aspects. According to the natural order of
things, I could only be near her for a couple of years, so I

clearly stated that concern for my continuing education would not permit me to do anything that would get in the way of our eventual separation. I knew that in this period she would not come along so far as to surmount the need to attach herself to a current male friend and that surely she would always be attached to me with esteem and friendship after my departure but sooner or later would of a certainty direct her love to another man – and often I prophesied this to her, half in jest, half in earnest.

Schleiermacher's lifelong intimate concourse with women, unexceptionably with the same pure intentions finally evidenced in his relationship with Frau Beneke, was to be a major factor in his development as a man and thinker. Young Friederike Dohna, who unknowingly first awakened romantic love and a sense for the nobility of woman;[19] the charming Jewish hostess Henriette Herz, with whom he shared half a lifetime of closest friendship; Frau Eleonore Grunow, who caused him six years of joy and agonized longing; and Henriette von Willich, the widow of his closest male friend, who had died in April 1807, and his precious wife from 1809 until death; these along with his sister Charlotte and a few others of lesser importance, were the women in his life, along with Frau Beneke. With such kindred souls he shared his deepest feelings and the bulk of his correspondence. "Only through knowledge of the inner spirit of women," he wrote in 1802, "have I gained knowledge of the true worth of man."[20] In 1804: "The nature of woman seems to me nobler and their life happier...."[21] Already in 1799: "It lies very deep in my nature that I should always attach myself more closely to women than to men, for there is so much in my spirit that men rarely understand...."[22] In any case, human life at its best is shared:[23]

> The quiet joys of common activity, of common feeling, remain the crown of my life! ... And when I think on all the manifold gifts of life and diligently analyze the value of each one, the most beautiful always remains the fact that one can be at home (häuslich).

It is no surprise, then, to find Schleiermacher writing to Alexander von Dohna on November 24, 1795 – three days after his twenty-seventh birthday – that during the half year that remains to him in Landsberg he will surely "break off many hours from my literary activities in order to spend them in friendship and household intimacy (*häuslichen Vertraulichkeit*)." Nor, if my thesis is correct, is there any doubt as to a key underlying meaning in the expectation he then indicates that when he leaves a new period of his scientific life will begin. The "highest intuition" to which he had in all likelihood attained by this moment would, of course, lead him to fresh affirmations of his being, first as one who is intimately "at home" and is truly himself there – a representative of humanity in his own way and an elect creation of the Godhead – then in the work to which he is called and for which he is especially suited.

During his 1793-94 stay in Berlin, Schleiermacher had experienced little intimate social intercourse and he had written practically nothing, though current movements of literature and politics had greatly stirred his thoughts and he had also read a Latin paper on the *Staatslehre* of Plato and Aristotle for the Gedike seminar. When he returned to the bustling, prosperous river-town of Landsberg an der Warthe in April 1794, after ordination in Berlin, he moved into a warm circle of relatives and cultured friends. Notably, besides the Benekes, he loved to visit the calmer, simpler home of Pastor Wedeke and his family in nearby Hermsdorf, and he made visits to his uncle in Drossen, a few hours' journey to the south.

Landsberg an der Warthe was some 150 kilometers directly east of Berlin as the crow flies. It had been chartered as a town in 1257 and had become a trade center; it was destroyed in the Thirty Years' War and had risen again in the eighteenth century. Since it had become the seat of a Roman Catholic bishop, the Marienkirche, situated by the marketplace, had long been the prominent feature of the town at a distance, as it is today. In Schleiermacher's day, a tower graced the small Schlossberg overlooking the town, which had some 6,000 inhabitants. The church where Schleiermacher worked was the Konkordienkirche, built in 1696-99, and so named according to the wish of Friedrich I, who had donated the materials. It was originally designated for both Reformed and Lutheran congregations, unusual at the time. By virtue of this tradition, in 1821 Landsberg was to be among the first churches to be united under the Prussian Kabinettsorder of September 9, 1817. The nave measured over 30 x 15 meters, and the two wings extended over 6 meters from the center, east and west. Inside the building was quite ornate. A raised pulpit stood over the alter on the east side, facing the main entrance on the west. Balconies stretched along the south and west sides, and there was an organ loft at the north end. Schleiermacher lived at Schloßstraße 4, in a simple room furnished only with a bed, two tables and three chairs.[24]

Here are the bare bones of his other activities in Landsberg. Because Schumann was ailing, Schleiermacher was asked to take over most of his duties. He preached regularly, spending much labor on his sermons and getting advice from his uncle and his father; he began catechetical work on October 13, 1794; and on his own initiative he spent some time instructing religion in the schools. He continued his studies during his spare time, including much occupation with English works and probably some with the Spinoza controversy, though not much is known about this activity; and he probably kept a journal, which has not survived (the first extant one is marked "no. 2" and begins in September 1796). Sermons by Joseph Fawcett he discovered in 1795; two years later he translated two volumes of them.[25] He suffered a long illness in mid-summer 1794. In late September of that year he learned from his uncle that his father had died on September 2. Between November 1794 and March 1795 he translated thirteen sermons by Hugh Blair, at the request of Bishop Sack.[26] In early June, 1795, Schumann died. The congregation requested that Schleiermacher take his place. The Reformed Church directorium in Berlin thought him too young at twenty-six, however, and decided to send uncle Stubenrauch instead – against the latter's protest. Schleiermacher stayed on a year longer, nevertheless.

His political perspective was already coming to fruition in a 1795 Landsberg sermon on "differences of political opinion" (Matt. 26:47-51) and in another on "righteousness as a foundation of civil welfare" (Prov. 14:13) in 1796 – the latter published in April, 1799 after a draft written out in October, 1796. This was his first published sermon.[27] He also preached on the Proverbs text again in 1832.[28]

The brand of individualism revealed in his later Landsberg sermons was not of an ingrown, self-centered variety. As was reflected in his later *Soliloquies* discussion, mentioned above, it was focused on the whole of humanity and on the individual's unique responsibilities within that whole. One sermon, for example, concentrated "on the ground of our hope for a better condition of people on earth." Its text was Jesus' answer to the Pharisees: "the kingdom of God is within you." Its message was: "first, that this hope does not rest on external circumstances, and second, that its fulfillment entirely depends on an inner improvement of human beings." Another sermon set forth love of neighbor – according to a person's inner worth, not one's external appearances – as a way of life "comprehending the whole kingdom of God with our understanding, our inclinations and our activity." Still another considered our respectful relation to people whose form of life is quite different from our own. The whole perspective was not only intra-personal. It was primarily inter-personal. However, there was a strong emphasis on the unique, individual development and responsibility of human beings.[29]

We turn again to Frau Beneke. As Schleiermacher himself indirectly speaks of what occurred in the relationship, it was not simply their intimacy that may have eased his vision of individuality but "separation" from her as well. Already in the summer of 1793 he had reportedly assumed the leading role in this separation, eschewing sexual intercourse and enabling her to stay in her marriage while remaining a close friend. These deeper meanings of their relationship would surely have been dramatized for Schleiermacher upon the death of his father in September 1794. His own mother had been dead eleven years by then, and there had been no other sustained, intensive relationship with a woman, save his sister. As a beloved first cousin on his mother's side, Frau Beneke had to have been a key figure in his life during the time of mourning.[30]

I believe that if further evidence becomes available – notably, from still unpublished sermons in the Berlin Archives – the timing of his "highest intuition" would be either in the next several months, if grieving permitted, most likely around the Advent to New Year's period of 1794-95, or a year later. In these years Schleiermacher regularly devoted concentrated time for reflection on his life and career from the time of his birthday (November 21) to the turn of the year. One year later he could easily have experienced an anniversary reaction to his being on his own, without his father. Moreover, on November 24, 1795, he reported to Alexander von Dohna that he had recently been "excited" (*entzückt*) in reading the first part of Goethe's *Wilhelm Meister*; he had also just read Schiller's *Agathon*. These works could have provided significant stimulus to, though not the specific content of, his new vision. It is well known that creativity – in fact, an entire creative career – frequently emerges out of loss and mourning. I believe that Schleiermacher presents a prime case of this phenomenon, though it did not occur so early in his life as is true for a great many creative figures.

In another essay,[31] I have attempted to show that Schleiermacher's considerable effort in English-to-German translation from the death of his Barby schoolmate, the Englishman Samuel Okely, in May of 1787 onward was a way both of keeping his dearest friend with him and of coping with the continual absence, then drastic rejection and eventual death of his father. Now it may be added that he got to know Frau Beneke but two years after those two initial heart-rending events of 1787 – in 1789, when he was only twenty years old and still quite alone; she was also prominently on hand at the death of his father in 1794. Ehrenfried von Willich, whom he met in May of 1801, was the successor to Okely as dearest male friend, and three months after Ehrenfried died in early April, 1807, Schleiermacher proposed marriage to his widow, whom he wedded a year later. The relationship with his father, then with Okely and von Willich, is but one component within his family constellation, however. The other major component is derived from his relationship with his mother and extends especially to Frau Beneke, his dearest female friend Henriette Herz, and his wife Henriette von Mühlenfels. Unfortunately, very few details are known about the relationship with his mother, but there is enough information to make the necessary links.

Toward her first-born son (sister Charlotte was born on March 25, 1765, he on November 21, 1768, so she was three-and-a-half at the time) – a rather short, sometimes sickly, somewhat deformed, extremely bright child – we know that she bore great affection, though she came to be overawed at his early budding scholastic interest, especially in languages, and that she left matters of regimen to her stern, though frequently absent husband. We also know that she was immediately occupied in his first years with two more infants: a sister, who died early, and his brother Karl. It appears, however, that the closer relationship, as Schleiermacher remembered it, was with his sister Charlotte. We know that the last time Schleiermacher saw his mother was when he and Karl were sent off to boarding school at Niesky in June of 1783, he aged fourteen-and-a-half, and that she died at age forty-seven on November 17, 1783, just before his fifteenth birthday. This loss, he later averred, he had been able to understand or feel only in an immature, fantastical way.[32] We know that the schooling decision was made during a marvelous eleven-week experience that the entire family had shared in the Herrnhuter Brethren community at Gnadenfrei from April to June 1783 – a time when Schleiermacher later said he had discovered "the higher world"[33] – and that the sequel for his sister Charlotte was that she became a lifelong member of the Brethren community, never marrying. (She lived most of her years at Gnadenfrei, then in Schleiermacher's house, and finally in a nearby Brethren house on Wilhelmstraße in Berlin, where she died in 1831.) The two siblings were bosom friends, corresponding often and at length, so that we can reasonably infer that for Schleiermacher his sister remained an essential, though partial, substitute for his mother.

As was indicated earlier, Schleiermacher was to affirm that it had ordinarily been easier for him to form close relationships with women, because so much that is extraneous to the most important features of intimacy tended to dominate concourse among men. Frau Beneke – and Henriette Herz and his eventual wife, Henriette von Mühlenfels, chief among her successors – gave him a chance to relate at the core of human feeling and interaction. More, she apparently occasioned his being able to affirm himself as a separate individual, distinctly different from his father and not bound to his mother or to any mother surrogate in the further development and expansion of his unique self. He was then free to draw from relationships of all kinds, while retaining in his case a deep continuing need for closeness and dialogue, especially with select married women. Fortunately for us, he did not become mired in the partly unresolved conflicts that were sure to accompany this situation but was able to gain from the inner struggle and to attain considerable autonomy, moral sensitivity and insight, and capacity for love. All this he used in the extraordinary corpus of writings we now study, as, inseparably, in the rest of his life.

It is time that we thanked Frau Beneke for her gift of self, while we celebrate Schleiermacher's being able to use that gift for his own growth.

Implications for Schleiermacher's Life and Thought

By September of 1796, probably before settling into Berlin, Schleiermacher wrote a remarkable essay-letter, very likely to Wilhelm von Dohna, on relations between "knowing," "having faith" and "having an opinion."[34] The essay was full of implicit comparisons with Kant's thinking and with his own earlier positions on rule-governed behavior. This is a part of what he wrote:

> To be sure, in general terms, you have laid out correctly the characteristic distinction between knowing, having faith, and having an opinion. However, this distinction is not expressed with sufficient exactness, nor is it applied with the fullness that the material permits.
>
> Knowing (*Wissen*) is taking something to be true (*Fürwahrhalten*) for objective reasons, of which I am conscious as sufficient and generally valid, and the consciousness of this taking something to be true is called conviction.
>
> Having faith (*Glauben*) is taking something to be true for subjective reasons, in that I cannot suppose either existence or attributes of an object that is outside myself because I know them in themselves or directly through other objects; rather, I do this because there is or is supposed to be something in me that stands in a necessary relation to the object. Now, the object or the idea of this subjective reason is the interest (*Interesse*) on which having faith rests.
>
> There is a still higher process of taking something to be true for subjective reasons, a process which on that account

relates itself not to an external object but to the very subject that is taking something to be true. This is immediate self-consciousness (*unmittelbare Selbstbewußtsein*). The interest that contains the basis of having faith must always rest on this immediate self-consciousness, and since it is of a twofold kind it too becomes the basis of having faith and therefore the faith itself.

Either I am self-conscious of my human nature and of that which immediately belongs to it, and a faith the interest of which is based on this self-consciousness is a necessary faith, which I can summon from every human being, or I am conscious in myself of certain modifications and of a certain condition of human nature in my *individuo*, and a faith the interest of which is related strictly to this is simply a subjective faith in the narrower sense of the word.

Finally, to have an opinion can as easily be an objective as a subjective taking something to be true but always accompanied by the consciousness of the inadequacy of the reasons – in the first instance if the objective grounds provide insufficient reason for a knowledge (*Erkenntnis*) which admits of being demonstrated and communicated, in the second instance if what is supposed does not stand in a demonstrably necessary relation to the interest on which I base it.

Now, the great question is this: in religion what is knowing? what within it is having faith? and what within it is mere opinion?

The response that he sketches out is then directly referred to his engagement with Kant, who had made the threefold distinction alluded to here in the *Critique of Pure Reason* (1781, 2nd ed., 1787). Against Kant, he here sees all religion to rest in an individual and subjective faith, not a general or necessary faith, however religion may be found in us – notably through consciousness of moral law and withal the striving for blessedness or of an external support for that law – whether relatively undeveloped as feeling (*Gefühl*) or developed as the insight of reason (*Vernunfteinsicht*); thus, whatever possibility of the reality referred to by reason is formed in us occurs not by general, purely objective means but by gaining an individual, self-conscious perspective (*anschaulich*). The nub of what Schleiermacher is saying, then, is that the ground of this immediate self-consciousness and of this faith is not in any merely external object of knowing, though nothing excludes the presence and stimulus of such objects, such as are referred to in communities of faith, but in an inner experience. Herein lies the basic inner-outer distinction and dialectic set forth in the *Soliloquies* and throughout all his writings to come. Furthermore, the new individual consciousness is here made the ground of religious faith in particular.

In his excellent historical work on *The Value of the Individual*, Karl Weintraub has argued that the momentous Socratic turn toward shared reasoning, toward a "spiritualizing of individual life," actually "impeded rather than promoted the growth of a sense of individuality."[35] Until Augustine (354-430), he contends, the few autobiographic writings that had appeared over the previous millenium tended to reveal very little of the inner life of their authors. This great, seminal thinker lived in a civilized world that had rapidly become Christianized over the previous century. Trained in classical culture, from 397 to 401, over a decade after his conversion in August 386 at age thirty-two, Augustine told the dramatic story of how his own spiritual development had brought him into conflict with moral and spiritual ideals in that culture. As the presentation of a life course, these *Confessions* were a first, unique event in history, unparalleled until modern times. Even so, the confession was not that of one who saw himself to be a singular being. His life was only supposed to be representative of "the typical life of all Christians," as Weintraub perceptively indicates.[36] Augustine's thought bears a profound witness to God's concern for every single soul and has room for vast differentiation among souls. Moreover, he had derived from Hebraic thought a sense of divine processes in history, fundamentally viewed as salvation-history. However, these features were not enough to create anything like the growing awareness of the historical dimension in human life or of attendant individuality that began to emerge with the Renaissance and Reformation and that came to their first great flower in Rousseau (1712-1778) – to some extent in Goethe (1749-1832) as well.

Like many recent interpreters of Rousseau's life, Weintraub points to his life-changing vision of October 1749 on the road to Vincennes, where he was to visit Diderot in prison.[37] Overcome by the hot sun, he had sat down in the shade of a tree, and he happened to read in the *Mercure de France* an announcement of a prize essay contest by the Academy of Dijon. The assigned question was: Had the progress of the arts and the sciences contributed more to the corruption or to the purification of morals? "In that instance," he reports in the *Confessions*, "I saw another universe and became another man." He felt impelled by his new vision to affirm that the illusions and artifices purveyed by European civilization had in fact alienated people from their true nature, had opposed the formation of true virtue. He developed this theme in his two famous "discourses" on arts and sciences in 1750 and on inequality in 1755 and then in three great works, *La Nouvelle Héloïse* in 1761 and both *Émile ou de l'Éducation* and *Du Contrat Social* in 1762 – between ages thirty-eight and fifty. Unlike many others, Weintraub also emphasizes that Rousseau was the first among the great autobiographers to think of childhood and youth as essentially formative of one's personality. Thus, his *Confessions* aim to portray, defend and offer lessons from the development of his own distinctive life, which he believed had displayed a unique closeness to the basics of human nature. Unfortunately, he did not positively value the individuality of others or even of himself very highly, because he could not place a high value on the historical context in which his life took shape; he could neither accept the necessity of self-limitation nor appreciate the interplay between himself and that world. Rather, he felt forced to condemn what the world had done to him and to withdraw. Given this overall account of Rousseau's achievement and its flaws, with which I agree, I think it is too much to claim of the man as John Lyons does that "the self was largely his invention."[38] Nevertheless, the self-reflective memory and sense of personal development present soon after in a Goethe or a Schleiermacher is almost unthinkable without his influence.

What distinguishes Schleiermacher from both Rousseau and Goethe is his retaining an Augustinian awareness of human finitude and sin but viewing both solely in relation to an everlasting, widespread gift of divine grace in the creation, preservation and redemption of the world. Likewise, in non-theological terms, he speaks understandingly of human frailty and lack of development, but this too is seen in the wider perspective of a gift by which each person is enabled through the mediation of others to represent humanity in one's own way. Lewis Hyde has demonstrated in his extraordinary anthropological study on gifts[39] that "unlike the sale of a commodity, the giving of a gift tends to establish a relationship between the parties involved. Furthermore, when gifts circulate within a group, their commerce leaves a series of interconnected relationships in its wake, and a kind of decentralized cohesiveness emerges." This is the way Schleiermacher saw both the church and the world as a whole.

There is another major difference which distinguishes Schleiermacher not only from Augustine but also from some other notable modern thinkers. Both Marx and Freud began with philosophy in reflecting on self and world but tried to leave it for science, thus disavowing the origins and foundations of their thought. Schleiermacher never did this, and his scientific efforts were the richer for his continual attempt to keep them philosophically in good tune. Therein lies another story, but it is closely allied with the acceptance of a self historically determined yet free critically to accept, use and transform the gifts received within one's historical world, both seeking the whole truth and representing humanity in one's own way.

As his later works would more clearly show, the frame for self-consciousness, religious or otherwise, was thoroughgoingly, unremittingly social and deterministic for Schleiermacher. He was not purveying "individualism," as such. There was still room for pervasive interpersonal, social and political commitment – in fact, such would constantly be called forth and demanded. However, the profound respect for individuality in persons and in all historical entities and processes was inextricably present as well, from this point on.

Schleiermacher's insight has won through to others, independently, from time to time, in some form or other. It is part of our inheritance now. Just the other day, for example, the American poet William Meredith penned these lines, which express aspects of Schleiermacher's intuition well.[40]

Perhaps we misuse
the word about nature.
Suppose
this is not violence that nature works
but something else,
call it the stating
and then the restating of terms –
inexorable, arbitrary, playful,
and for any given one of us, beyond appeal.
But terms to be responded to in character.

No one ever promised us more.

Notes

1. A shorter version of this essay was prepared for the Schleiermacher Colloquium at Herrnhut, June 25-26, 1988. I already identified Landsberg an der Warthe as the site of this key ethical discovery by Schleiermacher in *Schleiermacher's Theological Method* (Th.D. dissertation, Princeton Theological Seminary, 1961), with some supporting evidence. I have come to understand the background, import and implications of this discovery better through subsequent investigation, however. The shorter version lacked much of the discussion about Landsberg, Schleiermacher's activities there, his relationship with Frau Beneke, and comparisons with other thinkers.

2. See Gregory Vlastos, *Platonic Studies* (Princeton, N.J.: Princeton University Press, 1973), xvi, 437 p.

3. An adequate biography of Descartes is not yet available. I have referred to this identity-focusing event in my *Research Guide to Philosophy* (Chicago: American Library Association, 1983), p. 80, having already developed an account in *Ideology Old and New*, Philosophy Dissertation, University of Michigan, 1970, pp. 24-26.

4. The finest account of Marx's life from this perspective is Jerrold Siegel's *Marx's Fate: The Shape of a Life* (Princeton, N.J.: Princeton University Press, 1978), x, 451 p.

5. See Peter Gay, *Freud: A Life for Our Time* (New York: W.W. Norton, 1988), xxi, 810 p.

6. I present a detailed account and critique of Barth's views regarding Schleiermacher, within its historical context, in my chapter, "Interviews with Karl Barth and Reflections on His Interpretations of Schleiermacher," in *Barth and Schleiermacher: Beyond the Impasse?* ed. by James O. Duke and Robert F. Streetman (Philadelphia, Pa.: Fortress Press, 1988), 43-62.

7. Ordinarily I would translate Schleiermacher's general uses of *Anschauung* "perception" or "perspective," the more specific use referring to a basic religious outlook "perspectivity." Here I think he intends to be directly reflective of Kant. He still speaks of something clearly and directly observed, however, not transcendental and not posited and not a product of demonstrative reasoning, though subject to reasoned explanation; but the perception is inwardly achieved, not attached to specific objects, places or events. In 1822 he replaces "what is my highest intuition" with "what has since then advanced me most of all" (*was seitdem am meisten mich erhebt*).

8. This statement is from the unpublished 1793 essay "Über den Wert des Lebens," first made available only through excerpts by Wilhelm Dilthey, *Leben Schleiermachers* (Berlin:

Reimer, 1870), in a section entitled "Denkmale der inneren Entwicklung Schleiermachers: Anhang," p. 54. This material was omitted from the second edition of 1922. The essay and quote also appeared in Friedrich Michael Schiele, *Friedrich Schleiermacher: Monologen nebst den Vorarbeiten*, Kritische Ausgabe (Leipzig: Meiner, 1902) and in its second edition of 1914 (same publisher), p. 182. The full text of the essay only first appeared in *KGA* I/1 (1984), the quote on p. 418. See also note 39 below.

   9. My translation from Schiele (1914), *op cit.* (note 8), p. 28.

   10. Schiele (1914), *op. cit.* (note 8), p. 30. It would take another essay fully to explicate what this intuition meant to Schleiermacher, who already spelled this out in some detail in the *Soliloquies*. Such an essay would flesh out his evolving views on freedom and determinism, to a considerable extent marked out for the early period by Albert L. Blackwell, *Schleiermacher's Early Philosophy of Life: Determinism, Freedom, and Phantasy* (Chico, Cal.: Scholars Press, 1982), xi, 327 p. It would include his understanding of relations between individuality and community. Finally, it might fruitfully compare his views on all these matters with those of other seminal thinkers like Marx, Freud, Charles Sanders Peirce, John Dewey and their closer successors. If the reference to Peirce seems puzzling, see *The Sign of Three: Dupin, Holmes, Peirce*, ed. by Umberto Eco and Thomas A. Sebeok (Bloomington: Indiana University Press, 1988), xi, 236 p. – especially on Peirce's method of "abduction."

   11. For recent works on his conception of ethics see my *Schleiermacher Bibliography (1784-1984): Updating and Commentary* (Princeton, N.J.: Princeton University Press for Princeton Theological Seminary, 1985), 119 p.; and "Schleiermacher Bibliography: Update 1987" in *New Athenaeum/Neues Athenaeum*, Vol. One (1989), 280-350.

   12. See note 8 above. This essay and related sermons are currently being translated by Edwina Lawler, with my assistance; the volume is a companion to a new edition of *Soliloquies*, which I am translating with her assistance.

   13. This first appears in a letter probably written to Wilhelm von Dohna in or just before September, 1796; this is quoted at length in the final section below.

   14. Quoted in Wilhelm Dilthey, *Leben Schleiermachers*, hg.v. Martin Redeker, Bd I.1 (Berlin: de Gruyter, 1970), 542-544; and Blackwell, *op. cit.* (note 10), p. 240, refers to the key moment indicated here.

   15. In my first *Schleiermacher Bibliography* (Princeton, NJ.: Princeton University Press for Princeton Theological Seminary, 1966), see items ##164, 165, 173 and 868.

   16. In *KGA* V/1, #121, lines 11-46; also in Heinrich Meisner, *Schleiermacher als Mensch: Sein Werden – Familien- und Freundesbriefe 1783 bis 1804* (Gotha: Perthes, 1922), 45-46.

   17. See *KGA* I/3 and item #55 in my bibliographies, also *KGA* I/1.

   18. In Meisner, *op. cit.* (note 16), 225-227, and noted earlier by Dilthey, *op. cit.* (1922 edition, note 8), 31-82.

   19. Aug. 19, 1802. In *Aus Schleiermachers Leben in Briefen*, Bd 1 (Berlin: Reimer, 1860), 319 (abbrev.: *Br.*), and Meisner, *op cit*, (note 16), 260.

   20. *Loc. cit.*

   21. Aug. 4, 1804. In *Br.* (note 19), 403, and Meisner, *op. cit.* (note 16), 348.

   22. Mar. 23, 1799. In *Br.* (note 19), 207, and Meisner, *op cit*, (note 16), 136.

   23. See note 8.

   24. The town, still situated in beautiful, slightly hilly and wooded surroundings, is now called Gorzów Wielkopolski, and its population is entirely Polish today. A part of Poland after 1945, the city had been 50 percent destroyed in the war. The 1939 population was 48,043, that in 1946 was 19,796; it is still rather small today, sporting several large parks. The spire of the Marienkirche still stands, and the Konkordienkirche now also has a tower. The town is a rail junction within a lignite-mining region, and it has been known for its textiles and materials, woodworking, soap, chocolate and bricks. In 1848 a bronze bust of Schleiermacher was

erected on a tall post surrounded by four doric columns supporting a large roof, itself well over a meter high, an assemblage referred to as a "Baldachin-Tempel." A commemorative plaque was also affixed to his house. Sources: (a) A 1977 map of Gorzow in the New York Public Library (not yet catalogued). (b) *Columbia Lippincott Gazeteer of the World* (1962 ed.), p. 1016. (c) *Wege zueinander: Landsberg (Warthe) Gorzow Wlkp. Herford*, hg.v. Hans Beske und Ernst Handke (Berlin: Westkrauz, 1982), 176 S. (d) In *Landsberg an der Warthe, 1257, 1945, 1978*, Bd II: *Aus Kultur und Gesellschaft im Spiegel der Jahrhunderte*, hg.v. Hans Beske und Ernst Handke (Bielefeld: Gieseking, 1978): Otto Kaplick, "Schleiermachers Landsberger Jahre," 83-86; Klaus Jürgen Laube, "Landsbergs evangelische Kirchengeschichte," 68-80 [71-73 on Schleiermacher]. I am very grateful to Pfarrer Peter Keller of Frankfurt am Main for sharing items (c) and (d) with me.

25. *Joseph Fawcett's Predigten, aus dem English übersetzt* von F. Schleiermacher, mit einer Vorrede von F. S. G. Sack, 2 Theile (Berlin: August Mylius, 1798). xxx, 366; iv, 361 S. In my essay on "Schleiermacher as Translator" for a forthcoming volume on that subject, I provide a first study of Schleiermacher's activity as a translator from English and of his reasons for undertaking these efforts.

26. *Hugo Blairs Predigten, aus dem Englischen übersetzt*, Bde 4-5 (Leipzig: Weidmannischen Buchhandlung, 1795, 1801), viii, 319; vi, 385 S. Schleiermacher translated sermons 1-10 and 18-20 in the fourth volume and all of the fifth volume. Schleiermacher's accuracy and style were already very good in 1795, superb by 1801.

27. In his collected works, *SW* II,4, 1-15; originally published in *Predigten von protestantischen Gottesgelehrten, Siebente Sammlung* (Berlin: Mylius, 1799).

28. For outlines and discussions of both sermons, see Johannes Bauer, *Schleiermacher als patriotischer Prediger* (Giessen: Töpelmann, 1908), 309-315.

29. Sermons X-XI and XIII-XIV (*SW* II.7, Zweite Sammlung), written in Landsberg, together with his initial sermon at Charity Hospital in September, 1796, obviously display the new slant, but the earlier ones do not. A similar development is suggested in the sermon outlines published so far. See note 16 above.

30. In an August 22, 1808 letter from Landsberg to his bride-to-be he reports spending a night in the Beneke house, "where I stood in a similar relationship as Ehrenfried to Johanna. She loved me and without being able actually to requite that love I nevertheless brought something worthwhile into her life that she would not otherwise have had. Old memories of many sorts have encompassed me; all this has found me unchanged." *Friedrich Schleiermachers Briefwechsel mit seiner Braut*, hg.v. Heinrich Meisner (Gotha: Perthes, 1919), 118-119.

31. See note 25 above.

32. In *Br.* (note 19), 130-134, and Meisner (note 16), 82-83, then *KGA* V/l, #278: a letter to his sister Charlotte on Oct. 13, 1794 regarding his father's death.

33. In *Br.* (note 19), 295: letter while in Gnadenfrei to Georg Reimer, April 30, 1802. This is where he also says that he has become "a Herrnhuter, only of a higher order."

34. *KGA* V/1, #326. Johannes Bauer found this letter among Wilhelm von Dohna's papers.

35. Karl Joachim Weintraub, *The Value of the Individual: Self and Circumstance in Autobiography* (Chicago: University of Chicago Press, 1978), xix, 439 p. The quote is on p. 11-13.

36. Moreover, as Elaine Pagels has recently emphasized in *Adam, Eve, and the Serpent* (New York: Random House, 1988), xxviii, 189 p., especially on p. 105, whereas Augustine's contemporary John Chrysostom, like Clment of Alexandria and some earlier Christian theologians, had proclaimed the human's freedom to constitute and rule one's own being (*autexousia*), Augustine offered the diametrically opposite viewpoint of humanity's

bondage to sin. (See also p. 74, 98-99.) His view held the center of Western Christian tradition from that time on.

37. Jean Jacques Rousseau, *Confessions*, Book 8.

38. John O. Lyons, *The Invention of the Self: The Hinge of Consciousness in the Eighteenth Century* (Carbondale: Southern Illinois University Press, 1978), 268 p. The quote is on p. 111.

39. Lewis Hyde, *The Gift: Imagination and the Erotic Life of Property* (New York: Vintage Books, 1983), xvii, 327 p. The quote is on p. xiv. See also his comment that in American society labor that attends to the sharing of gifts, thus to the inner life and community, has come to be seen as a mark of the female gender, exploitation of gifts as that of the male (108). Schleiermacher's perspective works against that trend.

40. William Meredith, "The Three Sorts of Violence," in his *Partial Accounts: New and Selected Poems* (New York: Knopf, 1987), p. 178.

III

WAS IST EIN MONOLOG?

Erwin Quapp

Wir stellen die Frage unseres Themas an die Schleiermachersche Frühschrift *Monologen* von 1800. Wir benutzen den Text in der Edition von Hayo Gerdes; dabei beziehen wir unsere Seitenangaben auf die Seitenzählung der 1. Ausgabe, die H. Gerdes in seiner Edition angibt[1].

Wir gehen nun so vor, daß wir den Inhalt eines Monologs wiedergeben, – so haben wir schon eine erste, einfache Antwort auf unsere Frage des Themas, – dann befragen wir den Monolog auf seine leitende Frage; ferner stellen wir sein Thema heraus; schließlich geben wir eine Antwort auf die leitende Frage und stellen zum Schluß an jeden Monolog die Frage nach der Zeitstruktur des Sprechstils. Aus diesen Wiedergaben des sprachlichen Gehaltes und den Strukturanalysen ergibt sich eine vorläufige Antwort am Ende eines jeden Monologs. So werden wir insgesamt drei Antworten auf unsere thematische Frage: Was ist ein Monolog? – bekommen. Einige Ausführungen zur Sprache, zur Theorie der "ewigen Jugend" und zum Freiheitsverständnis werden unsere Überlegungen abrunden.

Wir geben zunächst den Inhalt des ersten Monologs wieder:

I. Die Reflexion. Gliederung.

Einleitung A 1. S. 5-6: Äußere wie innere Welt strahlen unser Wesen auf uns zurück. So lehrt schon der Jahreswechsel in rätselhafter Gestalt, daß eine Teilung des Lebens möglich ist.

A 2. S. 6-10: Das Dasein des Menschen in der Zeit läßt sich
mechanisch nicht hinreichend erklären. Vielmehr enthält
jeder Zeitpunkt, jedes Lebensmoment die Möglichkeit, sich
auf das Unendliche zu beziehen: ewig ist der Mensch nur im
Augenblick da. Nur der Genuß des Ewigkeits-Augenblicks
macht frei von der Zeit. Dieses höhere oder Unsterblichkeits-
leben verliert sich nicht selbst durch Produktion oder
Konsumption im ständigen Lebensfluß.

Hauptteil. S. 10-14 (Selbstbetrachtung): Das innere Wesen des
Geistes ist Selbstbetrachtung außerhalb des Gebietes der Zeit.
Diese Selbstbetrachtung schaut also nicht die äußere
Erscheinung der Geistestätigkeit an (etwa Sorge, Lebens-
kampf, Wissenszuwachs), sondern die innere Geistestätigkeit,
"die sich verborgen in seiner Tiefe regt" (12). Selbstentwürfe
oder sonstige Selbstobjektivationen hängen immer vom Inhalt
der Zeit ab: daher herrscht hier noch Notwendigkeit.

S. 14-15 (Freiheit): Demgegenüber ist nur das innerste Handeln
des Menschen frei. Darin besteht sein wahres Wesen: sich
selbst anzuschauen und jeden Zeitmoment als Element der
Ewigkeit herauszugreifen und in ein höheres Leben zu
verwandeln.

S. 15-19 (Weltanschauung): Freiheit und Unendlichkeit gibt's nur
für den, der die Trennung wie das Zusammenwirken von Welt
und Mensch vornehmen kann. Einen Leib gibt's nur, weil und
wann der Geist ihn braucht. So ist der Geist das Erste, der
eigene und der gemeinschaftliche Leib der Menschheit das
Zweite. Durch dieses Zweite verkündigt sich das Erste. Welt
ist die ewige Gemeinschaft freier Geister, "ihr Einfluß
aufeinander, ihr gegenseitiges Bilden, die hohe Harmonie der
Freiheit." Das Wirken in dieser Welt folgt ewigen Gesetzen.
In allen wohnt Freiheit; Notwendigkeit ergibt sich von dieser
Welt und den andern her, die sich die Freiheit nehmen zu
bilden und so meine Freiheit zu beschränken.

S. 19-22 (Selbstanschauung): So ist nur die Freiheit in allem das Erste, Ursprünglichste und Innerste. Die innere Anschauung der Freiheit läßt den Geist seines schöpferischen Wesens inne werden. Hier gibt es keine Determination durch das eigene Handeln in der Zeit. Vielmehr herrscht hier das Selbstgefühl des Geistes vor. Dieser Geist lebt innerlich; dies zeigen Schmerz und Lust an, die die freie Tat des Geistes sind. So wird der Mensch; er wird sich selbst bestimmter und eigener und bildet endlich auch Welt (indem er der Gemeinschaft freier Geister ein eigenes, freies Handeln darbietet).

S. 22-24 (Selbstwissen): Das Wissen darum, wer man selbst ist, trennt inneres Handeln und äußere Welt. Nur im inneren Handeln findet man sein Selbst. Hier sind Freiheit und Freiheitsgefühl zu suchen. Nur die Selbstanschauung hebt über alle Schranken des Einzelnen hinaus. Hier stellt jedes innere Tun das ganze Wesen des Menschen dar. Die Selbstanschauung verweist über sich hinaus auf die Menschheitsanschauung und diese wiederum auf das unermeßliche Gebiet des reinen Geistes.

S. 24-26 (Selbstbetrachtung): Die Selbstbetrachtung alleine ermöglicht es uns, unsterblich und d.h. göttlich zu leben. Erkenntnis und Gefühl sind im Fluß; nur beim Blick ins innere Selbst bin ich im Reich der Ewigkeit. Hier genieße ich das Ewige und lebe so in der höheren Welt.

Schluß. S. 26-30 (Einheit von Leben und Denken): So sollen Leben und Denken Eins sein: äußeres Handeln in der Welt kann sein ein inneres Denken des Handelns. So "stelle Dein Eigentümliches dar und zeichne mit Deinem Geist, was Dich umgibt" (27)! Durch sein bloßes Sein erhält sich der Geist die Welt und durch Freiheit gibt er sich die das Handeln hervorbringende Tätigkeit. So kann man schon hier sein ewiges Leben in steter Selbstbetrachtung beginnen (29).

Offenbar ist die leitende Frage des 1. Monologs: "Wer bin ich?" Die thematische Überschrift: "Reflexion muß als Methode gewertet werden, mit der die Frage: "Wer bin ich?" bearbeitet wird; insofern handelt es sich um eine Selbst- Reflexion. Die so methodisch, d.h. selbstreflexiv gewonnen Antwort lautet: ich bin ein selbstdenkendes Menschenleben. Die Zeitstruktur, in der dieser innere Monolog abläuft, ist die Ewigkeit im Augenblick.

Wir kommen zum zweiten Monolog. Wiederum gebe ich den Inhalt in aller Kürze wieder:

Inhaltsangabe des zweiten Monologs (Prüfungen):

S. 31-33. Einleitung: Selbsterkenntis wird aus Scheu gegenüber der Menschenerkenntnis zurückgestellt. Dabei irrt doch das Selbsturteil nie! Grund der Scheu vor der Selbsterkenntnis: Welt- und Lebensbindung! Den anderen erkenne ich nur aus seinen Taten; aber wie unsicher ist diese Fremderkenntnis verglichen mit der Selbsterkenntnis!

S. 33-35. Hauptteil: Sie − die anderen − sorgen sich um ihr inneres Tun, die Grundlage ihres Lebens. Aber bei ihnen ist der Faden des Menschheitsbewußtseins zu oft zerrissen. Demgegenüber die Menschheit in sich zu betrachten und stets anzuschauen, ist das sicherste Mittel, um den Boden der Menschheit nie zu verlieren. Nur menschliches Handeln erzeugt Menschheitsbewußtsein. Ein einziger, freier Entschluß gehört dazu, um unverlierbar Mensch zu sein.

S. 35-38. In einem hellen Augenblick kam von innen die Offenbarung, durch die ich (sc. Schl.) die Menschheit fand. Seitdem habe ich nie mehr mich selbst verlassen. Das Bewußtsein der Menschheit führe ich ununterbrochen in mir in stiller Ruh, in wechselvoller Einfalt.

Höher über der Menschheit ist ein anderes Ziel: Selbstbildung, höhere Sittlichkeit, Menschennatur; tiefer unter der Menschheit ist die Tierheit. Aber eine gleichmäßige Menschheitsmasse ist für den Menschheitsgedanken nicht genug, weil darin nur die Gleichheit des Einen Daseins als das einzige angebetet wird. Der einzelne Mensch soll dabei überall derselbe sein.

S. 38-39. Der allgemeinen Menschheit ist übergeordnet der individuelle Mensch mit der höheren Bildung und Sittlichkeit und mit der selbsterwählten Menschennatur. Nur der hat den Gedanken des höheren Daseins erfaßt.

S. 39-42. Dies ist meine höchste Anschauung: jeder Mensch soll auf eigene Art die Menschheit darstellen. Nur so offenbart sich die Menschheit auf jede Weise. So wird jeder von der Gottheit zu einem höhere Werk gestaltet und gebildet. Nur spät gelangt der Mensch zum vollen Bewußtsein seiner Eigentümlichkeit. Er hält viel lieber am Gemeinbesitz der Menschheit fest. Aber der Wille muß die Trägheit zähmen, die Übung den Blick schärfen: "ich denke mich in 1000 Bildungen hinein, um desto deutlicher die eigene zu erblicken!"

S. 43-44. Die ruhige Selbstbetrachtung muß sich absichtlich öfter das ganze Tun und Streben und die Geschichte des Selbst vergegenwärtigen. Nur so ist das Selbstverständnis die Brücke zur individuellen Menschheitsgestaltung, zum besseren Leben!

S. 44-46: Zwei Berufe des Menschen gibt es: die individuelle Menschheitsgestaltung oder die äußerliche, künstlerische Menschheitsabbildung. Dies ist die Trennungslinie der verschiedenen Naturen. Man kann nur eins von beiden sein. Schl. ist nicht der Künstlertypus, sondern der Bildungsbeflissene, der nur die Befestigung seiner Bildung zum Ziel hat.

S. 46-49: Schl. erblickt in jedem Kunstwerk nur die darin abgebildete Menschheit. Die freie Muße ist seine Göttin. Da lernt der Mensch sich selbst begreifen, da gründet der Gedanke seine Macht. Doch Schl. vermittelt sich dies über die Gemeinschaft: beim inneren Denken, beim Anschauen, beim

Aneignen des Fremden bedarf er eines geliebten Wesens Gegenwart. So will er sich auf seinem Felde der Bildung vollenden.

S. 49-55: Das Gebiet der Anschauung der Menschheit bewohnen nur die, die sich selbst bilden. So hat Schl. den Sinn geöffnet für alles, was nicht er ist. Hier ist das Gebiet der höchsten Sittlichkeit. Individuelle bewußte Unterscheidung zwischen eigenem Handel und Handeln des Nächsten verletzt den Nächsten nicht. Nur durch Entgegensetzung wird das Eigene erkannt. Die höchste Bedingung der eigenen Vollendung ist allgemeiner Sinn und Liebe. Liebe ist das Erste und Letzte: Keine Bildung ohne Liebe und ohne eigne Bildung keine Vollendung in der Liebe. Eins ergänzt und vollendet das andere.

Schl. ist gesonnen, sich selbst zu bilden und nicht die Wissenschaft. Ist sein "Sinn" beschränkt? Nein, nur: er füllt seinen Sinn gleichförmig und erweitert ihn. Der Streit mit Freunden dient dazu, die eigene Ansicht zu gewinnen.

S. 55-58: Gleichmut und Harmonie sind der Grundton des Wesens Schl.s. Sie erlauben es nicht, alles auf einmal ergreifen zu wollen. Neu Gelerntes muß mit Altem ins Spiel kommen. Selbstbildung und Tätigkeit müssen sich das Gleichgewicht halten.

S. 58-61: Inneres Wertbewußtsein, erhöhtes eigenes Lebensgefühl werden durch die Selbstbetrachtung vermittelt. Was ihn am stärksten bewegt, ist der Trieb zur Selbstoffenbarung. Unbedeutend ist das, was an ihm Welt ist, und aus heiliger Ehrfurcht vor der Freundschaft, aus zarter Sorgfalt hält er sich zurück, "das mitzuteilen, was er selbst noch nicht versteht".

"Wie mich selbst lieb ich den Freund, sobald ich etwas für mich erkenne, geb ich's hin." "Es ist das helle Bewußtsein des Gegensatzes zwischen Welt und Mensch der Grund, worauf die Achtung gegen mich und das Gefühl der Freiheit ruht".

S. 61-64: Liebe und Freundschaft sind der Freiheit reinste Tat und auf das eigene Sein des Menschen gerichtet. Sein eigentümliches Sein sucht er, und dessen Verhältnis zur Menschheit versteht er; dementsprechend hat er auch Liebe für ihn.

S. 64-66: Schluß: Wer sich selbst bildet, hat verschiedene Elemente der Menschheit in sich, gehört mehr als nur einer Welt an: der Gebildete verbindet verschiedene Weltsysteme. Nur die Freundschaft, das Ideal, ist gleich vollendet nach beiden Seiten: nach Sinn und nach Liebe.

Die leitende Frage des zweiten Monologs scheint zweifach zu sein. Einmal: "Was soll ich tun?" Zum andern: "Was soll ich sein?" Beide Fragen werden dem Monolog – Thema "Prüfungen" überantwortet. Auch dieses Thema erweist sich wieder als die Methode der Bearbeitung der Fragen, wobei die Prüfungen in hohem Maße Selbstprüfungen sind. Auf die zuerst gestellt Frage antwortet Schleiermacher: "Bildung des Geistes mit Sinn und Liebe"; die zweite Frage wird so beantwortet: Ich soll sein: eine individuelle oder künstlerische Darstellung der Menschheit. Die Zeitstruktur dieser "Prüfungen" verläuft in der Vergangenheit und im Augenblick.

Der Analyse des dritten Monolgs schicken wir zunächst den Inhalt des dritten Monologs voraus:

Inhaltsangabe über den dritten Monolog: Weltansicht:

Einleitung: Das Verhältnis Alter-Jugend ist mit dem Verhältnis Klage-Lachen falsch bestimmt. Auch die Mitte beider (Ruhe) spiegelt nicht das wahre Weltverhältnis wider. Wer sich in der Jugend nicht selbst geschmeichelt, wer wenig tat, um die Welt zu bilden, der schmeichelt auch der Welt nicht. Was soll auch Weltverbesserung, wo die eigene Bildung fehlt, wo nichts in Freiheit atmet, wo man zu wenig von der menschlichen Natur weiß, diesem "dunklen Nachtstück, und wo die Eigensucht

eben noch kein geselliges Haustier" ist. Zudem: das wahre
Ziel der Menschheit liegt noch in unbekannter Ferne!

**S. 70-74: Hauptteil (Das falsche Verhältnis Körper-Geist.
Dementsprechende Tugend, Gerechtigkeit und Liebe!):** Die
Herrschaft über die Körperwelt darf dem Menschen nicht
genügen. So sehr ist der Mensch Herr der Erde, daß der
Begriff der Unmöglichkeit sich immer mehr verengt. Über den
ganzen Erdkreis fördert sich das Werk der Menschen
gegenseitig. So erscheint die Gemeinschaft als kunstreiche
Kooperationsmaschine zur Beherrschung der Erde. –
Lebendiger wohnt das Gefühl des gemeinsam erhöhten Lebens
in jenen, die nicht das gleiche Maß des Lebens verbreiten, die
dem Geiste mehr als dem Leibe dienen. Sorge für das eigene
körperliche Wohlbefinden oder Sorge für das gleiche
Wohlbefinden für alle können nicht als Tugend, Gerechtigkeit
und Liebe hinausgeschrien werden.

S. 74-79 (Die Seele und die gegenwärtige Welt): Die
Gemeinschaft mit solcher Welt wird die Seele immer nur als
Beschränkung erfahren. Sklavendasein ist das Schicksal der
Besseren, die nie bei den unbekannten Freunden sein können,
und die in ihnen fremder Nähe bei schlechtem Dienst ihr
inneres Leben verschmachten müssen. Es kränkelt in sich
gekehrt die Fantasie, es muß in träumerischem Irrtum der
Geist sich verzehren. Allein muß jeder stehen; der Darstellung
der Menschheit, dem Bilden schöner Werke fehlt die
Gemeinschaft der Talente! Für den kommt die Menschheit
ihrem Ziele nicht näher, der mit blöder Fantasie nur an dem
Wirklichen und dessen nächsten Folgen haftet. Das aber ist
nicht erlaubte Beschränkung der Zukunft!

S. 79-84 (Die bessere Welt): Frei sollte jeder <u>Freund</u> den anderen
Freund gewähren lassen, wozu ihn der Geist treibt. So fände
jeder in jedem Nahrung und Leben, und was er werden könnte,
würde er ganz.

Die <u>Liebe</u> bindet Mann und Frau. "Wie eigene Wesen aus ihrer Liebe Schoß hervorgehen, so soll aus ihrer Naturen Harmonie ein neuer gemeinschaftlicher Wille sich erzeugen". Das stille Haus soll als freie Tat sein Dasein bekunden. "Macht beide nichts so glücklich, als wo einer dem anderen sich aufopfern kann?" Der <u>Staat</u> ist der höchste Grad des Daseins des Menschen. Jeder Mensch ist ein Teil von seiner (sc. des Staates) Vernunft, Fantasie und Stärke. Jeder liebt dieses selbstgeschaffene Dasein. Jeder paßt auf, daß dem Staat keine Verführung naht. Jeder Staat verkündigt sich durch einen eignen Charakter. Der Staat ist das schönste Kunstwerk des Menschen, wodurch er sein Wesen auf die höchste Stufe stellt. Der Staat ist kein Maschinenwerk, um die Gebrechen der Menschen zu verbergen und unschädlich zu machen.

S. 84-86: (Zukunftsaussichten von wahrer Freundschaft, Ehe, Staat): Vermehrten, äußern Besitz des Habens und des Wissens, Schutz und Hilfe gegen Schicksal und Unglück: das nur suchet der Mensch von Heute in Freundschaft, Ehe und Vaterland, nicht jedoch Hilfe und Ergänzung der Kraft zur eigenen Bildung und Gewinn an innerem Leben. Sittlichkeit und Bildung <u>mit</u> der Welt; Leben und freies Handeln; dieser besseren Zukunft sichere Ahndung vermittelt die göttliche Fantasie.

S. 87-88: Bildung und Leben sind die Elemente des besseren Lebens. Aber jetzt bewegen wir uns ja noch in den Kinderjahren der Menschheit. Gleichwohl wird das erhabene Reich der Bildung und Sittlichkeit kommen.

S. 89-91: Schleiermacher ist der Denkart und dem Leben des jetzigen Geschlechts ein Fremdling. Dieser späteren Welt gehört jeder Gedanke und jede Tat. Es nahet sich in Lieb und Hoffnung ein jeder, der wie Schleiermacher der Zukunft angehört. So erweitert sich das freie Bündnis der Verschworenen für die bessere Zeit.

S. 91-92 (Geist-Welt Mißdeutung): Die aus den heiligsten Ideen entspringende Tat ist Mißdeutungen in Richtung auf ein Handeln aus dem Sinn der Welt ausgesetzt. Gleichwohl soll jede Handlung den Stempel des Geistes tragen.

S. 91-94 (Sprache): Die Sprache ist der reinste Spiegel der Zeit, ein Kunstwerk, worin ihr Geist sich zu erkennen gibt. Die Sprache soll ein gemeinsames Gut für die Söhne des Geistes und für die Kinder der Welt sein.

S. 94-97 (Sitte): Sitte und Individualität sollen einander angepaßt sein. (Sitte = Gewand der Individualität). Auch die Sprache sei das Gewand des individuellen Geistes.

S. 97-98 (Zusammenfassung zu Sitte und Sprache): Harmonisch in schöner Sitte und Sprache lebt nur der sich selbst Bildende.

S. 98: Schluß: Aus diesem Gefühle stiller Allmacht muß endlich die Ehrfurcht vor dem Höchsten hervorgehen: vor der Menschheit!

Wiederum gehen wir als Erstes auf die leitende Frage ein. Sie lautet: Wofür lebe ich? Das Thema des dritten Monologs "Weltansicht" gibt darauf die methodische Antwort: für die bessere Welt. Damit ist das Reich der Selbstbildung und der Sittlichkeit gemeint. Sitte und Sprache sind dabei die vermittelnden Vorarbeiter auf die bessere Welt hin. Die Zeitstruktur dieser Weltansichts- Untersuchung ist Vergangenheit und Gegenwart.

Der vierte Monolog sticht in seinem Umfang gegenüber den anderen hervor. Wir geben den wesentlichen Inhalt wieder:

Inhaltsangabe und Gliederung des IV. Monologs.

S. 100-102 (Schicksal?): Wandeln wir nur abhängig von dunkler Zukunft oder blinder Schicksalsmacht? Nein!
Wenn Entschlüsse nur Wünsche sind, so ist der Mensch des Zufalls Spiel. Dann, wenn der Mensch nur im Wechsel flüchtiger Empfindungen und einzelner Gedanken, die die Wirklichkeit erzeugt, sich selbst zu finden weiß. Nur dann,

wenn er nicht tiefer in sein Wesen eindringt. Nur dann, wenn er von Augenblicksempfindungen geleitet ist. Nur dann erscheint ihm als ein dichter Schleier die eigene Blindheit, wenn das Licht der Freiheit nicht scheint. Nur dann fragt man danach, ob dieser Wechsel sich dem Willen Gottes oder dem Synchronismus verschiedener Kräfte verdankt. Schrecklich muß es den Menschen ergreifen, der nie dazu gelangt, sich selbst zu fassen. Denn nur dann ist er ein unfreies Wesen und fühlt sich als Zahn im großen Rade, das sich, ihn und alles bewegt. Nur dann kann er wider alle Erfahrung zum Trotz auf höheres Erbarmen hoffen.

S. 102-106 (Freiheit!): O geliebtes Bewußtsein der Freiheit! Durch sie ist die Zukunft mein Eigentum! Dem Schicksal unterliegen nur die Götter und die Sterblichen, die nichts in sich wirken wollen. Wer sein Handeln auf sich selbst richtet, kennt kein Schicksal. Es gibt keine Grenze für seine Kraft. Unmöglichkeit liegt nur in der Beschränkung meiner Natur durch die erste Tat meiner Freiheit, als ich bestimmte, was ich werden wollte, und dadurch anderes von mir ausschloß. So lebe ich im Bewußtsein meiner ganzen Natur. Mein einziger Wille ist, immer mehr zu werden, was ich bin. "So lang ich alles auf diesen ganzen Zweck beziehe, . . . so lange des Geistes Auge auf dieses Ganze allgegenwärtig gerichtet ist, . . . solange beherrscht mein Wille das Geschick, und wendet alles, was es bringen mag, zu seinen Zwecken mit Freiheit an". Beim Denken eines solchen Willens verschwindet der Begriff des Schicksals. "Es komme die Zeit und bringe, wie sie kann, zum Handeln, zum Bilden und zum Äußern meines Wesens mir mannigfachen Stoff" (106). Was aus der übrigen Menschen gemeinschaftlichem Handeln hervorgeht, will ich in der Art behandeln, daß ich meine Freiheit finde und meine Eigentümlichkeit äußere und bilde.

S. 106-107 (Freiheitsgefühl, bewährt durch Freiheitstat!): Dies Freiheitsgefühl ist kein Ohnmachtsgefühl; wer solches urteilt,

wird in jedem Augenblick durch die Tat gerichtet. Was andere
als äußere Gewalt bejammern, war doch nur innere Trägheit!
Nichts konnte Bildung in Vergangenheit hindern! Seitdem die
Vernunft sich meines Wesens bemächtigt hat und Freiheit und
Selbstbewußtsein in mir wohnen, bin ich die wechselreichen
Bahnen des Lebens durchwandert. Ich habe die große Tat
vollbracht, das lange mühsame Werk der frevelnden Erziehung
als falsche Maske wegzuwerfen. "Im fremden Hause ging der
Sinn mir auf für schönes, gemeinschaftliches Dasein. Freiheit
erst veredelt die zarten Geheimnisse der Menschheit, die
dadurch mehr sind als nur Bande der Natur." Ich habe die
innere Natur betrachtet, alle Zwecke, die der Menschheit
durch ihr Wesen aufgegeben sind, und alle Verrichtungen des
Geistes in ihrer ewigen Einheit angeschaut. "Alles, was mich
betraf, hat mir dazu gedient, meinem Wesen Neues
anzueignen und Kraft zu gewinnen, die das innere Leben
nährt!

S. 110-114 (**Die Zukunft meiner Welt liegt in meinem Wesen!**):
Die Vergangenheit sei Bürge für die Zukunft, denn sie ist ja
dasselbe dadurch, daß ich derselbe bin. Ich weiß, worin meine
Individualität besteht. "Durch gleichförmiges Handeln nach
allen Seiten mit der ganzen Einheit und Fülle meiner Kraft
werde ich mir dies erhalten. Leid und Freud erfüllen gleichviel
den Zweck, weil sie meines Wesens Verhältnisse offenbaren.
Ich kenne die Stellen, wo ich den Mangel eigener Ansicht
schmerzlich fühle, Wissenschaften sind noch zu ergründen,
Gestalten der Menschheit, Zeitalter und Völker sind mir noch
fremd. Die schönste Aussicht darauf breitet sich vor mir aus.
Kenntnisreiche Menschen verpflanzen die Gewächse ferner
Zeiten und Zonen in unser Vaterland. Diesem Ziele nähere
ich mich. Ich trotze dem Schicksal, das Tausende gebeugt,
denn nur durch Selbstverkauf gerät der Mensch in Sklaverei.
Nichts lockt mich von dem Orte weg, wo meinem Geiste wohl
ist: mit Fleiß habe ich ihn mir errungen, mit Bewußtsein habe

ich mir die eigne Welt gebildet, in der mein Geist gedeihen kann.

S. 114-118 (Die neue Welt des höheren Lebens): Ich sehne mich nach einer neuen Welt. Die heiligste Verbindung muß mich auf eine neue Stufe des Lebens heben. Auf die schönste Weise will meine Menschheit auf die Menschheit wirken. Ich will wissen, wie das verklärte, höhere Leben nach der Auferstehung der Freiheit sich in mir bildet, wie der alte Mensch die neue Welt beginnt. Ich will als Vater zeigen, wie, wer an Freiheit glaubt, die junge Vernunft bewahrt. – Oder wird mich hier nicht beim liebsten Wunsch des Herzens das Schicksal ergreifen? Wo wohnt die, mit der das Band des Lebens zu knüpfen mir ziemt? (115) Hier steh ich an der Grenze meiner Willkür durch fremde Freiheit, durch den Lauf der Welt, durch die Mysterien der Natur (116). Käme es nicht zustande, so würde ich die Welt bedauern, die wohl ein schönes und seltenes Beispiel dann verlöre. Aber: uns trägt auch unbekannt die Phantasie ins schöne Paradies. So kenne ich die Unbekannte, "und in dem Leben, das wir führen würden, bin ich eingewohnt!" (117) Würde ein Zauberschlag uns glücklich zusammenführen, nichts würde uns fremd sein. Anmutig und leicht würden wir in der neuen Lebensweise wandeln. Nur die äußere Darstellung entgeht der Welt.

S. 119-123 (Die Götterkraft der Phantasie): Die Phantasie trägt über jede Gewalt und Beschränkung hinaus. Der Mensch bleibt ungebildet, der nur auf Anstöße von außen wartet. Das wäre falsche Selbstbeschränkung. Demgegenüber ersetzt das innere Spiel der Phantasie, was der Wirklichkeit fehlt. Kraft des inneren Handelns nehme ich von der ganzen Welt Besitz. Das äußere Leben bringt dazu nur die Bestätigung und Probe. "Über des Schicksals Trägheit klage ich nicht mehr als über seinen schnellen und krümmungsvollen Verlauf". So lebe ich jetzt schon auf dem tatenreichen Schauplatz der Welt; jetzt schon in der Ehegemeinschaft.

S. 123-125 (Wider die falsche Liebe): Mir ist nicht schöne Gestalt verliehen. Nur was ich selbst hervorgebracht und immer wieder erwerbe, ist für mich Besitz. Die sind mir sicher, die mein inneres Wesen lieben wollen. Nur sie haben mich erkannt.

S. 125-127 (Wahre Liebe): Ich habe noch keinen verloren, der mir je in Liebe teuer ward. Diese Liebe überbrückt den Tod, den Raum, die Zeit in Richtung auf die Gemeinschaft freier Geister. Was ist denn Tod anderes als größere Entfernung? Wo solche Gemeinschaft ist, da ist mein Paradies!

S. 127-130 (Der Zusammenhang von Leben und Tod durch die Freiheit): Das Leben der Freundschaft ist eine schöne Folge von Akkorden. Stirbt der Freund, so stirbt der gemeinschaftliche Grundton ab. Zweifach ist des Menschen notwendiges Ende: Einmal muß der vergehen, dem das Gleichgewicht zwischen innerem und äußerem Leben zerstört ist. Zum anderen muß der vergehen, der nichts mehr in sich zu handeln hätte, der vollendet wäre. Also ist der Tod notwendig! Man muß es also zu einem Werk der Freiheit machen, sich dieser Notwendigkeit zu nähern. So wird aus dem Sterben-Müssen das Sterben- Wollen- Können. In einem Werk der Kunst will ich den Gedanken von meinem Wesen, und die Ansicht, die die Menschheit mir gab, zurücklassen. Ich werde ihn unreif aus meinem Inneren lösen, sonst würde mein Wesen vergehen, wenn dieser Gedanke vollendet wäre.

Als leitende Frage für diesen Monolog läßt sich die Frage ausmachen: Was bestimmt mich? Entsprechend dem Thema des Monologs: "Aussichten" fällt die Antwort auf diese Frage aus: nicht Schicksal noch Zukunft bestimmen mich, sondern mein Freiheitswille und die Phantasie an den Grenzen der Freiheit. Die Zeit, in der die Aussichtsthematik behandelt wird, ist die Vergangenheit und die Zukunft. Dem fünften Monolog schicken wir, – wie auch bei den anderen Monologen vorgehend, zunächst seinen Inhalt voraus:

V. Monolog. Jugend und Alter.

S. 131-132 (Verhältnis Jugend – Alter – Tod): Mit der Summe der gelebten Jahre und Stunden lebe ich immer näher dem Tode entgegen. Auch dem Alter? Nein, denn mag auch die Lust der frohen Jugend, mag auch die innere Gesundheit und mag auch endlich das übermütige Gefühl der Fülle schwinden, so können doch dem Geist die engeren Grenzen nicht genügen, leiser und bedächtiger einherzugehen. Man kann nur Reue empfinden über ein so verkümmertes, nüchternes Leben. Und in der Tat: auf den ersten Ruf kehrt ja auch die freundliche Jugend zurück! Lieber den Freitod wählen, als aus Furcht vor dem sicheren Übel sich jegliches Gute bitter vergellen lassen!

S. 132-135 (Der Wille, das Fundament der ewigen Jugend!): Das Leben des Geistes als freies und ungemessenes verrinnt nicht wie das irdische Leben. Durch des Willens Kraft wird die ewige Jugend festgehalten. Des Geistes Kraft nützt sich nicht ab durch die Tat, im Gegenteil! Es wird nicht jener alt, der mit dem Leben in der Jugend geizt; vielmehr ist jener zu verachten.

S. 135-136 (Der Geist wird stärker durch die Tat!): Nichts kann die Gewalt des Geistes brechen, wenn der Geist handelt und sich mitteilt. "Klarer und reicher fühl ich mich jetzt nach jedem Handeln, stärker und gesünder: denn bei jeder Tat eigne ich etwas mir an von dem gemeinschaftlichen Nahrungsstoff der Menschheit. Wachsend bestimmt sich so genauer meine Gestalt."

S. 136-139 (Das Verhältnis Geist-Körper wird vom Geist bestimmt!): Man ist es selbst schuld, wenn Mut und Kraft schwinden, denn der Geist hängt nicht vom Körper ab. Andere haben besseren Leib und schärfere Sinne. "Daß ich trauern soll über des Leibes Verfall, wäre mein Letztes!" Das

Bewußtsein der großen heiligen Gedanken hängt nicht vom
Körper ab. Der Sinn für die wahre Welt hängt nicht von der
äußeren Glieder Gebrauch ab. Für die Menschheitsanschauung brauche ich nicht das Auge. Hängt der Mut am
Gefühl der Gesundheit? Doch wohl nicht! Die Schmerzen
drücken den Geist nicht nieder, ihnen widerstehen ist ja sein
Handeln!

S. 139 (Selbst-Eid): Der frische Lebensmut soll mir nie vergehen!
Das Feuer der Liebe soll mir nie verlöschen! Ewige Jugend
schwöre ich bei mir selbst!

S. 139-142 (Blüte wie Reife in Jugend wie Alter!): Ist das Alter
nur Schwäche? Oder soll die Reife des Alters gepriesen
werden? Nein, schon in der südlichen Sonne gibt es Blüte
neben Frucht. So aber soll's beim Geist sein wie bei der
Natur! Weil es kann, soll es das auch!

S. 142-148 (Alter vermählt sich mit der Jugend bis zur Bildung
und Vollkommenheit): Weisheit und reife Erfahrung: "Ich
fühle, wie ich sie jetzt erwerbe, es ist das Treiben der Jugend
und das frische Leben des Geistes, das sie hervorbringt!" Nie
soll der Geist von mir weichen, der den Menschen vorwärts
treibt! Das ist des Menschen Ruhm zu wissen, daß das Ziel
unendlich ist. Auf seinem Wege kommt eine Stelle, die ihn
verschlingt. Der Jugend Kraft soll mir bis zum Ende bleiben.
Bis zum Ende will ich stärker werden und lebendiger im
Handeln. Die Jugend will ich mit dem Alter vermählen.
Doppelt sei die Vermählung: Das Leben verträgt nicht die
Trennung der Elemente Jugend-Alter. "Ein doppeltes
Handeln des Geistes soll es sein, vereint zu jeder Zeit; und das
ist die Bildung und die Vollkommenheit."

S. 148-150 (Jugend und Lebensfrucht): Für die Pflanze ist das
Höchste die Blüte. So ist auch für den Menschen das muntere
Leben der Jugend das Höchste. Ordne dir das Leben einmal
für immer: Was du der Welt bietest, das sei Frucht! Opfere
nicht den kleinsten Teil deines Wesens in falscher Großmut!

Was nicht für dich selbst ist Wachstum oder Bildung neuer
Organe, das sei wahre Frucht!

S. 150-151 (Jugend und Geistestätigkeit): Im Augenblick soll eine
Frucht reifen, wie eine Blüte sich entfaltet in der Nacht!
Damit die Jugend mir nicht entfliehe, will ich sie nicht
mißbrauchen. Im Reich des Geistes soll sie walten in
ungestörter Freiheit. Kein Gesetz soll mir das Leben
beschränken!

**S. 151-154 (Handeln, Werden, Leben, Lieben trage der Jugend
Farbe!):** Alles Handeln trage der Jugend Farbe! Werd' immer
nichts als Du! Wolle ja nicht mäßig sein im Handeln! Nur die
ungebrauchte Kraft geht verloren. Laß Dir nicht gebieten von
der Welt. Laß Dir keine Grenzen setzen in deiner Liebe; ist sie
doch dein Eigentum. Schäme Dich der falschen Scham!

S. 154-155 (Schluß): Frei und froh ist mein inneres Leben. Dem
Bewußtsein der inneren Freiheit entsprießt ewige Jugend und
Freude. Frisch bleibt der Puls des inneren Lebens bis an den
Tod.

Die leitende Frage dieses Monologs lautet: "Wohin gehe ich?"
Entsprechend dem Thema des 5. Monologs: "Jugend und Alter" fällt denn
auch die Antwort auf die leitende Frage aus: Ich gehe mit wachsenden
Geisteskräften und Tugenden der ewigen Jugend entgegen. Die Zeitform, in
der dieser Monolog argumentiert, ist die Gegenwart und der Augenblick.

Die Brücke zwischen den fünf Monologen ist der Mensch in seiner
Identität. Schleiermacher formuliert diese Identität des Menschen mit sich
selbst im 4. Monolog wie folgt: ich bin derselbe in der Zukunft wie in der
Vergangenheit. Diese Identität ist genau genommen ein Identifizierungs-
wille: der Mensch will in der Zukunft derselbe bleiben, der er schon in der
Vergangenheit gewesen war[2]. Der 4. Monolog bringt dies auf den Satz:
"Immer mehr zu werden was ich bin, das ist mein einziger Wille"[3]. Am
prägnantesten artikuliert sich dieser Zusammenhang von Identitäts-
bewußtsein des Subjektes und Zeit an folgender Stelle: "So sei denn die

Vergangenheit mir Bürge der Zukunft, sie ist ja dasselbe, was kann sie mir anders thun, wenn ich derselbe bin?"[4]

Nachdem wir so inhaltlich wiedergegeben haben, was ein Monolog ist, bringen wir das nochmals kurz auf den Begriff in Form dreier Antworten:

Erste Antwort: Ein Monolog ist ein wortwerdendes Selbstverhältnis. Dadurch konstituiert das Subjekt seine Kontinuität im inneren Handeln der Freiheit.

Zweite Antwort: Ein Monolog ist ein menschwerdendes Selbstgespräch. Dadurch wird der Mensch immer mehr das, was an Menschheit in ihm angelegt ist.

Dritte Antwort: Ein Monolog ist ein "für- sich- allein- Reden". Dies geschieht unter Beachtung der individuellen Sprachschöpfung des 3. Monologs, eine Sprachschöpfung, die die neue bessere Welt über die Sprache heraufführen hilft, an der auch die Sprachgenossen der alten Welt kommunizieren. Die dritte Antwort rekurriert vornehmlich auf den dritten Monolog. Eine Zeichung verdeutlicht diesen Vorgang wie folgt:

Wir fassen unsere Analysen nochmals in einer Übersicht zusammen:

Proprium und Zusammenhang der Monologen I-V

	Leitende Frage	Thema	Antwort	Zeitstruktur
I.	Wer bin ich?	Reflexion	ein selbstdenkendes Menschenleben	Ewigkeit im Augenblick (=Augenblick)
II.	Was soll ich tun? Was soll ich sein?	Prüfungen	Bildung des Geistes mit Sinn und Liebe. Individuelle oder künstlerische Darstellung der Menschheit.	Vergangenheit und Augenblick
III.	Wofür lebe ich?	Weltansicht	Für die bessere Welt – das Reich der Selbstbildung und der Sittlichkeit. Sitte und Sprache sind vermittelnde Vorarbeiter auf die bessere Welt hin.	Vergangenheit und Gegenwart.
IV.	Was bestimmt mich?	Aussicht	Nicht Schicksal noch Zukunft, sondern Freiheitswille und Phantasie (an den Grenzen der Freiheit)	Vergangenheit und Zukunft
V.	Wohin gehe ich?	Jugend und Alter	Mit wachsenden Geisteskräften und Tugenden der ewigen Jugend entgegen.	Gegenwart und Augenblick

Brücke zwischen den Zeiten: die Identität des Menschen mit sich selbst (Schleiermacher: ich bin derselbe in der Zukunft wie in der Vergangenheit).

Drei mögliche Antworten auf die Frage: Was ist bei Schleiermacher ein Monolog?

1. ein wortwerdendes Selbstverhältnis
2. ein menschwerdendes Selbstgespräch
3. für-sich-allein-reden (unter Beachtung der individuellen Sprachschöpfung des III. Monologs, die die neue bessere Welt heraufführen hilft über die Sprache, an der auch die Sprachgenossen der alten Welt kommunizieren)

Nachdem die Sprachtheorie schon entfaltet worden ist, bleibt uns nun noch die eingangs gestellte Aufgabe, das Freiheitsverständnis zu erhellen und die Theorie der "ewigen Jugend" zu entfalten. Im I. Monolog bezeichnet Schleiermacher die Freiheit als ein "heiliges Gebiet der Freiheit" (12), als einen Boden der Freiheit (14). Das Gebiet umfaßt das innere Handeln des Menschen (14), genauer: jegliches Gefühl ist ein freies Tun (17). Insofern wohnt Freiheit in allen (17); und im äußern Tun ist Freiheit nicht zu finden (22). So ist die Freiheit das Erste und Ursprünglichste und Innerste (19). Beim Anblick der Freiheit geht das Licht der Gottheit auf (19). Mich selbst kann ich nur als Freiheit anschauen (18); Notwendigkeit ist der schöne Ton vom Zusammenstoß der Freiheit (18). Durch Freiheit gibt sich der Geist die Tätigkeit (28).

Um ein Mensch zu werden, bedarf es eines einzigen freien Entschlusses (35), so formuliert Schleiermacher im II. Monolog, "wer den einmal gefaßt, wird's immer bleiben" (35). Durch das Bewußtsein der Freiheit wird die Zukunft zum eigenen freien Eigentum (102). Was sie ist und bringt, unterliegt der Tat der Freiheit. Unmöglichkeit liegt nur in dem, was durch die erste Tat ausgeschlossen wurde (103). Dabei ist der Wille als ein Herrscher über das Geschick gedacht; alles, was das Geschick bringt, wendet der Wille zu seinem Zweck mit Freiheit an (105). Die eigene Freiheit finden, heißt aber, der Aufgabe nachgehen, die eigene

Eigentümlichkeit zu bilden (106). So bildet sich in jedem das verklärte höhere Leben nach der Auferstehung der Freiheit (115). Die Grenze der eigenen Willkür ist gesetzt durch fremde Freiheit, durch den Lauf der Welt und durch die Mysterien der Natur (116). Hier kommt die Notwendigkeit des Todes in den Blick, doch auch dieser Notwendigkeit ist mit Freiheit zu begegnen: "Notwendig also ist der Tod, und dieser Notwendigkeit mich näher zu bringen, sei der Freiheit Werk, und sterben wollen können mein höchstes Ziel" (129).

Überblickt man das weite Feld der Aussagen zur Freiheit, so ist als Kern des Freiheitsverständnisses die Freiheit zur Bildung eines eigentümlichen Menschseins zu entdecken mit der Spitze der Vollendung der Individualität im Tod.

Nun noch einige Beobachtungen zur "ewigen Jugend", die unmittelbar mit dem Freiheitsverständnis zusammenhängt: Die schönste Frucht der Freiheit ist die ewige Jugend (140). Es ziemt dem Menschen, in der sorglosen Heiterkeit der Jugend zu wandeln (145). Der wird nicht alt, der sich noch nicht fertig weiß, der weiß, was er will und was er soll (145). Durch jedes Handeln wird der Mensch stärker und lebendiger, denn dieses Handeln ist Bilden an sich selbst (146). So gesellt sich zur Jugend das Alter: "Jetzt schon sei im starken Gemüte des Alters Kraft, daß sie dir erhalte die Jugend, damit später die Jugend dich schütze gegen des Alters Schwäche" (117). Das Leben verträgt nicht die Trennung von Jugend und Alter (147). Die Früchte der Reife des Alters soll schon die Jugend hervorbringen (148). So setzt die Blüte des Lebens aus freiem Willen eine Frucht an (148), sie ist aus der inneren Liebe des Geistes gezeugt (148). So trägt alles Handeln in mir und auf mich als ewiges Werden ewig der Jugend Farbe (151), so entsprießt der inneren Freiheit und ihrem Handeln ewige Jugend und Freude (154).

Damit setzt Schleiermacher im inneren Leben ein Übergewicht gegen alles äußere Leben an, und er kann ausrufen: "So frei und fröhlich bewegt sich mein inneres Leben." (154).

Abschließend läßt sich die Theorie der "ewigen Jugend" als eine Bildungs- und Alternstheorie bezeichnen. Gegenüber der heute häufig verwendeten Disengagemant- Theorie mit ihren Implikaten: Nachlassen der intellektuellen Kraft, Nachlassen der körperlichen Kraft, Rückgang der

Vitalität insgesamt,- darf sie als Aktivitätstheorie charakterisiert werden: Dem Bewußtsein innerer Freiheit und ihres Handelns entsprießt ewige Jugend und Freude. Dadurch werden auch das Sterben und der Tod zu einem Werk der Freiheit, denn indem ich meine Individualität immer stärker ausbilde, bringe ich mich dem Tode immer näher. Und was ist der Tod? Schleiermacher fragt zurück: "Aber Tod? Was ist denn Tod, als größere Entfernung?" (127)

Weil aber Jugend und Alter nicht getrennt werden dürfen, muß auch das Handeln des Geistes ein doppeltes sein: Bildung und Vollkommenheit, und wenn man so den Tod betrachtet, ist er die höchste Bildung und Vollendung der Individualität (147).

Anmerkungen

1. Friedrich Schleiermacher, Kleine Schriften und Predigten. 1800-1820. Bearbeitet von Hayo Gerdes. Berlin 1970. Der Text der Monologen von 1800 findet sich S. 21-75 = 1. Ausgabe S. 3-155. Unsere Seitenangaben beziehen sich, -analog zum üblichen Vorgehen bei den "Reden"-zitationen- auf die Seiten der 1. Ausgabe. Bloße Zahlen geben diese Seitenzahl wieder.
2. Monologen, S. 110.
3. Monologen, S. 104.
4. Monologen, S. 110.

IV

SCHLEIERMACHER'S 1800 "VERSUCH ÜBER DIE SCHAAMHAFTIGKEIT": A CONTRIBUTION TOWARD A TRULY HUMAN ETHIC

Ruth Drucilla Richardson

Introductory Remarks

This paper will investigate an essay entitled "Versuch über die Schaamhaftigkeit" which Schleiermacher inserted into the middle of his anonymous 1800 book *Vertraute Briefe über Friedrich Schlegels Lucinde* (Lübeck/Leipzig: Friedrich Bohn) [*Confidential Letters on Friedrich Schlegel's "Lucinde"*].[1] This largely unexplored essay will be examined in relation to the discussion of the term *Schaamhaftigkeit* in the writings of Rousseau, Kant, Campe, Hippel, and Fichte.[2]

In his essay, Schleiermacher enters into the discussion of the term *Schaamhaftigkeit* [shamefacedness, sense of shame] and exposes the dangers of the one-sided ethical systems of those thinkers who have defined *Schaamhaftigkeit* as an a priori ontological quality that is gender specific to women alone and which, either implicitly or explicitly, stands juxtaposed to the "reason" [*Verstand; raisonnement*] of men. Through their definitions, *Schaamhaftigkeit* qua unreason is employed as a concept that prevents women's access into the educational and political spheres. Schleiermacher's redefinition of *Schaamhaftigkeit* as a "human" quality has the effect of removing the most significant roadblock in women's path to increased participation in larger spheres of activity.

This essay was both relevant then and is still relevant today because of the anthropological starting point Schleiermacher used in his ethical analysis. In place of an anthropology that sets women and men apart as ontologically distinct, Schleiermacher's opening analysis focuses on male and female common traits. In the creed to his 1798 "Outline of a Reasonable Catechism for Noble Women" he had called this common trait "infinite humanity" [*unendliche Menschheit*]. This starting point, "infinite humanity," is the only truly ethical one for, both formally and teleologically, it contains a higher point of judgment within itself. Therefore, I hope, first, to contribute to a better understanding of the ethics of the "early Schleiermacher" through the contextual and historical explication of his use of the term *Schaamhaftigkeit*. Second, I hope to suggest that Schleiermacher has left us with the only viable ethical anthropological starting point that should be applied in contemporary theological and ethical systems.

Schleiermacher's 1800 *Vertraute Briefe* was written to help explain certain themes (that were then seen as offensive) found in his friend Friedrich Schlegel's 1799 novel *Lucinde*.[3] In *Lucinde*, a new literary theory known as "universal poetry" and the new Romantic doctrines of friendship, love, marriage, and the relation between the sexes were put forth. Schlegel believes that the love between a man and woman is the most important force in human life, because only through it can the religious secrets of the universe be illumined and mediated. Love is to be composed both of the spiritual and the sensual. Love no longer is to be seen as a merely spiritual moment, as was the case in the eighteenth century as typified in Jacobi's *Woldemar*.[4] Love is, in short, to reflect both sides of the universe, both *Geist* and *Natur*.

It is in relation to Schlegel's discussion of love that women's roles receive a new definition. "*Menschheit*," which women impart to men in a love relationship, rather than "*Weiblichkeit*" or "*Männlichkeit*," becomes the goal of human life and the path to the infinite. Women are to strive to take on the attributes of men, their activity, their capacity for philosophy. Further, women no longer are to be relegated to the sphere of the household but are to accompany men in all moments and tasks in life. Women are not to be just the daughters, wives, and mothers of men. Instead, they are to be their friends. In addition, women no longer are to be fearful of the sensual but rather are to incorporate it into their beings and lives in a healthy manner. Indeed, it is over against the "prudes" whom Schlegel criticizes as having corrupted the sensual within them that he presents the the two-year-old Wilhelmine (who kicks up her skirts in the sheer enjoyment of life) as a model of one who has expressed both sides of the universe, both the spiritual and the sensual, in a natural, healthy, and completely innocent way.[5]

When *Lucinde* failed not only to gain the high praise that Schlegel had expected but also made him either into the laughing stock of the literary world or an immoral beast in the eyes of others, he asked his friend Schleiermacher to step in to defend his work. This Schleiermacher agreed to do, anonymously publishing his *Vertraute Briefe über Friedrich Schlegels Lucinde* in 1800. The *Vertraute Briefe* are cast in the form of an epistolary novel. In it two men and three women correspond with one another in nine letters, providing what Schleiermacher calls "variations on the main theme in Lucinde."[6] Each of the letters, in which we learn what Schleiermacher's own opinions really are, represents an exploration of some aspect of *Lucinde*. These themes include among others: the literary form in which *Lucinde* was cast, love, marriage, and the possibility of friendship between men and women.

Cast awkwardly within the middle of the nine letters is an essay entitled "Versuch über die Schaamhaftigkeit." This essay on *Schaamhaftigkeit* takes up twenty-four pages of the original 152 page book and is written in a cumbersome, tedious, and difficult tone that contrasts sharply with the lighter, conversational style of the letters.[7] Like Schlegel's essay "Apprenticeship for Manhood,"[8] which was inserted into the center of *Lucinde* and held the most significant position casting luminous meaning over the whole, Schleiermacher's insertion of the essay on *Schaamhaftigkeit* in a prominent position indicates his own estimation of its prime importance to the issues at stake.

At first sight this essay appears to be out of place in Schleiermacher's *Vertraute Briefe*. One wonders how an essay on *Schaamhaftigkeit* could warrant the position of centrality that Schleiermacher has attributed to it. The main issues, after all, are those of love, marriage, friendship, and the relation between the sexes. What does *Schaamhaftigkeit* have to do with these? Why did he not write an essay on marriage instead?

What is even more puzzling is the fact that *Schaamhaftigkeit* was not only not the central issue for Friedrich Schlegel but he had used this word only one single time in the four works he had devoted to the question of women during the six year period from 1794 to 1799: "Über die weiblichen Charaktere in den griechischen Dichtern" [1794]; "Über die Diotima" [1795]; "Ueber die Philosophie. An Dorothea" [1799]; and *Lucinde* [1799]. Schlegel's sole use of the word *Schaamhaftigkeit* appears in his 1795 essay "Über die Diotima" where he praises Laconian men and women for their momentary overcoming of the limitations of gender in their quest for *Menschheit*. While the Laconian women had incorported "männliche Kraft und Selbständigkeit" into their beings, the Laconian men had incorporated "weibliche Bescheidenheit [modesty], Schamhaftigkeit [shamefacedness] und Sanftmut [gentleness]."[9] Other than this single usage of the word *Schamhaftigkeit* Schlegel is strangely silent. Since the *Vertraute Briefe* are a response to Schlegel, it thus becomes even more puzzling that Schleiermacher would write this particular essay.

Interpretation further is hindered because secondary sources discussing this essay are lacking. This is perhaps the least explored of all of Schleiermacher's works. Even the few commentators who have examined the *Vertraute Briefe* have paid scant attention to it.[10] Dilthey, for example, who devoted an entire chapter to a discussion of *Lucinde* and the *Vertraute Briefe* devotes a mere two paragraphs to it in his *Leben Schleiermachers*.[11] Kluckhohn, still the primary source for an understanding of the interpretation of love, marriage and friendship during this period, does not even mention it within the body of his text but merely refers to it within a footnote.[12]

The reaction of most to this essay, which in part may explain the absence of any commentaries on it, was probably similar to that of Schleiermacher's close friend Dorothea Mendelssohn Veit ["Lucinde"] who wrote him shortly after the *Vertraute Briefe* had appeared. She told him that the "others" had been "delighted" by this essay on *Schaamhaftigkeit*. Writing from Jena these "others" would have included Ludwig Tieck, Friedrich Schlegel, August Wilhelm Schlegel, and Caroline. Yet, she frankly stated that she had not understood this essay, although she hoped that enlightenment would come with time. She was unclear about Schleiermacher's new definition of *Schaamhaftigkeit*. Didn't it have something to do with the consciousness of nakedness at the Fall? Her reaction points to the fact that, although the term *Schaamhaftigkeit* was current within the German *Sprachgebiet* of that time, it had vague connotations and had not been defined precisely. On June 16, 1800, Dorothea wrote Schleiermacher:

> I . . . must thank you for the *Letters on Lucinde*, for it is true that you have taught me better to understand several things in *Lucinde* . . . they are a refreshing, ripe fruit that has sprouted from *Lucinde's* blossom, and Eleonore's fragments were the sweet kernel for me. It seems to me that you have never written anything so penetrating, and so light and clear; Friedrich also praised the religious conscientiousness. But should I make a confession to you? . . . The others are very delighted with the essay on *Schamhaftigkeit*; I, however, do not want to be too ashamed [*schamhaft*] to admit to you that I still do not thoroughly understand it; it probably will come to me. It seemed to me as though you dragged discretion and modesty [*Bescheidenheit*] into it; I always thought of *Schamhaftigkeit* as the consciousness of nakedness, the completely natural feeling, which stands in the Bible, which human beings received at the same time as reason through the Fall. Therefore, the more reason one has, the more inner Schamhaftigkeit one also has because of the well-known consciousness. In no case is it a virtue. Do you mean it in this way? Or how?[13]

This essay hopes to shed some light on the topic, moving the reader away from the confusion that Dorothea experienced toward the "delight" of the "others." It would appear, at first glance, that Schleiermacher's essay is but a confusing pontification on the term "*Schaamhaftigkeit*," which bears little if any relation to the issues at stake in *Lucinde* and the "Frauenfrage" in Schleiermacher's society at large. This essay, in actuality, exposes the most dangerous demon preventing women from moving into greater spheres of activity in human society. In short, this largely ignored and misunderstood essay is a brilliant and insightful work which, when properly understood, makes a significant contribution to the "Frauenfrage" of his day. It is also hoped that, through this study, new light will be shed on the "early Schleiermacher" and his early ethics.

The road to a correct interpretation of the essay on *Schaamhaftigkeit* is not an uncomplicated task. The interpretative must be preceded by the historical task. Schleiermacher's essay on *Schaamhaftigkeit* was written during a specific historical milieu, within which certain issues, books, and events were discussed. This is the general/historical framework that needs to be examined. But the personal/historical must also be seen in conversation with the general/historical. The personal/historical includes Schleiermacher's own aspirations for women at this time. I, therefore, will begin by taking the reader through two steps: first, a brief analysis of Schleiermachers own aspirations for women at the time that he wrote this essay;[14] and second, an analysis of the concept of *Schaamhaftigkeit* in the writings of a number of thinkers with whose works Schleiermacher was familiar (Rousseau, Kant, Campe, von Hippel, Fichte). Having done this Schleiermacher's new definition of *Schaamhaftigkeit* will be outlined.

Schleiermacher's Aspirations for Women

Schleiermacher's aspirations for women can be seen most clearly in a fragment entitled "Outline of a Reasonable Catechism for Noble Women" along with its "Creed," which Schleiermacher anonymously included in the 1798 edition of *Athenaeum*.[15] This "Catechism" sets forth, in a concise form, views Schleiermacher would expand upon two years later in his *Vertraute Briefe*. For convenience I will use this as a summary statement for Schleiermacher's aspirations for women at that time.

In the ten commandments and confession of the "Reasonable Catechism for Noble Women" Schleiermacher asserts, with Friedrich Schlegel, that more important and primary than the universe's bifurcation into the polarities of male and female is "infinite humanity, which existed before it assumed the cloak of manhood and womanhood."[16] Maleness and femaleness, masculinity and femininity are partial, limiting, and finite. The goal of human life should consist in transcending and becoming "independent of the limitations of gender."[17]

Two questions must be raised. First, what in Schleiermacher's opinion are the behaviors that keep women imprisoned within the limitations of gender? Second, what constructive behaviors can women engage in to move beyond these limitations to "infinite humanity"? Schleiermacher notes two destructive behavior traits. Both of these build up walls between men and women and perpetuate dishonesty between them. These activities are (1) coquetry and (2) idolizing. In his first two commandments Schleiermacher writes:

> [1.] You shall have no other lover beside him, but you shall be capable of being a friend without playing in the various hues of love and without coquetry or idolizing. [2.] You shall not make any ideal for yourself, either of an angel in heaven or of a hero out of a poem or novel, or one that you have dreamed of or created in your imagination; but you shall love a man as he is.[18]

Both idolizing and coquetry perpetuate the wall-building already so prevalent between men and women. Through idolizing, women impose unrealistic expectations upon men, subtly manipulating them to present an identity not indicative of their true self. Women not only are responsible for removing their utopian preconceptions when viewing men but they also must assume responsibility for the way that they are viewed by men. Women hide themselves behind a cloak of coquetry. Coquetry, which always has an ulterior motive, involves the snaring game-playing of women. It also involves an unethical use of one's sensual nature, which Schleiermacher believes to be holy. Schleiermacher is adamant in his assertion that to become closer again to the primordial "infinite humanity" each needs to try to see the other as he or she truly is. Men and women are to face one another honestly and to try to be realistic in their expectations. This is best done by disengaging from idolizing and coquetry, the two destructive behaviors that keep women imprisoned within the limitations of gender.

Schleiermacher does not stop here. He also outlines two behaviors that he believes will help women move closer to "infinite humanity" and broaden their spheres of activity. These are: (1) the assertion of the will and (2) an education. As Schleiermacher writes in his "Creed":

> (1) I believe in infinite humanity [*unendliche Menschheit*], which existed before it assumed the cloak of manhood and womanhood. (2) I believe that I live not in order to obey or to seek amusement but rather to be and to become; and I believe in the power of the will [*die Macht des Willens*] and of education [*Bildung*] to bring me close to the infinite again, to deliver me from the chains of miseducation, and to make me independent of the limitations of gender.[19]

When Schleiermacher uses the word "education" he does not mean the sort of activities that were usually granted women under the guise of "education" in his day, such as learning needlework and cooking. Rather, he makes it quite clear that he intends for women to be the recipients of the same education that men receive. He writes: "Covet the education, art, wisdom, and honor of men."[20] When Schleiermacher uses the term "will" he does so in the sense of an outward activity through which one shapes one's own destiny and impresses one's own God-given individuality upon the world. Because it was generally assumed that women were only passive, Schleiermacher's encouragement to women to assert their will entails a decisive move beyond the usual feminine spheres of activity.[21] All of these goals are reiterated in the *Vertraute Briefe über Friedrich Schlegels Lucinde.* These goals should be kept in mind as we turn to a discussion of the general historical horizon within which Schleiermacher wrote his "Versuch über die Schaamhaftigkeit." We next will examine the term *Schaamhaftigkeit* in books found in Schleiermacher's library.

Schleiermacher's Library

When we examine the Rauch listing of the books sold from Schleiermacher's library, we find that Schleiermacher owned a number of books that were key contributions to the debate over the "Frauenfrage" and in which the concept of *Schaamhaftigkeit* is discussed. We can reasonably assume that these works would have informed Schleiermacher's own analysis as he wrote his "Versuch über die Schaamhaftigkeit." These works were: Rousseau's *Complete Works* which contained his 1762 *Émile*,[22] Kant's *Beobachtungen über das Gefühl des Schönen und Erhabenen* [1764],[23] Campe's *Väterlicher Rath für meine Tochter* [1789],[24] Hippel's *Über die bürgerliche Verbesserung der Weiber* [1792],[25] Fichte's *Grundlage des Naturrechts* [1796][26] and *System der Sittenlehre* [1798].[27] These works, along with those of Friedrich Schlegel, form the intellectual horizon and conversation partners for Schleiermacher's "Versuch über die Schaamhaftigkeit."

While we have found the concept of *Schaamhaftigkeit* to be surprisingly absent from the works of Friedrich Schlegel, we will see that *Schaamhaftigkeit* is a central concept for Rousseau, Kant, Campe, Hippel, and Fichte. The use of *Schaamhaftigkeit* will now be examined in these works. Our study will begin with Rousseau.

The Swiss philosopher Rousseau's *Émile*, published in 1762, is perhaps the most significant book from the eighteenth century to discuss the role of women. It was the single most important stimulus for the subsequent debate over the status of women that emerged in late eighteenth-century Germany. This debate revolved around three issues in particular: first, a philosophical debate which explored whether or not there are any a priori ontological differences ["characteristics of sex"/*Geschlechtscharaktere*] between men and women; second, a pedagogical debate centering on women's need for and right to education; and third, a political debate revolving around the legal rights of women. The three were highly interrelated issues. The focus, however, was the philosophical question because women's access to the pedagogical and political spheres was contingent upon the a priori ontological characteristics that male philosophers assigned to women.

During this age, concepts were not merely words tossed around in the salons, which had no bearing on real life. Concepts, rather, drawn from the realm of ideas and applied to women as gender-specific ontological qualities could become dangerous weapons that either shut or opened the pedagogical and political doors for women. They usually had the effect of slamming the door shut in women's faces. *Schaamhaftigkeit*, we will see in what follows, was

just such a concept. Indeed *Schaamhaftigkeit* was the most powerful conceptual tool that men had for keeping the power structure intact. It preserved
an impenetrable wall both between men and women, and between women
and the pedagogical and political spheres.

In what follows we will see that *Schaamhaftigkeit* served a double
function. For Rousseau, *Schaamhaftigkeit* perpetuated the coquetry of
women through his definition of it as a "charm" that women used to
manipulate men. For Fichte and others, *Schaamhaftigkeit* was the final card
drawn from their loaded decks to keep women from spheres of greater
learning and political involvement. Women's frail *Schaamhaftigkeit* might be
harmed were they to receive an education or assert their political rights. It
will become clear why the concept of *Schaamhaftigkeit* necessarily became a
central concept that Schleiermacher needed to exegete since it perpetuates
negative behaviors (idolizing, coquetry) and prevents women from engaging
in those positive behaviors (assertion of the will, education) that he believed
would help women move closer to the goal of "infinite humanity."

Rousseau's 1762 "Émile"

Rousseau's 1762 *Émile* sets forth a new pedagogical model for both
boys and girls by promoting an educational method in which each sex is
encouraged to develop freely in accordance with nature, as opposed to
having foreign artificial constructs imposed upon them from without.[28]
Book V of *Émile* is devoted to an analysis of what the education of girls
should be, through its depiction of a young woman named Sophy, who later
becomes the ideal wife of Émile, the primary character of the book.

Rousseau begins his discussion of women in the philosophical realm.
He differentiates between the "characteristics of the species" and "characteristics of sex."[29] By "characteristics of the species" Rousseau refers to those
qualities that men and women share in common. By "characteristics of sex"
Rousseau refers to those a priori unalterable ontological differences between
men and women that are gender specific. This differention was to become
the standard way by which men and women were categorized in relation to
each other in the decades that followed.[30] Schleiermacher, too, was to

distinguish between these two, referring to the "characteristics of sex" with the term "*Geschlechtscharakter.*"[31]

For Rousseau, the "characteristics of sex" reside not only in the physical order but in the moral order as well.[32] Men receive the moral "characteristics of sex" of being bold, strong, and active; women, those of being timid, weak, and passive.[33] These ontological traits then determine the spheres of life to which each is allotted. Men's sphere is that of the outer world, participation in education and in politics. Based upon a woman's ontology, her sphere is defined as only that of the household, her roles being those of daughter, wife, and mother.[34] Furthermore, men are given the task of ruling over women; women, the task of pleasing men.[35]

Both men and women find themselves in life's arena as sensual, passionate beings, continually at war with themselves and others. Nature has given men and women each a special gender-specific attribute as a tool to cope with this problem in the spheres in which they find themselves. For each it is this special tool that distinguishes human beings from beasts, acting as a humanizing agent within them. Men are given the ontological tool of "reason"; women are given that of a "sense of shame" or "modesty." Rousseau writes:

> The Most High has deigned to do honour to mankind; he has endowed man with boundless passions, together with a law to guide them, so that man may be alike free and self-controlled; though swayed by these passions man is endowed with reason by which to control them. Woman is also endowed with boundless passions; God has given her modesty to restrain them.[36]

This ontological trait of a "sense of shame" or "modesty" is alluded to throughout this chapter.[37] Rousseau uses it in two different senses. It is first described as a "negative instinct,"[38] a "sense of shame"[39] or a "secret shame" that women feel whenever sensual desire stirs in them.[40] It is a limiting voice of conscience that helps women restrain their "boundless passions."[41]

Note the important fact that Rousseau has juxtaposed the "sense of shame" or "modesty" of women with the "reason" of men. Does it then also follow that women are not as "reasonable" as men? Rousseau poses the question himself as follows: "Are women capable of solid reason; should they cultivate it, can they cultivate it successfully?"[42] No, women are not capable of "solid reason" and there is no sense in cultivating it, for as Rousseau writes: "The search for abstract and speculative truths, for principles and axioms in science, for all that tends to wide generalisation, is beyond a woman's grasp; their studies should be thoroughly practical."[43] This "thoroughly practical" education should "be planned in relation to man" since, of course, we have already learned that women's purpose in life is to please men and to be their cheerful companions.[44] Thus, in his first definition Rousseau defines *Schaamhaftigkeit* as a "sense of shame" that, juxtaposed with reason, eventually works against a woman, by keeping her within the household and away from the pedagogical and political spheres.

Yet while, in Rousseau's first definition, a woman's *Schaamhaftigkeit* may appear to be a limiting and negative virtue only, in its secondary definition this same *Schaamhaftigkeit* can be used by a woman against a man. Rousseau admits that women stand in a position of great subordination to men. This, however, does not mean that women do not have any influence over men at all. A woman can get a man to do what she wants, Rousseau believes, through the skillful manipulation of her charms. He writes that "her strength is in her charms, by their means she should compel him to discover his strength."[45] Rousseau also writes that nature has given women these charms to be used as "weapons in their hands to make up for their lack of strength and to enable them to direct the strength of men."[46] The primary charm that nature has given women secretly to control the behavior of men is "the shame and modesty with which nature has armed the weak for the conquest of the strong."[47] This sense of shame or modesty, understood in this second sense, consists in a certain type of manipulative game-playing, which Rousseau describes as "coquetry."[48] A woman's outward appearance of dependency, weakness, sense of shame and modesty are but a means to an end. Rousseau even argues that this coquetry is moral: "Yes, I maintain that coquetry, kept within bounds, becomes modest and true, and out of it springs a law of right conduct."[49]

Rousseau paints the charm of *Schaamhaftigkeit* at great length in *Émile* in his depiction of the game-playing between Émile and Sophy that continues until they finally confess their love for each other and marry. Rousseau not only implicitly shows *Schaamhaftigkeit* at work but even explicitly sanctions Sophy's manipulative, coquettish behavior in which *Schaamhaftigkeit* is her primary tool. For example:

> When you see her [Sophy] you say, "That is a good modest girl," but while you are with her, you cannot take your eyes or your thoughts off her, and one might say that this very simple adornment is only put on to be removed bit by bit by the imagination.[50]

After months of displaying a modest front and utilizing all her charms Sophy finally gets Émile to behave exactly as she wants him to. She turns him into her ideal male, modeled after the hero in a novel she had read entitled *The Adventures of Telemachus.*[51] Rousseau summarizes Sophy's satisfaction at having shaped Émile into her ideal through her coquettish *Schaamhaftigkeit* with these words: "Yet unknown to him, Sophy, with all her pride, is observing him closely, and she is smiling to herself at the pride of her slave."[52]

Hence we have seen *Schaamhaftigkeit* defined in two ways. It is first juxtaposed to the "reason" of males as the ontological tool given to women to survive in the sphere of life assigned to them. Through this juxtaposition Rousseau implicitly is stating what women do not possess – reason. This lack of reason bars them from the pedagogical and political realms. Because *Schaamhaftigkeit* stands in the way of women's attaining an education, it contradicts Schleiermacher's own aims for women. *Schaamhaftigkeit* also is a "charm" given to women by Nature. It is almost a spell that a woman can cast on a man to manipulate him. *Schaamhaftigkeit*, understood in this second sense, also stands diametrically opposed to Schleiermacher's own aspirations for women. Rousseau explicitly sanctions what Schleiermacher explicitly bans – idolizing and coquetry. Consequently, *Schaamhaftigkeit* stands as a wall preventing women from passing into spheres of greater activity, through which alone they can attain "infinite humanity."

Kant's 1764 "Beobachtungen über das Gefühl des Schönen und Erhabenen"

In 1764, two years after Rousseau's *Émile* appeared, Kant wrote a treatise on aesthetics entitled *Beobachtungen über das Gefühl des Schönen und Erhabenen* [*Observations on the Feeling of the Beautiful and the Sublime*], in which he sought to derive statements about the ontological characteristics of women through inductive and empirical observation.[53] Kant's work, which shows evidence of the influence of Rousseau in its discussion of women, was found in Schleiermacher's library.[54] Here *Schaamhaftigkeit* is assigned to women as a significant ontological *Geschlechtscharakter*, which functions as their moral guide in the place where ethical principles of universalization based on reason function in men. Hence, like Rousseau, *Schaamhaftigkeit* is juxtaposed to "reason." This led Kant to deny that women are capable of abstraction. Women, consequently, have no need for an education.

In the *Beobachtungen*, Kant seeks to examine two particular kinds of finer feelings of pleasure that manifest themselves throughout the universe: the feeling of the sublime [*das Gefühl des Erhabenen*] and the feeling of the beautiful [*das Gefühl des Schönen*]. Of interest to us here is the fact that Kant (even though he might like us to think otherwise) does not believe that the two different feelings are equal. It is obviously the case that the feeling of the sublime, which is linked with a feeling of awe and admiration and which "moves" us, is superior to the feeling of the beautiful, which evokes a feeling of joy and happiness and "charms" us.[55]

Kant equates men with the feeling of the sublime, women with the feeling of the beautiful. It is, as Kant states, a "charming distinction that nature has chosen to make between the two sorts of human being[s]."[56] It is in the ethical realm that one can see the differences between the sexes most clearly. For Kant, only a moral decision based upon principles of universalization falls into the category of the sublime and can be called a "genuine"[57] or a "noble virtue" [*edele Tugend*].[58] A genuine, noble virtue can only be found in a person who has a "profound feeling for the beauty and dignity of human nature and a firmness and determination of the mind to refer all one's actions to this as to a universal ground. . . ."[59]

The capacity for universalization is gender specific and is attributed to men alone. Women lack this ability. The virtues of women cannot be based on such principles of universalization, yet women do demonstrate the capacity for ethical, virtuous behavior. How can this be explained? Kant writes that women possess an "adoptive" or a "beautiful virtue" [*schöne Tugend*].[60] Nature has not neglected women but has left them with the means by which to engage in ethical behavior. Juxtaposed to men's capacity for universalization, Nature has endowed women with *Schamhaftigkeit* as a moral guide. Kant writes:

> The virtue of a woman is a *beautiful virtue*. That of the male sex should be a *noble virtue*. . . . I hardly believe that the fair sex is capable of principles. . . . But in place of it Providence has put in their breast kind and benevolent sensations, a fine feeling for propriety, and a complaisant soul. . . . Sensitivity to *shame* [*Schamhaftigkeit*] is a secrecy of nature addressed to setting bounds to a very intractable inclination, and since it has the voice of nature on its side, seems always to agree with good moral qualities even if it yields to excess. Hence it is most needed, as a supplement to principles. . . . But at the same time it serves to draw a curtain of mystery before even the most appropriate and necessary purposes of nature, so that a too familiar acquaintance with them might not occasion disgust, or indifference at least, in respect to the final purpose of an impulse onto which the finest and liveliest inclinations of human nature are grafted.[61]

Schamhaftigkeit, for Kant, relates to a "sense of honor" along with its reverse in "shame" to counterbalance selfish tendencies and to assure ethical behavior.[62] It is a negative virtue, a feeling of shame in relation to excesses of sensuality, desire, or selfishness, or an exceeding of those boundaries or spheres of life that "Nature" or "Providence" has allotted to women.

Kant never praises coquetry as had Rousseau and, therefore, might agree with Schleiermacher that both idolizing and coquetry are destructive behaviors. Nevertheless, his use of *Schamhaftigkeit* still remains a stumbling block because it prevents women from receiving an education. One would expect that the juxtaposition of *Schamhaftigkeit* with principles of universalization based on "reason" in the ethical realm would imply a concomitant belittling of women's overall use of their powers of rationality in life at large. We find that this, indeed, is the case.

While Kant states that women are also "rational beings," he argues that their reason is ontologically different from that of men, writing: "The fair sex has just as much understanding as the male, but it is a *beautiful understanding* [*schöner Verstand*], whereas ours should be a *deep understanding* [*tiefer Verstand*], an expression that signifies identity with the sublime."[63] The deep [sublime] understanding of men is one that is guided by "reason" and "cold and speculative instruction."[64] By contrast, the beautiful understanding of women is guided by what Kant terms "sense" and "feelings" [*Empfinden*].[65] As in the ethical sphere where women are not capable of "principles of universalization," in the intellectual sphere women are not capable of "deep meditation and a long-sustained reflection . . . laborious learning or painful pondering."[66] The outcome of this is that women are denied access to the educational sphere.[67]

Campe's 1789 "Väterlicher Rath für meine Tochter"

The concept of *Schaamhaftigkeit* also was central in a book written by the pedagoge Joachim Heinrich Campe in 1789 entitled *Väterlicher Rath für meine Tochter. Ein Gegenstück zum Theophron*. This book, which Schleiermacher owned, represents the most prevalent popular view of *Schamhaftigkeit* at that time.[68] Campe distinguishes between the "characteristics of the species," which he calls an "allgemeine menschliche Bestimmung" that men and women share in common, and the "characteristics of sex/*Geschlechtscharaktere*," which he calls a "besondere Bestimmung" that is gender specific.[69] In Campe's view, women only can fulfill their general, human calling when they fulfill their particular, female calling in life. The vocation of women is defined as that of "wife, mother, and manager of the home."[70] Like Rousseau, Campe believes that in all three of these roles the woman's energies should always center on pleasing her husband and maintaining his interest.[71] It is a "will of nature"[72] that women are so destined for the household alone because they are ontologically determined as "weak, small, delicate, sensitive, fearful, and narrow-minded."[73] In this they differ greatly from men who are "strong, stable, bold, enduring, large, noble, and vigorous in body and soul."[74]

These ontological characteristics determine women's calling entirely, limiting them to the sphere of the household alone. To operate effectively in this sphere of life no education at all is necessary. Indeed, an education may actually be harmful and prevent one from fulfilling these tasks. This is because once one becomes exposed to the larger world through reading, the tasks within the household might appear to be insignificant and mundane.[75]

Although women have no need for an education, Campe argues that they were born with enough "good common sense"[76] to perform their household duties. Yet three virtues are necessary in addition to this, both to maintain a good household and to please their husbands.[77] These three essential qualities that every woman should strive to nurture within herself to help her fulfill her vocation in life are: (1) "purity of the heart and the sentiments: the foundation of all ethical perfection, the only fountain of all true happiness that never dries up!";[78] (2) True and enlightened piety [*Frömmigkeit*], i.e., childlike love and trust in God . . .;[79] and (3) "Chastity [*Keuschheit*] and *Schamhaftigkeit* – one of the first and most indispensable requirements for the purity of the heart recommended to you above."[80] *Schamhaftigkeit* is the most important of these because it is part and parcel of both the first and the third virtues.

Campe assigns at least three characteristics to *Schamhaftigkeit*. By relating the first and the third virtues Campe indicates that *Schamhaftigkeit* has to do with the inward purity of the heart, i.e., with one's thought processes. Sensual thoughts should not be given free reign in the imagination but should be fought against and expelled. *Schamhaftigkeit*, according to Campe, also includes outer behavior. This can be seen both through Campe's coupling of *Schamhaftigkeit* with chastity in his third virtue and in the following statement, which is the fourth of eleven commandments written for his daughter:

Be modest [*schamhaft*] to the highest degree both in relation to others and in relation to yourself. Your virgin body must be a

sanctuary both for you and for others, covered and protected
from degrading stares and disgraceful touches.[81]
Campe warns his daughter that *Schamhaftigkeit* further consists in refraining
from arousing sensual feelings in others. Consequently, *Schamhaftigkeit* is
defined as a responsibility not only toward oneself but also toward others.

Theodor von Hippel's 1792 "Über die bürgerliche Verbesserung der Weiber"

Theodor von Hippel's 1792 *Über die bürgerliche Verbesserung der
Weiber* [*On Improving the Status of Women*] also was found in
Schleiermacher's library.[82] Hippel's book, appearing the same year as Mary
Wollstonecraft's *A Vindication of the Rights of Woman*,[83] was along with the
latter, the most radical plea of his day for the emancipation of women.
Indeed, it was so radical that many believed that Hippel intended it to be a
satire. While France and England already were debating the civil rights of
women, Germany was years away from seriously addressing this question.
Hippel attempted to launch a discussion over women's rights in Germany
with his book. He himself promotes a position in favor of the civil equality of
women:

> Let us look forward to the time when the day of redemption
> for the fair sex will arrive; when people will no longer hinder
> others who are qualified for equal rights from exercising those
> rights; and when no discrimination is made between things
> which are obviously equal to each other.[84]

Hippel examines the causes of the inequality of the sexes in society
and proposes reforms to bring women nearer to the eventual goal of civil
equality. Hippel first analyzes and then rejects the two traditional arguments
for the inequality of the sexes: the argument from natural law (men are
stronger than women) and the argument from divine law (women led to the
Fall). Hippel combines methods drawn from the fields of anthropology,
classics, and history to account for the subjugation of women. He believes
that while men and women originally were equal, hunted together, and bore
the same hardships, the six or so hours when a woman gave birth to a child
led her, as a result of her natural instinct to protect both herself and her

child, to begin to store away food for this period. Preserving food was seen to be valuable and began to take up more of a woman's time. This activity, combined with women assuming the tasks of agriculture and fishing, kept them either in or near the home. As her spheres of activity became increasingly relegated to the home, the man, out on the hunt, continued to expand his horizons and to grow in courage and self-confidence. With the growth in population and the beginnings of settlements, men also took weapons into their hands to protect their settlements and property. Women began to be understood as part of this property belonging to men.

Accidentally initiated through the division of labor, men soon began to understand this differentiation between men and women to be hierarchical and the result of natural and divine law. Legislation was written to enforce what men believed was the natural superiority of men over women. Hippel maintained that the continued perpetuation of this inequality by men through the legal code could not be explained so much through the ignorance of men as through their fear that women might actually rule over them were they granted equality.

It was men's fear of women, Hippel believed, that led "enlightened" men in the *Aufklärung* to seek subtle philosophical arguments to preserve this power structure. The most important of these arguments were those that attributed the virtue of *Schamhaftigkeit* to women as a gender-specific quality. Keeping women's *Schamhaftigkeit* pure and intact was essential. Their *Schamhaftigkeit* might be tainted were they allowed to be involved in the civil and political spheres. In a particularly illuminating passage Hippel writes:

> In conformity with the diversity of laws pertaining to women there also exist, it is said, diverse motives for granting them – and it is within each law itself that we would seek with the greatest certainty the reason why it was made. To be sure, it is not always that reason which Their Majesties the legislators would have us believe it is; and indeed, we need not bother ourselves here with the flourishes and flowery language of the alleged reason. . . . Modesty [*Schamhaftigkeit*] is also given – *nota bene*, by the law itself – as an authentic reason

for the repression of women's rights. Are we really to
understand that the fair sex is denied due process of law simply
for reasons of feminine modesty? How generous the laws are
– as if one's modesty were in danger, or could even be lost
entirely in a court of justice! What is it here that could lead to
illicit passions and inflame a heart which is so far removed
from such things? Before either sex decides upon adopting this
virtue of modesty and demanding from every seductive word in
the language that it give account of itself, we must ask the
question: is there such a thing as modesty? And what is its
value as a unilateral virtue? Modesty is a virtue, if I may be
permitted to say so, which lives in a state of matrimony; that is,
if it is not practiced by both men and women equally, it
degenerates into affectation and feminine legerdemain.[85]

Hippel is wary of "feminine *Schamhaftigkeit*" because it is attributed to
women as a gender-specific ontological trait. He understands *Schamhaftigkeit*
as something that should apply both to men and to women within the
marriage relation. He fails to understand how, as a virtue, it protects women.
In his view, *Schamhaftigkeit* was one of the most dangerous weapons that
men used to control women and to prevent them from achieving civil
equality. He further interprets *Schamhaftigkeit* to be an empty, meaningless
virtue. His reasoning rests upon his notion of "virtue." In his view, a virtue is
known in its confrontation with, opposition to, and overcoming of
temptation. Thus, a virtue enables its bearer successfully to exercise self-
discipline in the face of temptation. Women, however, are not even given
the chance to exercise this virtue of *Schamhaftigkeit* in the larger sphere of
life.

The following passage also uncovers what Hippel believes to be men's
dishonesty in fostering this groundless belief in women's *Schamhaftigkeit*:

Let us be honest! Every means by which human beings can
distinguish themselves has been taken from the women. A
conspiracy among their enemies debases this sex as deeply as
an unavenged insult does a husband, expelling it to the class of
servants and menials by means of the bugbear that the limits of

feminine modesty [*Schamhaftigkeit*] might otherwise be transgressed – when in truth it is only so that we may remain secure from their challenge to a duel.[86]

Thus Hippel exposes *Schamhaftigkeit* as a convenient male ploy to debase women. His vision of a world in which women and men are equals, in which women have equal access to the pedagogical and political realms, left no room for *Schamhaftigkeit* as defined by previous interpreters. That Hippel was not merely interjecting his own thoughts into the writings and actions of others, that Hippel had exposed a genuine enemy in the *Geschlechtscharakter* of *Schamhaftigkeit*, that *Schamhaftigkeit* was a male weapon used for the oppression of women and to maintain the hierarchical power structure, and that concepts derived from the sphere of philosophy were then used to bar women from the pedagogical and political spheres – all of these will be seen quite clearly in our examination of Fichte's 1796 *Grundlage des Naturrechts* and his 1798 *System der Sittenlehre*.

Fichte's Use of 'Schamhaftigkeit' in his 1796 "Grundlage des Naturrechts" and his 1798 "System der Sittenlehre"

Fichte's analysis of *Schaamhaftigkeit* is delineated in two books, his 1796 *Grundlage des Naturrechts* and his 1798 *System der Sittenlehre*.[87] Schleiermacher not only owned these books[88] but also would have been thoroughly acquainted with the views contained therein because during the late 1790s Fichte and Schleiermacher shared meals together in the home of Dorothea Veit, where they also were joined by Friedrich Schlegel.[89] Because the views on men and women set forth in these two books are essentially the same, I will discuss both books together.

In Fichte's view, men and women possess differing *Geschlechtscharaktere*. The most important of these for a correct understanding of Fichte's theory of male-female relationships and marriage are the differing sexual urges [*Geschlechtstrieb*] of men and women. Fichte believes that only men possess an actual physical sexual urge [*Geschlechtstrieb*]. It is this urge that drives men toward marriage, for it is only in the marriage relation that this sexual urge can be expressed in an ethical manner. Women, on the other hand, should not possess such a sexual urge at all. Indeed, sensuality is something that Fichte finds abhorrent in women and unnatural to their being. As he writes: "In its crudity the sexual urge of a woman is the most repugnant and most disgusting thing that there is in nature; and at the same time it points to the absolute absence of all morality."[90]

Sensuality or sexual drive is immoral, according to Fichte, because it is directly opposed to the foundational gender-specific *Geschlechtscharakter* of women – *Schamhaftigkeit*. Fichte explains:

> The man, without giving up his worth, can admit to having a
> sexual urge and seek its satisfaction. . . . The woman cannot
> admit to having this sexual urge. . . . All the other differences
> of both of the sexes are based upon this single distinction.
> Female *Schamhaftigkeit*, which does not appear in this manner
> in the male sex, arises from this law of nature.[91]

Schamhaftigkeit, which is not so much a bridling of one's passions as it is not allowing sexual urge to surface at all, becomes the cornerstone of his discussion of women. All the other *Geschlechtscharaktere* are deduced from this single concept of *Schamhaftigkeit*.

If sexual urge, which *Schamhaftigkeit* forbids, does not lead women toward marriage, what then does? Fichte must posit a second foundational *Geschlechtscharakter* to explain this – love. It is this love that leads a woman to marry a man. Fichte writes: "*Love*, therefore, is the form under which sexual urge emerges in the woman."[92]   Only women contain love immediately within themselves. It is their vocation to try to awaken this love in men.

What is love and how can a woman awaken it in a man? Love, according to Fichte, is not some vague feeling but rather it consists in self-sacrifice. Fichte defines love as follows: "It, however, is love when one sacrifices oneself for the sake of the other, not because of a concept, but rather because of an instinct."[93] To awaken this counter-love in her husband a woman must sacrifice herself to her husband. She sacrifices herself entirely and for all eternity. Consequently, Fichte ascribes to a woman the *Geschlechtscharakter* of being "*unterworfen*" or standing in subjugation to a man. He writes:

In giving herself, she gives herself totally, with all her
property, her strength, her will, in short, her empirical I; and
she gives herself up for all *eternity* . . . Only under the condition
that she herself has completely lost her life and her will to her
lover, without reservation, and can be no other than his, does
her submission occur out of love and exist next to morality.[94]

After having deduced a woman's complete subjugation to a man from
the concept of *Schamhaftigkeit*, Fichte goes on to apply this ontological
category to the political and educational spheres, entirely to the detriment of
women. Fichte writes that only men, unmarried women beyond marriagable
age, and widows are allowed to vote. Young women, who stand under the
protection of their parents, are not allowed to vote at all. Lacking civil
liberties while living with their parents, they lose them entirely once they
marry, for then they belong to their husbands unconditionally. He explains:

The most unlimited subjection of the woman to the will of the
man lies in the concept of marriage; . . . The woman does not
belong to herself but rather to the man. . . . The man takes her
place totally; through her marriage she is completely
annihilated in the eyes of the state, as a result of her own,
necessary will, which the state has guaranteed. The man
becomes her guarantee within the state; he becomes her legal
guardian; he lives her public life in every respect; and, at last,
she retains a domestic sphere of activity alone.[95]

From this it follows that women are not allowed to vote. Aware of the
arguments for political equality promoted in his day by men such as Hippel
in his *Über die bürgerliche Verbesserung der Weiber*, Fichte feels compelled to
argue his case even further.[96] Women only want to vote, Fichte maintains,
out of a desire for recognition and outer appearance! But this desire, Fichte
argues, contradicts one of the most essential gender-specific traits of women
– *Schamhaftigkeit*. The ontological *Geschlechtscharakter* of *Schamhaftigkeit*
is, therefore, used to prevent a woman's move into the political sphere. We
read:

What do the women and their defendents really desire? . . . It
can only be the outer appearance of which they are desirous.

They do not want simply to take action but that others shall
know that they have taken action. They do not merely want
that what they wish should occur, but it shall also be known
that *they, precisely they* have carried it out. They seek celebrity
in their life, and after their death they seek celebrity in history.
. . . However, what is even more significant, is that in doing this
they sacrifice the lovable *Schamhaftigkeit* of their sex,
regarding which nothing can be more loathesome than for it to
be exhibited. For the man the thirst for glory and vanity is des-
picable, but for the woman it is fatal: it erradicates that *Scham-*
haftigkeit and surrendering love for her spouse, on which her
entire worth is based. A rational and virtuous woman can only
be proud of her husband and children, not of herself. . . .[97]

Only reluctantly does Fichte allow single older women and widows, who are
not subject to any man, the right to vote. Fichte, however, is not happy about
them doing so. Why not? Because these women will be acting against their
"obliging *Schamhaftigkeit*."[98]

Fichte not only uses the *Geschlechtscharakter* of *Schamhaftigkeit* to
keep women out of the political arena but he also uses it to prevent them
from participation in the academic community. He argues that there is a
significant difference between men who are writers or academics and their
female counterparts. Fichte believes that male academics do not learn for
themselves but rather for others.[99] Women, on the other hand, only wish to
learn or to become writers to show off. When they write it is but a "tool of
coquetry," which completely destroys *Schamhaftigkeit* and virtue within
them.[100]

Fichte especially is adamant that women not become serious
writers.[101] Should a woman decide to become a writer her marriage
necessarily would be destroyed. This is because, through writing, she might
gain an independent source of income and the feeling of having achieved
something on her own. This would undermine the absolute submission to
and dependence upon her husband that is foundational for marriage and that
the *Geschlechtscharakter* of *Schamhaftigkeit* requires. Fichte writes that if a
woman "is married she obtains an autonomy independent of her husband

through her literary fame, which necessarily debilitates the marital relation and threatens to dissolve it."[102]

Consequently, like his predecessors Rousseau, Kant, and Campe, Fichte has used what he deduces to be the *Geschlechtscharaktere* of women as conceptual tools to prevent them from claiming their political and pedagogical rights. Like these writers, Fichte makes *Schamhaftigkeit* play the most important role in keeping women locked within the domestic sphere. Hippel was right to warn his reader of the dangers of that little word "*Schamhaftigkeit*." Fichte has taken it to an extreme both in definition and in application. By definition it makes women hostile toward their own sexuality. Women, to be *schamhaft*, must completely scourge themselves of all sensual desire. *Schamhaftigkeit* further becomes, for Fichte, the single starting point from which everything relating to women is deduced. The outcome of this deduction for women is threefold: first, her total subjugation to a man by giving herself up to him completely and for all eternity; second, her being denied all political rights, if married; and third, her being stripped of her moral worth should she attempt to enter the academic community.

Schleiermacher's Redefinition of "Schaamhaftigkeit"

From the foregoing discussion we see that the concept of *Schaamhaftigkeit* was a loaded term. It was a concept that had the potentiality of continuing to keep women from entering into larger spheres of activity unless it could be redefined. While at first glance it might seem that Schleiermacher should have devoted his central essay in the *Vertraute Briefe* to a more pertinent topic such as an analysis of marriage, love or friendship between men and women, it is clearly the case that there is no concept more central to the "Frauenfrage" than that of *Schaamhaftigkeit*. *Schaamhaftigkeit* is, indeed, a crucial factor in all of the topics that *Lucinde* and the *Vertraute Briefe* address. It influences and determines an understanding of the ontological nature of women, friendship, love, marriage, and a woman's right to participate in the pedagogical and political spheres.

Not only is *Schaamhaftigkeit* central to the primary themes of *Lucinde* but it also was used by the writers just discussed in a manner that significantly hindered Schleiermacher's own aspirations for women. Sanctioned by Rousseau as a charm, *Schaamhaftigkeit* perpetuated both women's idolizing of men and their coquetry. As that ontological *Geschlechtscharakter* that corresponded in women to the analogous attribute of reason in men, *Schaamhaftigkeit* prevented women from seeking an education that would help them move beyond the limitations of gender to "infinite humanity." Finally, by defining *Schaamhaftigkeit* in a manner that was negative to sensuality, these writers were opposed to a central tenet of Schleiermacher and Schlegel – the union of the sensual and the spiritual in love.

Schleiermacher focused on what Hippel before him had seen: *Schaamhaftigkeit* was the most dangerous demon of all and it needed to be exorcised. Until its dangers were exposed and it was redefined theorists could continue to conjure up the little word *Schaamhaftigkeit* at their convenience to the complete detriment of women. It was the job of Hippel to call for an exorcist; it was Schleiermacher who was to perform the exorcism. This Schleiermacher was successfully able to do in his 1800 essay "Versuch über die Schaamhaftigkeit." The remainder of this essay will be devoted to an explication of Schleiermacher's reconception and redefinition of the term *Schaamhaftigkeit*, followed by a brief summary of what I believe its contemporary relevance to be.

Schleiermacher opens his essay by defining the reference of *Schaamhaftigkeit.* He writes that "*Schaamhaftigkeit* depends upon certain conceptions that relate to the mysteries of love."[103] He stands within the mainstream of the interpretation with this reference. Rousseau, Kant, Campe, Hippel, and Fichte also had discussed *Schaamhaftigkeit* in relation to certain mysteries of love, i.e., in relation to sensuality. The question Schleiermacher wants to answer is whether *Schaamhaftigkeit* refers to the not-having [*Nichthaben*] or the not-communicating [*Nichtmitteilen*] of thoughts about the mysteries of love. To demonstrate *Schaamhaftigkeit* must one "avoid thoughts as the distant determining cause of sin"?[104] The initial part of his essay attempts to answer this question.

Schleiermacher affirms that *Schaamhaftigkeit* can include the actual conceiving [*Vorstellen*] of the mysteries of love. He uses various arguments throughout his essay to prove this point. First, he argues from common sense.

If *Schaamhaftigkeit* forbids certain conceptions from entering one's mind it would be a completely empty, negative virtue: "it would be the only virtue that would choke because of lack of air."[105]   Second, Schleiermacher believes that the universe consists of the two interconnected forces of *Geist* (spiritual) and *Natur* (sensual). Each is an essential component of life, and each is holy. We are part of this natural order composed of and influenced by *Geist* and *Natur*. It, therefore, is impossible to prevent thoughts concerning love's mysteries from entering our consciouness. Everywhere in life ("from the isolated conversation with the most innocent boy or girl to the noisiest and most mixed society, from the bedroom to the pulpit, from the most thoughtful to the most passionate mood"[106]) the sensual and the spiritual intertwine. One can never find oneself in a situation devoid of either of these. Consequently, it would be absurd to assert that possessing *Schaamhaftigkeit* would entail what Fichte had demanded: that sensual thoughts never, ever enter one's *Gemüth*.

Third, if *Schaamhaftigkeit* is a virtue that society would like to see manifest, it somehow must be passed on and taught to others. But *Schaamhaftigkeit* cannot be illustrated through example alone. People can look at the example of others but only see their outer behavior and altogether miss their inner motivation. Therefore, *Schaamhaftigkeit* is a quality that must be taught to others through instruction. Yet to instruct presupposes that one can "abstract the concept of virtue."[107]   To abstract one needs the freedom to discuss where sensuality might transgress the boundaries of ethical behavior. Discussion presupposes allowing conceptions of love to enter into the minds both of the speaker and of the listener.

Schleiermacher's main argument that *Schaamhaftigkeit* does not refer to the not-having of thoughts finally occurs when he compares the two terms *"Schaam"* and *"Schaamhaftigkeit."* While they are linguistically related, they are accorded different meanings by Schleiermacher. *Schaam*, for Schleiermacher, is "the feeling of displeasure about something that has proceeded in the mind and heart [*Gemüth*], whether it be something damnable according to its essence or only according to its mode of existence."[108] *Schaam*, therefore, concerns itself with mental conceptions, with a displeasurable state of mind. Even if one does not communicate these mental conceptions to others, one still can feel ashamed that there is something at work within one that has allowed these conceptions to enter into one's consciousness in a certain displeasurable way. Hence *Schaam* becomes, in Schleiermacher's essay, a primary component of what Rousseau, Kant, Campe, and Fichte had understood by the term *Schaamhaftigkeit* – a purity of thoughts and sentiments.

In Schleiermacher's understanding, *Schaamhaftigkeit* no longer shares in this definition of *Schaam*. It leaves behind all fears of sensual thoughts entering into one's consciousness. But what then is *Schaamhaftigkeit*? To understand what *Schaamhaftigkeit* is and should be, Schleiermacher turns away from the inner mental processes and consciousness of individuals and takes his starting point within human society. It is at this point that his essay shows its relation to an essay he published a year earlier that bears a similar title, his 1799 "Versuch einer Theorie des geselligen Betragens," which appeared in the January and February issues of the *Berlinisches Archiv der Zeit und ihres Geschmacks*."[109] Our understanding of Schleiermacher's use of *Schaamhaftigkeit* will be helped by turning briefly to this essay.

In his "Versuch einer Theorie des geselligen Betragens," which very likely mirrors the goals of the Berliner salons he frequented, Schleiermacher seeks to define the boundaries of appropriate ethical behavior in that realm he terms *freie Geselligkeit [free sociality]*. The sphere of *freie Geselligkeit* is that place in human society where the concerns of the job and home are put aside for people to meet together reciprocally to affect mutual *Bildung*. Leaving behind these worldly cares, each is to bring into the social group the gift of one's own individuality, one's own individual intuition of the universe. Schleiermacher writes: "I shall bring along my individuality, my character."[110] The gift that each receives is that which each other person brings into the group. *Freie Geselligkeit* consists in this give [*Selbstthätigkeit*] and take [*Selbstbeschränkung*] of the individuality of each, or what Schleiermacher terms "reciprocal activity" [*Wechselwirkung*]. *Bildung* occurs through this interaction. Hence this social sphere is described as a "free play of thoughts and feelings through which all members mutually excite and stimulate one another. . . . All is to be reciprocal activity."[111]

Yet there is a certain law that needs to be followed for such *freie Geselligkeit* to function ethically. Schleiermacher summarizes this law as follows: "Your social activity shall always contain itself within the boundaries through which alone a certain society can exist as a whole."[112] What are these boundaries that should govern group behavior? Schleiermacher writes that it is important to recognize and respect the individuality of each human being. Each lives in a definite sphere of thoughts, feelings, and actions which is unique and shared by no other person completely. The focus of *freie Geselligkeit*, however, is not upon the individual person but rather upon the well-being of the group as a whole. Each time someone says or does something that excludes someone else the "society stops functioning as a whole."[113] When two people engage in a discussion to which a third cannot relate they are violating this law of social behavior. Schleiermacher defines this law more precisely as the "law of decency" [*Gebot der Schicklichkeit*] whose message reads: "that nothing shall be suggested that does not belong in the common sphere."[114]

When Schleiermacher discusses the term *Schaamhaftigkeit* in his "Versuch über die Schaamhaftigkeit" he also is referring to this sphere of *freie Geselligkeit* and he also is writing for the same audience. The term *"Schaamhaftigkeit"* functions for him in the individual sphere in a manner that is similar to the way that the term *"Schicklichkeit"* functions for the group. While it is the group that needs to be protected through *Schicklichkeit*, and the individual becomes subordinated to it, in his "Versuch über die Schaamhaftigkeit" the group becomes subordinated to the individual and it is the individual that needs to be protected through *Schaamhaftigkeit*. One might say that the "Versuch einer Theorie des geselligen Betragens" provides us with Schleiermacher's view of a public ethics while his "Versuch über die Schaamhaftigkeit" presents his view of a private ethics. Yet there is no contradiction between them. Both operate together. For example, an immodest statement is not only a statement that offends one individual, breaking the law of *Schaamhaftigkeit*, but since that individual thereby becomes excluded and is momentarily unable to participate wholeheartedly in the group, it also violates the law of *Schicklichkeit*.

In turning back to the "Versuch über die Schaamhaftigkeit" we find that Schleiermacher's starting point is the individual. The unique individuality of each person is stressed. Each person lives in one's own private realm of freedom. This sphere of freedom consists of a person's thoughts, feelings, actions, and aspirations.[115] It is a sphere that must be respected and that also is fragile and vulnerable to an attack from others.

Schaamhaftigkeit, in Schleiermacher's view, consists in respecting each person's sphere of freedom. In the definitive statement about *Schaamhaftigkeit*, Schleiermacher writes: "That upon which *Schaamhaftigkeit* insists is actually the respect for the state of mind of another, which should prevent us from interrupting it, as it were, in a forcible manner."[116] In another place he writes that "making some kind of an impression upon the mood and state of mind of human beings should be avoided."[117] When Schleiermacher says this he is referring to the disrespectful invasion of another's sphere of freedom without the other person's consent. In so doing, certain unwelcome and harmful impressions are forced upon a person in a manner that alters one's state of consciousness in a disagreeable manner.

What are the impressions that one should avoid imposing upon another? One should not force those impressions upon persons that have the potentiality of moving them into a state of pure desire.[118] When Schleiermacher says this he is presupposing a situation in which the spiritual is dominant. Yet Schleiermacher does not believe that one should view *Schaamhaftigkeit* from the perspective of the spiritual alone. One also must look at it from the perspective of the sensual. Schleiermacher believes that something can violate the boundaries of *Schaamhaftigkeit* which interrupts a sensuous moment shared between two lovers. He writes:

> It is very one-sided if one only wants to condemn something where a condition of quiet thinking generally is interrupted through the stimulus of the sensual or desire: the state of enjoyment and the prevailing sensuality also has something holy and demands equal respect, and it must likewise be shameful forcibly to interrupt it.[119]

The message proclaimed in the *Vertraute Briefe* is the unity of the sensual and the spiritual in love. There is a certain *Schaamhaftigkeit* which consists in respecting the state of mind of another and not trying to induce it into a crude state of desire. Yet there also is a *Schaamhaftigkeit* that operates within the state of desire and sensuality itself.[120] This *Schaamhaftigkeit* entails respecting the sweet and holy union of the sensual and the spiritual, never allowing the sensual to become torn from its spiritual element. In this situation the introduction of something immodest would entail causing the transition from a state in which the spiritual and the sensual are combined in love to a state in which crude sensuality alone prevails. Schleiermacher explains:

> Love shyly withdraws from this physiological view and cannot endure it when that which is connected with the highest in it is isolated and degraded as mechanism. To feel and to keep this intrusion into its free play at a distance is, therefore, the *Schaamhaftigkeit* of the lovers with each other. Their concern – and especially the woman's holiest concern – is that the service of the great Goddess not be desecrated; whatever is given from love, from longing, from the consciousness of enjoyment belongs as a beautiful surrounding to its condition; every charming intimation, every witty play that the imagination produces is acceptable, and because of *Schaamhaftigkeit* there is no excess and there are no boundaries.[121]

Schleiermacher's redefinition of *Schaamhaftigkeit*, as the respect for the state of mind of another, also has a general application. It consists in having the correct perception and assessment of the state of mind of other human beings and then in being sensitive to their moods and vulnerabilities so as not to hurt them. It involves knowing what is proper and decent [*schicklich*]. For example, joking when a person is mourning the death of a loved one would be shameful. This, too, would be an invasion of another person's sphere of freedom. Schleiermacher writes:

> Some sort of jest brought in at the wrong time, a cutting joke in the middle of a serious investigation, a seed to some kind of another passion thrown into the still river of a quiet mood,

seem to me to be just as unseemly and must excite the same feeling.[122]

Consequently, *Schaamhaftigkeit*, in its redefinition, becomes a sensitivity that each brings to each other, knowing where a person might be especially vulnerable and where one's sphere of freedom might be violated. Schleiermacher continues:

> The task of *Schaamhaftigkeit* remains becoming acquainted with every human being, in every mood which is common to one or to several, in order to know where one's freedom is most defenseless and vulnerable, in order to protect one there.[123]

Of course, it is impossible always to know where a person is vulnerable and defenseless. One, therefore, has to operate on a more general knowledge of human nature and use one's own powers of discretion in dealing with human beings. Schleiermacher writes that it is always best to treat human beings as a little better than they actually deserve to be treated, i.e., to treat human beings as though they are far frailer and more vulnerable than they really are. By invoking this simple principle one can be reasonably sure not to offend most people. It is in relation to this calling forth of principles relating to a general knowledge of human beings that Schleiermacher's concept of *Schaamhaftigkeit* is given a sure ethical foundation as a virtue.[124]

With this new definition Schleiermacher makes a clean break with previous theories of *Schaamhaftigkeit*. While he nowhere calls people by name, he is highly critical of previous ethical theories of *Schaamhaftigkeit* because of their obsession with the evils of the sensual. He speaks of a "fearful and narrow-minded *Schaamhaftigkeit*, which is now the character of society, having its foundation only in the consciousness of a great and universal perversity and a deep corruption."[125] In another place he writes that such *Schaamhaftigkeit* reminds him of the prudish Englishwomen "who withdraw whenever the wine is put out."[126] If one followed the precepts of *Schaamhaftigkeit* as defined by others one would have to "segregate the sexes."[127]

Schleiermacher fears that should this perverted, prudish *Schaamhaftigkeit* continue, society eventually will rebel and become truly shameful. Any one-sidedness necessarily must pass over into its opposite on the path to a healthy balance. A stress on the spiritual alone will eventually pass over into an overemphasis on the sensual. Schleiermacher phrases his fear in the following manner:

> . . . our society will end up like our women who, when good manners control them more and more strictly to the extent that it eventually becomes improper even to point a fingertip, suddenly turn the other way out of despair and again reveal the neck, shoulders, and bosom to the rough air and the inquiring eyes, or like caterpillars cast off their old skin with a resolute motion.[128]

What, then, is to be done? How can society free itself from this false *Schaamhaftigkeit* that oppresses the human spirit and threatens to destroy the proper balance of the universe? Schleiermacher believes that there are two great teachers who can lead human society back to a proper understanding of what true *Schaamhaftigkeit* should entail: [1] women and [2] works of art. Schleiermacher calls for the help of women with the following words:

> The first thing that is necessary to get the topic back on the right track is the help of women; . . . everything from which they distance themselves becomes crude . . . it is they who, through deed, must sanctify everything which until now was outlawed through false delusion. Only when they show that it has not offended them can the beautiful wit be released.[129]

Women, especially, play a crucial role as teachers because historically they alone have had to present a modest front to the world. Consequently, Schleiermacher believes that if women can exhibit behavior expressive of true *Schaamhaftigkeit* – i.e., respecting the individual sphere of freedom of others and refraining from forcible attacks upon others in which the healthy balance between the spiritual and sensual becomes unhinged or in which insensitivity is shown toward the mood of another – men likewise can learn what true *Schaamhaftigkeit* should entail. By asking women to define the standards of *Schaamhaftigkeit* Schleiermacher goes completely against the grain of the tradition. Instead of men defining the *Schaamhaftigkeit* that women alone should exhibit, women now are to define that *Schaamhaftigkeit* that both men and women are to practice.[130]

Next to women it is works of art – paintings, sculpture, literary works – which can teach us what true *Schaamhaftigkeit* should be. They can act as teachers, Schleiermacher argues, because they can harmonize the sensual and spiritual in an ethical manner. The spiritual always can shimmer through the sensual in art. Novels especially are adept at this. By saying this Schleiermacher implies that works like Schlegel's *Lucinde* can "through their example, restore for those the correct discretion and tone, that which is the tenderest and most beautiful in the art of living."[131] It is with these words that Schleiermacher's "Versuch über die Schaamhaftigkeit" comes to an end.

Concluding Reflections

Friedrich Schlegel relates that his brother August Wilhelm Schlegel had marveled at Schleiermacher's redefinition of *Schaamhaftigkeit*. He also wrote that his brother felt that Schleiermacher had "chased [previous ethical theories of *Schaamhaftigkeit*] like a rabbit . . . out of every corner until it finally had to tumble out into the open."[132] Old conceptions of *Schaamhaftigkeit* had indeed been chased from corner to corner until they finally had no choice but to jump out of the ethical arena. The three definitions of *Schaamhaftigkeit* that Schleiermacher had driven out were: first, *Schaamhaftigkeit* as a prudish, negative, empty virtue preoccupied with ridding the mind and heart of sensuous, desirous thoughts [Rousseau, Kant, Campe, Fichte]; second, *Schaamhaftigkeit* used as a charm by women to manipulate men [Rousseau]; and third, *Schaamhaftigkeit* as a *Geschlechts-charakter* of women, juxtaposed either explicitly or implicitly to the "reason" of men [Rousseau, Kant, Campe, Fichte]. These three definitions are excluded from Schleiermacher's redefinition of *Schaamhaftigkeit*. In their place comes a startling new interpretation of *Schaamhaftigkeit* as "the respect for the state of mind of another, which should prevent us from interrupting it, as it were, in a forcible manner."[133]

We have seen that Schleiermacher was able to dispose of the first definition of *Schaamhaftigkeit* (forbidding sensuous thoughts from entering one's consciousness) by employing the term *"Schaam"* where previous ethical theorists had used the term *Schaamhaftigkeit*. While these previous theorists had lumped a variety of attributes together under the one term *Schaamhaftigkeit*, Schleiermacher is careful to distinguish nuances of meaning and uses numerous words to define exactly what he intends. For example, besides the term *Schaam* [inner displeasurable feelings and thought processes], he also employs the term *Reue* [remorse] to depict the displeasure over something that has actually happened in reality.[134]

Schaam refers to the inner mental processes of human beings. Schleiermacher makes a great distinction between an inner mental process [*Schaam*] and the outer communication to another [*Schaamhaftigkeit*]. *Schaamhaftigkeit* is no longer defined as something that battles against intrusions and onslaughts of sensuous thoughts. The sensual has an important place within Schleiermacher's ethical theory. Indeed, it represents one component of the universe. One cannot say that one element of the universe, namely *Geist*/spiritual is holy, while the other, namely *Natur*/sensual, is unholy. Each is a sacred and necessary component of the universe. A profane, immodest state is one in which the two sides of the universe, which should always be interconnected, become separated and the sensual alone prevails. *Schaamhaftigkeit*, therefore, does not consist in shunning the sensual but rather in not doing anything that might destroy the delicate balance between the sensual and the spiritual. The *Schaamhaftigkeit* between lovers makes certain that the spiritual is always part and parcel of the sensual.

Schleiermacher also spurns the second (*Schaamhaftigkeit* as a manipulative charm) and third (*Schaamhaftigkeit* as non-reason) definitions of *Schaamhaftigkeit* through its redefinition as a <u>human</u> virtue. By doing so Schleiermacher makes his greatest contribution. It is obvious that if *Schaamhaftigkeit* had been defined as a virtue that both men and women are to practice it never could have been used against women in the way that it was. There never could have been a logical move from *Schaamhaftigkeit* to denying women educational opportunities or civil liberties. Quite clearly, a redefinition of *Schaamhaftigkeit* would have to entail the move of *Schaamhaftigkeit* from being categorized as a gender-specific "characteristic of sex/*Geschlechtscharakter*" assigned to women alone to a virtue to be practiced by men and women alike. It was precisely this move that Schleiermacher made.

We have seen that it was *Schaamhaftigkeit* defined as a manipulative charm and *Schaamhaftigkeit* defined over against reason that had enabled Rousseau, Kant, Campe, and Fichte to argue against the move of women into greater spheres of human activity. All of these men employed *Schaamhaftigkeit* within their philosophies as a female "characteristic of sex/ *Geschlechtscharakter.*" In Schleiermacher's view, *Schaamhaftigkeit* is not an ontological "characteristic of sex/*Geschlechtscharakter.*" *Schaamhaftigkeit* is a virtue that is to be shared and practiced both by men and by women. All human beings, regardless of gender, are to be responsible for demonstrating sensitivity toward the vulnerabilities and spheres of freedom of other human beings.

Because *Schaamhaftigkeit* is understood as a human virtue it cannot be used as a manipulative charm by women against men nor can it be juxtaposed over against reason. The positing of *Geschlechtscharaktere* presupposes an either/or situation. Either one has reason capable of abstraction and understanding principles based on universality or one has *Schaamhaftigkeit*. By attributing *Schaamhaftigkeit* both to men and to women Schleiermacher has freed us from an either/or situation. Women can now be defined as possessing both *Schaamhaftigkeit* and powers of rationality. Men are now to practice the virtue of *Schaamhaftigkeit* previously attributed to women alone.

Schleiermacher not only uses an anthropological starting point that stands at variance with those of Rousseau, Kant, Campe, and Fichte but he also uses one that stands at variance with some theological and ethical systems today. Their starting point I will simply term an "anthropology of division." Such an anthropology of division takes its starting point in separations within human life. Rather than starting from what all human beings share in common, or what Schleiermacher called "infinite humanity" in the Creed to his "Catechism for Noble Women," these systems start from divisions within human society. Rousseau, Kant, Campe and Fichte did not start their analyses with what men and women share in common ("characteristics of the species") but rather with what makes them distinct ("characteristics of sex/*Geschlechtscharaktere*").

We have seen in our examination where such an "anthropology of division" can lead. The most extreme case is that of Fichte. By setting women and men apart as ontologically distinct and by playing deductive tricks through whose logic he hopes to convince his readers of inalterable a priori truths, Fichte has reduced women to being the mere slaves of men, who give up their "empirical I's" entirely and for all eternity.

Some contemporary feminist theologians also start with such an "anthropology of division." Here again the starting point is not the "characteristics of the species" but rather the "characteristics of sex," i.e., what makes women different from men. Rightly infuriated by the misogyny of men such as Fichte, they have wrongly adopted an ethical system that will inevitably repeat Fichte's mistakes because it is Fichte's own system only clothed in twentieth-century garb. Women versus men or men versus women, it does not matter. The failure surely will result because there is no ethical criterion for judgment that stands above this division. Because the wrongs of human society are addressed from a partial point of view, they themselves become demonic. They lack a higher point of reference from which they themselves can be judged.

There are other contemporary systems that also start with such an anthropology of division. Rather than starting with shared "infinite humanity," some liberation theologies begin by dividing the world into the rich and the poor. Some black theologies start out by dividing the world into blacks and whites. Some feminist theologians divide the world into male and female. The concerns of feminist theology, black theology, and liberation theology are all legitimate ones. There are no problems more pressing in our society than those of poverty, racism, and the oppression of women and minorities. Yet how can change be effected if we lack the proper anthropological starting point in what Schleiermacher calls "infinite humanity"?

At first sight the "Versuch über die Schaamhaftigkeit" appears to be but an insignificant little essay. After a more careful examination, however, it must be claimed as one of Schleiermacher's greatest ethical works. Examined solely within its own historical context and the issues posed during Schleiermacher's own day, it must be upheld as the greatest contribution from the discipline of philosophical ethics to the "Frauenfrage" in early nineteenth-century Germany. Seen within the context of late twentieth-century theology, some of which is attempting conceptually to battle the continued wrongs performed against women, Schleiermacher can remind us of the only correct formal principle from which all anthropological analysis must begin. This starting point is "infinite humanity." It alone can lead to a truly ethical theology and a truly moral ethics. This is because "infinite humanity," as an anthropological starting point, is not only definitional but is also teleological, containing its own ethical point of judgment within itself.

Schleiermacher has been criticized for failing to fight for women's rights in the political sphere. It is true that the early Schleiermacher's contributions to the "Frauenfrage" were on a philosophical level alone. Yet this was the most primary and foundational work that needed to be carried out at that time. I believe that he made an important contribution in his "Versuch über die Schaamhaftigkeit" and that the "early Schleiermacher" of the 1797-1806 period should be extolled as an early harbinger working toward bettering women's conditions.[135] There is still much left to be done on this conceptual level. Theologians and ethicists who are working on this conceptual level in an attempt to provide the intellectual framework within which the rights of women can be discussed should remember where Fichte's anthropology of division led. Instead of perpetuating such anthropologies of division, they should consider adopting the following creed written by Schleiermacher in 1798: "I believe in infinite humanity, which existed before it assumed the cloak of manhood and womanhood."[136]

Notes

1. I cite using the pagination both from the original 1800 text and from the Kritische Gesamtausgabe. The page number from the 1800 edition will be put in [ ]. [{Friedrich Schleiermacher}, "Versuch über die Schaamhaftigkeit," *Vertraute Briefe über Friedrich Schlegels Lucinde* (Lübeck/Leipzig: Friedrich Bohn, 1800), pp [50-74]. Friedrich Schleiermacher, "Versuch über die Schaamhaftigkeit", *Vertraute Briefe über Friedrich Schlegels Lucinde*, in F.D.E. Schleiermacher, *Schriften aus der Berliner Zeit 1800-1802*, hg.v. Günter Meckenstock, Kritische Gesamtausgabe 1/3, hg.v. Hans-Joachim Birkner et al. (New York: Berlin: Walter de Gruyter, 1988), pp 168-178 (hereafter cited as *KGA* I/3).]

    Starting with the Gutzkow edition of the *Vertraute Briefe* in 1835 most editors of the text have modernized the spelling of *Schaamhaftigkeit* to "Schamhaftigkeit." Throughout I use the original spelling used by the authors.

2. *Schaamhaftigkeit* is a difficult term to translate into English. It is a term infrequently used in German, and today it is seen as outdated and quaint. Its root, *Schaam*, is derived from the Anglo-Saxon *scamu* meaning to "cover up." *Schaam* carries with it a variety of meanings including shame, modesty, bashfulness, decency, and chastity. Anatomically it refers to the genitals of human beings [e.g., *männliche Scham*, *weibliche Scham*]. Within a biblical context it refers to "nakedness." The term *Schaamhaftigkeit* has been variously translated into English either as "modesty" or as a "sense of shame." Usually the word "modesty" has been used. While *Schaamhaftigkeit* does connote a sense of modesty, the word modesty bears no etymological relation to the word *Schaamhaftigkeit*. From the French *modestie* or the Latin *modestia*, modesty refers more to a moderation in behavior that may or may not relate to the feelings of guilt and uneasiness that occur in conjunction with a state of shame. A "sense of shame" is much closer to the meaning of *Schaamhaftigkeit*. Both are derived from the same root – *scamu*. Yet "sense of shame" is better translated by the German *Schamgefühl*. Perhaps the best English translation is a word that, like the German, also is outdated – "shamefacedness." Shamefacedness originally was (mis)derived from the Middle English word *schamefast* which, in turn, was derived from the Anglo Saxon *scam* meaning "shame" and *faest* meaning "fast" or "firm." It meant being "restrained by shame." Because the German has been translated variously into English I will usually use the German original *Schaamhaftigkeit* throughout. (In my discussion here I follow the Oxford English Dictionary.)

    Shame, as a psychological phenomenon, has recently become a focus of attention in the field of psychotherapy. See, for example: John Bradshaw, *Healing the Shame That Binds You* (Deerfield Beach, Florida: Health Communications, 1988).

3. Friedrich Schlegel, *Lucinde. Ein Roman*, Erster Teil (Berlin: Heinrich Fröhlich, 1799). Critical reprint edition: Friedrich Schlegel, *Lucinde. Ein Roman*, in *Dichtungen*, hg.v. Hans Eichner, Kritische Friedrich-Schlegel-Ausgabe Bd. V, hg.v. Ernst Behler et al. (Paderborn/München/Wien: Ferdinand Schöningh; Zürich: Thomas-Verlag, 1962), pp. 1-92 (hereafter cited as *KFSA* V).

4. See Friedrich Schlegel's review of *Woldemar*: Friedrich Schlegel, *Charakteristiken und Kritiken I (1796-1801)*, hg.v. Hans Eichner, Kritische Friedrich-Schlegel-Ausgabe Bd. II, hg.v. Ernst Behler et al. (Paderborn/ München/Wien: Ferdinand Schöningh; Zürich: Thomas-Verlag, 1967), pp. 57-77 (hereafter cited as *KFSA* II).

5. Friedrich Schlegel, *Lucinde*, *KFSA V*, pp. 13-15. Also see Schlegel's discussion of false shame in an earlier work where he praises the Spartan men and women who, after winning a battle, threw off their clothes and celebrated their victory naked. See Friedrich Schlegel, "Über die Diotima" [1795], *Studien des klassischen Altertums*, hg.v. Ernst Behler, Kritische Friedrich-Schlegel-Ausgabe Bd. I, hg.v. Ernst Behler et al. (Paderborn/

München/Wien: Ferdinand Schöningh; Zürich: Thomas- Verlag, 1979), pp. 89-90 (hereafter cited as *KFSA* I). Schlegel also employs the term "falsche Scham" to depict this situation.

    6. Schleiermacher, *Vertraute Briefe*, p. 144 [3].

    7. Schleiermacher writes that this essay was an earlier attempt. See the *Vertraute Briefe*, pp. 167-168 [49-50]. He had originally planned to include an essay on "respectability." In a notation Schleiermacher made while preparing to write the *Vertraute Briefe* he wrote: "In den Brief über die Prüderie muß ein polemisches Gespräch über den Begrif des Anständigen eingewebt werden." [Friedrich Schleiermacher, *Schriften aus der Berliner Zeit 1796-1799*, hg.v. Günter Meckenstock, Kritische Gesamtausgabe 1/2, hg.v. Hans-Joachim Birkner et al. (Berlin/New York: Walter de Gruyter, 1984), #67, p. 135 (hereafter cited as *KGA* I/2).] Schleiermacher changed his mind, including the essay on *Schaamhaftigkeit* instead. He did go on to finish his essay on "respectability," entitling it "Über das Anständige. Zwei Gespräche." It is found in *KGA* I/3, pp. 73-99.

    8. Schlegel, *KFSA* V, pp. 35-58.

    9. Schlegel, "Über die Diotima," *KFSA* I, p. 91.

    10. Short discussions are found by Karl Barth, *The Theology of Schleiermacher*, ed. Dietrich Ritschl, trans. Geoffrey Bromiley (Grand Rapids: Eerdmans, 1982), p. 122; Kurt Lüthi, *Feminismus und Romantik. Sprache, Gesellschaft, Symbole, Religion* (Wien/Köln/Graz: Hermann Böhlaus, 1985), pp. 97-98; Kurt Nowak, *Schleiermacher und die Frühromantik* (Weimar: Hermann Böhlaus, 1986), pp. 282-283; D.A. Twesten, hg., *Friedrich Schleiermachers, Grundriß der philosophischen Ethik* (Berlin: G. Reimer, 1841), pp. lxxxi-lxxxii. The lengthiest and most detailed analysis of Schleiermacher's essay on *Schaamhaftigkeit* can be found in: Klaus Mollenhauer, "Der frühromantische Pädagoge," in *Friedrich Schleiermacher 1768-1834. Theologe-Philosoph-Pädagoge*, hg.v., Dietz Lange (Göttingen: Vandenhoeck & Ruprecht, 1985), pp. 193-216.

    11. Wilhelm Dilthey, *Leben Schleiermachers*, hg.v. Martin Redeker 3.A. (Berlin: Walter de Gruyter, 1970), Bd. I, pp. 512-513.

    12. Paul Kluckhohn, *Die Auffassung der Liebe in der Literatur des 18. Jahrhunderts und in der deutschen Romantik*, 3.A. (Tübingen: Max Niemeyer, 1966), pp. 439-441.

    13. Friedrich Schleiermacher, *Aus Schleiermacher's Leben. In Briefen*, Zum Druck vorbereitet von Ludwig Jonas nach dessen Tode herausgegeben von Wilhelm Dilthey (Berlin: Georg Reimer, 1861), Vol. III, p. 188. Cf. Ibid., 173, 177, 186-187, 196 for other responses to the "Versuch über die Schaamhaftigkeit." The four volumes of Schleiermacher's correspondence will be cited hereafter as *Br.* I, *Br.* II, *Br.* III, *Br.* IV.

    14. My comments are limited to this specific early period of Schleiermacher's life. Schleiermacher did not bring to fruition the revolutionary potential in these ideas in works written after 1806. His later psychological and pedagogical works and *Household Sermons* reveal that his later assessment of women was not as emancipatory.

    15. "Idee zu einem Katechismus der Vernunft für edle Frauen," in *Athenaeum. Eine Zeitschrift* 1/2, von August Wilhelm Schlegel und Friedrich Schlegel (Berlin: Friedrich Vieweg dem älteren, 1798; reprint ed., Darmstadt: Wissenschaftliche Buchgesellschaft, 1983), pp. [109-111], 285-287. Also found in: Friedrich Schleiermacher, *KGA* I/2, pp. 153-154.

    16. Ibid.

    17. Ibid.

    18. Ibid.

    19. Ibid.

    20. Ibid.

    21. The best introduction to the characteristics attributed to men and women can be found in: Karin Hausen, "Die Polarisierung der 'Geschlechtscharaktere' – Eine Spiegelung der Dissoziation von Erwerbs- und Familienleben," in *Sozialgeschichte der Familie in der Neuzeit Europas*, Neue Forschungen, hg.v. Werner Conze (Stuttgart: Ernst Klett, 1976), pp.

363-393. ET: Karin Hausen, "Family and Role-Division: The Polarisation of Sexual Stereotypes in the Nineteenth Century – An Aspect of the Dissociation of Work and Family Life," trans. Cathleen Catt, in *The German Family. Essays on the Social History of the Family and Nineteenth- and Twentieth-Century Germany*, ed. Richard J. Evans and W.R. Lee (London: Croom Helm; Totowa, NJ: Barnes & Noble, 1981), pp. 51-83.

22.   D. Rauch, ed., *Tabulae librorum e bibliotheca defuncti Schleiermacher . . .* (Berolini: Typis Reimerianis, 1835), p. 88, #433-447.

23.   Ibid., p. 86, #361.

24.   Ibid., p. 102, #32.

25.   Ibid., p. 100, #314.

26.   Ibid., p. 86, #381.

27.   Ibid., p. 86, #380.

28.   Jean-Jacques Rousseau, *Émile*, trans. Barbara Foxley, introduced by P.D. Jimack (London/Toronto: Dent; New York: Dutton, 1974). I cite from this edition throughout.

29.   Ibid., p. 321.

30.   See note 21.

31.   Friedrich Schleiermacher, *Brouillon zur Ethik (1805/06)*, hg.v. Hans-Joachim Birkner (Hamburg: Felix Meiner, 1981), p. 54. It is important to note that Schleiermacher, while believing in "*Geschlechtscharaktere*," i.e., the ontological characteristics of the sexes, understood these as limiting. He pleads for the "Extinction des Geschlechtscharakters" (Ibid., p. 57). For a discussion of Schleiermacher's assertion that true humanity consists in "psychological androgyny" see Ruth Drucilla Richardson, *The Role of Women in the Life and Thought of the Early Schleiermacher (1768-1806): An Historical Overview* (Lewiston/Queenston/Lampeter: Edwin Mellen Press, 1990).

32.   Rousseau, *Émile*, p. 322.

33.   Ibid.

34.   Ibid., p. 324.

35.   Ibid., p. 322.

36.   Ibid., p. 323; cf. p. 322.

37.   See Ibid., pp. 325, 328, 334, 338, 348, 349, 353, 360, 361, 366, 378, 384.

38.   Ibid., p. 322.

39.   Ibid.

40.   Ibid., p. 377.

41.   Ibid., p. 323.

42.   Ibid., p. 345.

43.   Ibid., 349.

44.   Ibid., p. 328.

45.   Ibid., p. 322.

46.   Ibid., p. 327.

47.   Ibid., p. 322.

48.   Ibid., pp. 328-329.

49.   Ibid., p. 348.

50.   Ibid., pp. 356-357.

51.   Ibid., p. 377.

52.   Ibid., p. 387.

53.   M. Immanuel Kant, *Beobachtungen über das Gefühl des Schönen und Erhabenen* (Königsberg: Johann Jacob Kanter, 1764). ET: Immanuel Kant, *Observations on the Feeling of the Beautiful and Sublime*, trans. John T. Goldthwait (Berkeley/Los Angeles/London: University of California Press, 1960). I cite from Goldthwait's English translations throughout.

54.   See note 23.

55.   Kant, *Observations*, p. 47.

56. Ibid., p. 77.
57. Ibid., p. 63.
58. Ibid., p. 81.
59. Ibid., pp. 62-63.
60. Ibid., p. 81.
61. Ibid., p. 81, 84.
62. Ibid., p. 61.
63. Ibid., p. 78.
64. Ibid., p. 81.
65. Ibid., p. 79, 81.
66. Ibid., p. 78.
67. Only after a woman has lost her physical attractiveness is a limited education allowed to her. In this undertaking it is her husband who is to be her teacher. (Ibid., p. 92.) Kant speaks out harshly against learned women again in his 1798 *Anthropologie*, stating: "Was die gelehrten Frauen betrifft: so brauchen sie ihre Bücher etwa so wie ihre Uhr, nämlich sie zu tragen, damit gesehen werde, daß sie eine haben; ob sie zwar gemeiniglich still steht oder nicht nach der Sonne gestellt ist." [Immanuel Kant, "Der Charakter des Geschlechts," *Anthropologie in pragmatischer Hinsicht*, hg.v. Wolfgang Becker, Nachwort Hans Ebeling (Stuttgart: Reclam, 1983), p. 261.] Kant's analysis of women also can be seen in: Immanuel Kant, "Das Eherecht," *Die Metaphysik der Sitten. Metaphysische Anfangsgründe der Rechtslehre* [1797], Erster Teil (Leipzig: Felix Meiner, 1945), §§24-27, pp. 91-94.
68. Joachim Heinrich Campe, *Väterlicher Rath für meine Tochter. Ein Gegenstück zum Theophron* [1789], (Frankfurt/Leipzig, 1790). See note 24 for Rauch's listing of the book. Schleiermacher's sister had loved Campe's book, writing: "Campens Väterlicher Rath, hatte ich auch von ihr, welches ich zu meiner MorgenLecture den Herbst machte, o! hätte ich es in jüngern Jahren gelesen dis lehrreiche schöne Buch für die Jugend unsers Geschlechts.'" [Friedrich Schleiermacher, *Briefwechsel 1774-1796*, hg.v. Andreas Arndt und Wolfgang Virmond, Kritische Gesamtausgabe V/1, hg.v. Hans-Joachim Birkner et al. (Berlin/New York: Walter de Gruyter, 1985), #241, lines 151-154.
69. Campe, *Väterlicher Rath*, pp. 5-6.
70. Ibid., p. 37; cf. pp. 14-15.
71. Ibid., p. 70.
72. Ibid., p. 21.
73. Ibid., p. 20.
74. Ibid.
75. Ibid., pp. 49-51; 64-65.
76. Ibid., p. 48.
77. Ibid., p. 70.
78. Ibid., p. 136.
79. Ibid., p. 138.
80. Ibid., p. 141.
81. Ibid., p. 159.
82. Theodor Gottlieb von Hippel, *Über die bürgerliche Verbesserung der Weiber* (Berlin: Voßischen Buchhandlung, 1792). ET: Theodor Gottlieb von Hippel, *On Improving the Status of Women*, trans. Timothy F. Sellner (Detroit: Wayne State University Press, 1979). I use Sellner's translation throughout. For Rauch listing see note 25.
83. Wollstonecraft devotes an entire chapter to an analysis of "modesty," a term similar to *Schaamhaftigkeit*, in: Mary Wollstonecraft, "Modesty. – Comprehensively considered, and not as a sexual virtue," in *A Vindication of the Rights of Woman: With Strictures on Political and Moral Subjects* (London: J. Johnson, 1792; reprint ed. New York: Source Books, 1971), pp. 149-161.

84. Hippel, *Improving the Status of Women*, p. 58.

85. Ibid., pp. 106-107.

86. Ibid., pp. 112-113.

87. Johann Gottlieb Fichte, *Grundlage des Naturrechts nach Principien der Wissenschaftslehre* (Jena/Leipzig: Christian Ernst Gabler, 1796; reprint ed. Berlin: Walter de Gruyter, 1971). Johann Gottlieb Fichte, *Das System der Sittenlehre nach den Principien der Wissenschaftslehre* (Jena/Leipzig: Christian Ernst Gabler, 1798; reprint ed., Berlin: Walter de Gruyter, 1971). These will be cited as *NR* and *SL* throughout. I will be citing from the de Gruyter edition, using their pagination.

88. See notes 26 and 27.

89. See for example his letter to Brinkmann of January 4, 1800, in *Br.* IV, p. 53.

90. *SL*, p. 330.

91. *NR*, p. 309.

92. *NR*, p. 310.

93. *NR*, p. 310.

94. *SL*, p. 330.

95. *NR*, pp. 325-326.

96. *NR*, 346, 350. He does not directly name women's "Schutzredner" but it is clear whom he means.

97. *NR*, p. 347.

98. *NR*, p. 347.

99. *NR*, p. 350.

100. *NR*, p. 353.

101. Fichte does, however, allow women to write popular books for other women on useful subjects. See *NR*, p. 352.

102. *NR*, p. 353.

103. Schleiermacher, "Versuch über die Schaamhaftigkeit," in *Vertraute Briefe*, in *KGA* I/3, p. 168 [50].

104. Ibid., p. 168 [51].

105. Ibid.

106. Ibid., p. 171 [57].

107. Ibid., p. 169 [52].

108. Ibid., p. 169 [54].

109. Friedrich Schleiermacher, "Versuch einer Theorie des geselligen Betragens [1799]," in *KGA* I/2, pp. 165-184.

110. Ibid., p. 173.

111. Ibid., p. 170.

112. Ibid., p. 171.

113. Ibid.

114. Ibid.

115. Schleiermacher's discussion of a person's individual sphere of freedom should be seen in conjunction with his 1800 *Monologen*, written at about the same time.

116. *Vertraute Briefe*, p. 172 [60].

117. Ibid., p. 171 [58].

118. Ibid.

119. Ibid., p. 173 [63].

120. Schleiermacher also discussed this in an unpublished fragment:
Doppeltes Princip bei der Schamhaftigkeit die Sinnlichkeit nicht zu profanieren und einen der Sinnlichkeit fremden Gemüthszustand nicht durch Sinnlichkeit zu profaniren. Wer nur die lezte hat fürchtet sich vor seiner eignen Lascivitaet. Wer nur die erste hat ist ein sentimentaler

Wollüstling. Die erste für sich allein ist den Frauen sehr eigen, die zweite den Mädchen. Eine neue Frau besizt die höchste Schaamhaftigkeit weil sie nothwendig beide vereinigen muß. In Rüksicht des ersten Princips besteht die Schamhaftigkeit in Vermeidung des groben animalischen, in Rüksicht des lezteren in Vermeidung des anschaulichen und des genetischen. Je ethischer ein Zustand ist je gröber kann man von allen Obiecten der Schaamhaftigkeit reden ohne sie zu verlezen je erotischer er ist: desto üppiger darf man seyn aber ja nicht plump. Hieraus ergeben sich zugleich die Regeln für die Individuen. So wie bei der vollkomnen Unschuld keine Schaam ist so bei der vollkomnen Corruption auch keine. In der Art wie Männer und Frauen hierin miteinander umgehn liegt ein [vollstaendiger] [ ]. (Schleiermacher, *KGA* I/3, #6, pp. 132-133.)

121. Ibid., p. 175 [66-67].
122. Ibid., p. 172 [60-61].
123. Ibid., p. 172 [61].
124. Ibid., p. 173 [62].
125. Ibid., p. 176 [70].
126. Ibid., p. 175 [66].
127. Ibid., p. 176 [70].
128. Ibid., pp. 176-177 [70-71].
129. Ibid., pp. 177-178 [72-73].

130. Also to be noted is the fact that Schleiermacher wrote in the *Vertraute Briefe* that the ideas contained in the "Versuch über die Schaamhaftigkeit" were born out of conversations that he had with Ernestine. See the third letter by Ernestine where she reminds him of the important role she had played in the creation of the essay on *Schaamhaftigkeit*. Ibid., p. 160 [34-35].

131. Ibid., p. 178 [74].
132. *Br.* III, p. 187.
133. *Vertraute Briefe*, p. 172 [60].
134. Ibid., p. 170 [54].
135. See note 14.
136. See note 15.

V

SCHLEIERMACHER'S "BROUILLON ZUR ETHIK, 1805/06"

John Wallhausser

I. The Setting

Schleiermacher's 1805/06 lectures on ethics (*Brouillon zur Ethik*) at the University of Halle provide the first comprehensive statement of his ethical system. The lectures were given during a brief interlude between his earlier self-imposed exile at Stolp, which ended with his appointment to the University of Halle in 1804, and the closing of the University by Napoleon in 1806. The extant lecture notes give us a tight, sometimes cryptic, always striking insight into Schleiermacher's unique grasp of the scope and nature of ethical thinking. The title for these dense lecture notes (*Brouillon zur Ethik*) characterizes them as an important initial step toward the formulation of his own ethics – they are a "Rough Outline for Ethics."

Schleiermacher arrived at the university town on October 12, 1804, to take up his dual post as professor and University preacher. However, the opportunity of combining academic study with preaching – a union for which he had longed – was initially obstructed. The ostensible reason for the delay was that facilities were not available, although it would appear that the suspicions of some University officials and local clergy about his religious views were also involved. Only after repeated insistence were some meager facilities made available and permission for beginning worship services given. (For Schleiermacher's account of the difficulties see *Briefe* II, 54-57, 65-67.)

In addition to this inauspicious beginning, many of Schleiermacher's new colleagues in philosophy and religion also found his views (and reputation) unacceptable; the faculty was still dominated by an older eighteenth-century supernaturalism or rationalism. He once again found himself in an ambiguous situation, wryly noting that within a quarter of an hour he was called a mystic, a materialist, and a narrow follower of orthodoxy. The one exception to this cool reception was Heinrich Steffens, a young professor of natural science and philosophy. Schleiermacher found in Steffens' philosophy of nature a companion for his own conception of ethics. Steffens' conception of "physics" (the philosophy of nature) provided that partner in dialogue with ethics Schleiermacher had asked for in his review of Schelling's *Lectures on the Method of Academic Studies*. I shall return to the argument in that review shortly.

Schleiermacher had planned to begin with lectures on Christian ethics. Upon arriving at Halle, however, "various circumstances have forced me to begin with the philosophical ethics and perhaps it is just as well that I should lay the foundations in this way" (*Briefe* II, 8). He lectured twice on ethics, in 1804-05 and again in 1805-06. Of the first set only the lecture notes on virtue remain; the 1805-06 notes, the *Brouillon zur Ethik*, contain Schleiermacher's typical threefold division into theories of the highest good, virtue, and duty. Early in the winter of 1804 Schleiermacher expressed satisfaction with the first set of lectures: "The ethics bring me the greatest pleasure and if I can lecture on them once more I expect they will turn out quite well. This alone is worth all the trouble in having come to Halle" (*Briefe* IV, 105). At the same time he began planning for the publication of his ethics, writing his friend Brinkmann, "The best I can say about my professorship is that I can certainly learn a great deal and that perhaps in a few years my own ethics will be ready" (*Briefe* IV, 109).

During the following academic year the second set of lectures proceeded even more smoothly. In retrospect, he was critical of "the stiff formalistic nature evident in the first year's lectures"; the *Brouillon*, he believed, exhibited more grace and life (*Briefe* II, 70). He also wrote to his publisher Reimer that he wanted to lecture three times on ethics before submitting the results for publication. This schedule, Schleiermacher noted, would put the earliest publication date at 1807 (*Briefe* IV, 117). However, the Napoleonic invasion undid his plans, the third lecture series never occurred, and thus began the first of the postponements which eventually left

Schleiermacher's ethics unpublished. Many other projects, however, were published during the brief time at Halle including the first volume of his Plato translation, his *Critique of Previous Ethical Theories*, the 1806 revised edition of the *Speeches on Religion*, a "little dialogue" on celebrating Christmas Eve (*Weihnachtsfeier*), and a commentary on the first letter to Timothy.

The University was closed by Napoleon in 1806. As Redeker suggests, it is interesting to compare Schleiermacher's response to Napoleon's presence with Hegel's: Schleiermacher refused to witness the conqueror's entry into the city (1973, 87). Schleiermacher stayed at first out of a sense of duty, although he existed under conditions of near poverty. With the Peace of Tilsit he left Halle and returned to Berlin in May 1807. Dilthey has dated the end of Schleiermacher's *Lehrjahre* and the beginning of the mature years and works after 1808 and his return to Berlin.

Although Schleiermacher's later lectures on ethics would bring changes in the schematic frame work and terminology, they did not basically alter the organization found in the *Brouillon*. An observation on the style of the *Brouillon* is in order: the lectures weave a massive, intricate web of unalleviated abstraction. The formalism of Schleiermacher's method makes an even more stark impression in that the manuscript of the lectures consists of highly concentrated and formal propositions and fragments. As in his preaching, Schleiermacher would write out only the outline of his topic in brief propositions, filling them in and expanding them spontaneously while speaking. The lecture notes provide only the stark internal skeleton, each joint presupposing and requiring the organic whole; the muscle of concrete commentary is largely absent. Less sympathetic interpreters find this style but another reflection of an extreme deductive and formalistic *Drang* to abstract system in Schleiermacher's thought. Others, myself included, hold that despite the obtrusive foreground of the conceptual schema, the goal of the ethics is to provide a flexible heuristic guide for discovering how concrete communities of history develop into the objective organs and agencies of the moral world: "It is not the particular concepts of the 'framework' which bring the proper grasp of the becoming moral world, but the presence and openness of the fundamental moral intuition in all the parts" (Ungern-Sternberg, 1931, 336).

II. Preparations for the "Brouillon"

Two works decisively prepared for his first systematic lectures on ethics: his brief review of Schelling's *Lectures on the Method of Academic Studies* (1804) and his extraordinarily dense and obscure *Critique of Previous Ethical Theories* (1803). Both wrestle with complex dialectical issues while seeking to identify the place, scope, and nature of ethics as a discipline; yet both yield intriguingly simple insights. These insights into the foundational principles of ethics and the relation of ethics to the other academic disciplines Schleiermacher, in the *Brouillon*, calls his "original intuition [*ursprüngliche Anschauung*]" (Braun II, 82). The aim of this "intuition" is to grasp structures of the whole, foundational patterns. Today in philosophy and theology we would say that Schleiermacher discovered a concrete **metaphor** which contains the whole and which he delineates in a descriptive and – what he even calls a – narrative method (Braun II, 80). This metaphorical grasp of the whole he first clearly worked out in the two works just preceding his ethics lectures at Halle.

The Review of Schelling's "Lectures on the Method of Academic Studies"

It was in Schelling's work that Schleiermacher found the schema of the sciences for which he had been searching in his own *Critique*. In Schelling's *Lectures* the inner structure of Identity philosophy set the pattern for the organization of the sciences. The forms of knowing cluster about three points. They are the two poles of Ideal and Real being and the center or identity of both. The distinctions between Ideal and Real are relative for they presuppose "the point of indifference in which the Ideal and the Real worlds are viewed as one" (The review is found in *Briefe* IV, 587-593). The Absolute Identity appears under the conditions of finite life as predominantly natural and predominantly spiritual being.

The sciences are organized according to their objects (Ideal or Real) and the manner in which knowing is related to the manifestations of Being, i.e., speculatively and empirically. Physics (the philosophy of nature) and History (the philosophy of Spirit) are the two contrasting "speculative" sciences distinguished by their objects but the same in their method (the "speculative" development of general laws). In contrast, the empirical sciences share their respective objects with the speculative sciences, but differ in their method. In Schelling's presentation the corresponding empirical study of Ideal being is jurisprudence or forms of Right by which the State organizes the life of culture. The empirical science of Nature which corresponds to the speculative philosophy of physics is medicine. Briefly formulated, the division of the sciences follow this pattern:

Forms of Knowing	The Known:	Ideal Being	Real Being
speculative (predominantly formal)		History	Physics
empirical (predominantly positive)		Jurisprudence	Medicine

No one of the sciences objectifies the whole of Being. Philosophy as the highest form of knowing, which considers the unity of being and knowledge, must exist through all these forms of knowing and dialectically comprehend their interrelatedness. Each of the sciences must be understood not as independent but as a disciplined effort to grasp reality viewed from a certain angle, or preponderant perspective. I find Schleiermacher's discussion of the forms of knowing in his *Critique* virtually identical with Schelling's.

With one major exception! Agreeing with this polar construction of the sciences, Schleiermacher saw the area marked out for his own ethics in Schelling's concept of "History": Ethics "is properly the historical construction of morality" (*Briefe* IV, 589). In the first lecture hour of the *Brouillon* one now consequently reads:

> Ethics is also one entire side of philosophy. Everything appears in it as a producing, just as it appears in the science of nature as product. Each must accept something positive from the other. For even Knowing and Doing are natural powers and must be shown as such. Accordingly, all real knowing

divides into these two sides. Therefore, ethics is the science of
history, i.e., intelligence as appearance. (Braun, II 80)
Ethics is to be the descriptive study of Reason's organization of Nature into
social organs, although for Schleiermacher these organs were not subsumed
alone under the idea of the State. By the time of the Halle lectures, ethics
had, for Schleiermacher, become part of the cosmological process of
interacting forces, physical and spiritual, in which physics describes the action
of nature upon reason and ethics describes the purposive action of reason
upon nature, shaping nature into forms of human community.

"The Critique of Previous Ethical Theories"

The conception of the polar construction of finite being and forms of
knowing did not first derive from Schleiermacher's reading of Schelling. One
finds such a polar model already at work, for example, in the literary
structure of the *Speeches on Religion*. But it was in preparing the *Critique*
that Schleiermacher first hit upon the exact geometrical metaphor for
presenting his ethics. A letter to his publisher Reimer in 1803 illustrates the
prominence of this polar metaphor in his thinking. Schleiermacher included
a "freely drawn symbolic vignette" which he wanted Reimer to put on the title
page of the *Critique*. The drawing was a mathematical figure of two
interwoven ellipses of the same axis but of differenct foci with the
characteristic lines for each ellipse" (*Briefe* III, 333). A few months later
Schleiermacher again wrote Reimer withdrawing the figure, declaring it "too
mystical," but adding that he wanted to save it for his own ethics which he
was already planning (*Briefe* III, 349). We next hear of the intertwined
ellipses in a letter of March 30, 1818 to F. H. Jacobi where Schleiermacher
refers to the symbol as the "universal form of all finite existence" in which the
oscillation between the foci represents "the entire fullness of earthly life"
(Cited by Keller-Wentorf, 1984, 7-8, from letters collected in *Schleiermacher
als Mensch*, ed. H. Meisner: Gotha, 1922-23, 274). Schleiermacher's
constant use of the image of "life oscillation" and his insistence in the
Brouillon on always developing parallel distinctions wherein the two sides
consistently modify each other are rooted in the metaphor of the interwoven

ellipses. The four foci of the two ellipses provide a fourfold organization for interpreting the structure of consciousness and phenomena; the most inclusive statement of this fourfold is found in the contrasts of nature and reason (consciousness) and universal and particular. Accordingly, in the ethics, there is no universal practical reason-in-itself apart from the individuation of reason in particular, concrete moral agents, whether this individuation is the moral person or a particular community; moral reason is to be found at work only in its interaction with nature in the shaping of organs into moral agents and in forming individuations of personality and community.

A second mathematical-geometrical metaphor appears in *The Critique of Previous Ethical Theories* when he argues for the connectedness of the three "ideas" necessary to ethics: the highest good, virtue, and duty. To illustrate the relatedness of this triad, Schleiermacher draws on his earliest student essay, *On the Highest Good* (1792), written while still a professed follower of Kant's ethics. In the youthful essay he suggested the following metaphor: the moral law comes to us as an algebraic formula which, when applied, draws a curved line, representing the highest good. We again find an allusion to this analogy in the *Brouillon* (Braun II, 84). There is nothing present in the idea of the highest good (the geometric curve) that does not follow from the decisions of a will thoroughly conformable to the commands of practical reason (the algebraic functions). In appropriating this analogy for his *Critique*, Schleiermacher includes a new element: the idea of virtue. Virtue is likened to the sensitive instrument that is able to draw the curved line from the functions or to derive the algebraic formula from the shape of the line (Braun, I, 71-72). The idea of virtue introduces the agent of moral action, the artist, the living continuum within which particular decisions occur. The idea of virtue also mediates between the algebraic functions and the curved line; the "wise one" is "the living law and the power productive of the Highest Good" (71).

The three "ideas" of ethics refer to different aspects of the same moral process and correspond to the formal, efficient, and final causes of moral activity. All are equally necessary for ethics and there is no **logical** priority or subordination possible among them. Nevertheless, he argues, for a system to become individualized as an historical tradition it will have to take its character and style from one of the ideas made dominant. In other words, while the structure of dialectical reasoning is polar, the structure of ethical systems is **triadic**; one idea stands at the apex of the triad as its leading motif, the other two form the base. Consequently, as an ethical tradition is formed, a practical (decisional) subordination or "reduction" does occur among the ideas. No system is ever absolute, and every system in becoming concrete also enters and belongs to the age and culture in which it appears. Whether the idea of the highest good, virtue, or duty is the dominant motif depends upon "life" rather than "idea," upon the actual interests, the *praxis*, character and ethos of the thinker and communities. In the *Critique* Schleiermacher requires that ethical reasoning be rigorously systematic. But he also argues that morality is related not simply to the system of moral abstractions (the Ideal) but to the concrete historical life and existing interests of the thinker and the community (the Real). His own decision was to make the idea of the highest good the dominant theme of his own ethics; the image of the interwoven ellipses are, I suggest, his way of grasping and structuring the highest good as a whole, an image he had wanted to turn into the symbolic frontispiece for his ethics. The two metaphors, triad and interwoven ellipses, lead us directly into the *Brouillon zur Ethik*.

III. The Fundamental Intuition

Reason, Nature, Moral World

Schleiermacher sought for ethics a comprehensive moral vision which would exclude no human activity, relationship, or product. Ethics as the theory of the highest good "is the cosmography" of culture with the task of "expressing the whole of organized life" (Braun II, 84, 87). Yet this diversity of human activity and its products requires some unifying character as it is brought to ethical reflection. Is there, in other words, some unifying character underlying and connecting all scientific, practical, technological, and artistic reasoning? Schleiermacher selected the teleological principle in which all human reasoning is purposive; the common activity present in morals, art, science, language, statecraft is moral reasoning carried on under a goal with ends in view. Ethics, thus conceived, is not a separate discipline alongside other areas of activity. Ethics, rather, becomes that comprehensive inquiry into the structures of purposive reasoning present in the very diversity and individuality of human interests and communities. Ethics, as a unifying vision, should be so constituted that "all social relations must arise from within it, according to the same laws, and by which the conduct within these relationships is also regulated" (Braun II, 79).

The initial intuition of his ethics is that "reason should become soul" (Braun II, 85). Purposive reasoning enters and takes possession of body (nature), producing organs and symbols of its presence, transforming nature into a new level of moral being and consciousness. The highest intuition of ethics "affirms as its broadest contour the ensouling of human nature by reason" (Braun II, 87).

> Reason should become soul. The ensouling principle forms, takes unto itself organs and supports body and life: we must also discern Reason as adopting human nature and maintaining itself as soul in reciprocity with the whole. This conceived in its entirety is the teaching of the highest good (Braun II, 85).

The basic metaphor present in this intuition is that of growth and transformation through a process of interaction among the polarities of life. The thinking that seeks to grasp moral being is in constant movement, oscillating between the poles of finite reason and life. "Oscillation" expresses abstractly the to and fro movement, the play, the dialogical structure of life and thought. (There is, consequently, no absolute vantage point within finite being and consciousness for constructing a perfect and finished ethical system, an issue I shall return to later.)

The whole of the moral vision is contained within the original (or fundamental) intuition. The "manysidedness" of this intuition cannot be articulated in just one proposition (Braun, 82). The explication of the original intuiton into an artistic and dialectical whole occurs within an hermeneutical circle in which the beginning presupposes the whole and the whole is found in each part. The systematic unfolding of the ethical theory is itself the process of explicating the original intuition, a "narrating" of the growth of moral consciousness from its initial simplicity into an increasingly intricate vision of human activity and its products. The accusation that Schleiermacher develops a rigid deductive system in the lectures misses the mark. It is more appropriate to refer to his method as a phenomenology of moral spirit and the "world" it has produced (i.e., "world" as the secondary environment of human making: history, culture.)

Nature permeated and shaped by reason becomes something new in the creative process of life. Nature is transformed into the moral world, into history, culture [(Braun II, 109.) Keller-Wentorf traces how the term culture becomes increasing recessive in Schleiermacher's later lectures on ethics, disappearing finally in the 1816 lectures. (1984, 26-27).] But even the earlier writings turn to this new level of moral being arising from human creativity. It is this "world" of culture Schleiermacher so rhapsodically identified in his earlier *Soliloquies*:

> What the multitude calls the world, I call man, and what they
> call man, I call world . . . For what I take to be the world is but
> the fairest creation of spirit, a mirror in which it is reflected.
> To me all this is but the giant body of Humanity, belonging to
> us even as an individual's body does to him, made possible by
> Humanity alone, to which it is given in order that the human
> spirit may master it and be revealed therein. The creative
> freedom of Humanity is exercized upon this body, to sense all
> its pulsations, to mold and transmute all its features into
> organs of human life. (41)

Let this extended passage illustrate how the starkly abstract, often cryptic phrasing of the *Brouillon* can be translated back into the lyric of the youthful writings. Even in this earlier work we discern the shape of the "world" arising from the interaction and permeation of nature by reason; already we can discern the organ-forming and symbolizing power of reason Schleiermacher delineated in his Halle lectures. Through the creativity of purposive reason nature is transformed into "world," itself a new mode of human consciousness. It is the task of ethics to describe this consciousness and this process. Keller-Wentorf summarizes this way of thinking about the foundations of ethical theory: morality is both structure and process which

> . . . in the striving of the physical to human life the prepared elevation of nature into the spiritual is not the dissolution of the natural into the purely spiritual. Rather, reason and nature are so related to each other that they require each other: reason penetrates nature and enables it thereby to attain a higher, spiritual life; but reason itself can become actuality only in nature. (1984, 45)

Contrasting Types (Traditions) of Ethical Theories

The interactive process by which nature is elevated by reason to become the human world of history presupposes significant ontological issues and commitments. In the *Brouillon* Schleiermacher does not inquire deeply into the questions belonging to the "highest philosophy," Dialectics. Yet his allusions to these issues make sense when the *Brouillon* is read in light of *The Critique of Previous Ethical Theories* wherein he does elaborate these questions. Furthermore, in his *Critique* he develops a schema of three types of ethical thought built upon the foundations of prior ontological and epistemological assumptions. In almost excruciating detail Schleiermacher extracts two types of ethics, reflecting either rationalist or empiricist traditions in philosophy. In the *Brouillon* they are referred to simply as "systems of conformity to universal laws" and systems of "happiness." In the *Critique* he referred to all eudaemonistic or hedonist ethics as traditions of "feeling," while the Stoics, Kant, and Fichte (the "neo-Stoics") present theories of "obligation." Schleiermacher treats eudaemonistic and obligation (we would say deontological) ethics as equally one-sided and incomplete in their mutual exclusion. His basic objection to eudaemonism is its failure to draw a clear line between the moral and the natural; it tends to collapse the ethical into descriptions of natural impulses rather than positing a distinct sphere and power of its own (reason/spirit). In the *Critique* he again protests such a reduction in ethics and here agrees with Kant in recognizing that the natural and conventional cannot produce the "ought" of reason. While rejecting the conventional-empirical in the name of a reason that transcends nature, Schleiermacher also identifies what to his mind is the opposite error: the isolation and separation of the rational moral self from the empirical self and natural world. In the *Brouillon* he is even more confrontational with the Kantian traditon: "The formula of the Ought in ethics is totally unacceptable" (Braun II, 81). This tradition in ethics "bifurcates" reality. In it nature and reason are put at odds with each other.

Schleiermacher presents a third type or tradition, claiming it as his own. He refers to it variously as the tradition of "God-likeness" or "perfectibility." In the *Critique* only Plato and Spinoza, the chief representatives of this type of ethics, found favor in his otherwise harsh judgments. Schleiermacher presents this ethics not simply as a third alternative but as a mediating philosophy between rationalism and empiricism. In the *Critique* the pattern becomes clear (although he claimed to have allowed his own views to shine through only "obliquely"). Schleiermacher opposes an ethics derived from the concrete given as well as one derived from an abstract transcendence of reason. The empirical and the rational need to be brought into productive relationship with each other. Schleiermacher's alternative to those traditions is an ethics of the indwelling of reason in nature, transforming and elevating nature into new being. He requires a distinction between nature and purposive reason, yet rejects a dualism in which reason transcends but does not reenter nature to shape and transform it. Reason must become soul. The following formula applies consistently to the distinction drawn throughout the *Brouillon*: the contrast between nature and reason (consciousness) is real but relative, for consciousness emerges from nature (there is no "pure" reason in abstraction from nature) and returns to it in the shaping process of *Bildung*, which is itself history.

> Life everywhere appears in various functions which stand together in relative contrasts, but which as [isolated] particulars can neither be understood nor exist alone; rather they stand in a necessary connection. In such a manner we must also discover the life of ensouling reason; we must observe it in singlars [*Einzelheiten*], which organically and

necessarily belong together. That is to say, it is the theory of history. (Braun II, 88)

Each ethical type also has its own "style" or method: obligation requires the imperative, eudaemonism the "consultive," and his own the "narrative"/descriptive (Braun II, 80). At the conclusion of the *Critique* he also had added an appendix on the "style" of prevailing ethical systems and developed parallel distinctions: the rationalistic method is "dogmatic" and "seeks to begin science with a fixed point," proceeding deductively in a single direction; the empirical method in ethics he calls "rhapsodic," dealing only with aggregates of particulars, lauding the merely conventional. In contrast to both Schleiermacher refers to his own method as heuristic, not beginning at a fixed point but "consistently presents general principles and the particular simultaneously and then combines them both as if by an electric spark" (Braun 1, 338-339).

This third ethical alternative Schleiermacher sees as a much needed ethics of the future. It arises from a tradition renewing itself and beginning to speak again to the present age: an ethics of *Bildung* as the modern extension of the Platonic ethics of *paideia*. Schiller and Schelling pursued *Bildung* as an aesthetic vision for the future; Schleiermacher wanted to present the new *Bildung* as a moral possibility, as the most fruitful and comprehensive ideal for his "total vision." [In the *Brouillon* Schleiermacher discovered three historical images expressing this idea of the Highest Good: Biblically in the image of God in human beings exercising active dominion over the earth, Greek philosophy's contemplative use of the mythical representation of "eternity in time," and in the "recent idea of a perfected culture" – i.e., *Bildung* (Braun II, 92).]

IV. The Functions of Ethical Reason and the Organs of the Moral World

Schleiermacher's doctrine of the highest good brings together the two sides of his ethical reasoning: a) the formal structure of reason (represented by the symbol of the interwoven ellipses) discerned in the organs (the moral agencies) within which it dwells; and b) the actual communities (organs) within and through which individuals come to know and express their identity and purpose. In short, his theory of the highest good develops the social context for moral activity and knowing.

The Functions of Ethical Reason

Schleiermacher's fourfold ordering of the functions of reason consists of: organ formation (*Organbilden*) and organ use (*Organgebrauch*), "self-contained existence" (*abgeschlossenes Dasein*) and "community with the whole" (*Gemeinshaft mit dem Ganzen*). (One of the difficulties with the *Brouillon* is the constant rephrasing of these central functions in order to introduce different shades of meaning. In the later lectures on ethics the terminology becomes less amorphous.)

Organ forming expresses the predominantly active function of shaping communities into agents of moral reason; Organ using is allied to the contemplative function of recognizing and revealing the presence of reason in body. (The term *Brauch* implies not simply use of an instrument or tool in a utilitarian sense but also "custom" and "tradition," with the accompanying respect for the heritage of language, symbols and agencies historically shaped by moral reason.) In short, it is a kind of *anamnesis*, not in a mythological, but in the historical form of exercising our respect for the origins and traditions of our intellectual and spiritual inheritance.) Organ use is further broken down into two additional functions expressing the rhythm of "setting-forth" and of "taking-into" one's self and community, the breathing out and the breathing in of both physical and moral life, a rhythm first found in the movements of the first speech in the *Speeches on Religion*. This rhythm reappears in the ethics as a "manifesting", "expressing" (*Darstellen*) of consciousness and as a conceptual "knowing" (*Erkennen*) through the symbols and language formed by spirit. (*Darstellen* is also translated by Richard R. Niebuhr as "self-impartation." July, 1960, 163). *Darstellen* is the setting forth of purposive reason in organs functioning as objective symbols of indwelling reason. "Knowing" (*Erkennen*) is the appropriative taking into self of communal reason, internalizing the symbols and ideas of the culture. The reciprocity of knowing and expressing is the first "life oscillation" of ethics:

This reciprocity of knowing and expressing is the oscillation of the moral life and neither of the two can be thought without the other . . . The World has for ethics no other significance than this: it is the object for knowledge or the symbol for self-expression or the organ for both (Braun II, 89).

In short, the basic divisions of Schleiermacher's formal outline are:

1) *Organbilden*: reason actively functioning to rationalize nature and form organs of the moral World and

2) *Organgebrauch*: reason functioning reflectively by using the organs for

    (a) *Erkennen*: the intellectual conveying and receiving communal knowledge

    (b) *Darstellen*: the symbolic self-imparting of individual and community.

The asymmetrical character of *Organbilden* and *Organgebrauch* may be noted, the former having only one function, the latter two. In later lectures Schleiermacher introduced a formal symmetry by simplifying the functions simply into only "organizing" and "symbolizing" activity.

The second major polarity describes the mutual involvement of self and community in moral action and thought. Although the most general and predominant expression of this polarity is "self-contained existence" and "community with others," another set of parallel terms is used to establish its meaning, individual and identical. This polarity is basis for the second "life oscillation": reason is posited in the individual person and yet transcends the private and unique to enter into community. Schleiermacher here incorporates two images into the framework of his ethics. "Self-contained existence" (individual) operates with the self-other distinction: differences between rational beings are real, individuated by their time, place, and that distinctiveness in each which is not transferable to an other (*Eigentümlichkeit*). "Community with the whole" (identical) belongs to the . part-whole image; participation in larger communities brings about shared symbols and goods. Here we touch on a crucial problem in this discussion: what and where is the locus of action and this ideal structure of consciousness? Is the self-other distinction simply a more primitive form of consciousness in the ethical process which is then overcome and elevated

into some metaphysical group mind? Schleiermacher's answer is a clear "no"
to such an alternative:

> If one is permitted to speak of a higher and lower in ethics,
> then individuality is the higher and community is the lower.
> The drive toward community presupposes the consciousness of
> individuality in a way that the drive toward individualization
> does not presuppose the consciousness of community (Braun
> II, 122).

Communal consciousness must become real only in the consciousness of
individual beings.   At the same time, Schleiermacher insists that the
individuality of which he speaks is not an isolated particular; to come to full
individuality one will enter into relation with others and share common
symbols. "Naturally ethics does not relate to every singular (*Einzelne*) but
always to the ethically construed singular" (Braun II, 8l).   Communal
consciousness, then, is real but only in its presence within the totality of
persons: "The relation of an activity of reason itself is revealed not merely
through going beyond persons, which would only be a negative idea, but
rather is revealed in its relation to the totality of persons" (Braun II, 111.
Also see his remarks about the character of the Academy which begin: "[The
task of Knowing] is falsified if it views individuality as merely accidental and
wishes to dispense with it in order correctly to hold to the universal. . . ."
Braun II, 169).

The Organs of the Moral World

The final step in the theory of the highest good consists in filling the
abstract dialectical framework of reason's functions with actual communal
forms of historical life.   Schleiermacher's ethics is finally a method of
correlation, heuristically combining the intellectual ("Ideal") side of analysis
of consciousness with the organic world of actual relationships (the "Real").
Schleiermacher's goal is to reveal how this correlation of Ideal and Real
yields the fourfold structure of moral organs (goods) in history.   Not only
does he show these social goods embodying distinctive forms of reason in
history/culture, but also, through his organization, how they mutually and

reciprocally nurture each other and the individual lives within them. The four organs of historically embodied reason are: 1) the **state** as economic community and organ of justice; 2) communities of **free association** in friendship and fellowship; 3) the **Academy** as the community of public inquiry and science; 4) the religious community (**Church**) founded on the disclosure of humankind's relation to God and world.

The four types of goods are not communities of "nature." They extend the natural communities of family, race, and people into a new quality of historical being. The family is itself presented as the transition from natural to historical (ethical) being. However, it has no specific place within Schleiermacher's framework of the moral agencies. It is not one sphere among others but the nexus of all communities, natural as well as historical, and hence a microcosm of the entire ethics. All the polarities of reason are so integrated into this "complete individuum" that it becomes "a perfect manifestation of the Idea of Humanity." As primal community it expresses "eternity in time." The family not only recapitulates the past but anticipates the future, containing all functions which will be extended through it to form the moral world. (Schleiermacher's *Weihnachtsfeier* is a vivid portrayal of the structure and dynamic he found in the manysidedness of the extended family unit.)

The four organs of the moral world are identified through these dialectical permeations of reason and nature:

Organ Forming	Identical (Community with others)	Individual (Self-contained)
	The State: Identical organ formation creating goods of commerce and justice; relations of Right.	**Free Sociality**: individuals creating goods of friendship based on privacy and uniqueness; relations of freedom between individuals.
Organ Using	**The Academy**: Identical organ use resulting in exchange of knowledge; relations of trust and criticism.	**Church**: individual organ use resulting in the communication of feeling through symbols expressing relations of self with others and with God.

Recall that the discussion of Organ Use received an even more complex structure than Organ Formation; the complication results from contrasting the modes of those "speculative" and empirical disciplines of knowing in science (*Erkennen*) with more immediate and existential experience communicated in symbols (*Darstellung*). The organization of the work reveals that the structure of reason is not grasped apart from its externalization in outward forms. That is, Schleiermacher speaks about thought or feeling not "in-themselves" but only as found in objectified structures in language and symbols and the appropriate agencies (communities of knowledge and contemplation) in which they are formed and expressed.

Identical (universal) Organ-Use: perfected in the moral organ of the **Academy** (schools).

1. Knowing (*Erkennen*):	2. Self-Imparting (*Darstellung*):
a. Objective, conceptual form of consciousness; thought as Intuition (*Anschauung*).	b. Language as prose and dialectics.

Individual (concrete) Organ-Use: perfected in the moral organ of the **Church** (religious community).

1. Knowing (*Erkennen*)	2. Self-Imparting (*Darstellung*)
a. Subjective, immediate form of self-consciousness given in Feeling (*Gefühl*).	b. Art as symbol, including language as poetry.

This introduction to the *Brouillon zur Ethik* is not the place to develop the detail of Schleiermacher's discussion of the organs of the moral world. However, some comments on his distinctive treatment of each follow. The

State is discussed as a corporate individuality which functions to promote justice and regulate commerce (*Recht* and *Verkehr*). Contract, the binding of individuals into common pursuits, is based on two products within a national community: <u>Coin</u> and <u>Language</u> are both modes of exchange, of goods and of ideas. As there is no universal language, so there can be no universal state or, for that matter, a single universal philosophy (Braun II, 169). **Free sociality** is the realm of personal assets (*Eigenthum*) which establishes each individual as uniquely one's own (*Eigenthümlichkeit*), even as each reaches beyond the private to develop fellowship with others. This organ of individuated reason is Schleiermacher's way of establishing a distinct sphere and good in society for Platonic *philia*, the free association of friends equally sharing and expressing full humanity; this *philia* is not limited to the older friendship of men but projects a new vision of friendship and equality among men and women as belonging to the objective structures of the social world. I also understand free sociality to contain Schiller's idea of culture as play; the free play of human powers (reason and sense) is set into motion for its own sake without regard for the social utility of the product.

The **Academy** is the organ of objectifiable knowledge and science. It presupposes language and free sociality. Claims to knowledge must be made public and tested in a universal community. Schleiermacher asserts, "In every act of knowing we posit a Thou for our I" (Braun II, 167); acquisition of knowledge requires collegiality, trust relations, a dimension of free sociality in which the community of learning exhibits *philia* as its very basis. **Church** refers to the distinctive character of religious community and its mode of "knowing" and "expression." Human beings are, for Schleiermacher, religious beings with a distinctive form of religious consciousness, the general structures of which the ethics discerns and explicates. That is, in the ethics distinctions are drawn between consciousness as a form of doing (forming nature into organs), consciousness as thinking and knowing, and now religious consciousness as a contemplative, receptive act. He designates that mode of consciousness as Feeling, a term often disputed and misunderstood. Feeling is not a narcissistic emotion but a manner of experiencing relatedness in an immediacy apart from conceptual mediation. This religious consciousness presents itself objectively in symbols and poetic language.

> As there is no objective knowing without the subjective, so
> there is no manifestation (*Darstellung)* without the subjective,
> and this must reveal itself in language as poetry – in the plastic
> element of the word and the musical element of the rhythm
> (Braun II, 188).

If the "highest form" of the objectified language of the Academy is dialectics,
its corrolary in subjective speaking is poetry and dialogue: "Thus posey in its
highest cultivation is dialogue" (Braun II, 188). Intriguingly, each of the four
social spheres discussed in the ethics share yet uniquely develop language
according to their own distinctive grasp of ethical being. Language, as does
the family, reaches into each sphere, shaping and being shaped by the
distinctive use in each, bringing the whole to completion.

Schleiermacher's "fourfold" goods of state, free sociality, academy, and
church round out his picture of the highest good as life in communities
reciprocally supporting one another, receiving and allowing traditions of the
past to come alive again in the present, endowing the future with a fullness
and richness of life. One organ does not encroach on or dominate others,
each fulfills its own distinctive function, while mutually, with the others,
contributing to the whole, the highest good, the moral world. It is not
difficult to discern the beloved Plato in the background of this teaching; as
Plato derived the good polis from the distinctive functions of the soul, so
Schleiermacher unfolds the good of culture from the distinctive functions of
reason interacting with nature. To the theory of the highest good
Schleiermacher appends theories of virtue and duty in a manner totally
conformable to the dominant idea of his ethics.

V. A Phenomenology of Moral Consciousness

We have surveyed the first systematic statement of Schleiermacher's
philosophical ethics. He calls his ethics a "philosophy of history." In an age
soon to be dominated philosophically by Hegel what does Schleiermacher
mean by "philosophy of history?" The ethics of both lead to a theory of
Objective Spirit in which the social forms are deposited into the world
independent of the producing consciousness. However, Schleiermacher's

ethics is not finally a system in which actual historical change and the structure of reason are identical, yielding an absolute, unconditioned viewpoint from within history/reason itself. Schleiermacher's philosophical ethics no more produces the actual content of history than his theory of general religious consciousness produces the content of positive Christianity. In describing the limits of reason and knowing in his interpretation of the academy Schleiermacher insists, "the usual formulas of transcendental philosophy, which seek to establish a universal knowing abstracted from all individuality but which in this way can only reach a contentless and indeterminate form, turn away from [our point of view]" (Braun II, 175). The philosophical ethics of Schleiermacher is open to empirical history, but does not produce or duplicate it. Rather, we discover here a phenomenology of moral consciousness in which the general structures of practical reason's involvement with the world are explicated. But to approach these patterns ("essences") one must reflect on concrete manifestations of reason within social consciousness: "There is no intuition of ideas except in actual knowledge" (Braun II, 170). The abstract Ideal alone is not sufficient for grounding this new theory of ethics. In *The Critique of Previous Ethical Systems*, written a few years before these lectures, Schleiermacher developed the same point at greater length: the possibility of ethical thinking depends upon the "Real" of ethics, upon the objectified consciousness within historical communities (Braun I, 262).

In this survey we recognized Schleiermacher's use of a method of correlation. His ethics correlates the intellectual (Ideal) side of consciousness with the organic (Real) side of actual relationships. He dialectically brings the two sides together as reason interacts with nature to produce the moral world. But the correlation does not produce an identity. We never grasp the Ideal-Real in its center and unity. We can only grasp its finite movements and receive partial glimpses; yet they are glimpses of something, they are perspectives of an objective horizon. The conclusion of *The Critique of Previous Ethical Theories* provides a key for understanding Schleiermacher's dialectical movement between the Ideal and the Real in his ethics. The last paragraph of the book recapitulates the entire movement of ethical thinking and summarizes the prospects of moral inquiry in both its promise and its limits. [There is in this concluding paragraph a summary of the organization of this dense and difficult book. *The Critique* should be read in light of this conclusion to make it come together into a whole.] A perfectly actualized consciousness of humanity is the necessary condition for a perfect descriptive ethics. Perfect consciousness of humanity is the final goal of ethics, but our view is too limited and our culture too incomplete to permit universal formulae expressing the perfect equilibrium and symmetry of this goal.

> But where and so long as this consciousness is not yet present, ethics is not yet becoming as a science but only as its idea. But this kind of becoming cannot be symmetrical and offers the appearance of being fortuitous in that first one and then the other side stands out in approximation of their symmetry. First there is the sense of the Ideal intuited merely in the laws of the form taken from the higher Real but which leaves reality behind; but then the Real hurries forth in the actuality of that which is present in the science even without having been acknowledged by it. And thus there appears, partly progressive, partly regressive, that moral being which is not yet given in its center and in its law; for only in perfect truth and in clear self-consciousness is the proportion and the order unmistakably proclaimed (Braun I, 345-346).

This passage unlocks the dialectical correlations of the lectures, the to and fro movement, the constantly shifting distinctions of the lectures. It admits the relativity of ethics and yet affirms that each moral perspective, while only partial, still grasps an objective goal and end: the truth of what it means to be human with other selves and communities. "Where that consciousness is present," he concludes, there too "in the same measure is the germ of the true ethics" (Braun I, 345).

References

Schleiermacher, Friedrich
1911   *Schleiermachers Werke: Auswahl in vier Bänden.*
                O. Braun and D.J. Bauer (ed.). Leipzig: Meiner.
                Vol. I contains the *Grundlinien einer Kritik der bisherigen Sittenlehre.*
                Vol. II contains the lectures, *Brouillon zur Ethik.*

1858-1863   Aus *Schleiermachers Leben in Briefen.* W. Dilthey (ed.). Berlin:
                Reimer.
                Referred to as *Briefe.*

1926   *Schleiermacher's Soliloquies.* Horace Leland Friess
                (trans.). Chicago: Open Court.

Keller-Wentorf, Christel
1984   *Schleiermachers Denken: Die Bewußtseinslehre in Schleiermachers
                philosophischer Ethik als Schlüssel zu seinem Denken.* Berlin:
                Walter De Gruyter.

Niebuhr, Richard R.
1960   "Schleiermacher on Language and Feeling." *Theology Today* 17
                (July). 150-169.

Redeker, Martin
1973   *Schleiermacher: Life and Thought.* John Wallhausser (trans.).
                Philadelphia: Fortress Press.

Ungern-Sternberg, Arthur
1931   *Freiheit und Wirklichkeit, Schleiermachers philosophischer Reiseweg
                durch den deutschen Idealismus.* Gotha: Leopold Klotz.

VI

DIE ESOTERISCHE KOMMUNIKATIONSSTRUKTUR DER "WEIHNACHTSFEIER" ÜBER ANSPIELUNGEN UND ZITATE

Hermann Patsch

Ruth Drucilla Richardson
gewidmet

Das Wort 'esoterisch' soll hier nicht im geheimnisvoll-mystischen Sinn gebraucht sein, etwa als ob Schleiermachers *Weihnachtsfeier* eine nur dem geweihten Auge sichtbare, geheime Bedeutung neben der allgemeinen offenbaren habe, sondern im streng literaturhistorischen, der sich auf die unmittelbaren Rezipienten bezieht, also den begrenzten geselligen Kreis, der in stärkerem Maße für die Lektüre disponiert war und von Schleiermacher disponiert wurde, als dem gegenwärtigen Leser unmittelbar deutlich werden kann. Zur exoterischen Struktur, also zu den Winken an die gewünschten und erhofften Leser Goethe, Jean Paul, A.W. Schlegel, habe ich in meinem Aufsatz "Die zeitgenössische Rezeption der *Weihnachtsfeier*"[1] Stellung genommen. Hier geht es darum zu zeigen, daß die *Weihnachtsfeier* sich als ein dichtes Gewebe von Beziehungen und Anspielungen auf den geselligen Kreis, dem das Werk entstammt, erweist, auf zeitgenössische ästhetische und religionsphilosophische Diskussionen und politische Ereignisse. Dieser ausgeprägte Leserbezug muß – neben der theologisch-christologischen Thematik – als ein kommunikatives Strukturmerkmal der ersten Ausgabe gelten.

Im Folgenden werde ich zunächst die eher biographischen Anspielungen besprechen, dann kulturell-ästhetische Bezüge untersuchen, schließlich allgemeinere bis politische Aspekte. Abschließend werde ich, mit

Blick auf den genius loci dieses Vortrags, der Frage nachgehen, ob sich in der *Weihnachtsfeier* eine Konnotation mit Herrnhut feststellen läßt. (Daß ich bei all diesen Problemen auf frühere Forschung angewiesen bin, braucht als selbstverständlich hier nur erwähnt zu werden[2]).

I.

Der biographische Hintergrund der Personen und Geschehnisse ist den Lesern aus dem Freundeskreis Schleiermachers bekannt gewesen und ist auch aus den Äußerungen des Autors selbst belegt. Mit den Worten des engen Hallenser Schülers Adolph Müller gesagt: " (...) das Ganze ist voller großer und kleiner Beziehungen, was ihn auch bewog, seinen Namen für's erste nicht auf dem Titel bekannt zu machen"[3]. Müller erwähnt dabei die Tatsache, daß Schleiermacher, der wie bei fast allen seinen frühen Werken eigentlich auch bei der *Weihnachtsfeier* "strengste Anonymität" hatte walten lassen wollen, bei den in Halle und Berlin zu verausgabenden Exemplaren den Namen des Verfassers nicht hatte setzen lassen[4]. "Kleine Streiche" nennt August Varnhagen von Ense das, die Schleiermacher "heimlicher" als Goethe in seinen Schriften mache und die ihm sehr gefielen – auch er ein Hallenser Schüler und Intimus[5]. Ob die "großen und kleinen Beziehungen" persönlicher und – das besonders – sachlicher Art noch alle aufgeklärt werden können, steht dahin. Die jetzt noch erkennbaren Hinweise und Winke jedenfalls lassen ein dichtes Netz von Bezügen auf Personen, zeitgenössische Geschehnisse und Gedanken erkennen, das die angestrebte Anonymität als ein grundsätzlicheres Strukturmerkmal des Schleiermacherschen Kommunikationswillens erscheinen läßt, als es die Selbstauskunft "Scherz" (an Gaß) wahrhaben will. Es mache doch, bemerkt er später selbst, "einen großen Unterschied in der Art die Sachen zu sagen", wenn man anonym schreibe: "Wie man manches von einem Andern spricht hinter seinem Rücken, ganz unbesorgt darum, ob er es wieder erfahren wird oder nicht, was man ihm doch um keinen Preis selbst grade so in's Gesicht sagen würde, so scheint es mir auch hiemit"[6]. Zu den Frauengestalten in der *Weihnachtsfeier* hat sich Schleiermacher selbst enthüllend geäußert, wie ich sogleich belegen werde. Die

Hauptfrage biographischer Neugier bis auf den heutigen Tag aber, wer denn die drei Redner Leonhardt, Eduard und Ernst seien, die den abschließenden Teil bestreiten, hat sich freilich weder aus den Namen, den personalen Anspielungen noch aus den von ihnen vertretenen philosophisch-theologischen Positionen im Lauf einer langen Interpretationsgeschichte beantwortet. Allzu gern hätte man gewußt, in welchem Redner sich Schleiermacher selbst verkörpert – romantisch gesagt: poetisiert – habe[7]! Schleiermacher hat dazu geschwiegen, sicher nicht zufällig. Das Versagen der biographischen Herleitungsfrage an dieser zentralen Stelle muß tiefere Gründe haben, die in der intellektuellen Struktur des Werkes selbst liegen.

So verdient auch die erst 1982 bekannt gewordene Vermutung Achim von Arnims, der das Weihnachtsfest 1805 im Hause Johann Friedrich Reichardts verbracht hatte und bei der Lektüre der *Weihnachtsfeier* die dortige Szenerie wiederzuerkennen meinte, Leonhardt entspreche dem Naturphilosophen Henrik Steffens, wenig Vertrauen – wenngleich eine nähere Prüfung hier noch aussteht[8]. Interpretatorisch interessanter könnte Arnims Auskunft sein: "(...) die letzte Rede darin [sc. in der *Weihnachtsfeier*] hörte ich von ihm [sc. Schleiermacher] am ersten Weihnachtsfeyertage", was wahrscheinlich auf die – nicht erhaltene – Weihnachtspredigt Schleiermachers zu beziehen ist[9]. Oder sollte Schleiermacher in geselliger Runde so geredet haben? Hier wäre eine Brücke zwischen Eduard und Schleiermacher zu konstruieren. Aber Arnim scheint in der *Weihnachtsfeier* insgesamt eine Abspiegelung der Weihnachtstage des Jahres 1805 zu vermuten[10], was den Entstehungsdaten widerspricht[11]. Achim war wohl nicht kompetent genug, um Schleiermachers Feinheiten zu verstehen; es ist nicht ratsam, allzuviel aus dieser kurzen Bemerkung zu schließen.

Schelling meinte in seiner Rezension, daß Schleiermacher in dem Werk selbst nicht erscheine, sondern, "wenn er die bestimmten und wirklichen religiösen Ansichten von Individuen unserer Zeit mit ihren Gegensätzen und Eigenheiten darzustellen die Absicht hatte, eben durch den reinen Ausdruck subjectiver Denkweisen am meisten die Gewalt objectiver Darstellung erprobt" habe[12]. Das wird sachgemäß sein.

Mehr Erfolg verspricht die Betrachtung der Frauengestalten. Daß Schleiermacher sich hier so häufig selbst geäußert hat, läßt im Rückschluß

das biographische Schweigen über die Redner umso bedeutsamer
erscheinen. Zu den Anspielungen, auf deren Entschlüsselung durch die
befreundeten Leser Schleiermacher wartete und die er in seinem
Briefwechsel selbst enthüllte, gehört die Erzählung Karolines, die als dritte
der kleinen Novellen der Frauen an einem deutlichen Höhepunkt vor den
Reden der Männer steht (S. 88-95). Das Schicksal Charlottes, der
"herrlichen seltenen Frau" (S. 95), der am Weihnachtsabend das todkranke
Kind dem Leben wiedergegeben wird, ist Charlotte von Kathen (1777-1850)
und deren Sohn Gottlieb Ferdinand Ehrenfried (geb. 22. Mai 1804)
nachgestaltet[13]. Die Krankheit des Knaben hatte Schleiermacher seinerzeit
erschüttert[14]. Nun wundert er sich in seinem späten, aufklärenden Brief
vom 20. Juni 1806 an Charlotte von Kathen, daß diese seine Verfasserschaft
nicht sofort erraten habe, "weil doch Niemand Ihr Leiden so erzählen konnte
als ich", aber er ist zufrieden damit, daß es ihr recht sei, "einige Züge von
Ihrem Bilde dort aufbewahrt zu sehn" : "Sie waren gleich mit Ihrem kleinen
Liebling so in die Idee des Ganzen eingewachsen, daß es mir unmöglich
gewesen wäre Sie nicht hineinzubringen. Auch weiß meine Kunst nichts
schöneres zu thun, als zusammenzuflechten, was sich vor mir in schönen
Gemüthern entfaltet hat, und grade diese Erzählung hat Mehrere ganz
vorzüglich gerührt. Es ist also nicht ein Geschenk, was ich Ihnen mache,
sondern was Sie mir machen, was ich mir im Vertrauen auf Sie von Ihnen
genommen habe"[15].

In das sich hier äußernde nur bedingt realistische Erzählkonzept
gehört der Hinweis auf das Vorbild der Ernestine: "Die Ernestine in den
[vertrauten] Briefen [sc. über die Lucinde] und die in der Weihnachtsfeier
sind gewissermaßen dieselbe Person. Ich kann nicht sagen daß ich Jemanden
bestimmt damit gemeint; ich weiß nur, daß mir ein Bild dabei vorgeschwebt,
was ich mir, bloß nach Erzählungen die vielleicht nicht die getreuesten waren
entworfen habe von einer Schwester von [sc. Friedrich] Schlegel in Dresden
[sc. Charlotte Ernst]. Wenn er mir von ihr erzählte gestaltete sich diese
Figur in mir die ich hernach so ausgeführt habe"[16]. Der Ehe-Name der
Schwester Schlegels – die Schleiermacher erst bei seinem Aufenthalt in
Dresden im September 1810 kennenlernen sollte[17] – klingt, subtil versteckt,
in dem Vornamen wider. Die äußeren Anregungen werden innerlich

angeeignet und transformiert; Detailtreue bei der Porträtierung im Sinne des späteren Realismus wird nicht angestrebt, könnte bei der Vagheit der Informationen auch gar nicht erreicht werden.

Das würde in gleichem Maße auch gelten, wenn – wie vermutet wurde – das Kind Sophie eine Anspielung auf die "Sophie" im *Heinrich von Ofterdingen* und damit auf Sophie von Kühn, die Braut des Dichters Novalis, sein sollte, die Schleiermacher gleichfalls nur vom Hörensagen kannte[18]. Doch hieß auch Reichardts jüngste Tochter Sophie; sie war, geboren 1795, Ende 1805 "noch immer ein kleines, schelmisches Kind" (wie Oehlenschläger in seinen Memoiren erinnert)[19]. Wie alt genau sich Schleiermacher das "Kind" (S. 7) gedacht hat, wird nicht deutlich. Aus den Namen allein, die durchweg Modenamen sind (Ernestine, Charlotte, Friederike, Sophie, Karoline, Agnes, Luise), kann man so gut wie nichts schließen.

Daß der gesellige Kreis, der Weihnachten feiert, das gastfreie Haus Johann Friedrich Reichardts auf dem Giebichenstein bei Halle als äußerliches Vorbild hat, ist den befreundeten Lesern deutlich gewesen. "Es sind darin sichtbare Züge von mir bekannten Personen, und die Umgebungen und das Aeußere darin des geselligen Lebens mag wohl Spuren an sich tragen, daß Schleiermacher nicht selten in Reichardt's Hause gewesen", heißt es bei Adolph Müller, leider ohne näheren Hinweis[20]. "(...) das Weihnachten war in Reichardts Hause", vermutete Achim von Arnim denn auch allzu direkt[21]. Schleiermachers häufige und geschätzte Anwesenheit im Haus des bedeutenden Kapellmeisters, Komponisten und Musikjournalisten Johann Friedrich Reichardt (1752-1814)[22] ist durch eigene briefliche Erwähnungen vielfach belegt, spielt aber auch in den biographischen Zeugnissen und Erinnerungen seiner Freunde und Schüler eine Rolle[23]. Hier also ist das eigentliche Anspielungspotential zu suchen; doch zeigt der Brief an Charlotte von Kathen, daß Schleiermacher auch an den Freundeskreis auf Rügen dachte, zeigen Bemerkungen gegenüber Henriette Herz, daß auch Berlin im Blickfeld stand. "Ich wollte sehn, ob meine Freunde mich erkennen würden in dem kleinen Werkchen, das doch so manches eigene hat, wodurch es wol den andern ungleichartig scheinen kann", heißt es in dem schon angeführten Brief an Charlotte von Kathen[24]. Damit ist der esoterische Kreis im engeren Sinne genannt, der allein die

Biographika erkennen und genießen kann. Daß die anderen Leser hier ausgeschlossen sind, hat Schleiermacher deutlich gesehen.

Daß der esoterische Leserbezug bis zum Einzel-Leser geht, belegt der beiläufige Hinweis auf den englischen satirischen Dichter Charles Churchill (1731-1764), dessen Werke und Lebensbeschreibung 1804 erschienen waren[25]. Von ihm heißt es anläßlich der Geschenke für den Täufling, zu dem auch ein Uhrband gehört: "wenn er am Uhrband spielt, wenn er in den Zähnen stochert kommt ein Gedicht heraus" (S. 81). Das scheint kein Autorzitat zu sein, sondern ein Aperçu der Henriette Herz, die sich ja bekanntlich als Übersetzerin mit englischer Literatur befaßte. Schleiermacher wundert sich brieflich jedenfalls, daß diese ihn, der ihr ein anonymes Exemplar der *Weihnachtsfeier* zugespielt hatte, nicht sogleich "an der Kathen [i.e. an der Erzählung Karolines], am Churchill und an andern solchen Kleinigkeiten" erkannt habe[26]. Wenn Henriette Herz Schleiermacher an diesem Zitat hat enttarnen sollen, dann muß dieses Aperçu in einem Gespräch unter vier Augen gefallen sein, wohl von H. Herz selbst.

Was mögen die "andern solchen Kleinigkeiten" sein? Etwa das Amusement über die Fremdwort-Verdeutschung "Zierbold" (für Elegant) als "Kampisch" kurz darauf (S. 82) – also über Joachim Heinrich Campe (1746-1818), dessen *Wörterbuch zur Erklärung und Verdeutschung der unserer Sprache aufgedrungenen fremden Ausdrücke* 1801 erschienen war? Dort werden allerdings "Schmuckebold" und "Hageprunk" als veraltet durch "Zierling" ersetzt – erst die zweite Auflage 1813 bucht "Zierbold" als Vorschlag eines anderen Sprachreinigers[27].

Vielleicht hat Henriette Herz oder hat ein Leser aus Rügen die Anspielung auf "Tante Kornelie" verstanden und den "Schmerzenssohn", den "schönen Jüngling", "der so heldenmüthig und so vergeblich für die Freiheit gestorben ist" (S. 76f) – wir können es nicht [28]. Die "herrliche tragische Gestalt" (S. 75) ist ohne Zweifel keine literarische Fiktion; die huldigende Bezeichnung muß in Schleiermachers unmittelbarer Umgebung verständlich gewesen sein.

Natürlich sind auch Anspielungen auf die Hallenser Theologenschaft denkbar, gerade und besonders in den Reden der Männer. Sattler hat vorgeschlagen, den Satz Leonhardts über die Prediger, die sich "rühmlich

beeifern, auf der Kanzel die Bibel möglichst entbehrlich zu machen" (S. 39f),
auf Schleiermachers Kollegen August Hermann Niemeyer (1754-1828) zu
beziehen[29]. Aber der angeführte Beleg deckt eine solche einseitige Sentenz
nicht ab[30], so daß der personale Bezug als nicht nachgewiesen gelten muß.

Insgesamt zeigt sich, daß überzeugende Zuschreibungen nur dort
gelingen, wo sie mit Hilfe zeitgenössischer Autoren vorgenommen werden
können, also aufgrund von brieflichen Zeugnissen, besonders von
Schleiermacher selbst. Hier waltet der Zufall der Überlieferung. Esoterik hat
ihren Preis!

II.

Der Kreis der gemeinten, angesprochenen, ja erhofften Leser
vergrößert sich, schaut man auf die kulturphilosophischen, ästhetischen
Anspielungen und Zitate. Auch sie beziehen sich zurück auf Schleiermachers
Gesprächs- und Lebenspraxis in den verschiedenen geselligen Kreisen, aber
sie schließen nun alle die ein, denen die angesprochenen Themen gleichfalls
Lebenselixier waren, die produktiv oder rezipierend an der geistigen Bildung
der Zeit teilhatten.

In diesem Lichte muß man die Huldigung an Johann Friedrich
Reichardt lesen, die das Lob der *Wei[h]nachtskantilene* enthält, in der – wie
es heißt – "die Freude und das Gefühl der Errettung und die demüthige
Anbetung so schön ausgedrückt ist" (S. 21). Der andächtigen Gesellschaft
"geschah es, wie immer, daß religiöse Musik zuerst eine stille Befriedigung
und Zurükgezogenheit des Gemüthes bewirkt. Es gab einige stumme
Augenblikke, in denen aber Jeder wußte, daß eines Jeden Gemüth liebend
auf die Uebrigen und auf etwas noch Höheres gerichtet war".
Schleiermacher wird die 1786 gedruckte Weihnachtsmusik in Reichardts
Haus gehört haben, wie in der *Weihnachtsfeier* in der Klavierfassung[31].
Neben dieser Referenz ist zugleich Stellung genommen zu der sehr
lebendigen Diskussion über Kirchenmusik, zu der der Kreis um Reichardt
einen eigenen Beitrag geleistet hat und die Schleiermacher in Giebichenstein
kennengelernt haben wird[32]. Die Anregungen gehen bis in den Wortschatz;
wahrscheinlich ist es Giebichensteiner Redeweise, Dur männlich und Moll

weiblich zu nennen (S. 53)[33]. Man darf bei dem überschwenglichen Lob der *Weihnachtskantilene*, das sich in der Geschichte der Musikbeurteilung und in der Aufführungspraxis keineswegs bestätigt hat, natürlich nicht übersehen, daß Bachs *Weihnachtsoratorium* noch nicht wiederentdeckt war!

Auch die nur Eingeweihten verständliche Anspielung auf Händels *Messias* ("Vom Chor der Engel ward Jesus empfangen, und so begleiten wir ihn mit Tönen und Gesang bis zum großen Hallelujah der Himmelfahrt" S. 51f – entprechend Nr. 15: Chorus 'Ehre sei Gott' und Nr. 42: Chorus 'Hallelujah'), die erst in der zweiten Ausgabe von 1826 namentlich enthüllt wurde ([2]S. 57), zeigt keineswegs eine originäre Entdeckung Schleiermachers an, sondern deutet auf die Wichtigkeit dieser Musik für den Kreis um Reichardt[34]. Nur in diesem Leserkreis kann eine solche kryptische Bemerkung ohne nähere Aufschlüsselung verständlich sein. An dieser Stelle wird Schleiermachers Lesererwartung besonders deutlich!

Auf der gleichen Ebene liegt die Auswahl der Lieder des Novalis, die Friederike und Sophie als von ihrem "Lieblingsdichter" singen: 'Ich sehe dich in tausend Bildern' (S. 76) und 'Wo bleibst du Trost der ganzen Welt' (S. 87) aus den 1802 erschienenen *Geistlichen Liedern*[35]. Auch hier ist an eine Anregung aus der Musizierpraxis des Reichardtschen Hauses, näherhin durch Louise Reichardt, zu denken[36]. Reichardt und seine Töcher gehörten zu den ersten Komponisten, die romantische Poesie – besonders von Tieck, Arnim, Novalis – vertonten; Louise Reichardts Vortragsweise wird in den Autobiographien stets als einer "reineren Welt" angehörig hervorgehoben[37]. Schleiermacher schätzte die "Lieder" Hardenbergs freilich schon seit 1800, d.h. vor deren Druck[38]; bekanntlich hat er noch 1829 dafür gesorgt, daß einige von ihnen in das neue Berliner Gesangbuch aufgenommen wurden[39]. In der *Weihnachtsfeier* scheint er an geistliche Melodien zu den Texten zu denken, ohne daß die "schöne Kirchenmelodie" (S. 76) bzw. die "heitere klare Kirchenmelodie", die "wenig mehr gehört" werde (S. 87), erkenntlich wären[40]. Daß bei dem Lied 'Wo bleibst du Trost der ganzen Welt' "natürlich" diejenigen Strophen ausgewählt werden, "die dem weiblichen Sinn die verständlichsten sein mußten" (S. 87f), deutet dem Kenner eine leise Kritik an der Sexualmystik des Liedes an.

Es liegt nahe, auch an der folgenden Stelle auf ein geflügeltes Wort
aus dem Reichardtschen Kreis zu schließen, wenn Schleiermacher Eduard
sagen läßt: "Es ist auch gewiß wahr, was Jemand gesagt hat, daß die
Kirchenmusik nicht des Gesanges, wol aber der bestimmten Worte
entbehren könnte" (S. 51). Wer ist der "Jemand"? Ein direkter Nachweis hat
sich nicht finden lassen. Ich schlage eine überraschende Lösung des Rätsels
vor: Es ist denkbar, daß Schleiermacher sich hier schalkhaft selbst als
Aphoristiker einführt! Ganz ähnlich klang es ja schon in den *Reden* von 1799:
"(...) so wie eine solche Rede Musik ist auch ohne Gesang und Ton, so ist
auch eine Musik unter den Heiligen, die zur Rede wird ohne Worte, zum
bestimmtesten verständlichsten Ausdruk des Innersten. (...) In heiligen
Hymnen und Chören, denen die Worte der Dichter nur lose und luftig
anhängen, wird ausgehaucht was die bestimmte Rede nicht mehr faßen kann,
und so unterstüzen sich und wechseln die Töne des Gedankens und der
Empfindung bis Alles gesättigt ist und voll des Heiligen und Unendlichen"[41].
Eduard entfaltet an dieser Stelle jedenfalls Schleiermachers Musik-
Theologie. Sollte Schleiermacher sich in dieser doppelten Weise – durchaus
romantisch – literalisiert haben, wäre noch einmal deutlich, daß nur ein eng
umgrenzter Kreis einen solchen Scherz goutieren konnte.

Literatursoziologisch ist nach dem bisher Aufgezeigten sichtbar
geworden, wen Schleiermacher sich – über die biographisch mit ihm
Verbundenen hinaus – als Leser vorstellt, für wen er schreibt: für den
"Gebildeten", der Anspielungen versteht, der Winke schätzt, mit dem sich
über Literatur, Musik, Philosophie und eben auch über Religion "reden" läßt.

Wer sonst etwa sollte den andeutenden Hinweis auf den zuletzt
erschienenen Roman von Jean Paul *Flegeljahre* verstehen, wenn es heißt: "Ich
erinnere mich (...) an etwas ohnlängst Gelesenes; ihr werdet gleich rathen,
wem es angehört. Nie über einzelne Begebenheiten, so lauten etwa die
Worte, weint oder lacht die Musik, sondern immer nur über das Leben
selbst" (S. 52)? Auch wenn der Name Jean Pauls fällt, ist die Anspielung auf
das Kapitel 'Smaragdfluß. Musik der Musik' mit seinen neuplatonisch
klingenden musikphilosophischen Reflexionen nur dem ganz in der
gegenwärtigen Diskussion stehenden Leser nachvollziehbar[42].

Daß Schleiermacher gerade diese Stelle aus Jean Pauls Roman anführt, läßt eine weitere, geheime Dimension erahnen, nämlich die seiner eigenen Hörerfahrung nicht nur, sondern einer subtilen Kritik an dem zitierten Autor. Bekanntlich hat Schleiermacher den Keimentschluß für das Schreiben der *Weihnachtsfeier* in einem Konzert des blinden Flötenvirtuosen Friedrich Ludwig Dülon (1769-1826) empfangen[43]. In der angezogenen Stelle der *Flegeljahre* nun werden die Höreindrücke des Flötenspiels des Flautotraversisten Vult wiedergegeben, der sich, bewußt Dülon imitierend, blind stellt und in dessen empfindsamer Manier spielt. Was allerdings aus dem längeren Text von Schleiermacher zitiert wird, ist nicht das neuplatonisch getönte "Heimweh in der Menschenbrust" nach der jenseitigen Welt, ist nicht die "Ewigkeit (...), deren Tantalus der Mensch ist" – vor dieser die irdische Existenz abwertenden Folgerung wird das Zitat abgebrochen. Schleiermacher nimmt nur das Stichwort "Leben" auf[44]. Nicht die Musik als solche hat himmlische Dignität, sondern das "Leben selbst", der Mensch in seiner individuellen Fülle, in dessen "Gemüth" die Harmonie der Musik lediglich ein Analogon für das "religiöse Gefühl" (S. 49), für die "frommen Stimmungen" (S. 53) darstellt[45]. Daß also die Verkürzung des Zitats zugleich eine Kritik an der Musikauffassung Jean Pauls bedeutet, kann der Leser – bloß – der *Weihnachtsfeier* nicht erkennen, sondern nur der gebildete Kreis, der – mit Schleiermacher? – Jean Paul diskutiert hat.

Ein erhebliches Maß an Bildung verlangt es, die beiden Anspielungen auf Platons *Symposion* zu erkennen, wenn Ernst die Reden der Männer nach "alter Weise" begründet – die zweite Ausgabe verdeutlicht: nach "griechischer" (^{2}S. 103), – einen Gegenstand zu wählen, "über welchen Jedem obläge etwas zu sagen" (S. 98), oder wenn Eduard bescheiden auf einen "Besseren, als ich bin" – nämlich Sokrates – verweist, der bei einer ähnlichen Gelegenheit angemerkt habe, "daß die Lezten am übelsten daran sind, wo über einen Gegenstand, welcher es sei, auf diese Weise geredet wird" (S. 123)[46].

An der Grenze der Nachvollziehbarkeit steht Eduards etwas dunkle Rede vom "Erdgeist" (S. 126f. 130). Hier ist wohl ein Wink zu Schelling hin zu sehen, der diese religionsphilosophische Metapher einmal in seinen *Vorlesungen über die Methode des academischen Studium* von 1803 gebraucht

hat, wo er von der "Einheit des allem eingebohrnen Erdgeistes" spricht[47].
Schleiermacher hat diese Metapher in seiner Rezension dieser Schrift
rezipiert[48] und in der *Weihnachtsfeier* sowie im *Ethik-Brouillon* von 1805
wiederholt[49]. Schelling jedenfalls hat, als exemplarischer gebildeter Leser,
dieses Metaphern-Zitat in seiner Rezension der *Weihnachtsfeier* bemerkt und
diskutiert[50].

Auch die folgenden Belege können noch unter "Bildungsanspielung"
gebucht werden, gehen aber in ihrer Stellungnahme zu den einstigen
romantischen Lebensgenossen über eine solche hinaus. Auch hier überrascht
Schleiermachers Erwartung, daß seine Leser – über die Angesprochenen
hinaus – ihn verstehen werden.

Das gilt zunächst für Schleiermachers Anspielung auf Correggios
'Nacht', wenn er Sophie sich als "ein zweiter Correggio" fühlen läßt für eine
gelungene Krippen-Komposition der Heiligen Familie: "Alles ist dunkel in
der ärmlichen Hütte, nur ein verborgenes starkes Licht bestrahlt das Haupt
des Kindes, und bildet einen Widerschein auf dem vorgebeugten Angesicht
der Mutter" (S. 18f). Schleiermacher kannte das Werk aus der Dresdner
Gemälde-Galerie – wo es sich jetzt noch befindet – nicht selbst, sondern
lediglich aus der Beschreibung im Gespräch 'Die Gemählde' von August
Wilhelm (und Caroline) Schlegel im *Athenaeum* von 1799[51] und aus
Schilderungen von Henriette Herz[52]. Im Anschluß an das genannte
Gespräch entwickelte Friedrich Schlegel, nicht zuletzt unter Bezug auf
Correggio, in der Zeitschrift *Europa* seine antiklassische Theorie der
christlichen Kunst, mit der er große Wirkung auf die religiöse Malerei seiner
Zeit hatte[53]. Schleiermacher hatte zwar, wie er Henriette Herz gegenüber
andeutet, im Stillen eine "Theorie" entwickelt, in der *Weihnachtsfeier* wagte
er aber noch kein eigenes öffentliches Urteil; er deutet vielmehr auf sehr
dezente Weise lediglich seine Belesenheit an.

Nicht zufällig wird – aber auch hier nur dem Kenner bemerkbar –
aus dem soeben 1805 erschienenen klassizistischen Gegenwerk, dem von
Goethe herausgegebenen *Winkelmann und sein Jahrhundert*, zitiert, das
natürlich jeder Gebildete kennen mußte. Das Zitat Leonhardts ("[...] wenn
das wahr ist was Göthe sagt, daß immer ein Makel auf einer Person haftet,
die ihre Ehe aufgelöst oder ihre Religion geändert hat" S. 29) hat freilich mit

Kunst nichts zu tun; Schleiermacher hat sehr gezielt aus den 'Skizzen zu einer Schilderung Winkelmanns' den Unterteil 'Katholicismus' angeführt[54]. Dabei ist freilich anzumerken, daß das Zitat in diesem Kontext Goethes Meinung genau in ihr Gegenteil verkehrt: Schleiermacher läßt seinen Protagonisten, wenn auch im Eventualis, positiv aufführen, was Goethe bitter ironisch abwehren wollte! Die harte Abfertigung des Konfessionswechsels (vgl. auch S. 35f) ist allerdings Schleiermachers Meinung, wie der 'Zusaz' in der zweiten Ausgabe der *Reden* aus dem Jahr 1806 zeigt [55].

Die verhältnismäßig scharfe Kritik an August Wilhelm Schlegels erkünstelter Begeisterung für die christliche Religion – "Ich mag die steife Kirche nicht, die uns Schlegel in seinen steifen Stanzen geschildert hat", sagt Leonhardt (S. 44) – setzt bei den Lesern die Kenntnis der *Gedichte* von 1800 mit dem umfänglichen Gedicht in Stanzen 'Der Bund der Kirche mit den Künsten' voraus[56], also keineswegs Selbstverständliches. Sie ist wohl ein Beleg für die während des Schreibens noch geplante Anonymität der *Weihnachtsfeier*. Die als Redebeitrag Leonhardts poetisch ermöglichte Direktheit entsprach Schleiermachers persönlicher Auffassung[57], die er aber dem älteren Schlegel "um keinen Preis selbst grade so in's Gesicht" (s.o.) hätte sagen können. Damit ist zugleich eine wichtige Tendenz der Jenaer Romantik – wo das inkriminierte Gedicht als "Meisterstück" galt[58] – getroffen, die auf eine eigentümliche Weise die Religion poetisieren und Schleiermacher in ihr Bestreben einbinden wollte. (Die Novalis- Zitate in der *Weihnachtsfeier* und die Änderungen in der zweiten Ausgabe der *Reden* zeigen, daß Schleiermacher nur Friedrich von Hardenberg auf dem richtigen Wege sah[59]). Offenbar hat diesen sehr deutlichen Wink nur Friedrich Schlegel verstanden[60].

Noch einmal zeigt sich, daß Schleiermachers Rezeptionserwartung über die Biographica hinaus auf die Diskussionskreise zielte, in denen er selber lebte und in deren geselliger Unterhaltung all die Themen der Kulturphilosophie und Theologie, die er anspricht – also des "höchsten Gutes", um in der Terminologie seiner Hallenser Ethik zu reden – , eine prägende Rolle spielten. Musik, Dichtung, Malerei, Religion – das sind nicht so sehr die Themen des Rügener Familien- und Freundeskreises, eher des Salons der Henriette Herz, gewiß aber der romantischen Lebens- und

Gesprächszirkel in Halle und Jena. Deren Mitglieder sind nun allerdings keine "gebildeten Verächter" mehr, aber doch solche, die – in einem Gewitter von Anspielungen, Winken, Zitaten – einer tieferen Belehrung über christlich-protestantisch-kirchliche Lebensweise bedürfen.

III.

Es gehört zur esoterischen Struktur des Werkes, daß die äußeren, politischen Verhältnisse nur am Rande, dann aber doch unüberlesbar aufscheinen. Von dem "schönen Jüngling", der "als eins der lezten Opfer der blutdürstigsten Zeit" "so heldenmüthig und so vergeblich für die Freiheit gestorben ist" (S. 77), haben wir schon gehört, ohne daß der historische Zusammenhang aufgehellt werden kann.

Anders ist es mit der Anspielung auf Napoleon, die mitten in die gesellschaftliche Konversation die politische Wirklichkeit des Dezember 1805 mit ihrer Kriegsfurcht und -hoffnung einbrechen läßt: "(...) es können Euch andere Prüfungen bereitet sein, daß Ihr sie bestehet." sagt Leonhardt zu den Frauen. "Die Anstalten sind schon gemacht. Ein großes Schiksal geht unschlüssig auf und ab in unserer Nähe, mit Schritten unter denen die Erde erbebt, und wir wissen nicht wie es uns mit ergreifen kann. Daß sich dann nur nicht das Wirkliche mit stolzer Uebermacht für Eure demüthige Verachtung räche!" (S. 56)

Welche genauen Kenntnisse über die geschichtlichen Ereignisse beim Schreiben dieser Zeilen Schleiermacher hatte, ist ungewiß. Wahrscheinlich kannte er über die Schlacht bei Austerlitz am 2. Dezember 1805, in der Napoleon die Heere Österreichs und Rußlands schlug und als deren Folge Preußen Mitte des Monats einen – von Schleiermacher als schimpflich empfundenen[61] – separaten Vertrag schloß, zunächst nur Gerüchte. Die preußischen Zeitungen verschwiegen den Ausgang der Schlacht bis zur Mitte des Monats, berichteten vielmehr von der Mobilmachung der preußischen Armee[62]. Das mag die vorsichtige Formulierung erklären.

In der 'Vorerinnerung zur zweiten Ausgabe', datiert "am Ende des November 1826", hat Schleiermacher seine politische Andeutung zitiert ("Das große Schicksal, welches damals drohend einherschritt, hat seine Rolle ausgespielt" S. I), aber unpolitisch weitergedeutet auf den Kampf der "religiösen Verschiedenheiten", den er schlichten möchte. Hier sind die Berliner kirchenpolitischen Querelen im Blick, die esoterische Perspektive hat sich grundlegend gewandelt.

IV.

Zu den großen Rätseln der Interpretation der *Weihnachtsfeier* gehört die Gestalt des Josef, die – lang erwartet (S. 97) – nach Abschluß der Reden der Männer zu der Weihnachtsgesellschaft stößt und in einer gar nicht so kurzen Rede darlegt, daß sie nicht gekommen sei, Reden zu halten, sondern sich mit der Gesellschaft zu freuen. "Der sprachlose Gegenstand verlangt oder erzeugt auch mir eine sprachlose Freude, die meinige kann wie ein Kind nur lächeln und jauchzen. Alle Menschen sind mir heute Kinder, und sind mir eben darum so lieb". "Auch ich selbst bin ganz ein Kind geworden zu meinem Glükk" (S. 133). Ein tiefer, unvergänglicher Schmerz sei heute besänftigt: "Ich fühle mich einheimisch und wie neugeboren in der besseren Welt, in der Schmerz und Klage keinen Sinn hat und keinen Raum". Wie bei Christus sei das Herz nun "voll himmlischer Liebe und Freude" (S. 134), und so lautet die abschließende Forderung: "(...) laßt uns heiter sein und etwas Frommes und Fröhliches singen" (S. 135).

Es gibt keinerlei biographische Hinweise aus Schleiermachers Kreis, obgleich doch diese Josefs-Gestalt kompositorisch so eindrücklich am Ende steht[63]. Walther Sattler nun hat – und das würde in der Tat den Gipfel der Esoterik darstellen – gemeint, in Josef die Idealgestalt des Herrnhuter Brüderbischofs August Gottlieb Spangenberg (1704-1792) sehen zu dürfen, zu der Schleiermacher von Goethe angeregt worden sei[64]. Diese doppelte These gilt es sorgfältig zu prüfen.

Sattler hat sich mehrfach bemüht, allerdings durchweg nicht überzeugend[65], Goethe-Anspielungen in der *Weihnachtsfeier* aufzufinden, vor allem aus dem Epos *Hermann und Dorothea*. Er hat den Mut gehabt, seiner Edition einen feinsinnigen, aber völlig mißverständlich übertitelten Essay "Goethe als Interpret der *Weihnachtsfeier*" beizugeben, in dem er das Werk im Goetheschen Geist interpretiert. Daß die *Weihnachtsfeier* aus dem geistigen Klima der klassisch-romantischen Zeit heraus und darum auch im Hinblick auf Goethe gedeutet werden muß, soll dabei positiv festgehalten werden. So kann der Motivhaushalt der *Luise* von Johann Heinrich Voß und von Goethes *Hermann und Dorothea*, wie Sattler es tut, durchaus zum Vergleich mit herangezogen werden. Abhängigkeiten aber müssen philologisch bewiesen werden, und das gelingt nicht.

Was hat Goethe mit Spangenberg und dieser mit der *Weihnachtsfeier* zu tun? Daß Goethe gelegentliche Beziehungen zur Herrnhuter Brüdergemeinde hatte und sich zeitweilig in höchstem Maße für sie interessierte, ist bekannt[66]. Er hat in den berühmten 'Bekenntnisse(n) einer schönen Seele' in *Wilhelm Meisters Lehrjahre(n)* – die Schleiermacher natürlich nicht entgingen[67] – die Freundin seiner Mutter, Susanna Katharina von Klettenberg, als "eine herrnhutische Schwester auf (...) eigene Hand" dargestellt[68]. Lokalkenntnisse hatte er, wie er in *Dichtung und Wahrheit* berichtet, durch die Teilnahme an einer Synode in der Herrnhuter Gemeinde in Marienborn in der Wetterau am 21./22. September 1769 erlangt[69], also im Alter von 20 Jahren. Dort hörte er eine Predigt des Brüderbischofs Spangenberg. Dieser wird in den zeitgenössschen Quellen, seit er 1744 in den von Zinzendorf 1743 gegründeten "Närrchenorden" eingetreten war – hier sollte das Evangelium für die "Unmündigen" (Mt 11,25) gelebt werden – , "Bruder Joseph" genannt; ein Name, der ihm bis ins hohe Greisenalter blieb[70]. So heißt er auch in dem Diarium der Gemeinde, in dem der Besuch Goethes festgehalten ist: "Am 21. hielt uns unser l. Bruder Joseph die letzte Gelegenheit, redte sehr herzlich und eindrücklich über die Losung, fiel sodann mit uns auf die Knie etc. . . . Der H. Legationsrath Moritz, und H. Rath Göthe aus Frankfurt Sohn, ein junger Student, die von Frankfurt zum Besuch hier waren, wohnten dieser Versamlung bey"[71]. Goethe hat Jahrzehnte später geäußert, daß er sich an den "nachherigen Bischof Spangenberg" auf dieser Synode "noch recht gut" erinnere[72].

Auch 1776 war Goethe in einer Herrnhuter Gemeinde, und zwar – mit dem Herzog von Sachsen-Weimar – in Barby. Auch hier wohnte er, wie das Diarium der Gemeinde vermeldet, "einer Rede des Br. Josephs über die Loosungen in der Gemeindestunde mit vieler Satisfaction bei"[73]. Das Tagebuch des ebenfalls anwesenden Goethe-Freundes Christoph Kaufmann, gestorben 1795 in Herrnhut, enthält dazu folgende Notiz: "(...) es (blieb) Goethe Hypothese, wie Spangenberg so einfältig kindisch, so vergnügt und so weise und klug beisammen sein könnte"[74].

An dieser Stelle setzt Sattler, der offenbar keine Schrift Spangenbergs gelesen hat, seine Hypothese an: Die Namensgleichheit – obwohl in der *Weihnachtsfeier* das Beiwort "Bruder" fehlt – und die "kindische Freude" (S. 134) der Figur lassen ihn vermuten, daß diese "nicht ohne besondere Rücksicht auf Goethe und seine persönlichen Beziehungen zur Brüder- gemeine" dem 'Gespräch' eingefügt worden sei[75]. Als nämlich Schleier- macher, der Ostern 1805 Barby wieder besucht hatte[76], im Juli und August 1805 in Friedrich August Wolfs Haus in Halle mehrfach mit Goethe zusammen traf und dabei freundlich aufgenommen wurde[77], seien, meint Sattler, die gemeinsamen Erinnerungen an die Brüdergemeinde "wohl nicht unerörtert geblieben"[78]. In dieser Weise habe Goethe produktiv auf die Entstehung und Ausführung der *Weihnachtsfeier* gewirkt.

Ich muß gestehen, daß mich diese Argumentation in ihrem Hauptaspekt überzeugt, nämlich daß in dem "Josef" eine Herrnhutische Gestalt intendiert sei. Daß Goethe dafür anregend gewirkt habe, ist Spekulation, obwohl durchaus wahrscheinlich ist, daß er mit Schleiermacher nicht nur über dessen Mitarbeit an der neuen Jenaischen Allgemeinen Literaturzeitung gesprochen haben wird[79], sondern auch Herrnhutisch- Barbysche Erfahrungen ausgetauscht hat. Das könnte bei dem Treffen "ohne andre Gesellschaft" am 26. August 1805 gewesen sein, von dem sich Schleiermacher versprach, daß sich "mehr reden lassen" werde als bei den vorherigen Malen; über dieses Treffen ist aber kein Echo überliefert[80].

Wahrscheinlich kann man biographisch und onomatologisch noch einen Schritt weiterkommen. Bei dem Gespräch mit Goethe könnte Schleiermacher daran erinnert worden sein, daß er 20 Jahre früher den damals 81-jährigen Spangenberg selbst kennengelernt hatte, nämlich bei der Reise der Barbyer Kandidaten im September 1785 nach Herrnhut[81]. Spangenbergs Biograph Risler berichtet, daß der greise Bischof während der Visitation der Gemeinde Erwachsenen wie Kindern "mit Herzenswärme und freudigem Aufthun seines Mundes" "Versammlungen" gehalten habe[82], also wohl auch der zu Besuch weilenden Kandidatenschar. Die Sammlungen der

Kinderpredigten aus dieser Zeit[83] enthalten leider keine Predigt aus dem September 1785. Ein Echo Schleiermachers ist nicht erhalten; er erwähnt Spangenberg in seinen Briefen (und Werken ?) meines Wissens niemals. Im Rauchschen Nachlaß-Katalog der Schleiermacherschen Bibliothek aber ist Rislers *Leben August Gottlieb Spangenbergs, Bischofs der evangelischen Brüderkirche* (Barby 1794) verzeichnet[84], vielleicht bei dem Osterbesuch 1805 erstanden und folglich im Jahr der Entstehung der *Weihnachtsfeier* gelesen.

Spangenberg war ein fruchtbarer Liederdichter; seine Lieder müssen Schleiermacher im *Gesangbuch zum Gebrauch der evangelischen Brüder-gemeinen* (Barby 1778) oder im *Gesangbüchlein für die Kinder in den Brüdergemeinen* (Barby 1789) vielfach begegnet sein. In ihnen herrscht ein Ton, den man – mit der *Weihnachtsfeier* gesprochen – "fromm" und "fröhlich" nennen kann. Von hier her wie auch aus den posthum 1797 und 1799 in Barby gedruckten Kinderpredigten[85] ließe sich das auffällige semantische Umfeld der vielfachen Kind-Metapher in der Sprache "Josefs" erklären.

Schließlich wird man auf den auffälligen Namen selbst hinweisen müssen. Dem ehemaligen Herrnhuter Schleiermacher mußten bei "Josef" mit Sicherheit Herrnhutische Konnotationen mitschwingen. Während alle anderen Männernamen in der *Weihnachtsfeier* in der Goethe-Zeit konven-tionell waren, kann man das – jedenfalls im protestantischen Bereich – von "Josef" nicht sagen[86]; in Schleiermachers unmittelbarer Umgebung trug, glaube ich, niemand diesen biblischen Namen. Dieser "poetische" Name ist – für den Kenner, freilich nur für diesen – "redend"[87].

Der Wortschatz "Josefs" – noch niemals untersucht, wie überhaupt Schleiermachers Sprache nicht – ist allgemein pietistisch gehalten (Herz voll Liebe und Freude, voll himmlischer Liebe und Freude, sprachlose Freude, kindischer Schmerz, kindische Freude, langer tiefer unvergänglicher Schmerz[88], Braut Christi, Freunde Christi, neugeboren, Frommes und Fröhliches), Herrnhutisch-Zinzendorfische Sexual-Mystik klingt an, ganz arglos ("Es war Ein langer liebkosender Kuß, den ich der Welt gab, und jezt meine Freude mit Euch, sollte der lezte Drukk der Lippe sein" S. 134f), mehrfache Anspielungen auf die Johannes-Apokalypse begegnen[89], so daß ein eschatologischer Klang nicht zu verkennen ist.

Ohne in die anachronistische Forderung des literarischen Realismus zu verfallen, daß Schleiermacher intendiert haben müsse, in der Gestalt des Josef eine historisch-biographisch genau zu umreißende Person darzustellen, kann Sattler doch insgesamt zugestimmt werden. Die Gestalt des Josef ist deutlich genug von den Männern und Frauen der Weihnachtsgesellschaft unterschieden, sie gehört nicht der "gebildeten" Gesellschaft an, sie kommt von außen: aus einem – poetischen – Herrnhut.

Wenn Schleiermacher eine herrnhutische Gestalt kompositorisch so betont an das Ende der *Weihnachtsfeier* stellt – nachdem in der kritischen Debatte um die herrnhutische weibliche Frömmigkeit das Thema "Herrnhut" längst abschließend behandelt schien (S. 28, 33ff) – , muß hier ein besonderes Anliegen des "höheren Herrnhuters" verborgen sein, das in der Gesamtdeutung des weihnachtlichen 'Gesprächs' erschlossen und gewürdigt werden muß.

Blickt man abschließend auf die Dimensionen der esoterischen Schreibweise in der *Weihnachtsfeier* zurück, so wird man sagen können, daß Schleiermacher diese sehr bewußt und offenbar sehr gezielt gehandhabt hat. Er stellte sich über den unmittelbar mit ihm biographisch verbundenen Kreis hinaus eine "gebildete" Leserschar vor, mit der er thematisch universal kommunizieren konnte und die darum auch Interesse für die inhaltliche, theologische Thematik hatte. Beides gehört für den religiösen "Redner" zusammen. In diesem Sinne ist das Werk von strenger Zeitbezogenheit. Aber ebenso deutlich erwies sich die Grenze dieser Schreibweise, die die zeitgenössische Rezeption – und nicht nur diese – erschwerte. Ging die Esoterik so weit, daß sie in der Andeutung verblieb, nur mehr die geistige Atmosphäre wiedergab, hat sie Schleiermachers Leser nicht mehr erreicht. Zu vielfältig war das Anspielungspotential, als daß die angesprochenen "gebildeten" Kreise einen umfassenden Genuß der Komposition hätten erlangen können. Ob, aus dem Abstand der Zeiten, philologisch-historische Kommentierung diesen dem gegenwärtigen Leser schaffen kann, steht dahin.

Anmerkungen

1. Kurt-Victor Selge (Hg): Internationaler Schleiermacher Kongreß Berlin 1984 (Schleiermacher-Archiv Bd. 1). Berlin-New York 1985, S. 1215-1228.
Im Folgenden kürze ich ab: Aus Schleiermachers Leben. In Briefen. 4 Bde 1860-1863 (ND Berlin 1974) mit Br. I-IV; Heinrich Meisner (Hg): Schleiermacher als Mensch. Sein Wirken. Familien- und Freundesbriefe 1804-1834. Gotha 1923 mit M II; H. Meisner (Hg): Friedrich Schleiermachers Briefwechsel mit seiner Braut. Gotha 1919 mit M III; mit Gaß-Br.: Fr. Schleiermacher's Briefwechsel mit J.Chr.Gaß. Mit einer biographischen Vorrede hg.v. W. Gaß. Berlin 1852.
Ich zitiere folgende Ausgaben: Die Weihnachtsfeier. Ein Gespräch. Von Friedrich Schleiermacher. Halle 1806, bei Schimmelpfennig und Kompagnie. Die Weihnachtsfeier. Ein Gespräch. Von Friedrich Schleiermacher. Zweite Ausgabe. Berlin, 1826. Gedruckt und verlegt bei G. Reimer.
2. Eine erste Zusammenstellung gibt Hermann Mulert in seiner Ausgabe (Friedrich Schleiermachers Weihnachtsfeier. Kritische Ausgabe. Mit Einleitung und Register von H.M. Philosophische Bibliothek Bd. 117. Leipzig 1908, S. 73.) Neuere Zusammenstellungen: Christmas Eve. Dialogue on the Incarnation. By Friedrich Schleiermacher. Translated, with Introduction and Notes, by Terrence N. Tice. Richmond, Virginia 1967, p. 87f; Friedrich Schleiermacher. Kleine Schriften und Predigten Bd. 1: 1800-1820. Bearb.v. Hayo Gerdes. Berlin 1970, S. 454-458; Fr.D.E. Schleiermacher. Theologische Schriften. Hg.u. eingeleitet v. Kurt Nowak. (Texte zur Philosophie u. Religionsgeschichte) Berlin 1983, S. 459f.
Zu wenig beachtet geblieben sind die für historisch-philologische Arbeit wichtigen Studien von Walther Sattler: Beiträge zur Schleiermacher-Forschung (Theol. Studien und Kritiken 89, 1916, S. 402-416. 529-554, hier S. 402ff. 531f); Eine extemporierte Taufrede am Heiligabend [I]. Marginalien zu Schleiermachers 'Weihnachtsfeier' (Monatschrift f. Gottesdienst und kirchl. Kunst 26, H.7/8, 1921, S. 249-254); Eine extemporierte Taufrede am Heiligabend. II. (Monatschrift f. Gottesdienst und kirchl. Kunst 27, 1922, S. 14-20); Goethe als Interpret der 'Weihnachtsfeier' (S. 72-88 seiner Edition Leipzig 1923). Vgl. noch Erich Gülzow: Schleiermachers 'Weihnachtsfeier'. Pommerns Anteil an ihrer Entstehung. (In: E.G.: Menschen und Bilder aus Pommerns Vergangenheit. Stralsund 1928, S. 36-45) sowie Gunter Scholtz: Schleiermachers Musikphilosophie. Göttingen, 1981, S. 31-45. Die vielen Studien zur Interpretation brauchen hier nicht aufgeführt zu werden.
3. In einem Brief v. 18. Februar 1806 an den Vater Wilhelm Christian Müller (Aus dem Nachlaß Varnhagen's von Ense. Briefe von der Unversität in die Heimath. Leipzig 1874, S. 284)
4. Vgl. die Briefe an Gaß vom 5. Jan. und 6. Febr. 1806 (Gaß-Br. S. 41f).
5. Varnhagen an Rahel Levi, 25. Dezember 1808 (Aus dem Nachlaß Varnhagen's von Ense. Briefwechsel zwischen Varnhagen und Rahel. Erster Band. Leipzig 1874, S. 229 = Rahel-Bibliothek. Rahel Varnhagen. Gesammelte Werke. Hg. v. Konrad Feilchenfeldt, Uwe Schweikert und Rahel E. Steiner. Bd. IV. München 1983). Zu Varnhagens Verhältnis zu Schleiermacher vgl. mein Buch: Alle Menschen sind Künstler. Friedrich Schleiermachers Poetische Versuche (= Schleiermacher-Archiv Bd. 2). Berlin - New York 1986, S. 164f.
6. an Brinckmann, Br.v. 1. März 1808 (Br. IV, S. 149 - mit kleiner Textänderung nach der Kollation von Albert Leitzmann: Rudolf Haym zum Gedächtniss. Neue Briefe von Karoline von Humboldt. Halle a.S. 1901, S. 142-150: Mitteilungen aus Brinckmanns handschriftlichem Nachlass. 4. Schleiermacher, hier S. 149), anläßlich der 'Gelegentlichen Gedanken über deutsche Universitäten' von 1808. Anonym zu schreiben, war im übrigen zeittypisch, besonders im Bereich der erzählenden Literatur (vgl. Gerhard Schulz: Die deutsche Literatur zwischen Französischer Revolution und Restauration. Erster Teil. Das

Zeitalter der Französischen Revolution 1789-1806 [Geschichte der deutschen Literatur von den Anfängen bis zur Gegenwart Bd. VII/1] , München 1983, S. 284), so daß Schleiermachers Bestreben nicht nur biographisch erklärt werden darf.

7.   Zur Interpretationsgeschichte vgl. Mulerts Erwägungen (a.a.o. S. XII-XXIX); E.H.U. Quapp: Barth contra Schleiermacher? Die "Weihnachtsfeier" als Nagelprobe. Marburg 1978; Ruth Drucilla Richardson: Friedrich Schleiermacher's "Weihnachtsfeier" as 'Universal Poetry': The Impact of Friedrich Schlegel on the Intellectual Development of the Young Schleiermacher. Phil.Diss. Drew University Madison, New Jersey 1985!

8.   Schwerlich hätte wohl Schleiermacher die erste Rede "ihrer Natur nach eigentlich frivol" nennen können (an Henriette Herz, 17. Jan. 1806, Br. II, S. 50/ M II, S. 51), wenn er hätte Steffens reden lassen wollen. Doch müßten Steffens' frühe Werke gegengehalten werden. Über St.s Reaktion äußert sich Schleiermacher nur andeutend (ebd. und Gaß-Br. S.42/ M II, S. 54).

9.   Arnims Briefe an Savigny 1803-1831. Hg. und kommentiert von Heinz Härtl. Weimar 1982, S. 33 (Brief v. 17. Februar 1806). Schleiermachers Predigten aus dieser Zeit sind nicht überliefert.

10.   Arnims weitere briefliche Berichte über seinen Weihnachtsbesuch (Brief o.D., Januar 1806, an Clemens Brentano [Achim von Arnim und die ihm nahe standen. Hg.v. Reinhold Steig und Herman Grimm. Erster Band: Achim von Arnim und Clemens Brentano. Bearb.v. R. Steig. Stuttgart 1984, S. 154]; Brief an Goethe vom 20. Februar 1806 [Goethe und die Romantik. Briefe mit Erläuterungen. 2. Theil. Hg.v. Carl Schüddekopf und Oskar Walzel. Schriften der Goethe-Gesellschaft Bd. 14. Weimar 1899, S. 83f]) erwähnen Schleiermacher nicht, als ob dieser bei dem Geschenkakt nicht dabei gewesen wäre. Anderseits schreibt Schleiermacher aber an Henriette v. Willich: "(...) ich habe den Weihnachtsabend recht schön zugebracht bei Reichardts in Giebichenstein mit Steffens, habe geschenkt und mir schenken lassen" (Ende Dez. 1805, M III, S. 56).

11.   Das im Dezember 1805 entstandene Werk sollte, wie die 'Monologen' eine "Neujahrsgabe", eine Weihnachtsgabe werden (vgl. Gaß-Br. S. 42; Br. IV, S. 122), wurde aber nicht rechtzeitig fertig: "Grade am Morgen des Weihnachtsabends schikte ich das lezte in die Drukkerei" (an Ehrenfried von Willich, 20. Juni 1806. Mitteilungen aus dem Litteraturarchive in Berlin. N.F.9. Briefe Friedrich Schleiermachers an Ehrenfried und Henriette von Willich geb. von Mühlenfels 1801-1806. Berlin 1914, S. 160).

12.   Jenaische Allgemeine Literatur-Zeitung 1807. Erster Band. Num. 58 + 59 v. 9.+ 10. März, Sp. 457-467, hier Sp. 466 (= Friedrich Wilhelm Joseph von Schellings sämmtliche Werke, 1. Abth. 7.Bd, Stuttgart 1860, S. 498-510).

13.   Vgl. E. Gülzow, a.a.O., S. 38f. Zu Charlotte von Kathen vgl. - neben den vielfältigen Bezügen in Schleiermachers Briefwechsel - Erich Gülzow (Hg.): Ernst Moritz Arndts Briefe an eine Freundin. Stuttgart - Berlin 1928.

14.   Vgl. Henr.v. Willichs Brief an Schleiermacher vom 26. Dez. 1804 und S.s Antwort o.D. (Januar 1805) (M III, S. 27 und 29f) sowie - bei einem Rückfall der Krankheit - S.s Briefe an Charl.v.Kathen vom 5. Mai 1805 (Br.II, S. 22/ M II, S.35) und an Charl. Pistorius, vor dem 10. Juni 1805 (Br. II, S. 28/ M. II, S. 39 - Datum nach der Handschrift).

15.   Br. II, S. 63/ M II, S. 63.

16.   an Henriette v. Willich, 21. Febr. 1809 (M III, S. 346 - Textverbesserungen nach der Handschrift). Durch dieses Selbstzeugnis ist zugleich Arnims Behauptung widerlegt, Ernestine sei nach Louise Reichardt gestaltet (a.a.o. Anm.9, S. 33). Zeitgenössische rühmende Zeugnisse über Charlotte Ernst sammelt Josef Körner: Krisenjahre der Frühromantik. Briefe aus dem Schlegelkreis. Dritter Band Kommentar. Bern 1958, S. 332f.

17.   Das geht aus dem (noch unveröffentlichten) 'Erinnerungsbüchlein für das Jahr 1810' hervor, aus dem Karl-Ludwig Hoch September-Eintragungen zitiert (Friedrich

Schleiermacher und Caspar David Friedrich. Deutsches Pfarrerblatt 84, 1984, S. 167-171, hier S. 167).

18. So etwa Sattler: Goethe als Interpret der 'Weihnachtsfeier' a.a.O., S. 79.

19. Meine Lebenserinnerungen. Ein Nachlaß von Adam Oehlenschläger. 2.Bd. Leipzig 1850, S. 11.

20. a.a.O. Anm.3, S. 284.

21. a.a.O. S. 33.

22. Walter Salmen: Johann Friedrich Reichardt. Komponist, Schriftsteller, Kapellmeister und Verwaltungsbeamter der Goethezeit. Freiburg i.Br./Zürich 1963.

23. Neben Adolph Müller, a.a.O., vgl. Varnhagen von Ense. Denkwürdigkeiten des eigenen Lebens. 2. Aufl. 1. Theil. Leipzig 1843, S. 363ff. (= Karl August Varnhagen von Ense Werke in fünf Bänden. Bd.1-3: Denkwürdigkeiten des eigenen Lebens. Erster Band (1785-1810). Hg.v. Konrad Feilchenfeldt. Frankfurt a.M. 1987, S. 350ff); Henrich Steffens: Was ich erlebte. Aus der Erinnerung niedergeschrieben. Breslau 1842. Bd.V, S. 144; Bd. VI, S. 91, 96; Karl von Raumer's Leben von ihm selbst erzählt. Stuttgart 1866, S. 43-46; Adam Oehlenschläger, a.a.O., S. 10f.

24. Br. II, S. 62/ M II, S. 63.

25. The Poetical Works of Charles Churchill, with explanatory notes; and an authentic account of his life. [By William Tooke] London 1804. 2 vols.

26. Br. v. 17. Jan. 1806 (Br. II, S. 50/ M II, S. 51).

27. Vgl. Joachim Heinrich Campe: Wörterbuch zur Erklärung und Verdeutschung der unserer Sprache aufgedrungenen fremden Ausdrücke. Braunschweig 1801, Bd.I, S. 324 (Artikel 'Elegant') mit der Neue(n) starkvermehrte(n) und durchgängig verbesserte(n) Ausgabe Braunschweig 1813, S. 282! Henriette Herz' Umgang mit Campe ist von ihr selbst bezeugt (Henriette Herz in Erinnerungen, Briefen und Zeugnissen. Hg. v. Rainer Schmitz. Leipzig und Weimar 1984, S. 162f); Schleiermacher hat 1801 ein pädagogisches Werk von Campe rezensiert (KGA I/3, 1988, 433-448).   In der 1804 erschienen 'Vorschule der Aesthetik' von Jean Paul, die Schleiermacher mit Sicherheit zur Kenntnis kam, gilt ein ganzer Paragraph (§ 84) "Campens Sprachreinigkeit", wobei auch "Zierling" erwähnt wird (Jean Paul. Werke in zwölf Bänden. Hg.v. Norbert Miller. Bd.9 München/Wien 1975, S. 307-318). Wahrscheinlich ist in Schleiermachers Kreis auch Campes verteidigender Aufsatz nicht übersehen und diskutiert worden (J.B.Campe: Zu Hrn Johann Paul Richter's Vorlesung über Campe's Sprachreinigkeit. In: Neue Berlinische Monatsschrift. Hg.v. Biester. 13. Bd. Februar 1805, S. 81-121).

28. Der Ausdruck "eins der lezten Opfer der blutdürstigsten Zeit" (S. 77) kann sich noch nicht auf den Kampf gegen Napoleon beziehen. Die zwei "Gemälde", die den Abschied des Helden und die Rückkehr aus der Schlacht darstellen (S. 77), werden schwerlich Fiktion sein.   Eine "Tante Kornelie" scheint es weder im Rügenschen Familien- und Freundeskreis noch in Berlin zu geben; ob in Halle, steht dahin.

29. Sattler, Taufrede I, a.a.O., S. 251.

30. Niemeyer meint an der angezogenen Stelle (D. August Hermann Niemeyers (...) Handbuch für christliche Religionslehrer. Zweyter Theil. Homiletik, Pastoralwissenschaft, und Liturgik. Fünfte verbesserte Auflage. Halle 1807, S. 40) lediglich, zum Wesen einer Predigt gehöre ein einzelner biblischer Text nicht notwendig, vielmehr könne ein Vortrag sehr schriftmäßig sein, der das Resultat mehrerer miteinander verglichener biblischer Stellen enthalte. "(...) eh man biblische Worte blos des Herkommens wegen einer Predigt vorausschickt, ohne hernach den mindesten Gebrauch davon zu machen, wäre es gewissermaßen besser, es gar nicht zu thun." Insgesamt aber hält N. die Einrichtung, die hl. Schrift den "Religionsvorträgen" zugrunde zu legen, für "löblich und nützlich" (S. 41).

31. Weinachts=Cantilene von Mathias Claudius, in Musik gesetzt von Johann Friederich Reichardt, Königl. Preuß. Capellmeister. Berlin, Auf Kosten des Autors, 1786. (In

dem Exemplar der Bayer. Staatsbibliothek München findet sich eine handschriftliche Widmung, offenbar von Reichardt selbst: Zeile 1 "Für Herrn Mathias Claudius", Zeile 2 nicht mehr entzifferbar.)

Der Druck von 1786 gibt keine Instrumente an. Doch siehe Reichardt selbst in der Berliner Musikalischen Zeitung (BMZ), 1 Jg. 1805, Nro.26, S.101: "In der Weihnachts= Cantilene sind nicht größtentheils nur Blasinstrumente angebracht; sie ist für ein ganz vollständiges Orchester componirt". Einen Klavierauszug stellte Louise Reichardt kurz vor ihrem Tode her (Leben der Luise Reichardt. Nach Quellen dargestellt von M.G.W. Brandt. Zweite erweiterte Aufl. Basel 1865, S. 37).

32. Vgl. Reichardts Aufsatz 'Kirchenmusik' aus dem 'Musikalischen Kunstmagazin' Bd. I v. 1782 (Johann Friedrich Reichardt: Briefe, die Musik betreffend. Berichte, Rezensionen, Essays. Hg. v. Grita Herre und Walther Siegmund-Schultze. Leipzig 1976, S. 170-174), seine Bemerkung in der BMZ in seinem Artikel über 'Die berlinische Singe-akademie' (l.Jg. 1805, Nro. 8, S.31) und die vielen Beiträge aus dem Mitarbeiterkreis. Vgl. auch Salmen, a.a.O. Anm. 22, S. 284ff.

33. Vgl. BMZ l.Jg. 1805, S. 267. Zu einem historischen Verständnis der Auffassung Schleiermachers gehört die Kenntnisnahme der zeitgenössischen Musikästhetik unbedingt hinzu. Vgl. auch Scholtz, a.a.O. Anm.2, S. 19-56. Zu erwähnen wäre als zeitgenössischer Musikroman noch Wilhelm Heinses 'Hildegard von Hohenthal' (1795/6), der nach Heinses Tod als Restauflage mit neuem Titelblatt 1804 in Berlin erschien.

34. Vgl. etwa die Besprechung der Mozartschen Bearbeitung durch Z. [= Carl Friedrich Zelter] in BMZ 1.Jg. 1805 Nro. 11+12, S. 41-48 und durch M. [= C.F.Michaelis] in Nro.32, S. 126-128 sowie die Diskussion um eine deutsche Ausgabe der Werke Händels in Nro. 85+86, S.335-341, etwa in der Zeit der Entstehung der 'Weihnachtsfeier'. Eine Aufführung in Halle - zu spät für eine Anregung Schleiermachers - ist für den 26. Dezember 1805 belegt (kritische Besprechung in BMZ 2.Jg. l806, Nro.6, S.24). In Heinses 'Hildegard von Hohenthal', a.a.O., gilt die erste ausführliche Analyse dem 'Messias'.

35. Novalis Schriften. Herausgegeben von Friedrich Schlegel und Ludwig Tieck. Berlin 1802. Band II, S. 157f. 150 (ff).

36. Zu Louise Reichardts. Brandt, a.a.O.; Luise Reichardt. Ausgewählte Lieder. Hg. und eingeleitet v. Gerty Rheinhardt. München 1922 (Musikalische Stundenbücher [18]); Walter Salmen in: Musik in Geschichte und Gegenwart Bd. XI, Mainz 1963, Sp. 160f. Schleiermachers Beziehungen zu L.R. hat Dilthey erörtert (Wilhelm Dilthey: Leben Schleiermachers. Erster Band. Auf Grund des Textes der l. Aufl. von 1870 und der Zusätze aus dem Nachlaß hg. v. Martin Redeker. Zweiter Halbband. 1803-1807 [=Ges. Schr. XIII/2]. Göttingen 1970, S. 121-125. 221-229).

37. Karl von Raumer's Leben, a.a.O., S.71, vgl. S. 47; vgl. auch Oehlenschläger, a.a.O., Bd. 2, S. 11, zur romantischen Stimmung Joseph von Eichendorff: Erlebtes. II. Halle und Heidelberg (Werke Bd. I. Gedichte.Versepen.Dramen. Autobiographisches. München 1970, S. 929).

38. an Brinckmann, 22. April 1800 (Br. IV, S. 65). Schleiermacher besaß eine Abschrift der ersten 'Geistlichen Lieder', die ihm Friedrich Schlegel gesandt hatte (Br. III, S. 134). In dem Teildruck im Musen-Almanach für das Jahr 1802. Hg. v. A.W. Schlegel und L. Tieck. Tübingen 1802, kommen die von Schleiermacher zitierten Lieder noch nicht vor.

39. Gesangbuch zum gottesdienstlichen Gebrauch für evangelische Gemeinen. Mit Genehmigung Eines hohen Ministerii der geistlichen Angelegenheiten. Berlin o.J. [1829]. Vgl. Novalis. Schriften. Die Werke Friedrich von Hardenbergs. Dritte, nach den Handschriften ergänzte, erweiterte und verb. Aufl. Bd. I: Das dichterische Werk. Hg.v. Paul Kluckhohn und Richard Samuel unter Mitarbeit v. Heinz Ritter und Gerhard Schulz. Revidiert v. R. Samuel. Darmstadt 1977, S. 125.

40. Ob Schleiermacher die Vorlage zu 'Wo bleibst du Trost der ganzen Welt', nämlich 'O Heyland, reiß den Himmel auff' von Friedrich von Spee (1591-1635) (s. den Kommentar in Novalis. Schriften 1, a.a.O., S. 619f) ahnte und an die bekannte Kirchenmelodie dachte, muß offen bleiben. Nicht datierbar ist Louise Reichardts Vertonung von 'Ich sehe dich in tausend Bildern' (Zwoelf Gesänge mit Begleitung des Piano=Forte. Componirt und ihrer Freundin und Schülerin Fräulein Louise Sittem zugeeignet von Louise Reichardt. Drittes Werk. Hamburg o.J., No: 11. S. 22; Wiederabdruck bei Gerty Rheinhardt, a.a.O., S. 30f), doch kann diese ersichtlich nicht gemeint sein.

41. Über die Religion. Reden an die Gebildeten unter ihren Verächtern. Berlin 1799. Vierte Rede. S. 183 (KGA I/2, S. 269,40-270,6). Vgl. zu dieser Stelle auch Scholtz, a.a.O. Anm.2, S. 37ff, der auf die Nähe zu Gedanken Herders verweist, und Albert L. Blackwell: The Role of Music in Schleiermacher's Writings. Internationaler Schleiermacher-Kongreß Berlin 1984. Hg.v. Kurt-Victor Selge. Berlin-New York 1985 (= Schleiermacher-Archiv 1), S. 439-448!

42. Flegeljahre. Eine Biographie von Jean Paul Richter. Zweites Bändgen. Tübingen 1804, S. 110. Die Enttarnung dieser Stelle gelang Scholtz, a.a.O., S. 34. Daß S. um diese Zeit die 'Flegeljahre' diskutierte, ist auch aus einem Brief Oehlenschlägers belegt, wohl aus dem Dezember 1805: "Ad velamfacientem. / Habe doch o vortreflicher Mann die freundliche Güte / Flegeljahre Jean Pauls, oder besser: von Friedrich Richter / Die ich gestern Abend vergass, mit Eile zu senden; / Denn ich sehne mich innig danach, was er weiter geflegelt.(...) " (Breve fra og til Adam Oehlenschläger Januar 1798 - November 1809 udgivet af H.A.Paludan. Daniel Preisz . Morten Borup. Bd. I. København 1945, S. 225).

43. Br. an Reimer v. 10. Febr. 1806 (Br. IV, S. 122), in dem S. selbst von einer "Empfängniß" spricht.

44. Das genaue Zitat lautet: "O ihr unbefleckten Töne, wie so heilig ist euere Freude und euer Schmerz! Denn ihr frohlockt und wehklagt nicht über irgend eine Begebenheit, sondern über das Leben und Sein und eurer Thränen ist nur die Ewigkeit würdig, deren Tantalus der Mensch ist". Vgl. zu dieser Stelle auch Scholtz, a.a.O., S. 39f!

45. Quapp, a.a.O. Anm. 7, S. 32 hat hier gegen Barth recht gesehen, auch wenn er den Bezug auf Jean Paul nicht erkannte.

46. Siehe Symposion 176e-177a sowie l98a-199a.

47. Vorlesungen über die Methode des academischen Studium. Von F.W.J. Schelling. Tübingen 1803, S. 32.

48. Br. IV, S. 579-593, hier S. 590.

49. Schleiermacher. Brouillon zur Ethik (1805/06). Auf der Grundlage der Ausgabe von Otto Braun hg. und eingeleitet von Hans-Joachim Birkner. (Philosophische Bibliothek 334) Hamburg 1981, S. 73. 77. 79. 99.

50. Jenaische Allgemeine Literaturzeitung 1807 Num. 58, Sp. 463f. 466. Vgl. zum Thema insgesamt meinen Aufsatz: Metamorphosen des Erdgeistes. Zu einer mythologischen Metapher in der Philosophie der Goethe-Zeit. New Athenaeum/Neues Athenaeum Jg.I, 1989, S. 248-279.

51. Athenaeum. Eine Zeitschrift von August Wilhelm Schlegel und Friedrich Schlegel, Zweiten Bandes Erstes Stück. Berlin 1799, S. 39-151, hier S. 92-95 sowie S. 138 (Sonett 'Christi Geburt'), vgl. S. 142 [Paginierung des Fotomech. Nachdr. Darmstadt 1960]. Zur 'Nacht' heißt es da: "Eben so scheint mir in seiner Nacht das Licht ganz einzig gemacht, um die Armuth und Einfalt der umgebenden Gegenstände wunderbar zu erleuchten" (S. 95).

52. Siehe Schleiermachers Brief an Henriette Herz v. 9. Juli 1803 (Br.I, S. 371/ M I, S. 307f, gebessert nach der Handschrift), in dem er auf den Aufsatz im 'Athenaeum' hinweist und gern wissen möchte, ob Henriette bei ihrem Besuch in der Dresdner Galerie "einige Ähnlichkeit" der Schlegelschen Sonette "im Charakter und im Eindruck mit den Gemälden selbst" finde. "Mir ist diese Art von Uebersetzung eine Hauptsache für meine Theorie und ich

mögte wohl wissen wie es damit gelungen ist. Auch Friedrichs Gedanken über die Malerei in der Europa, besonders auch über Raphael und Corregio studiere doch recht durch. Hernach will ich sehen ob ich von meinen Gedanken über die Sache etwas aufs Klare bringen und mittheilen kann". Der weitere Hinweis bezieht sich auf Friedrich Schlegel: 'Nachricht von den Gemählden in Paris'. In: Europa. Eine Zeitschrift, Hg.v. Friedrich Schlegel, Erster Band [H. 1]. Frankfurt a.M. 1803, S. 108-157, hier S. 124ff. 147ff [Fotomech. Nachdr. Darmstadt 1973].

53. Vgl. Friedrich Schlegel: Ansichten und Ideen von der christlichen Kunst. Hg. und eingeleitet v. Hans Eichner. Kritische Friedrich Schlegel Ausgabe Bd. IV, München etc. 1959, S. XXII-XXX.

54. Winkelmann und sein Jahrhundert. In Briefen und Aufsätzen herausgegeben von Goethe. Tübingen 1805, S. 387-470, hier S. 402-405, mit Zitat aus S. 404. Da diese 'Skizzen' keinen Verfassernamen tragen und es im Vorwort lediglich "Aufsätze von drey Freunden" heißt (S. 389) [nämlich Goethe, H. Meyer und F.A. Wolf], hat Schleiermacher den Verfasser - zutreffend - erraten, der aber wohl kein Geheimnis war.

55. Über die Religion. Reden an die Gebildeten unter ihren Verächtern. Zweite Ausgabe, Berlin 1806, S. 363-372. Auf wen direkt gezielt ist, bleibt unklar. An Konversionen aus diesen Jahren sind bekannt die von Friedrich Stolberg (1800), Philipp Veit (1803), Friedrich und Johann Riepenhausen (1804), Adam Müller (1805).

56. August Wilhelm Schlegel: Gedichte. Tübingen 1800, S. 143-156.

57. s. Br. IV, S. 65 (an Brinckmann, 22. April 1800).

58. Caroline Schlegel an Gries, 27. Dezember 1799 (Caroline. Briefe aus der Frühromantik. Nach Georg Waitz vermehrt hg. v. Erich Schmidt. Leipzig 1913, Bd. I, S. 592); vgl. Friedrich Schlegel: Literatur (Europa Bd. I/1, 1803, a.a.O., S. 41-63, hier S. 57).

59. Reden, Zweite Ausgabe, a.a.O., S. 68f. Vgl. Patsch: Alle Menschen sind Künstler, a.a.O. Anm. 5, S. 14f.

60. Vgl. Patsch: Die zeitgenössische Rezeption, a.a.O. Anm.1, S. 1220f.

61. Br. an Gaß v. 25. April 1806 (Gaß-Br. S. 45/ M II, S. 62).

62. Vgl. dazu etwa die Nachrichten aus den Berliner Zeitungen in der Kaiserlich und Kurpfalzbairisch privilegirte(n) Allgemeine(n) Zeitung 1805, Sp. 1373. 1388. 1393. 1400. 1404f. 1409. 1413. 1425!

63. Lediglich Arnim hat ironisch gemeint: "(...) ich möchte am liebsten der Josef seyn, der zu lezt sagt, es könnte das alles auch wohl unbesprochen geblieben seyn" (Br. an Savigny v. 17. Februar 1806. A.a.O. Anm.9, S. 33).

64. Taufrede I, a.a.O. Anm.2, S. 251f; Goethe als Interpret S. 77f. Auch Nowak, a.a.O. Anm.2, S. 26 bezeichnet, ohne Kenntnis Sattlers, Josef als "Herrnhuter" und weist auf Spangenberg.

65. Sattler hört (Taufrede I, S. 251f) in Josefs Rede Goethes "Weihnachtsgedicht" 'Ich komme bald, ihr goldnen Kinder' (Goethes Werke. Hamburger Ausgabe in 14 Bänden, hg.v. Erich Trunz. Hamburg ⁵1960 [=HA] Bd. 1, S. 25) "deutlich" wiederklingen - obgleich doch dieses erst 1840 (!) gedruckt wurde (HA 1, S. 424)! Auch die Beziehung in den Worten der Agnes (S. 54) auf Goethes 'Hermann und Dorothea' III, 47ff kann philologisch nicht bewiesen werden; das Gleiche gilt für "das Bild des Todes" (S. 92), das nicht notwendig auf "Des Todes rührendes Bild" (Hermann und Dorothea IX, 46) zurückgehen muß (bei beiderseits ganz unterschiedlichem Kontext !), sondern eine geläufige Wendung darstellt (Beiträge zur Schleiermacherforschung, a.a.O. Anm.2, S. 403).

66. Vgl. John Becker: Goethe und die Brüdergemeine. Zeitschr. f. Brüdergeschichte 3, 1909, S. 94-111 (Nachdr. Hildesheim - New York 1973) (= J.B.: Goethe und die Brüdergemeine. Mit einem Geleitwort v. Friedrich Lienhard. Neudietendorf/Thür. 1922). Wenig ergiebig ist Peter Meinhold: Goethe zur Geschichte des Christentums. Freiburg/München 1958, S. 16f.

67. Br. an Charlotte Schleiermacher v. 16. Juni 1798 (Br.I, S. 178).

68. Siehe HA Bd. 7, S. 398 sowie 'Dichtung und Wahrheit' II, 8 (HA Bd.9, S. 338f)!

69. Siehe HA Bd. 10, S. 43 sowie S. 604 (Kommentar)!

70. Vgl. Gerhard Reichel: August Gottlieb Spangenberg, Bischof der Brüderkirche. Tübingen 1906, S. 170f.193; allgemein auch Theodor Bechler: August Gottlieb Spangenberg und die Mission (Hefte zur Missionskunde. Herrnhuter Missionstudien Nr.28/29). Herrnhut 1933 (zu Goethe S. 134).

71. Becker, a.a.O. S. 98.

72. Br. an J.F.H. Schlosser v. 15. Jan. 1813 (Goethes Werke. Weimarer Ausgabe. IV. Abth. Goethes Briefe 23. Bd., Weimar 1900, S. 249).

73. Becker S. 103.

74. ebd, S. 104.

75. Goethe als Interpret S. 78.

76. s. M II, S. 36f.

77. Vgl. dazu die Briefe an H. Herz Br. II, S. 35f/M II, S. 41f.

78. Taufrede I, S. 252.

79. Vgl. Goethes Liste "An Eichstädt. Recensenten betreffend. (...) 7. Stolpe in Pommern. Hofprediger Schleiermacher. (...) einzuladen mit Bezug auf mich" (Karl Bulling: Die Rezensenten der Jenaischen Allgemeinen Literaturzeitung im ersten Jahrzehnt ihres Bestehens 1804-1813. Claves Jenenses 11. Weimar 1962, S. 3l; Goethes Werke WA IV, Bd.16, Weimar 1894, S. 308f, aus dem Sept. 1803 - der ebd. S. 313f im Concept abgedruckte Brief Goethes an Schleiermacher ist wohl nicht abgesandt worden; jedenfalls fehlt ein Echo S.s.)!

80. Br. II, S. 36/M II, S. 42.

81. Zu dieser Reise siehe Friedrich Schleiermacher Kritische Gesamtausgabe V. Abt. Bd 1: Briefwechsel 1774-1796, hg. v. Andreas Arndt und Wolfgang Virmond, Berlin/ New York 1985, S. XXVIII, in Verbindung mit Rislers Bericht über Spangenbergs Visitationsaufenthalt in Herrnhut (Leben August Gottlieb Spangenbergs, Bischofs der evangelischen Brüderkirche, beschrieben von Jeremias Risler. Barby 1794, S.477ff).

82. S. 480.

83. Sammlung einiger Reden, gehalten an die Kinder in Herrnhut von August Gottlieb Spangenberg. Barby 1797; Einige Reden an die Kinder, gehalten in verschiedenen Brüdergemeinen von August Gottlieb Spangenberg. Zweyte Sammlung. Barby 1799.

84. D. Rauch: Tabulae librorum e bibliotheca defuncti Schleiermacher (...), Berlin 1835, S. 97.

85. Siehe Anm. 83. Weder in den Predigtsammlungen und Liedern Spangenbergs noch in der Biographie Rislers ließen sich wörtliche Zitate oder Anklänge auffinden.

86. Die streng biblisch-christlich begrenzte Bedeutung dieses Namens im gleichen protestantisch begrenzten Milieu zur gleichen Zeit kann man im zweiten Kapitel von Goethes 'Wilhelm Meisters Wanderjahre' "Sankt Joseph der Zweite" studieren (HA Bd. 8, S. 13-28), in dem dieser Name die gesamte "Lebensweise" des Namensträgers bestimmt (S. 17). Goethe diktierte dieses Kapitel im Mai 1807, es wurde 1810 vorabgedruckt (ebd. S. 572f).

87. Vgl. zur Theorie der Namengebung im Kunstwerk Hendrik Birus: Poetische Namengebung. Zur Bedeutung der Namen in Lessings "Nathan der Weise". (Palaestra Bd. 270) Göttingen 1978, bes. S. 31-53!

88. Hier schließt Sattler: Goethe als Interpret S. 85 auf den Schmerz um Eleonore Grunow und vermischt damit literarische und biographische Gesichtspunkte. Die biographische Anknüpfung an Schleiermachers Beziehung zu E.G. findet sich auch bei anderen Autoren.

89. Apk 21,4.9; 22,17. Darauf hat Tice, a.a.O. Anm.2, p. 88 aufmerksam gemacht. Daß das Werk insgesamt von biblischen Zitaten durchzogen ist, erklärt sich aus dem Thema.

SECTION TWO

THE MATURE SCHLEIERMACHER

VII

RELIGION UND ERZIEHUNG: NOTWENDIGKEIT UND GRENZEN DES RELIGIONSUNTERRICHTS BEI SCHLEIERMACHER

Erich Schrofner

Einleitung: Zur Religionspädagogischen Aktualität Schleiermachers

Die Religionspädagogik zählt nicht zu den Schwerpunkten der Schleiermacher-Forschung und der Schleiermacher-Literatur. Das deutschsprachige Standardwerk mit dem entsprechenden Titel "Religionspädagogik bei Schleiermacher" von Wißmann[1] wurde 1934 veröffentlicht, im selben Jahr wie das englischsprachige Gegenstück "Schleiermacher and Religious Education" von Osborn[2]. Selbstverständlich gibt es auch jüngere Veröffentlichungen zu diesem Thema[3], aber zum Rang eines Standardwerkes hat es bisher keines von ihnen gebracht. Die Gründe für diesen Sachverhalt liegen auf der Hand: Schleiermacher selber hat über Religionspädagogik weder Vorlesungen gehalten noch Schriften veröffentlicht. Seine diesbezüglichen Äußerungen müssen in verschiedenen, oft weit auseinanderliegenden thematischen Zusammenhängen[4] aufgesucht werden und lassen sich nur schwer zu einer überzeugenden Synthese bringen.

Trotz dieser Schwierigkeiten ist Schleiermacher in der modernen religionspädagogischen Literatur allgegenwärtig, ausgesprochen oder unausgesprochen, ausführlich oder nur nebenbei. Es ist hier offensichtlich genauso schwer, sich seinem Einfluß zu entziehen, wie dies in vielen anderen Disziplinen der Fall ist. Auch die Gründe für Schleiermachers Anziehungskraft dürften überall ähnlich sein. Am Anfang steht jeweils der starke Eindruck, daß in der historischen Distanz von annähernd zwei Jahrhunderten verblüffende Entsprechungen zu gegenwärtigen aktuellen Problemen hervortreten[5]. Dazu kommt die Faszination durch das hohe Niveau, den weiten Horizont und die Differenziertheit, die Schleiermachers Behandlung der jeweiligen Themen auszeichnen.

Diese Vorzüge sind jedoch häufig mit Verstehens- und Interpretationsproblemen verbunden, welche die anfängliche Begeisterung in zunehmende Ratlosigkeit verwandeln. Infolge der oft verwirrenden Komplexheit des Gegenstandes, widersprüchlich erscheinender Aussagen[6] und der sich abzeichnenden Unbrauchbarkeit der Ergebnisse zur Lösung gegenwärtiger Probleme kann die aufkommende Frustration gelegentlich sogar in Aggressivität umschlagen. Für unser Thema kommt erschwerend hinzu, daß Schleiermacher dem schulischen Religionsunterricht ausgesprochen negativ gegenübersteht, an dessen Stelle aber fast selbstverständlich mit einem kirchlichen Religionsunterricht operiert, der bei uns höchstens in bescheidenen Ansätzen existiert und auch in näherer Zukunft keine größere Entfaltung erwarten läßt.

In dieser Situation liegt es nahe, Schleiermachers Argumente gegen den schulischen Religionsunterricht zu sichten, ihre Überzeugungskraft zu prüfen und die möglichen Konsequenzen für unsere eigene Situation ins Auge zu fassen. Aus praktischen Gründen empfiehlt es sich, als erstes die Argumente im Umkreis des Religionsbegriffs aufzusuchen, danach jene im Zusammenhang des Erziehungsbegriffs, wobei sich von der Quellenlage her eine Schwerpunktsetzung bei den Reden "Über die Religion" und bei den Pädagogischen Schriften Schleiermachers ergibt.

I. Religionspädagogische Implikationen des Religionsbegriffs

Trotz mancher Präzisierungen und Akzentverschiebungen in den späteren Auflagen der Reden und in der Einleitung zur Glaubenslehre hat Schleiermacher seine Grundkonzeption von Religion, wie er sie in der ersten Auflage der Reden entwickelt hat, zeit seines Lebens beibehalten. Für unser Thema sind vor allem die zweite Rede, "Über das Wesen der Religion", und die dritte, "Über die Bildung zur Religion", relevant.

1. *Religion ist nicht lehrbar*

Als eines der Grundübel im Religionsverständnis seiner Zeit diagnostiziert Schleiermacher die Verwechslung der Religion mit Metaphysik und Moral bzw. die Vermischung von Religion, Wissen und Tun. Daher setzen seine Erörterungen über das Wesen der Religion mit deren scharfer Abgrenzung vom Bereich der philosophischen Erkenntnis und des sittlichen Handelns ein. Die dezidierte Zuordnung der Religion zum Bereich des Gefühls[7] soll ihr eine "eigene Provinz" in der geistigen Landschaft sichern. Eine große Zahl eindringlicher Hinweise und plastischer Formulierungen verstärkt den Eindruck, daß Religion und Lehre nach Schleiermachers Theorie unvereinbar sind.

Alle Bemühungen der Aufklärungsphilosophie, aus verschiedenen Elementen der Metaphysik und der Moral eine zeitgemäße Religion herzustellen, sind nach Auskunft der zweiten Rede genauso zum Scheitern verurteilt wie entsprechende Versuche auf dem Gebiet der organischen Natur. So wie hier "wird es Euch mit der Religion nicht gelingen, wenn Ihr Euch ihre einzelnen Elemente auch noch so vollkommen von außen an- und eingebildet habt" (R 77)[8]. In der dritten Rede wendet Schleiermacher für die Zurückweisung alles Lehrhaften fast ebensoviel Mühe auf wie für die Darlegung der richtigen Bildung zur Religion. Belehrung ist offensichtlich unvereinbar mit einer Religion, die als "Anschauen des Universums" oder als "Sinn und Geschmack fürs Unendliche" charakterisiert wird. "Was durch Kunst und fremde Tätigkeit in einem Menschen gewirkt werden kann, ist nur dieses, daß Ihr ihm Eure Vorstellungen mitteilt und ihn zu einem Magazin Eurer Ideen macht, daß Ihr sie soweit in die seinigen verflechtet, bis er sich ihrer erinnert zu gelegener Zeit: aber nie könnt Ihr bewirken, daß er die, welche Ihr wollt, aus sich hervor bringe. Ihr seht den Widerspruch, der schon aus den Worten nicht herausgebracht werden kann. Nicht einmal gewöhnen könnt Ihr jemand, auf einen bestimmten Eindruck, sooft er ihm kommt, eine bestimmte Gegenwirkung erfolgen zu lassen, viel weniger, daß Ihr ihn dahin bringen könntet, über diese Verbindung hinauszugehen und eine innere Tätigkeit dabei frei zu erzeugen. Kurz, auf den Mechanismus des Geistes könnt Ihr wirken, aber in die Organisation desselben, in diese geheiligte

Werkstätte des Universums, könnt Ihr nach Eurer Willkür nicht eindringen, da vermögt Ihr nicht irgendetwas zu ändern oder zu verschieben, wegzuschneiden oder zu ergänzen, nur zurückhalten könnt Ihr seine Entwicklung und gewaltsam einen Teil des Gewächses verstümmeln" (R 138 f).[9] Nur wenig später äußert sich Schleiermacher ausdrücklich über das Verhältnis von Religion und Unterricht: "Alles was, wie sie, ein Kontinuum sein soll im menschlichen Gemüt, liegt weit außer dem Gebiet des Lehrens und Anbildens. Darum ist jedem, der die Religion so ansieht, Unterricht in ihr ein abgeschmacktes und sinnleeres Wort. Unsere Meinungen und Lehrsätze können wir andern wohl mitteilen, dazu bedürfen wir nur Worte, und sie nur der auffassenden und nachbildenden Kraft des Geistes: aber wir wissen sehr wohl, daß das nur die Schatten unserer Anschauungen und unserer Gefühle sind, und ohne diese mit uns zu teilen, würden sie nicht verstehen, was sie sagen und was sie zu denken glauben. Anschauen können wir sie nicht lehren. . . ." (R 139 f).

Mit der verbalen Mitteilung eigener Erfahrungen ist auf dem Gebiet der Religion wenig gewonnen. Notwendig wäre eine Übertragung jener Kraft und Fertigkeit, die in allem einzelnen "das ursprüngliche Licht des Universums" (R 140) wahrzunehmen erlaubt. Durch Belehrung ist nach Schleiermachers Überzeugung diese Fähigkeit genauso wenig zu wecken wie das Verständnis für die Kunst. Daher weiß er sich in seiner Ablehnung der Lehrbarkeit der Religion in voller Übereinstimmung mit seinen gebildeten Adressaten. "Zeigt mir jemand, dem Ihr Urteilskraft, Beobachtungsgeist, Kunstgefühl oder Sittlichkeit angebildet oder eingeimpft habt; dann will ich mich anheischig machen, auch Religion zu lehren" (R 141). Nicht nur eine Anerziehung von Religion ist ausgeschlossen, sondern auch jede Anleitung zu religiöser Selbstbildung. "Das Universum bildet sich selbst seine Betrachter und Bewunderer" (R 143), lautet einer der am häufigsten zitierten Sätze aus der dritten Rede.[10] Schleiermachers Kritik an der zeitgenössischen Kirche in der vierten Rede hat fast ausschließlich die "Lehrkirche" im Visier. Sein Hauptvorwurf geht dahin, daß sie mit ihrer Fixierung auf Begriffe, Meinungen und Lehrsätze lediglich dürre Abstraktionen an die Stelle der lebendigen Religion setze. Die Mitteilung religiöser Begriffe und Erkenntnisse führt aber nicht zum Ziel einer eigenständigen Religiosität und ist somit auch hinderlich für die Ausbildung der wahren Kirche.

2. *Religion ist auf Bildung angewiesen*

Die Verneinung der Lehrbarkeit der Religion ist nicht Schleiermachers einziges oder letztes Wort zur Sache. Die Religion ist für ihn nicht eine isolierte Sonderwelt, sondern eine anthropologische Grundgegebenheit, die trotz aller Abgrenzungsbemühungen in der zweiten Rede mit allen anderen Lebensvollzügen in Verbindung steht und in den wechselvollen Strom der Entwicklung des menschlichen Lebens eingebunden ist. Daher gibt es für Schleiermacher eine Bildung zur Religion, welche das Thema seiner dritten Rede ausmacht, und deshalb muß es auch religiöse Erziehung und sogar Unterricht und Lehre auf religiösem Gebiet geben.

Schleiermacher führt die Religion zuletzt auf eine angeborene Anlage zurück, so daß sie keinem Menschen vollkommen fremd sein kann. Wie jede Anlage müßte sich auch die Religion "in jedem unfehlbar auf seine eigene Art entwickeln" (R 144)[11], wenn sie nicht durch störende Einflüsse von außen daran gehindert würde. "Mit Schmerzen sehe ich es täglich, wie die Wut des Verstehens den Sinn gar nicht aufkommen läßt, und wie alles sich vereinigt, den Menschen an das Endliche und an einen sehr kleinen Punkt desselben zu befestigen, damit das Unendliche ihm soweit als möglich aus den Augen gerückt werde" (R 144). Die Hauptschuldigen für diese Beeinträchtigung sieht er nicht in den Zweiflern und Spöttern gegen die Religion oder in den unmoralischen Zeitgenossen, sondern in einem völlig harmlos erscheinenden Menschentyp: "Die verständigen und praktischen Menschen, diese sind in dem jetzigen Zustande der Welt das Gegengewicht gegen die Religion, und ihr großes Übergewicht ist die Ursache, warum sie eine so dürftige und unbedeutende Rolle spielt. Von der zarten Kindheit an mißhandeln sie den Menschen und unterdrücken sein Streben nach dem Höheren" (R 144 f).

Wenn die Entfaltung der religiösen Anlage des Menschen durch äußere Einflüsse gehemmt wird, dann muß es auch Mittel und Wege geben, diese Störung auszugleichen. Die Grundlage dafür bildet der ursprüngliche

Gemeinschaftsbezug der Religion selber. Sie ist für ihre Entfaltung auf Gemeinschaft angewiesen und bringt ihrerseits neue Gemeinschaft hervor. Durch die Wahrnehmung religiöser Aktivität bei anderen kann die eigene Religiosität angeregt werden, wie umgekehrt der religiöse Mensch einen unüberwindlichen Drang verspürt, sich vernehmbar zu äußern und sich anderen mitzuteilen.

Schon in der zweiten Rede streicht Schleiermacher mittels einer Paraphrase der biblischen Schöpfungsgeschichte die Unverzichtbarkeit der Mitmenschen für die religiöse Anschauung des Universums heraus. Der betreffende Abschnitt schließt mit der Feststellung: "Denn um die Welt anzuschauen und um Religion zu haben, muß der Mensch erst die Menschheit gefunden haben, und er findet sie nur in Liebe und durch Liebe" (R 89). Die vierte Rede könnte man geradezu als eine Apotheose der religiösen Gemeinschaft interpretieren, neben und trotz aller harten Kritik am gegenwärtigen Zustand der Kirche. Die religiöse Gemeinschaft ist auch der Ort für Mittlerschaft, Priestertum und Jüngerschaft in der Religion. "Jeder Mensch, wenige Auserwählte ausgenommen, bedarf allerdings eines Mittlers, eines Anführers, der seinen Sinn für Religion aus dem ersten Schlummer wecke und ihm eine erste Richtung gebe" (R 121). Es ist für Schleiermacher undenkbar, daß die Religion "die einzige menschliche Angelegenheit sein" soll, "in der es keine Veranstaltungen gäbe zum Behuf der Schüler und Lehrlinge" (R 200). Seine nach der Kritik umso überzeugendere Verteidigung der Kirche beschränkt sich keineswegs auf die ideale Kirche einer fernen Zukunft. Sie bezieht auch die vielgeschmähte Lehrkirche der Gegenwart ein, welche das notwendige Bindeglied zwischen den Virtuosen und den Schülern auf religiösem Gebiet darstellt. Als Lehrkirche ist die religiöse Gemeinschaft auf klar definierte Begriffe angewiesen. Theologische Grundbegriffe wie Wunder, Offenbarung, Weissagung, Gnadenwirkung "bezeichnen auf die eigentümlichste Art das Bewußtsein eines Menschen von seiner Religion; sie sind umso wichtiger deswegen, weil sie nicht nur etwas bezeichnen, was allgemein sein darf in der Religion, sondern gerade dasjenige, was allgemein sein muß in ihr" (R 120). Auf diesem Hintergrund ist es weniger befremdlich, wenn Schleiermacher in der vierten Rede das mangelhafte Wissen der Menschen über die Religion für deren schlechten Zustand verantwortlich macht. "Weil sie von der wahren und lebendigen Religion weder Begriff noch Anschauung haben", suchen sie ständig an der falschen Stelle nach einer Verbesserung ihrer Situation, anstatt sich auf ihre eigene Innerlichkeit zu konzentrieren (R 196 f). Die Ausschaltung des Verstandes ist nicht nur keine religiöse Tugend, sondern das Tor zu Irrtümern und Fehlverhalten auf religiösem Gebiet.

Zusammenfassend wäre festzuhalten, daß Schleiermachers Religionsbegriff zwar die Lehrbarkeit der Religion ausschließt, daß aber gezielte Maßnahmen der Bildung und Erziehung auf religiösem Gebiet nicht nur erlaubt, sondern um der Religion selber willen notwendig sind.

II. Religionspädagogische Implikationen des Erziehungsbegriffs

Es ist in diesem Zusammenhang weder möglich noch notwendig, Schleiermachers Erziehungsbegriff systematisch zu entfalten oder seine wissenschaftstheoretische Begründung der Pädagogik[12] detailliert wiederzugeben. Wir beschränken uns vielmehr auf einige für unser Thema relevante Gesichtspunkte.

1. Religiöse Erziehung als Aufgabe der Familie und der Kirche

Indem Schleiermacher als Grundlage der Pädagogik das Verhältnis der Generationen zueinander bzw. die Einwirkung der älteren Generation auf die jüngere wählt, legt er sich auf die Familie, die ursprünglichste Gemeinschaft verschiedener Generationen, als den primären Ort der Erziehung fest. Ihr allein soll die Erziehung des Kindes von der Geburt bis zum Schuleintritt vorbehalten sein. Der Schulbeginn markiert den ersten Übergang von der Geborgenheit der Familie in das öffentliche Leben und setzt das Kind dem Einfluß zusätzlicher Erziehungseinrichtungen aus. Im Hinblick auf das Endziel aller Erziehung, die selbständige Existenz als erwachsener Mensch in der Gesellschaft, schreibt ihnen Schleiermacher eine wachsende Bedeutung zu, während er die vorschulische Familienerziehung als "rein propädeutisch" (PS I, 152)[13] charakterisiert. Ihre vorrangige Aufgabe besteht darin, den jungen Menschen auf das Leben in den vier ethischen Gemeinschaften, nämlich Staat, Kirche, freie Geselligkeit und Wissenschaft, vorzubereiten, die mit fortschreitendem Alter des Kindes sich zunehmend an dessen Erziehung beteiligen.

Im Unterschied zu den verschiedenen Formen öffentlicher Erziehung ist die Familienerziehung nicht von einer bestimmten Theorie geleitet. Folglich besteht auch kein Bedarf, aber auch keine Möglichkeit, eine solche in der Pädagogik zu entwickeln. Man könnte diese erste Phase der Erziehung charakterisieren als spontanes Mitleben des Kindes mit dem Leben der ganzen Familie, soweit ihm dies möglich ist. "Es ist alles aus dem Hauptgesichtspunkt zu betrachten, daß das Zusammenleben mit den Kindern gleichsam ein Lebenhelfen sein soll, ein unterstützendes, entwickelndes Zusammenleben, aus dem sich erst die Prämissen zu einer bestimmten Organisation absichtlicher Tätigkeit in der zweiten Periode entwickeln müssen" (PS I, 167).

Ähnlich selbstverständlich und theoriefrei wie die übrige Erziehung soll auch die früheste religiöse Erziehung in der familiären Atmosphäre erfolgen. Sie beschränkt sich auf eine angemessene Beteiligung der Kinder am religiösen Leben der Familie. Schleiermachers Sorge konzentriert sich auf die Vermeidung von Schäden, die aus einer frühzeitigen religiösen Indoktrination wie auch aus der gänzlichen Fernhaltung der Kinder vom religiösen Leben der Familie resultieren können. Angesichts der unaufhebbaren Verschiedenheit der jeweiligen Umstände beschränkt er sich auf eine Empfehlung zu einem möglichst ungezwungenen Verhalten aller Beteiligten. "Wenn man nun in allen diesen Beziehungen mit Vorsicht zu Werke geht, so wird aus der naturgemäßen Entwicklung des religiösen Elements in der Periode der Kindheit niemals ein Nachteil entstehen" (PS I, 228).

Wie auf allen anderen Gebieten muß auch die religiöse Erziehung wegen der Begrenztheit der familiären Möglichkeiten etwa ab dem Schulalter eine Ergänzung von außen erfahren. Unter der Voraussetzung der Existenz der vier großen Gemeinschaften, die nach Schleiermachers Ethik alle gemeinschaftsfähigen Belange des menschlichen Lebens abdecken, fällt die außerfamiliäre religiöse Erziehung in die Kompetenz der Kirche. Dies gilt auch für die Theorie dieser Erziehungstätigkeit. Folglich beläßt es der

Pädagoge Schleiermacher bei einigen allgemeinem Hinweisen auf die richtige Verteilung der pädagogischen Gewichte zwischen Familie und Kirche. Über die Einzelheiten des kirchlichen Religionsunterrichts äußert sich der Theologe Schleiermacher im Zusammenhang der zuständigen theologischen Disziplinen, vor allem der Enzyklopädie, der Christlichen Sittenlehre und der Praktischen Theologie.

Der auffälligste, wenn auch mit Schleiermachers Gesamtkonzeption[14] völlig konforme Grundzug dieses Unterrichts ist seine konsequente Hinordnung auf die kirchliche Gemeinschaft. Als Einrichtung dieser Gemeinschaft hat er keine andere Aufgabe, als deren Fortbestand und ständige Selbsterneuerung zu fördern. Die entscheidende Voraussetzung dafür ist die Weckung der religiösen Gesinnung des Kindes im familiären Bereich. Die kirchliche Gemeinschaft kann nur daran anknüpfen, um die religiöse Gesinnung in der kirchlichen Öffentlichkeit weiter zu pflegen und zu vertiefen. Ihre Bemühungen laufen hauptsächlich in zwei Richtungen. Die eine geht auf die direkte Betätigung der religiösen Gesinnung aus, die vorwiegend im Gottesdienst geschieht. Die andere konzentriert sich auf die Ausbildung der religiösen Gedanken und Vorstellungen der neuen Kirchenmitglieder mit Hilfe von Lehre und Unterricht. Bezüglich der pädagogischen Detailfragen hat sich der kirchliche Unterricht an der allgemeinen Pädagogik zu orientieren.

2. Die Unzuständigkeit der Schule für die religiöse Erziehung

Schleiermachers Aufteilung der religiösen Erziehung auf Familie und Kirche geht zu Lasten der Schule als einer Bildungseinrichtung des Staates. Seine Ablehnung des schulischen Religionsunterrichts ist zwar nicht starr und kompromißlos, aber in der Grundtendenz eindeutig und konsequent.

Am klarsten äußert er sich diesbezüglich gegen Ende seiner Pädagogik-Vorlesung aus dem Jahre 1826: "Was nun den Religionsunterricht, der in öffentlichen Anstalten erteilt wird, betrifft, so bin ich der Meinung, daß dieser ganz erspart werden kann" (PS I, 339). Schleiermacher beläßt es nicht bei der bloßen Meinungskundgabe, sondern fügt eine Reihe von Argumenten unterschiedlichen Charakters hinzu. Ein historisches

Argument charakterisiert den Religionsunterricht als Relikt aus den kirchlichen Anfangszeiten des Schulwesens überhaupt, das seit der Ablösung der staatlichen Schule vom kirchlichen Bildungswesen seine ursprüngliche Basis verloren habe. Unter institutionellem Gesichtspunkt kritisiert Schleiermacher die Zweigleisigkeit und das Konkurrenzverhältnis zum kirchlichen Konfirmandenunterricht. In methodischer Hinsicht gibt die übliche Vermischung von Paränese und Theologie, vor allem auf der Stufe des Gymnasiums, Anlaß zu Kritik. Auch die Wirkung des Religionsunterrichts bei den Schülern stellt keine Empfehlung für ihn dar. Schließlich befürchtet Schleiermacher innerkirchliche Konflikte, wenn in der Schule eine andere theologische Richtung vertreten wird als in den Gemeinden[15].

Zu diesen eher pragmatisch ausgerichteten Argumenten, die im Kontext der höheren Schule (Bürgerschule und Gymnasium) auftreten, gesellt sich bezüglich der Volksschule noch eine grundsätzlichere Überlegung, die in engem Zusammenhang mit einem Grundgedanken der Reden steht. Den Rahmen bildet eine Erörterung über die Zuständigkeiten von Familie und Schule in der Kindererziehung. Auf der Grundlage der Zweiteilung aller Erziehungsbemühungen hinsichtlich der allem Handeln zugrundeliegenden Gesinnung einerseits und der Fertigkeit in der Umsetzung der Gesinnung in die Tat andererseits weist Schleiermacher der Schule schwerpunktmäßig die Übung der Fertigkeiten neben dem eigentlichen Unterricht in den Grundkenntnissen zu. Entgegen der Annahme, die Entwicklung der Gesinnung sei zur Gänze der Familie vorbehalten, beansprucht Schleiermacher die Schule auch für die Gesinnungsbildung. Er betrachtet sie somit auch als Erziehungsanstalt neben ihrer Funktion als Unterrichtsanstalt. Er beschränkt ihren Erziehungsauftrag jedoch streng auf das Gemeinschaftsbewußtsein der Schüler, den sogenannten Gemeingeist, während er die ethische und religiöse Erziehung ausschließlich der Familie (bzw. Kirche) vorbehalten möchte. Schleiermacher lehnt aus diesem Grunde auch eine vollständige Überlassung der Kinder an die Schule entschieden ab, "denn die Entwicklung und Fortbildung der Gesinnung aus dem religiösen Standpunkt und aus dem allgemein ethischen kann nur in der Familie erfolgen" (PS I, 238). Zur Begründung seiner Auffassung rekurriert Schleiermacher auf einen Gedanken, den er in der dritten Rede ausgeführt hat. Demnach geschieht religiöse Kommunikation ausschließlich zwischen Individuen und beansprucht diese in ihrer Totalität. Schulischer Unterricht aber kann sich nur in seltenen Ausnahmefällen mit dem einzelnen Schüler befassen. Andererseits ist er notgedrungen auf einzelne Lebensfunktionen bzw. Wirklichkeitsbereiche beschränkt. Der Mensch als ganzer in seiner Beziehung zur Totalität der Wirklichkeit ist somit kein möglicher Gegenstand des Unterrichts. Infolgedessen kann es schon aufgrund der pädagogischen Struktur des schulischen Unterrichts einen Religionsunterricht im strengen Sinn nicht geben.

III. Verlagerung des Religionsunterrichts von der Kirche zur Schule

Wer sich trotz des überwältigenden Textbefundes nicht damit abfinden will, daß die Gegner des schulischen Religionsunterrichts Schleiermacher einfachhin für sich in Anspruch nehmen, der befindet sich keineswegs in einem Argumentationsnotstand. Zum einen gibt es Äußerungen Schleiermachers, welche für einen solchen Unterricht sprechen, zum anderen lassen sich seine Einwände weitgehend entkräften und teilweise sogar positiv wenden.

1. *Bildung der Gesinnung unter der Form des Lehrens*

Das Hauptdokument einer Befürwortung des schulischen Religionsunterrichts durch Schleiermacher ist sein "Allgemeiner Entwurf zum Religionsunterricht auf gelehrten Schulen" aus dem Jahre 1810, den er im Auftrag der von ihm geleiteten Wissenschaftlichen Deputation im Hinblick auf die damals geplante Unterrichtsreform in Preußen verfaßt hat. Von grundsätzlichen Bedenken gegen den schulischen Religionsunterricht ist in diesem Gutachten überhaupt nicht die Rede. Obwohl einleitend allen Unterrichtsstunden auch ein Beitrag zur Gesinnungsbildung abverlangt wird, spricht es sich für einen gesonderten Religionsunterricht aus, der in konzentrierter und systematischer Weise "unter der Form des Lehrens" (PS II, 141) auf die Bildung der Gesinnung ausgerichtet ist. Eine Einschränkung gibt es lediglich für die zweite Bildungsstufe wegen der Kollision mit dem kirchlichen Konfirmandenunterricht. Immerhin wird neben der Aussetzung des schulischen Religionsunterrichts auch ein Verzicht auf den Konfirmandenunterricht erwogen. Beachtung verdient auch die Begründung des Religionsunterrichts in der Oberstufe des Gymnasiums mit der Notwendigkeit einer Ergänzung und Korrektur des kirchlichen Unterrichts für die gehobenen geistigen Ansprüche der gebildeten Jugendlichen.

Zurecht wird in der Literatur darauf hingewiesen, daß dieses Gutachten nicht Schleiermachers persönliche Überzeugung wiedergibt, sondern einen Kompromiß zwischen den gegensätzlichen Standpunkten aller Kommissionsmitglieder darstellt. Trotzdem ist nicht zu bestreiten, daß Schleiermacher diese Stellungnahme persönlich formuliert und offensichtlich auch vertreten hat. Dazu kommt, daß er schon in seinem eigenen Vorentwurf dazu den bekannten Bedenken auch einige Argumente zugunsten des Religionsunterrichts gegenübergestellt hat. "Die Auflösung des scheinbaren Streites" sieht er darin, "daß bei dem Religionsunterricht auf gelehrten Schulen die Einsicht die Hauptsache sein muß und die Belebung der Gesinnung die Nebensache" (PS II, 144), während im kirchlichen Bereich offensichtlich die umgekehrte Schwerpunktsetzung gelten soll. Sein abschließendes Plädoyer für einen Unterricht "in der Form einer allgemeinen historischen Darstellung der christlichen Lehre und Kirche" (PS II, 144) fällt ihm umso leichter, als das "Zusammensein verschiedener Religionsgenossen" und die Qualifikation der vorgesehenen Lehrer unter dieser Voraussetzung keine Probleme aufwirft.

2. *Unterscheidung von Religion und Unterricht in Religion*

Ein beträchtlicher Teil der Argumente gegen den schulischen Religionsunterricht muß auf eine mangelhafte Unterscheidung zwischen religiösem Leben und religiösem Unterricht zurückgeführt werden. Dies gilt auf jeden Fall für die Polemik gegen Lehre und Unterricht in den Reden, welche nicht auf den Religionsunterricht, sondern auf die innerkirchliche (und außerkirchliche) Verwechslung der christlichen Botschaft mit einem philosophischen Lehrgebäude gemünzt ist. Ähnliches gilt für den Gegensatz zwischen den Grundstrukturen des Religiösen und jenen des Schulunterrichts in der Pädagogikvorlesung. Dieser Gegensatz käme nur dann zum Tragen, wenn es im Religionsunterricht tatsächlich um den religiösen Vollzug bzw. um die Betätigung der religiösen Gesinnung ginge. Tatsächlich ordnet aber auch Schleiermacher den Religionsunterricht sowohl im schulischen wie im kirchlichen Rahmen nicht unmittelbar der religiösen Praxis zu, sondern der Lehre[16], der Vermittlung von Grundkenntnissen, zu denen auch eine Verständigung über die Eigenart der religiösen Praxis gehören mag. Erstaunlich ist, daß Schleiermacher in seinen theologischen Schriften diese Unterscheidung sehr klar vornimmt und konsequent durchhält, im pädagogischen Kontext hingegen vernachlässigt und daraus ein Argument gegen den schulischen Religionsunterricht schmiedet.

Jedenfalls leistet das in sich überzeugende Konzept eines kirchlichen Religionsunterrichts die wirksamste Widerlegung derartiger Argumente gegen den schulischen Religionsunterricht, wenn es sich in beiden Fällen um eine vergleichbare Art von Unterricht handelt, was für Schleiermacher zweifellos zutrifft[17]. Somit verbleibt als Haupteinwand gegen den schulischen Religionsunterricht die exklusive Zuständigkeit der Kirche für einen religiösen Unterricht, dessen Notwendigkeit zusätzlich zur religiösen Familienerziehung für Schleiermacher außer Frage steht.

3. Vertretung der Kirche durch die Schule

Gegen Schleiermachers Konstruktion der vier ethischen Gemein-schaften lassen sich verschiedene Einwände erheben. Man kann die Adäquatheit und Vollständigkeit der von ihm getroffenen Einteilung bezweifeln[18], man kann seine Sicht der Familie als einer Art Mikrokosmos der ganzen Gesellschaft der Idealisierung[19] oder der Überschätzung ihrer Möglichkeiten zeihen[20], man kann auch die von ihm vertretene Trennung von Kirche und Staat als praktisch undurchführbar ansehen. Die auf den ersten Blick gewiß plausible Zuweisung des Religionsunterrichts an die Kirche kann aber zumindest für unsere Zeit vor allem deshalb nicht überzeugen, weil die Kirchen heute noch weniger als zur Zeit Schleiermachers das religiöse Leben der Menschen öffentlich repräsentieren und auch keinen den gesellschaftlichen Bedürfnissen angemessenen Unterricht praktizieren. Umgekehrt läßt sich die Schule heute weniger denn je auf die Vermittlung von Kenntnissen und Fertigkeiten einengen. Sie ist vielmehr einer ganzheitlichen Förderung der Schüler auf breiter anthropologischer Basis verpflichtet. Infolge der prinzipiellen Gleichberechtigung der kognitiven und affektiven Komponenten des Unterrichts hat auch die Bildung der "Gesinnung", auch und gerade auf ethischem und religiösem Gebiet, ihren legitimen und unverzichtbaren Platz in der modernen Schule, zu deren Wegbereitern Schleiermacher mit seiner Konzeption eines von der unmittelbaren Glaubensvermittlung unterschiedenen Religionsunterrichts ohne Zweifel gehört[21].

Anmerkungen

1. Wißmann, Religionspädagogik bei Schleiermacher. Gießen 1934
2. A.R. Osborn, Schleiermacher and Religious Education. Montreal 1934
3. An erster Stelle wären zu nennen R. Fischer, Religionspädagogik unter den Bedingungen der Aufklärung. Studien zum Verhältnisproblem von Theologie und Pädagogik bei Schleiermacher, Palmer und Diesterweg. Heidelberg 1973, sowie H.H. Wilke, Religionspädagogik, wissenschaftliche Bildung und Theologie am Beispiel der religionspädagogischen Fragestellungen in Schleiermachers System der Wissenschaften. Diss. Hannover 1977
4. Neben philosophischen (Ethik), theologischen (Enzyklopädie; Praktische Theologie; Theologische Ethik) und pädagogischen Schriften müssen auch die Predigten herangezogen werden.
5. Für unser Thema wäre vor allem die Frage des Verhältnisses zwischen Familie, Schule und Kirche in der religiösen Erziehung zu nennen.
6. Vgl. die diesbezüglichen Klagen bei Wißmann 31 f., 262 f. u.ö.
7. Durch die Gleichsetzung von "Gefühl" und "unmittelbares Selbstbewußtsein" in Glaubenslehre und Dialektik sollte ein sentimentales Mißverständnis des Gefühlsbegriffs endgültig ausgeschlossen sein.
8. Alle mit "R" versehenen Seitenangaben im Text beziehen sich auf die Paginierung der ersten Auflage der Reden "Über die Religion", welche in alle neueren Ausgaben aufgenommen ist.
9. Der erwähnte Widerspruch liegt offensichtlich in dem Gegensatz von "mitteilen" und "aus sich hervorbringen".
10. Aufschlußreich ist ein Vergleich mit der theologischen Fassung dieses Grundsatzes in der "Praktischen Theologie": "Den Glauben kann der Geistliche nicht mitteilen, sein Entstehen ist Werk des göttlichen Geistes und dieser wirkt aus der Gesammtheit des Lebens" (PrTh 349).

11. Weitere Belege für diese Auffassung aus späteren Werken Schleiermachers sind bei Wißmann 49 f. aufgeführt.

12. W. Sünkel, Friedrich Schleiermachers Begründung der Pädagogik als Wissenschaft. Ratingen 1964

13. Die mit "PS" beginnenden Seitenangaben beziehen sich auf die zweibändige Ausgabe der Pädagogischen Schriften Schleiermachers, hrsg. v. Th. Schulze und E. Weniger, Düsseldorf 1957.

14. Vgl. E. Schrofner, Theologie als positive Wissenschaft. Prinzipien und Methoden der Dogmatik bei Schleiermacher. Frankfurt a.M. 1980

15. Vor allem in seiner Glaubenslehre ist es Schleiermacher um die Überwindung des Gegensatzes zwischen Rationalismus und Supranaturalismus in Theologie und Kirche zu tun.

16. Der Charakter auch des kirchlichen Religionsunterrichts als öffentlicher Unterricht wird von H. Wilke (s. Anm. 3) überzeugend herausgestellt (S. 153-156).

17. Vgl. den Hinweis in der "Kurzen Darstellung des theologischen Studiums", wonach "die Katechetik überhaupt auf die Pädagogik als Kunstlehre zurückgeht" (§ 294 Anm.). Demnach prägt der "techne-Charakter" den kirchlichen Unterricht genauso wie den schulischen und kann nicht einseitig gegen letzteren ins Treffen geführt werden wie bei W. Sommer, Der Zusammenhang von Pädagogik und Praktischer Theologie in Schleiermachers Religionspädagogik, in: Der Evangelische Erzieher 30 (1978) 321-341, 328 u. 340 f. Die ebenfalls didaktisch begründete Entgegensetzung des kirchlichen und schulischen Religionsunterrichts bei I. Lohmann (Lehrplan und Allgemeinbildung in Preußen. Eine Fallstudie zur Lehrplantheorie F.E.D. (so auch durchgängig im Literaturverzeichnis S. 461 f.) Schleiermachers. Frankfurt a.M. 1984. S. 247 f.) ist wohl nur durch die konsequente Ausklammerung der theologischen Schriften Schleiermachers zu erklären.

18. Vgl. W. Klafki, Das pädagogische Problem des Elementaren und die Theorie der kategorialen Bildung. Weinheim 4. Aufl. 1964. S. 166.

19. R. Fischer (s. Anm. 3) S. 57 u. 73; H. Friebel, Über den Begriff der öffentlichen Erziehung in der Pädagogik Schleiermachers, in: B.Gerner (Hg.), Schleiermacher. Interpretation und Kritik. München 1971. S. 103-121, 107.

20. W. Weishaupt, Religionsbegriff und Religionsunterricht. Eine historisch-systematische Untersuchung zur Funktion des Religionsunterrichts in ausgewählten religionspädagogischen Entwürfen. Frankfurt a.M. 1980. S. 31.

21. Nach Schulze "bleibt Schleiermacher einsam in seiner Zeit gegenüber den Bekehrungsbemühungen der Pietisten auf der einen und dem Gesinnungsunterricht der Herbartianer auf der anderen Seite. Heute beginnt man wieder einzusehen, daß Schleiermachers nüchterne Beschränkung vielleicht die einzige Form ist, den Religionsunterricht vor Verfälschungen und den Religionslehrer vor Überforderung zu schützen" (Th. Schulze, Stand und Probleme der erziehungswissenschaftlichen Schleiermacher-Forschung in Deutschland, in: Paedagogica Historica I, 2 (1961) 291-326, 325).

VIII

THE EPISTEMOLOGY OF FRIEDRICH SCHLEIERMACHER FROM A DIPOLAR PERSPECTIVE

Michael Nealeigh

It is not uncommon when discussing epistemological concerns to become embroiled in the issue of methodology. This fact is nowhere more evident than when discussing the epistemology of Friedrich Schleiermacher. What method does one employ to properly understand the epistemology of this pivotal 19th century thinker? The answer to this question may be found in the dipolar theory of Charles Hartshorne. The notion of applying the dipolar model of Charles Hartshorne's process thought to the epistemology of Friedrich Schleiermacher has its origin in three different and independent sources. First, Karl Barth, in his history of Protestant thought, describes Schleiermacher as a theologian of mediation, "mediating . . . not only between this and that opposite, but ultimately between all, even the most pronounced opposites."[1] He describes Schleiermacher's method as one where truth is found, not in the synthesis of two opposites as in Hegel, but in some indefinable center between contrasting poles.[2] Although Barth did not pursue this motif in organizing his interpretation of Schleiermacher's thought, he did provide a definite point of contact between Schleiermacher's theological method and the concept of contrasts integral to the dipolar model of Charles Hartshorne. Second, Robert Williams, in a 1978 monograph on Schleiermacher's doctrine of God, compares him to Nikolas Cusanus and describes his doctrine of God as "bipolar."[3] Third, a study of Schleiermacher's *Dialektik* reveals the two pole structure of his thought. This evidence, albeit tentative, provides the impetus for the current study. It is the contention of the current study that the application of dipolar theory to Schleiermacher's fundamental method will greatly enhance an understanding of this particular aspect of his thought and of his larger theological system as a whole. After reviewing the background and nature of dipolar theory its principles will be applied to a study of Schleiermacher's theory of knowledge.

The Di-polar Model

For Hartshorne, the crisis of modern theology is at least in large measure a conceptual one. How is theology to deal with the apparant contradictions within the structures and arguments of classical theism? Hartshorne reconstructs the traditional doctrines of theology around his theory of dipolar theism. Although the dipolar model pervades Hartshorne's effort, it is nowhere set down in systematic fashion. Thus, it becomes necessary to glean the dipolar model from its application in his theory of dipolar theism. It is important to the current study to understand dipolarity as a method, separated as much as is possible from the context of its origins in process thought. Several distinct principles make up the dipolar model.[4]

1. The dipolar model is built on the foundation of Morris Cohen's "law of polarity." Under the law of polarity, principles that are usually conceived as distinct and competitive are brought into harmony, the apparant incompatibility being reduced to contrast within unity. Cohen states:

> ... we must be on our guard against the universal tendency to simplify situations and to analyze them in terms of only one of such contrary tendencies. This principle of polarity is a maxim of research. ... It may be generalized as the principle ... of the necessary co-presence and mutual dependence of opposite determinations.[5]

Hartshorne spends a great deal of his time defending his application of this principle to his doctrine of God. He insists, however, that its alternative, monopolarity, whether applied to God or any less supreme aspect of reality, renders reality weak and stinted. The tendency in classical theism, he points out, has been to favor one pole over the other. This one-sided bias, as Hartshorne calls it, results in God being viewed from the perspective of only one pole of ultimate conceptual contrasts such that he is seen as being absolute but not relative, cause but not effect, absolute but not relative, and so on. Hartshorne overcomes the limitations of the traditional monopolar viewpoint, while at the same time avoiding both contradiction and dualism, in his explanation of the relationship between the poles of ultimate contraries.[6]

2. The law of polarity requires that the poles, or ultimate contraries, be related as either part to whole, or as two different aspects of the same reality. An example of the poles relating at two different logical dimensions of reality is Hartshorne's concept of God as both necessary and contingent. His perspective can be diagrammed as follows:

NECESSARY •————————→ GOD ←————————• CONTINGENT
(character)   (experience)

At the level of his character God is necessary, i.e., his character is such that it will exist exactly as it is irrespective of any contingent reality. At the level of God's experience of the world, however, he is contingent, i.e., his experience of the world is dependent upon finite humanity's response to him (if subject A worships God, God experiences the world one way; if subject A refuses to worship God, God experiences the world another way).

An example of the poles relating as part to whole is Hartshorne's concept of reality as both abstract and concrete. Diagrammed it looks like this:

ABSTRACT •————————→ REALITY ←————————• CONCRETE

For Hartshorne, abstractness and concreteness are related as part to whole. The concrete represents reality as it exists, while the abstract represents that concrete reality as it is "abstracted" or removed for the sake of noetic consideration. The concrete contains the abstract, the abstract being a part of, or another way of looking at, the concrete whole. Ultimately, for Hartshorne, the poles relate in a way reflected in the merging of these two criteria. The two logical aspects of reality are themselves related as part to whole. Any set of ultimate contraries relate in a concrete manner and in an abstract manner. Put another way, the two logical dimensions at which the poles relate are themselves related as part to whole. For example, the relative aspect of a subject is related to the absolute aspects of a subject as different aspects of the same reality, the one being concrete (the relative) and the other being abstract (the absolute). These different aspects of reality, however, are related also as part to whole since the relative is the whole from which the absolute is abstracted and of which it is a part. It is sufficient for the current study, however, to understand that the relationship between the poles is such that each pole contributes to the knowledge of the subject without falling into either contradiction or dualism.

Both contradiction and dualism are avoided in a proper understanding of the relationship between the poles. Hartshorne maintains that the law of contradiction has been incorrectly formulated when it states that no subject can have predicate P and not-P at the same time. The missing element, he insists, is the insertion "in the same respect."[7] Thus, contrary poles can both be true as long as they refer to the same reality in different aspects of its characters or are related as part to whole. Dualism is avoided in the same way. As long as the poles are referring to distinct aspects of the same reality, the charge of dualism cannot apply.

3. It is important in Hartshorne's system that the poles of the ultimate contraries remain distinct. The theory of dipolarity goes beyond the notion that in every opposite there is some truth that must be incorporated into the larger body of truth. Likewise, he is not saying that opposite poles are "synthesized" into some definable third which is more true than the first two. Dipolarity involves neither the choosing between mutually exclusive alternatives nor the combining of these alternatives (at least not in the strict Hegelian sense). The poles are genuine aspects that go together to make up the subject without abrogating their distinctiveness. This relationship between the poles constitutes the distinct nature of dipolar theory and distinguishes it from a view which merely advocates that reality be understood with an appreciation for opposites. The poles are vitally related. This point cannot be overemphasized. Polar aspects of a given reality can best be described in terms of the conjunction of the two. Together they constitute that reality. In popular language this relationship is one of "both/and" in contrast to "either/or."

The threefold criteria of dipolarity can be seen in the diagram previously discussed.

NECESSARY •————————→ GOD ←————————• CONTINGENT
(character)   (experience)

The diagram itself expresses the two pole nature of Hartshorne's model. The points reflect the distinctiveness of the poles. Each pole has a separate identity which is not lost in the process of coming together to form or express the reality under consideration. The arrows represent this process and underscore the joining of the two in conjunction. The poles (or contraries) are in capital letters while the qualifications that specify their relationship to each other are in parentheses.

It should be understood that this study is not an effort to prove that Schleiermacher was a nineteenth-century dipolar theist. Rather, the application of the dipolar model is an attempt at elucidation and clarity. It is felt that the dipolar model can provide the framework needed to clarify and organize the structure and content of Schleiermacher's complex epistemological system. In a matter as complex as this, clarification is no meager goal.

Preliminary Considerations: The "Dialektik"

The primary source for a study of Schleiermacher's epistemology is the *Dialektik*. During his tenure at Berlin, Schleiermacher lectured six times on *Dialektik* in the years 1811, 1814, 1818, 1822, 1828, and 1831. The *Dialektik* was published postumously in 1839 by his student and friend Ludwig Jonas. In the Jonas edition the lectures of 1814 form the basis of the text, although these are supplemented by the lectures of 1818. The extant material from the other lectures as well as Schleiermacher's introduction are included as appendices. It is clear that Jonas seeks to provide a representative cross-section of the extant material. The text itself is modeled after Schleiermacher's theological encyclopedia, *Kurze Darstellung des theologischen Studiums*. First published in 1811, this work is more an outline of his thought than is the more extensive *Glaubenslehre*. The sketchy form of the Jonas edition has prompted two efforts to arrange the material differently. Isidor Halpern, in his 1903 edition, structures the *Dialektik* along the lines of the lectures of 1831.[8] Though the lectures of 1831 are neither as complete nor as precise as the lectures of 1814, Halpern considers them to be the mature and final expression of Schleiermacher's doctrine. On the other hand, Rudolf Odebrecht, in his 1942 edition, concentrates on the lectures of 1822.[9] Odebrecht supplements Schleiermacher's lecture notes with notes from students who attended his lectures that year. The chief weakness of this edition, however, is its exclusion of the lectures of 1811, 1814, 1818, 1828, and 1831. As John Thiel points out in his very good summary of the redaction of the *Dialektik*, this exclusion makes it impossible to follow the development of Schleiermacher's thought throughout the history of the lectures.[10] More recent efforts by Andreas Arndt have resulted in critical editions of the lectures of 1811 and 1814.[11] Nonetheless, in spite of its unsatisfactory form, the Jonas edition has retained its primacy for two reasons. First, it is the work of a man intimately acquainted with Schleiermacher's thought and way of thinking. Schleiermacher himself commissioned Jonas to edit his notes when it became evident that poor health would keep him from preparing his lectures for publication. Second, the Jonas edition preserves the integrity of each lecture plan, thereby permitting the reader to perceive and analyze the development of Schleiermacher's thought from one lecture to the other.[12]

Over the course of Schleiermacher scholarship the *Dialektik* has been studied in one of two ways. The first method, utilized by Halpern, traces the development of Schleiermacher's thought by a historical examination of the lectures themselves. The second approach is much less specific in its analysis of the individual lectures and presents the issues raised in the *Dialektik* in general terms based on an interpretation drawn from all the lectures. This methodology has been employed in more recent scholarship by Falk Wagner and John Thiel.[13] It rests on the presupposition that the fundamental stance of the *Dialektik* is the same in all of its historical expressions. This latter approach will be adopted in the current effort. The goal will be to present a lucid outline of Schleiermacher's epistemology as it is developed in the Trancendental Part of the Jonas edition of the *Dialektik*.

Limited Nature of Schleiermacher's Epistemology

Schleiermacher's epistemological quest is indeed a limited one. On the one hand, his goal is specific and practical as he seeks to determine the nature of proper thinking.[14] How does one move from the relativity of thinking to the certainty of knowing? On the other hand, his goal is general and metaphysical as being concerned with justifying his presupposition of a transcendent ground of knowing. Since all thinking is relative, a final consummate unity beyond thinking is required for knowing to take place. The search for this transcendent ground of knowing consumes the majority of Schleiermacher's epistemological effort. In this sense, Martin Redeker is correct in describing the first part of his *Dialektik* as a "metaphysics of knowledge."[15] Yet, the speculation in which Schleiermacher engages is not for the purpose of advancing a body of knowledge about God, humanity, or the world, but rather it is an attempt to justify the presupposition of the transcendent ground. This presupposition and his search for its justification is clearly in the interest of epistemology, not ontology.

Schleiermacher's quest for a transcendent ground of knowing that will ensure the possibility of the universal movement from thinking to knowing is not an attempt to arrive at a formal ontology. Rather, throughout his discussion, Schleiermacher presupposes the givenness of being and provides only a descriptive explanation of the processes of being by asking the limited epistemological question of how being is related to knowing.[16] Although his goal to justify the presupposition of a transcendent ground of knowing inevitably involves a consideration of the ontological counterpart of the individual's cognitive experience, it does so only in the interest of epistemology. Schleiermacher does not regard being as an object of speculation.[17] Yet, he does give specific ontological status to the transcendent ground of knowing – the absolute unity of thinking and being. The nature of the transcendent ground will be discussed in detail below. It is sufficient at this point to understand that, for Schleiermacher, the transcendent ground is not deduced from speculative principles but is presupposed in contrast to the relativity of knowing. Metaphysics, therefore, provides the formal tools or the methodology for determining how thinking becomes knowing.[18] The transcendent ground serves a heuristic function. In fact, Schleiermacher insists, the methodology of the *Dialektik* cannot be developed if the transcendent ground is not presupposed. Since the existence of this ground cannot be established logically, all that can be offered is justification for its presupposition. For Schleiermacher, this justification proceeds by a process of discovering, not by a process of establishing. Metaphysics, the fruit of speculative activity, facilitates the development of epistemological theory by offering evidence, albeit tentative evidence, for the formal possibility of knowing.

In the process of pursuing these two goals, it is clear that Schleiermacher is firmly grounded in the epistemology of Immanuel Kant. Like Kant, he asks the question of what can and cannot be known. Indeed, he builds on Kant's system and then takes it one step further. For Kant, God cannot be the direct source of any physical thing since the category of causality cannot be applied to that which is outside the spaciotemporal realm of phenomena.[19] As the current study unfolds it will become clear that, although Schleiermacher agrees with Kant that God is outside the realm in which knowledge is possible, God nevertheless does exert an influence on knowing, an influence that goes beyond that of being a "regulatory principle."[20]

Although Schleiermacher's epistemological quest is limited in its scope and purpose, it must be considered as a whole. It cannot be properly understood if its parts are studied in isolation or from a strict phenomenological approach. Each aspect of his theory of knowledge fits into a cohesive whole whose parts cannot be completely understood until the project is complete and his entire theory delineated.

Philosophical Background for Polarity

The basis for the polar nature of Schleiermacher's approach to epistemology can be traced to the philosophical revolution initiated by René Descartes. Simply stated, Descartes divided reality into two metaphysically distinct substances, matter and mind. He sought to establish a firm philosophical foundation for eighteenth-century physics, one that would free science to proceed unfettered by theological assumptions and at the same time exclude scientific mechanism from the realm of religion. The tendency among eighteenth-century thinkers was to choose one of the two and carry it to its logical extreme. The Continental rationalists ignored sensual perception and the material world (the real) in favor of propositions put together and interrelated in the mind by the categories of reason (the ideal). Locke and his followers, on the other hand, concentrated on the sensible and held that ideas in the mind (the ideal) were caused by external material objects (the real) and that these objects constituted the essence of reality.[21] The Cartesian compromise had evolved into a dichotomy of mind and matter, of subject and object, of the ideal and the real.

Kant, inspired by the skepticism of David Hume, insisted that knowledge is a mixture of rationalism and empiricism, of the ideal and the real. He ageed with the empiricists that the "raw material" of knowledge (his synthetic element) comes from the sensible "manifold," the realm of matter outside the reasoning mind. Yet the mind also plays a part in processing that material by means of its own built-in categories (his a priori element).[22] Schleiermacher was thoroughly schooled in Kant's philosophy and thus began his epistemological quest with this distinction already in place.

Schleiermacher's Epistemology: The Nature of Proper Thinking

Like Kant, Schleiermacher develops his theory of knowing from the human experience of thinking. He begins his task by defining the limits of thinking itself. Thinking, he states, may take shape in one of three modes: practical (*geschäftliches*), artistic (*künstlerisches*), or pure (*reines*). Practical thinking is all thinking that is for the sake of something else. It is thinking that culminates in concrete action. This mode of thinking is the proper object of ethics.[23] Artistic thinking involves all thinking that reflects on the feeling of pleasure at the moment of its occurrence. Artistic thinking is the proper object of aesthetics.[24] Pure thinking is defined in contrast to both practical and artistic thinking. It is neither other-directed nor limited by the temporal experience of sensible feeling. Pure thinking is "thinking for the sake of knowing," thinking "which elevates itself toward immutability and universality."[25] Consequently, pure thinking is the proper object of epistemology. Although pure thinking tends to become knowing, it is not in itself true knowledge. Yet, inherent in pure thinking is the desire to know (*Wissenwollen*) that drives thinking toward the goal of the certainty of knowing.[26]

The polar nature of Schleiermacher's theory is evident in his criteria for distinguishing true knowing from mere thinking. First, knowing is thinking which "is necessarily conceived in such a way that it is produced in the same way by all possessing the ability to think." Second, true knowing is thinking which "is conceived as corresponding to the being that is the object of thought."[27] He seeks to validate epistemic agreement both from the standpoint of human subjects and in terms of the connection between thinking and being. True knowledge exists when there is *agreement* among thinking minds and when there is *agreement* between thought and its object. For Schleiermacher these criteria constitute the fundamental poles of epistemology.

Agreement among subjects is based on the *ideal* side of human thinking which contributes to the formation of knowledge through what Schleiermacher describes as the intellectual function or the activity of reason (*Vernunftthätigkeit*). Objective agreement is based on the *real* side of human thinking which adds to the constitution of knowledge through what Schleiermacher describes as the organic function or the faculty of organization (*Organisation*). Simply put, the organic function is the human capacity for sensibility; the intellectual function is the human activity of reason. It is possible for thinking to become true knowing only when the ideal and the real aspects of thinking come together in the conjunction of reason and sensibility. This first step toward knowing Schleiermacher calls "proper thinking" (*wirkliches Denken*)[28] Proper thinking takes place in the conjunction in experience of the intellectual and the organic functions, of reason and sensibility. The polar nature of proper thinking can be diagrammed as follows:

IDEAL   REAL
•————————→ PROPER THINKING ←———————•
Intellectual Function   Organic Function
(reason)   (sensibility)

Both poles are required if thinking is to provide the depth and expanse necessary for true knowing. The activity of the organic function "without any activity of reason is not yet thinking," while "the activity of reason without any activity of organization would no longer be thinking."[29]

Proper thinking, and thus knowing, originates in the organic function. As the human capacity for sensibility, the organic function is the source of the raw data of thinking and ultimately, of knowing. Schleiermacher describes this raw data in Kantian fashion by the term "manifold" (*Mannigfaltigkeit*). It is the body of unrefined and disordered sensible impressions prior to their being ordered by the activity of reason. The organic function can be expressed in the polar relationship between the self and the world (or between internal consciousness and external consciousness) and can be diagrammed as follows:

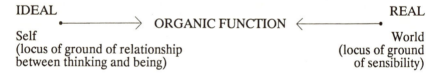

IDEAL   REAL
•————————→ ORGANIC FUNCTION ←———————•
Self   World
(locus of ground of relationship   (locus of ground
between thinking and being)   of sensibility)

The organic function represents the agreement between thinking and being and thus involves the proper relating of subject and object. The self reflects the subject side of the manifold and represents the subjective pole of human experience (internal consciousness). The world reflects the object side of the manifold and represents the objective pole of human experience (external consciousness). Elevated to the level of the noetic, internal consciousness, or self-consciousness, is the context of proper thinking and the locus in experience of the ground of the relationship between thinking and being. In the same way, external consciousness, or the world, is the experiential locus of the ground of sensibility. There can be no doubt that Schleiermacher firmly grounds thinking in human experience. As will be discussed later, this is not to say that he grounds knowing in the same way.

Just as the organic function is the source of the real pole of thinking, the intellectual function, or the activity of reason, is the source of the ideal pole. The activity of reason contains the cognitive categories that structure the raw data of sense experience. Unlike Kant, however, Schleiermacher does not elaborate a detailed classification of the categories of the mind. Rather, he designates only two: unity (*Einheit*) and multiplicity (*Vielheit*).[30] The relationship between these categories can also be described in polar terms.

IDEAL   REAL

•————————⟶ INTELLECTUAL FUNCTION ⟵————————•

Unity   (activity of reason)   Multiplicity

The category of unity represents the ideal side of thinking. Unity reflects the agreement between thinking minds and between thought and its object, toward which all thinking strives and on which true knowledge is based. In contrast, multiplicity is rooted more deeply in the sensual matter of thinking and thus represents the real side of thinking. It expresses the initial organization by the mind of the raw sensual data of the manifold in which all the distinctives or multiplicities of the data are maintained. Admittedly, Schleiermacher's classification of the various modes of order that the intellectual function imprints on experience is simple, especially when compared to Kant's twelve-fold delimitation of understanding in his *Critique of Pure Reason*. Yet, for Schleiermacher, the categories of unity and multiplicity define the noetic poles between which thinking constantly oscillates. Each category presents to the other its unique perspective on the proper constitution of thinking and knowing – unity at the level of fundamental agreements and multiplicity at the level of specific content.

The Forms of Knowledge

According to the *Dialektik*, knowledge can occur only under the forms of concept and judgment.[31] Proper thinking becomes knowing that is either

of an object or *about* an object. A concept is the refined cognitive representation of the sensible image (*Bild*) of a given object. Concepts are rooted in
the ideal side of the activity of reason and express the unity of being.[32] They
operate on a hierarchy implied by the different levels of conceptual
precision. Schleiermacher considers those concepts "higher" that more
faithfully mirror the unity of being and uses the term "power" (*Kraft*) to
describe them. In turn, he considers those concepts that mirror the unity of
being less successfully as "lower" and uses the term "manifestation" or
"phenomenon" (*Erscheinung*) to describe them. The dipolar nature of
concept can be diagrammed as follows:

IDEAL   REAL
•————————————> CONCEPT <————————————•
Power   Manifestation

Judgments, on the other hand, build on the unity of the concept to
augment knowledge. They produce knowledge by joining different concepts
and are essentially knowledge *about* objects. Through the propositional
linking of subject and predicate, judgments express being as dynamic. The
dipolar nature of judgment can be diagrammed as follows:

IDEAL   REAL
•————————————> JUDGMENT <————————————•
(Subject)   (Predicate)

For Schleiermacher, concept and judgment are correlative and
mutually interdependent. Concept requires a multiplicity of logical
affirmations in order to define its unity more precisely. Judgment requires
the unity of both subject and predicate in order to maintain the authenticity
and integrity of its construction.[33] The one without the other is devoid of
meaning.

From Schleiermacher's perspective on the forms of knowledge it is
possible to trace his understanding of the relativity of knowledge. For
Schleiermacher, knowledge, whether in the form of concept or judgment, is
only possible under the conditions of time and space. Only in the finite world
to which sensibility is bound can an object of thinking become an object of

knowing. The relativity of thinking and, thus, of knowing is established in the subject-object antithesis inherent in self-consciousness. Thinking and knowing forever hover between the poles of the intellectual and the organic functions, between reason and sensibility, between subject and object. This polar dynamic can never be completely dissipated and defines all knowledge as relative.

The Transcendent Ground of Knowing

Schleiermacher recognizes that an analysis of proper thinking and even of the forms of knowledge cannot in themselves explain how one moves from the relativity of thinking to the certainty of knowing. For Schleiermacher, the missing ingredient is found in the presupposition of a transcendent ground of knowing. This transcendent ground, Schleiermacher insists, is what determines proper thinking as knowing. The transcendent ground of knowing makes it possible for proper thinking to become knowing. Yet, Schleiermacher does not deduce a ground of epistemic agreement from the realm of knowledge. Rather, he presupposes that such a ground exists and attempts to justify his presupposition. As a presupposition the principle of an absolute, transcendent unity cannot be posited in terms of either concept or judgment. Although it is reflected in all knowing it cannot be grasped in these terms and thus eludes knowing. Schleiermacher maintains there must be a ground or basis for knowing that transcends human experience and the limits of the finite. He concludes that the transcendent ground of agreement between thinking and being can be found in the principle of absolute unity, a unity above the relativity and oscillation inherent in thinking. Such a ground is necessary if knowledge is to be both universal and meaningful. Schleiermacher identifies this principle of absolute unity with God.[34]

In this respect, he differs sharply from Kant. Kant grounds knowledge in the transcendental unity of apperception and thus essentially maintains the grounding principle within the organic and the finite. Unlike Kant, however, Schleiermacher seeks the metaphysical foundation for the categories of the mind. He agrees with Kant that metaphysics cannot be considered a science in the sense that it adds content to a body of knowledge. Yet, he insists, metaphysical speculation can serve as a methodology for justifying the presupposition of a transcendent ground of knowledge. The Transcendental Part of the *Dialektik* is taken up with the two-fold task of discovering the point of contact of the transcendent ground in human experience and of justifying its original presupposition.

Schleiermacher travels the ideal and real paths of proper thinking in search of a point of contact in human experience with the fundamental principle of epistemic agreement. Because knowing originates in the organic function, he begins his quest by examining the two poles of human experience, self-consciousness and the world. As previously stated, Schleiermacher holds that self-consciousness is both the internal pole of the manifold and the experiential locus of the relationship between thinking and being. It is both a source of the raw data to be structured by the activity of reason and the context in which proper thinking takes place. As the meeting point of thinking and being in human experience, self-consciousness serves as the principle guaranteeing the *relationship* between thinking and being, but cannot in itself provide the *ground of agreement* between thinking and being. Although it is possible to ground *thinking* in self-consciousness, the agreement between thinking minds and between thought and its object requires a ground outside the self. Indeed, self-consciousness, rather than being the source of agreement, is the source of the subject-object antithesis and the consequent relativity that charactierizes all thinking. Knowing must transcend the relativity of doubt and contention in order to achieve the goal of certainty. This task cannot be completed, Schleiermacher contends, within self-consciousness since the constant oscillation between conflicting truth claims, inherent in the process of thinking, results from the antithetical nature of thinking and being rooted in self-consciousness.

Likewise, the world, although it serves as the ground of sensibility, is unable to ground epistemic agreement between thinking and being. The world is the objective side of the subject-object dichotomy and, as such, is caught up in the relativity of thinking. Schleiermacher seeks a ground of knowing that is reflected in, but which exists apart from, all concrete occasions of specific agreement. The ground of epistemic agreement must be free from the relativity that plagues the subject-object antithesis. Consequently, Schleiermacher does not find the transcendent ground for knowing in the world. Rather, he insists, the ground of knowing must lie beyond the realm of the anthithetical and must be an absolute unity of thinking and being.[35] In fact, the *real*, at the point of either its objective (the world) or its subjective (self-consciousness) pole, is precluded, by virtue of its organic limitations, from being the point of contact in experience for the transcendent ground of knowing. Schleiermacher is compelled to proceed beyond the conditions of concrete experience in his quest for the basis of knowing.

As stated above, all proper thinking, on which true knowledge is based, rests on the noetic conjunction of the real and the ideal – that is, the union in experience of sensibility and reason. The real pole of thinking fails at the outset to meet Schleiermacher's fundamental criterion that the ground of knowing be free from the relativity inherent in the thinking process. Schleiermacher concludes, therefore, that the ideal pole of thinking (*Vernunftthätigkeit*), focused as it is in the intellectual category of unity, provides the necessary point of contact in thought with the ground of knowing. Indeed, the presupposition of a transcendent ground of knowing is itself the foundation of the order imposed on sense experience by the activity of reason.[36] However, even though knowing, as opposed to thinking, is grounded in the absolute unity of thinking and being it is not absolute. Knowing cannot furnish the ground of agreement between thinking and being. It is not self-validating. Schleiermacher insists that even knowledge grounded in the infinite is not free of the relativity inherent in thinking.

Schleiermacher's presupposition of a transcendent ground of knowing is itself based on several assumptions. First, Schleiermacher assumes the relationship between thinking and being constructed in self-consciousness into proper thinking is an insufficient ground for knowing. Second, he assumes the principle grounding epistemic agreement must be a transcendent, absolute unity of thinking and being. And lastly, he identifies this principle with God. The first two presuppositions are more understandable in light of the third. Schleiermacher begins with rather than arrives at his position that the unity of knowledge reflects the unity of God.[37]

He insists on making both an epistemological and an ontological connection between the infinite and the finite. He states:

> ... by positing this higher being we ascend to the absolute, to the deity, the transcendental source of all being and, in an ideal way, of all knowing, so that everything exists in us as being and thinking only as rooted in the deity (*Gottheit*).[38]

As Thiel points out, Schleiermacher's presupposition cannot stand alone. There is no sound logical basis for it. But this apparent dilemma is not an indication of an immature philosophy. Rather, it specifies the role played in Schleiermacher's epistemology by the experience of feeling.[39] Thus, Schleiermacher's presupposition of God as the transcendent ground of knowing cannot be fully understood until his system is fully expressed. Following a discussion of his quest to justify this presupposition the role he gives to feeling in the process of knowing will be discussed in detail. Indeed, as will be seen, Schleiermacher considers feeling to be his most convincing evidence for the transcendent ground. In addition, the dipolar nature of Schleiermacher's theory of knowledge will become evident as he examines the areas of ontology, the forms of knowledge and ethics in search for justification for his foundational principle.

Having postulated the transcendent ground of knowing Schleiermacher searches the structure of proper thinking for justification for his original presupposition. He isolates the intellectual and organic functions that make up proper thinking in order to ascertain the ontological foundation of each. His goal, however, is not to arrive at a formal ontology but to establish the boundaries of thought and in so doing to find evidence for the presupposition of a transcendent ground of knowing. He establishes the ontological mode or boundary of the real side of proper thinking, the organic function, through an abstractive process of imagining the removal of the ordering activity of reason from sensibility. The result is the ontological source of the organic function (the manifold). He calls this real boundary of thought *Chaos*. Because it lacks the activity of reason, it cannot be the object of proper thinking. In the same way, he approximates the ontological mode or boundary of the ideal side of proper thinking by imagining the removal of the influence of sensibility upon reason. The result is the ontological source of the intellectual function (reason). He calls this ideal boundary of thought *Gott* or *Gottheit*. Because it lacks sensibility it too cannot be the object of proper thinking. The relationship of these boundaries of thought, or ontological modes of being, can be diagrammed as follows:

IDEAL   REAL

$\bullet \longrightarrow$ Ontological Modes of Being $\longleftarrow \bullet$

GOTT   (boundaries of thought)   CHAOS

Gott and *Chaos* are the ontological principles on which the intellectual and organic functions, respectively, are based. They define the boundaries of thought and establish the ontological roots of all thinking and being. By uncovering the common roots of thinking and being in *Gott* and *Chaos* Schleiermacher feels he has supplied at least tentative justification for his presupposition of an absolute unity of thinking and being as the transcendental ground of knowing. He finds this justification most clearly at the ideal boundary of thought where thinking unites with being without the corruption of sensibility. Indeed, the unity brought by the intellectual function to the organic in the construction of knowledge reflects, Schleiermacher maintains, this absolute unity of thinking and being, i.e., the ideal boundary of thought.[40]

It is noteworthy that Schleiermacher must violate the rules of proper thinking in order to establish its boundaries and ontological foundations. Since *Gott* and *Chaos* do not involve their polar extremes, neither can be the object of proper thinking and thus knowing. Indeed, Schleiermacher calls this abstractive isolation of the ideal-real poles of proper thinking "fictional" (*fictionsweise*). According to the lectures of 1822, the search for the boundaries of thought can only be pursued by means of abstraction ("*durch Fiction*").[41] In concrete experience the boundaries of thought and their ontological foundations cannot be known. Abstraction is necessary in order to identify the extremes of thought beyond which knowledge cannot go and to discuss the foundational relationship between thinking and being which is itself beyond knowing and available only through metaphysical speculation. Schleiermacher also applies this abstractive analysis to the forms of knowledge. He questions whether concept and judgment do not also point to an origin in the transcendental unity of thinking and being.

Recall that, for Schleiermacher, concept produces knowing by the noetic assimilation of various attributes into a unity, while judgment produces knowing through the joining of different concepts.[42] He examines the ideal and real boundaries of each in search of a justification for his presupposition of a transcendent ground of knowing. Schleiermacher establishes the ideal boundary of concept as power without manifestation and identifies it with God (*Gott*). It is the precise representation of subject without the possibility of multiple manifestations. In contrast, he identifies the real boundary of concept as mere manifestation without any power (*Chaos*). It is possible manifestations without any unity of precision.

IDEAL   REAL
[Gott] •————————————→ CONCEPT ←————————————• [Chaos]
Power   Manifestation

Schleiermacher establishes the boundaries of judgment by the same abstactive process. The ideal boundary of judgment is subject without predicate; the real boundary is predicate without subject. The absolute subject, one needing no qualifications or predicates, Schleiermacher identifies with God (*Gott*). Predicates with no subjects he identifies with *Chaos*.

IDEAL   REAL
[Gott] •————————————→ JUDGMENT ←————————————• [Chaos]
Absolute subject   Predicate with
with no predicate   no subject

In this abstractive, or hypothetical, way Schleiermacher is able to establish a connection between the forms of knowledge and the transcendental unity of thinking and being he defines as God. The process itself, however, isolates the functions of thinking and determines the boundaries of concept and judgment as unknowable. Would the same be true if this abstractive process was not involved? Schleiermacher investigates this possibility by examining the polar extremes of concept and judgment while maintaining the integrity of proper thinking. He does this not by the process of positing the one pole prescinded from the other, but by calculating each polar extreme in terms of the continuum of precision that constitute concept and judgment separately.

For Schleiermacher, the gradation of concepts into those higher and lower, more or less precise, suggests the polar extremes that define the expanse of the conceptual hierarchy. The upper or ideal boundary of concept, considered noetically, is the idea of an absolute unity of being which embraces all concepts within itself. This ideal boundary of concept, however, transcends the subject-object antithesis and, thus, cannot be framed as a concept.[43] The lower or real boundary of concept is "the possibility of a manifold of judgments" that are totally undetermined and completely lacking in conceptual unity.[44] The lower boundary of concept, Schleiermacher states, is "the inexhaustible multiplicity of the perceivable."[45] According to Schleiermacher, both boundaries of concept, thus derived, elude the grasp of knowing. The upper limit, however, does point in the direction of Schleiermacher's original presupposition:

> The idea of the absolute being as the identity of concept and object is, consequently, not knowledge. . . . It is, however, the transcendental ground and the form of all knowing.[46]

Though the ideal boundary of concept does not prove the ground of knowing it offers justification for its presupposition.

In a similiar way, Schleiermacher defines the upper boundary of judgment as the absolute subject of which nothing more is predicable. He defines the lower boundary as an infinity of predicates for which there are no determined subjects, or as "an absolute communality of being" (*Gemeinschaftlichkeit*).[47] It is important to understand that, for Schleiermacher, these upper and lower boundaries of judgment transcend the subject-object antithesis common to proper thinking and reflect respectively the ideal and real modes of being. He feels he has found additional justification for the presupposition of the transcendent ground of knowing as the absolute unity of thinking and being in the ontological understanding of the ideal boundary of judgment. In the lectures of 1814 he states:

> . . . [the] more ontological determination is posited in a subject, the less ontological determination is excluded from it and, consequently, the less ontological determination is posited as

predicable of it. And the absolute subject is that in which all being is posited and of which, therefore, nothing can be predicated.[48]

In the final analysis, concept and judgment should not be considered separately. The upper and lower boundaries of each represent the same transcendent modes of being.

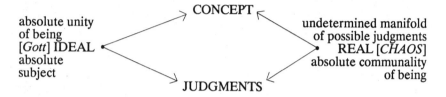

absolute unity of being [*Gott*] IDEAL absolute subject — CONCEPT — undetermined manifold of possible judgments REAL [*CHAOS*] absolute communality of being — JUDGMENTS

At the upper and lower boundaries concept and judgment merge into either the transcendental unity of *Gott* or the transcendental multiplicity of *Chaos*. Schleiermacher's analysis of the forms of knowledge demonstrates the unknowability of the transcendent ground, while providing tentative evidence for its presupposition

Schleiermacher next turns to a consideration of ethical knowledge in his quest to justify his presupposition of a transcendent ground of knowing. He distinguishes ethical knowledge from the "physical" knowledge of concept and judgment. In physical knowledge the subject is in a passive state of being influenced sensibly by a given object of experience. Ethical knowledge, however, originates when the subject is transforming the external world of objects by his actions.[49] Strictly speaking, ethical knowledge is "knowing" in the form of "willing" (*Wollen*). Ethical knowledge also requires a ground for the agreement it posits between willing and being. For Schleiermacher, this ground "cannot be different" from the ground of physical knowledge and is just as elusive to ethical as it is to physical knowledge.[50] Thus, ethical knowledge also provides justification for, but not proof of, the transcendent ground of knowing.

Schleiermacher is aware of the tentative nature of his justification for the presupposition of a transcendent ground of knowing. He realizes just how scant the evidence is and mades no claims for its final conclusiveness.

At the outset he stated that the ground of epistemic agreement could not be deduced logically. He accepted the relativity of thinking and knowing. His speculation, therefore, has been limited to seeking warrant in thinking for the presupposition of the transcendent ground.

Although his analysis of the ideal-real antithesis does not prove the transcendent ground, it does specify both the nature and the limits of proper thinking. Proper thinking hovers between the noetic and the sensible, between the boundaries of thought, and between the boundaries of concept and judgment. It is the noetic point at which the ideal and real lines of thinking and being intersect. This delimitation of proper thinking is perhaps the most important contribution of the *Dialektik*.[51]

Feeling as the Experience of the Transcendent Ground

What is the relationship between the transcendent ground of knowing and human experience? Indeed, since human experience is plagued by the relativity inherent in the subject-object dichotomy, can there be a relationship at all? Schleiermacher claims that the final ground of knowing, which itself evades knowing, may be experienced directly in feeling (*Gefühl*).[52] It is feeling, which Schleiermacher also calls immediate self-consciousness, that overcomes, at least to a degree, the subject-object dichotomy on which thinking and knowing is structured. He implies that there is a kind of experiential indifference between subject and object in feeling that is analogous to the divine in human beings.[53] This analogy constitutes, for Schleiermacher, experiential justification for the pre-supposition of the transcendent ground of knowing. On this basis, he redefines the epistemological task as the process of discovering what thinking, on the basis of the presupposed ground of agreement between thinking and being experienced in feeling, may be properly determined as knowing.

Feeling eludes the activities of thinking and willing but may be apprehended in the conjunction of these activities. The dipolar relationship between thinking and willing may be diagrammed as follows:

WILLING •————————————→ FEELING ←————————————• THINKING

At the point of conjunction between willing and thinking the passive subject becomes active. This point "exists in the oscillation [between these activities] as the final end of thinking and the beginning of willing."[54] Yet, feeling both embraces and cancels the antithesis between thinking and willing. Schleiermacher defines it as "the relative identity of thinking and willing."[55] Only in the experiential identity of feeling can the presupposed transcendent ground be present to human consciousness. In feeling the absolute unity of the ideal and the real, merely presupposed in thinking and willing, is actually accomplished. There the unity is immediate consciousness, or, as he also calls it, original consciousness. The thought of this unity, however, insofar as it can be possessed, is only mediated through feeling. In this regard, feeling is only an imitation of the transcendent ground.[56] Schleiermacher regards this conjunction of thinking and willing, however, as an experiential analogy of the transcendent ground in the human subject.[57]

In the lectures of 1822, Schleiermacher distinguishes feeling from ego (*Ich*) and sensation (*Empfindung*). The ego is the reflective consciousness which "expresses only the identity of the subject in different experiential moments and, consequently, is based on the combining of these moments, a combining which at all times is something mediated."[58] Sensation is the experience of the manifold of sense impressions which is personal and determined at a moment of experience. Both together constitute the ingredients of proper thinking.

Intellectual Function •————→ Proper Thinking ←————————• Organic Function
(Ego)   (Sensation)

They are mediate experience grounded in the subject-object antithesis. Feeling, however, transcends the subject-object antithesis and is the immediate experience of the ideal boundary of thought. In the unity of immediate consciousness the contraries merge in an experiential identity, which Schleiermacher considers to be the most cogent evidence possible for the existence of the presupposed transcendent ground. There is more justification for the presupposed ground, he states, in feeling than in proper thinking. By overcoming the antithetical nature of proper thinking, feeling mirrors the transcendental unity of thinking and being, which is God. Although God cannot be properly thought or known, God can be experienced in the immediacy of feeling.

Feeling, however, cannot finally escape the relativity characteristic of all human experience. The ambiguities of thinking and knowing are not removed in the identity of feeling. Feeling gives only further evidence for the presupposed transcendent ground. The evidence is strong but mitigated and thus inconclusive. Feeling imitates the unity of the transcendent ground, he states, but feeling is not that ground. Schleiermacher stresses this point by saying that "feeling is the immediate, although only relative, identity of thinking and willing."[59] The relativity of feeling results from the antithetical nature of the poles that define it. As already stated, feeling oscillates between the poles of thinking and willing and constitutes the experiential point of conjunction between these poles. It cannot help but be at least touched by the subject-object antithesis on which thinking and willing are based.[60] Feeling is also limited in as much as it is mediated in self-consciousness. Feeling does not have an object in the manifold, in either the self or the world. Yet, its experiential locus, its context, is human self-consciousness. Feeling is unavoidably connected to forms of experience which are grounded in the subject-object dichotomy. "We can say," he states, "that with our consciousness, the consciousness of God is also given to us as a constituent of our self-consciousness as well as our external consciousness."[61] To isolate the consciousness of God in feeling from mediate self-consciounesss would result in what Schleiermacher describes as "consciousness brooding."[62] Without the concrete context of mediate self-consciousness the immediate consciousness of God would be vague and ephemeral.

Mediate self-consciousness and immediate feeling can only be distinguished by abstraction.[63] In actual (concrete) experience, feeling and mediate self-consciousness are inseparable and mutually determining. In its concrete experience in time the immediate consciousness of God dwells in the determinateness of proper thinking. Yet, by imitating the unity of the transcendent ground, it draws proper thinking toward the unity of knowing.

Therefore, it is the experience of the transcendent ground (the absolute unity of thinking and being) through feeling *and* the determination of proper thinking that constitutes knowing.

FEELING •————————————→ KNOWING ←——• PROPER THINKING
(experience of   (determinative
transcendent ground)   content)

Feeling represents the ideality of knowing because it reflects the transcendent ground and is *relatively* free from organic involvment. Proper thinking represents the reality of knowing in as much as it reflects the process of structuring sensible experience.   In the final analysis knowing, for Schleiermacher, is a divine-human process. It takes place in and employs the mechanisms of human experience (internal and external consciousness). Yet, it would remain merely thinking (reflections and sensations) were not the divine experienced in self-consciousness through feeling.

Summary and Conclusions

Schleiermacher begins his epistemological quest with the human experience of thinking and from there attempts to discover and justify a ground of knowing that transcends the relativity of human thought. Such is the dipolar nature of his epistemological system. Knowing forever hovers between the poles of proper thinking and the transcendent ground. At the real pole, proper thinking reflects the relative and finite nature of sensible experience. Thinking not only has its origin in the human capacity for sensibility but takes place in the context of human self-consciousness. From proper thinking comes both the desire to know and the relativity that hinders thinking from becoming knowing. At the ideal pole, the transcendent ground reflects the absolute unity of thinking and being mediated in self-consciousness by feeling. The transcendent ground apart from proper thinking is devoid of definitive content. Thinking apart from the transcendent ground is reduced to mere perception or reflection devoid of certainty. Both are needed if true knowing is to take place. In human experience the transcendent ground is experienced through the mode of feeling. Yet, this feeling, although it provides immediate experience of the transcendent ground, is itself mediated through self-consciousness. Thus, the relativity of thinking, grounded as it is in the sensibility of self-consciousness, can never be completely eliminated.

The polar dimension of Schleiermacher's thought can also be seen in his treatment of the relationship of the real and the ideal. Rather than forcing a choice between the two he insists that both are necessary if reality is to be known. He is a realist in his conviction that a sensible manifold exists irrespective of human perception. He is an idealist in his resolve to structure that manifold of raw sensible data by the activity of reason. For Schleiermacher there is no dichotomy between the real and the ideal, between mind and matter, between reason and intuition. They are mutually correlative poles that together determine the knowable.

Several other conclusions are possible on the basis of the current study. Schleiermacher does not ground his system in the merely human. Although the absolute ground is absolute, knowledge about it, even the experience of God in feeling, is mediated through self-consciousness and is thus relative. Yet, Schleiermacher is clear in his distinction that the consciousness of God comes *through*, not *from*, human self-consciousness. Barth's claim that Schleiermacher was attempting to talk about God by saying man in a loud voice is refuted by his epistemology. One has to talk about God from the context of the self and, for this reason, all such talk will forever be relative and lacking in absolute certainty. Even the experience of God in feeling provides only relative certainty. Yet, the source of God-consciousness comes from beyond the realm of the finite and the relativity of the subject-object antithesis inherent in human thinking. Understanding his use of the word "transcendent" for the ground of knowing is essential. God is above the human process even though knowledge about him is mediated through self-consciousness. The distinction is essential.

In addition, the assertion that Schleiermacher fails to abide by his own dictum that speculation has no place in the content of dogmatics is also refuted by his theory of knowledge. Although he has a high regard for the contributions of philosophy, Schleiermacher does not regard dogmatics to be a product of philosophy. The influence of philosophy on theology is formal rather than material. Logical and metaphysical interests regulate not the "what" but the "how" of theological expression.

Finally, it can be concluded from the current study that Schleiermacher's system possesses the dynamism necessary to insure its compatibility with dipolar theory. The interaction between the poles of proper thinking and between proper thinking and feeling is dynamic. His epistemology completely lacks the mechanical overtones of either enlightenment physics or the religious scholasticism of the late eighteenth century. Schleiermacher's system is vitally interrelated and cannot be understood properly without considering the interaction of its polar aspects. In addition, the conjunction of the poles implied in his system requires that they be dynamically related. They together make up, to the extent possible, the unity and certainty of knowing.

Notes

1. Karl Barth, *Protestant Thought: From Rousseau to Ritschl,* Essay Index Reprint Series (Freeport, NY: Books for Libraries Press, 1971), 331.

2. Ibid., 333-334.

3. Robert R. Williams, *Schleiermacher the Theologian: the Construction of the Doctrine of God* (Philadelphia: Fortress, 1978), xi, 15.

4. It is noteworthy that in tracing the development of the polar principle Hartshorne cites, among others, Plato and Schelling. Schleiermacher was familiar with the writings of both men. Charles Hartshorne, *The Divine Relativity: A Social Conception of God* (New Haven: Yale University Press, 1948), xi.

5. Morris Cohen, *Preface to Logic* (New York: Henry Holt, 1944), 74-75.

6. Although Hartshorne defines his ultimate contraries as a specific set of metaphysical categories, the rules applied to these can be also applied to any set of contraries that reflect a polar relationship, whether that relationship is ontological or epistemological, or whether that relationship is stated in terms of one of those categories. It is sufficient that the contraries under consideration reflect a genuine metaphysical contrast. The specific application of this principle will become clear as the dipolar model is applied to Schleiermacher's theory of knowledge. For a list of his metaphysical contraries see: Charles Hartshorne, *Creative Synthesis and Philosophic Method* (La Salle, IL: Open Court, 1970), 100-101.

7. Santiago Sia, *God in Process Thought: A Study in Charles Hartshorne's Concept of God* (Dordrecht, The Netherlands: Martinus Nijhoff, 1985), 48-49.

8. Friedrich Schleiermacher, *Dialektik*, herausgegeben von Isidor Halpern (Berlin: Mayer & Müller, 1903).

9. Friedrich Schleiermacher, *Dialektik*, herausgegeben von Rudolf Odebrecht (Leipzig: J. C. Hinrichs, 1942).

10. John E. Thiel, *God and World in Schleiermacher's Dialektik and Glaubenslehre: Criticism and the Methodology of Dogmatics* (Bern: Peter Lang, 1981), 9-16.

11. Friedrich Schleiermacher, *Dialektik (1811)*, herausgegeben von Andreas Arndt (Hamburg: Felix Meiner, 1986); Friedrich Schleiermacher, *Dialektik (1814/15)*, herausgegeben von Andreas Arndt (Hamburg: Felix Meiner, 1988).

12. Thiel, 13.

13. Falk Wagner, *Schleiermachers Dialektik: Eine kritische Interpretation* (Gutersloh: Gerd Mohn, 1974).

14. *Dial.*, Introduction (Appendix F), 609-610.

15. Martin Redeker, *Schleiermacher: Life and Thought*, trans. by John Wallhausser (Philadelphia: Fortress, 1973), 155.

16. Gerhard Spiegler, *The Eternal Covenant: Schleiermacher's Experiment in Cultural Theology* (New York: Harper & Row, 1967), 43-44.

17. Ibid.

18. *Dial.*, Lectures of 1814, 22.

19. Immanual Kant, *Critique of Pure Reason*, trans. by N. Kemp Smith (Macmillan: London, 1929), 623-27.

20. Ibid., 670-686.

21. W. T. Jones, *A History of Western Philosophy*, vol. 4: *Kant and the Nineteenth Century*, 2nd ed., revised (New York: Harcourt Brace Jovanovich, 1975), 15-16.

22. Kant, *Critique of Pure Reason*, 26-28.

23. *Dial.*, Introduction (Appendix F), 569

24. Ibid., 569-570.

25. Ibid., 570-571.

26. Ibid.

27. Ibid., Lectures of 1814, 43.

28. Ibid., 52.

29. Schleiermacher's implication here is that organic activity without the influence of reason is merely sensation, while intellectual activity without sensibility is merely reflection. Neither of these aspects of thought constitutes proper thinking when isolated from the other.

30. Ibid., 63, 64.

31. Ibid., 81.

32. Ibid., 63, 85.

33. Ibid., 82-83: "Urtheile sind daher auch desto vollkommner, je mehr die Begriffe schon gebildet sind. . . . Der Begriff ist desto vollkommner, je mehr er auf einem System von Urtheilen ruht. . . . Wenn also das Wissen in gleichmässig producirten Begriffen bestehen soll: so müssen diese auf gleichmässig gebildeten Urtheilen beruhen, und umgekehrt; nnd (sic.) wir sind in einem Kreise befangen."

34. He uses the terms *Gott* and *Gottheit*. See, for example, *Dial.*, Lectures of 1814, 69, 188, 120-121.

35. Ibid., 54.

36. Ibid.

37. Spiegler recognizes the enigmatic nature of Schleiermacher's presupposition at this point. Spiegler, 73-74; 99-103.

38. *Dial.*, Lectures of 1811, 319.

39. Thiel, 99-100.

40. *Dial.*, Lectures of 1822, 389-390.

41. Ibid.

42. *Dial.*, 400-401.

43. *Dial.*, Lectures of 1814, 86. "Nur die Idee der absoluten Einheit des Seins, in wiefern darin der Gegensaz von Gedanke und Gegenstand aufgehoben ist, ist kein Begriff mehr."

44. Ibid., 85.

45. Ibid.

46. Ibid., 87.

47. Ibid., 90-91.

48. Ibid., 91.

49. Ibid., 147.

50. Ibid., 150.

51. Thiel, 106-107.

52. *Dial.*, Lectures of 1814, 151. "Dem gemäss nun haben wir auch den trans-cendentalen Grund nur in der relativen Identität des Denkens and Wollens, namlich im Gefühl."

53. *Dial.*, Lectures of 1822, 429.

54. *Dial.*, Lectures of 1814, 151.

55. Ibid.

56. *Dial.*, Lectures of 1818, 151.

57. Ibid., 155.

58. *Dial.*, Lectures of 1822, 429.

59. *Dial.*, Lectures of 1818, 154.

60. *Dial.*, Lectures of 1822, 429.

61. *Dial.*, Lectures of 1814, 151-152.

62. *Dial.*, Lectures of 1818, 153.

63. Schleiermacher hints here of an understanding of the concrete similiar to that of Hartshorne. In concrete experience no distinction is possible. The idea must be abstacted from the concrete before a distinction can be seen and evaluated.

IX

EINIGE GESICHTSPUNKTE ZUR PROBLEMATIK DER DENKGRENZE IN DEN VERSCHIEDENEN ENTWÜRFEN DER DIALEKTIK SCHLEIERMACHERS

Peter Weiß

1. Literaturbefund

Wenige Arbeiten widmen sich dem Problem. Jonas hat gemessen an seiner sonstigen, der Edition angepaßten Kommentierung, relativ ausführlich die Konstellation der Denkgrenze innerhalb der Dialektik behandelt.[1] Seine Anmerkungen zählen weiterhin zu den bemerkenswertesten Erkenntnissen in diesem Bereich.

Georg Weißenborn geht in seiner Darstellung und Kritik der Schleiermacherschen Dialektik überhaupt nicht auf die Denkgrenze ein.[2] Bei Bruno Weiß finden sich wenige Hinweise. Allerdings erklärt er, daß "diese Grenzen kein Denken mehr sind", sondern "die transcendentalen Wurzeln alles Denkens".[3]

Ungenau und fehlerhaft erwähnt Georg Wehrung die Denkgrenze. Er hält den Begriff für "zweideutig" und schillernd.[4]

Die wenigen Untersuchungen zur Dialektik seit dem Anfang der 50iger Jahre sehen zwar das Problem, geben es fast alle in seinen Grundzügen wieder, aber behandeln es als unwesentlich. So bezeichnet Karl Pohl die Grenzen in Schleiermachers Dialektik als "formale Regulative".[5] Rothert sieht in der Grenze nur den Ausdruck der "Individualität".[6] Auch Marlin E. Miller beläßt es nur bei Andeutungen in seiner ansonsten tiefgründigen Erörterung der Dialektik.[7] So, wie Robert Stalders ausgezeichnete Arbeit über die Grundlinien der Theologie Schleiermachers fast unbeachtet blieb, so auch dessen Einsicht, daß "die Grenzformeln des

Denkens und Wollens, wie sie Schleiermacher in der Dialektik ableitet . . .
den Weg zum Glauben, zur Theologie frei" legen.[8]

Die eigentlich erste umfassende Darstellung der Grenzproblematik
bei Schleiermacher geschieht durch Falk Wagner. Nur, so, wie, allgemein
geurteit, er den Zugang zur Dialektik nicht erstellt, sondern verstellt,
geschieht es auch bei seiner Erörterung der Grenze. Sicher steht diese
Arbeit in der Tradition der Hegelkritik an Schleiermacher, durchaus
vergleichbar mit der Ablehnung der Werke Schleiermachers durch Chr.F.
Baur. Deshalb sollte es von allen, die vom Schaffen Schleiermachers
gefangen gehalten werden, als Korrektiv herangezogen werden. Nur
Wagners Darstellung der Grenze vernachlässigt bei aller korrekten Wiedergabe Schleiermachers Intention.[9]

H.R. Reuter, der Wagners Interpretation scharfsinnig widerlegt,
widmet sich angemessen der Darstellung der Grenze. Er erkennt, daß "die
Näherbestimmung der Grenze" bei Schleiermacher der Idee entsprach, "auf
die die Vernunft als Organ des Vernehmens gekommen ist, und zwar des
Vernehmens der elementaren Einheit des Satzes".[10]

Manfred Frank, dessen Untersuchung zur Textstrukturierung bei
Schleiermacher zwei Jahre vorher erschien, sieht die Grenze in der Dialektik
bei dem Versuch, Verstehen zu erlangen, nur als Ausdruck der Grenze
unserer Existenz an.[11]

Udo Kliebisch folgt weitgehenst der Interpretation Wagners. Er wirft
Schleiermacher vor, daß dieser "die gefundenen Grenzbestimmungen zu
Unrecht als die Grenzen des Denkens selbst ausgibt".[12]

Ulrich Barth's schwierige und mir rätselhafte Untersuchung geht nur
einmal auf den Begriff Grenze ein. Für ihn gibt es bei Schleiermacher
offensichtlich nur den "Grenzbegriff des reinen Seins."[13] Erst die Arbeit von
Michael Eckert scheint den Durchbruch bei der Interpretaion und der
Erforschung der Grenzproblematik bei Schleiermacher zu bringen". Es ist
nach meiner Meinung die bisher einzige Untersuchung, die aus der
Darstellung der Grenze die Konsequenz für das theologisch-philosophische
System Schleiermachers in dessen Kern, der Setzung des religiösen Gefühls,
ableitet und dabei die Bedeutung der Denkgrenze und der Grenzformeln des
Denkens erkennt.[14]

2. Der Befund.

"Die Denkgrenzen sind die allgemeinen Bedingungen der Wahrheit". Dieser bemerkenswerte Satz findet sich im zweiten "technischen" Teil der Dialektik an der Stelle, an der die Theorie der Urteilsbildung entwickelt wird.[15] Er ist der Ausgabe der Dialektik entnommen, die Odebrecht herausgegeben hat. Er stammt also aus einer Vorlesungsnachschrift. Es darf nicht unbeachtet bleiben, daß die vorliegenden Texte zur Dialektik eine unterschiedliche Wertigkeit. besitzen. Entwürfe, Randnotizen, Anmerkungen und Ausführungen von Schleiermachers Hand sind sicher gewichtiger als Vorlesungsnachschriften. Außerdem wird zu wenig bedacht, daß Odebrecht an Hand der ihm vorliegenden Nachschriften "das Wagnis einer Rekonstruktion unternommen" hat.[16] In Odebrechts Ausgabe tritt das Wort Grenze zudem in allen seinen Kombinationen gehäuft auf, bei weitem mehr als in den anderen Textquellen. Sollte der Satz von Schleiermacher so in der Vorlesung im Jahre 1822 formuliert worden sein, dann hätte, abgesehen von der Tragweite der Aussage, die Denkgrenze innerhalb der Dialektik und folgerichtig auch im theologisch-philosophischen System Schleiermacher eine derart bedeutende Funktion, daß man deren Konsequenz ausreichender als es bisher erfolgt ist, untersuchen sollte.

Welche Vorstellungen verbindet Schleiermacher mit dem Wort Grenze und wann und mit welcher Absicht kombiniert er das Denken mit der Grenze? Ein knapper Überblick in der Form von Gesichtspunkten soll einige vorhandene Textstellen beleuchten und soll helfen, die Problematik zu erhellen.

2.1. Die Endlichkeit des Denkens (Entwurf A).

Die erste Erwähnung des Wortes Grenze findet sich in den Belegen zu der ersten Vorlesung Schleiermachers über Dialektik aus dem Jahre 1811. Außer dem Text, den Jonas unter dem Buchstaben A wiedergegeben hat[17], verfügen wir über die Studienausgabe zur Dialektik von 1811, herausgegeben von Andreas Arndt, in der die Nachschrift von August Twesten und dessen

Ausarbeitung zur 1. - 11. Vorlesungsstunde enthalten sind.[18] In der 10. und
11. Stunde, wie Arndt belegen kann, entfaltet Schleiermacher vier Formen
der Grenze. Für Begriff und Urteil setzt Schleiermacher jeweils eine obere
und eine untere Grenze als gegeben. Für den Begriff ergibt sich nach oben
die Grenze der "Identität des Wissens und Seins", nach unten, die der
"unendlichen Mannigfaltigkeit" von Urteilen. Für das Urteil ist die obere
Grenze "das absolute Subject", von dem nichts mehr "prädiziert werden
kann". Die untere Grenze ist "die absolute Gemeinschaftlichkeit alles
Seins".[19] Diese formale vierfache Setzung der Grenze läßt sich letztlich auf
zwei Grenzen zurückführen, einmal nach oben auf die Identität alles Seins,
in dem alles gewollte Wissen aufgeht, auch beschreibbar mit der Formel vom
absoluten Subjekt und zum anderen stellt sich nach unten die Grenze der
absoluten Gemeinschaftlichkeit oder der unendlichen Mannigfaltigkeit dem
Denken entgegen. In Varianten behält Schleiermacher bei allen folgenden
Dialektikvorlesungen diese Setzung bei.

Es hat nur den Anschein, als bewege sich Schleiermacher bei diesen
ersten Festlegungen über die Funktionsweise von Begriff und Urteil im
ausschließlich formallogischen Bereich. Ab der 7. Stunde stellt er seine
Ausführungen unter die Überschrift "Transcendentaler Theil".[20] Begriff und
Urteil, die Formen unter denen Denken allein möglich wird und Gedachtes
verknüpft werden kann, sind für Schleiermacher als die formalen
Funktionsträger des Wissen-Wollenden-Denkenden ebenso transzendent-
transzendental, d.h. in ihrem Wesen unerkannt, wie der Ursprung und das
Ziel des Denkens, Wollens und Wissens überhaupt. Die wechselseitige
Ersetzung von transzendent und transzendental soll nicht befremden. Nach
meiner Auffassung sind beide im Sinne Schleiermachers austauschbar, weil
das Denken, das er sucht, "über jede mögliche bestimmte Erfahrung und
jedes mögliche bestimmte Denken hinaus(geht)."[21] Zahlreiche Stellen.
innerhalb der Dialektik belegen außerdem, daß Schleiermacher sehr wohl
die Festlegungen Kants zum exakten Gebrauch der Wörter transzentent und
transzendental bekannt waren.[22]

Der Entwurf von 1811 ist in der Bewertung umstritten. Keineswegs ist
er ein erster mißglückter Versuch voller Mängel und Ungenauigkeiten, wie.
Kritiker Schleiermacher nachweisen wollen.[23] Als Schleiermacher im Jahre

1811 zum ersten Mal eine Vorlesung über spekulative Philosophie hält, steht kein Anfänger auf dem Katheder. Die Problemstellung der Dialektik, der Versuch, die transzendentale Aufgabe lösen zu wollen, ist in ihren Grundzügen klar erkennbar. Dialektik bleibt für Schleiermacher zeitlebens wie er 1811 wohl in der Vorlesung formuliert hat "die vollständige Analyse der Idee des Wissens"[24] und die unter "Prinzipien" gestellte "Kunst zu philosophieren".[25]

Außer in seiner verbalen Funktion findet sich der terminus der Grenze nur einmal in diesem Manuskript. Die von Arndt herausgegebene Vorlesungsnachschrift von Twesten weist den Begriff nicht aus. Allerdings steht die Formulierung Grenze in einem gewichtigen Zusammenhang. "So bestimmt die Idee der Welt auch die Grenze unseres Wissens. Wir sind an die Erde gebunden. Alle Operationen des Denkens, auch das ganze System der Begriffsbildung muß darin gegründet sein."[26] Die tragische Endlichkeit menschlichen Seins behindert die Seinserkundung. Wir sind an die Erde gebunden, d.h. wir sind in einem endlichen begrenzten Denken befangen. Unsere Versuche, Wissen zu erringen, es streitfrei zu übermitteln, sind Bedingungen unterworfen, die hemmend den Denkprozeß begleiten. Dieser Gesichtspunkt darf bereits jetzt festgehalten werden, wir müssen in Grenzen denken. Unsere Menschlichkeit bedingt diese Tatsache. So nachteilig diese Konsequenz für die Aufgabe der Philosophie erscheinen mag, so vorteilhaft ist sie für diejenigen, die sich dem Zugriff totalitärer Ideologien entziehen wollen. Die schwer kontrollierbaren reinen Geist-Theorien, wie sie Fichte und Hegel im Umkreis Schleiermachers konstruiert haben oder die späteren reinen Materie-Lehren entsprechen nicht der Seinsverfassung des Menschen. Das In-Grenzen-denken-müssen trägt der Endlichkeit unseres Daseins Rechung.

2.2. Der transzendent-transzendentale Ursprung des Wissens.

In Schleiermachers Manuskript von 1814, das Jonas zu Recht zur Grundlage aller Bemühungen erhob, um Schleiermachers Dialektik zu verstehen und das bis zum Erscheinen einer kritischen Neuauflage der Dialektik im Rahmen der "Kritischen Gesamtausgabe" auch Grundlage und

Rahmenbedingung für die Heranziehung der anderen hellen sein sollte, tritt die Formulierung der Grenze relative spät auf. Erst im #135 findet sich die Formulierung zum ersten Mal. Bei der Erklärung des höchsten Gegensatzes bestimmt Schleiermacher diesen als "die Grenze des transcendentalen und immanenten".[27] Ab dem #147 im Bereich der transzendent-transzendentalen Erkundung über das Wesen des Begriffs und des Urteils finden sich die Grenzbestimmungen in ähnlicher Form wieder, nahezu so, wie sie Schleiermacher in der 10. und 11. Vorlesungsstunde im Jahre 1811 in ihren Grundzügen erstellt hat, wohlgemerkt nur in der Kombination von Begriffs- und Urteilsgrenzen. Schleiermacher ist bemüht, die Beziehung dieser beiden Wissensformen von Begriff und Urteil im Blick auf deren transzendenten Ursprung ersichtlich werden zu lassen. Noch nicht geklärt ist die wechselseitige Austauschbarkeit der Grenzen und das Ineinandergehen der beiden Wissensformen, ihre jeweilige Ergänzung und Austauschbarkeit beim Erfassen des Seins. Eines ist aber bereits deutlich geworden, die Konstruktion des Wissens kann aus dem Rahmen, den ihr Begriff und Urteil setzen, nicht heraus. Ein wichtiger Gesichtspunkt muß im Zusammenhang der Grenzbestimmungen von Begriff und Urteil im Manuskript von 1814 festgehalten werden. Die Behauptung von der Identität des Seins, die trotz der unterschiedlichen Funktion der Wissensformen von Schleiermacher getroffen wird, die sich 1811 nur andeutete, stützt sich auf die Erkenntnis von der Begrenzung von Begriff und Urteil. In einer Randbemerkung zum #174a, bei der ich mir nicht sicher bin, ob sie aus dem Jahre 1814 stammt, schreibt Schleiermacher: "Weil beides Wissen dasselbe ist, sind auch beide Grenzen dasselbe".[28] Gemeint ist von ihm einmal das absolute Subjekt und zum anderen die absolute Einheit des Seins. Nun geht aber aus den Ausführungen Schleiermachers von 1814 im #163 nur hervor, daß "das Gebiet des Urtheils . . . auf der einen Seite durch das Sezen eines absoluten Subjectes" "begrenzt" wird.[29] Die absolute Einheit des Seins wird nicht benannt. Weshalb wird sie von Schleiermacher behauptet? Wende ich den Satz der Randbemerkung und formuliere in der Umkehrung, weil beide Grenzen im oberen Bereich dasselbe sind, ist auch beides Wissen dasselbe, dann erhalte ich zuerst das eigenartig anmutende Ergebnis, daß sich trotz der Teilung des Seins nach der Grenzbestimmung des Urteils nach oben in das absolute Subjekt und nach unten in "die unerschöpfliche Mannigfaltigkeit des Wahrnehmbaren" die absolute Einheit des Seins herausstellt.[30] Gestützt wird diese Festlegung durch die von Jonas wiedergegebenen Auszüge aus der Dialektikvorlesung von 1818, die er kommentierend zu dem Schleiermacher-manuskript von 1814 unter den Text stellt.

2.2.1. Die Transzendenz des Seins.

Zugegeben, es ist schwierig, die jeweilige Beziehung zu erkennen, auf die Jonas mit dieser Kommentierung abzielt. Zum Befund der Grenze sind diese Einfügungen von Bedeutung. Sie erhärten die Hypothese, daß die Grenzbestimmungen von Begriff und Urteil allein der Erkundung des transzendent-transzendentalen Ursprungs des Wissens dienen. Auch an dieser Stelle kann nur auf weniges hingewiesen werden. Auf der Seite in der Jonasausgabe, auf der sich die Randbemerkung findet, bringt Jonas den Vorlesungstext von 1818 als Erläuterung. Darin heißt es: "Das Wissen nämlich ist nur ein Wissen vermöge seiner Uebereinstimmung mit dem Sein, und wir sagen, Es ist dasselbe Sein, was jezt unter der Form des Begriffs jezt unter der Form des Urtheils gedacht ist. Was an der Grenze des Begriffs ist, ist seiner Form nach kein Begriff mehr, weil wir keine Mannigfaltigkeit von Merkmalen davon aufstellen können."[31] Einige Zeilen weiter heißt es: "Am Ende (hier könnte im Sinne der Ausführungen statt Ende das Wort Grenze eingesetzt werden) des Urtheils ... finden wir das absolute Subject, von dem nichts mehr prädicirt werden kann." Schleiermachers Schlußfolgerung; "So fehlt die Form des Urtheils."[32] Die Form, oder wie Schleiermacher ansonsten in der Dialektik formuliert, die formale Seite des Wissens scheitert in ihrer Zielsetzung. Begriff und Urteil stoßen bei ihrem Bemühen, streitfreies Wissen erstellen zu wollen, an eine undurchdringliche Grenze. Übrig bleibt für Schleiermacher nur das Sein als Inhalt des Wissens, durchaus als Folge der Begriffs- und Urteiloperationen des Denkens in seiner Grenzsetzung gesehen. Was für Schleiermacher in den Blick kommt, ist ein Sein, von dem weder ein Begriff noch ein Urteil erstellt werden kann, das aber beiden Wissensformen stets zu Grunde liegt und das Denken in Gang bringt.

3. Die Einheit von Denken und Sein.

Ab dem Jahre 1822 finden sich in den Bemerkungen von Schleiermachers Hand zu seiner Vorlesung, von Jonas als Beilage C abgedruckt und in der Ausgabe von Odebrecht nach der Terminierung der Vorlesungsnachschriften unter den Text gestellt, die Termini Grenze in der Kombination von Begriffs-, Urteils- , Vorstellungs- und Gedankengrenze in dichter Folge. Die Operationen im transzendent-transzendentalem Bereich, die mit Hilfe der Einführung der Grenzsetzung erfolgen, basieren ohne wesentliche Korrektur auf den Ergebnissen der vorangegangenen drei Vorlesungen. Eine Variante der Grenzsetzung tritt ab dem Jahre 1822 beherrschend hervor. In seinen Bemerkungen zur Vorlesung verwendet Schleiermacher ab XXXV zum ersten Mal die Formulierung der Denkgrenze.[33] Sie wird zur Leitformulierung, um sowohl die Begriffs als auch die Urteilsgrenzen zu kennzeichnen. Dem Leser der Odebrechtausgabe ist diese Formulierung vor allem durch die Überschriften vertraut.[34] Was bezweckt Schleiermacher mit dieser Wortkombination? Will er den Begriff der Grenze aus der Bestimmung des Seins herausnehmen? Denn die Assoziation, daß nicht nur unser Denken, sondern das Sein an sich, in Grenzen gesetzt ist, drängt sich zunehmend auf. Ich halte diese Absicht für möglich. Einmal charakterisiert Schleiermacher mit dieser Formulierung präziser als in den Jahren zuvor die menschliche Denkfähigkeit als in Grenzen gesetzt und zum anderen kann er den transzendent-transzendentalen Ursprung der formalen Wissenserstellung durch Begriff und Urteil besser aufzeigen. Um die Transzendenz der formalen Wissensformen von Begriff und Urteil noch deutlicher hervorzuheben führt Schleiermacher die negative Vorstellung der Denkgrenze ein. So verstanden ist sie immer nur das dem wirklichen Denken "Vorangehende".[35] Nach der Vorlesungsnachschrift von 1822 stellt Schleiermacher angesichts dieser Schwierigkeit die Frage "nach dem Wert unserer Denkgrenzen" im Hinblick darauf, "inwiefern ihnen etwas im Sein entspricht". Ganz im Sinn des identitäts-philosophischen System fällt Schleiermachers Antwort positiv aus. Unter den Voraussetzungen "einer Analogie des Zusammenhangs des Seins und Denkens im wirklichen

Denken" und weil "es dasselbe Sein sei, welches das Gedachte ist im Verhältnis des Wissens unter der Form des Urteils", verbunden mit der anderen Voraussetzung, daß "die Grenzen des Denkens unter der Form des Begriffs und des Urteils identisch sind", gelangt Schleiermacher zu dem Resultat, daß dem "wirklichen Sein" ein "Entsprechendes zugrunde Liegendes gesetzt werden" muß und daß "dieses Entsprechende" letztlich "identisch sein" muß.[36] Die Einheit von Denken und Sein und der fortwährende Zugang des Denken-Wollenden zum Wissen bleiben positiv gesetzt. Der Prozeß der Denkbewegung verbleibt trotzt der einen negativen Setzung der Grenze im Positiven. Deutlicher wird diese Denkbewegung angesichts der Denkgrenze bei der Sicht auf die positive Zielstellung, wenn sie als Hinwendung zum Sein, Be- und Ergreifen des Seins verstanden wird. Nachdem Schleiermacher die vorhandenen Formeln für eine mögliche Fassung des transzendenten Grundes, höchste Kraft, Materie, Gott, Freiheit und Notwendigkeit, Vorsehung und Schicksal kritisch diskutiert hat,[37] Formeln, die Odebrecht als erster als "Grenzformeln" tituliert[38], gelangt er nach der Vorlesungsnachschrift von 1822 zu folgendem Ergebnis: "Wir sehen, wie alle unsere Formeln unvollständig waren. Doch haben sie alle einen wahren Gehalt. Das absolute Subjekt, von dem nichts mehr prädiziert werden kann, in seiner Identität mit der absoluten Gemeinschaftlichkeit des Seins, als in jenem absoluten Subjekt eingeschlossen, und ebenso die höchste Kraft, wovon das ganze System der Kräfte die natürlichen Erscheinungen sind – , diese Formeln enthalten alle die Idee der Welt, denn sie sprechen die Totalität des Seins aus. Wenn wir sagen: Wir kommen an der Grenze des Denkens auf die Vorstellung von einem absoluten Subjekt, so heißt das: die Idee der Welt ist die Grenze unseres wirklichen Denkens, der transzendente Grund liegt außerhalb dieser Grenze. Und so haben wir an jenen Ausdrücken nur einen Weg, vom wirklichen Denken aus dorthin zu kommen."[39] Einer der Wege ist die Approximation, das sich dem Sein und damit dem Wissen Annähern. Möglich wird dieser Weg, wenn er als Philosophieren und als Theologisieren, als ein lebendiger Prozeß der Seinsaneignung verstanden wird, aber nur unter der durch die Denkgrenze erwiesenen strikten Voraussetzung, daß die Idee der Welt, so, wie die Idee der Gottheit dem Wissen nicht zugänglich ist. Sie bleiben beide transzendent. So gesehen ist die Tiefe des einzelnen Satzes, daß "die Denkgrenzen . . . die allgemeinen Bedingungen der Wahrheit" sind[40], den ich an den Anfang setzte, einsehbar.

Schleiermacher vollzog mit der Erörterung der Denkgrenze keinen methodischen Trick oder eine formallogische Spielerei, er wollte das Denken in seiner Struktur, die ein der Seinsverhaftung der Endlichkeit entspricht, die nur dem Menschen eigen ist, auffinden. Weiter einsichtig wird dieser Gesichtspunkt an einer der Bemerkungen Schleiermachers unter LIV. Eingeleitet wird sie mit der Feststellung "Nachdem wir nun die Grenze gefunden (haben) für das Bestreben in dem Ausdruck des transzendenten Grundes auch das ihm als Sein entsprechende auszudrücken, so kommen wir nun zurück zu der Identität der transzendentalen und formalen Seite und fragen, wie sich beide Werte in dieser Hinsicht verhalten".[41] Unter dem Verweis, daß "die Formeln, welche den terminus a quo ausdrücken, . . . auf die Idee der Welt bezogen, rein negativ" sind, betont Schleiermacher den Wert der Idee der Welt unter der Formel des terminus ad quem, ohne dabei die Idee der Gottheit, die er mit der Formel a quo fixiert, in ihrer Funktion für die approximative Wissenserstellung aus den Augen zu verlieren. Beide, terminus a quo und terminus ad quem, lassen sich verknüpfen und bewegen die Approximation. Schleiermacher schreibt: ". . . jedes wirkliche Denken, sofern es durch Approximation der Idee des Wissens entspricht, ist ein Teil der Welt, wenngleich diese niemals vollständig wird; sie wird aber doch durch jedes Hinzufügen mehr ausgefüllt."[42] Unverzichtbar bei der approximativen Erreichung von Wissen ist die Idee der Gottheit. Sicher, sie steht, wie Schleiermacher schreibt, "in gar keinem Verhältnis . . . zum Fortschreiten, sondern nur zu jedem einzelnen Denken an und für sich", aber kein wirkliches Denken kann zustande kommen, ohne daß es durch den terminus a quo, also letztlich durch Gott, bewegt wird.[43]

2.4. Denkgrenze – Seinsgrenze

Die Niederschrift Schleiermachers zu seinem Vorlesungsentwurf von 1822 enthält eine wichtige vertiefende Erörterung zu der Problematik, inwieweit das religiöse Gefühl den transzendenten Grund vermitteln kann.

Die Funktion der Denkgrenze bedenkt Schleiermacher so, daß die Möglichkeit eine ihr entsprechenden Seinsgrenze stärker in's Auge gefaßt wird als in den vorangegangenen Jahren. In der 51. Stunde der Dialektikvorlesung gelangt Schleiermacher zu seinen Einsichten über die Struktur des Selbstbewußtseins und dessen Fähigkeit, als denkend-wollendes und wollend-denkendes Sein mit Hilfe des Gefühls Unmittelbarkeit zu haben. "Unmittelbares Selbstbewußtsein = Gefühl", diese These scheint die Lösung der transzendentalen Aufgabe, die sich Schleiermacher gestellt hat, zu erbringen.[44] An dieser Stelle der Dialektik faßt Schleiermacher den transzendenten Grund. Es ist der Bereich einer Grenzüberschreitung. Nicht Begriff und Urteil, deren Begrenztheit Schleiermacher aufgewiesen hat, können das Transzendente formal und transzendental darstellen, sondern nur das religiöse Gefühl. "Das religiöse Gefühl als Repräsentation des transzendenten Grundes"[45], – eine Randbemerkung, die bei Jonas fehlt und Odebrecht im Manuskript liest – , erklärt die "transzendente Bestimmtheit des Selbstbewußtseins".[46] Im Zusammenhang seiner Ausführungen setzt Schleiermacher den transzendenten Grund und das "höchste Wesen", also Gott gleich.[47] Wie nun erscheint dieser transzendente Grund oder das höchste Wesen im Selbstbewußtsein des Menschen? An diesem Punkt seiner Erörterung nimmt Schleiermacher seine Hypothese vom Übergang zur Hilfe. Im Übergang vom Denken zu Wollen und umgekehrt "finden wir auch das Gefühl als beständig jeden Moment, sei er nun vorherrschend denkend oder wollend, immer begleitend".[48] In der Vorlesungsnachschrift, die Odebrecht redaktionell bearbeitet hat, wird dieses Begleiten als "zeitlos" erklärt. "Der transzendente Grund . . . begleitet das wirkliche Denken auf zeitlose Weise" und "begleitet . . . auch das wirkliche Sein auf eine zeitlose Weise als unmittelbares Selbstbewußtsein". Für Schleiermacher bedeutet "auf zeitlose Weise", daß "dieses Begleiten nicht in der Zeit erscheinen und daher nicht wahrgenommen, also auch nicht nachgewiesen werden" kann. Innerhalb der "organischen Funktion", die diesem Erkenntnisakt beibehalten bleibt, "soll kein Korrelat" auffindbar sein.[49] Abgesehen davon, ob es dem Denkenden überhaupt möglich ist, einen Denkakt in irgendeiner Weise außerhalb der Zeit, also zeitlos zu vollziehen, muß im Sinn Schleiermachers festgehalten werden, daß in einem bestimmten Bereich des Bewußtseins sich diese

Erfahrung der Transzendenz unabhängig von der Begrenztheit der
Wissensformen von Begriff und Urteil niederschlägt. Eine weitere Erörterung dieser Hypothese muß unterbleiben, Verwiesen sei nur auf die
umfassende Diskussion des Übergangs in der Arbeit von Marlin E. Miller.[50]
Wichtig zur Problematik der Denkgrenze ist in diesem Zusammenhang die
Faktizität, daß in allen Entwürfen und Nachschrifen vor 1828 die Relation
zwischen Denkgrenze und Grenzüberschreitung unerwähnt bleibt. Auch die
nur bei Jonas noch auffindbare Vorlesungsnachschrift von 1818 kennt an
dieser Stelle nicht die Formulierung der Denkgrenze, auch wenn diese
sinngemäß angedeutet wird.[51]

Worin besteht die Bedeutung der Niederschrift von 1822? Es scheint
auf dem ersten Blick so, als relativiere Schleiermacher seine getroffenen
Einsichten von 1814 und 1818, den transzendenten Grund im religiösen
Gefühl zu haben. Tatsächlich vertieft er die Begründung, indem er
speculativ-mystische Erwägungen abwehrt. Das in Funktion getretene
religiöse Gefühl, das den transzedenten Grund signalisiert, ist kein elitäres
Wissen. Nüchtern verweist Schleiermacher auf die "ursprüngliche Gestalt"
seiner Einsicht, "daß das die Wahrheit des Denkens und die Realität des
Wollens bedingende außer unserer Selbstthätigkeit gesezt ist."[52] Das
denkend-wollende und wollend-denkende Selbstbewußtsein hat seinen
Ursprung in Gott. Letztlich kann Gott "als das absolute Denkend-wollen und
Wollend-denken gesezt" werden.[53] Der Problematik dieser Festlegung ist
sich Schleiermacher durchaus bewußt. Gott in dieser Weise auszusagen, um
den Durchbruch zum transzendenten Grund zu veranschaulichen, ist ein
Ausdruck des Anthropodeisirens. Schleiermacher verbleibt im Rahmen der
von ihm von Anfang an getroffenen Gottesbestimmung.[54] Nach dem
Entwurf von 1814 ist Gott als Begriff ein Schema, "die Anschauung Gottes
wird nie wirklich vollzogen.[55] Diese Aussage Schleiermachers verweist auf
die dem endlichen Bewußtsein des Menschen auferlegten Grenzen. Das
vollzogene Bewußtsein von Gott ist "immer an einem anderen", d.h. das
Unmittelbare der Transzendenz wird mittelbar in den Grenzen der
endlichen Vernunft sichtbar.[56] Die Grenzformel für den transzendenten
Grund, damit für Gott, wie Schicksal und Vorsehung, belegen die Mittel-
barkeit endlich geprägter Vorstellungshilfen.[57] In der Randschrift von 1828

erfolgt eine Präzisierung der zentralen Festlegungen Schleiermachers über die grenzüberschreitende Funktion des religiösen Gefühls. Bei seinem Bemühen spekulatives oder ethisches Streben nach Unmittelbarkeit "in unseren Grenzen zu halten",[58] fordert Schleiermacher die Beachtung einer Relation.

Gesehen werden muß, "wie sich nun das gemeinsame Resultat (gemeint ist von Schleiermacher das Haben des transzendenten Grundes im religiösen Gefühl) zu demjenigen verhält, was im Sein unsern Denkgrenzen entspricht".[59] Schleiermacher ventiliert in diesem Zusammenhang die beiden Ideen von Gott und Welt. Im Blick auf die "Totalität der Erscheinungen", die "in dem Complexus der festen Formen des Seins" aufgeht, die wir trotz der Grenzen von Begriff und Urteil denken können, wird die Idee der Welt konstruiert. Sie ist "die Identität des absoluten Subjects und der absoluten Gemeinschaftlichkeit des Seins". Bei dieser für ihn zwingenden Setzung stellt Schleiermacher eine Identität der Denkgrenze und der Welt in Bezug auf die Transzendenz fest. Es ist die "Aufgabe" des Menschen, Welt "zu denken". In diesem Prozeß ist er der Welt immer hinterher. Sie bleibt für ihn Idee. Denn ihr Sein ist durch die Kopplung an das absolute transzendente Subjekt Gottes ein unendliches. Schleiermacher formuliert, daß sie "immer nur wird". Das werdende Sein der Welt wird allein von dem transzendenten Sein her letztlich ein wirkliches. Im unmittelbaren Selbst-bewußtsein besitzt menschliches Sein durch das religiöse Gefühl, dann, wenn es durch den konsequenten Gebrauch der Wissensformen von Begriff und Urteil an die Denkgrenze herangeführt worden ist, einen "Theil an dem nicht wirklichen Denken", ähnlich wie die "Welt an dem transcendenten Sein".[60] Der Durchbruch zur Transzendenz, die mögliche vollziehbare Grenzüberschreitung, bleibt aber in den wirklichen denkbaren, also "anthropoeidische"[61], Begriffen und Urteilen gebunden.

So verstehe ich die komplizierte Erläuterung der Relation, die Schleiermacher an das Ende seiner Niederschrift zur 51. Stunde setzt, sicher von ihm zu seiner eigenen Selbstverständigung geschrieben und nur im Zusammenhang mit seinen anderen, in den vorangegangenen Jahren in der gleichen Stunde getroffenen Festlegungen verstehbar: "Wie nun das transcendente und die Denkgrenze am nächsten verwandt sind: so ist also die Aufgabe das Verhältniß zwischen Gott und Welt zu bestimmen so, daß die Reduction des anthropoeidischen aufgegeben bleibt ohne daß der Ausdrukk für das transcendente aufgelöst Werde. *Die Welt ist nicht ohne Gott, und Gott nicht ohne die Welt.*"[62] Es erübrigt sich, darauf zu verweisen, daß mit dieser Formulierung jeder Vorwurf des Pantheismus gegenüber Schleiermacher gegenstandslos wird. Für unsere Aufgabe, die Funktion der Denkgrenze im System Schleiermachers zu erhellen, ergibt sich eine andere wesentlichere Einsicht, der Durchbruch zur Grenzüberschreitung in der Funktion des religiösen Gefühls, das von Gott her im Selbstbewußtsein gesetzt wird, eröffnet eine beispiellose Energie zum Denken, die in der Hinwendung zur Welt, als einer Werdenden und damit zu Gestaltenden in der umfassenden Ethik Schleiermachers Raum gewinnt.

2.5. Werdendes Sein.

Ohne Zweifel ist Halpern's Ausgabe der Dialektik vom Jahre 1903 ein mißglückter Versuch. Sie ist nicht, wie Halpern meint, "eine vollständige, geschlossene Gestalt der Dialektik in ihrer reifsten Ausbildung".[63] Auch seiner Beurteilung der einzelnen Entwürfe mit ihrer jeweiligen Wertschätzung muß widersprochen werden. Seiner Bewertung der Zettelnotizen Schleiermachers aus dem Vorlesungsjahr 1831 sollte allerdings wieder mehr Beachtung geschenkt werden. Tatsächlich finden sich in den Aufzeichnungen Schleiermachers und in den von Jonas edierten Vorlesungsnachschriften Aussagen, die verdichtet wesentliche Einsichten aus den vorangegangenen Vorlesungen wiederholen und vertiefen.[64]

So dominiert in "E" die These vom "werdenden Wissen".[65] Gestützt wird diese durch Schleiermacher weiterentwickelte Einsicht in die Funktion der Denkgrenze. Bereits im Jahre 1814 sah Schleiermacher, daß der "transcendente Begriff" und das "transcendente Urtheil dasselbe sind".[66] Angedeutet ist innerhalb seiner Begriffs- und Urteilslehre bereits das Ineinanderübergehen beider Grenzen.[67] Begriff und Urteil an die Grenze ihrer Denkmöglichkeit geführt, gehen ineinander über, so daß auch Begriffsgrenze und Urteilsgrenze "dasselbe" sind. Zettelnotiz und

Vorlesungsnachschrift aus dem Jahre 1831 belegen diese Prazisierung.[68] Sicher ist "E" ein Torso. Nur Konturen der möglichen Gestaltung können erkannt werden. Unter Berücksichtigung dieser Einsicht sollte aber die von Schleiermacher erst in diesem Jahr entwickelte Folgerung vom "Uebergang", der sowohl "dem wissen-wollenden Denken" als auch dem "transcendenten Grunde" wie Schleiermacher formuliert "zum Grunde liegt" eingehender beleuchtet werden. Sie dient ihm als ein weiterer Beweis für seine Theorie vom werdenden Wissen. Bereits Jonas hatte im Textbereich von dem Entwurf des Jahres 1814 in einer Anmerkung auf diese Besonderheit von "E" verwiesen.[69]

Zum Problem der Denkgrenze gilt festzuhalten, daß deren tragende Bedeutung bei der Erstellung von Wissen für Schleiermacher genau so wichtig ist, wie deren Rolle bei der Hinführung zu grenzüberschreitenden Funktion des religiösen Gefühls. Unter der Voraussetzung, daß "Begriff und Urtheil die einzigen Formen des werdenden Wissens sind" und deren Grenzen letztlich "dieselben" sind, behauptet Schleiermacher, daß diese Grenzen des Denkens auch "die des werdenden Wissens überhaupt" sind.[70] Keineswegs darf daraus der Schluß gezogen werden, als blockiere Schleiermacher den Prozeß der Wissenserstellung. Im Gegenteil, im Blick auf die ständig sich entgegenstellende Denkgrenze bei jedem "Ausgangs- und jede(m) Endpunkt" des werdenden Wissens, verweist Schleiermacher auf "die Bildungs-regeln der Denkacte" beider Formen der Wissens-produktion von Begriff und Urteil. Durch die Denkgrenze entstehen gleichsam im Rückstoß-effekt "Regeln der Production" für das werdende Wissen. Diese von Schleiermacher im technischen oder formalen zweiten Teil der Dialektik 1831 notierten Einsichten entfaltet er offentsichtlich intensiv in der Vorlesung des gleichen Jahres. Das Rudiment dieser Vorlesung, von Jonas als Anmerkung unter die Notizen gesetzt, belegt, daß Schleiermacher aus der Behauptung der Denkgrenze im Prozeß des werdenden Wissens die "Construction oder Production des einzelnen Wissens" als ein "Zurükk- und Fortschreiten" begreift, also nicht Stagnation, die sich aus dem ständigen Zurück aus der erfahrenen Grenze des Denkens ergeben könnten, sondern Fortschreiten mit einem ständig neuen Anlaufnehmen, ergibt sich für Schleiermacher aus der Existenz der Denkgrenze.[71] In der im Jahre 1831

von ihm entfalteten Theorie der Begriffsbildung wird daher sehr klar auf die
nicht Fixierbarkeit der Begriffe Wert gelegt, d.h. aber nichts anderes, als eine
ständige Korrektur von bereits erreichtem Wissen und eine stete Weiter-
entwicklung von gesichertem Wissen. Wieder tritt im Komplex dieser
Aussagen der Vorlesung der Begriff der Denkgrenze auf. Sie ist es, die dieses
Werden und Weiterentwickeln der Wissenskonstruktion im Bereich der von
Schleiermacher so formulierten Heuristik und Architektonik in Gang hält.[72]
Nur angedeutet werden kann, daß vor allem in "E" in dem Komplex der 58.
Stunde, belehrt von der Erfahrung der Denkgrenze, Schleiermacher die wohl
klarsten Aussagen über die Rolle des Irrtums bei der Erstellung von Wissen
trifft.[73]

3. Schlußbemerkungen.

Diese Skizze, die nur Gesichtspunkte zur Problematik der
Denkgrenze innerhalb Schleiermachers Dialektik aufzeigen wollte, muß
genügen. Sie soll zu einem weiteren Eindringen in das komplizierte
Gedankengebäude der Schleiermacherschen Philosophie ermutigen. Denn es
ist nach wie vor erforderlich, die Interpretation zu betreiben und diese trotz
der noch nicht vorliegenden Ausgabe der Dialektik im Rahmen der
"Kritischen Gesamtausgabe" an Hand der vorhandenen Quellen durchaus im
Sinne Schleiermachers von irgendeinem der Anknüpfungspunkte innerhalb
des Werkes in Gang zu bringen. Die unterschiedliche Beleuchtung eines
Teilkomplexes, wie dem der Denkgrenze, führt in jedem Fall in das Innere
des schwierigen philosophischen Entwurfs. Andere Gewichte werden
spürbar. Bisher für sicher gehaltene Deutungen verlieren an Wertigkeit.
Sicher ist die Dialektik kein verschlossenes Buch mehr, wie es Rothert
formuliert hat.[74] Keineswegs aber sind ihre Untiefen ausgelotet und die
Rätselhaftigkeit vieler ihrer Aussagen entschlüsselt worden. Eine
umfangreiche wissenschaftliche Arbeit, durchaus von verschiedenen nicht
immer zustimmenden Positionen aus, muß noch geleistet werden.
Unsystematisch, wiederum nur als Skizze aufzufassen, soll auf einige
Konsequenzen, die sich aus dem Bedenken der Denkgrenze ergeben,
verwiesen werden.

1. Der Zusammenhang von Dialektik und Hermeneutik bei Schleiermacher gilt als unbestritten. Wie Odebrecht richtig gesehen hat, sind "Hermeneutik und Dialektik . . . polar gekoppelt".[75] Schleiermachers Versuch, den transzendenten Grund zu fassen und sichere Ergebnisse im Gebiet des reinen Denkens erbringen zu wollen, bedingt das Verstehen dieses Versuches und aller schrittweise gewonnene Erkenntnisse. Die Grenze des Verstehens ist für Schleiermacher begleitendes Problem aller hermeneutischen Bemühungen. Auf dem Hintergrund dieser gegebenen Verstehensschwierigkeiten sehe ich das Divinations-Theorem. Sollte die Divination, die Schleiermacher meint, eine vom religiösen Gefühl getragene menschliche Fähigkeit des tieferen und reinen Verstehens sein, die aus der Grenzüberschreitung auf den transzendenten Grund hin, wie es vor allem die Niederschrift von 1822 aufweist, erwächst, dann wäre die Erfahrung der Denkgrenze im Bereich des üblichen Umgangs mit Begriff und Urteil im Prozeß des Verstehens der Ansatz um die Fähigkeit der Divination zu entwickeln. Die Konsequenzen für die Sprachtheorie, vor allem im Reden über Gott, sind unübersehbar.

2. Das Bedenken der Denkgrenze vermittelt die Einsicht in die Struktur der endlichen Vernunft. Eingefügt in eine endliche Welt ist das dieser Endlichkeit unterworfene menschliche Geschöpf zwar in der Lage um diese Endlichkeit zu wissen und den Versuch zu unternehmen, Unendlichkeit zu tangieren, es kann aber nicht mit Hilfe seiner Vernunft eine Wissenstheorie gestalten, die, mit einem Absolutheitsanspruch versehen meint, ein für allemal das ideologische System gefunden zu haben, mit dem die Welt und Gott erkannt und erfaßt werden können. Damit würde eine Immunität gegenüber vorhandenen philosophisch oder theologisch bestimmten Ideologien geschaffen, die zu einem stärkeren Hinterfragen dieser Systeme und letztenendes zu deren Korrektur führen würde. Eine dem Menschen nicht restlos verfügbare Welt; die als Gottes Schöpfung allein diesem gehört, kann nicht mit der Hybris einer grenzenlosen Vernunft beherrscht werden. Die mit Hilfe der Denkgrenze erfolgte Einsicht in die Endlichkeit der Vernunft würde einer extrem rationalistisch-naturwissenschaftlich auf wirtschaftliche Expansion getrimmten Welt ethische Maxime bereitstellen, die in einem Rückgriff auf die Ethik Schleiermachers, die von diesem

geforderte Humanisierung der Natur und Naturalisierung des Humanum zum Wohle der Menschheit voranbringt.

3. Das Bedenken der Denkgrenze führt im Sinne Schleiermachers zu einer Relativierung der Philosophie und der Theologie. Allgemeine Verbindlichkeit oder gar Totalitätsanspruch eines jeweilig auftretenden Systems ist angesichts der Denkgrenze unmöglich. Für Schleiermacher ist der Versuch, in beiden Bereichen allgemein gültiges, streitfreies und damit sicher übertragbares Wissen zu erlangen, unabgeschlossen, d.h. es kann z.b. sowohl notwendig werden, ein vergangenes fast vergessenes Wissen zurückholen zu müssen, als auch ein gegenwärtiges zu verwerfen. Wir unterliegen ständig dem Vergessen von Seinswahrheiten und der Verstrickung in den Irrtum. Unter diesem Aspekt ist Philosophie immer Philosophieren und Theologie Theologisieren. Gerade die letztere sollte angesichts der Denkgrenze, die bei der Erstellung theologischer Sätze mit Hilfe von Begriff und Urteil formal durchaus mit dem Bereich der Philosophie vergleichbar ist, sich darüber im klaren sein, daß die Verbindlichkeit der jeweiligen Theologie gegenüber der Heilswahrheit der Offenbarung Gottes mangelhat bleibt. Der Anspruch der Theologie in einer Zeit bleibt gemessen an der Wirklichkeit und Wahrheit der zeitlosen Offenbarung Gottes in Christo ungenügend. Theologisieren als Folge des vom religiösen Gefühl bestimmten Menschseins hat das Ziel, Glauben so zur Sprache zu bringen, das er mitteilbar wird. Theologisieren ist ein nahezu unendlicher Prozeß, der jede statische, formal gewordene Bekenntnisstruktur verhindert und der Erstellung von Glaubenssätzen jene Dynamik verleiht, die notwendig ist, um in der Geschichte Christus zu verkündigen.

3.1. Für die Dogmatik im herkömmlichen Sinn verstanden, gelangt jedes Aussagen über Gott in einen Grenzbereich. Jede Gotteslehre sollte deshalb stets und ständig ihre Grundfrage bedenken, inwieweit überhaupt gültige Aussagen über Gott möglich sind. Die Leichtfertigkeit vieler theologischer Systeme im Umgang mit dem 1. Artikel, die Banalität frömmelnder Esoterik bei dem Versuch, Gott zur Sprache zu bringen, wäre angesichts der Schleiermacherschen Denkstruktur der Grenze unmöglich. Hier soll wiederum auf den gelungenen Versuch von M. Eckert verwiesen werden, der unter Thematik "Gott – Glauben und Wissen" bei der

Untersuchung der philosophischen Theologie Schleiermachers einem verantwortlichen Reden über Gott Bahn brechen will.

3.2. Für ein Philosophieren im Sinne Schleiermachers ergeben sich Detailprobleme, die innerhalb der Dialektik mit der Bezeichnung der Approximation, der Lehre vom Irrtum und vom Übergang, um nur drei der wichtigsten herauszugreifen, immer im Zusammenhang mit der Denkgrenze dargestellt werden.

3.2.1. Approximation versteht Schleiermacher als die Annäherung an das streitfreie Wissen. Sie gilt für alle Wissensbereiche. Wichtige Untersuchungen zur Dialektik, wie die von Reuter und Wagner verweisen nur auf dieses Problem. Eine ausführliche Diskussion zu dieser Thematik steht noch aus.[76]

3.2.2. Im Zusammenhang mit der Denkgrenze entwickelt Schleiermacher im technisch-formalen Teil der Dialektik Ansätze zu einer Theorie des Irrtums. Deutlich wird dieser Zusammenhang in der Vorlesungsnachschrift von 1831.[77] Die Theorie des Irrtums kann mit Hilfe der aus der Denkgrenze entstandenen Einsichten in die Fähigkeit des Denkens strukturmäßig erfaßt als Kontrolle der Denkergebnisse methodisch entwickelt und zur Wissenschaft ausgebaut werden.

Bisher blieb auch unerörtert, daß die Manuskripte Dilthey's, die Martin Redeker erstmals veröffentlicht hat, immer wieder die Thematik des Irrtums behandeln.[78] In ihnen finden sich wichtige Hinweise über die Entwicklung der Irrtumstheorie bei Schleiermacher ab dem ersten Entwurf zur Dialektik im Jahre 1811. Für Dilthey ist es kennzeichnend, daß gerade identitäts-philosophische Systeme sich dem Problem widmen, "wie der Irrtum entstehe".[79] Soweit unbearbeitete Manuskripte, wie die von Redeker veroffentlichten, einen solchen Schluß zulassen, zeigt sich, daß Dilthey besonders davon beeindruckt war, daß Schleiermacher Irrtum und Wahrheit miteinander in Beziehung gesetzt hat, ". . . , ja der Irrtum ist nur an der Wahrheit, wie das Böse nur am Guten ist".[80]

3.2.3. Unter dem Gesichtspunkt der Denkgrenze würde eine Erörterung der These Schleiermachers vom Übergang zu neuen Einsichten führen. Ist der Übergang tatsächlich eine Grenzüberschreitung oder ein sich Bewegen im Grenzbereich des Denkens? Die Beantwortung dieser Frage, die man bei Miller findet, ist nicht eindeutig. Miller sieht als Ausdruck der symbolisierenden Wirksamkeit der Vernunft im unmittelbaren Selbstbewußtsein den "Übergang von einem zum nächsten zeitlichen Moment des Selbstbewußtseins" als gegeben an.[81] Die interessante Untersuchung Millers ist bisher die einzige umfassende Studie zum Problem des Übergangs. Die weiteren Arbeiten zur Dialektik widmen sich zwar der Problematik, aber mit Ausnahmen von H.R. Reuter erfassen sie nicht die Tiefe der Problemstellung.[82]

Zum Schluß sollte einem möglichen Vorbehalt begegnet werden. Ist es die Aufgabe eines Gemeindepfarrers, denn aus dieser Situation ist die Beschäftigung mit dieser Problematik entstanden, sich, einer kräfte- und zeitraubenden Arbeit zu widmen, die eigentlich außerhalb des Verkündigungsdienstes liegt und vielleicht mehr dem Bereich der Philosophie als dem der Theologie angehört? Die Antwort ist einfach. Die Existenz des Predigers erfordert nahezu täglich, gültige Aussagen über Gott treffen zu müssen. Alles Sagen in diesem Dienst, die Kirche erklärt es als Verkündigen, – ein großes Wort – , geschieht in den Formen von Begriff und Urteil, auch die Sprache des Glaubens kann davon nicht absehen. So, wie Schleiermacher Philosophie als Philosophieren verstand, d.h. nach den Prinzipien der Dialektik als ein Unterwegsseins zum Wissen, so verstehe ich die Theologie als ein Theologisieren, d.h. als ein Unterwegsseins zum Glauben, das letztlich die totale Existenz, des Menschen vor Gott zum Ziel hat. Mit allem möglichen Einsatz in diesen Prozeß hineingestellt zu sein, die Geheimnisse der Offenbarung Gottes in Christo durchdenken zu müssen, ist die Eigenart dieses Theologisierens. Sie erfordert von demjenigen, der im akademischen Bereich Gott bedenkt, genau so viel Mühe und Kraft, wie von demjenigen, der im Verkündigungsdienst der Gemeinde steht und verpflichtet ist, sich die Arbeit der akademischen Theologie anzueignen. Das Einüben und Praktizieren in eine Form des Denkens, das die Problematik der Glaubenswahrheiten zum Inhalt hat, war sicherlich eines der Ziele Schleiermachers. Sein Bedenken der Denkgrenze geschah in der gelebten spannungsreichen Einheit als akademischer Lehrer und Gemeindepfarrer. Allein dieses Vorbild könnte genügen, um dieses Problem in die gegenwärtige theologischphilosophische Diskussion zurückzuholen. Eine letzte

Schlußbemerkung, es hat nur den Anschein, als beende die Denkgrenze den Prozeß des Denkens, indem sie mitteilt, daß unserem Versuch, letzte gültige Wahrheit zu errringen, eine undurchdringliche Schranke gesetzt ist, daß eine endliche Vernunft niemals den von ihr erahnten unendlichen Bereich des Transzendenten ergründen kann. Das mögliche durch die Erfahrung der Denkgrenze entstandenen Wissen um, das Nichtwissen führt nicht zum Stillstand oder zur Resignation, sondern bewirkt eine ständige Bewegung zum Denken, einem Willen zur Grenzüberschreitung, in derem Vollzug die Einbettung des Menschen in die Welt zu deren aktiven Aneignung und Gestaltung führt, ohne die erfahrene Bindung an die Transzendenz Gottes aufzugeben.

Anmerkungen

1. Friedrich Schleiermacher, Dialektik. Aus Schleiermachers handschriftl. Nachlasse ed. von L. Jonas, in Werke Schleiermachers, Berlin 1839 (WW III, 4,2), weiter abgek.: DJ, S. 79-81, 93-94, 101, 115, 118, 145-146, 161.

2. Georg Weißenborn, Darstellung und Kritik der Schleiermacherschen Dialektik, Leipzig 1847.

3. Bruno Weiß, "Untersuchungen über F. Schleiermachers Dialektik", in: Zeitschrift für Philosophie und philosophische Kritik 74 (1879), S. 69.

4. Georg Wehrung, Die Dialektik Schleiermachers, Tübingen 1920, S. 119 und S. 126.

5. Karl Pohl, Studien zur Dialektik Friedrich Schleiermachers, Mainz 1954, S. 78.

6. H.J. Rothert, Die Endlichkeit des Menschen bei Fr. Schleiermacher. Eine systematische Untersuchung zur Dialektik aus dem unmittelbaren Selbstbewußtsein, Tübingen 1954, S. 145.

7. Marlin E. Miller, Der Übergang. Schleiermachers Theologie des Reiches Gottes im Zusammenhang seines Gesamtdenkens, Gütersloh 1970, S. 31, 38-50.

8. Robert Stalder, Grundlinien der Theologie Schleiermachers, Wiesbaden 1969, S. 345.

9. Falk Wagner, Schleiermachers Dialektik. Eine kritische Interpretation, Gütersloh 1974, S. 93 ff..

10. Hans-Richard Reuter, Die Einheit der Dialektik Friedrich Schleiermachers, München 1979, S. 120.

11. Manfred Frank, Das individuelle Allgemeine. Textstrukturierung und Interpretation nach Schleiermacher, Frankfurt/M. 1977, S. 114.

12. Udo Kliebisch, Transzendentalphilosophie als Kommunikationstheorie, Bochum 1980, S. 175.

13. Ulrich Barth, Christentum und Selbstbewußtsein. Versuch einer rationalen Rekonstruktion des systematischen Zusammenhangs von Schleiermachers subjektstheoretischer Deutung der christlichen Religion, Göttingen 1983, S. 53.

14. Michael Eckert, Gott – Glauben und Wissen. Friedrich Schleiermachers Philosophische Theologie, Berlin 1987, S. 47ff..

15. Friedrich Schleiermachers Dialektik, hrsg. von Rudolf Odebrecht, Leipzig 1942, weiter abgek.: DO, S. 408.

16. DO XXV.

17. DJ 315-361.

18. F.D.E. Schleiermacher, Dialektik (1811), hrsg. von Andreas Arndt, Hamburg 1986 weiter abgk.: DA.

19. DJ 316. DA 94.

20. DJ 315, DA 89.

21. DJ 38 (aus der Vorlesung von 1831).

22. Die Formulierung transzendent-transzendental wurde im Vortrag so angewendet. In einem anschließenden Gespräch mit Prof. Dr. Sergio Sorrentino ließ ich mich von dessen Auffassung überzeugen, daß Schleiermacher innerhalb der Dialektik durchaus im Kantschen Sinn transzendent dann gebraucht, wenn das Ziel der Denkbewegung benannt wird. Das Denken selbst, das auf die Transzendenz abzielt ist auch bei Schleiermacher transzendental, d.h. alle Formulierungen innerhalb der Dialektik, in der Schleiermacher das Wort transzendental gebraucht, sind Sprachbildungen des Philosophierens, die das Transzendente in der. Form von Begriff und Urteil ergründen wollen. In seinem Vortrag "Schleiermachers Philosophie und der Ansatz der transzendentalen Philosophie," erklärt Sorrentino transzendental als die Fähigkeit des Denkens "die Bedingung der Möglichkeit des selbstbegründeten Wissens" darzustellen. (S.9). Insofern ist "das unmittelbare Selbstbewußtsein" der Ort an dem der "transzendentale Grund des Wissens (bzw. des Wollens)" zur Rede gelangt. In gleicher Weise erläutert Sorrentino den Gebrauch von transzendental bei Schleiermacher in seinem Buch: Ermeneutica e Filosofia transcendentale. La filosofia di Schleiermacher come progetto di comprensione dell'altro, Bologna 1986, S.259 ff..

23. So Odebrecht DO XX. So Georg Wehrung, Die Dialektik Schleiermachers, Tübingen 1920, S. 65. Auch H.R. Reuter übernimmt das Urteil von Odebrecht, H.R. Reuter, Die Einheit der Dialektik Friedrich Schleiermachers, München 1979, S.26.

24. DJ 315

25. DA 4

26. DJ 333, DA 35. Erst in seinen Bemerkungen zu der Vorlesung, die er 1822 hält, relativiert Schleiermacher die Schwere des Satzes. Da heißt es unter XLII, wir sind "nicht ganz an die Erde gebunden." DJ 416, DO 243.

27. DJ 77.

28. DJ 99.

29. DJ 91.

30. DJ 92.

31. DJ 99.

32. DJ 99-100.

33. DJ 407, DO 207.

34. Z.B. "Die Denkgrenzen als Primär- und Finalvoraussetzungen". (DO 218). Oder: "Identität der Denkgrenzen" (DO 213), "Die Denkgrenzen und das wirkliche Denken" (DO 219). Es ist verständlich, daß Interpreteten und Kritiker zur Problemstellung der Denkgrenze auf die Odebrechtausgabe zurückgreifen.

35. DJ 412, DO 228.

36. DO 229-230.

37. DJ 422 ff., DO 265 ff..

38. DO 265. ff..

39. DO 299.

40. DO 408.

41. DJ 434, DO 304.

42. DJ 434, DO 305.

43. DJ 434, DO 305.

44. DJ 428 ff., DJ 475-476, DO 288ff..

45. DO 289.

46. DJ 430, DO 290.

47. DJ 430, DO 290.

48. DJ 429, DO 289.

49. DO 291.

50. Marlin E. Miller, Der Übergang. Schleiermachers Theologie des Reiches Gottes im Zusammenhang seines Gesamtdenkens, Gütersloh 1970, S. 19, 54, 68, 73, 80, 86-89, 107, 111-112, 121, 124, 128, 131, 133.

51. DJ 153.

52. DJ 475.

53. DJ 475.

54. DJ 152.

55. DJ 152.

56. DJ 152.

57. DJ 422 ff., DO 265 ff..

58. DJ 475.

59. DJ 475-476.

60. DJ 476.

61. DJ 476.

62. DJ 476.

63. F. Schleiermachers Dialektik, Berlin 1903, hrsg. von Isidor Halpern, S. XXXIII.

64. DJ 480-567.

65. DJ 503.

66. DJ 93.

67. DJ 91 f..

68. DJ 506.

69. DJ 94.

70. DJ 506.

71. DJ 536.

72. DJ 544.

73. DJ 539 ff.. Schleiermachers durchformulierte "Einleitung in die Dialektik", wahrscheinlich von ihm erst unmittelbar vor seinem Tod vollendet, ist sicher eine wertvolle Hilfe, um an das Werk selbst herangeführt zu werden. Das Wort Denkgrenze findet sich in der Einleitung nicht. Nur einmal verwendet Schleiermacher in einem für die Sachproblematik unwesentlichen Zusammenhang den Begriff Grenzen. (DO 38, DJ 605). Die von Schleiermacher in's Auge gefaßte "Hemmung des reinen Denkens" (DO 9, DJ 573), könnte die Problematik der Denkgrenze enthalten, ausgeführt wird sie in der Einleitung von Schleiermacher nicht.

74. H.J. Rothert, "Die Dialektik Friedrich Schleiermachers. Überlegungen zu einem immer noch wartenden Buch", ZThK 67 (1970), S.183.

75. Friedrich Schleiermachers Dialektik, hrsg. von Rudolf Odebrecht, Leipzig 1942, S. XXIV.

76. H.R. Reuter, Die Einheit der Dialektik Friedrich Schleiermachers, München 1979, S. 261. Falk Wagner, Schleiermachers Dialektik. Eine kritische Interpretation, Gütersloh 1974, S. 234.

77. DJ 544.

78. Wilhelm Dilthey, Leben Schleiermachers, Berlin 1966, Bd.II, 1, S. 167 ff..

79. Ebd. S.167.
80. Ebd. S.169, DJ 188, DJ 540 f..
81. Marlin E. Miller, Der Übergang. Schleiermachers Theologie des Reiches Gottes im Zusammenhang seines Gesamtdenkens, Gütersloh 1970, S. 68.
82. H.R. Reuter Die Einheit der Dialektik Friedrich Schleiermachers, München 1979, S. 214ff. und S. 247 ff..

X

SCHLEIERMACHERS PHILOSOPHIE UND DER ANSATZ DER TRANSZENDENTALEN PHILOSOPHIE

Sergio Sorrentino

I. Schleiermacher und die Philosophie überhaupt

Schleiermachers Philosophie ist allzu oft als Randgebiet seines Denkens und gedanklichen Schaffens betrachtet worden. Auf der einen Seite ist sein philosphisches Schaffen verstanden worden als dilettantische Tätigkeit im Felde des philosophischen Denkens, indem man einen berühmten Ausdruck von Schleiermacher selbst aufnahm (vergl. Sendschreiben an Lücke, SW I/2, S. 650), der allerdings m. E. in jenem bestimmten Zusammenhang einen eigentümlichen Sinn hatte (etwa ironisch), und kann daher keineswegs Schleiermachers gesamtes Bemühen um Themen und Probleme der Philosophie qualifizieren. Auf der anderen Seite hat man Schleiermachers philosophischen Diskurs als Erarbeitung einer Methode des Denkens betrachtet, besonders als Erarbeitung einer formellen Topologie der Wissenschaften und des Wissens. Das ist vor allem geschehen unter Berufung auf die *Dialektik*, zu deren zentralen Themen allerdings die "Verknüpfung" des Denkens gehört. Nach Kant, der mit der Methodenlehre der *Kritik der reinen Vernunft* die Methodenfragen des Denkens nachdrücklich bewußt gemacht hatte, ist die Frage nach der Methode kein sekundäres Geschäft des Denkens, sondern gehört zu dessen Grundlage. In dieser Hinsicht folgt Schleiermacher Kant, und dieser Bereich des gedanklichen Schaffens von Schleiermacher, nämlich die Philosophie, ist immer wieder unterschätzt worden. Natürlich hat es durchgehend auch eine umgekehrte Interpretationsrichtung gegeben, die das ganze Schleiermachersche Denken auf philosophische Grundsätze zurückführen wollte und auch Schleiermachers Theologie als verkleidete Philosophie interpretiert hat (so z. B. W. Bender). Doch letzten Endes hat auch solch eine Richtung der Interpretation nicht viel dazu beigetragen, den selbständigen Rang des philosophischen Denkens Schleiermachers hervorzuheben; es hat vielmehr, so paradox solche Folgerung auch sein mag, zu einer Unterschätzung der Philosophie Schleiermachers beigetragen. Wir können die Sache mit den Ausdrücken aus Schleiermachers Brief an Jacobi aussprechen: Das Denken Schleiermachers lebt ganz und gar aus der unüberwindlichen Spannung von Verstand und Herz, Philosophie und gläubiger Existenz, sie stellen zwei Pole dar, die aufeinander bezogen sind. Die Reichweite und Produktivität solcher gedanklichen Welt, die auch noch innerhalb eines von uns gelebten geschichtlichen kulturellen Standes ein durchgehendes Interesse zu beanspruchen vermag, kann nur bewahrt werden, wenn die Eigenständigkeit jener beiden Pole festgehalten wird, wenn man also darauf verzichtet, die Antriebs- und Ausbildungskraft der beiden selbständigen und doch im Verhältnis zueinander befindlichen Sinnwelten unrechtmäßig zu verkürzen. Eine ganz andere Frage ist freilich der Stand der Texte. Überwiegend ist Schleiermachers philosophische Arbeit aus Vorlesungen hervorgegangen und in Schriften dokumentiert, die vom Urheber selbst nicht veröffentlicht worden sind. Sie stellen uns vor schwierige kritische Probleme, die auch das Unternehmen einer *Kritischen Gesamtausgabe* der Werke Schleiermachers betreffen. Aber ich bin der Meinung, daß solche Schwierigkeiten nicht davon abhalten dürfen, zu einem angemessenen Verständnis und Umgang mit der Philosophie Schleiermachers zu kommen. Dies umso mehr, als die große Philosophie es von jeher vorzog, eher die Form der dialogischen Fassung und der lebendigen Mitteilung zu suchen, als die exoterische Bearbeitung von Gedanken und die texttreue Überlieferung von Ideen zu befördern.

II. Grund- und Ansatzproblem im Felde der Philosophie Schleiermachers

Zunächst muß betont werden, daß Schleiermachers Philosophie selbst noch eine Reihe schwer lösbarer Aufgaben bietet und immer noch ein offenes Interpretationsfeld darstellt. So hat z. B. neuerdings M. Welker diese

Philosophie aus ihrem Grundproblem her problematisiert. Ohne Zweifel ist Schleieimachers Grundproblem das Problem der Ethik. In seiner Perspektive erfährt die Ethik eine äußerste Erweiterung bis dahin, daß sie alles das umgreift, was den Geisteswissenschaften zugehört. Aber das Problem des Ansatzes (nämlich die *Dialektik*) wirft Fragen auf, die das Grundproblem der Philosophie Schleiermachers (nämlich der Ethik) ausmachen. Bei seiner Suche nach einem angemessenen Weg für das richtige Verständnis der Philosophie Schleiermachers bietet M. Welker eine Typisierung der verschiedenen in der Forschung vorkommenden Annäherungsversuche. Es gibt einmal, so sagt er, eine Darstellung der Philosophie Schleiermachers, die sich an denjenigen Problemen orientiert, die sich in der Rezeption der Philosophie Schleiermachers durchgesetzt haben. Das ist der hermeneutische Versuch; hier wird Schleiermachers Philosophie auf seine Hermeneutik konzentriert. Das ist aber eine ungerechtfertigte Einschränkung, vor allem wird nicht dem gesamten Bezugrahmen solcher Hermeneutik Rechnung getragen.

Es gibt einen weiteren Interpetationsversuch, der den Akzent darauf legt, wie solches Denken die Prinzipien des Philosophierens ansetzt. Dann konzentriert man sich vor allem auf die *Dialektik*. Endlich gibt es noch eine Darstellungsweise, die auf das Grundproblem der gesamten Philosophie Schleiermachers ausgerichtet ist; damit steht das ethische Problem zur Diskussion, das immer wieder Schleiermachers Interesse hervorgerufen und ihn überhaupt seit Beginn seiner philosophischen Arbeit beschäftigt hat. Nun scheint der Grund, den Welker anführt, um seine Wahl zu motivieren, nämlich die Ethik als Darstellungsachse der Philosophie Schleiermachers anzusetzen, dahin zu führen, die Aufmerksamkeit vom Grundproblem auf das Ansatzproblem zu verschieben. Und so hat es uns veranlaßt, die *Dialektik* als den Hauptort und das Hauptwerk zu wählen, um an Schleiermachers Philosophie die Fragen zu stellen und daraus Anregungen zu empfangen. Denn in der *Dialektik* werden nicht nur formelle Prinzipien des philosophischen Denkens erarbeitet, sondern es wird etwas ehrgeiziger und durchaus qualifizierter versucht (eben in dem Sinne, daß es um die Ansatzproblematik philosophischer Rede geht) – in den Ausdrücken von

Welker – die Exekutions-Prinzipien samt dem angebbaren Operationsfeld
zu erstellen.

Tatsächlich knüpft Schleiermachers *Dialektik* an ein von Kant in
Beziehung auf die Philosophie entwickeltes grundlegendes Problem an.
Denn in Kantischer Perspektive hat die Philosophie ein besonderes
Operationsfeld, worin Kategorien und Prinzipien diskursive Funktionen sind
(und so bedeutungsvoll sind), indem sie die mögliche Erfahrung
vorwegnehmen. Als solches Operationsfeld (die philosophische Diskur-
sivität) ist es mit Exekutions-Prinzipien versehen, die den Bedeutungsbereich
selbst aufbauen und so die "Bedingungen der Möglichkeit" des fraglichen
Feldes bilden. Eben darum sind die philosophisch aufgestellten Grundsätze
Exekutions-Prinzipien, nicht etwa Theoreme, da sie das bedeutungsreiche
Operationsfeld konstituieren, innerhalb dessen sie vorkommen; oder, wie
Kant sich ausdrückt, weil jeder solcher Grundsätze "die besondere
Eigenschaft hat, daß er seinen Beweisgrund, nämlich Erfahrung, selbst zuerst
möglich macht, und bei dieser immer vorausgesetzt werden muß" (B 765).
Indem Schleiermachers *Dialektik* dieses <u>Problem</u> wiederaufnimmt, unterliegt
es darin einer bedeutungsvollen Umwandlung, als sie die Problemstellung
der Philosophie thematisch als Diskurs und Sprache versteht: die Philosophie
wird das durch eigene sprachliche Funktionen bzw. Leistungen bestimmte
Operationsfeld; ihre Sagbarkeit, d.h. ihr Funktionieren, ist durch Exekutions-
Prinzipien geleitet, die eben von der *Dialektik* her zu entwickeln sind, doch
keinem übersprachlichen Gebiet angehören können. Sie bestimmen eben
die Protokolle bzw. die Bedingungen der Möglichkeit, für die Bedeutung
(und die Sagbarkeit) philosophischer Rede.

III. Die Lage und Aufgabe der Philosophie
in der Perspektive Schleiermachers

Ich möchte den Ansatz der Philosophie Schleiermachers erörtern, um
zu beweisen, daß für diese die Transzendentalphilosophie von fundamentaler
Bedeutung ist. Denn Schleiermachers philosophisches Denken stellt insofern
eine besonders interessante Fassung der Transzendentalphilosophie dar, als
sie sich in den Aufbau einer der Modernität betreffenden Theorieanlage

einordnet. Der hervorstechende Zug solcher Theorieanlage ist die Wahrnehmung der Endlichkeit des menschlichen Daseins und seiner Vernunft, und solche Wahrnehmung verbindet sich entweder mit der Endeckung der Antonomie (wie bei Kant) oder mit der Anschauung der ursprünglichen Beschränktheit des Ichs (wie bei Fichte); oder mit der Feststellung des Gegensatzes zwischen Idealem und Realem (wie bei Schelling). Schleiermachers Philosophie geht aus einer scharfen Konfrontation mit all diesen Theorieansätzen hervor, die den Nährboden des deutschen Idealismus ausmachen. Sie schlägt einen anderen Weg ein, der sich nicht auf den Boden jener philosophischen Kultur zurückführen läßt. Schleiermachers Philosophie darf deshalb auch nicht auf dem Boden des deutschen Idealismus angesiedelt werden und etwa "von innen" heraus interpretiert werden (wie es A. Arndt in seiner neuerdings erschienenen Einführung in die *Dialektik 1814/15* tut). Vielmehr kann sie dem ursprünglichen Kantischen Ansatz nähergebracht werden, wenn man ihn jedenfalls außerhalb eines subjektivistischen Musters deutet. Von Anfang an ist die von Schleiermacher eingeschlagene Richtung die einer "Vereinigung des Idealismus und Realismus" (Brief an Schwarz vom 28.3.1801) bzw. die eines "höheren Realismus"; d. h. ein kritischer, unnaiver, unmetaphysischer Realismus. So darf man es ausdrücken, wenn man sowohl den Ansatz der Philosophie Schleiermachers als auch ihre Folgen in den Blick nimmt. Im negativen Sinne zielte diese Forderung – quasi als erkenntnis-theoretischer Weg für eine selbständige und konsistente Philosophie – darauf ab, die Einseitigkeiten des idealistischen Grundsatzes zu vermeiden, ohne den ihn beseelenden transzendentalen Anspruch zu entwerten. Im positiven Sinne dagegen handelte es sich für Schleiermacher darum, sich darüber Rechenschaft zu geben, daß jene Einseitigkeiten aus der Konzentration auf nur jeweils einen Pol dieser Antinomie herrühren, sich also der Vernachlässigung jener Lage verdanken, die für das Wissen und Denken (als ursprüngliche Fähigkeit des menschlichen Daseins, sich in der Gesamtheit des Seins zu orientieren) infolge jener Antinomie unausweichlich ist. Eben die Bestimmung dieser Lage des menschlichen Daseins und seiner Orientierungsfähigkeit (d. h. Denken und Wissen) in der Antinomie bezeichnet den Standort des von Schleiermacher eingeschlagenen Weges, d.h. Schleiermacher will entweder die Zurückführung des menschlichen Daseins auf die Natürlichkeit und damit letztlich auf die Unsinnigkeit vermeiden (wenn man sich darüber klar wird, daß die Identität von Natürlichkeit und Vernunft, Realem und Idealem, dem Nihilismus das Tor öffnet), oder der Zurückführung des menschlichen Daseins auf den metaphysisch unbedingten Grund aus dem Wege gehen (bedenkt man, daß solche Zurückführung die Autonomie und also die Konsistenz des menschlichen endlichen Daseins aufsaugt und sie letzten Endes der Heteronomie preisgibt, dann ist das eine nicht weniger zerstörende Fassung des Nihilismus).

Die Position die sich aus der Vermeidung solcher Missverständnisse ergibt, bezeichnet Schleiermachers Ansatz als einen transzendentalen.

IV. Der transzendentale Ansatz

In Schleiermachers Anschauung des menschlichen Wesens bilden seine philosophische Reflexion, seine religiös-philosophische Betrachtung und schließlich seine theologische Ausarbeitung eine Einheit. Man darf nicht vergessen, daß das hervorragende Kennzeichen des Schleiermacherschen Denkens bzw. seiner Ausführungen im Bereiche des Wissens und der Wissenschaft in der Kohärenz liegt (in der *Dialektik* nennt er das die Zusammengehörigkeit), die für die doppelte Wahrheit oder Zusammenhangslosigkeit keinen Raum läßt, gleichwohl aber offen ist für die Verschiedenheit, Eigentümlichkeit und Selbstständigkeit auseinandergehender Perspektiven.

Nach solcher Anschauung ist der Mensch ein Wesen, das im Ungleichgewicht, im Gegensatz existiert; der Gegensatz zwischen Idealem und Realem, Natur und Vernunft (sozusagen ihre Ungleichmäßigkeit) gehört zur Konstitution des menschlichen Seins. Das menschliche Wesen, das zu diesem Wissen nicht fähig ist, kann den Gegensatz, den Bruch nicht überwinden. Ein mögliche Überwindung befindet sich immer nur im Werden, (d.h. in der Näherungslinie; das ist kein zufälliger Zug, sondern macht die Struktur des Menschen aus): es qualifiziert das Verhältnis dieses Wesens (und seines Wissens, d.h. seines Orientierungsvermögens) zum

Absoluten. Dies Verhältnis ist nie unmittelbar, sondern immer nur mittelbar; d. h. dem menschlichen Wesen ist niemals die Möglichkeit eines unmittelbaren Verhältnisses zum Absoluten gegeben, weder auf der Ebene des Theoretischen (der Erkenntnis, sei es im Sinne der kritischen oder der strategischen Erkenntnis), noch auf der Ebene des Praktischen (sei es des Ethischen oder gar des Poietischen). Allerdings muß hinzugefügt werden, daß es im menschlichen Wesen ein Unmittelbares als ursprüngliche Quelle jeder sowohl theoretischen als auch praktischen Vermittlung gibt; darin besteht das Paradox, mit dem Schleiermachers Philosophische Reflexion durchgehend gerungen hat. Das Unmittelbare ist eben das unmittelbare Selbstbewußtsein, das im Bereiche der philosophischen Reflexion von Schleiermacher als Konstitutionsprinzip sowohl der erkennenden als auch der ethisch-geschichtlichen Gesamtheit gilt, die allerdings in der Perspektive dieses Philosophierens die beiden wesentlichen Seiten der menschlichen Welt ausmachen. Darüber hinaus bezeichnet solches Unmittelbare des menschlichen Wesens eine Dimension bzw. eine Funktion (ohne aber das Ungleichgewicht, den Gegensatz aufzuheben, oder die diesem Wesen eingeborene Antinomie zu schwächen), worin ebenfalls ein mit eigener Struktur versehenes Verhältnis zum Absoluten wirkt. Auch in diesem Falle handelt es sich auf der einen Seite um eine transzendentale Modalität, die es zu erhellen gilt, und tatsächlich wird sie in der Einleitung der *Glaubenslehre* von Schleiermacher auf zusammenfassende Weise äußerst klar beleuchtet; auf der anderen Seite bedarf die eigene Art solcher Struktur einer besonderen Bezeichnung; deshalb wird Schleiermacher dazu genötigt, einen eigenen begrifflichen Wortschatz anzueignen, der sich auf die Kategorie des Gefühls stützt, und eine musterhafte, für die religiöse Erfahrung und ihren Mitteilungsbereich angewandte Sprache veranlaßt. Diese eigene Struktur des menschlichen Wesens legt kein Verhältnis mit Richtung vom menschlichen Dasein auf das Absolute hin fest, sondern ein Verhältnis mit umgekehrter Richtung, vom Absoluten auf das menschliche Dasein hin; und zeichnet letzten Endes nicht das Selbstsein des menschlichen Daseins, sondern sein Her-Sein (sein ex-sistere), etwa seine existentiale dezentrierte Beschaffenheit; sie veranlaßt eine die absolute Initiative Gottes bezeichnende Sinnerzeugung, die letztlich auf einen geschenkten Sinn zuläuft. Wenn

manche Interpreten von Schleiermacher das Gefühl richtig als
transzendentale Kategorie der Konstitution der religiösen Welt verstanden
hätten, würde man wahrscheinlich niemals so weit gekommen sein,
Schleiermachers Theologie als eine Umkehrung der Theologie in Anthropologie zu deuten; und man würde noch deutlicher das Mißverstehen
durchschauen, das durch diesen Ausdruck veranlaßt worden ist. Ich denke
hier an Hegels kritische Irreführung, an seine Kritik der Gefühlstheologie!
Ich würde mich statt dessen auf den Anspruch von Feuerbach beziehen, eine
Grundforderung von Schleiermacher zu übernehmen, nämlich im Gefühl in
Schleiermachers Sinn eine wesentliche Stütze seiner eigenen Aussagen über
die Beschaffenheit des Religiösen zu finden

V. Das unmittelbare Selbstbewußtsein als transzendentaler Grund des Wissens (bzw. des Wollens)

1. Der Prozeßcharakter des Wissens

Hier befinden wir uns im Herzen der Philosophie Schleiermachers,
und an dieser Zentralstelle ihres Ansatzes gilt es, die Sache näher zu
erhellen. Schleiermacher teilt mit der ganzen zeitgenössischen Kultur die
heute fraglich gewordene und nur durch einen kritischen Weg wieder-
herzustellende Voraussetzung, daß die Philosophie den Kern der
menschlichen Suche nach Wissen und Wissenschaft darstellt. Nun ist für ihn
das Wissen, vor allem das wissenschaftlich charakterisierte Wissen, das die
Philosophie bildet, nicht eines absoluten Zustandes fähig; es kann nicht die
Gesamtheit endgültig umgreifen. Das beleuchtet den dem Wissen eigenen
Prozeßcharakter, den die ganze zeitgenössische Kultur anerkennt, wenn dies
auch in unterschiedlicher Bedeutung geschieht; Hegel z.B. thematisiert
solchen Prozeßcharakter des Wissens, interpretiert ihn aber in einem
logischen Sinne und mit logischen Kategorien.

2. Wissen als apodeixis

Schleiermacher freilich versteht das Wissen als Prozess, dem der Prozeßcharakter der ethischen Praxis entspricht. Beiden liegt der gleiche philosophische Ansatz und die gleiche Problemstellung zugrunde, worauf sich die Erhellung des Wissens stützt, indem die philosophische transzendentale Untersuchung, nämlich die Untersuchung nach den Bedingungen der Möglichkeit, sich sowohl dem Wissensprozeß als auch dem Wollensprozeß zuwenden kann. Deswegen ist für Schleiermacher das Wissen je aufgeschlossen, nie fähig, sich in ein Wissen des Absoluten zu verwandeln; in Bezug darauf eignet sich Schleiermachers Philosophie sowohl den apophatischen Vorbehalt der Tradition der negativen Theologie an, als auch die Kantische Restriktion in Bezug auf die Unkennbarkeit des Unbedingten. In diesem Zusammenhang darf man sowohl Schleiermachers Ablehnung anführen, die Kategorie der Persönlichkeit für Gott anzuwenden, als auch seine Betonung des unausweichlichen Anthropomorphismus unserer Rede über Gott nennen.

Doch solch ein Prozeßcharakter vereinigt sich gleichwohl mit einem scharfen epistemischen Anspruch: das Wissen ist fähig, eine epistemische Schärfe anzunehmen, die Bedingung der Möglichkeit universaler Mitteilung unter den Menschen ist, indem solche Mitteilung (und diese Universalität) der Niederschlag der menschlichen Denkfähigkeit und des vernünftigen Vermögens ist, sich im Meer des Seins zu orientieren. Aber was ist der Grund dieses Wissens als apodeixis, nämlich jenes Wissens, das ein apodiktisch strenges Erkennen zustandezubringen vermag? Die Frage nach der Apodeixis, nach unwidersprechlichem Wissen, wird durch Schleiermachers Philosophie nicht fallengelassen; vielmehr wird sie geltend gemacht, wenn auch in neuem grundlegenden Zusammenhang. Andererseits ermöglicht das apodiktisch angesetzte Wissen erst recht die Überwindung des im Bereich des Denkens vorkommenden Streits; es ist eben das angestrebte Ziel der dialektischen Praxis und der durch die *Dialektik* ausgeführten Kunstlehre. Insofern schließt dies Wissen das Feld der universalen Mitteilung auf und bewahrheitet die Vernunft als eigene

Seinsweise (die dem menschlichen Wesen eignet). Die Antwort auf die eben
erhobene Frage erlaubt uns, den transzendentalen, den die Schleiermachersche Philosophie stützenden Ansatz, zu erklären, und sie in die
Tradition der transzendentalen Philosophie zu stellen (dennoch auf
eigentümliche Art, ihrer ursprünglichen Ausführung entsprechend).

3. Das in sich selbst begründete Wissen: transzendenter und transzendentaler Grund

Schleiermachers philosophische Untersuchurg strebt nach der
Möglichkeit intersubjektiver Einstimmung, worauf das wirkliche Wissen in
seiner vielfältigen Gliederung zu gründen ist; denn die Wissenschaften
unterscheiden und beteiligen sich untereinander, ohne ihren Zusammenhang
zu verlieren, der allerdings das Zeichen ihrer Wissenschaftlichkeit ist.
Insofern identifiziert Schleiermacher diese Möglichkeit nicht auf der Linie
des Unbedingten, sondern auf der Linie des Transzendentalen, indem er
damit die Bedingung der Möglichkeit des selbstbegründeten Wissen vollzieht
(worin noch eine weitere Bedingung der Wissenschaftlichkeit besteht). Der
Grund, auf dem Schleiermachers philosophische Rede den Hebel ansetzt,
soll also nicht mit dem transzendenten Grund identifiziert werden, der zwar
in der dialektischen Rede in Frage kommt, dennoch mit einer immer wieder
problematischen Rede. Solche Rede weist auf die Thematisierung des
Gefühls hin, das seinerseits eine die Bedingung der Möglichkeit religiöser
Erfahrung zusammenfassende Kategorie bildet, und daher ihre
transzendentale Struktur erhellt. Diese Unterscheidung zwischen
transzendentalem Grund (des selbstbegründeten Wissens) und transzen-
dentem Grund (dieser entgeht grundsätzlich der begrifflichen Auffassung,
gleichwohl wirkt er noch in der Rede über die Konstitution des selbstbegründeten Wissens mit: eben in seiner postulierenden Funktion, die aber
näher zu erörtern und zu erklären wäre) weist eine große Tragweite für das
Verständnis der Philosophie Schleiermachers auf. Sie ist oft durch manche
Interpreten mißverstanden worden. Indem solche Interpreten sich meistens
auf die in Schleiermachers Texten und noch mehr in den Nachschriften
vorkommenden Ausdrucksschwankungen stützen, verwechseln sie zu eilig

und folgenreich beide Arten von Grund: der transzendente Grund, der auf die Seite des Unbedingten und des "Übersinnlichen" bzw. "Überweltlichen" gehört; und der transzendentale Grund, der auf die Seite des Daseins und des in-der-Welt-seins gehört. Das geschieht noch einmal in der Einleitung zur *Dialektik 1814/15* von A. Arndt (vgl. S. X, fg und Anm. 11, wo es heißt, daß "Schleiermacher in seiner Dialektik durchgängig transzendent und transzendental synonym gebraucht" und wo es noch weiter zu Unrecht heißt, daß "die Präsenz dieses Grundes im Wissen des (endlichen) Subjektes zum zentralen Problem seiner Dialektik" gehört.

4. Die unaufgebbaren Bedingungen des Wissens

Eine als Wissen geltende Erkenntnis, die nämlich durch formale Verknüpfung auf ein selbstbegründetes Wissen zurückzuführen ist, und zugleich Verständigungsboden unter ursprünglich abweichenden Subjekten sein kann, eine Erkenntnis also, die zu Recht als wissenschaftlich gilt und dem Zustand des Meinens (dennoch durchaus nicht dem unzerstörbaren Band mit ihm) entgeht, soll transzendental aus der Verbindung eines "gemeinsamen ursprünglichen Wissens" mit gemeinsanen Regeln der Combination" (DJ 46) konstituiert werden (vergl. DO 55, 94-97). In dieser Verbindung wird zugleich die Bedingung der Möglichkeit des Denkens und seiner Sagbarkeit erkannt, indem der mitteilende Vollzug des Denkens und seiner Sagbarkeit sich strukturell mit den Bedingungen der Möglichkeit der Intersubjektivität verbindet; diese findet im Wissen (oder besser in den Wissen) ihren vorzüglichen Realisierungsort, da Wissen der wesentliche Ort der Verständigung unter den Menschen und der Überwindung des streitenden Zustandes der Meinung ist. Daher gibt es ein primum, einen Grundsatz im Sinne der transzendentalen Ontologie, und ein einzelnes, in dem das Denken wurzelt und sich seine Sagbarkeit begründet; doch dies primum ist weder das Unbedingte noch ein einziger Deduktionsgrundsatz (der einzige Grundsatz, wonach die Philosophie gleich nach Kant strebte), sondern ein transzendentales: nämlich ein jedem wirklichen Wissen vorhergehendes Wissen, das fähig ist, die formellen Verfahren des Zusammenhanges und der Unterscheidung des wirklichen Wissens sowie der streitenden oder einstimmigen Erkenntnisse in ihre ontologische Kraft einzusetzen. Solches jedem empirischen Bewußtsein vorhergehendes und jedes wirkliche Wissen vorwegnehmendes Wissen ist ein Wissen eigener Art (sui generis), indem es keinen bestimmten Bewußtseinsinhalt (keine bestimmte Vorstellung) gliedert, sondern die Zusammenhangs- und Verknüpfungsverfahren mit ontologischer Gegebenheit durchdringt; und insofern als Bedingung der Möglichkeit für die Konstitution der Wissensarten, für deren intersubjektive Sagbarkeit gilt, Bedingung für die Feststellung der Protokolle ist, die Verständigung unter den auf der Ebene des Erkennens und Meinens voneinander abweichenden Subjekten bewirken. In solchem problematischen Zusammenhang, der im Zentrum der *Dialektik* steht, kehrt die berühmt Frage wieder, die in der *Kritik der reinen Vernunft* die transzendentale Deduktion der Kategorien zum Problem gemacht hatte: die Frage nämlich nach dem Prinzip der synthetischen Tätigkeit des Verstandes, die eben Kant Verbindung bzw. conjunctio nennt. In jenem problematischen Bereich wurde diese Frage gelöst, indem Kant die synthetische Tätigkeit des Verstandes in der ursprünglichen Apperzeption verankerte. Bei Schleiermacher nun wird die Frage aufs neue gestellt; vom Kantischen Ansatz wird ausschließlich das transzendentale Muster bewahrt; d. h. die Identifizierung des letztgültigen bzw. grundsätzlichen Grundes mit dem unbedingten Grund wird abgelehnt mit der Intention, den Grund an die bedingte Notwendigkeit zu binden.

5. Die Art der transzendentalen Grundlegung

Das Neue besteht nun darin, daß das "Urwissen, die arché, das Prinzip, wovon das Wissen ausgeht" (DO 115), aus der aufsteigenden Reihe der grundsätzlichen Begründung herausgenommen und als unabdingbar geltendes Postulat in die absteigende Reihe eingerückt wird, die den intersubjektiven Horizont der einstimmenden oder abweichenden Subjekte ausmacht. Damit wird jener Ansatz abgelehnt, der das Prinzip, aus dem das Wissen hervorgeht, als einzigen Grundsatz versteht, aus dem man das gesamte wirkliche Wissen deduktiv erschließen könnte. Es ist vor allem diese zweite Art von Ansatz, die Schleiermacher im Blick auf die zentralen

Probleme der *Dialektik* ausschließt. Dies aus zwei Gründen: zuerst, weil solches philosophische Muster in der zeitgenössischen Philosophie weitgehend das herrschende war, sodann weil es sachlich eine abgeänderte Fassung des metaphysischen Musters darstellt. Wir können diesen neuen Ansatz der *Dialektik* Schleiermachers in folgender Formulierung ausdrücken: an die Stelle des <u>Ich denke</u> als Schlüsselkategorie der kantischen Grundlegung tritt hier ein <u>Wir denken</u> des intersubjektiven und sprachlichen Horizonts, sei es im Zustand der Unstimmigkeit, der dennoch ein "ursprüngliches gemeinsames Wissen" (DO 114) postuliert (im Sinne zwar des Postulats, nicht der Petitio), weil man sonst den Zustand der streitenden Meinungen sprachlich gar nicht ausdrücken oder mitteilen könnte; sei es im Zustand der Einstimmigkeit und der Verständigung, der eine "gleichmäßige Methode der Fortschreitung" (DO 114) postuliert, nicht aber einer ableitenden Deduktion gleichgestellt werden kann.

6. Das unmittelbare Selbstbewußtsein

Mit seinem transzendentalen Ansatz versucht Schleiermacher also, in abweichender Weise das Motiv der Begründung zu verwerten; dieses Motiv liegt selbst der "verstehenden Vernunft" und der gesamten von ihr beseelten hermeneutischen Forderung zugrunde, für die Schleiermacher gleichwohl den transzendentalen Grund in Anspruch nimmt: Und so wandelt sich die Frage nach dem Grund, aus einer Frage nach dem transzendenten Grund, in eine Frage nach dem transzendentalen Grund. Das wird an einer entscheidenden Stelle der DO erklärt, wo der "transzendentale Rückgang" auf das unmittelbare Selbstbewußtsein zur Diskussion steht. In diesem unmittelbaren Selbstbewußtsein ist zwar die Bedingung der Möglichkeit für die Bildung des "begründeten" Wissens enthalten, das heißt jenes Wissens, das den Charakter der Intersubjektivität und der Zusammenstimmung hat, und daher imstande ist, die Unstimmigkeit und Streitigkeit unter den Gesprächspartnern aufzuheben. "Der Grund des Mißlingens unserer Unternehmung (so drückt sich Schleiermacher aus) liegt also darin, daß wir uns das Transzendente <u>denken</u> wollen. So kommen wir aus dem Gegensatz nicht heraus und gelangen zu einer Vielheit statt zur Einheit. Wir müssen also von der Identität des Seins und Denkens in uns ausgehen, um zu jenem transzendenten Grunde alles Seins aufzusteigen" (DO 270). Und kurz vorher erklärt er dieses "in uns" mit einer den gesamten transzendentalen Ansatz des dialektischen Verfahrens zusammenfassenden Formel: "Die Identität des Seins und Denkens tragen wir in uns selbst; wir selbst sind Sein und Denken, das denkende Sein und das seiende Denken" (ebd.). Insofern ist das unmittelbare Selbstbewußtsein eben der Ort, an dem die Darlegung des Grundes erfolgt (in dem bestimmten Sinn, auf den wir schon hingewiesen haben, und in dem Schleiermacher den Begriff nimmt); Kraft dieses Grundes gelingt dem Wissen seine eigene Selbstbegründung, und zugleich öffnet es sich zusammen mit dem Wollen für den transzendenten Grund (ein "mangelhafter" Grund), indem es in jenem erkennenden und praktischen Inbegriff wurzelt, der das unmittelbare Selbstbewußtsein ist.

Dieses Geöffnetsein, das auf der einen Seite den Raum des "Gefühls" aufschließt (und das tranzendental den Bereich der religiösen Erfahrung konstituiert), bezeichnet auf der anderen Seite die eigene Endlichkeit jenes endlichen realen Seienden das im Unmittelbaren des Selbstbewußtseins vorgestellt und zusammengefaßt wird.

VI. Schlußbetrachtungen

Jetzt geht es darum, etliche Bemerkungen als Schluß meiner Betrachtungen über Schleiermachers Philosophie darzustellen. Es handelt sich vor allem um das neu bestimmte Verhältnis zwischen Philosophie und Religion. Es ist folgendermaßen zu erörtern.

1. Schleiermacher arbeitet ein neues Muster der Idee der Philosophie und der Religion bzw. des Glaubens aus. Er ist durch ihre gegenseitige Selbstständigkeit und Autonomie gekennzeichnet. Die Philosophie ist wesentlich erkennende Dialektik der Konstitution eines weltlichen Korrelats. Die Religion (und der Glaube) ist wesentlich schlechthinniges Abhängigkeitsgefühl.

Welche Funktion ist es denn beiden zuzuschreiben in dieser Hinsicht? [A] Der Philosophie eine erkennende Funktion: d.h. die Funktion der

Öffnung der Welt und dem Anderen. [B] Der Religion (dem Glaube) eine Funktion in Bezug auf die Bestimmung (Qualifikation) des Selbst: das Gefühl qualifiziert die *Individualit*ät (im Sinne des Wortes Jesu: vgl. Lk. 9; 25).

2. Welches Verhältnis besteht denn zwischen den beiden, d.h. zwischen Philosophie und Religion? [A] Die Religion (als Glaubenserfahrung) *donne à penser* (erregt zum Denken): daher kommt der hermeneutische Ansatz der Reflexion auf den Glauben (und insbesondere der Theologie). [B] Die Philosophie den Logos der universellen Kommunikation bietet; denn sie leistet die dialektischen Sprache für die Reflexion auf die Religion (auf den Glauben), verbindet die religiöse Erfahrung mit der übrigen Gesamterfahrung des Menschen, versteht den Glauben als geschichtsbildende Kraft, also als Dimension des Ethischen (vgl. in diesem Sinne den Begriff der religiösen Gemeinschaft als ethischen Gemeinschaft).

3. Welcher Zusammenhang verbindet denn Philosophie und Theologie? Wir können die Sache mit drei Stichworten erklären, die des weiteren eine ausführlichere Betrachtung verdienten. [A] Hermeneutischer Ansatz der Theologie (vgl. oben den Punkt 2.A). [B] Religionsphilosophie: sowohl als spekulatives Fach (=Ethik), als auch als kritische Disziplin (=Phänomenologie des Religiösen). [C] Philosophische Theologie (Apologetik und Polemik): es handelt sich um eine Art Fundamentaltheologie.

XI

FRIEDRICH SCHLEIERMACHERS SÄKULARISIERUNG DER CHRISTLICHEN THEOLOGIE

Michael D. Ryan

Übersetzung von Astrid Petrascheck Posegga

I. Säkularisierung gemäß Schleiermacher?

Soll der Knoten der Geschichte so auseinandergehen; das Christentum mit der Barbarei, und die Wissenchaft mit dem Unglauben.[1]

Mit dieser ergreifenden, sogar prophetischen Frage drückte im Jahre 1829 der sechzigjährige Schleiermacher die Hauptsorge seiner reiferen Jahre aus. Er glaubte an Gott den Schöpfer. Er glaubte an Jesus Christus als seinen Erlöser. Für ihn war die christliche Gemeinschaft die Trägerin seines Heils; das alles wollte er glauben, ohne all das zu vergessen, was er über die Welt und die weltlichen Bedingungen der Übermittlung des christlichen Glaubens gelernt hatte. Kurz gesagt, er wollte sich zu einem Glauben bekennen, für den er weder seine Intelligenz noch seine Gefühle aufopfern mußte.

Während viele Zeitgenossen Schleiermachers von der Tatsache ausgingen, daß eine Zunahme der Erkenntnisse automatisch zu einer Abnahme des Glaubens führen mußte, lautete Schleiermachers Rechnung, daß eine Zunahme der Erkenntnisse eine Veränderung der Bedingungen, unter denen er als Christ glaubte, liebte und hoffte, darstellte. Die erste Ausgabe von *Der christliche Glaube*, 1821 veröffentlicht, – er war 53 Jahre alt – bringt sein Verständis für den christlichen Glauben in seinen reiferen Jahren zum Ausdruck und integriert somit seine Fähigkeit zu lernen und seine

Frömmigkeit in eine Identifizierungshandlung mit der historischen christlichen Glaubensgemeinschaft.

Aber das soll nicht heißen, daß Schleiermacher niemals wankte, wenn es sich um seine Identifizierung mit dem Christentum handelte. Wie viele Studenten von damals bis heute brach Schleiermacher mit der Religionsgemeinschaft, die ihn von Jugend an aufgezogen hatte. Er besuchte die Herrnhuterschule von seinem 14. Lebensjahr an, bis er 1787 auf die Universität ging. Aber dann fand er, daß er nicht länger ernsthaft "nach den übernatürlichen Gefühlen und dem was in der Sprache jener Gesellschaft der Umgang mit Jesu hieß"[2], jagen konnte. Da er gemäß der Lehre der Herrnhuter von christlicher Vollkommenheit erzogen worden war, war der junge Schleiermacher zutiefst enttäuscht über die Diskrepanz, die zwischen den geistigen Ansprüchen herrnhuterischer Frömmigkeit und der Realität der unvollkommenen menschlichen Natur herrscht. Diese letztere sollte er – gemäß der Herrnhuterdoktrin – geringschätzen. Er erkannte die Schwächen menschlicher Natur, aber er konnte es schließlich nicht über sich bringen die Entfremdung von seiner eigenen menschlichen Natur durch das was ihm durch die Lehre der Herrnhuter und das orthodoxe Christentum beigebracht worden war, zu akzeptieren. Er verwarf die traditionelle Lehren von Sünde und Heil:

Ich kann nicht glauben, daß der ewiger, wahrer Gott war, der sich selbst nur den Menschensohn nannte, ich kann nicht glauben, daß sein Tod eine stellvertretende Versöhnung war, weil er es selbst nie ausdrücklich gesagt hat, und ich nicht glauben kann, daß sie nöthig gewesen; denn Gott kann die Menschen, die er offenbar nicht zur Vollkommenheit sondern nur zum Streben nach derselben geschaffen hat, unmöglich darum ewig strafen wollen, weil sie nicht vollkommen geworden sind.[3]

In einem früheren Essay "Des jungen Friedrich Schleiermachers religiöse Identifikation" argumentierte ich, daß sein Bruch mit der Herrnhuter-interpretation von christlicher Vollkommenheit ihn für einen Skeptizismus gegenüber allen Ansprüchen auf menschliche Vollkommenheit, sei sie ethischer Natur, wie des philosophischen Moralisten Immanuel Kant, oder auf der Erkenntnistheorie des Absoluten eines Fichte oder Hegel beruhend, empfänglich machte.[4]   Die Kritik von Kants moralischem Idealismus, wie sie in seinen Jugendessays "Freiheitsgespräch", "Über das höchste Gut" und "Über die Freiheit" enthalten ist, offenbaren eine überraschend nüchterne Resignation über die menschliche Fehlbarkeit und Endlichkeit von seiten eines jungen Universitätsstudenten.[5] In diesen Essays drückte er positive Beurteilung der Sinnlichkeit als notwendigem Lehrer und Quelle der Weisheit für die Menschheit und die gesamte Welt aus und warnt vor der Vernachlässigung der Rolle der Sinnlichkeit beim Studium.

Nachdem er für sich selbst geklärt hatte, was er nicht glauben konnte, verbrauchte der junge Friedrich Schleiermacher in den nächsten Jahren den größten Teil seiner Energie, um sich eine Meinung über die Welt und die Natur des Menschen, und über die Voraussetzungen derselben für die Rolle der Religion in der Natur des Menschen zu bilden. In diesen Jahren pries er die Sinnlichkeit und die endliche Kreatürlichkeit als das Mittel zur Erlangung religiösen Bewußtseins. Die Frucht dieser Überlegungen reifte in der Diskussion *Über die Religion: Reden an die Gebildeten unter ihren Verächtern* [1799], die die Philosophen der Ideen der Freiheit beleidigten, da er sich weigerte das Wesen der Religion mit menschlicher Freiheit als durch praktische Gründe bestimmt gleichzusetzen. Er befand hingegen, daß sie unter einem mittelbaren Einfluß der Sinnlichkeit stehe; in seinen Worten: "Religion ist Sinn und Geschmack fürs Unendliche."[6]

In einer mit Gefühl und Metaphern überladenen Prosa beschreibt Schleiermacher eine Art Umarmung des Universums, eine Identifizierung mit dem pulsierenden Leben über sich selbst hinaus und dann den Augenblick des Ausbruchs und die Rückkehr zur Trennung mit der Erfahrung von Einswerdung und einer unauslöschlichen Erinnerung.[7]   All dies gibt zu verstehen, daß er daran als eine endliche Erfahrung des Unendlichen dachte, für das der menschliche sexuelle Akt gleichzeitig eine Metapher und Realität ist. In weit nüchterneren Worten schrieb er in der zweiten Ausgabe der *Reden*:

> Denn aus zwei Elementen besteht das ganze religiöse Leben,
> daß sich der Mensch hingebe dem Universum und sich erregen
> lasse von der Seite desselben, die es ihm eben zuwendet, und

dann, daß er diese Berührung, die als solche und in ihrer Bestimmheit ein einzelnes Gefühl ist, nach innen zu fortpflanze und in die innere Einheit seines Lebens und Seins aufnehme; und das religiöse Leben ist Nichts Anderes als die beständige Erneuerung dieses Verfahrens.[8]

Hier drückt Schleiermacher die Bedeutung der Religion in philosophischen Worten aus und es ist klar, daß er an die Frömmigkeit als einen Akt von religiöser Identifizierung mit dem Universum dachte, so als ob die endliche Kreatur in einem Augenblick eins wird mit der Unendlichkeit. Aber die hier gebotene Beschreibung religiösen Lebens enthält das Rationale des Aktes einer religiösen Identifizierung, die er als christlicher Theologe vollzogen hat. Der erste Augenblick eines religiösen Lebens kulminiert in dem Sicherregenlassen von der Seite des Universums, die es einem eben zuwendet.

Nach Schleiermacher ist die Seite des Universums, die es einem zuwendet, immer die wahrgenommene Einheit der physikalischen und geschichtlichen Welt. Das bedeutet sich zu unterwerfen und beeinflußt zu werden durch die historische Gemeinschaft des Glaubens, insbesonders des Christentums, in dem sein religiöses Gefühl entstanden war, und in dem es genährt wurde. Aber gerade wie er den Einfluß der historischen christlichen Gemeinschaft auf sein Bewußtsein verstand, verlangt eine Untersuchung seines Standpunktes über Denken und Sprache im menschlichen Bewußtsein.

Ehe wir weiter in die Diskussion eintreten, lassen Sie uns bei der Betrachtung verweilen, ob diese Sicht der Welt und des menschlichen Wesens in dieser Welt eine Säkularisierung ist. Vom Standpunkt des orthodoxen und römisch-katholischen Glaubens aus, der ausdrücklich die Heiligung auffaßt als ein Teilhaben am göttlichen Leben, würde Schleiermachers Resignation auf die Endlichkeit und seine Bejahung des religiösen Gefühls einer unvollkommenen endlichen Psyche, die die grundlegende Realität einer geistigen Entwicklung ist, als radikale Säkularisierung, sogar als eine Art von Stoizismus erscheinen.

Vom Standpunkt der protestantischen Reformer, Luther und Calvin, ist die Verneinung der Vollkommenheit in diesem Leben die wahre Lehre, da beide die Heiligung im Sinne einer Vergöttlichung als wichtigste Gabe

des Altarsakramentes ablehnten. Luthers Formel "*simul iustus et peccator*"[9]
rechtfertigt sowohl den Sünder als christlichen Gläubigen vor Gott, als es
auch einen Bruch mit der traditionellen Heiligung darstellt, ebenso wie
Calvins Verneinung der Vollkommenheit in diesem Leben.[10] Was
ketzerisch und vielleicht ungeeignet "weltlich" oder säkular für die klassische
Reformationstheologie erscheint, ist Schleiermachers Einsatz fur die
Sinnlichkeit und das Gefühl als Mittel der Offenbarung, und diesen mißt er
in einem höheren Maße Bedeutung bei, als dem Wort Gottes in dem Neuen
Testament.

Von seinem Standpunkt aus betrachtet Schleiermacher die Welt und
das Ich als sakral und darin wird die Welt der Gefühlserfahrung das Mittel
zur Kommunikation für den Sinn des Heiligen oder das "Himmlische und
Ewige"[11] und das Ich, das diese Kommunikation erfährt, wird ein "wahrer
Priester des Höchsten", welches dann das wirkliche Leben als ein Geschenk
Gottes annimmt ohne daß es auf eine Doktrin von übernatürlichen
Ereignissen, wie Wunder oder außernatürliche Kenntnisse, wie die Lehre
von wörtlicher Inspiration, zurückgreifen muß.

II. Schleiermachers Historisierung des Denkens und der Sprache.

In seiner Beschreibung der Hermeneutik definiert Schleiermacher die
historisierende Betrachtung der Sprache und des menschlichen Verstandes
die später die Denker Wilhelm Dilthey und Ernst Troeltsch so sehr
schätzten. Seiner Meinung nach ist Sprache kein Universum, das über der
Geschichte steht, sondern sie ist vielmehr das was menschliche Geschichte
ausmacht, da sie erst einer Person Geschichte verleiht.

Sprache ist Rede, und Rede ist erst einmal ein "Lebensmoment des
Redenden in der Bedingtheit aller seiner Lebensmomente".[12] Diese
anderen "Lebensmomente" sind hingegen nur im Zusammenhang mit dem
auslösenden Effekt in der Entwicklung und Erhaltung des Lebens des
Sprechers erfahrbar, – d.h. nur veständlich aus der Zeit und dem Ort, der
historischen Gemeinschaft, in der der Sprecher lebte und dem
Entwicklungsstadium dieser Gemeinschaft. Sprache ist ein konstituierendes
Element der Geschichte, denn sie stellt das Mittel dar, durch die die

Lebensmomente der Individuen und Gemeinschaften zusammengehalten wurden. So ist daher die Hermeneutik eine formale Beschreibung des ethischen oder historischen Prozesses selbst.

In Schleiermachers Phänomenologie des Geistes, die sich immer auf den menschlichen Geist unter den Bedingungen von Zeit und Raum bezieht, wird das Bewußtsein durch eine reziproke Bewegung zwischen der Aufnahmefähigkeit in der Welt, als durch die Sinne erfahren, und die Aktivität, als einem Ausdruck des Bewußtseins in verschiedenen Richtungen in der Welt dargestellt. Was das Bewußtseinsstadium bei Schleiermacher angeht, so ist die Rezeptionsfähigkeit ein Gefühl relativer Abhängigkeit und die Aktivität, vom Willen geleitet, ein relatives Gefühl der Freiheit.[13] Was das Denken angeht, so war diese Reziprozität in seiner Dialektik zwischen zwei Arten des Denkens angesiedelt: das abbildliche Denken, in der aufnehmenden Form und das vorbildliche Denken, in der aktiven Form.[14] In seiner Hermeneutik wird dies ein wechselseitiges Verhältnis zwischen dem Verstehen in der receptiven Form und dem Sprechen in der aktiven Form. So konnte Schleiermacher sagen:

> Nun aber hat die Sprache ihre Naturseite: die Differenzen des menschlichen Geistes sind auch bedingt durch das Physische des Menschen und des Erdkörpers. Und so wurzelt die Hermeneutik nicht bloß in der Ethik, sondern auch in der Physik. Ethik und Physik führen wieder zurück auf die Dialektik, als der Wissenschaft von der Einheit des Wissens.[15]

Nicht so wie Immanuel Kant, der versuchte die Identität menschlichen Denkens und Seins im menschlichen Willen anzusetzen, fand hingegen Schleiermacher sie in einer Wechselbeziehung zwischen Denken und Wollen. In jeder Bewegung des Bewußtseins, entweder bei der Rezeption oder der Aktion, tritt eine Bewußtheit über den Unterschied zwischen Denken und Sein auf.[16] Die Einheit des Selbstbewußtseins, z.B. die Identität von Denken und Sein kann daher nicht im abbildlichen, noch im vorbildlichen Denken gefunden werden. Diese Einheit muß in einem direkten Selbstbewußtsein gefunden werden, das streng gesprochen nicht objektiviert werden kann.

Man wird dabei der nicht-objektiven, transzendentalen Einheit des
Ich gewahr, wobei das Ich sein Selbstverständnis bewahrt, auf sich selbst
setzend beim Übergang von einer Form des Denkens und Seins in eine
andere.[17] Das menschliche Selbstbewußtsein ist nicht faßbar – laut
Schleiermacher – in Begriffen, die über die Bewußtseinsaktivität
hinausgehen. Die Einheit oder die Identität des direkten Selbstbewußtseins
ist immer eine Einheit, bedingt durch die verschiedenen Stadien und
Bewegungen des Bewußtseins.

So ist das menschliche Ich, wie die Welt, eine Einheit, die
Verschiedenheit mit einschließt, aber das Ich noch spezifischer angeordnet,
ist eine endliche Einheit.[18] Genau gesagt, erfolgt die Erfahrung der Einheit
durch das Gefühl und nicht durch Wissen; das Problem der Einheit des Ich in
der Beziehung zu der Vielfalt des Bewußtseins ist direkt vergleichbar mit
dem Problem des transzendentalen Grundes für die Einheit der Welt in
Beziehung zur Verschiedenheit der Welt im weiteren Sinn.

In Schleiermachers Hermeneutik sind Denken und Sprache
gleichgesetzt. Denken ist Sprechen in innerlicher oder geistiger Form und
Sprache ist Sprechen in äußerer oder natürlicher Form.[19] Das Ziel des
Prozesses ist die Kommunikation oder wie er sagt:

> Das Reden ist die Vermittlung für Gemeinschaftlichkeit des
> Denkens, . . . Reden ist freilich auch Vermittlung des Denkens
> für den Einzelnen. Das Denken wird durch die innere Rede
> fertig und insofern ist die Rede nur der gewordene Gedanke
> selbst. Aber wo der Denkende nötig findet, den Gedanken
> sich selbst zu fixieren, da entsteht auch die Kunst der Rede,
> Umwandlung des ursprünglichen und wird hernach auch
> Auslegung nöthig.[20]

Das Verstehen ist ein Akt des Menschen und zwar die Umkehrung
eines Aktes des Redens, wodurch die äußerliche Form der Rede wieder zur
innerlichen Form einer Rede, nämlich der des Denkens, umgewandelt
wird.[21] Als ein "Akt des Verstehens" geschieht es im Bewußtsein des
Auslegers, wo als "Denkakt" es die Rede in einen ganz neuen historischen
Zusammenhang hineinführt. Nun wird es zum Ereignis im Leben des
Auslegers.[22]

Schleiermachers Verständnis des Sprechvorganges als eine Wechselwirkung zwischen Sprechen und Verstehen führt ihn zu folgendem Schluß
über die menschliche Erkenntnis: "Sonach gibt es in der Realität kein reines
Wissen, sondern nur verschiedene konzentrische Sphären der Gemeinsam-
keit, der Erfahrung und der Prinzipien".

Und so darf er sagen, "Kein Wissen in zwei Sprachen kann als ganz
dasselbe angesehen werden, auch Ding und a = a nicht".[23] Schleiermacher
meinte damit alle Aussagen, die man im Zusammenhang mit der Welt
macht, da diese aus der Polarität von Natur und Geschichte besteht.

Aber damit wollte er nicht sagen, daß jeder allgemeine Begriff
unmöglich sei, nur daß die "allgemeinen Begriffe" nicht ohne die Bedingung
organischer Aktivitäten entstehen. Ohne diese Aktivitäten wären sie keine
Begriffe mehr. Sie werden nur "als Zeichen" gebraucht.[24] Jeder eigentlich
allgemeine Begriff ensteht aus einem Verhältnis "einer vernünftigen
Organisation zu einem Umgebenden", also zur Welt des Realen. Die direkte
Folgerung, die er daraus zog, war die, daß die historische Voraussetzung jede
Sprache, jedes Denken gewissermaßen besonders und eigentümlich gestaltet,
was er für die philosophischen Systeme als spezifisch wahr ansah.[25] Dies
trifft selbstverständlich auch auf theologische Systeme und Religions-
gemeinschaften zu, soweit sie miteinander durch die Sprache kommunizieren.

III. Schleiermachers neue Auffassung der christlichen Theologie.

Mit diesen Ansichten der Welt und des menschlichen Denkens und
Seins, die er impliziert durch Sprache und Geschichte sah, wollte
Schleiermacher als Professor der christlichen Theologie an der eben im
Jahre 1810 gegründeten Universität in Berlin, sich der Seite des Universums
hingeben, die es ihm zuwandte. Der christliche Glaube war für ihn nicht, –
wie er es ausreichend klar in seinen Reden äußerte – vorrangig eine Sache
der Lehre. Er war vielmehr die Äußerung einer Gemeinschaft, die durch
eine gemeinsame Vorstellung für den Sinn des Göttlichen und ein
gemeinsames Gottesbewußtsein miteinander verbunden war, welches man
durch den Verlauf des sprachlichen Ausdruck in der Geschichte bis Jesus

von Nazareth verfolgen kann. Für Schleiermacher ist das Christentum vorrangig ein Gottesbewußtsein mit Geschichte. Als Pastor und Theologe in der calvinistischen Tradition, verstand er seine theologische Aufgabe nicht darin, eine Beschreibung der metaphysischen Realität der göttlichen Macht der Sakramente unter der Verwaltung einer Priesterschaft abzugeben. Andererseits würde man erwarten, daß er eine klare Darstellung über die Wahrheit des Glaubens, so wie sie in den Lehren aus der Heiligen Schrift dargestellt ist, abgegeben hätte. Schon immer seit Justinus Martyr hat die Proklamation des biblischen Glaubens Fragen bei Gläubigen und Ungläubigen aufgeworfen, die nach der Anwendung der Philosophie riefen, um eine Darstellung für die Beziehungen zwischen Himmel und Erde zu geben, wie sie in den Schriften überliefert werden. Schleiermacher ging anders zur Tagesordnung über.

Er wollte nicht die metaphysischen Ansprüche des traditionellen Glaubens überprüfen, sondern vielmehr aufzeigen, wie diese Ansprüche und die verschiedenen Glaubensdoktrinen der sprachliche Ausdruck eines religiösen Bewußtseins sind, welches, da es zur Struktur menschlichen Bewußtseins gehört, unerwartetes sich Wohlbefinden bietet, was zu entdecken eine ebensolche Freude ist, wie das Anschauen von Blumen in einem Feld. Ein Kenner der Religion kann dieses Bewußtsein veredeln. Schleiermacher, der Theologe und Lehrer, der Diener Christi, betrachtete es als seine Aufgabe, die Diener für die Pflege eines vitalen christlichen Gottesbewußtseins auszubilden.

Hatte er metaphysische Postulate und Ansprüche für sich selbst? Selbstverständlich. Hielt er sich selbst für verantwortlich gegenüber dem Anspruch auf Wahrheit und dem Unterschied zwischen Tatsache und Gleichnis? Wiederum – selbstverständlich! Aber seine metaphysischen Postulate führten ihn dazu seine Frömmigkeit zu pflegen, aber nicht für sein Heil im Jenseits, sondern für ein Leben hier, mit allen menschlichen Fähigkeiten, im Bewußtsein ein Mitglied einer Glaubensgemeinschaft mit Geschichte und einer Bestimmung zu sein.

a. Ein neuer Fokus und Aufgaben für die Theologie.

Was bedeutet das für die Pflege eines christlichen Gottesbewußtseins? Erst sollte man sich des eigenen bewußt werden, dieses Wechselspiels mit dem Bewußtsein der Welt, der Natur, der Geschichte und der Gesellschaft und seines verschieden artigen Ausdrucks in Taten und in Sprache. Schleiermachers *Kurze Darstellung des theologischen Studiums*, – veröffentlicht als das Ergebnis einer jahrelangen Beschäftigung mit diesem Thema [1811], als er 41 Jahre alt war, – setzte von da an einen Verlauf für die Pflege eines Gottesbewußtseins in der Kirche fest.

Er erarbeitete zuerst drei Hauptteile der Theologie: philosophische Theologie, historische Theologie und praktische Theologie. Die philosophische Theologie versucht das eigentümliche Wesen des Christentums auf allgemeine Weise zu bestimmen.[26] Dafür benützt sie "die Ethik als Wissenschaft der Geschichtsprinzipien", um die Art und Weise des christlichen Werdens als ein geschichtliches Ganzes zu zeigen.[27] Er verwendete hierfür eine vergleichende Methode, um dadurch das Wesentliche des Christentums in den Ausdrücken der positiven historischen Gemeinschaften zu bestimmen.[28] So erfährt man, was in der Entwicklung des Christentums reiner Ausdruck seiner Idee ist, und was hingegen als Abweichung hievon, mithin als Krankheitszustand angesehen werden muß.[29] Also prüft man die Ansprüche, die die vielen christlichen Gemeinden für sich erheben, "christlich" zu sein. Mit seinen Grundsätzen der Apologetik und der Polemik hat Schleiermacher eine wissenschaftliche Grundlage für die fruchtbare Auseinandersetzung zwischen christlichen Kirchengemeinschaften und zwischen christlichen und nichtchristlichen Gemeinden gelegt.[30] Die historische Theologie ist der Hauptteil der Theologie und "ist ihrem Inhalte nach ein Teil der neueren Geschichtskunde, und als solche sind ihr alle natürlichen Glieder dieser Wissenschaft koordiniert".[31] Der positive Charakter der Theologie besteht auch in der Anwendung dieses historischen Materials und der Methode von der praktischen Theologie zur Erledigung "aller unter den Begriff Kirchenleitung zu bringenden Aufgaben".[32] Wenn die Kenntnisse, die hier dargestellt werden, nicht von der Kirchenleitung für ihre Aufgaben gebraucht werden, "hören sie auf theologische zu sein und fallen jede der Wissenschaften anheim, der sie ihrem Inhalte nach angehören".[33]

Die historische Theologie hat drei Hauptabteilungen, von denen jede eine spezielle Untersuchung betreibt. Er listet sie in umgekehrter Reihenfolge auf, also genau andersherum, als sie angewendet werden sollten. Erstens nennt er "die geschichtliche Kenntnis des gegenwärtigen Momentes, welche in dem unmittelbarsten Bezug auf die Kirchenleitung steht".[34] Das ist dogmatische Theologie, die sich mit der zukünftigen Entwicklung des Glaubens befaßt. Zweitens, nennt er das Studium der Gegenwart "als Ergebnis der Vergangenheit", d.h. "die Kenntnis des gesamten früheren Verlaufs", nämlich die Kirchengeschichte.[35] Es ist klar, daß Schleiermacher hier zwei verschiedene Richtungen der Untersuchungen im Auge hat: die erste betrachtet die Gegenwart als den Nährboden für die zukünftige Entwicklung und die zweite die Gegenwart als das Ergebnis der Vergangenheit. Diese Ergebnisse werden in Relation zueinander gebracht und miteinander verglichen, um ein Konzept für die ganze Christenheit hervorzubringen, und um neue normative Festellungen und Beschreibungen des Glaubens zu entwickeln.

Die dritte Disziplin der historischen Theologie ist die exegetische Theologie, die das eigentümliche Wesen des Christentums in "dem Zeitraum" sucht, . . . worin Lehre und Gemeinschaft in ihrer Beziehung aufeinander erst wurden und noch nicht in ihrer Abschliessung schon waren".[36] In jeder Disziplin stellte sich Schleiermacher die notwendige analytische und kritische Arbeit vor, um zu einer Beurteilung der Beziehung des christlichen oder sprachlichen Ausdrucks zu gelangen, dem christliche Frömmigkeit oder Gottesbewußtsein zugrundeliegt. Die Kenntnisse von Sprachen, der Hermeneutik und sozialer und historischer Zusammenhänge – d.h. das gesamte Repertoire der historischen Methodologie ist in jedem Fall Voraussetzung.

Mit dieser allzu knappen Skizze der *Kurzen Darstellung* möchte ich nur Schleiermachers Säkularisierung der Theologie durch seine neue Auffassung der historischen Theologie und seine Anwendung der geschichtlichen Wissenschaften für die Zwecke der Theologie darstellen. Genauer gesagt, Schleiermachers Säkularisierung der Theologie besteht hauptsächlich aus der Anwendung der weltlichen Wissenschaften für die Aufgaben der Theologie, sowohl für die Auslegung der Schrift, als auch für das Selbstverständnis der Kirche als eine in der Geschichte gewordene Gemeinde. So durfte **Karl Barth** bemerken: "Es müßte also nach ihm [Schleiermacher] nicht nur eine 'profane Kirchengeschichte', sondern auch eine 'profane Bibelerklärung' . . . im Bereich des Möglichen liegen, aber auch eine profanhistorische Dogmatik wäre theoretisch nicht ausgeschlossen" (Karl Barth, *Gesamtausgabe*, Bd. II, S. 272-273). Eben darum muß man sagen, verdient er den Ehrentitel "Vater der modernen Theologie." Wie er sie tatsächlich angewandt hat, sieht man in seiner Glaubenslehre.

b. Dogmatik als Kritik der christlichen Sprache

Elf Jahre nach dem Erscheinen der *Kurzen Darstellung*, veröffentlichte Schleiermacher seine eigene Dogmatik *Der christliche Glaube*, die er selbstbewußt als einem Wiederaufbau des christlichen Glaubens und zum Heil der Entwicklung des Christentums in einem zukünftigen wissenschaftlichen Zeitalter geschrieben hat. In einer langen Einführung beschreibt er noch einmal seine Theorie des menschlichen Bewußtseins, seine Postulate als Vorschläge, übernommen aus den Lehren der Ethik, Religionsphilosophie und Apologetik und seine analytische und kontruktive Methodologie.

In einem Versuch den Platz und die Rolle der Religion im menschlichen Bewußtsein zu klären, beschreibt er drei Stufen des menschlichen Selbstbewußtseins. Die erste und unterste nennt er eine "tierartig verworrene", in welcher der Gegensatz "zwischen einem einzelnen und einem anderen noch nicht hervorgerufen werden kann".[37] Diese Stufe ziehe sich in die träumerischen Momente zurück, "welche die Übergänge zwischen Wachen und Schlaf vermitteln, wogegen in der hellen und wachen Zeit Gefühl und Anschauung sich klar voneinander sondern, und so die ganze Fülle des im weitesten Umfange des Wortes verstandenen sinnlichen Menschenlebens bilden".[38]

Die zweite oder Mittelstufe des Selbstbewußtseins ist die des menschlichen Alltagsbewußtseins, worin die Subjekt-Objekt Spaltung herrscht. Er nennt es auch "das sinnliche Selbstbewußtsein," um die Gegenwartsbezogenheit des Selbstbewußtseins in und zu der Welt durch die Sinne zu betonen.

In der dritten oder der höchsten Stufe, der des schlechthinnigen Abhängigkeitsgefühl oder des religiösen Selbstbewußtseins, verschwinde der Gegensatz der mittleren Stufe, "und alles, dem sich das Subjekt auf der mittleren Stufe entgegensetzte" werde jetzt "mit ihm identisch zusammengefaßt".[39] Schleiermacher hätte nicht deutlicher die Wiederholung der Auffassung des in seinen *Reden* beschriebenen Aktes der religiösen Identifizierung mit dem Weltall ausdrücken können, als er es hier getan hat. Dieser Akt der Identifizierung mit Weltall dürfte wohl ein "Bewußtsein des Geschöpftwerden" genannt werden, denn er meint damit ein Bewußtsein "von uns als einzelnem endlichen Sein überhaupt"[40] und als "Teil der Welt"[41], was er dann in Paragraph 35 als das "in jenem Selbstbewußtsein gesetzte Verhältnis zwischen dem endlichen Sein der Welt und dem unendlichen Sein Gottes" auslegt.[42]

Da dieses religiöse Bewußtsein sich unvermeidlich in der Sprache, in Symbolen, in liturgischen Riten und religiösen Institutionen ausdrückt, kann man das Gottesbewußtsein jeder einzelnen Religion durch diese Ausdrucksformen nachvollziehen. So reflektiert die christliche Dogmatik, die Ausdrucksformen des christlichen Gottesbewußtseins in der Geschichte und auch der Gegenwart. Man versucht das religiöse Gefühl zu verstehen, das zu dieser Sprache, Mythos und Symbol geführt hat. Dann versucht man es klarer und genauer in einer zeitgenössischen Sprache auszudrücken. Es wäre Schleiermachers Konzeption keineswegs fremd gewesen, die Dogmatik einen Prozess der "Umsetzung in Sprache" zu nennen, die die Funktion von Kritik und Klärung einer anderen Sprache zur Aufgabe hat. In seinen eigenen Worten:

> Wenn aber die Dogmatik ihre eigentliche Bestimmung erfüllen
> soll, nämlich die Verwirrungen, welche auf dem Gesamtgebiet
> der Mitteilungen aus dem unmittelbaren christlich frommen
> Leben immer entstehen wollen, teils aufzulösen, teils auch
> durch die Norm, welche sie aufstellt, soviel an ihr ist zu
> verhüten: so ist ihr, indem sie den Inbegriff der Lehre aufstellt,

außer der dialektisch gebildeten Sprache auch eine möglichst
strenge systematische Anordnung unerläßlich. Denn das
unbestimmtere und unvollkommener Gebildete jeder
fragmentarischen Mitteilung kann nur an dem völlig
Bestimmten und Organisierten eines abgeschlossenen
Inbegriffs richtig geschätzt und auch nur danach rektifiziert
werden; in dem auch die bestimmteste Vorstellung und der
reingebildeste Satz alles Schwankende nur verlieren, wenn sie
zugleich in einen absoluten Zusammenhang gestellt sind, weil
nämlich der Sinn eines jeden Satzes nur in einem
Zusammenhang völlig gegeben ist.[43]

Das Wichtigste sind hier die gegebenen Fakten christlichen
Bewußtseins und nicht einfach eine private Beichte, sondern vielmehr eben
als "das christliche Gesamtbewußtsein" das eine erlebte innere Erfahrung
ist.[44] Das heißt, daß die dogmatische Sprache eine kirchliche Funktion
erfüllen muß. Der kirchliche Wert eines dogmatischen Satzes bestehe nach
Schleiermacher in seiner "Beziehung auf Christum als Erlöser, in dem Maß,
wie sie (die Beziehung) in dem frommen Bewußtsein selbst hervortritt".[45]

Weil ein Vorschlag auf einer religiösen Emotion beruht, hat er eine
"eigentümliche Modifikation" erfahren, wenn er sprachlich ausgedrückt
werden soll. Es kann dann der Glaube eines kleineren oder größeren Kreises
von Christen dargestellt werden, wobei dies von der Kraft des religiösen
Impulses und der Vermittlungsqualität gegenüber der Außenwelt abhängt.
Es ist diese Ausdrucksfähigkeit, die für eine Gruppe von Christen in ihrer
Semantik der Boden und der Ursprung ihres Glaubens sind, und so die
empirische Basis für dogmatische Thesen darstellt. Der wissenschaftliche
Wert eines dogmatischen Satzes beruht auf seiner "Bestimmtheit", also auf
der möglichst genauen und bestimmten Erklärung der vorkommenden
bildlichen Ausdrücke"[46], und auch auf seiner "Fruchtbarkeit," d.h. "wie
vielseitig er auf andere verwandte hinweist," und zwar "in kritischer Hinsicht,
weil nämlich um so leichter die Probe gemacht werden kann, wie gut der
eine dogmatische Ausdruck mit dem anderen zusammenstimmt".[47]

C. Die Sprache Jesu und sein Gottesbewußtsein.

Schleiermachers Anwendung seiner hermeneutischen Prinzipien zur Auslegung des Neuen Testaments, besonders zum Johannesevangelium, bietet dem heutigen Leser etwas fast Überraschendes, was seine neue Auffassung des christlichen Glaubens zu einer Fehlkonstruktion für die kritischeren Neu-Testamentler seiner und auch unserer Zeit macht.

Er ging von einigen Orientierungsbeurteilungen aus, die noch immer Gültigkeit haben – insbesonders, daß die Sprache des Neuen Testamentes zu einer besonderen Zeit und einem geographischen Raum gehört, in denen ein schlechtes Griechisch gebraucht wurde[48]; und daß die Verfasser des Neuen Testamentes meist zweisprachig waren, und daß das Neue Testament eine eigene Grammatik und Hermeneutik verlangt.[49] So weit, so gut, aber wenn er dann seine eigene Theorie über den gewöhnlichen Verlauf der Entwicklung der historischen Sprache in der Geschichte hinzufügt, und wie und aus welch besonderen Gründen dieser Verlauf in der Entstehungszeit des Christentums nicht eingehalten wurde, dann wird das ganze Verfahren verdächtig.

Gemäß Schleiermacher verläuft die normale Entwicklung einer religiösen Sprache so, daß das religiöse Bewußtsein sich erst in der Poesie ausdrückt.[50] Die Poesie drückt Gefühle "rein von innen heraus" aus, wird dann eine rhetorische Sprache, bis eine Stimulans von außen, sei es entweder der Widerstand oder das Interesse von anderen, eine Proklamation oder eine Empfehlung hervorruft. Die religiöse Sprache erreicht ein drittes Stadium, wenn sie konfessional wird; dies ist dann die Sprache, die beides verbindet, den poetischen Ausdruck von innen heraus und den didaktischen Ausdruck, der durch das Äußere stimuliert wird. Er nannte es "das Didaktische, darsstellend Belehrende".[51] So könnte man davon ausgehen, daß die Entwicklung der christlichen Sprache von der Poesie, über die Doktrin zur Bekenntnis sich vollzogen hat. Nicht so, laut Schleiermacher.

In dem nächsten Absatz von *Der christliche Glaube* argumentiert Schleiermacher, daß die christliche Sprache in Wirklichkeit mit der "Selbstverkündigung Christi," begann, der als Subjekt der göttlichen Offenbarung, einen Unterschied starker und schwacher Erregung nicht in sich tragen, sondern an demselben nur vermöge des gemeinsamen Lebens mit anderen teilnehmen konnte".[52] Also war die Sprache Christi von Anfang an "das Didaktische, darstellend Belehrende", weil er immer "von seinem sich selbst immer gleichen Selbstbewußtsein" und zwar von seinem stetigen Gottesbewußtsein aus sich heraus gesprochen hat. Dabei habe er "zugleich sein allein richtiges objektives Bewußtsein von dem Zustand und der Beschaffenheit der Mensche im allgemeinen" mitgeteilt.[53] Das war sein Bewußtsein menschlicher Sündhaftigkeit oder der allgemeine zu akzeptierende Widerstand, oder, klar gesagt, die eigene unverfälschte Abhängigkeit von Gott. Diesen drei Vorschlägen aus dem *Christlichen Glauben* liegen folgende exegetische Annahmen von Schleiermacher zugrunde, die er später in seinen "Vorlesungen über Einführung in das Neue Testament"[54] bestätigt hat, die aber in seinen Vorträgen über *Das Leben Jesu*, die er zuerst 1819 hielt,[55] praktischer Natur waren. Die synoptischen Evangelien Mathäus, Markus und Lukas wurden von Menschen geschrieben, die mindestens zwei Generationen nach Jesus gelebt haben, und die gesammelten Aussprüche und Gleichnisse von Jesus in längere Reden zusammengestellt haben, so wie Mathäus dies in den Kapiteln 5 bis 7 und 13 gemacht hat.[56] In dieser Hinsicht war Schleiermacher sehr modern, ja sogar seiner Zeit weit voraus.

Gleichzeitig war er jedoch absolut davon überzeugt, daß das Evangelium von Johannes von einem Augenzeugen geschrieben worden war, der wahrheitsgemäß die echten Worte Jesu überliefert hat.[57] So beurteilte Schleiermacher die Worte Jesu nach dem Johannes Evangelium als "beschreibend belehrende" oder als eine höhere Form von dialektischer Sprache, die den Ausdruck seines perfekten Gottesbewußtseins darstellt. Das bedeutet, daß er im Johannes-Evangelium eine normative Sprache sah, mit der die wahre Bedeutung des Gottesbewußtseins ausgedrückt wurde und so war dies für ihn die ultimative Norm für jede Form der Kirchenpredigt.

Wie konnte Schleiermacher dies wissen? Seine Antwort lautete, daß er es intuitiv aus seinem direkten Eindruck von diesem Evangelium erfahren hat.

> das Evangelium des Johannes trägt so unverkennbare Spuren der Echtheit und athmet so sehr auf jedem Blatt den

Augenzeugen und persönlichen Teilnehmer, daß man sehr von
Vorurteilen eingenommen sein muß und aus der natürlichen
Richtung hinausgeschoben, um an der Echtheit zu zweifeln.[58]

Als er mit den Beweisen konfrontiert wurde, die seine Ansichten
widerlegten, wies er dieselben einfach zurück. Zum Beispiel, er fand nichts
Zwingendes in der Frage, warum Papias, Bischof von Hierapolis in
Kleinasien von den synoptischen Evangelien wußte, aber gar nichts von dem
Johannesevangelium schrieb, wenn dieses urprünglicher, und also weit älter
wäre als jene? Seine Antwort war nur, daß ihm "solch äußere Gründe"
unwichtig waren

denn die inneren Gründe sind für mich so stark, daß zehn
solcher äußeren Gründe nichts für mich gelten würden.[59]

Schleiermacher ging sogar soweit, zu behaupten, daß das Johannes-
Evangelium die wahren Worte Jesu auf Griechisch enthalte, da Jesus
wahrscheinlich ein "Autodidakt" war.[60] Deshalb legte Schleiermacher die
Schrift wörtlich aus, d.h. er ordnete Jesu selbst alle berühmten Passagen, die
mit "*ego eimi*" oder "Ich bin" beginnen, zu, wie man sie nur im Johannes
Evangelium findet. Der sich selbst bekennende Christ aus dem Johannes-
Evangelium war der wahre historische Jesus für Schleiermacher. Es war
dieser "schlechte historische Teil" bei Schleiermacher, der David Friedrich
Straußens negative Reaktion und seine schriftliche Stellungnahme zu dem
was er kritisch für ein wahres *Leben Jesu* hielt[61] zur Folge hatte.

Dessenungeachtet, wenn auch die Aussprüche Jesu bei Johannes für
alle Ausdrucksformen in der Kirche Normcharakter haben, so bedeutet das
nicht, daß sie selbst nicht Interpretationen unterworfen sind, bei denen eine
präzisere Erklärung ihrer Absicht offenbar wird, und zwar durch das
Gottesbewußtsein ihres Interpreten, der in diesem Fall Schleiermacher ist.
So hat er Christi Worte durch eine theologische Neuinterpretation ausgelegt,
die für ihn im Sinne Jesu richtig war, der selbst wiederum bewiesen hatte,
daß er kein Schriftgelehrter war.[62]   Hier einige Beispiele aus seiner
Abhandlung:

. . . der Sohn kann nichts aus sich selbst tun. (Joh.5, 19) Nach
Schleiermacher, "er könne nichts aus sich thun, sondern müsse

immer auf den Vater sehen, d.h. sein Gottesbewußtsein sei stetig und außer demselben betrachtet sei er null".[63]

"...ich bin vom Himmel herabgestiegen." Joh. 6,38a

"Vom Himmel herabsteigen ist nur der angemessene Ausdruck seiner Sendung und hinaufsteigen, wo er vorher war, ist nur der Ausdruck für das zeitliche erfüllt haben den ewigen göttlichen Ratschluß".[64]

"... ich und der Vater sind Eins." Joh. 10,30 Sein Einssein mit dem Vater ist zu erklären aus unserem Einssein mit ihm, Ausdruck dafür daß er ganz vom Gottesbewußtsein bestimmt wurde".[65]

Die eindeutige Absicht von Schleiermachers Interpretation war es, ein Konzept von dem idealen Gottesbewußtsein von Jesu hervorzurufen. Das heißt, nur in Christus ist das Ideal historisch geworden[66], sodaß nur er den perfekten Sinn für die Abhängigkeit von Gott haben konnte, obwohl er auch zugestand, daß Jesus in anderen Dingen nicht perfekt gewesen sein mag.[67] Hier liegt eine große metaphysische Behauptung vor, die seine Rekonstruktion als ein Stück Spekulation erscheinen läßt, trotz seiner Absicht ein ausschließlich empirisches Werk zu schreiben.

d. Der Christus des christlichen Bewußtseins.

In seinen Versuchen die Formulierung vom Gottesbewußtsein mit spezifisch christlichen Inhalten zu füllen, sagte Schleiermacher, daß die christliche Erfahrung eine Antithese von Lust und Unlust besonderer Art war. Er wollte klar machen, daß die relativen Erfahrungen eines Gefühls absoluter Abhängigkeit nicht nur möglich sind, sondern sogar die einzige Form darstellen, die wir kennen. Er behauptet sogar, daß "das schlechthinnige Abhängkeitsgefühl an und für sich nie einen frommen Moment allein erfülle".[68] Das relative Gefühl von Abhängigkeit und

Freiheit des sensiblen oder mittelmäßig Bewußten wird eine variable Bezugsgröße für das Gefühl schierer Abhängigkeit. Da entsteht ein Pendeleffekt im menschlichen Bewußtsein. Wenn der Ausschlag sich gegen das Gefühl blanker Abhängigkeit richtet, ist es eine Erfahrung der Sünde. Wenn der Ausschlag damit in Einklang steht, ist es Gnade.

Für Schleiermacher hat diese Antithese zwischen Lust und Unlust einen direkten Bezug zu Christus für den christlichen Gläubigen, denn das christliche Gottesbewußtsein ist auch ein Christusbewußtsein. In seinen Worten:

> In der Wirklichkeit des christlichen Lebens ist also beides immer ineinander: kein allgemeines Gottesbewußtsein, ohne daß eine Beziehung auf das Christentum mitgesetzt sei, aber auch kein Verhältnis zum Erlöser, welches nicht auf das allgemeine Gottesbewußtsein bezogen wurde.[69]

Diese Feststellung ist der Ausgangspunkt für eine Doktrin von christlichem Bewußtsein, das die Christologie und die Kirchenkunde zusammenhält, wobei die erstere der historische Brennpunkt ist, und die zweitere der gemeinschaftliche Ausdruck eines gemeinsamen Gottesbewußtseins. Als solches ist es ein Gottesbewußtsein mit Geschichte und kann daher bis auf Jesus Christus zurückverfolgt werden, dessen Vermittlung seines eigenen Gottesbewußtseins so stark war, daß es in der christlichen Gemeinschaft widerhallte, deren Gottesbewußtsein sich mit ihrem Christusbewußtsein identifizierte. Schleiermacher faßte es als die Aufnahme der Gläubigen durch den Erlöser in die "Kraft seines Gottesbewußtseins auf".[70] Das ist das Werk Christi als Erlöser und Vermittler.

Der Gläubige wird bekehrt, wenn er des tiefen Eindrucks gewahr wird, den Christus auf die historische Gemeinschaft gemacht hat und findet ein "Gefühl der schlechthinnigen Abhängigkeit" vor, das einmal hervorgerufen, zu einer Gemeinschaft des Glaubens, der Hoffnung und der Liebe führt, die das Bewußtsein eines Gottes als Schöpfer und Christus als Erlöser teilt.[71] Es ergibt sich daraus, daß die Glaubensgemeinschaft der übrigen Welt einem so gegenübersteht, wie Christus, und ein neues gemeinschaftsbildendes Prinzip tritt in Kraft.[72]

Bei der Ausarbeitung seines Standpunktes über das gemeinschaftliche religiöse Bewußtsein der Christenheit, verwendet Schleiermacher die traditionellen Titel Christi: Prophet, Hoher Priester und König und deutet sie als Variationen desselben Gottesbewußtseins, das bei der heutigen Glaubensgemeinschaft herrscht.[73]

Es liegt aber ein wichtiger neuer Anfang vor gegenüber der traditionellen Kirchenlehre, die eine Beteiligung der spirituellen Kraft und Autorität von Jesus Christus beansprucht.

Die Kirche, die in der Geschichte als eine öffentliche Einrichtung auftritt, teilt nach Schleiermacher nicht die Kraft der Vollkommenheit Christi, der erst einmal die Kirche gegründet hat. Die sichtbare Kirche, oder sollte man besser sagen "die sichtbaren Kirchen" – denn die Pluralität der Kirchen ist evident, – sind fehlbar. Und als solche ist da immer Raum für Besserung vorhanden, für den, laut Schleiermacher, der für die Theologie die grundlegende Verantwortung hat.

Par. 153. Wie in Jedem Teil der sichtbaren Kirche ist der Irrtum möglich, mithin auch irgendwie wirklich: so fehlt es auch in keinem und der berichtigenden Kraft der Wahrheit.[74]

Und genauso wie er sagt, daß es keine absolute oder vollkommene Erkenntnis auf dieser Welt gibt, und daher auch keine Philosophie des Absoluten, so gibt es keine absolute oder vollkommene Äußerung des christlichen Glaubens.

Par. 154. Keine von der sichtbaren Kirche ausgehende Darstellung christlicher Frömmigkeit trägt die lautere und vollkommene Wahrheit in sich.[75]

Angefangen von seinen anthropologische Vorstellungen über den Willen und Geist des Menschen, bis zu seiner Kosmologie und seiner Ansicht über das System der Natur und die Beziehungen zwischen den menschlichen Gemeinschaften auf diesem Planeten, bis zu seiner Meinung über die christliche Gemeinschaft und Lehre, lebte und erlebte Schleiermacher – von seiner Studentenzeit an, bis zu seinem letzten Atemzug – das Leben, das ihm gegeben war, als das einzige Leben, das er kannte, – das endliche Leben.

IV. Schleiermachers Erbe, oder warum man ihn ernst nehmen soll.

Wörtlich genommen paßt das deutsche Wort 'Fehlgriff' zu Schleiermachers Rekonstruktion der christlichen Theologie.

Gemäß der heutigen Bibelwissenschaft basiert Schleiermachers Christologie auf einem Fehlgriff. Sein Verständnis des Johannesevangeliums als der Arbeit eines Augenzeugen, der den wirklichen historischen Jesus hörte, wie er seine Jünger auf Griechisch lehrte, kann heute niemandem dienen. Für ihn war es die historische Quelle und der Ursprung des Stromes christlichen Glaubens. Also warum und wie soll man seine Theologie ernstnehmen?

Was bleibt von seinem Unternehmen, wenn erst einmal die Struktur dieser Rekonstruktion zusammengebrochen ist? Die Antwort auf diese Frage lautet: "Ein großer Teil bleibt erhalten, und das meiste davon ist methodologisch!". Schleiermachers Erbe wird meist in dem Satz zusammengefaßt: "Der Vater der modernen Theologie", was noch umfassender als "der Gründer der modernen Theologie" ausgedrückt werden kann. Er war dies in der Tat, denn er sah und versuchte sich mit so vielen Problemen und Streitfragen auseinanderzusetzen, an denen die moderne Theologie noch immer arbeitet. Viele Fäden von Untersuchungen und Betrachtungen über die Religion und Theologie und Philosophie können bis zu ihm zurückgesponnen werden. Von der zeitgenössischen vergleichenden und historischen Religionswissenschaft von Mircea Eliade und Wilfred Cantwell Smith angefangen, über die Phänomenologiestudien von Rudolf Otto, bis zu den zeitgenössischen hermeneutischen und ontologischen Theorien, die Sprache mit dem menschlichen Sein in der Welt gleichsetzen von Heidegger und Husserl; bei allen Fäden, die nicht direkt zu Hegel zurückgehen, finden wir einen Kreuzungspunkt in dem alternativen geistigen Feld des Friedrich Schleiermacher.

Aber diese sind meist sein philosophisches Erbe; was verbleibt von seiner Theologie? Schleiermachers Leistung und sein größtes Erbe war die Schaffung einer christlichen liberalen Theologie. Aber dies im heutigen Meinungsklima zu sagen, kommt einem Todesstoß gleich, da das Wort "liberal", sei es in der Politik oder in der Religion, Grund für eine augenblickliche Ablehnung ist.

Im Zusammenhang mit theologischen Studien in einer Universität wollen wir diese Gefahr auf uns nehmen.

Leider hat die liberale Theologie mehr unter der Verachtung der Theologen und Gläubigen gelitten, als irgendwelche anderen Gruppen. Wenn Schleiermacher mit den "Gebildeten unter den Verächtern der Religion" in seiner Zeit konfrontiert wurde, so müssen sich seine Anhänger heute den "theologischen Verächtern einer liberalen Theologie" stellen, worunter man "Schleiermachers Theologie" versteht. Besonders drei sehr verschiedene Kritiken sind für diesen schlechten Ruf verantwortlich.

Liberale Theologie wurde durch den Barthianismus mißbilligt, da sie mit Anthropologie und Kosmologie beginnt und sich so außer Hörweite für das ewige Wort Gottes begibt, das menschliche Sündhaftigkeit mit dem göttlichen "Nein" verdammt und den Sünder mit dem göttlichen "Ja" im Evangelium Jesu Christi erlöst.[76] Daraus ergibt sich, daß liberale Theologie als solche zur menschlich sündhaften Anmaßung gehört, die durch das göttliche Wort verdammt wird. Sie stammt nicht wirklich von Gott.

Die amerikanische Version der Neo-Orthodoxie in der christlichen Theologie – zusammen mit Reinhold Niebuhr – mißbilligt liberale Theologie wegen ihrer naiven optimistischen, manchmal perfektionistischen Sicht der menschlichen Natur. In dieser Hinsicht bietet die liberale Theologie simplifizierende Analysen des Menschen, wobei sie davon ausgeht, daß menschliche Handlungen und Lösungen in der Lage sind, einen Ausweg zu finden. Es fehlt die Einschätzung der komplexen Natur sozialer Probleme in der Menschheit und wenn diese erkannt werden, bestand eine Tendenz sie zu optimistisch, ja zu utopisch in der Denkweise der marxistischen Tradition zu beurteilen.

Der reife Reinhold Niebuhr schrieb als Antimarxist, der erst einmal durch die Versuchung des marxistischen Denkens gegangen war, diese Kritik.

In Schleiermachers Denken sah er einen "romantischen Relativismus", der im letzten Ende selbstzerstörerisch sei, weil er logischerweise zum Polytheismus führen müsse.[77] Also Reinhold Niebuhr wie auch Karl Barth, mußten glauben, er habe einen irgendwie gearteten absoluten Standpunkt, von dem aus der seine Theologie betreiben konnte. Da er sich mit einer fehlbaren, menschlichen Endlichkeit abfand, konnte Schleiermacher ohne einen solchen Standpunkt auskommen.

Letztendlich wurde liberale Theologie wegen ihres Mangels an Pflichtbewußtsein von den Fundamentalisten und konservativen evangelischen Christen (gerade die letzteren sollten hervorgehoben werden) getadelt. Die Meßeinheit für solch mangelnde Engagiertheit sind das numerische Wachstum, oder sein Fehlen, der liberalen Kirchen und der Geldbetrag, der für diese Kirchen aufgebracht wird. Diese konservativen Gruppen tendieren dazu, ihren eigenen Erfolg in diesen Bereichen als Beweis Gottes für die Wahrheit ihrer Theologie und ihrer prophetischen Arbeit zu sehen, und dies insbesonders bei der Verurteilung von weltlichem Humanismus, als der Arbeit des Satans in unserer Kultur, unseren Gerichten und Schulen.

Vom Standpunkt Schleiermacherscher Theologie stellt die Streitfrage über den anthropologischen Standpunkt keinen Nachteil im Vergleich zur Doktrin von Karl Barth über das Wort Gottes dar, da das Sprechen über Gott und das Handeln eindeutig ein anthropologischer Ausgangspunkt ist, insbesondere die Vorstellung von Gott in menschlichen Begriffen. Hier deutet sich die anthropomorphische Zwangsvorstellung der orthodoxen christlichen Theologie an.

Sprache ist, wie der Hl. Augustinus lehrte, eine menschliche Konvention und wenn Barth herausstreicht, daß Theologie nichts anderes tut, als in menschlichen Worten alles das zu wiederholen, was Gott durch Gott über Gott sagt, und daß daher die Offenbarung eine geistige Form von Sprache ist, in der Gott über Gott durch den Heiligen Geist lehrt, dann drücken alle diese Konzepte die Voraussetzung einer menschlichen Kultur aus, die ihre wirkliche Quelle ist.

Schleiermacher gesteht so, daß der Ausgangspunkt für seine Lehre von Gott im menschlichen Bewußtsein liegt, aber daß dieses Bewußtsein durch die Kraft seiner Beziehung durch Sprache und natürliche Bilder über sich selbst hinaus zu dem Heiligen als unvorstellbarem Ort alles endlichen Seins weist. Karl Barth würde er entgegnen, daß seine Doktrin von Gott ernsthafter und besser fundiert sei, weil sie vom menschlichen Bewußtsein ausgehe, wo alle Theologie in der Geschichte, sei sie nun jüdisch, christlich, islamisch oder sonstwie, ja sogar die des Karl Barth wirklich beginnt.

Was die Niebuhrsche Anklage des anthropologischen Optimismus angeht, so hängt diese wiederum von einer Einschätzung der grundlegenden Voraussetzung die menschliche Natur betreffend ab. Für Schleiermacher ist die menschliche Natur, das menschliche Sein und Geist endlich. Man mag nach Vollkommenheit oder Besserung im moralischen Verhalten streben, man kann jedoch keine Perfektion erwarten, denn jede rationale Maxime, die eine Aktion leitet, wird durch Vielfalt des sinnlichen Bewußtseins bedingt. Schleiermacher hat sich im Prinzip darauf festgelegt, daß unser Denken, sei es philosophisch oder theologisch, ebenso wie unser moralisches Verhalten unvollkommen ist. Er konnte überzeugender als die meisten seiner philosophischen und theologischen Gegner die Worte des Paulus aus dem Ersten Korinther 13 zitieren: "All unser Wissen ist Stückwerk und all unser Weissagen ist Stückwerk" (v.9). Ja in dieser Hinsicht ist sogar christliche Prophezeiung und Predigt unvollkommen; dies aber ist kein Grund solches Predigen abzuwerten oder zu verachten.

Dies ist, so scheint es, der wahre Stein des Anstoßes Schleiermachers liberaler christlicher Theologie; die Tatsache sich mit der Endlichkeit menschlichen Seins und Geistes, bis hin zur Endlichkeit der Welt und der christlichen Kirche, als Teil der Geschichte, abzufinden. Hier hätte Schleiermacher besser daran getan im menschlichen Bewußtsein nach den Gründen für die Verweigerung der Anerkennung der eigenen Endlichkeit, der eigenen Ablehnung der Begrenztheit und dem was man von der letzten Wahrheit und Wirklichkeit wissen kann, zu suchen. Dies geschieht philosophisch im Deutschen Idealismus und theologisch in der christlichen Orthodoxie und in der Neo-Orthodoxie, wo der Anspruch erhoben wird, daß Gott unsere Bedingtheit überwindet, in dem er uns die Gnade der absoluten Wahrheit schenkt. Hätte sich Schleiermacher direkter dem Problem des Dilemmas des Menschen genähert, wie dies Reinhold Niebuhr getan hat, hätte er in diesen Forderungen nach Vollkommenheit in der Erkenntnis, in der Religion oder im moralischen Ausdruck, menschliche Wesen gefunden, die sich von ihrer eigenen Endlichkeit entfremdet haben.

Hier muß Sünde als menschliche Hybris bezeichnet werden, oder als das, was Dietrich Bonhoeffer "*sicut Deus*" genannt hat, das menschliche Wesen, das Gott spielt oder versucht über die Grenzen der endlichen Natur hinauszugreifen, da es die eigene Kreatürlichkeit nicht erträgt. Aus Schleiermachers Sicht kann jeder alle Forderungen nach Vollkommenheit, philosophischer oder religiöser Art, stellen, als Ausdruck der Verweigerung das Leben und das Wesen, das Gott durch die Schöpfung gegeben hat, zu akzeptieren; er weigert sich, die Seite des Universums anzunehmen, die es ihm zuwendet. Für Schleiermacher bringt dieses Sichergeben die Erlösung und eine gesundere Haltung im Leben, wenn man den Haß gegen die Endlichkeit und die Begrenztheit überwindet, der dazu führt, die Erreichung des Absoluten zu fordern, sei es durch Philosophie oder durch Religion; diese Forderungen beinhalten die unvermeidlichen Mittel, jene zu manipulieren, die diese Forderungen annehmen.

Ihnen gegenüber kann Schleiermacher nur die Kritik durch Vernunft vorbringen, daß er das Endliche und Fehlbare zugelassen hat. Wie kann man aber wirklich jemandem entgegnen, der von der Möglichkeit der Vollkommenheit überzeugt ist? Schleiermacher war sich bewußt, daß Erkenntnis "wirklich" wird und dies der geeignete Bezug ist, zu dem, was man von der Welt und dem menschlichen Bewußtsein wissen kann, wenn man es an seinem Platz in der Welt anerkennt und akzeptiert. Aber man muß erst die Wirklichkeit und den Wert der Überlegungen unter diesen Bedingungen erkennen, um eine solche Erkenntnis zu erlangen. Und es beunruhigte ihn nicht wenig, wenn er die zukünftigen Beziehungen des Christentums zu dieser Art Endlichkeit oder wirklichen Erkenntnis der Welt betrachtete.

Das Christentum wird es vielleicht niemals lernen die endliche Vernunft richtig einzuschätzen. Es baut in der Tat eine Barrikade dagegen auf, um die Erkenntnis über die Endlichkeit aus seiner Mitte zu verbannen, wodurch "der Knoten der Geschichte so auseinandergehen würde: das Christentum mit der Barbarei und die Wissenschaft mit dem Unglauben."

Hat er ein wirklich bedeutendes Problem gesehen? Schauen Sie nur nach dem heutigen Amerika, insbesonders die Angriffe durch die fundamentalistischen Christen auf die Schulen und die Gerichte und ihre Bemühungen eine Mauer in unserer Kultur gegenüber der Erkenntnis, die durch die endliche Vernunft gewonnen wurde, zu errichten. Sie nennen es: säkularer Humanismus. Aber es reicht an einen Versuch heran, dem Einfluß der Erkenntnis, die durch die endliche Vernunft erlangt wurde, in unserer Gesellschaft eine Grenze zu setzen. Diesgeht so weit, daß sie erfolgreich sind, und daß die amerikanische Gesellschaft ihre Rolle bei der rationalen Untersuchung der Welt abzuschließen droht.

Für die, die auf dem Besitz der absoluten Erkenntnis durch die Philosophie oder durch ihren religiösen Glauben beharren, für die, die auf der Hoffnung bestehen, ewig zu werden, als dem einzigen bedeutungsvollen Ausdruck ihrer Philosophie oder ihrer Religion, muß Schleiermachers Phänomenologie des endlichen Geistes und die Hoffnung nach einer gesunden Haltung im Leben, einem Wohlbefinden, – man könnte sagen, eines Shalom – unter den Bedingungen des Daseins, nur wie ein endliches Krümmel erscheinen, verglichen mit dem Brotlaib des ewigen Lebens. Aber selbst wenn sie dieses Krümmel vom Diskussionstisch fegen wollten, ist klar, daß Schleiermacher es aufheben würde, da es die Basis und der Gehalt menschlichen Lebens ist, so wie es als Geschenk Gottes gefeiert werden muß. Es wäre eine ontologische Undankbarkeit es nicht zu tun.

Anmerkungen

1. Friedrich D. E. Schleiermacher, "Über seine Glaubenslehre an Herrn Dr. Lücke," *Theologische Studien und Kritiken*, 2 (1829), 255-284; 481-532. Hier werden Schleiermachers *Sämmtliche Werke*, Band I.2, S. 614, zitiert.

2. Schleiermacher, *Briefe* 1, S. 10; zitiert von William A. Johnson, *On Religion: A Study of Theological Method in Schleiermacher and Nygren*, (Leiden: E.J. Brill, 1964), S. 7, Fußnote 5.

3. Ebenda.

4. Michael D. Ryan, "Young Friedrich Schleiermacher's Act of Religious Identification," *New Athenaeum/Neues Athenaeum* 1 (1989), S. 142-172.

5. Ebenda, S. 145-156.

6. Friedrich Schleiermacher, *Über die Religion: Reden an die Gebildeten unter ihren Verächtern*. (Berlin: bei Johann Friedrich Unger, 1799) Sechste Auflage 1967 bei Vandenhoeck & Ruprecht, Göttingen, S. 51.

7. Ebenda, S. 64f. In der zweiten Auflage hat Schleiermacher eine erklärende Version der Beschreibung des flüchtigen Moments des Einswerdens des religiösen Geistes mit dem Universum eingeführt, und liess die folgende, viel poetischere Version wegfallen:
"Schnell und zaubrisch entwickelt sich eine Erscheinung, eine Begebenheit zu einem Bilde des Universums. So wie sie sich formt die geliebte und immer

gesuchte Gestalt, flieht ihr meine Seele entgegen, ich umfange sie nicht wie
einen Schatten, sondern wie das heilige Wesen selbst. Ich liege am Busen
der unendlichen Welt: ich bin in diesem Augenblick ihre Seele, denn ich
fühle alle ihre Kräfte und ihr unendliches Leben wie mein eigenes, sie ist in
diesem Augenblicke mein Leib, denn ich durchdringe ihre Muskeln und ihre
Glieder wie meine eigenen, und ihre innersten Nerven bewegen sich nach
meinen Sinn und meiner Ahnung wie die meinigen. Die geringste
Erschütterung, und es verweht die heilige Umarmung, und nun erst steht die
Anschauung vor mir als eine abgesonderte Gestalt, ich messe sie, und sie
spiegelt sich in der offenen Seele wie das Bild der sich entwindenden
Geliebten in dem aufgeschlagenen Auge des Jünglings, und nun erst arbeitet
sich das Gefühl aus dem Innern empor, und verbreitet sich wie die Röthe der
Scham und der Lust auf seiner Wange. Dieser Moment ist die höchste
Blüthe der Religion. Könnte ich ihn Euch schaffen, so wäre ich ein Gott –
das heilige Schicksal verzeihe mir nur, dass ich mehr als Eleusische
Mysterien habe aufdecken mussen. – Er ist die Geburtstunde alles
Lebendigen in der Religion."
[Vgl. Kritische Ausgabe, *Schleiermachers Reden über die Religion*, Braunschweig: C.A.
Schwetschke und Sohn, 1879, S. 55 für die zweite Auflage, und S. 78f. für die erste Auflage.]

  8. *Reden*, Kritische Ausgabe, 1879, S. 72.

  9. Martin Luther, *Werke*, Weimar Ausgabe, Bd. 39, S. 523.

  10. Johannes Calvin, *Unterricht in der christlichen Religion*, Institutio Christianae
Religionis, Dritter Band, (Buch IV), nach der letzten Ausgabe übersetzt und bearbeitet von
Otto Weber (Buchhandlung des Erziehungsvereins Neukirchen Kreis Moers, 1938), Kap. 1,
Par. 16, Seiten 25-26, "Die falsche Vollkommenheitsforderung kommt aus verkehrter
Gesinnung." In Par. 20, S. 30 druckt sich Calvin so aus:
    "Ich gebe nun zwar zu, daß man nicht etwa lässig oder kalt sein soll, wenn
    man sich bemüht, auf Vollkommenheit zu dringen, und noch viel weniger
    davon ablassen darf; aber ich behaupte: es ist ein teuflisches Hirngespinst,
    wenn man, solange wir noch im Laufe sind, die Herzen mit dem Vertrauen
    auf solche Vollkommenheit erfüllt. Deshalb wird im Glaubensbekenntnis die
    Vergebung der Sünden durchaus sinnvoll und die Lehre von der Kirche
    angeschlossen."

  11. *Reden*, (1799), 1967, S. 25.

  12. Schleiermacher, *Hermeneutik*, S.W., III.7, (Berlin bei G. Reimer), S. 13.

  13. Schleiermacher, *Der christliche Glaube* (Berlin: Walter de Gruyter & Co., 1960),
§4, S. 24-25.

  14. Schleiermacher, *Dialektik*, p. 517, zitiert von Marlin E. Miller, *Der Übergang*:
Schleiermachers Theologie des Reiches Gottes im Zusammenhang seines Gesamtdenkens,
(Gerd Mohn: Gutersloher Verlagshaus, 1970), p. 30f.

  15. *Hermeneutik*, S. 10.

  16. *Dialektik*, S. 518, zitiert von M. Miller, S. 31.

  17. Ebenda. S. 483, 488, 507, zitiert von M. Miller, S. 34. Vgl. auch Seiten 36 bis 47,
wo Millers vortreffliche Auslegung von Schleiermachers Begriff vom unmittelbaren
Selbstbewußtsein durch eine Seinsanalogie zwischen dem transzendenten Grunde der Identität
und dem transzendenten Grunde der Welt zu finden ist. Miller stellt ganz überzeugend den
"Übergang" von Passivität zu Aktivität und umgekehrt, der den Mittelpunkt des ganzen
Systems Schleiermachers bildet. Daß Schleiermacher auch dieses Modell von Einheit/
Vielheit bei der Beschreibung des Welt- und Selbstbewußtseins hinüber zu seiner Lehre von
Gott übertragen hat, hat Dr. Robert Streetman in seiner Dissertation, "Friedrich
Schleiermacher's Doctrine of the Trinity and its Significance," Drew University, 1975,

aufgezeigt; besonders auf Seite 222 bis 229, wo er die göttliche *monas*, die Einheit der Gottheit, im Unterschied zur göttlichen *trias*, der Dreieinigkeit Gottes, diskutiert.

18. M. Miller, S. 37.

19. *Hermeneutik*, S. 9.

20. Ibid., S. 10.

21. Ebenda.

22. Schleiermacher wußte Bescheid, daß man den ursprünglichen historischen Zusammenhang einer Rede aus dem Altertum nicht einfach wiederherstellen kann. Eben darum hat er gelehrt, daß man jenen Zusammenhang durch eine Analogie zwischen der Gegenwart und jener Vergangenheit herstellen muß (*Hermeneutik*, p. 215). Hier hat der Historiker in Schleiermacher über den Philosoph gesiegt.

Obwohl er wußte, daß es unmöglich ist, die Vergangenheit ganz wie sie war, genau zu erkennen – ja, bekannte sich zu der Fehlbarkeit des Geistes in allem menschlichen Wissen und Tätigkeiten – versuchte er sie doch zu rekonstruieren, weil er sich so sehr für die Eigentümlichkeit und die Partikularität der Menschen in ihrer eigenen Faktizität interessierte, wie sie die Welt sahen, und wie sie darin handelten.

In seinem sehr einflußreichen Buch, *Wahrheit und Methode* (Tübingen: J.C.B. Mohr, 1960) hat Hans-Georg Gadamer die Überlegenheit von Hegels Hermeneutik über diejenige Schleiermachers betont, weil Hegel "das klarste Bewußtsein von der Ohnmacht aller Restauration" habe (S. 166). Nach Hegel sei die Erforschung des Okkasionellen unmöglich, weil es "vom Baum gebrochene Früchte" blieben. Dadurch "gewinnt man kein Verhältnis des Lebens zu ihnen, sondern das der blossen Vorstellung" (Ebenda). Sie können nur durch "die Er-Innerung des in ihnen noch veräusserten Geistes" in die Gegenwart hinein kommen, und zwar "der Geist des tragischen Schicksals, das alle jene individuellen Götter und Attribute der Substanz in das Eine Pantheon versammelt, in den seiner als Geist selbstbewußten Geist" (S. 161).

Es ist jedoch ganz klar, daß Hegel (und auch Gadamer) wenig Interesse für das Leben und die Wirklichkeit eines vergangenen Volkes hatte, weil "der Geist des tragischen Schicksals" ihm eben nicht nur viel wichtiger war, als "das sittliche Leben und die Wirklichkeit jenes Volkes", sondern auch nur der Geist "denkende Vermittlung" mit jenem Volke schaffen könne (ebenda).

Wie oben gesagt, regte bei Schleiermacher die Erinnerung an die Vergangenheit die vorstellenden-geschichtlichen Denkprozesse an, was Hegel die "*der blossen Vorstellung*" nannte. Nach Hegel sei es der Moment, worin die historischen Tatsachen vom Geist hinauf auf die Ebene der universalen Vernunft aufgehoben werden. Also wurde Hegel ganz vom philosophischen Vorurteil beherrscht, welches höheren Wert auf den menschlichen Genus als auf menschliche Partikularität legt. Der Historiker aber interessiert sich immer mehr für "das Leben und Wirklichkeit jenes Volkes."

23. *Dialektik*, S.W. (Berlin, 1839) S. 68f.

24. Ebenda. S. 58f.

25. Heinrich Scholz, *Christentum und Wissenschaft in Schleiermachers Glaubenslehre* (Berlin: Arthur Glaue Verlag, 1909), S. 38, streicht den Unterschied zwischen Schleiermacher und Hegel ganz heraus:
"Hegel hatte schon 1801 behauptet: 'Wenn ein Eigentümliches wirklich das Wesen einer Philosophie ausmache, so würde es keine Philosophie sein. Denn wie sollte das Vernünftige eigentümlich sein?' [*Differenz des Fichtischen und Schellingschen Systems der Philosophie*, Hegel, W.W. I., p. 166 der zweiten Auflage.] Schleiermacher erklärte 1802, vor Philosophen von Fach, daß am Ende das philosophische System eines jeden von seinem Charakter abhängig sei. [In der Rezension von Asts Dissertation *De Platonis Phaedro* (Br. IV, S. 575).] Und im Vortrag der Ethik, vor seiner Studenten,

sprach er noch entschiedener aus: 'Ein philosophisches System ist allemal ein Individuelles aus allgemeinen Elementen.' [*Ethik*, S. 363]."

26. F. Schleiermacher, *Kurze Darstellung des theologischen Studiums zum Behuf einleitender Vorlesungen*, Kritische Ausgabe von Heinrich Scholz (Nachdruck der dritten, kritischen Ausgabe, Leipzig, 1910, Hildesheim, Georg Olms Verlagsbuchhandlung, 1961), S. 13.

27. Ebenda, S. 15.

28. Ebenda, §32. "Da das eigentümliche Wesen des Christentums sich ebensowenig rein wissenschaftlich konstruieren lässt, als es bloss empirisch aufgefasst werden kann: so lässt es sich nur kritisch bestimmen (vgl. §23) durch Gegeneinanderhalten dessen, was im Christentum geschichtlich gegeben ist, und der Gegensätze, vermöge deren fromme Gemeinschaften können voneinander verschieden sein." S. 13.

29. Ebenda, §35, S. 15.

30. Ebenda, §44. "Auf den Begriff des Positiven zurückgehend, muß dann für das eigentümliche Wesen des Christentums eine Formel aufgestellt und mit Beziehung auf das Eigentümliche anderer frommen Gemeinschaften unter jenen Begriff subsumiert werden." Also hatte Karl Barth völlig Recht, als er in seiner Vorlesung 1923/24 sagte, "Ich brauche kaum zu sagen, daß wir hier an der methodischen Quelle der modernen Religionswissenschaft stehen." K. Barth, *Gesamtausgabe*, Bd. 11, S. 266.

31. Ebenda, §69, S. 30. Vgl. K. Barth, *Gesamtausgabe*, Bd. 11, S. 273. Schleiermacher habe das Primat der Historiker begründet.

32. Ebenda, §260, S. 100.

33. Ebenda, §6, S. 3.

34. Ebenda, §81, S. 35.

35. Ebenda, §82, S. 35.

36. Ebenda, §87, S. 37.

37. *Der christliche Glaube*, §5, S. 32f.

38. Ebenda, §5, S. 31-32.

39. Ebenda, S. 33.

40. Ebenda, S. 32. Cf. §34, S. 181, "Erweitern wir es zum Bewußtsein der menschlichen Gattung, oder sind wir uns gar unsrer selbst als endlicher Geist schlechthin bewußt, so ist uns nichts mehr entgegengesetzt, als nur, was der Geist nicht hat."

41. Ebenda, §34, S. 180.

42. Ibid., §35, p. 140.

43. Ebenda, §28, S. 157f. Schleiermachers Interesse in der Vielheit der möglichen Ausdrucksweisen, die den Menschen zu ihrer Verfügung in der Sprache besonders für philosophische und theologische Zwecke stehen, hat Dr. Ruth Drucilla Richardson in ihrer Dissertation, "Friedrich Schleiermacher's *Weihnachtsfeier* as 'Universal Poetry': The Impact of Friedrich Schlegel on the Intellectual Development of the Young Schleiermacher" (Drew University, 1985) gezeigt. Beeindruckend ist ihre Behandlung der Versuche des jungen Schleiermacher in verschiedenen literarischen Genres zu schreiben.

44. *Sendschreiben an Lücke*, (neu herausgegeben von Lic. Hermann Mulert, Giessen: Verlag von A. Töpelmann: 1908), S. 57.

45. *Der christliche Glaube*, §17, S. 113.

46. Ebenda, S. 114.

47. Ebenda.

48. *Hermeneutik*, (hg. Kimmerle, Heidelberg, 1959), S. 70.

49. Ebenda, S. 93.

50. *Der christliche Glaube*, §15, S. 107.

51. Ebenda, S. 108.

52. Ebenda.

53. Ebenda, S. 109.

54. Schleiermacher, *Einleitung ins Neue Testament*, S.W., I.8. Dieser Band enthält seine Manuskripte ergänzt durch Nachschriften von Sommersemester 1829 und Winter Semester 1831-32.

55. *Das Leben Jesu*, S.W., I.6, Berlin: G. Reimer Verlag, 1864. Schleiermacher las über "Das Leben Jesu" viermal zwischen 1819 und 1832.

56. *Einleitung ins Neue Testament*, S.W., I.8, S. 207f, S. 245, und S. 303.

57. Ebenda, S. 207.

58. Ebenda, S. 283.

59. Ebenda, S. 243.

60. *Das Leben Jesu*, S.W., I.6, S. 121.

61. David Friedrich Strauss' *Leben Jesu* erschien 1835, ein Jahr nach Schleiermachers Tode. Zu den vielerlei kritischen Reaktionen auf Strauss vgl. das Buch von Edwina G. Lawler, *David Friedrich Strauss and his Critics: The Life of Jesus Debate in Early Nineteenth-Century German Journals*, New York, Berne, Frankfurt am Main: Peter Lang, 1986.

62. *Leben Jesu*, S. 265, wo es heißt:
". . . alle Stellen des Pentateuch sind von einer ganz allgemeinen Art, und es lässt sich aus diesen Stellen sehen, daß Christus sagen konnte, Es ist da von mir die Rede, – ohne daß er behauptete, daß von einer bestimmten Vorstellung von ihm in dem Redenden gehandelt worden ist, sondern nur von der Idee, die in ihm realisirt worden ist. Dessenungeachtet kann er sagen, daß die Schrift diejenigen verklage, die an die Schrift glaubten, aber nun, nachdem er erschienen sei, die Anwendung nicht davon machten die er selbst macht. Also eine absolute Buchstäblichkeit ist hier nicht vorauszusetzen, und wenn sich Christus als den Verheissenen darstellt, gehört dazu nicht, daß er in seinem eigenthümlichen persönlichen Sein, oder in seinen eigenthümlichen Schikkungen und Lebensführungen sei vorhergesehen worden, sondern das wird nur behauptet werden können, wo er solches einzelne bestimmt anführt."

63. Ebenda, S. 281.

64. Ebenda, S. 287.

65. Ebenda.

66. *Der christliche Glaube*, Band II, §93, S. 42.

67. Ebenda, Bd. II, §93, S. 35.
"Nun aber handelt es sich in diesem Gesamtleben nicht um die tausenderlei Beziehungen des menschlichen Lebens, so daß er auch für alles Wissen oder alle Kunst und Geschicklichkeit, die sich in der menschlichen Gesellschaft entwickelt, urbildlich sein musste, sondern nur um die Kräftigkeit des Gottesbewußtseins, zu allen Lebensmomenten den Impuls zu geben und sie zu bestimmen, und weiter dehnen wir auch die Urbildlichkeit des Erlösers nicht aus."

68. Ebenda, §62, S. 342.

69. Ebenda, S. 344.

70. Ebenda, Band II, §100, S. 90.

71. Ebenda.

72. Ebenda, S. 91f.

73. Ebenda, Bd. II, §§102-105, S. 105-147.

74. Ebenda, S. 398.

75. Ebenda, S. 400.

76. Karl Barth, *Die Theologie Schleiermachers*, V, Bd. 2 der *Karl Barth Gesamtausgabe*, (Theologischer Verlag, Zürich, 1978), besonders "Nachwort" in Heinz Bolli

(Redaktor), *Schleiermacher-Auswahl,* München u. Hamburg, 1968, was auf englisch den Titel trägt, "Concluding Unscientific Postscript on Schleiermacher," *The Theology of Karl Barth,* ed. Dietrich Ritschl, Tr. Geoffrey W. Bromiley (Grand Rapids, William B. Eerdmans Publishing Co, 1982), wo zum Schluß Barth über die Zukunft der Theologie spekuliert (S. 279 der englischen Ausgabe). Interessant ist Barths Behauptung, Schleiermacher habe "aus einem anthropologischen Standpunkt" gedacht und gesprochen, als ob er vom heiligen Geist dazu ermutigt wurde, als ob der heilige Geist irgendjemand dazu ermutigen würde.

  77. Reinhold Niebuhr, *The Nature and Destiny of Man,* Bd. 1, (New York: Charles Scribner's Sons, 1941), S. 86.

SECTION THREE

SCHLEIERMACHER AND THE CHURCH

XII

LIEDERBLÄTTER – EIN UNBEKANNTES PERIODIKUM SCHLEIERMACHERS
ZUGLEICH EIN BEITRAG ZUR VORGESCHICHTE UND ENTSTEHUNG DES BERLINER GESANGBUCHS VON 1829

Wolfgang Virmond

Für Terrence Tice

In ihrer letzten Stunde bittet die alte Frau Nimptsch ihre Pflegetochter: "Lene, Kind, ich liege nicht hoch genug. Du mußt mir noch das Gesangbuch unterlegen. – Lene widersprach nicht, ging vielmehr und holte das Gesangbuch. Als sie's aber brachte, sagte die Alte: Nein, nich das, das ist das neue. Das alte will ich, das dicke mit den zwei Klappen [...] Das hab ich meiner Mutter auch holen müssen [...] Als ich ihr aber das Porstsche, das sie bei der Einsegnung gehabt, unterschob, da wurde sie ganz still und ist ruhig eingeschlafen. Und das möcht ich auch. Ach, Lene. Der Tod ist es nich... Aber das Sterben... So, so. Ah, das hilft."

Die Szene aus dem Berlin von 1878, die Fontane im 19. Kapitel von "Irrungen Wirrungen" so unvergleichlich schildert, macht das Schicksal des "Gesangbuchs zum gottesdienstlichen Gebrauch für evangelische Gemeinen", welches Schleiermacher im Verein mit mehreren Amtskollegen von 1818 bis 1827 erarbeitet hatte und das 1829 gedruckt und am 1.1.1830 eingeführt worden war, mit wenigen Worten deutlich: es stieß weithin auf Ablehnung und wurde vom Volk nie geliebt; es gelang ihm nicht, Johann Porsts "Geistliche und liebliche Lieder" aus dem Anfang des 18. Jh. zu verdrängen. Der "alte" Porst ist vielmehr bis zum Beginn des 20. Jh. immer wieder neu aufgelegt worden und hat das "neue" Gesangbuch Schleiermachers (dessen letzte Auflage 1883 nachweisbar ist) überlebt.

Entstehung, Gestalt und Rezeption von Schleiermachers hymnologischer Arbeit, die die Liebe des Volkes nicht zu gewinnen vermochte, sind
mehrfach dargestellt worden[1]; dagegen hat die Forschung nicht gefragt,
welches Gesangbuch Schleiermacher in den beiden Jahrzehnten von 1809 bis
1829 in seinen Gottesdiensten verwendet hat.[2]

Allerdings muß man noch genauer fragen: in welchen Gottesdiensten?
In der Dreifaltigkeitskirche wurde sonntags dreimal gepredigt: in der Regel
früh um 7, vormittags um 9 und nachmittags um 2 Uhr. In einem fürs ganze
Jahr aufgestellten Plan waren jedem der drei Prediger seine Termine
zugewiesen, und in den späteren Jahren bildete sich die Regel heraus, daß
der dritte Prediger die (weniger wichtige) Nachmittagspredigt hielt und
Schleiermacher und sein lutherischer Kollege Marheineke im Wechsel die
Früh- und Hauptpredigt, so daß also Schleiermacher mit einer gewissen
Regelmäßigkeit 14tägig die Frühpredigt und ebenso 14tägig die Haupt-
predigt hielt[3]. Über die Lieder der Hauptpredigten nun läßt sich einiges in
Erfahrung bringen.

So berichtet Friedrich Lücke 1834 in seinen Erinnerungen an Schleiermacher: "Da er Gesang und Predigt als ein lebendiges Ganzes betrachtete,
das damals eingeführte Gesangbuch aber der Anordnung eines solchen
Ganzen zum Theile hinderlich war, traf er die Einrichtung, wenigstens für
jeden Morgengottesdienst [Hauptgottesdienst] besondere Gesänge drucken
zu lassen, die er aus dem reichen Liederschatze unsrer Kirche, dem älteren
und neueren, sinnig und schicklich auswählte. So wurde seine Gemeinde
nach und nach mit den schönsten Liedern bekannt, und er selbst geübt und
geschickt, an dem Werke eines neuen Gesangbuches, welches dem
gegenwärtigen Zustande der christlichen Bildung angemessen sey, leitenden
Antheil zu nehmen."[4] – Aus diesem wichtigen Zeugnis ergibt sich, daß
Schleiermacher periodisch – nämlich 14tägig zu seinen Hauptgottesdiensten
– ein Blatt mit Kirchenliedern für seine Gemeinde herausgab, und das über
viele Jahre hinweg: eine Zeitschrift also, von der die Schleiermacher-
Forschung nichts weiß.

Auch andere Zeitgenossen kannten diese Blätter. Ein Ungenannter berichtet 1847 aus seiner Erinnerung: "Noch muß ich Schleiermacher
erwähnen. Ich ging eines Morgens nach der französischen Kirche neben dem

Schauspielhaus, wo er predigen sollte. Unter dem Thore mußte man sich für einen Groschen das eigens gedruckte Lied kaufen, und wieder für einen Groschen bekam man im Innern einen Stuhl"[5]. – 1857 notiert Friedrich Gustav Lisco: "Schleiermacher ließ seit 1817 für den Gebrauch beim Sonntags-Vormittags-Gottesdienste besondere Liedertexte drucken, die an den Kirchthüren vertheilt wurden; seit 1819 wählte er hierzu oft Lieder, die in der Gesangbuchs-Commission bearbeitet worden waren; mit der Einführung des neuen Gesangbuchs hörte dies aber auf."[6] – Karl Gutzkow erzählt 1869 aus seiner Berliner Zeit: "Schleiermacher war mir eine von frühester Kindheit an vertraute Erscheinung. Ich hörte seine Predigten schon als Knabe [...] An den Kirchtüren wurden die Gesangbuchlieder, die gesungen werden sollten, auf Zetteln verkauft, wie die Textbücher am Opernhause. Man hatte da die revidierten Gesänge vor sich, die eine zur Modernisierung, jedoch nicht Verflachung des Porstschen Gesangbuchs niedergesetzte Kommission zu verantworten hatte."[7] – Das letzte mir bekannte (und schon recht blasse) Zeugnis hat Siegfried Lommatzsch, ein Enkel Schleiermachers, 1889 drucken lassen: "Da Schleiermacher mit den vorhandenen Gesangbüchern wenig zufrieden war, so ließ er vor der Einführung des neuen für seine Gottesdienste besondere Liederzusammenstellungen drucken."[8]

Wie mag nun dieses in Vergessenheit geratene Periodikum ausgesehen haben, das 13 Jahre lang mit jährlich etwa 30 Nummern, also mit insgesamt fast 400 Ausgaben erschienen ist? Es müßte doch noch irgend etwas davon erhalten sein, – aber wie danach suchen, da es doch offenbar keinen Titel hat und ohnedies als ein Privatdruck für die Gemeinde (und für die vielen treuen Predigthörer aus andern Berliner Gemeinden) nur geringe Verbreitung gefunden haben kann.

Ich habe es gefunden, bevor ich danach suchte. Als ich mit meinem Kollegen Andreas Arndt vor vielen Jahren im Archiv des Verlags de Gruyter (in dem der Reimer-Verlag aufgegangen ist) die großen und völlig verstaubten Pakete mit Predigtnachschriften durchblätterte, fielen mir einige dieser gedruckten Blätter auf und ich machte mir eine Fotokopie, ohne zu wissen, was es damit auf sich habe. Erst sehr viel später bemerkte ich in der Schleiermacher-Bibliography von Terrence N. Tice als Nr. 107 einen rätselhaften Eintrag: "Am Neujahrstage 1817... (Berlin, 1817–1828). [a collection of German hymns, selected by Schleiermacher, and used for public worship in the Dreifaltigkeitskirche in Berlin, from 1817 to 1828]". Das mochten solche Blätter sein, es gab also eine ganze Sammlung (ohne Titel), aber wo? in welcher Bibliothek?

Nach langer Zeit bin ich im Katalog der Londoner British Library, der ehemaligen Bibliothek des British Museum, auf die Quelle gestoßen, die Tice abgeschrieben hat, offenbar ohne eine Vorstellung damit zu verbinden: "*Begin.* Am Neujahrstage 1817. [A collection of German Hymns, selected by F.D.E. Schleiermacher, and used at public worship in the Dreifaltigkeitskirche at Berlin.] [1817–28.] 12°. 3436. h. 29." Am Ende steht die Signatur, und so konnte ich sofort einen Mikrofilm aus London bestellen. – Es *waren* die gleichen Blätter wie die im Verlag de Gruyter: ein starker Sammelband mit insgesamt 310 Nummern in chronologischer Ordnung vom 1.1.1817 bis zum 27.1.1828, aber bei weitem nicht vollständig, denn es fehlten die Jahre 1818, 1828 (nur eine Nummer) und 1829, und auch in den übrigen Jahren waren offenbar mehrere Lücken.

Doch damit ist die Fundgeschichte noch nicht zu Ende. Da ich weder Theologe noch Kirchenmusiker bin, bat ich meinen kirchenmusikalisch gebildeten Freund Eckhart Altemüller, den Fund zu bearbeiten und zunächst für eine Examensarbeit auszuwerten: dieser entdeckte in einer Bibliothek in Hannover einen weiteren starken Sammelband, welcher nach dem Kirchenjahr geordnet ist: es liegen also z.B. 5 Blätter zum Ostersonntag aus verschiedenen Jahren beisammen. Mit den Fotokopien dieses Bandes läßt sich nun der Londoner Sammelband ergänzen; dennoch bleiben deutliche Lücken (die wohl nie ganz gefüllt werden können).

Das Wichtigste an dem Hannoveraner Sammelband ist jedoch, daß – im Gegensatz zum Londoner Sammelband – auf vielen Blättern gar kein Jahr angegeben ist: sie gehören offenbar in die Zeit *vor* 1817, ohne daß man ein bestimmtes Blatt einem bestimmten Jahr zuordnen könnte. Hier ist also noch eine große Schwierigkeit für die künftige Forschung.

Jedenfalls hat Schleiermacher schon lange vor 1817 dieses Periodikum herausgegeben; aber seit wann? Glücklicherweise gibt es dafür einen Hinweis. – Schleiermacher kaufte bei seinem Verleger Reimer viele Bücher, aber auch Cognac, Butter, Gänse usw., was nach Möglichkeit mit den

Honoraren für seine zahlreichen Publikationen verrechnet wurde; er hatte also bei Reimer (wie auch die andern Verlagsautoren) ein Konto, und die Kontoführung ist im Reimerschen Hauptbuch (im Verlagsarchiv) seit 1809 überliefert. Hierin heißt es unter dem 6. Dezember 1813: "für Druck u. Papier der Lieder von 1812 – 13 ... 67 rth / zahlte er [Schleiermacher] hierauf ... 50 rth / ab als Beitrag zum Druck ... 17 rth". Das Ganze ist nur eine Notiz; die Zahlen sind nicht in die Zahlenspalten eingetragen, und es ergibt sich daraus, daß Reimer für die Jahrgänge 1812 und 1813 zunächst 67 Reichstaler in Rechnung gestellt hat, Schleiermacher in bar (!) 50 Taler bezahlt hat und die verbleibenden 17 Taler offenbar von Reimer getilgt wurden (als ein Beitrag zum Gemeindeleben; er war ja Gemeindemitglied).

Nun führt gewöhnlich auch Schleiermacher (in seinem Tagebuch) Buch über seine Einnahmen und Ausgaben, doch leider sind von 1812 bis 1819 keine Tagebücher erhalten. Aber aus späteren Jahrgängen wissen wir, daß er tatsächlich eine "Liederkasse" hatte, in die die Einnahmen aus dem Verkauf der Blätter flossen und aus der er die jeweilige Rechnung bei Reimer (bar) bezahlte. Allerdings ist diese Liederkasse auch bei Schleiermacher außerhalb der eigentlichen Buchführung, denn es ist ja nicht sein eignes Geld, sondern fremdes, das er nur verwaltet und bei Reimer abliefern muß. Nur wenn er kurzfristig etwas aus der Liederkasse entnimmt oder später wieder einlegt, dann macht er sich zur Erinnerung eine Notiz im Tagebuch.

Nachdem wir also wissen, daß zumindest 1812 schon Liederblätter gedruckt wurden, sind die Tagebücher von 1809 bis 1811 von höchstem Interesse; doch bei der Durchsicht hat sich kein Hinweis auf die Liederkasse gefunden. Somit ist der Druck von Liederblättern auch vor 1812 zwar möglich, läßt sich aber weder aus dem Reimerschen Hauptbuch noch aus Schleiermachers Tagebuch wahrscheinlich machen, und vorläufig können wir also feststellen, daß dieses Periodikum von 1812 bis 1828 erschienen ist (aus dem Jahr 1829 hat sich nur ein Blatt gefunden, und dies ist möglicherweise ein ärgerlicher Druckfehler für 1828), – also 17 Jahre lang.

Der Plan für solche Liederblätter freilich ist gewiß älter. Im Zusammenhang mit der Berliner Universitätsgründung hat Schleiermacher am 25. Mai 1810 einen Entwurf für den (dann doch nicht zu Stande gekommenen) Universitätsgottesdienst vorgelegt und darin vieles gesagt, was für die Gottesdienste in der Dreifaltigkeitskirche gleichermaßen galt. "Da kein bekanntes Gesangbuch", heißt es da, "noch weniger ein hier eingeführtes den Bedürfnissen des Universitäts-Gottesdienstes völlig entsprechen dürfte, so müßte die wenig kostspielige Veranstaltung getroffen werden, daß die Gesänge jedesmahl auf einem besondern Blatte gedruckt und an den Kirchenthüren ausgegeben würden, bis man auf diese Weise allmählig und ohne etwas zu übereilen zu einem zweckmäßigen Gesangbuch gelangte."[9]

Noch im selben Jahr hat Schleiermacher seine am 5. August gehaltene Gedächtnispredigt für die Königin Luise drucken lassen; in der *Vorerinnerung* sagt er, er gebe nicht nur die "Predigt, sondern fast den ganzen Verlauf des Gottesdienstes. Es wäre zu wünschen, daß dies häufiger geschehen könnte, und daß dabei auch noch den Lesern anschaulich würde, wie die andern Theile des Gottesdienstes nicht minder kräftig als die Predigt selbst zu einer bestimmten Art der Erbauung mitgewirkt haben. Dies war hier in einem hohen Grade der Fall [...]. Möchten wir doch je länger je mehr dahin kommen, die Bedeutsamkeit des Kirchengesanges, sowol der Gemeine als kunstreicherer Chöre, wieder herzustellen, und seine erbauende Kraft zu empfinden." Tatsächlich umfaßt der Druck den *Gesang* der *Gemeine* ("Wie fleucht dahin der Menschen Zeit!..."), das *Gebet*, dann den *Gesang* des *Chors* ("Staub bei Staube ruhst Du nun ...") und der *Gemeine* ("Herr, Du unsre Zuversicht!..."); dann eine kurze Ansprache über die verstorbene Königin mit einer anschließenden Liedstrophe ("An uns stirbt nichts als Sterblichkeit...") und dem Vaterunser; sodann die dreiteilige Predigt (über Jesaja 55, 8−9) und abschließend ein Gebet.[10] − Ob Schleiermacher schon vor der Predigt diese Lieder auf Blätter hat drucken lassen, wissen wir nicht; es ist aber gut möglich, zumal er bereits zur Hallenser Antrittspredigt vom 3. August 1806 sich notiert hat: "Gesänge gedrukt"[11].

Nun zur Erscheinungsweise und zum Vertrieb von Schleiermachers zumindest seit 1812 erschienenen Zeitschrift. Wir haben schon erfahren, daß die Blätter am Eingang der Kirche verkauft wurden; in den frühen Jahren hatten sie noch keinen Preis, sondern vom Besucher wurde eine Spende erwartet. So heißt es am Ende des Blattes "Am Sonntage Sexagesimä", einem Blatt ohne Jahresangabe und darum aus dem Hannoveraner Sammelband:

"Was beim Empfang der Gesänge in die Büchsen gegeben wird ist zu Deckung der Kosten bestimmt. Wer etwa wünscht ein vollständig Exemplar zu erhalten pränumerirt auf das laufende Jahr 12 Gr[oschen] Cour[ant] und erhält es dafür zugeschickt; Pränumeration nimmt Herr Prediger Pischon an." Da Pischon von 1811 bis 1815 Hilfsprediger an Dreifaltigkeit war, ist das Blatt in diesen Zeitraum zu datieren. Aus demselben Zeitraum stammt das Blatt "Am Sonntag Exaudi" mit der Notiz: "Die Druckkosten können nur dadurch bestritten werden, daß beim Empfang etwas in die Büchsen geworfen wird. Vollständige Exemplare sind für 12. Gr. Cour. zu erhalten, die Bezahlung nimmt Hr. Prediger Pischon an". – Auf dem undatierten Hannoveraner Blatt "Am vierten Advents Sonntage" (vielleicht vom Jahre 1816) heißt es am Ende: "Es wird wieder Vorausbezahlung auf das nächste Jahr angenommen. Auch werden noch Exemplare des ablaufenden Jahrgangs von Neujahr an geheftet zu haben sein." Und am Ende des 2. Blattes im Londoner Sammelband ("Am ersten Sonntage nach Epiph. 1817") heißt es ganz kurz: "Vorausbezahlung wird auf den neuen Jahrgang wie gewöhnlich angenommen."

Diese Hinweise sind von größter Bedeutung. Sie zeigen, daß es sich schon vor 1816 nicht etwa um gelegentlich verteilte Zettel handelt, sondern um ein Periodikum, das man im Abonnement (und im Versand) erhalten konnte, und von dem man auch nachträglich komplette Jahrgänge *geheftet* kaufen konnte. Dies ist nicht zu verwundern, denn der Herausgeber Schleiermacher war ein erfahrener Publizist (er hatte z.B. lange Zeit das *Athenaeum* der Brüder Schlegel redigiert) und der Drucker/Verleger Reimer gehörte zu den Großen seiner Branche.[12]

Die Zeitschrift erschien gewöhnlich 14tägig zu Schleiermachers Hauptgottesdiensten, wobei die Festtage (Weihnachten, Neujahr, Karfreitag, Ostern, Bußtag, Himmelfahrt, Pfingsten) notwendig zu Abweichungen von der Regel führten. Nun sagte man von Schleiermacher, er habe sich oft erst auf dem Weg zur Kirche zurechtgelegt, was er predigen wolle[13]; das eng mit der jeweiligen Predigt zusammenhängende Liederblatt aber mußte schon gedruckt vorliegen, und das war natürlich nur möglich, wenn das Manuskript dazu schon früher abgeschlossen und zur Druckerei gegeben worden war. Einen Tag vorher? eine Woche vorher? einen Monat vorher?

Die in 17 Jahrgängen erschienene Zeitschrift war auch in ihren einzelnen Nummern kein Tagesprodukt, und es war gewiß nicht so, daß Schleiermacher am Freitag (oder gar am Samstag) schnell aus mancherlei
Gesangbüchern einige Lieder abschrieb und dies Manuskript zu Reimer
schickte, der den Text in aller Eile setzen und drucken ließ (und wohl gar am
Sonntag kurz vor dem Gottesdienst mit den druckfrischen Exemplaren
herbeieilte). Zunächst einmal war es gar nicht üblich, solche kleinformatigen
Zettel einzeln zu drucken: im Buchdruck werden ja gewöhnlich 4 oder 8 oder
12 oder 16 Druckseiten auf jede Seite eines Bogens gedruckt, der dann
gefaltet (in unserm Fall: zerschnitten) wird; und so kann man auch hier
davon ausgehen, daß mehrere Nummern gleichzeitig gedruckt wurden: daß
also Schleiermacher sein Manuskript oft mehrere Wochen, wenn nicht
Monate vor dem entsprechenden Gottesdienst abliefern mußte.[14]

Diese Überlegung wird gestützt durch eine weitere Beobachtung. Der
Jahres-Predigtplan war ja nur ein Schema, von dem immer dann abgewichen
werden mußte, wenn Schleiermacher krank oder verreist oder sonst
verhindert war zu predigen. Die Abweichungen vom Predigtplan ersehen wir
einerseits aus Schleiermachers Tagebüchern und andererseits aus dem
Berliner "Kirchenzettel", jenem Periodikum, worin jeden Samstag für alle
Berliner (deutschen) Kirchengemeinden die Vormittags- und Nachmittags-
prediger des folgenden Sonntags genannt waren.[15] Es zeigt sich nun, daß
auch bei längeren Reisen Schleiermachers die Liederblätter dennoch erschienen; z.B. sind vom 22. September und 6. Oktober 1822 Blätter erhalten,
obwohl Schleiermacher nicht in Berlin, sondern in Schmiedeberg und in
Niesky war; zum 18. September und 2. Oktober 1825 sind ebenfalls Blätter
überliefert, obwohl er verreist war, und so öfter.

Es ist mithin offenkundig, daß Schleiermacher die redaktionelle Arbeit
an diesen Blättern tatsächlich meist lange im Voraus abgeschlossen hatte
und daß die gedruckten Exemplare entsprechend dem Jahres-Predigtplan
erschienen, unabhängig davon, ob ihr Urheber den vorgesehenen Gottesdienst wirklich halten konnte. Das heißt aber, daß Schleiermacher auch für
seine (Haupt-)Predigten lange im Voraus ein Konzept haben mußte: sei's im
Kopf, sei's auf dem Papier. Und dies widerspricht gar nicht der
Überlieferung, daß er seine Predigten extemporiert habe – Thema,

Bibelstelle, Schwerpunkte, wohl auch die Hauptgliederung wurden bereits Wochen oder Monate zuvor festgelegt: die Untergliederung und die besondere Ausprägung der einzelnen Teile mochten dann kurz vor dem Gottesdienst im Kopf (und Herzen) zurechtgelegt werden: die Worte und Sätze jedenfalls entstanden erst auf der Kanzel.

Ob nun, wenn Schleiermacher abwesend war, sein Vertreter (meist ein Candidat, dessen Namen wir aus Tagebuch oder Kirchenzettel erfahren) das Liederblatt verwendet und also auch Schleiermachers Predigtthema aufgenommen hat, – darüber wissen wir bis heute nichts. Immerhin mußte es seltsam erscheinen, wenn die Abonnenten ein Liederblatt zugeschickt bekamen und die Besucher am Kircheneingang ein Liederblatt erwarben, das im Gottesdienst dann gar keine Verwendung fand.

Wie sehen nun diese Blätter aus? Es sind meist Einzelblätter (zu besonderen Festtagen auch Doppelblätter), sie haben keinen gemeinsamen Titel, sondern nur die Bezeichnung des Festtags als Einzeltitel; darauf folgen die Texte der Lieder mit dem Hinweis, nach welcher Melodie sie zu singen seien[16], sowie der Angabe des liturgischen Ortes: *Vor dem Gebet – Nach dem Gebet – Unter der Predigt – Nach der Predigt*, wovon allerdings das dritte Lied (unter der Predigt) in den späteren Jahren wegfällt[17]. Besondere Gottesdienste haben natürlich auch eine eigne Liturgie: so wird beim Einsegnungsgottesdienst "Am Grün-Donnerstag 1824" fünfmal gesungen, und zwar *zum Anfang, nach der Vorbereitungsrede, nach dem Gebet, nach der Einsegnung, Schlußgesang.*

Oft ist am Ende eines Liedes sein Dichter genannt oder aber das Gesangbuch, dem Schleiermacher es entnommen hat, also *Jauersches Gesangbuch, Bremer Gesangbuch, Freylingshausens Gesangbuch, Gesangbuch der Brüdergemeine* usf. Dies erleichtert natürlich die Aufgabe, den von Schleiermacher hergestellten Text mit seiner Vorlage zu vergleichen. Als Beispiel wähle ich das erste Blatt des Londoner Sammelbandes: "Am Neujahrstage 1817". Als Quelle zu dem *vor dem Gebet* zu singenden Lied ist "Mohn" angegeben. Schleiermacher hat das Lied ohne Zweifel aus dem von ihm oft benutzten Jauerschen Gesangbuch von 1813 entnommen, aus der "Sammlung christlicher Lieder für die kirchliche Andacht evangelischer

Gemeinen. Zunächst derer zu Jauer. Breslau und Jauer, im Verlage bei
Groß und Barth"; dort ist als Dichter *Mohn* genannt. Von den 7 Strophen des
Liedes (Nr. 31) hat Schleiermacher nur die Strophen 1 bis 3 und 7
verwendet. Um den Vergleich zu erleichtern, sind unten beide Texte
nebeneinander gedruckt und alle Abweichungen hervorgehoben.

[Mohn:]

    Heilig ist der Gott der Götter!
    Erbebt, er*bebt* ihr frechen Spötter,
    die ihr des Herrn Gesetz verhöhnt!
    Mit gerechten Abscheu siehet
5   er den, der Licht u. Wahrheit fliehet
    und knechtisch *bösen Lüsten* fröhnt.
    Fluch und Verderben ruht
    auf dem, der Böses thut.
    Gott ist heilig! Der Frevler Schaar umringt Gefahr
10   und Schrecken Gottes immerdar.

    Heilig war sein Sohn auf Erden!
    Ihm täglich ähnlicher zu werden
    ist unser *heiliger* Beruf.
    Ehren sollen wir im Stillen,
15   gleich ihm, des großen Vaters Willen,
    der zur Vollkommenheit uns schuf.
    Wer *spricht: ich* kenne ihn:
    muß *jedes Laster* fliehn.
    Gott ist heilig! Wie glänzt am Thron des Christen Lohn,
20   der heilig lebt, wie Gottes Sohn.

Dabei ist leicht zu sehen, daß Schleiermacher den Text nicht nur abgeschrieben, sondern ihn dabei bewußt verändert und umgedichtet hat. Manche Änderungen sind stilistische Verbesserungen, so ist in Vers 2 das monotone *erbebt erbebt* differenziert in *erbebt erblaßt*; auch Vers 31 ist in Schleiermachers Fassung weniger hölzern.

[Schleiermacher:]

Heilig ist der Gott der Götter,
Erbebt, er*blaßt* ihr frechen Spötter,
Die ihr des Herrn Gesez verhöhnt!
Mit gerechtem Abscheu siehet
5   Er den, der Licht und Wahrheit fliehet,
Und knechtisch *nur der Sünde* fröhnt.
Fluch und Verderben ruht
Auf dem der Böses thut,
Gott ist heilig! der Frevler Schaar umringt Gefahr
10   Und Schrecken Gottes immerdar.

Heilig war sein Sohn auf Erden;
Ihm täglich ähnlicher zu werden,
Ist unser *göttlicher* Beruf.
Ehren sollen wir im Stillen
15   Gleich ihm des großen Vaters Willen,
Der zur Vollkommenheit uns schuf.
Wer *sagt, er* kenne ihn,
Muß *alles Böse* fliehn.
Gott ist heilig, wie glänzt am Thron des Christen Lohn,
20   Der heilig lebt, wie Gottes Sohn!

Heilig ist der Geist der Gnade,
der auf der Wahrheit lichtem Pfade
dem *hohen* Ziel uns näher führt!
Glücklich wer des Geistes Triebe
25   zu Gottesfurcht und *Menschen*liebe
und *edlen* Werken in sich spürt!
Sein Herz ist fromm und rein,
und Jesus nennt ihn sein.
Gott ist heilig! O folge gern dem Geist des Herrn!
30   Sein Licht, o Mensch, ist dir nicht fern!

Auf laßt uns als Christen ringen,
nur edle Thaten zu vollbringen,
wie Christus uns ein Beispiel gab!
Frommer Sinn macht unsre Herzen
35   *im Glück vergnügt,* getrost in Schmerzen,
u. *söhnt uns aus* mit Tod und Grab.
Zur *bessern* Welt erhebt
Gott den der heilig lebt.
Gott ist heilig! Ihm ähnlich seyn vermag allein
40   uns ewig, ewig zu erfreun.

Umfangreicher sind jene Änderungen, bei denen man inhaltliche Motive vermuten kann. Schleiermacher ersetzt die *Menschenliebe* durch die *Bruderliebe* (25); *die edlen Werke* durch die *frommen Werke* (26); die *edlen Thaten* durch den *Kampf des Glaubens* (32); und er läßt die Herzen nicht im *Glück,* sondern in *Gott* vergnügt sein (35). Es sind Elemente der Aufklärungstheologie, jener Natur-Religion, die – um 1800 noch sehr lebendig – inzwischen mit der Entfaltung der Erweckungsbewegung obsolet geworden war und gegen die Schleiermacher sich schon im alten Jahrhundert in seinen Predigten und seinen *Reden über die Religion* gewendet hatte.[18]

Heilig ist der Geist der Gnade,
Der auf der Wahrheit lichtem Pfade
Dem *höhern* Ziel uns näher führt.
Glücklich wer des Geistes Triebe
25   Zu Gottesfurcht und *Bruder*liebe
Und *frommen* Werken in sich spürt.
Des Herz ist fromm und rein,
Und Jesus nennt ihn sein.
Gott ist heilig! O folge gern dem Geist des Hern!
30   Sein Licht, o Mensch, ist dir nicht fern!

Laßt uns *denn* als Christen ringen,
Den Kampf des Glaubens zu vollbringen,
Wie Christus uns ein Beispiel gab.
Aehnlich ihm sein unsre Herzen,
35   *Vergnügt in Gott,* getrost in Schmerzen
Und *ausgesöhnt* mit Tod und Grab.
Zur *besten* Welt erhebt
Gott den, der heilig lebt.
Gott ist heilig! ihm ähnlich sein vermag allein
40   Uns ewig, ewig zu erfreun.

Auch die vereinzelten und allzu sinnlichen *bösen Lüste* und die *Laster* ersetzt Schleiermacher durch die dogmatisch korrekten Begriffe der *Sünde* und des *Bösen* (6;18).

Das Lied, das Schleiermacher am Neujahrstag 1817 in seinem Gottesdienst hat singen lassen, ist eigentlich ein nur wenig anspruchsvolles Produkt der Aufklärungszeit; sein Dichter (Friedrich Mohn, 1762 bis um 1830, Prediger zu Ratingen im rheinischen Herzogtum Berg) war mehrfach mit Gedichten an die Öffentlichkeit getreten; im Jahre 1800 wurden im Bergischen Gesangbuch sechs geistliche Lieder von ihm – darunter das obige – erstmals gedruckt[19]. Daß Schleiermacher dieses Lied gewählt hat, ist symptomatisch für sein in den Liederblättern offenkundiges Bestreben, auch neuere und zeitgenössische Dichter zu Wort kommen zu lassen. Im Gesangbuch von 1829 ist dies nicht immer so deutlich, und das Mohnsche Lied ist dort nicht aufgenommen.

Viele andere Texte der Liederblätter erscheinen aber auch – oft erneut umgearbeitet – im Gesangbuch, und die künftige Forschung wird also rückwärtsblickend den Vergleich mit Schleiermachers Quellen durchführen und zugleich vorwärtsschauend die späteren Gesangbuchfassungen heranziehen müssen, die freilich nur zum (größten) Teil von Schleiermacher allein herrühren, zum Teil von andern Mitgliedern der Gesangbuch-Commission hergestellt wurden, welche in jedem Fall als ganze die Verantwortung trug[20].

Worin liegt nun die Bedeutung dieser äußerlich so unscheinbaren Liederblätter? – Zunächst einmal sind sie ein unentbehrliches Hilfsmittel bei der Analyse des Gesangbuchs von 1829, insbesondere bei der Zuweisung der einzelnen Liedbearbeitungen an die Herausgeber. – Zum andern ist die Zeitschrift ein Werk Schleiermachers, das er – anders als das Gesangbuch – allein ausgewählt, zusammengestellt, bearbeitet und umgedichtet hat[21]. – Zum dritten gewinnen wir aus der Zusammenstellung der überlieferten Predigten mit den zugehörigen Liederblättern ein volleres (wenn auch kein vollständiges) Bild von Schleiermachers einzelnen Gottesdiensten sowie von seiner liturgischen Praxis und ihrem Wandel. – Schließlich können die Blätter bei der Datierung bisher undatierter Predigten hilfreich sein und die künftige Edition der Predigten nach der liturgischen Seite hin bereichern.

Die wissenschaftliche Bearbeitung der Zeitschrift ist in drei Stufen geplant: zunächst hat Frau Seibt eine theologische Dissertation in Angriff genommen, mit deren Abschluß in etwa 2 Jahren zu rechnen ist; sodann sollen die Blätter in (soweit möglich) chronologischer Folge in einem fotomechanischen Nachdruck vorgelegt werden; schließlich ist – falls Interesse daran besteht – an eine Edition mit umfassenden Quellennachweisen etc. zu denken.

Dabei halte ich es für wahrscheinlich, daß noch weitere Sammelbände oder Einzelnummern dieser bisher nur unvollständig nachweisbaren Zeitschrift, die weder Titel noch Herausgeber nennt, in Archiven und Bibliotheken oder auch in privatem Besitz sich befinden, ohne bisher beachtet worden zu sein. Die beigegebene Abbildung eines Blattes soll vor allem auch die Identifizierung solcher weiteren Exemplare ermöglichen; entsprechende Hinweise werden erbeten an den Verfasser (Schleiermacherforschungsstelle, Leuchtenburgstraße 39-41, D – 1000 Berlin 37, Federal Republic of Germany).

Anmerkungen

1. Zum Einzelnen vgl. J.F.Bachmann: Zur Geschichte der Berliner Gesangbücher. Ein hymnologischer Beitrag. Berlin: Schultze 1856. – Reprint Hildesheim: Olms 1970.

2. In einem Göttinger Universitätsvortrag von 1984 (in: Friedrich Schleiermacher 1768-1834. Theologe – Philosoph – Pädagoge. Hg. D.Lange. Göttingen: Vandenhoeck 1985, S.11) resümiert der bedeutendste Kenner von Schleiermachers Predigten, Wolfgang Trillhaas, den Forschungsstand: "Wurde eigentlich in diesen Gottesdiensten viel, wurden die Lieder (und welche) vollständig gesungen? Wir wissen es ebenso wenig, wie wir etwas wissen über die Gebete und Lesungen, die dann in irgendeinem, wenn auch noch so bescheidenen Sinne, eine Liturgie bedeutet hätten."

3. Im Reglement der Union der beiden Dreifaltigkeitsgemeinden vom 10.1.1822 heißt es: "Beide Pastoren halten auch in Zukunft wie bisher abwechselnd die Hauptpredigten. Wegen der Früh- und Nachmittagspredigten einigen sie sich mit dem dritten [dem Hilfsprediger]." Eine genaue Aufstellung aller Schleiermacherschen Predigten nach Ort, Datum, Uhrzeit, Bibelstelle und Überlieferung werde ich demnächst in einer Monographie geben.

4. Theologische Studien und Kritiken 7 (1834), S.791.

5. Jahrbücher der Gegenwart 1847, S.745; hier zitiert nach Christoph Albrecht: Schleiermachers Liturgik. Göttingen 1963, S.37f Fußnote. – Während der Renovierung der Dreifaltigkeitskirche fand der Gottesdienst über längere Zeit in der französischen Kirche ("Dom") statt.

6. Lisco: Zur Kirchen-Geschichte Berlins. Berlin: Hayn 1857, S.278.

7. Zuerst in: Der Salon (1869); hier zitiert nach Karl Gutzkow: Werke, hg. R.Gensel, Berlin usw.: Bong um 1910, Teil 8, S.20.

8. Lommatzsch: Geschichte der Dreifaltigkeits-Kirche zu Berlin. Im Zusammenhange der Berliner Kirchengeschichte dargestellt. Festschrift zum Hundertundfunfzigjährigen Jubiläum der Kirche. Berlin: Reimer 1889, S.97. – Auch dieses Zeugnis ist bei Albrecht (S.47) zitiert.

9. Rudolf Köpke: Die Gründung der Königlichen Friedrich-Wilhelm-Universität zu Berlin. Berlin: Schade 1860, S. 215.

10. "Zwei Predigten am 22sten Julius und am 5ten August in der Dreifaltigkeitskirche zu Berlin gesprochen von D.F. Schleiermacher. Berlin, im Verlage der Realschulbuchhandlung. 1810." (S. 4 und 25 – 52); auch in Schleiermachers Sämmtlichen Werken 2,4 (Neue Ausg. 1844, S. 42 und 52 – 64)

11. "Predigt-Entwürfe beim Akademischen Gottesdienst. 1806." Handschrift im Zentralen Archiv der Akademie der Wissenschaften der DDR, Schleiermacher-Nachlaß Nr.56, S.3. – Bisher ist dieser Lieder-Druck nicht bekannt. – Die Predigt (ohne die Lieder) erschien als Einzeldruck: "Predigt bei Eröffnung des akademischen Gottesdienstes der Friedrichs-Universität. Am Geburtstage des Königes den 3ten August 1806. gesprochen von

F.Schleiermacher, Berlin im Verlag der Realschulbuchhandlung, 1806."; auch in Schleiermachers Sämmtlichen Werken 2,4 (1844), S.16–28.

12. In ähnlicher Weise hat Reimer die vielen Einzeldrucke Schleiermacherscher Predigten, die er verlegt hatte, später auch komplett angeboten.

13. Es gibt viele Berichte, daß Schleiermacher sich z.B. am Vorabend des Gottesdienstes für kurze Zeit von einer Gesellschaft zurückgezogen habe, um über seine Predigt zu meditieren.

14. Wenn von dem abgelaufenen Jahrgang auch *geheftete* Exemplare verkauft wurden, so kann man dies dahin verstehen, daß es sich um unzerschnittene, vielmehr gefaltete (halbe?) Bogen à 4 oder 6 Blatt handelte, der ganze Jahrgang bestehend aus ca. 5 halben Bogen bzw. aus 2 und einem halben Bogen. Denn Einzelblätter zu "heften" war keine fabrikmäßige Arbeit,–dies mußte der Käufer selbst mit Nadel und Faden erledigen (wie der Besitzer des Hannoveraner Sammelbandes), oder aber der Buchbinder. Über den Londoner Sammelband läßt sich hierüber natürlich aus dem Mikrofilm nichts ersehen. Gewiß ist nur, daß er – wie Katherine M. Padilla dankenswerterweise am Ort aus den Akten ermittelt hat – 1858 in die Bibliothek gelangte als Teil einer Sammlung von über 500 Gesangbüchern und liturgischen Werken aus dem Besitz der Familie von Bunsen. Als Vorbesitzer kommen in Frage Christian Karl Josias von Bunsen (1791–1860) und sein Sohn Ernst (1819–1903); da jedoch der Vater von 1816 bis 1834 in Rom (und seit 1842 in London) weilte, läßt sich der Sammler der einzelnen Liederblätter nicht namhaft machen. Wahrscheinlich hat der Vater (der selbst 1846 ein "Allgemeines evangelisches Gesang- und Gebetbuch" herausgab) den Sammelband aus privater Hand erworben.

15. Der Kirchenzettel ist heute meines Wissens leider nicht mehr vollständig überliefert; genauere Auskunft wird meine künftige Liste von Schleiermachers Predigten geben.

16. Auch in den Gesangbüchern der Epoche war der Abdruck der Melodien selbst nicht üblich, da nur wenige, allgemein bekannte Melodien in Gebrauch waren und die Kenntnis der Notenschrift wohl nicht allgemein war. Allerdings kannte man besondere Choralbücher zu den Gesangbüchern; so erschien schon 1830 in Berlin von August Wilhelm Bach das "Choralbuch zum gottesdienstlichen Gebrauch für evangelische Gemeinen", also zu dem Schleiermacherschen Gesangbuch von 1829 gehörig.

17. Von 1819 bis 1822 wird der Gesang *unter der Predigt* immer seltener; die Begründung dafür hat Schleiermacher in seiner *Praktischen Theologie* vorgetragen.

18. Statt vieler Zitate aus Schleiermachers Werken nur eine Stelle, derzufolge die "allgemeine Menschenliebe" zur "äußeren Sphäre" gehört und "auf dem eigenthümlich christlichen Gebiete" ihr die "brüderliche Liebe" entspricht (Die christliche Sitte. Sämmtliche Werke 1,12 [2.Aufl. 1884], S.514).

19. Christliches Gesangbuch für die evang. lutherischen Gemeinden im Herzogthum Berg. Mülheim am Rhein: Eyrich 1800, Nr.13, S.15f mit der Unterschrift *F.Mohn* (Vgl. K. Goedeke: Grundriß Bd.7, 2.Aufl., S.327). Der Text des Jauerschen Gesangbuchs weicht nur in Vers 24 von dieser Quelle ab, wo es heißt: *Wohl dem, der* (statt: *Glücklich wer*). – Beide Gesangbuchdrucke verzichten (wie damals üblich) auf eine Abgrenzung der Verse, die in der obigen Wiedergabe entsprechend der Schleiermacherschen Fassung vorgenommen wurde. Als Melodie ist in allen drei Fassungen die zu dem Lied *Wachet auf ruft uns die* angegeben.

20. Von dieser Commission wissen wir nur (aus Schleiermachers Tagebüchern), wann und bei wem sie getagt hat; irgendwelche Arbeitsprotokolle (wie Albrecht–S.120 Fußnote – sie ausfindig zu machen gesucht hat) sind wohl gar nicht angefertigt worden. Dagegen sind die von Albrecht (ebd.) als "verbrannt" bezeichneten Konsistorialakten zum Berliner Gesangbuch von 1829 im Evangelischen Zentral-Archiv erhalten. – Erhalten ist übrigens auch Schleiermachers Handschrift zu einem der Liederblätter, worüber ich an anderm Ort handeln werde.

21. Natürlich irrt Gutzkow (in dem oben angeführten Zitat), wenn er behauptet, auf den Liederblättern seien die von der Commission verantworteten Gesangbuchfassungen wiedergegeben; allenfalls erscheinen Schleiermachers Liederblatt-Fassungen bisweilen unverändert oder nur wenig verändert später auch im Gesangbuch: viele der Lieder aber sind hier gar nicht aufgenommen. – Gerade bei den kürzeren Liedtexten *nach der Predigt* muß man auch damit rechnen, daß Schleiermacher sie selbst gedichtet hat; genauere Vermutungen werden sich allerdings erst im Laufe jahrelanger Forschungsarbeiten ergeben. – Für vielerlei Hinweise habe ich nicht nur Eckhart Altemüller und Ilsabe Seibt, sondern auch Frauke Kesper, Andreas Reich und Katherine M. Padilla zu danken.

Am Neujahrstage 1817.

Vor dem Gebet.

Mel. Wachet auf ruft uns. ꝛc.

Heilig ist der Gott der Götter,
Erbebt, erblaßt ihr frechen Spötter,
Die ihr des Herrn Gesetz verhöhnt!
Mit gerechtem Abscheu siehet
Er den, der Licht und Wahrheit fliehet,
Und knechtisch nur der Sünde fröhnt.
Fluch und Verderben ruht
Auf dem der Böses thut,
Gott ist heilig! der Frevler Schaar umringt Gefahr
Und Schrecken Gottes immerdar.

Heilig war sein Sohn auf Erden;
Ihm täglich ähnlicher zu werden,
Ist unser göttlicher Beruf.
Ehren sollen wir im Stillen
Gleich ihm des großen Vaters Willen,
Der zur Vollkommenheit uns schuf.
Wer sagt, er kenne ihn,
Muß alles Böse fliehn.
Gott ist heilig, wie glänzt am Thron des Christen Lohn,
Der heilig lebt, wie Gottes Sohn!

Heilig ist der Geist der Gnade,
Der auf der Wahrheit lichtem Pfade
Dem höhern Ziel uns näher führt.
Glücklich wer des Geistes Triebe
Zu Gottesfurcht und Bruderliebe
Und frommen Werken in sich spürt.
Des Herz ist fromm und rein,
Und Jesus nennt ihn sein.
Gott ist heilig! O folge gern dem Geist des Herrn,
Sein Licht, o Mensch, ist dir nicht fern!

Laßt uns denn als Christen ringen
Den Kampf des Glaubens zu vollbringen,
Wie Christus uns ein Beispiel gab.
Aehnlich ihm sein unsre Herzen,
Vergnügt in Gott, getrost in Schmerzen
Und ausgesöhnt mit Tod und Grab.
Zur besten Welt erhebt
Gott den, der heilig lebt.
Gott ist heilig! ihm ähnlich sein vermag allein
Uns ewig, ewig zu erfreun.   [Mohn.]

Nach dem Gebet.

Chor.

Alle eure Sorgen werft auf den Herrn, denn er sorget für euch.
Treulich Herr auf deinen Wegen laß mich wandeln immerdar,
Sei bei mir auf deinem Stegen, rette Gott mich in Gefahr.
Gott ist unsre Zuversicht und Stärke, eine Hülfe in den
großen Nöthen, die uns troffen haben. Darum fürchten wir
uns nicht; wenn gleich die Welt unterginge, und die Berge
mitten ins Meer sänken.

Das erste Blatt des Londoner Sammelbandes von Schleiermachers Liederblättern

Gemeine.
Mel. Wie wohl ist mir o Freund.

Herr den die Sonnen und die Erden
Durch ihren Bau voll Pracht erhöhn,
Durch deffen Machtwort Welten werden
Und Welten wieder untergehn!
Dein Thron Gott bleibet ewig stehen,
Du bleibst derselbe; wir vergehen;
Wie schnell verströmet unsre Zeit!
Schon wieder ist von unserm Leben
Ein Jahr das deine Huld gegeben,
Im Abgrund der Vergangenheit.

Chor.
Kommt, dies sei uns ein Tag des Bundes!
Dem frommen Bunde bleibet treu,
Und den Gelübden eures Mundes
Stimm eure Seele redlich bei.
O Land! gelobe Gott zu dienen,
Und Du wirst wie ein Garten grünen,
Den er sich selbst gepflanzet hat.
Geht, Brüder, geht auf seinen Wegen;
Dann macht sein unerschöpfter Segen
Aus seiner Füll euch täglich satt.

Gemeine.
Gott schau herab von deinen Höhen,
Auf uns, als Kinder die Du liebst,
Erhöre, die in Christo flehen,
Gieb, wie Du Deinen Kindern giebst
Erhalte deiner Kirche Wächter,
Daß noch die spätesten Geschlechter,
Die Predigt deines Worts erfreu.
Durch sie laß Segen auf uns fließen,
Dem Pflanzen Herr und dem Begießen
Gieb Gnade, daß es stets gedeih.

Unter der Predigt.

Mel. Nun laßt uns gehn und rc.
Lob Dir, Du schenkst aufs neue
Uns deine Vatertreue!
Lob sei den starken Händen,
Die alles Unglück wenden.

Nach der Predigt.

Laß keine Seel ihr Heil verscherzen,
Und mache selbst die Thoren klug,
Gieb deine Kraft den schwachen Herzen,
Den dürftgen Muth und Trost genug!
Für Ihn flehn wir um Heil und Leben,
Den König den Du uns gegeben,
Durch Furcht vor Dir besteh sein Thron!
Laß ihn auf Licht und Wahrheit schauen
Durch Recht des Reiches Wohlfahrt bauen,
Der Herzen Liebe sei sein Lohn. [J. A. Schlegel.]

XIII

SCHLEIERMACHERS ERSTGEDRUCKTE PREDIGT IN IHREM URSPRÜNGLICHEN KONTEXT

Wichmann von Meding

Wer sich mit dem Werk eines Großen der Theologiegeschichte befaßt, hat Grund zu der Annahme, auf ein besonderes Interesse an dessen Frühwerk zu stoßen. Der junge Luther, der frühe Hegel, der angehende Prediger Schleiermacher sind Gegenstand der Forschung. Manuskripte, die sie nie veröffentlicht hatten, werden aufmerksam studiert. Doch die erste im Druck erschienene Predigt Schleiermachers blieb eigenartig unbeachtet.

Dies Faktum soll zunächst durch drei Beobachtungen belegt werden (I). Sodann soll der ursprüngliche Kontext der Predigt vorgestellt (II) und das Wichtigste zu ihrem historischen Ort und ihrer Thematik zusammengefaßt werden (III). Schließlich sollen einige hauptsächliche Einsichten angedeutet sein, die sich aufdrängen, wenn man die Predigt mit Schleiermachers gleichzeitig erschienenen Reden über die Religion zusammen liest (IV).

I.

Friedrich Schleiermachers erstgedruckte Predigt – es handelt sich selbstverständlich nicht um die erste von ihm gehaltene und auch nicht um seine erste uns erhaltene – findet sich zu Beginn des 1844 erschienenen Bandes 4 seiner gesammelten Predigten[1.] Dort erfährt der Leser, der Text sei ein Abdruck "Aus den 'Predigten von protestantischen Gottesgelehrten. Siebente Sammlung.' Berlin, bei A. Mylius, 1799"[2]. Das Vorwort des Bandes vermerkt darüber hinaus knapp, bisherigem Nachforschen sei sie "entgangen" gewesen[3]. In der Tat fehlt die fragliche Predigt in der 1835 zu Berlin heraus-gekommenen Erstfassung des 4. Predigtbandes der sämmtlichen Werke. Obwohl sie also 1799 in Berlin erstmals gedruckt worden war, blieb Schleiermachers Erstlingspredigt während seiner gesamten Berliner Wirk-samkeit und weit darüber hinaus gänzlich unbekannt. Darin liegt offenbar der ursprüngliche Grund für ihre auffällige Nichtbeachtung.

Doch auch mit der seit Mitte des 19. Jahrhunderts gegebenen problemlosen Erreichbarkeit setzte keine erkennbare Rezeption dieser Predigt ein. Dafür nur zwei Belege: die der Theologie des jungen Schleiermacher gewidmete Untersuchung Paul Seiferts von 1960[4] zieht zur Interpretation der Reden zwar zu Recht Schleiermachers frühe Predigten heran, unter ihnen sogar ungedruckte Predigtentwurfbücher – nicht aber die nun wirklich gleichzeitige erstgedruckte Predigt. Und die ist, im Unterschied zur Fülle der sonstigen Predigten Schleiermachers, seit 1844 offensichtlich nicht ein einzigesmal wieder nachgedruckt worden. Wie eine Bestätigung für das Aschenputteldasein der ersten veröffentlichten Predigt Schleiermachers will es da erscheinen, daß die gesamte siebenbändige Reihe "Predigten von protestantischen Gottesgelehrten", aus der 1844 der Abdruck erfolgte, als verschollen gelten mußte, bis sie 1986 in einer kirchlichen Bibliothek aufgefunden werden konnte[5].

Somit beschränkt sich der derzeitige Kenntnisstand zu der 1799 erst-gedruckten Predigt des jungen Schleiermacher auf viererlei:

1. liegt ihr Text im Band SW 2,4 von 1844 vor;

2. kennt man den Titel der ursprünglichen Predigtsammlung[6];

3. nennt man als ihren Herausgeber den Potsdamer Hof- und Garnison-Prediger Johann Peter Bamberger[7];

4. weiß man aus einer Briefäußerung Schleiermachers, er habe seine Predigt im September 1798 "gearbeitet"[8].

Das ist wenig genug und doch so viel, daß Interesse entstehen kann für die Frage, ob sich aus der neuerlichen Kenntnis der ursprünglichen Veröffent-lichung weitere Einsichten ergeben und welches die Stellung der Schleiermacherpredigt in ihrem bisher unbekannten Kontext sei.

II.

Geht man anhand des nun vorliegenden Sammelbandes von 1799 die genannten vier Punkte noch einmal durch, ergibt sich folgendes:

ad 1: Schleiermachers Redetext ist 1844 bis auf völlig unbedeutende Kleinigkeiten sauber aus dem Original in die sämmtlichen Werke übernommen worden. Das ist ein erneuter Beleg für die Qualität jener Werkausgabe.

ad 2: Der 1799 erschienene Band hat zwei verschiedene Titelblätter. Der Haupttitel lautet vollständig: "Auswahl noch ungedruckter Predigten von Ammon, Bartels, Diterich, Löffler, Marezoll, Sack, Schleiermacher, Spalding, Teller, Zöllner, Zollikofer. Berlin, bei August Mylius 1799." Der Vorbericht des Bandes vermerkt ausdrücklich, "diese Auswahl" werde "auch unter jenem Titel als siebente Sammlung ausgegeben", der in SW 2,4 als einziger Titel erscheint.

ad 3: Weder der Haupt- noch der Nebentitel nennen einen Herausgeber. Die elf Predigernamen des Haupttitels bezeichnen die eigenverantwortlichen Autoren des Bandes. Sie wurden von der Myliusischen Buchhandlung – so ist der Vorbericht unterzeichnet – lediglich nach dem Alphabet geordnet (II). Wie verträgt sich das mit Schleiermachers brieflicher Äußerung, in jener Vorrede habe sich "der B. . . . erdreistet, . . . zu sagen, ich sei in Berlin meiner Talente und Kenntnisse wegen allgemein geschätzt"[9], eine Äußerung, die in dem anonymen Vorwort tatsächlich enthalten ist? Wie vor allem verträgt sich diese Anonymität mit Diltheys Deutung jenes "B." auf Bamberger[10]? Um es in zwei Worten zu sagen: Überhaupt nicht. Bambergers Herausgeberschaft ist in sich ganz unwahrscheinlich, schon wegen seiner 1798 erfolgten Emeritierung[11]. Vor allem aber existiert Schleiermachers Brief noch in der Abschrift, die Henriette Herz Wilhelm Dilthey für den Druck zur Verfügung stellte. Dort aber lesen wir in aller Deutlichkeit, "der Buttmann" habe sich erdreistet, ihn als talentierten Berliner Prediger zu rühmen. Gemeint sein kann nur Philipp Buttmann[12], bedeutender Philologe und Bibliothekar in Berlin und Schleiermacher eng verbunden, beispielsweise durch Rat und Tat während seiner Platoübersetzung. Er erfreute sich, seit er in Berlin lebte und arbeitete, besonderer Förderung durch die Witwe des Buchhändlers Mylius[13]. In ihrem Verlag war auch seine bedeutende Griechische Grammatik erschienen, die zahlreiche Auflagen erleben sollte[14]. Von ihm also stammt das anonyme Vorwort der bei Mylius erschienenen Auswahl ungedruckter Predigten, die Schleiermachers erstgedruckte Predigt enthält[15]. In dieser Angelegenheit, so interessant sie ist, gilt sachlich jedoch noch mehr, was Spalding, einer der am gleichen Band beteiligten Prediger, 1788 über sich als anonymen Autor gesagt hatte: "im Grund thut der (Name) auch nichts zur Sache"[16].

ad 4: Das derzeitige Wissen zur Datierung der erstveröffentlichten Predigt Schleiermachers soll später erörtert werden, weil dabei der Inhalt der Rede eine gewisse Rolle spielt. Zuvor ist der ganze Band darzustellen. Das kann hier nur in einer äußerst eingeschränkten Andeutung dessen geschehen, was für die Interpretation der enthaltenen Schleiermacherrede von Bedeutung sein könnte.

Der Band der Myliusischen Buchhandlung von 1799, gespickt mit kleinen Druckfehlern, enthält auf 500 Seiten oktav 27 Predigten aus der Feder der elf genannten Gottesgelehrten. Jeder von ihnen hat zwei oder drei Reden beigesteuert, bei zwei Ausnahmen: aus dem Nachlaß Zollikofers wurden vier, von dem jungen Charité-Prediger Schleiermacher nur eine Predigt gedruckt[17]. Dies ist das erste, ganz äußerliche Faktum, das Schleiermacher im Kreis seiner Mitautoren kennzeichnet.

Ein großer Teil der elf Prediger amtierte in Berlin. Das mag bei einem Berliner Verlag zunächst nicht auffallen. Da aber die Berliner mehr als die Hälfte der Autorenschaft stellten[18], ohne daß nur ein einziger Preuße sonst ihnen zur Seite träte, ist Aufmerksamkeit am Platz. Ihre fünf Mitautoren verteilen sich recht gleichmäßig auf die nördlichen, nicht-preußischen Reichsterritorien und das Auslandsdeutschtum.

Daß Berlin für den untersuchten Predigtband mehr war als ein prinzipiell gleichgültiger Verlagsort, bestätigt sich an einer weiteren Beobachtung: sechs seiner elf Prediger waren in ihrer vita beträchtlich durch das Wöllnersche Religionsedikt von 1788 gezeichnet[19]. Unter ihnen sind vier der fünf Oberkonsistorialräte, die damals sofort dagegen protestiert hatten: Diterich, Sack, Spalding und Teller[20]. Außer ihnen ist Zöllner zu nennen, der des zurückgetretenen Spalding Nachfolger geworden war, und Löffler, der 1788 ins nichtpreußische Ausland ausgewichen war. Der einzige Berliner Prediger, der nicht den vom Wöllnerschen Konfessionszwang Betroffenen zuzuzählen ist, war der junge Schleiermacher. Dies ist sein zweites, nicht mehr ganz äußerliches Spezifikum unter den Predigern des Mylius-Bandes von 1799.

Ordnet man die elf Prediger nicht nach dem Alphabet, wie es im Mylius-Band versucht worden ist[21], sondern nach ihren Geburtsjahren, um einen sachgerechten Einblick in die Art und Weise zu gewinnen, wie sie auf die 1798 beendete Ära Wöllner reagierten[22], so tritt die dritte Besonderheit Schleiermachers an den Tag: er war der jüngste unter den Autoren. Von dem Ältesten, Spalding, trennten ihn 54 Jahre, fast zwei Generationen. Mit seiner relativen Jugend hängt wohl das Vierte zusammen, das Schleiermachers Rede im Rahmen der 27 zusammengestellten Predigten auszeichnet: ihre 26 Druckseiten machen sie zur längsten des Bandes. Der Durchschnitt aller Vorträge liegt bei 18 Seiten.

Wesentlich gewichtiger und von größerem Interesse als dies alles ist naturgemäß die Frage nach dem theologischen Profil der Schleiermacherpredigt, wie es sich in ihrem ursprünglichen Kontext zeigen mag. Um diese Frage zu erörtern, sind zunächst die Reden der zehn Kollegen, wenn auch in fast unverantwortlicher Kürze, theologiepositionell zu umreißen.

Die drei Reden Johann Joachim Spaldings[23] stehen am Ende des Bandes, da Spalding sich erst in letzter Minute zu einem Beitrag hatte entschließen können. Sein Amtsverzicht unter Wöllner scheint tiefe Spuren hinterlassen zu haben. Das Vorwort kommentiert dieses Faktum mit den Worten "das Ende krönet das Werk" (II). Dieser Satz zeichnet Spaldings Ansprachen ebenso aus wie er den ganzen Band 7 einer lange unterbrochenen Reihe kennzeichnet[24]. Damit werden sie gleichsam zu Repräsentanten des theologischen Programms, das der Herausgabe zugrunde lag. Thema der ersten und dritten Predigt ist der Glaube. Ihn habe man oft für einen Nachteil gehalten, der den Eifer eigener Besserung hindere. Andere hätten dem kaum mehr als die häufige Nennung des Glaubensbegriffes entgegenzuhalten gewußt. So beschreibt Spalding die neologische Normaltheologie und die dem Namen Wöllners verbundene

Reaktion darauf. Letzterem stimmt Spalding insofern zu, als er den Glauben eine der wichtigsten Religionslehrern nennt und für unverzichtbar erklärt. Aber auf seine rechte Bestimmung komme es an. Nur "der Glaube, der wirklich das Herz bessert, der uns zu gutgesinnten tugendhaften Menschen macht, (ist) durchaus unentbehrlich" (459). Das sei der Glaube, der sich an Jesu Vorschriften hält und sich seiner Lohnverheißung sicher ist. Spaldings Position ist also die, eine Vermittlung legitimer Elemente zwischen den bisherigen Extremkonzepten zu versuchen.

Ganz anders lesen sich die drei Predigten Johann Samuel Diterichs[25]. In ihnen tritt das Biblische auffallend zurück. Sie sind dem Nachdenken des Menschen über seine eigene Natur gewidmet. Strittiges spielt nicht die geringste Rolle. Es entsteht der Eindruck einer kirchlichen Überlebensstrategie durch Übergehen dessen, was Anstoß erregen könnte. Dabei ist zu bedenken, daß Diterich vor Ende der Ära Wöllner gestorben war[26].

In zeitlich geordneter Reihe ist Georg Joachim Zollikofer der erste Ausländer unter den Autoren des Berliner Predigtbandes, denn er wirkte als bedeutender Prediger der reformierten Gemeinde in Leipzig, und er ist der einzige, der die Ära Wöllner nicht einmal von dort aus miterlebte, da er 1788 starb[27]. Sein Beitrag kann also in keiner Weise Bezug nehmen auf das innere Thema der 1799 vorgelegten Predigtauswahl, wie es sich bisher herausgeschält hat. Aber aus seiner Feder bietet der Band vier Predigten, den umfangreichsten Anteil eines der elf Prediger. Ein hervorragendes Interesse an seiner Verkündigung deutet sich an. Es scheint sich darauf zu beziehen, daß Zollikofer weniger vermittelnd redet als Spalding, schon gar nicht ausweichend wie Diterich, sondern mit integrierender Kraft. "Die Stimme der Vernunft ist zugleich Stimme der Religion. Gott belehret uns durch jene, so wie durch diese; aber diese verstärket jene durch neue Belehrungen und Forderungen, und beide unterstützen einander gegenseitig" (390). Theologie wird im Blick auf Gott und darum im Blick auf das Ganze betrieben. Dabei fällt Zollikofers Fähigkeit auf, Gegensätze, mit denen sich die Zeitgenossen mühen, differenziert zu integrieren, ohne ihnen zuvor etwas abgemarktet zu haben. Aus diesem Grund könnte er in der Situation des Jahres 1798 als willkommenes Vorbild für die Bewältigung der zeitgemäßen kirchlichen Aufgabe verstanden worden sein.

Vom theologischen Niveau dieser Bibelauslegungen weit entfernt sind die Predigten Wilhelm Abraham Tellers[28]. Sein Kampf gilt dem "rohen Unglauben" wie dem "düstern Aberglauben" (272). Zu Beidem erscheint der "dreiste Glaube an Jesum" (267) wie eine Vorstufe. Wegen dieser Gefahr wird er eliminiert, sogar im Zitat von Joh 3,16 (274). An dieser Stelle drängt sich der Vergleich mit Spaldings Predigten auf, in denen versucht worden war, der neologischen Verkündigung das unverzichtbare Glaubensthema zurückzugewinnen, wenn auch in angepaßter Weise. Neben ihnen wirken Tellers Reden, obwohl von einem Jüngeren gehalten, wie Zeugnisse einer vergangenen Zeit, in denen weiterhin Gott verkündigt wird als der, der "vergelten (werde) einem Jeden nach seinen Werken" (285). Es ist reizvoll, diese Predigten zu lesen als Kommentar zu Tellers Gespräch mit den jüdischen Hausvätern Berlins über die Frage, ob man sich taufen lassen dürfe, um die vollen Bürgerrechte erwerben zu können, ohne dabei zugleich Christ zu werden[29]. Da die Taufe gewiß nicht zu den eigenen Tugendwerken rechnet, werde man fragen dürfen, ob sie nicht in tugendhafter Großzügigkeit den Juden freigegeben werden mag. Nach Tellers Ansicht benötigt Tugend nichts als einen Gesetzgeber (292)[30].

Hatte Spalding zu vermitteln gesucht zwischen dem Glauben und der Besserung der Menschen, hatte Diterich sich gleichsam zurückgezogen auf ein unangreifbares Terrain, hatte Zollikofer die integrierende Kraft der Religion hervorgehoben und Teller im Kampf gegen Aberglauben und Unglauben auch den Glauben als gefährlichen Schritt auf beide zu ausgeschieden, so findet sich Friedrich Samuel Gottfried Sack, der Förderer und Kritiker Schleiermachers, seinerseits an einer anderen Front tätig[31]. Sein Anliegen lautet, daß "in der Religion Erkenntniß und Empfindung verbunden sein müsse" (219). Dabei bleibt er Neologe: "Die Religion ist zuvörderst eine Sache des Verstandes" (219 und mehrfach) – aber "eben so gewiß ist es auch, ... daß das Gemüth dadurch in Bewegung gesetzt werde" (224). In der Einsicht, das bisherige Religionsverständnis sei ergänzungsbedürftig, steht er prinzipiell seinem Schwiegervater Spalding nahe. Dabei erscheint ihm, dem Jüngeren, die erhöhte Empfindsamkeit der Zeitgenossen als legitime Hilfestellung. Das Christentum "ist ganz eigentlich eine Wissenschaft des Herzens" (225). Zu ihr gehören auch die "herzerleichternden Thränen, wie jene die aus den Augen eines reuigen Petrus flossen. Ich weiß, was das Christenthum, das allein in Gefühlen besteht, für eine mißliche, gefahrvolle und fruchtlose Sache sey; aber ich beklage auch die Seele, die in der Religion nichts empfindet, und die das blos zu einer Beschäftigung des Verstandes oder zu einer Beobachtung äußerlicher Gebräuche macht, was doch mit dem Herzen . . . in so naher, natürlicher und unauflöslicher Verbindung ist" (226). Neologische Verstandesbeschäftigung und wöllnerischer Traditionalismus sind für Sack nicht mehr Gegensätze, sondern unterschiedliche Ausformungen eines nur äußerlichen Religionsverständnisses, dem das Empfinden "Gottes und seines in unserm Gewissen wirkenden Geistes" (228) zur Seite treten muß.

Deutet sich zwischen Schwiegervater und Schwiegersohn somit auch ein theologischer Generationenunterschied an, so beginnt die zweite Generation in dem vorzustellenden Predigtband doch erst bei dem elf Jahre jüngeren August Christian Bartels[32]. Seine drei Predigten verlassen die für die Neologie charakteristische anthropologische Engführung im Religionsverständnis, indem sie von Gottes Werken handeln statt den eigenen, und entfalten in ungewöhnlich eleganter Sprache eine reiche Theologie der Natur. Sie ist als fruitio dei konzipiert und wird in enger Anlehnung an Paulus entfaltet. So lesenswert diese über ein einziges Psalmwort gehaltenen Reden angesichts heutiger Probleme und Einseitigkeiten auch sind, für die Erfassung des Kontextes der ersten gedruckten Schleiermacherpredigt sind sie ohne Bedeutung. Sie vermögen in ihrer Andersartigkeit nur ein Hinweis darauf zu sein, daß der Predigtauswahl von 1799 ein Thema aus der Fülle dessen gemeinsam ist, was die Prediger am Ausgang des 18. Jahrhunderts beschäftigte.

Nur zwei Jahre jünger als Bartels war Josias Friedrich Christian Löffler[33]. Protest gegen die durch Wöllner proklamierte bekenntnisgebundene Verkündigungsaufgabe gestaltet die Gedanken jedenfalls der ersten, der Karfreitagspredigt Löfflers. Ihr stellt er die Überzeugung Jesu entgegen, "daß nur ein reines Herz, standhafte und durchgängige Tugend, und Vertrauen zu Gott, den Menschen wirklich veredeln und nie unglücklich seyn lassen" (134). Seinen Tod hingegen bewirkten "die Obern des Volks, welche jene verkehrte Lehrart beschützten" (135). Mit seinem Wort über die, die nicht wissen was sie tun, habe Jesus noch am Kreuz deutlich gemacht, nicht korrekte gottesdienstliche Riten, sondern Wissen um das eigene Tun und also Aufklärung seien geboten. Die Mächtigen und Weisen der Erde werden direkt aufgefordert: "höret eure Widerlegung aus dem Munde des sterbenden Erlösers" (142f). Jesus selber hat schon längst auch gegen Wöllner entschieden, der rationalistische Prediger braucht lediglich das reformatorische sola scriptura gegen ein konfessionell einseitiges Religionsverständnis zur Sprache zu bringen.

Dem Rationalisten Löffler folgt im Alter der zum aufkommenden Supranaturalismus tendierende Johann Friedrich Zöllner[34]. Er war 1788 Nachfolger Spaldings als Propst der Nikolaikirche in Berlin geworden, war also Nutznießer der Kirchenpolitik Friedrich Wilhelm II. Evangelium, Abendmahl, Vergebung und Gnade werden als Wohltaten dessen vorgestellt, der im Weihnachtsevangelium von Engeln bejubelt worden ist (320. 325). Eine Abrechnung mit der soeben durch Wöllners Entlassung beendeten preußischen Religionspolitik sind Zöllners Weihnachtspredigten also nicht. Sie enthalten sich jeder Stellungnahme zur eigenen Zeit. Linientreue im Sinne einer der umstrittenen Positionen wird man ihnen nicht unterstellen dürfen.

Die Behauptung, Reden aus zwei unterscheidbaren Predigergenerationen bildeten in dem 1799 erschienenen Berliner Auswahlband den Kontext zu Schleiermachers erster gedruckter Predigt, erhärtet sich an Johann Gottlob Marezoll[35]. Seit seinem Studium hat Marezoll Zollikofer als Lehrer und Predigervorbild verehrt[36]. Lehrer und Schüler sind als Autoren in diesem Band verbunden, ohne dort Ältester bzw. Jüngster zu sein. Obwohl Marezoll 1799 in Kopenhagen wirkte, fügen sich seine Reden nahtlos der Berliner Abrechnung ein: nur "in den Zeiten der tiefsten Barbarey und Unwissenheit (war man) verblendet genug . . . , die Vernunft zu verachten und zu unterdrücken . . . ; aber daß man selbst in unsern Tagen noch immer fortfährt, oder vielmehr wieder aufs neue anfängt, dieselbe Sprache zu reden und dieselben Forderungen zu machen, das setzt den unpartheyischen Beobachter in Erstaunen" (165f). Dieser Unparteiische wollte Marezoll jedoch keineswegs sein: "die Freunde und Vertheidiger des Wahren und Guten verdächtig machen, verfolgen, außer Wirksamkeit setzen: das heißt doch wohl Gottes Absichten widerstreben und sich gegen seinen Willen empören, das ist doch wohl das verworfenste, unseeligste Geschäft, welches ein Mensch, ein Christ, ein Bekenner dessen, der sich das Licht der Welt nannte, nur irgend treiben kann" (195). Das klingt wie ein Berliner Wutausbruch, denn unter mehr oder weniger freiwilligem Zwang außer Wirksamkeit gesetzte Prediger des Wahren und Guten hatte es vor allem in und um Berlin gegeben. Doch Marezoll war kein Berliner und hatte keine sonderlichen Beziehungen nach Berlin. Das ist ein Hinweis darauf, daß die Wöllnerischen Vorgänge in Preußen ihre eigenständigen Parallelen hatten in anderen Reichsterritorien[37]. Deswegen konnten auch nicht-preußische Predigten als Zeugnisse zur eigenen Sache in dem engagierten Berliner Band abgedruckt werden.

Durch Marezoll vergrößert sich die Zahl der mit staatlichen Maßnahmen gegen die neologische Kirchenwirklichkeit abrechnenden Theologen noch einmal. Nur zwei Prediger des untersuchten Bandes hatten sich bisher diesem Thema nicht unmittelbar eingefügt: der längst verstorbene Zollikofer und der auffallend Anderem zugewandte Bartels. Ihnen zur Seite tritt nun auf seine spezifische Weise der letzte der Mitautoren Schleiermachers, der Nachfolger Marezolls im Amt eines Göttinger Universitätspredigers, Friedrich Christoph von Ammon[38]. Seine 1799 veröffentlichten Predigten fallen auf durch ihr ausführliches Eingehen auf die französische Revolution (412). Neun ältere Prediger hatten kein Wort verloren zu den bewegenden Ereignissen im Nachbarland, die inzwischen so viel Enttäuschung hervorriefen. Das ist ein erneuter Hinweis darauf, wie konzentriert die Berliner Predigtauswahl von 1799 Stimmen zu fast nur einem Thema bietet.

III.

Nach diesem allzu oberflächlichen Blick in den thematisch konzentrierten, theologisch aber facettenreichen Predigtband wendet sich die Aufmerksamkeit seiner 13. Rede zu, der Bußtagspredigt des jungen Friedrich Daniel Ernst Schleiermacher[39]. Ihrer Interpretation soll die bisherige Betrachtung ihres ursprünglichen Kontextes ein Stück weit dienen.

Zunächst ist notwendig, die Predigt in die Biographie Schleiermachers einzuzeichnen und damit dem oben Angekündigten nachzukommen. Dafür ist zu erinnern, daß es sich selbstverständlich nicht um eine 1799 gehaltene Predigt handelt, da sie im September 1798 für den Druck ausgearbeitet worden ist[40]. Wann und wo sie jedoch gehalten worden war, ist dadurch noch nicht bestimmt. 1798 war Schleiermacher Krankenhausprediger in Berlin[41]. Die Predigt jedoch wendet sich an eine Landgemeinde. Sie warnt vor der "Sorglosigkeit womit ihr eure Gärten und Felder dem Ungeziefer überlaßt" (248) und erinnert: "Wie weise sind nicht unsere Häuser und Felder gegen die Gewalt des Feuers und Wassers geschützt!" (239). Die ländliche, hochwassergefährdete Gemeinde kann nur das Landstädtchen Landsberg an der Warthe sein, wo Schleiermacher nach seinem zweiten theologischen Examen, von 1794 bis 1796, als Adjunkt seines Onkels regelmäßig predigte[42]. Um die Zeit des Bußtags, der in Preußen auf den Mittwoch zwischen Jubilate und Kantate fiel, seitdem 1778 die anderen drei jährlichen Bußtage abgeschafft wurden[43], waren die Frühlingswasser gefallen. In Schleiermachers Landsberger Amtsjahre gehören die Bußtage des 15.5.1794, des 29.4.1795 und des 20.4.1796. Nun existiert für das letztgenannte Datum ein Predigtentwurf Schleiermachers[44]. Ihm liegt mit Prov 14,34 der gleiche Bibeltext zugrunde wie der 1799 veröffentlichten Predigt, und auch das formulierte Thema ist das gleiche: "Von der Gerechtigkeit als Grundlage des bürgerlichen Wohles" lautet es im Konzept von 1796, "Die Gerechtigkeit ist die unentbehrliche Grundlage des allgemeinen Wohlergehens" in der Druckfassung 1799.

Die Zugehörigkeit der hier untersuchten Predigt zum Termin des 20.4.1796 kann also nicht zweifelhaft sein, zumal schon der Herausgeber des Predigtentwurfs 1908 darauf verwiesen hat[45]. Schleiermachers erste veröffentlichte Predigt war somit noch zur Regierungszeit Friedrich Wilhelm II. in Landsberg gehalten worden, bevor sie im Herbst 1798 für den Druck ausgearbeitet wurde und im Frühjahr 1799 erschien.

Sogleich ihr erster langer Satz spielt kritisch auf die französischen Ereignisse an, durch die eine gesittete Nation beherrscht wird, ohne auf ihre Religion Wert zu legen. Solche Töne hatte es im ganzen Predigtband nur ein einziges Mal gegeben, bei Ammon, dem Zweitjüngsten neben Schleiermacher. Ebenso deutlich ist, daß Schleiermacher im Unterschied zu seinen Berliner Kollegen und denen, die ihnen vom Ausland her sekundierten, von den Fragen um Bekenntnistreue und gottesdienstliche Riten nicht betroffen und am Zusammenhang von Religion, Tugend und Seligkeit nicht besonders interessiert war. Der öffentliche Bettag fordere die Gemeinde auf "zu einer frommen Erwägung ihrer bürgerlichen Verhältnisse" (232) und lasse die Gerechtigkeit des Predigttextes verstehen "als die unentbehrliche Grundlage alles bürgerlichen Wohlergehens" (234 Predigtthema). Religion fordert nicht Tugend, der der verheißene Lohn korrespondiert, sondern ist die "reiche Quelle geselliger Tugenden" (232, vgl. 256). Ein solches Religionsverständnis läßt der gesamte Band in keiner seiner 26 sonstigen Predigten erkennen.

Entfaltet wird das in drei Predigtabschnitten. Der erste und längste handelt davon, wir müßten "gerecht seyn gegen die Obrigkeit" (235-244). Der zweite mahnt, "daß wir gerecht untereinander seyn" (244-249). Der dritte spricht von der Gerechtigkeit gegen Untergebene (249-255). In einem kurzen Schluß (255f) betont Schleiermacher, mit allem dem wolle er "mehr Dankbarkeit für den Beistand der göttlichen Gnade, als tiefe, beschämende Gefühle der Reue veranlassen" (256). In der Ablehnung beschämender Reuegefühle steht er sicher Löffler und wohl allen Neologen des gemeinsamen Buches nahe, scheint aber zugleich an das zu denken, was ihn von der Brüdergemeine trennte[46]. Im Hervorheben der Dankbarkeit steht er Bartels am nächsten – nur daß die göttliche Gnade nicht in der Natur genossen, sondern dankbar im Geselligen empfangen wird.

Schon diese knappe Skizze verführt also zum Vergleichen. Alles Vergleichen aber kann doch nur belegen, was sowieso selbstverständlich ist, daß nämlich auch der Landsberger Prediger ein Kind seiner Zeit, ein von sich aufdrängenden theologischen Problemen und Lösungen geprägter Theologe war. Wichtiger scheint zu sein, die Besonderheiten der Predigt näher zu bestimmen und ein wenig zu vervollständigen:

Schleiermachers Predigt unterscheidet sich von den 26 anderen durch konsequenten Gemeinschaftsbezug. Wie ausschließlich sonst das Individuum im Blick ist, zeigt sich besonders da, wo ausnahmsweise auch einmal Staat und Kirche in den Gedankenkreis aufgenommen sind, etwa bei Sack: "Handelt Jemand gewissenlos in der Verwaltung seines Amtes, . . . müßten wir . . . auf uns selbst zurückkommen" (208f). Schleiermacher dagegen argumentiert ganz um der Gemeinschaft willen. Diese Gemeinschaft ist der christliche, aber keineswegs der stets richtig handelnde, der idealisierte Staat (241). Das Verhalten gegen Gleichgestellte und Untergebene wird ihm nach – und damit eingeordnet. Innerkirchlich oder gar brüderisch predigt Schleiermacher nicht. Seine Ethik erweist sich als christlich nicht durch Beschränkung auf die Kirche, sondern durch die Totalität ihrer zu predigenden Geltung[47].

Schleiermacher spricht als preußischer Prediger. Das verbindet ihn nur auf den ersten Blick mit der Mehrzahl der zehn anderen Autoren. Denn sie verteidigten die wahren Rechte, die die Religion den Menschen gewährt, gegen den preußischen Eingriff. Schleiermachers Rede aber ist in mindestens dreifacher Hinsicht inhaltlich preußisch zu nennen:

In unmittelbarem Anschluß an den Predigttext erklärt Schleiermacher, Gerechtigkeit bedeute "die Bewahrung der Treue und Redlichkeit" und das sei "unsere Art zu reden" (233). Das könnte eine Anspielung sein auf den der seit 1797 von der Potsdamer Garnisonkirche erklingenden Mozartmelodie unterlegten Höltytext "Üb' immer Treu' und Redlichkeit. . .". Dann hätte Schleiermacher diese Passage erst 1798 bei der Ausarbeitung verfaßt. Das aber ist nicht nachweisbar[48]. Einfacher ist es daher, mit dem Grimmschen Wörterbuch[49] die Worte "Treue und Redlichkeit" als eine Verbindung zu verstehen, die "vor allem in der aufklärungszeit" häufig war.

Von größerem Interesse ist, daß Schleiermacher in einer der untersuchten zeitlich nahestehenden Predigt[50] deutlich macht, wie er die Wortverbindung "Treu und Redlichkeit" versteht. Ausgehend von der Feststellung, der Anblick eines Frommen mache Eindruck auf jedermann, wehrt er ab: "Ich möchte nicht sagen, daß es die unwandelbare Rechtschaffenheit des Frommen ist, was diesen Eindrukk hervorbringt". Vielmehr stehe fest, "daß auch unter denen, welche am Glauben Mangel leiden, nicht Wenige ihren Wandel in unbestechlicher Treue und Redlichkeit führen, und die Erfüllung ihrer Pflichten im ganzen Umfange ihr erstes und höchstes sein lassen" (151). Treue und Redlichkeit bezeichnen also zusammen die

Rechtschaffenheit eines Menschen in seiner Pflichterfüllung. Sie sind ausdrücklich kein Spezifikum des Frommen. Dies beschreibt Schleiermacher vielmehr so: "Der Gedanke an Gott begleitet den Frommen überall hin, nicht der bloße Gedanke, er sieht und empfindet überall das ewige Wesen... Alles legt hievon ein Zeugniß ab. Seine Treue und Redlichkeit hat eine ganz eigenthümliche Gestalt, weil durch diesen göttlichen Sinn alle Begierden, die ihn versuchen könnten, zum Schweigen gebracht sind" (152). Dies ruhevolle Gegründetsein spüre jedermann der Treue und Redlichkeit des Frommen ab, auch wenn er faktisch nicht anders handle als andere Rechtschaffene auch.

Der Blick in eine verwandte Predigt macht also deutlich, warum Schleiermacher in seiner 1799 gedruckten Predigt den Gerechtigkeitsbegriff seines Predigttextes bewußt einschränkend als Treue und Redlichkeit kennzeichnet: um deutlich zu machen, er wolle sich am staatlichen, allgemeinen Bettage nicht einem spezifisch christlichen Gerechtigkeitsverständnis zuwenden, sondern auf die allen Staatsbürgern wohl anstehende Rechtschaffenheit eingehen. Indem er dies eingeschränkte Gerechtigkeitsverständnis "unsere Art zu reden" nennt, weist er seine Gemeinde also nicht auf ein lokalspezifisches Ereignis, wie es Potsdams Glockenspiel sicherlich gewesen ist, sondern erinnert an die in anderen Territorien so nicht gepflegte preußische Aufklärung, die ihn mit seiner Gemeinde verbindet.

Zweites preußisches Element seiner Predigt ist ihr Gottesbild. Gott ist nicht so sehr Vater aller Menschen oder Schöpfer der Natur wie in anderen Predigten des Bandes, sondern "der Stifter . . . von Gesetz und Recht" (232). Nicht was die Vernunft, die Natur, das Gewissen sagen, sondern "alles gute und löbliche was das Vaterland von uns fordert, (ist) eine Pflicht . . . Gott" gegenüber (232). Die Belege sind zahlreich.[51]

Drittens zeigt sich sein Preußentum auch im Kritischen. "Wollten wir von jedem Fehler, der in dem Privatleben einer obrigkeitlichen Person wahrgenommen wird, glauben, daß er auch in den Geschäften ihres Amtes begangen werde, . . . so würden wir sehr Unrecht, ja wohl gar verläumderisch handeln" (241). Jeder Hörer wußte, daß hiermit das ärgerliche Privatleben

Friedrich Wilhelm II. gemeint war. Schleiermacher predigte konkret preußisch[52].

Schleiermacher spricht zu einer Gemeinde, die argwöhnisch die in Frankreich freiwerdenden Kräfte beobachtet. "Die irrige Meinung, der Ruhm eines Volkes bestehe in den siegreichen Fortschritten seiner Waffen, in dem Kriegsruhm seiner Beherrscher, . . . diese Meinung hat ihre täuschende Kraft seit langem verloren" (234). Bei dieser Feststellung aber bleibt er nicht stehen, sondern warnt seine Gemeinde vor dem Irrtum, "die Furcht vor den angemessensten Strafen" könne ähnlich gut oder gar besser als die Religion "zu einem rechtlichen und schuldlosen Verhalten" wirken (231). Schleiermacher zeigt seiner Gemeinde die zügellos gebrauchte Guillotine als miserablen Religionsersatz. Dies Anliegen verbindet ihn im gemeinsamen Predigtband nur mit Ammon. Der aber kritisierte sie nicht als Moloch, sondern als Aufruhr (412). Staatliche Tötung begriffen beide schon 1799 in verschiedenen Dimensionen. Im Unterschied zur Freude der Berliner Kollegen aber über das Ende einer reaktionären Kirchenpolitik zeigt Schleiermachers Kritik der Revolutions-Religion in nuce konservative Züge (z.B. 232)[53].

Sehr differenziert unterscheidet Schleiermacher zwischen Religion und christlicher Religion. Das kennzeichnet ihn vor sämtlichen Mitautoren und muß festgehalten werden, weil Schleiermacher gerade hier des schlechthinnigen Versagens geziehen worden ist. In der Tat trennt er nicht zwischen Mystik und Wort, Christus und Religion, weil "Ehrfurcht vor einem höhern Wesen" alle Religion auszeichnet (231). Dieser Übereinstimmung könne jedoch ein zureichender Begriff der christlichen Religion nicht entnommen werden. Denn gleich im nächsten Satz heißt es: "Wie viel mehr muß also nicht allen Völkern und ihren Regenten die christliche Religion theuer und heilig seyn, welche von ihren Bekennern nicht nur vorübergehende Handlungen fordert, sondern sie zu bleibenden Gesinnungen erhebt" (231f). Auch die christliche Religion fordert Handlungen. Auch die Handlungen der Christen gehen vorüber – Schleiermacher sagt das im Gegensatz zu Sack 227! Darüber hinaus jedoch werden die Christen zu bleibenden Gesinnungen erhoben. Diese passivische Formulierung fällt im Kontext des Mylius-Bandes auf, auch wenn sie mit

Ansätzen konvergiert, wie sie bei Spalding, Sack und vor allem Bartels erkennbar sind. Sie zeigt deutliche Nachbarschaft zu den im gleichen Jahr erschienenen Reden mit ihrem "sich in kindlicher Passivität ergreifen und erfüllen lassen"[54] – wie die Überschrift der vierten Rede "Über das Gesellige in der Religion" dem Thema der ganzen Predigt korrespondiert[55]. In vierfacher Hinsicht, so läßt sich jetzt zusammenfassen:

in ihrem Gemeinschaftsbezug,

in ihrer preußischen Ausrichtung,

in ihrer religiösen Revolutionskritik und

in ihrem in der passivitas gipfelnden Religionsverständnis

zeichnet sich Schleiermachers erste gedruckte Predigt vor allem aus, liest man sie neu in ihrem ursprünglichen Kontext. Nimmt man hinzu, was zuvor an mehr äußerlichen Besonderheiten im Vergleich zu den Mitautoren genannt war, nämlich daß Schleiermacher unter ihnen der jüngste war, daß er als einziger mit nur einer Predigt beteiligt wurde, daß er die mit Abstand längste Ausarbeitung vorlegte, die einzige vor einer Landgemeinde gehaltene Predigt beisteuerte und als einziger Berliner nicht so oder so der Wöllner-Ära verhaftet war, so ergibt sich das erstaunlich deutliche Profil eines während der Ausarbeitung seiner Rede doch erst dreißigjährigen Predigers. Viel stärker als in einer Sammlung, die nur Predigten aus Schleiermachers Feder enthält, tritt dadurch zutage, wie viel Schleiermacher jeder Kirche der Subjektivität zu sagen hätte.

IV.

Schleiermacher selber hat im Jahr 1799 seiner Verwunderung darüber Ausdruck verliehen, wie unterschiedlicher Art die Veröffentlichungen seien, mit denen er gleichzeitig und erstmals an die Öffentlichkeit treten werde. Unter dem 16.4.1799 schrieb er an Henriette Herz: "Daß zugleich mit der Religion auch eine Predigt von mir erscheint, ist wunderlich genug . . . Die Fragmente, die Predigt, die Religion und der Kalender machen zusammen eine wunderliche Entrée in die literarische Welt"[56]. Unter den vier hier genannten Projekten sind die Predigt und die Religion[57] am engsten aufeinander bezogen – schon alleine weil die Fragmente Torso blieben und

der Kalender, zu dem Schleiermacher eine Siedlungsgeschichte des
australischen Neuholland beisteuern sollte, nie erschien[58]. Dennoch
bestätigt eine vergleichende Lektüre zunächst einmal ganz deutlich
Schleiermachers eigene Einschätzung, auch diese beiden 1799 wirklich
erschienenen Texte bildeten ein wunderliches Gespann.

Schleiermachers Reden stellen sich als Apologie der Religion vor. Mit
Schärfe treten sie "den übelzusammengenähten Bruchstücken von Metaphysik und Moral, die man vernünftiges Christentum nennt," entgegen (25).
Sie berufen sich geradezu auf die Verachtung der Gebildeten für solch "eine
schlanke Religion" (21: Erste Rede) und bezeichnen als Wesen der Religion
"weder Denken noch Handeln, sondern Anschauung und Gefühl. Anschauen
will sie das Universum, in seinen eigenen Darstellungen und Handlungen
will sie es andächtig belauschen, von seinen unmittelbaren Einflüssen will sie
sich in kindlicher Passivität ergreifen und erfüllen lassen. So ist sie beiden in
allem entgegengesetzt," der Moral und der Metaphysik (50: Zweite Rede).

Nichts von alledem bestimmt die Ausführungen der gleichzeitig
gedruckten Predigt. Sie erläutert der Bettagsgemeinde unter betonter
Ausschaltung des christlichen Gerechtigkeitsverständnisses das Ziel bürgerlichen Zusammenlebens, "daß in tiefer Sicherheit jeder seine Hütte
bewohnen, und seinen Geschäften nachgehen könne, daß frecher Eigennutz
nicht den Bestrebungen anderer muthwillig Hindernisse in den Weg lege,
und daß alles, was menschliches Wohlbefinden vermehren kann, ruhige und
sichere Fortschritte mache" (234f). Hier ist des Menschen Aktivität im Blick.
Damit bestätigt sich Kurt Nowaks Eindruck eines "Doppellebens", das
Schleiermacher in frühromantisch-geselligen Kreisen einerseits, in amtlicher
Tätigkeit andererseits geführt habe[59]. Religionsschrift und Predigt sind
dann Dokumente dieser seiner beiden Lebenskreise. Schleiermacher predigt
also amtlich die Moral, der zu entsagen er als Redner der Religion aufruft.

Der Gegensatz ist in der Tat nicht zu übersehen und wunderlich
genug. Er läßt sich nicht nivellieren durch Hinweise darauf, die Predigt sei
doch beträchtliche Zeit vor den Reden gehalten worden, und die Reden
konzedierten dem Priester doch immerhin, nebenher auch "Moralist sein
(zu) dürfen im Dienste des Staates" (222: Vierte Rede). Beide Argumente
verfangen nicht. Schleiermacher hat zu eben der Zeit, da die Reden

entstanden, diese eine Predigt zum Druck ausgewählt und ausgearbeitet. Vor allem aber hat er in den Reden vor jedem "in und durcheinander sein" von Religion und Moral gewarnt (222) und ausgerufen: "Hinweg also mit jeder solchen Verbindung von Kirche und Staat – das bleibt mein Catonischer Ratsspruch bis ans Ende, oder bis ich es erlebe, sie wirklich zertrümmert zu sehen" (224). Jeder Vermittlungsversuch hätte also Schleiermacher gegen sich. Das aber bedeutet, daß Kurt Nowaks Darstellung noch um ein Stück präzisiert werden muß. Sein berechtigter Ausdruck "Doppelleben" klingt nach zwei voneinander völlig unberührten Bereichen. In Wahrheit aber ist das, was Schleiermacher predigte, gleichzeitig von ihm als Moral aus der Religion verwiesen worden. Da aber nun die Predigt unzweifelhaft eine wirkliche Predigt aus einem bestimmten christlichen Gottesdienst ist, geht es nicht an, die Reden über die Religion ihr gegenüber theologisch abzuwerten. Sie erweisen sich, von dieser Predigt aus gesehen, als fundamental-theologische Schrift. Das ist nicht alles, was über sie zu sagen wäre. In dem hier angestellten Vergleich aber ist es die notwendige Konsequenz aus dem allerdings Wunderlichen, das Schleiermacher zu gleicher Zeit erscheinen ließ.

Sind also Schleiermachers Reden, aus sich selbst verstanden, dem Wesen der Religion, wie es sich im Christentum überbietet und erfüllt (Fünfte Rede), in ganz anderer Tiefe zugewandt als die gleichzeitige Predigt, so überrascht es auch nicht mehr gar zu sehr, bei genauerer Lektüre der Predigt doch noch auf einiges zu stoßen, das in deutlicher Zurückhaltung auf die Reden hinweist, das den Hörern der Predigt unmöglich deutlich werden konnte – die Reden waren 1796 noch lange nicht erschienen[60] – und im Zusammenhang des Predigtbandes aus dem Verlag Mylius nicht auffallen muß. Allerdings war schon in jenem Kontext der Gemeinschaftsbezug der Schleiermacherpredigt hervorgetreten. Er ist auch der Religionsschrift nicht fremd, die in der Vierten Rede eine Gemeinschaft der Religionsvirtuosen untereinander und jedes von ihnen mit seinen Schülern skizziert. Dennoch liegt ihr ein subjektives und vereinzelndes Religionsverständnis zugrunde. Erst im Zusammenhang mit dieser vom Individuum getragenen Religions-gemeinschaft wird Schleiermachers Bejahung einer das Individuum

tragenden Staatsgemeinschaft als Predigtgegenstand deutlich werden
können. Wie sehr die staatliche Gemeinschaft der Bürger das Individuum
trägt, wird nun gerade da erkennbar, wo Schleiermacher in seiner Predigt –
wenn auch wesentlich weniger scharf als in den Reden – Staatskritik
aufgreift. Immerhin ist die zweite Hälfte des ersten Predigtabschnitts von ihr
durchzogen (240-244). Daß sie auch den preußischen König nicht ausläßt,
war oben gezeigt. Doch sie geht weit über ihn hinaus! Der obrigkeitliche
Staat ist der Bereich, "wo alles unvollkommen ist" und wo es "nicht möglich
(ist), daß alle, die einen Antheil an der höchsten Gewalt haben, immer die
tugendhaftesten seyn" (241). Gerade diese behutsame aber deutliche Kritik
wird nun zu der auch das obrigkeitliche Individuum tragenden Kraft der
Gemeinschaft. Denn jeder Bürger wird in dieser Predigt aufgefordert, seine
wohlgeprüfte Kritik gehörigenorts vorzutragen: "Strebst du aber nützlich zu
seyn durch deine Gedanken, über öffentliche Angelegenheiten, wohlan so
erwirb dir den Ruhm eines wohlgesinnten und einsichtsvollen Mannes . . .
und trage dann deine besten Einsichten da vor, wo sie nützlich werden, und
wirksam seyn können" (242f). Jeder Bürger, nicht nur der dazu bestallte, soll
ein "Rathgeber" seiner Obrigkeit sein. Jeder darf, ja sollte deren "Fehler
verhüten" und ihre "Schwachheiten unschädlich machen" (241). Was von der
Religion aus gesehen harsche Staatskritik sein mußte, hat im Staat selber
staatstragende Kraft.

Ein drittes gemeinsames Element verbindet die Reden und die
Predigt von 1799 neben dem Gemeinschaftsgedanken und der Staatskritik.
Denn der angedeutete Gegensatz zwischen der passiven, empfangenden
Religionskonzeption der Reden und der bürgerlich aktiven Moral der
Predigt umfaßt nicht alles, was Schleiermacher in seiner Predigt schrieb. Ihr
Eingang unterscheidet die christliche Religion von Religion überhaupt, da
sie "nicht nur vorübergehende Handlungen fordert" wie diese, sondern ihre
Bekenner "zu bleibenden Gesinnungen erhebt, welche nicht nur durch
unsichre Gefühle, und einen mit vielem Irrthum vermischten Glauben,
sondern durch die deutlichsten Einsichten und die unwiderstehlichsten
Empfindungen wirkt" (231f). Diese Unterscheidung klingt im kurzen
Predigtschluß noch einmal auf, wo Schleiermacher seinen Darlegungen

wünscht, "daß sie mehr Dankbarkeit für den Beistand der göttlichen Gnade, als tiefe, beschämende Gefühle der Reue veranlassen mögen" (256). Beschämende Reuegefühle beziehen sich auf das eigene Tun. Darum geht es auch dem Prediger Schleiermacher letztlich nicht. Göttliche Gnade aber empfangen zu haben kann der Christ nur dankbar sein. So zeigt die 1799 gedruckte Predigt Schleiermachers nicht nur im Kontext des von Buttmann bevorworteten Predigtbandes deutliches Profil, sondern läßt im Kontext seiner gleichzeitigen Religionsschrift erkennen, wie Scheiermacher sein Predigtamt vom Religionsverständnis aus neu zu gestalten begonnen hat.

Anmerkungen

1. Friedrich Schleiermacher's sämmtliche Werke. Zweite Abtheilung. Predigten. Vierter Band. Neue Ausgabe. Berlins 1844 (zitiert SW 2,4), 1-15.
2. A.a.O. 1 Anmerkung.
3. A.a.O. IV. Auch Wilhelm Dilthey, Aus Schleiermacher's Leben. In Briefen (zitiert: Briefe). Dritter Band, Berlin 1861, 116 Anmerkung gibt an, sie sei bis zu dieser Ausgabe übersehen worden.
4. BFChTh 49, Gütersloh 1960.
5. Der Bibliothek des Predigerseminars Hildesheim sei an dieser Stelle für alles freundliche Entgegenkommen herzlich gedankt. Die Wissenschaftliche Buchgesellschaft Darmstadt hat einen fotomechanischen Nachdruck vorgelegt unter dem Titel "Predigten von protestantischen Gottesgelehrten der Aufklärungszeit. Herausgegeben von Wichmann von Meding. Darmstadt 1989". Die Einleitung enthält auch zeitgenössische Predigerportraits, die für die Erfassung des Bandkonzeptes nicht ohne Bedeutung sind.
6. Sowohl SW 2,4 (1844) 1 als auch Günter Meckenstock, Friedrich Daniel Ernst Schleiermacher, Kritische Gesamtausgabe (zitiert: KGA) Band 1.2, Berlin 1984, XVI Anm. 28f nennen ihn, beide jedoch unvollständig.
7. Briefe III, 116 Anmerkung. Bamberger lebte 1722-1804 und war seit 1780 an der Garnisonkirche Potsdam tätig: Otto Fischer, Evangelisches Pfarrbuch für die Mark Brandenburg seit der Reformation, Band 2,1, Berlin 1971, 26. Schleiermacher versah die durch seine Emeritierung freigewordene Stelle 1799 für kurze Zeit.
8. Briefe III, 97. Es ist nicht ersichtlich, auf welche andere Predigt als diese sich die Äußerung beziehen könnte, da Schleiermacher seine Predigtvorbereitungen nicht als Arbeiten zu bezeichnen pflegte (vgl. SW 2,1, 5).
9. Briefe I, 220.
10. Siehe Anmerkung 7.
11. Siehe Anmerkung 7. Bamberger konnte nicht am 20.12.1798 um Dispens von seinen Amtspflichten bitten, da er "nicht mehr im Stande sey, mein Ammt zu versehen" (Evangelisches Zentralarchiv Berlin, Bestand 14/2344 Blatt 54) und im Frühjahr 1799 als Herausgeber eines Predigtsammelbandes vor die Öffentlichkeit treten.
12. Geboren 5.12.1764 in Frankfurt/Main, gestorben 21.6.1829 in Berlin. Über sein Leben und Wirken in Berlin Alexander Buttmann, ADB 3, Leipzig 1876, 656-659.

13. A. Buttmann a.a.O. 657.

14. Siehe GV22, München. New York. London. Paris 1980, 369f.

15. Buttmann hatte die Herausgeberschaft von Bamberger übernommen. Diltheys Angabe enthält also irrtümlich einen wahren Kern.

16. Vertraute Briefe, die Religion betreffend. Dritte Auflage mit einer Zugabe. Breslau 1788, Vorwort Blatt 2.

17. Der außerhalb Berlins noch unbekannte Charité-Prediger, der im Vorbericht des Verlages eigens vorgestellt wurde, fühlte sich selber ein wenig deplaziert zwischen den großen Kanzelrednern seiner Zeit: Briefe I, 220.

18. Diterich, Sack, Schleiermacher, Spalding, Teller und Zöllner.

19. Hanns Hubert Hofmann, Biographisches Wörterbuch zur deutschen Geschichte, Band 3, München 1975, 3229-3231; Fritz Valjavec, Das Wöllnersche Religionsedikt, HJb 72, 1953, 386-400 schildert Wöllners politische Bedeutung positiver als Emanuel Hirsch, Geschichte der neuern evangelischen Theologie, Band V, Gütersloh 1960, 7f seine theologische.

20. Der fünfte, Anton Friedrich Büsching (1724-1793) war seit 1766 Oberkonsistorialrat in Berlin und Leiter des Gymnasiums im Grauen Kloster. Er trat als vor allem geographischer Schriftsteller hervor: Georg Meusel, Lexikon der vom Jahr 1750-1800 verstorbenen teutschen Schriftsteller, Erster Band, Leipzig 1802, 700-721. Als Autor eines Predigtbandes kam er also kaum in Frage. Insofern läßt sich sagen, alle theologischen Berliner Oberkonsistorialräte seien, nachdem sie 1788 gemeinsam protestiert hatten, 1799 nach Wöllners Entlassung gemeinsam als Autoren dieses Bandes an die Offentlichkeit getreten.

21. Die Predigten Ammons und Spaldings mußten, da verspätet eingereicht, auf den letzten Bögen nachgetragen werden, wie das Vorwort ausdrücklich verzeichnet.

22. In das Jahr, in dem Friedrich Wilhelm III. den Minister seines Vaters entließ, fallen die Vorbereitungen zu dem hier untersuchten Band.

23. Geboren 1.11.1714 in Triebsees, seit 1764 Oberkonsistorialrat und Propst an St. Nikolai zu Berlin, 1788 emeritiert, gestorben 22.5.1804 in Berlin. Siehe Martin Schmidt RGG VI, 3. Auflage, Tübingen 1962, 221 und 222.

24. Die Bände 1 bis 6 waren 1771 bis 1776 regelmäßig Jahr für Jahr zur Leipziger Ostermesse erschienen: Nachricht zu Beginn des ersten Bandes Blatt 2.

25. Geboren zu Berlin 15.12.1721, 1754 Archidiakon an der Marienkirche, 1770 Oberkonsistorialrat, gestorben 14.1.1797 im Amt. Siehe Wolfgang Philipp RGG II, 3. Auflage, Tübingen 1958, 213.

26. Teller berichtet 296f ausdrücklich, Diterich sei am Tage nach der Königin Elisabeth Christine gestorben, die sein Beichtkind gewesen war.

27. Geboren 5.8.1730 St. Gallen, gestorben 22.1.1788 in Leipzig. Siehe Erich Beyreuther RGG VI, 3. Auflage, Tübingen 1962, 1928. Die in mancher Hinsicht vergleichbare Affäre um Reinhards Dresdener Reformationspredigt von 1800 (dazu Christian-Erdmann Schott, Möglichkeiten und Grenzen der Aufklärungspredigt. Dargestellt am Beispiel Franz Volkmar Reinhards, Göttingen 1978, 250-263) hat Zollikofer also erst recht nicht miterlebt.

28. Geboren 9.1.1734 in Leipzig, seit 1767 Oberkonsistorialrat und Propst zu Cölln an der Spree, seit 1786 auch Mitglied der Akademie der Wissenschaften, gestorben 9.12.1804 in Berlin. Siehe H. Hohlwein RGG VI, 3. Auflage, Tübingen 1962, 678.

29. Siehe G. Meckenstock a.a.O. (Anmerkung 6) LXXVIII-LXXXV.

30. Von Interesse ist hier Stubenrauchs briefliche Äußerung an Schleiermacher vom 27.4.1799, Teller sei "in eine etwas unangenehme Verlegenheit" geraten: Briefe III, 116.

31. Geboren 4.9.1738 in Magdeburg, 1777 Hof- und Domprediger in Berlin, 1793 Oberhofprediger, 1816 Bischof, gestorben 2.10.1817 in Berlin. Sack hatte, als der Mylius-Band erschien, das Vorwort zu Schleiermachers Fawcett-Übersetzung verfaßt. Vgl. K. H. Sack RE 17, 3. Auflage, Leipzig 1906, 321-323.

32. Geboren 9.12.1749 in Harderode im Braunschweigischen, gestorben 16.12.1826 in Wolfenbüttel als Nachfolger Jerusalems und erster Geistlicher Braunschweigs. Nicht nur der Registerband der RGG, 3. Auflage, erwähnt Bartels nicht, auch Emanuel Hirsch, Geschichte der neuern evangelischen Theologie, übergeht ihn. Doch siehe ADB 2, Leipzig 1875, 85 und 86.

33. Geboren 8.1.1752 in Saalfeld, gestorben 4.2.1816 als Generalsuperintendent von Gotha, wohin er 1788 aus dem preußischen Frankfurt/Oder gegangen war.

34. Geboren 24.4.1753 in Neudamme, gestorben 12.9.1804 in Frankfurt/Oder als Propst der Nikolaikirche Berlin.

35. Geboren 25.12.1761 zu Plauen im Voigtland, 1794 Hauptpastor der deutschen Petrikirche Kopenhagen, gestorben 15.1.1828 als Superintendent in Jena.

36. Siehe Heinrich August Schott, Homilien und einige andere Predigten in der neuesten Zeit gehalten von dem verewigten Herrn Consistorial=Rathe D. Johann Gottlob Marezoll, Superintendenten, Pfarrern der Stadtkirche und Theol. Prof. honor. zu Jena. Herausgegeben nebst einigen Nachrichten über das Leben und Wirken des Verewigten, Neustadt a. d. Orla 1829.

37. Hierher gehören die in das folgende Jahr fallenden sächsischen Ereignisse (siehe Anmerkung 27) ebenso wie das württembergische Vorgehen (dazu Fritz Valjavec, Anmerkung 19), der in Sachsen-Weimar auszustehende Atheismusstreit (siehe dazu das Kapitel "Johann Gottlieb Fichte und der Atheismusstreit" bei Emanuel Hirsch, Geschichte der neuern evangelischen Theologie, Band IV, Gütersloh 1952, 337-407), die schwedischen Maßnahmen in Vorpommern (Josias F. C. Löffler, Magazin für Prediger, IV. Bandes I. Stück, Jena 1808, 299) und anderes mehr. In dem Maße aber, wie Fremdherrschaft und Befreiung von Napoleon zum Thema der christlichen Gemeinden wurden, geriet der mit Vergangenem abrechnende Predigtband von 1799 in Vergessenheit.

38. Geboren 16.1.1766 in Bayreuth, gestorben 21.5.1849 in Dresden als emeritierter, einflußreicher Nachfolger Reinhards. Über ihn Martin Schmidt TRE 2, Berlin 1978, 453-455.

39. Siehe Anmerkung l.

40. Siehe Anmerkung 8.

41. Die Vermutung, bei der 1798 gearbeiteten Predigt könne es sich um eine Charité-Predigt Schleiermachers handeln, verbietet sich schon darum, weil Schleiermacher ausdrücklich erklärt hat, er wolle Arbeiten für die Charité-Gemeinde nicht veröffentlichen: SW 2,1,4.

42. Das Ende der Vakanzvertretung nach Schumanns Tod in Landsberg hat Kurt Nowak ThZ 41, 1985, 399f überzeugend geklärt. Siehe dazu die Dokumente KGA V,1 Nr. 308-310 und 318. Schleiermachers Aufstellungspredigt fand am 4.9.1796 in der Dreifaltigkeitskirche Berlin statt. Zwei Jahre danach, am 3.9.1798, schrieb Schleiermacher aus Landsberg, gestern habe er "auf meiner alten Kanzel" gepredigt, "als wären die zwei Jahre, die zwischen mir und der Gewohnheit hier zu predigen stehen, auf einen Schlag vernichtet" (Briefe 1,190). Diese Äußerung bestätigt präzis das Ende der ersten amtlichen Tätigkeit und hat zur Voraussetzung, daß Schleiermacher seit zwei Jahren nicht in Landsberg gepredigt hatte.

43. Carl Bertheau RE VI, 3. Auflage, Leipzig 1899, 58.

44. Johannes Bauer, Schleiermacher als patriotischer Prediger. Ein Beitrag zur Geschichte der nationalen Erhebung vor hundert Jahren, Gießen 1908, 309 und 310.

45. Bauer a.a.O. 310, vermischt allerdings mit Unzutreffendem.

46. E. R. Meyer, Schleiermachers und C. G. von Brinkmanns Gang durch die Brüdergemeine, Leipzig 1905, 22.

47. Darin zeigt sich der sachliche Zusammenhang mit den im gleichen Jahr veröffentlichten "Reden an die Gebildeten unter ihren (der Religion) Verächtern" und mit dem Programm, predigen zu wollen, "als gäbe es noch Gemeinen der Gläubigen" (SW 2,1,6).

48. Diese Vermutung hat ihren Reiz, solange man Dilthey folgend Bamberger für den Bandherausgeber hält (siehe Anmerkung 7 und 11) und Schleiermacher in Sachen seiner Predigt bei ihm sozusagen aus- und eingehen sieht. Doch sie fällt ohnedies in sich zusammen: zwar war Höltys Gedicht über die testamentarische Anrede eines alten Landmanns an seinen Sohn, bis an sein kühles Grab stets Treu und Redlichkeit zu üben, als erweiternde Veröffentlichung im Musenalmanach 1779 durch J. H. Voß bekannt gemacht worden (den Autographentext bietet Wilhelm Michael, Ludwig Heinrich Hölty's Sämtliche Werke, Erster Band, Weimar 1914, 197-199), doch Mozarts Zauberflöte erklang in Berlin erstmals am 12.5.1794 (Hermann Abert, W. A. Mozart, zweiter Teil, Leipzig 1956, 689). Seit wann dieser in Berlin ganz neuen Melodie Höltys älterer Text unterlegt wurde, ist nicht festzustellen. Aber es ist kaum vorstellbar, das sei schon ein Jahr nach der Installierung des dieses Lied vortragenden Glockenspiels auf dem Turm der Garnisonkirche (Bernhard Rogge, Die königliche Hof und Garnisonkirche zu Potsdam, Berlin 1882, 11) in so allgemeiner Verbreitung geschehen, daß ein Prediger von der Kanzel darauf anspielen konnte. Schließlich erlaubt das Predigtkonzept Schleiermachers von 1796 keine Aussage darüber, ob die Formulierung "Treu und Redlichkeit" erst nachträglich eingearbeitet wurde. Sicher ist nur dies, daß Schleiermacher 1796 in Landsberg nicht zitiert haben kann, was erst seit 1797 in Potsdam erklang.

49. Jacob und Wilhelm Grimm, Deutsches Wörterbuch 11.I.II, Leipzig 1952, 305.

50. SW 2,1, 151-166.

51. Hierher gehört auch, was Schleiermacher im dritten Predigtteil über das ostelbische Junkertum und die Leibeigenschaft andeutet.

52. Bauer a.a.O. (Anmerkung 44) 311 schränkt die Weite dieser Formulierung ein auf "Beamte". Schleiermacher jedoch spricht auf der gleichen Seite 241 sowohl davon, daß "jeder einzelne Obere über sich hat", als auch davon, "oder Rathgeber zur Seite, welche den Einfluß seiner Fehler verhüten und seine Schwachheiten unschädlich machen". Friedrich Wilhelm II. stand ihm also vor Augen.

53. Klaus Epstein, Die Ursprünge des Konservativismus in Deutschland, Frankfurt/Main und Berlin 1973, 410 definiert Konservativismus geradezu als kritische Reaktion auf die französisch- konsequente Aufklärung. Damit sind Wöllner und Bischofswerder "die ersten bewußt konservativen Politiker der deutschen Geschichte". In diesem (!) Sinne sind Ammon und Schleiermacher die beiden konservativen Theologen des untersuchten Sammelbandes.

54. Über die Religion. Reden an die Gebildeten unter ihren Verächtern. Berlin 1799, 50.

55. A.a.O. 174

56. Briefe I, 219f.

57. Siehe Anmerkung 54.

58. Günter Meckenstock (siehe Anmerkung 6), XII-XV.

59. A.a.O. (Anm. 42) 402.

60. Das nach dem Gottesdienst erstellte Predigtkonzept (s. Anm.44) scheint nahezulegen, daß Schleiermacher nicht nur die Predigtgliederung umgestaltet hat, sondern Eingang und Schluß neu konzipierte. In diesem Falle wäre einiges, was hier anzudeuten sein wird, erst 1798 verfaßt worden.

XIV

DIE BEDEUTUNG DER PRAKTISCHEN THEOLOGIE FÜR THEOLOGIE UND KIRCHE

Heinrich Fink

Seitdem Schleiermacher zu Beginn des 19. Jahrhunderts seine die traditionelle Pastoraltheologie schockierenden Thesen von einer der Heiligen Schrift, der Kirche und der säkularisierten Gesellschaft entsprechenden und verpflichteten Praktischen Theologie aufgestellt hat, ist die Diskussion um die Bedeutung der Praktischen Theologie nicht mehr abgerissen. Immer wieder wird nach ihrer Funktion an der Universität und außerhalb der theologischen Wissenschaft gefragt.[1] Namhafte Theologen haben versucht, die Praktische Theologie aus ihrem leider noch immer toten Winkel herauszuholen, aber trotz aller Reformvorschläge konnte die allgemeine Krise bisher noch nicht überwunden werden. Die Daseinsberechtigung einer Praktischen Theologie als wissenschaftliche Disziplin und ihre theologische Bedeutung bleibt also umstritten.[2]

Aber keiner der heutigen Reformvorschläge wagt eine so mutige Hochschätzung der Praktischen Theologie (nicht nur innerhalb der Theologischen Fakultät, sondern auch in ihrer Funktion im Vergleich mit anderen Fakultäten), keiner wagt, in Form der Beschreibung der Aufgaben, eine so scharfe Kritik an den übrigen theologischen Disziplinen und an Selbstverständnis und Praxis der Kirche, wie es Schleiermacher sein Leben lang getan hat. An Hand der Vorlesungen zur Praktischen Theologie, die Schleiermacher an der 1810 neu gegründeten Berliner "Friedrich-Wilhelm-Universität" gehalten hat, soll gezeigt werden, welche Bedeutung er dieser jüngsten theologischen Disziplin beimißt, worin er ihre wissenschaftliche Begründung und ihren Nutzen für die Kirche sieht.

"Das Allgemeine der Praktischen Theologie wird der am klarsten
sehen, der sich die philosophische Theologie am meisten angeeignet hat; das
Besondere und der Ausführung Nächste wird jeder um so sicherer finden, je
geschichtlicher er in der Gegenwart lebt", heißt es am Schluß der "Kurzen
Darstellung des Theologiestudiums zum Behuf einleitender Vorlesungen".
Schleiermacher, der für einen Theologen beispielhaft "geschichtlich" in
seiner Gegenwart lebte, hat das Verdienst, aus der traditionellen, nur in
innerkirchlichen Überlegungen befangenen Pastoraltheologie die Konzeption einer an Wissenschaft, Kirche und Gesellschaft gleichermaßen
interessierten und orientierten praktischen Theologie entwickelt zu haben.

Was Schleiermacher als Pastoraltheologie vorfand, war keine
geschlossene Disziplin. Sie verstand sich nur als "Anweisung für die
zweckmäßigste Art, das Geschäft der Belehrung aus dem göttlichen Wort
und die Verwaltung der Sakramente in seinen verschiedenen Formen
auszuführen." Homiletik und Katechetik standen neben den speziellen
Pastoralia beziehungslos zu der übrigen Theologie: Homiletik blieb ein
Spezialgebiet der Rhetorik, Katechetik war Teil der Pädagogik. Diese
Konzeption hielt Schleiermacher für unzureichend, weil sie völlig darauf
verzichtet, die geistlichen und organisatorischen Strukturen der Gemeinde
und die Gesellschaft, in der die Gemeinde lebt, zu berücksichtigen. Er
dagegen will innerhalb der Praktischen Theologie nicht nur diese
entsprechenden Strukturen untersuchen, er kritisiert auch die Strukturen der
bestehenden Kirche und versucht sie zu verändern.

Schleiermacher sieht, wie noch ausgeführt wird, die Aufgabe der
Praktischen Theologie darin, die theologischen Disziplinen zu koordinieren
und in eine aktive und verantwortliche Beziehung zur Kirche zu setzen. An
seinen Ausführungen über Praktische Theologie in der "Kurzen Darstellung",
erst recht in seinen eigenen Vorlesungen zur Praktischen Theologie, wird
deutlich, daß seine Praktische Theologie die Koordination der Erkenntnisse
und Ergebnisse seiner Vorlesungen in Philosophie, Pädagogik, Psychologie,
Staatslehre und Politik ist. Er hat sich nicht nur darum bemüht, die
Praktische Theologie als "krönenden" Abschluß des Theologiestudiums, als
eine die gesamte Theologie verbindende Disziplin aufzubauen, er wollte
außerdem auch eine Disziplin schaffen, die zu Beginn des Theologiestudiums

den Studenten einen Überblick von der Theologie vermittelt und ihnen das Ziel des Studiums deutlich macht.

Schleiermacher weiß, daß seine Maßnahmen zur Neuorientierung von Theologie und Kirche nur dann realisiert werden können, wenn das reale Handeln der Geistlichen von wissenschaftlichem Interesse gestützt wird. Darum möchte er erreichen, daß schon zu Beginn der Studienzeit das Urteilsvermögen der Studenten durch Einführung in Apologetik und Polemik geweckt und entwickelt wird. Bereits in der 1. Auflage seiner "Kurzen Darstellung des theologischen Studiums" hat er den Entwurf einer Philosophischen Theologie" vorgelegt, die allen anderen theologischen Fächern vorausgehen müßte.

I. Theologie als "positive" Wissenschaft, von der "Kirchenleitenden Verantwortung" der Theologie

1811 legt Schleiermacher in seiner "Kurzen Darstellung des theologischen Studiums zum Behuf einleitender Vorlesungen" den Entwurf seiner Konzeption einer auf die Kirche bezogenen Wissenschaft vor. Er ergänzte nicht nur die übliche Einteilung in exegetische, historische und systematische Fächer durch die "Praktische Theologie", er will die traditionellen theologischen Fachgebiete untereinander mit Hilfe dieser neuen Disziplin in eine positive Beziehung bringen und sie dann gemeinsam in Relation zur Kirche setzen.

Den Stoff der traditionellen Pastoraltheologie faßt Schleiermacher unter "Kirchendienst" zusammen und weitet die gängige Lehre vom Kirchenregiment zur "Theologie von den kirchenleitenden Funktionen" aus. Darin entfaltet er seine Meinung über die Beziehung von Kirche und Staat und die "notwendige Beziehung aller Theologie auf die Kirche in ihrer Bedeutung für die Praktische Theologie". Schleiermachers Interesse gilt also nicht nur der pastoralen Praxis am Ort XY, auf die der Student in der bisher üblichen Pastoraltheologie sowieso unzureichend vorbereitet wurde. Er will nicht nur die Pastoraltheologie "reformieren", sondern hält die Praktische Theologie für eine Disziplin, die die gesamte Theologie aus der traditionellen Definition einer "spekulativen" Wissenschaft befreit und ihr im

Rahmen des neuen Wissenschaftsbegriffs den Rang einer "positiven" Wissenschaft verschafft. Dieses gelingt Schleiermacher, indem er den Aufgabenbereich der Praktischen Theologie ausweitet. Nach seiner Definition von Kirchenregiment haben Theologie und theologische Lehrer entscheidende kirchenleitende Tätigkeit wahrzunehmen, d.h., daß Theologie, Lehrer und Pastor (ob sie sich so verstehen oder nicht) in einer engen Beziehung zur Kirche stehen. Damit erweist sich die Theologie als "positive" Wissenschaft, sie ist ebenso auf die Gesellschaft bezogen, wie Medizin, Staatswissenschaft und Jura durch ihre jeweils charakteristische Beziehung zur Gesellschaft "positive" Wissenschaften sind.

Für Schleiermacher steht die Theologie unter dem Aspekt der praktischen Aufgabe: "Eine Positive Wissenschaft überhaupt ist nämlich ein solcher Inbegriff wissenschaftlicher Elemente, welche ihre Zusammengehörigkeit nicht haben, als ob sie einen vermöge der Idee der wissenschaftsnotwendigen Bestandteile der wissenschaftlichen Organisation bildeten, sondern nur, insofern sie zur Lösung einer praktischen Aufgabe erforderlich sind. Wenn man aber ehedem eine rationale Theologie in der wissenschaftlichen Organisation mit aufgeführt hat, so bezieht sich zwar diese auch auf den Gott unseres Gottesbewußtseins, ist aber als spekulative Wissenschaft von unserer Theologie gänzlich verschieden."[3] Das Charakteristikum einer "positiven" Wissenschaft ist also, daß sie eine aufweisbare Funktion in der Gesellschaft habe: "Die Ärzte sind aber die, welche die Leitung der menschlichen Gesellschaft übernehmen in Beziehung auf den organischen Prozeß. Wenn jede dieser Beziehungen so auf sich selbst redigiert wäre und die ganze Gesellschaft in solch elementarischem Zustand, daß jeder für sich selbst zu sorgen hätte: so gäbe es keine solche Leitung und es gäbe keine medizinische Wissenschaft."[4] Für die Juristen gilt: "Wenn die Gesellschaften, worin das menschliche Geschlecht zerteilt ist, jede für sich isoliert wäre und sich in solch elementarischem Zustande fortbewegen könnte: so würde von keiner juristischen oder staatswissenschaftlichen Fakultät die Rede sein können." In der Analogie zu diesem Verständnis sieht Schleiermacher in dem überlieferten Begriff des Kirchenregimentes die Möglichkeit, der gesamten Theologie zu einem neuen Selbstverständnis in Form der "kirchenleitenden Verantwortung" für die Kirche zu verhelfen.

Die Praktische Theologie hat nun die Aufgabe, die Beziehung zwischen Kirche und den Disziplinen der theologischen Wissenschaft nicht nur einmalig herzustellen, sondern sie muß diese auch ständig aufrechterhalten. Zur Zeit Schleiermachers wurde Dogmatik als die eigentliche Theologie angesehen, Schleiermacher dagegen vertritt die Meinung, daß gerade die Dogmatik nicht in der Lage ist, das jeweils Geschichtliche der Kirche zu berücksichtigen. Eine "reine" Wissenschaft kann die Dogmatik aber wiederum nicht sein, weil sie nur ein Teil der Theologie und somit auf die exegetischen Disziplinen angewiesen ist. Darum sind die theologischen Disziplinen nur sinnvoll, wenn sie (untereinander verbunden!) in schöpferischer Beziehung zur christlichen Kirche stehen. Die Theologie, die, wie dargestellt, streng auf die Kirche bezogen ist, muß aber in gleicher Weise auf die Öffentlichkeit, die "Geselligkeit" ihrer Zeit orientiert und für sie interessiert sein.

Daß <u>dieses</u> geschieht, daß das Interesse geweckt wird und in der Praxis geschieht, <u>hat</u> die Praktische Theologie zu leisten. Schleiermacher kritisiert und ironisiert z.B., daß die allgemeine christliche Ethik die Gegenwart ignoriere und immer noch auf "Stände" orientiert sei, obwohl schon in den Anfängen des Pietismus die Notwendigkeit erkannt worden sei, die Veränderungen der gesellschaftlichen Zusammenhänge in der Ethik zu berücksichtigen. Auch Schleiermachers unermüdliche Hinweise, die bürgerliche Öffentlichkeit wahrzunehmen und ernst zu nehmen, sind von der Kirche nicht aufgenommen worden. Und so blieb es leider nur ein Versuch, die vorfindlichen gesellschaftlichen Zusammenhänge im Rahmen der Vorbereitung einer sachgemäßen Verkündigung analytisch zu erfassen und sie nicht nur "blind zusammenhängende Empirie" sein zu lassen. Für Schleiermacher ist der gesellschaftliche Hintergrund Kontext seiner Theologie: <u>Begriffe</u> in den Reden wie "Gefühl", "Sittlichkeit" und "Geselligkeit" haben darum auch einen bestimmten säkularen Stellenwert, der nur im Sprachgebrauch der Zeit Schleiermachers erschlossen werden kann. Die Theorie von der "totalen Abhängigkeit" und der "relativen Freiheit" eines jeden Menschen, seine Theorie vom "freien Verkehr der Gleichen im Gespräch" haben ihre Wurzeln in eigener Erfahrung sowohl in der Geselligkeit der Salons, seiner Lehrtätigkeit an der Theologischen und

Philosophischen Fakultät, als Prediger und als Bürger, der die wirtschaftliche Neuordnung nach der Französischen Revolution als einen Versuch erlebt und es begrüßt, eine politische, wirtschaftliche Sphäre des "freien Verkehrs" zu entwickeln.

II. Praktische Theologie als "Technik" zur Erhaltung und Vervollkommnung der Kirche

Wenn die Praktische Theologie nicht Einübung in das Pfarramt sein soll, was hat sie dann mit dem Wort "Technik" zu tun? Alle Disziplinen in der Theologie arbeiten an vorgegebenen Texten. Die Praktische Theologie hat zunächst nur eine bestimmte Aufgabe zu leisten; deshalb muß die Theorie einer Technik gefunden werden, aus der sich Regeln aufstellen lassen für die Kirche, die schon vor aller Theologie existierte – also vorgegeben ist und Bezugspunkt aller Theologie zu sein hat. Sowohl extensiv als auch intensiv müssen die Regeln zusammenhaltend und abbildend wirken. Weil die Theologie in allen Disziplinen sich anderer wissenschaftlicher Kenntnisse und Kunstregeln zu ihrem Zweck bedient, nimmt Schleiermacher aus der Ästhetik, die er als eine "Anweisung" versteht, wie, mit Gründen belegt, "etwas auf die richtige Weise hervorzubringen sei", die Kunsttheorie für seine Praktische Theologie. In seiner Vorlesung über Ästhetik heißt es darüber: "Die Praxis ist immer etwas früheres gewesen als die Theorie; wir finden überdem eine schöne Kunst schon in ihrer Vollkommenheit, ehe von einer wissenschaftlichen Disziplin darüber die Rede ist."

Für Schleiermacher ist also die Kirche die Praxis, die vor der Theorie = Theologie war. Technik ist bei Schleiermacher also nicht Handfertigkeit in Amtsführung, Lehr- und Sakramentsverwaltung, sondern "schöpferische Tun", das der Kunst nahekommt: ". . . aber wenn man von einer Technik redet, setzt dies nur voraus, daß man selbst Ereignisse hervorbringen will". Und in diesem schöpferischen Sinne gemeint, wird "Technik" in Schleiermachers Vorlesungen zur Praktischen Theologie ein zentraler Begriff. Diese Technik ist dynamisch zu verstehen und hat sich mit dem jeweilig zu erarbeitenden Gegenstand zu ändern. Deshalb kann die Technik in der Praktischen Theologie keinesfalls für alle Zeiten festgelegt werden, sie muß je neu gefunden werden. Der Gegenstand bestimmt die Technik und nicht die Technik den Gegenstand. Gegenstand ist die christliche Gemeinde, die vom Wort Gottes bestimmt ist. Dieses zu verkündigen, bedarf es einer Technik, die alle nur möglichen schöpferischen Kräfte in den Dienst der Sache stellt. Nicht die Technik gibt dem Handeln den Impuls, sondern der "göttliche Geist" selbst. Technik ist in den Dienst gestellte Ausführung. Daher ist sie nicht Selbstzweck, sondern gibt dem Gegenstand die Möglichkeit, seine Funktion richtig wahrzunehmen. "Es ist nicht in der Schrift gesagt, und alle Erfahrung, wenn man auf die Resultate sieht, selbst die Praxis der Kirche leugnet es, daß die Wirksamkeit des göttlichen Geistes der wissenschaftlichen Bestrebung und der Kunst entbehren könne."

III. Über das Kirchenregiment – ein verantwortlicher Beitrag zur Vervollkommnung der Kirche

In seiner Praktischen Theologie unternimmt Schleiermacher nun den Versuch, in der Freiheit eines kirchlichen Lehrers, der die "Unvollkommenheit der Zustände" erkennt, eine Theorie des Kirchenregimentes zu entwerfen, als einen verantwortlichen Beitrag zur Vervollkommnung der Kirche: "Der Inhalt der Theorie des Kirchenregimentes sind die Tätigkeiten der einzelnen, aus denen die Tätigkeiten des ganzen entstehen, die wieder Wirkungen auf die Vielheit der einzelnen ausüben; sonst wäre die Tätigkeit der einzelnen nicht Wirkung auf das ganze, wenn sie nichts im ganzen hervorbrächte".[5] Aus seiner Herrnhuter Tradition weiß Schleiermacher, daß einer hierarchisch-autoritär verwalteten Kirche eine entmündigte Gemeinde entspricht. Schleiermacher verspricht sich eine Gesundung der Kirche zu verantwortlicher Verkündigung in ihrer Gesellschaft, wenn die Verantwortung in der Kirche auf eine breite Basis gestellt würde. In seinen Vorlesungen über das Kirchenregiment bietet er also keine traditionelle Darstellung von der zweckmäßigsten Verwaltung der Kirche. Wenn er über die Verfassung des Kirchenregimentes spricht, über "Einfluß und Anteil des Kirchenregimentes an der Gestaltung und

Aufrechterhaltung des Gegensatzes zwischen Klerus und Laien", über
"Einfluß des Kirchenregimentes auf die Organisation der Gemeinde", "auf
den öffentlichen Gottesdienst" und die "Feststellung des Lehrbegriffes", so
sollen diese Darstellungen den Studenten Einblick in die inneren Funktionen
des Gemeinwesens Kirche und der schöpferischen Freiheit der gegenseitigen
Einwirkungen geben, die nicht nur innerkirchlich sind, sondern auch die
Beziehung der Kirche zum Staat, zur Wissenschaft und zum geselligen Leben
betreffen. Schleiermacher will mit seiner Theorie nicht die administrativen
Rechte des Konsistoriums rechtfertigen. Für ihn gehört es zum Wesen der
Kirche, daß streitig gemacht werden darf, was früher schon feststand. "Der
Heilige Geist wirkt überall in der Schrift als das Gemeingut, nicht als das
Gut der einzelnen in dem Ganzen verteilt und wirksam dargestellt".[6]
Schleiermacher sieht es als eine Notwendigkeit für die protestantische
Kirche an, daß sich ein Kirchenregiment herausgebildet hat. Zwei Gründe
sind wichtig: Der "eine ist der Metropolitanzusammenhang und die
Notwendigkeit zwischen allen Christen, die Möglichkeit der Gemeinschaft
festzustellen, die allgemeingültige Maßregeln voraussetzt; also ein
Zusammenhang, der sich von jedem relativen Zentralpunkt in eine
Peripherie entwickelt. Das andere ist ein Streben, von allen Punkten aus
einen Zentralpunkt zu bilden".[7] Das Kirchenregiment hat aber nicht die
Aufgabe, im Protestantismus konfessionelle Grenzen aufrechtzuhalten,
sondern soll vielmehr auf eine Verbandsgesellschaft hin wirken, deren
Funktion darin besteht, Gemeinden nicht vereinzeln zu lassen. Daraus
versteht sich, daß Schleiermacher den Unionsbestrebungen gegenüber sehr
aufgeschlossen war, wenn er die Gründe, aus denen die Union von Seiten der
Regierung betrieben wurde, öffentlich immer wieder kritisiert und karikiert
hat.

So wichtig für Schleiermacher das Kirchenregiment ist – es gehört für
ihn nicht zum Wesen der Kirche: "Denn wenn Kirche ohne Regiment
bestehen könnte, so wäre sie vollkommen; wo alles ohne Gesetze selbst geht,
da sind die Gesetze nicht nötig".[8] Schleiermacher hält es für die Aufgabe
von Kirchenleitungen, sich selbst überflüssig zu machen. Er weiß aber, daß
das nur möglich ist bei einer "idealen" Kirche. Kirche auf dieser Erde wird
aber niemals vollkommen sein, weil sie immer gesellschaftlichen Charakter

haben wird. Darum muß sie, um ihre Aufgaben möglichst gut wahrnehmen zu können, innerhalb der Gesellschaft ein möglichst gutes Kirchenregiment haben, um dem Staat gegenüber selbständig zu sein. Ein schlechtes Kirchenregiment bringt Kirche notwendig in Abhängigkeit, die die Kirche behindert, ihrem Auftrag gemäß Kirche zu sein. Gerade in diesem Zusammenhang sieht Schleiermacher für den akademischen Lehrer große Chancen der Verantwortung, die er als "ungebundenes Element des Kirchenregiments" und als "freie Geistesmacht" hat. Darauf macht Schleiermacher unermüdlich aufmerksam und will seine Studenten zu dieser Verantwortung erziehen. Er will nicht nur Wissen vermitteln, sondern sie in und mit den Vorlesungen auf ihr künftiges Amt vorbereiten: "Wenn auch unter ihnen solche wären, die künftig einmal ein großes Kirchenregiment leiten würden: so könnte ihnen diese Theorie treffliche Dienste leisten; aber das weiß ich freilich nicht. Indes habe ich mich doch absichtlich mit solcher Ausführlichkeit bei diesem Punkt verweilt. Aus zwei Gründen ist es nämlich notwendig, daß ein jeder in den Grundsätzen des Kirchenregimentes unterrichtet ist: erstens, weil viel daran gelegen ist, daß man das, was geschieht, durch sein Urteil entweder unterstützt oder ihm entgegen arbeitet; zweitens, weil auch für den Geistlichen überhaupt ein gewisser freier Spielraum gegeben werden muß, weil eine strenge Buchstäblichkeit nie und nimmer verpflichtend sein kann, und so können wichtige Fortschritte auch offenbar von unten heraus geschehen".[9] An anderer Stelle heißt es: "Die Aufgaben, zumal im Gebiet des Kirchenregimentes, wird derjenige am richtigsten stellen, der sich seine philosophische Theologie am vollkommensten durchgebildet hat. Die richtigsten Methoden werden sich demjenigen darbieten, der am vielseitigsten auf geschichtlicher Basis in der Gegenwart lebt."

IV. Kirchenpolitische Aspekte der Praktischen Theologie – Trennung von Kirche und Staat

Schleiermachers wichtigstes theologisches Anliegen und kirchenpolitisches Interesse war die Trennung von Kirche und Staat. Allerdings war dieses ein völlig unzeitgemäßer Gedanke, so daß er in den

Konsistorien und Kanzleien auf keinerlei Gegenliebe stieß. Die Initiative zu dieser Trennung habe, so meint Schleiermacher, von der Kirche auszugehen. Sie wird dazu allerdings erst dann in der Lage sein, wenn sie geistlich für eine presbyteriale Verfassung bereit ist. Schleiermachers Praktische Theologie ist darum den bestehenden kirchlichen Verhältnissen gegenüber stark polemisch, oft aggressiv. Die Bedeutung von Kirchenregiment und Kirchendienst kann darum in der Praxis auch erst dann erschlossen werden, wenn die Kirche, wie es nach Schleiermacher im eigentlichen Sinne evangelisch ist, presbyterial verfaßt ist. Schleiermacher will mit seiner Praktischen Theologie – und seiner literarischen Tätigkeit der Kirche – eine Möglichkeit zur Selbstbesinnung anbieten, aus der heraus sie ihre Position korrigieren könnte. Das Wichtigste ist die Lösung der Kirche aus den feudal-monarchischen Bindungen, denn damit würde sie überhaupt erst die Freiheit gewinnen, Kirche in der und für die bürgerliche Welt zu sein. Als Institution politisch neutral, könnten aber die kirchlichen Repräsentanten das Gespräch mit den "Gebildeten unter ihren Verächtern" neu beginnen. Vielleicht würden sie sogar zu Ratgebern in dem Ringen um Neuorientierung und gesellschaftliche Neuordnung, den Früchten der bürgerlichen Revolution. "Die evangelische Kirche bleibt nur eine evangelische, wenn sie die Beweglichkeit des Dogmas durch die Schrifterklärung annimmt; sie wird darum nicht in sich selbst verfallen, sondern durch den Geist eins sein".[10] Praktische Theologie hat daher der mobilste Teil der Theologie zu sein. Sie muß dafür sorgen, daß all die Sprach- und Bildungsgebiete integriert werden, die sich dadurch erschließen, daß sich die Gesellschaft fortschreitend entwickelt.

Der Fortgang der Ereignisse zeigt, daß z. B. die "Union" von Dauer war, Schleiermacher seinerzeit auch durchaus Impulse vermitteln konnte, aber seine Hauptanliegen, die Orientierung der Kirche auf Gegenwartsprobleme und die Neuordnung des Kirchenregiments um des Kircheseins der Kirche willen, von den romantisch-restaurativen Tendenzen in Kirche und Staat untergraben wurden. Neupietismus und erstarkender Konfessionalismus ließen die Kirche in ihrer Selbstgenügsamkeit erstarken. Das Wirken dieses unermüdlichen Kirchenkritikers und schöpferischen Denkers, der voller Optimismus und Phantasie das Evangelium mit der bürgerlichen Welt konfrontieren wollte, ist vielleicht ein Anlaß für uns, Schleiermacher neu zu entdecken. Bei unseren Gesprächen und Bemühungen um Neuorientierung und Neustrukturierung unserer Kirche heute könnte es ja sein, daß wir uns dankbar aus den Gedankenvorräten Schleiermachers beraten lassen.

Anmerkungen

1. H. Schröer, Theologia applicata, MPTh, 53 Jahrg., 1964, H.10, S. 389ff. dazu: M. Mezgers Rezension, Das Praktische und das Praktikable, Deutsches Pfarrerblatt, 65. Jahrg., Nr. 11, 1965, Sp. 320-325.
2. R. Bohren, Einführung in das Studium der Theologie als Problem der Seelsorge und der Enzyklopädie, München 1964, S. 149.
3. Kurze Darstellung, § 1, 2. Aufl.
4. Praktische Theologie, S. 11.
5. Praktische Theologie, S. 25.
6. Praktische Theologie, S. 566.
7. Praktische Theologie, S. 525.
8. Praktische Theologie, S. 521.
9. Praktische Theologie, S. 728.
10. Praktische Theologie, S. 641.

XV

ÜBER DIE NOTWENDIGKEIT VON UNORDNUNG UND ORDNUNG IN DER KIRCHE

Martina Kaiser

"Wenn die Kirche vollkommen in sich abgeschlossen wäre, so daß in allen zu ihr gehörigen nichts mehr der Welt angehörte, sondern die Seele eines jeden Christen dem ganzen System ihrer Kräfte nach ein vollkommnes Organ des heiligen Geistes wäre; So würde überall und immer in der Kirche alles nur so erfolgen und zwar von selbst, wie es diesem Geist gemäß ist. Und weil wegen der Selbigkeit dieses Geistes dann alles, was geschähe, auch von selbst zusammenstimmte: so gäbe es keine Differenz zwischen dem allgemeinen Willen und dem der Einzelnen, und nirgends wäre Veranlassung zu einem Gesez . . ."[1] Weil das aber nicht so ist, weil die Kirche immer noch in der Welt ist und in ihr zugleich Gerechtfertigte und Sünder leben, bedingt ihre Unvollkommenheit diesen Vortrag über Freiheiten und Ordnungen in der Kirche.

Schleiermacher entwirft in den Reden *Über die Religion* ein Idealbild der Gemeinschaft, an dem er trotz und wegen aller Bemühungen um kirchliche Praxis bis zu seinem Lebensende festhält. Nach dem Vorbild der literarischen Salons des 18. Jahrhunderts gestaltet er das Modell seiner idealen Gemeinde: eine Versammlung von Gleichen, die miteinander kommunizieren und sich ohne jede Beschränkung frei austauschen (Wem das Herz voll ist, dem läuft der Mund über). Da dies auf derselben Ebene geschieht (alle sind gleich gelehrt von Gott), sind alle Priester, keiner kann Laie bleiben. So hebt sich auf der Ebene der Gemeinde jegliche Notwendigkeit einer Lenkung und Leitung und verschiedener Amtspersonen, jegliche irdische Ordnung auf. Gleichzeitig wird der Begriff des Priestertums für den inneren Bereich der Kirche entwertet. Die "freien Regungen des

Geistes", der alle, zwar mit unterschiedlicher Akzentuierung, ergreift, führen
zur Harmonie untereinander.[2] Alle sind sich des inneren Antriebs auf ein
Ziel bewußt, "neues Gesamtleben" zu werden, auf das Reich Gottes
hinzuarbeiten.

Diese freie Verbindung, lediglich bestimmt durch den Geist als ihr
gemeinsames inneres Prinzip, bleibt als Norm gegenüber der existierenden
Kirche mit all ihren Gesetzen und Ordnungen bestehen (Antithese von Geist
und Zwangsordnung).

So wie das Vorhandensein des Geistes im Einzelnen die Bedingung
für seinen Anteil an der Gemeinschaft ist, so ist auch die Einzelgemeinde als
Teil der Gesamtkirche nur vom Geist her bestimmt. In dem Teil der
Glaubenslehre, der von der Kirche handelt, sind die Begriffe Gemeinschaft
und Kirche, Einzelgemeinde und Gesamtkirche austauschbar. Schleier-
machers "Kerngemeinde" kommt seinem Ideal nahe. Bei denjenigen, die vom
Glauben ergriffen sind, ist das *Was*, der freie Austausch der frommen
Gefühle, garantiert. *Wie* das geschieht, die Formen des Austausches und der
Gemeinschaft, hängen von den menschlichen Möglichkeiten ab. Hier
kommen Welt und Unvollkommenheit in den Blick. Halten wir fest: Im
Inneren der Gemeinschaft, was den vom Geist bestimmten Teil anlangt,
existiert zugleich das Element der Freiheit und der Ordnung. Die Art des
Göttlichen im Menschen zu sein ist immer dieselbe[3], und die Art der
Mitteilung geschieht immer geordnet (Redende und Hörende, gemeinsames
Bekenntnis). Das freie Wirken des Geistes aber ist unbegrenzt, die jeweilige
Akzentsetzung sowie die Gaben und Tätigkeiten für die Gemeinde sind
verschieden. Das Zeugnis von Christus ist immer dasselbe, die Erhaltung der
Gemeinschaft mit ihm beruht auf denselben Prinzipien, und der gegenseitige
Einfluß von Ganzem und Einzelnen ist immer geordnet. Variabel hingegen
ist die Art und Weise, in der dies geschieht.[4]

Lassen Sie mich das am Beispiel des "Dienstes am Wort"
verdeutlichen. Der "Dienst am Wort" meint bei Schleiermacher nicht nur die
Predigt, sondern bezieht sich auf alle Lebensbereiche. Es gibt also einen
förmlichen und geordneten Bereich des Dienstes (Predigt, Unterweisung)
und einen ungeordneten und zufälligen (Einzelgespräch, Seelsorge).[5] In
beiden Bereichen ist es derselbe Dienst und derselbe Geist spricht sich darin

aus. Die Art, in der dieser Dienst geschieht, ist jedoch verschieden. Die geordneten und damit festgelegten Momente sind in der Predigt jedoch größer als im Einzelgespräch, aber nicht für immer festgelegt und unwandelbar. Die Ordnung ist keine reine Formfrage. In der Form drücken sich bestimmte Bereiche des Glaubens (Schwerpunktsetzung) aus.

Die Notwendigkeit von Gesetzen ergibt sich daraus, daß die Kirche ein corpus mixtum ist. Alles was "Welt" ist – bei Schleiermacher der dem Glauben widersprechende, nicht aber von ihm unabhängige Teil – widerstrebt dem Wirken des Geistes. Da der weltliche Bereich nicht eigenständig existieren kann, wird er immer wieder vom geistigen angezogen und beeinflußt. Er ist aber gleichzeitig fremdbestimmt. Die Ordnungen sind zugleich Ausdruck der Geistwirkung und der weltlichen Realität. Sie sind an einen Zweck gebunden und dem Irrtum unterworfen. Dies betrifft im inneren Bereich der Kirche das ganze Gebiet der Kirchenleitung, und nach außen, gegenüber der Welt, das Gebiet der öffentlichen Verkündigung.

Schleiermacher erkennt in der *Kurzen Darstellung des theologischen Studiums*, daß seine Idealvorstellung einer "vollkommenen Gleichheit und Vernichtung aller irdischen Ordnung", wie er sie in den *Reden* dargelegt hat, eine eschatologische Hoffnung ist, und daß sie nur über die vorhandene Praxis und durch sie hindurch[6] zu erreichen ist. Deshalb ist die Leitung der Kirche als Ziel der Theologie angegeben. Kirchenleitung ist der Begriff, der sowohl die "unterste" Ebene der Kirche, die Gemeinde, als auch die "oberste", die Sorge um's Ganze, umfaßt.[7] Kirchenleitung ist gebunden an Ordnungen, nicht aber an hierarchische Strukturen. Bei Schleiermacher entspricht "Kirchenleitung", als Begriff für die gesamte Tätigkeit in der Kirche, dem Begriff "Seelenleitung" im Einzelgespräch.[8] Seelenleitung zielt auf die geistige Freiheit des Einzelnen, auf die Befähigung, Hemmungen und Störungen selbst zu überwinden, um am freien Austausch wieder gleichberechtigt teilzunehmen, zielt auf die Stärkung der Mündigkeit. Sobald das erreicht ist, ist Seelenleitung überflüssig.

Die Freiheit des Einzelnen und der Gemeinde bedingen einander. Kirchenleitung ist nur solange notwendig, wie bestimmte Bereiche der Ungleichheit bestehen. Kirchenleitung betrifft nicht den Bereich des Austausches, in dem es Gebende und Empfangende gibt. Sobald aber nur

einer der Gebende und viele Empfangende sind, setzt Kirchenleitung ein, um
den Unterschied zu beheben. Am Beispiel der Unterweisung der am Rande
der Gemeinde Stehenden, die zum inneren Kern gezogen werden sollen,
zeigt sich dies. Sobald die Ungleichheit der Bildung aufgehoben ist, und in
ihnen das Ziel, in der und für die Gemeinschaft zu wirken, ebenso
ausgeprägt ist wie bei den anderen, werden die Formen und Ordnungen der
Kirchenleitung, die diesen Bereich betreffen, überflüssig. Blieben sie weiter
bestehen, würden sie zur Einengung des Geistes führen, der nun frei fließen
kann. Kein Argument für die dauernde Notwendigkeit von Kirchenleitung ist
die Gemeindegröße. Wenn auch eine größere Anzahl von Individuen eine
Ordnung in Dienste und Aufgaben mit dem Ziel der Auferbauung der
Gemeinde erfordert, so sind diese Ordnungen doch jeweils zweckgebunden
und heben sich mit der Lösung der Aufgaben auf. Die Befähigung zur
Mündigkeit macht Unterweisung überflüssig. Die Aufhebung der bildungs-
mäßigen Ungleichheit (auch im Bereich der theologischen Wissenschaft)
führt zur Beteiligung aller, z.B. im Gottesdienst, hebt die Predigt des
Einzelnen auf. Auf die Wirkungsweise der Kirchenleitung im Bereich der
Gesamtkirche trifft dasselbe zu. Ihre Aufgaben, die Wirksamkeit der freien
Geistesmacht als Korrektiv zu sich selbst zu schützen,[9] die Einheit der
Kirche festzuhalten[10] und die Wissenschaftlichkeit zu sichern,[11] werden
organisiert und geordnet solange sie anstehen, heben sich auf, sobald die
Bedingungen für das Tätigsein aller Glieder in der Kirche gegeben sind. Daß
Kirchenleitung das oft verkennt und an Gesetzen, Ordnungen, Organisationsformen, Strukturen starr festhält, ist ihrer Beharrung in der Welt
zuzuschreiben. Daß sie an den Ordnungen als Begrenzungen leidet und sich
genügend voranbringende Arbeit in und neben diesen Ordnungen stehts
vollzieht, ist Ausdruck für die geistgewirkte "Unordnung" im Rahmen der
menschlich erstarrten "Ordnung".

Die Kirchenleitung in dem Bereich der Kirche, der sich dem
notwendigen Wirken in der Welt zuwendet, ist noch mehr an feste
Ordnungen gebunden. Ohne Ordnungen wäre jegliche Verkündigung
zufällig. Damit könnte die Aufgabe der Kirche, der Welt Christus zu
verkündigen, nicht erfüllt werden. Das Wirken der Gnade hängt bei
Schleiermacher daran, daß die Kirche da ist, denn im Wort von der

Rechtfertigung kommt das Ereignis der Rechtfertigung erst zustande. Die Kirche hat somit eine Mittlerposition in der Welt und für die Welt. In der Gesellschaft muß sie sich der vorhandenen Menschen, ihrer Organisationsformen und Normen bedienen, um verstanden zu werden. Das gesamte Gebiet der Verkündigung kann sie nur innerhalb geordneter Formen abdecken, denn sie strebt nach größter Vollkommenheit. Damit ordnet sie in gewissem Maße das freie Wirken der Einzelnen mit, kann es aber nicht kanalisieren und unterdrücken.

Die Regungen und Impulse des Geistes drücken sich in Gesetzen aus, sobald sich Widerstand vom weltlichen Bereich regt.[12] Ordnungen sind mit ausübender Macht der Kirche verbunden. Festzuhalten bleibt, daß alle Einwirkungen des Ganzen nach innen (auf Einzelne und Gemeinden) und außen (auf Welt, Einzelne) geordnet und strukturiert erfolgen, die Rückwirkungen der Einzelnen jedoch zumeist ungeordnet und unstrukturiert. Dies zu Ordnungen mit der gleichen Wirksamkeit zu machen, bleibt ein Problem.

Da Schleiermacher hofft, einmal die zeitliche Bindung des Geistes an die Einzelnen aufgehoben zu sehen und alle Welt im Inneren der Kirche zu finden, heben sich letztendlich alle unvollkommenen Ordnungen der Kirche auf. Der Geist jedoch wird in Ordnungen ungeordnet wirken.

Anmerkungen

1. Schleiermacher: Der christliche Glaube nach den Grundsätzen der evangelischen Kirche. 2. Aufl. Berlin 1831, Bd.2, S. 458, §144 (= Glaubenslehre).
2. Schleiermacher: Über die Religion. Reden an die Gebildeten unter ihren Verächtern. – In: Schleiermacher: Theologische Schriften, hg. Kurt Nowak. Berlin: Union-Verlag 1983, S. 146.
3. vgl. Glaubenslehre S. 340, §126.
4. vgl. Glaubenslehre S. 345, §127, Leitsatz.
5. vgl. Glaubenslehre S. 386, §133.
6. Christian Möller: Die Erbauung der Gemeinde aus der "lebendigen Circulation des religiösen Interesses" bei Friedrich Schleiermacher. – In: Pastoraltheologische Informationen 1/1985, S. 52-73, hier S. 55.
7. vgl. Schleiermacher: Die praktische Theologie nach den Grundsätzen der evangelischen Kirche. Hg. Jacob Frerichs. Berlin: Reimer 1850, S. 34.
8. ebd. S. 40.

9. vgl. Schleiermacher: Kurze Darstellung des theologischen Studiums zum Behuf einleitender Vorlesungen. 2. Aufl., §323. – In: Schleiermacher: Theologische Schriften, Berlin: Union Verlag 1983.

10. vgl. ebd. und Praktische Theologie S. 531.

11. vgl. Kurze Darstellung §328.

12. vgl. Glaubenslehre S. 458f, §144.

XVI

DIE UFERPREDIGTEN
GOTTHARD LUDWIG KOSEGARTENS (1758-1818)
AUF RÜGEN IM BEZUG ZU
SCHLEIERMACHERS "REDEN ÜBER DIE RELIGION"

Katharina Coblenz

Ich muß gestehen, daß mich die Theologie Schleiermachers während meiner theologischen Ausbildung nicht berührte, obwohl ich in den Bücherschränken meines Vaters die Hauptschriften Schleiermachers sowie Predigtbände von ihm finden konnte. Erst als ich zehn Jahre später in die Gemeinde Altenkirchen auf Rügen kam, begann ich mich mit Schleiermacher zu beschäftigen. Ich verdanke dies einem Vorgänger hier: Gotthard Ludwig Kosegarten.

Als ich seine Uferpredigten[1] las, entdeckte ich in ihnen den Geist der Reden Schleiermachers wieder. Es war für mich eine Überraschung, daß mich 200 Jahre alte Predigten existenziell ansprachen.

Kosegarten – zehn Jahre älter als Schleiermacher – entstammte ebenso einem Pfarrhaus, nicht reformierten, aber lutherisch orthodoxen Geistes in Mecklenburg in Grevesmühlen. Er studierte Theologie und ging den typischen Weg vom Hauslehrer über den Pfarrberuf ins Professorenamt der Universität in Greifswald.

Auch seine Liebesbeziehung scheiterte in jungen Jahren. Als Hauslehrer verliebte er sich in die Tochter des Hauses und wurde davongejagt. Fünfmal wechselte er die Stellung. In zahlreichen Gedichten und Romanen bearbeitete er diese Erfahrung. So ist er heute eher den Germanisten bekannt als den Theologen. Er gilt als "Künder der Schönheit Rügens".

Von Kindheit an war Kosegarten empfindsam für Naturgewalt und Schönheit. In seinem Naturgefühl wurde er durch die Dichtungen seiner Zeit beeinflußt und bestärkt. Mit Goethes Werther in der Tasche zog er einst zum Studium.

1784 veröffentlichte er eine Ekstase seiner frühen Jugend "Über die wesentliche Schönheit".[2] Diese Abhandlung stammt aus seiner letzten Hauslehrerzeit, wo er viel Muße hatte, in der freien Natur umherzuschwärmen. Er selbst wollte mit seinem Wirken – wie er das immer wieder betonte – zur Summe des Guten und Schönen einen Beitrag liefern. Dabei geht er vom Gefühl aus. "Wahres Gefühl . . . ist ein angebohrner, innerer, offener und reiner Geisterssinn für das Schöne, Edle, Große . . ."[3]

Nach der Auseinandersetzung mit den Schönheitsbegriffen seiner Zeit mündet Kosegarten in die Schlußfolgerung – in Anlehnung an Plato – "Schönheit ist das Göttliche in der Natur". Natur wird ihm zum Symbol Gottes. Als Wiederschein der Gottheit wird sie selbst Offenbarerin Gottes. "Heil uns" schließt er, "wenn wir . . . uns weiden können an lebendiger Natur, des Schöpfers Spuren aufspüren können im Geschöpf, von aller dieser irdischen Schöne uns emporflügeln können zur unanfänglichen Schönheit."[4] Im Grunde ist diese Schrift schon eine Frühform der romantischen Ästhetik. Die Flucht aus der Gelehrtenstube in die freie unbegrenzte Natur und die Sehnsucht nach der Unendlichkeit verbinden ihn mit den Romantikern. Die Maler der Frühromantik, Philipp Otto Runge und Caspar David Friedrich, erhielten durch ihn entscheidende Anregung für ihr Werk.

Daß Kosegarten nach seiner kräfteaufzehrenden Rektorentätigkeit an der Stadtschule in Wolgast (1784-1792) Gelegenheit bekam, auf Wittow unter freiem Himmel zu predigen, erscheint wie der lebendige Beweis seiner theoretischen Anschauung. In seinen schöpferischsten Jahren, von 1792-1808, wirkte er auf Wittow, der nördlichsten Halbinsel Rügens. Altenkirchen galt als eine der reichsten Pfründe Pommerns und die Pfarrstelle wurde – da Rügen seit dem dreißigjährigen Krieg zu Schweden gehörte – vom schwedischen König verliehen. War es ein Kunstgriff Kosegartens, daß er dem vierzehnjährigen Kronprinzen 1792 seine Übersetzung der römischen Geschichte von Oliver Goldsmith widmete?

Wenn man vom Pfarrhaus 2,4 km übers Feld geht, steht man am Steilufer über der Tromper Wiek. Dieser Anblick, "diese Buchten, diese Ufer, diese verschwiegenen Uferschründe, dieses herrliche Arkonavorgebirge, die silberweißen Dünen . . . diese ganze erschütternde Majestät der Natur" verbürgten ihm, daß seine geistigen Flügel niemals sinken und der Funke der Begeisterung in ihm nicht erlöschen werde, als mit dem Funken des Lebens selber.[5]

Hier fand er die Sitte der Uferpredigten vor. Schon seit undenklicher Zeit hielt man in Vitt, dem Fischerdorf, unter freiem Himmel Gottesdienst. In dem schönen geräumigen Tal oberhalb des Meeres ersammelte sich die Gemeinde an acht Sonntagen in den Monaten September und Oktober zur Zeit des Heringsfangs. Wahrscheinlich ist dieser Gottesdienst in der freien Natur schon so alt wie das Christentum auf der Insel. Und man könnte fast vermuten, daß hier sogar schon in slavischer Zeit die Rahnen dem Gott Svantevit opferten und sich dadurch einen reichen Fischfang erhofften. Denn schon zur Zeit der Eroberung der slavischen Tempelburg Arkona, dem Sturz des Gottes Svantevit unter dem Dänenkönig Waldemar I mit seinem Feldherrn Absalom, dem Bischof von Roskilde, im Jahre 1168 wird dieses Dorf erwähnt. Das Christentum machte mit Aberglauben und Götzenkult gewaltsam Schluß. Die Uferpredigten bekamen nun einen pragmatischen Zug. Denn nach der Zerstörung der Tempelburg Arkona verlagerte sich mit dem Bau der Altenkirchner Kirche vor 1200 das religiöse Zentrum ins Innere der Halbinsel Wittow. Für die Fischer von Vitt bedeutete das nun einen Fußmarsch von zwei Stunden zum Gottesdienst. Diesen weiten Weg scheuten sie zur Zeit des Heringsfangs. Wenn die Heringsschwärme am Ufer vorbeizogen, so daß die See silbern blitzte, mußten sie mit ihren Booten zum Fang hinaus. So kam der Pfarrer Sonntags zu ihnen.

Kosegarten belebte diese Gottesdienste in seiner gefühlvollen naturbetrachtenden Art und es strömten Hörer aus allen Teilen des Landes herbei. Es wurde zum geflügelten Wort – die See bei Rügen – das ist: Wo Kosegarten wohnt.[6] Hier predigte er Schönheit als das Göttliche in der Natur den einfachen Fischern, der Masse der Leibeigenen, sowie den adligen Herrn. Er empfand schon die soziale Diskrepanz und setzte sich mit seinem

Vermögen auch öffentlich für die Aufhebung dieses menschenentrechtenden Übels ein.

Doch er selbst wollte den Menschen in seinem Alltag erheben. Dabei ist Gottes Wort für Jedermann leicht verständlich. Auf die Frage eines dreijährigen Kindes "Wer hat die Sonne gemacht?", erklärt er einmal zum Erstaunen seines gebildeten Begleiters, nachdem er die Frage des Kindes beantwortet hatte: "Was wir von Gott zu wissen brauchen, das kann ein Kind fassen. Das übrige haben nicht Sie, nicht Aristoteles ... nicht Kant begriffen und werden es nie begreifen."[7]

So griff er bei seinen Predigten den Ausdruck der lebendigen Volkssprache auf, eine sehr bildreiche und gleichnishafte Sprache, die den Hörer leicht mitgehen läßt. Ich empfinde die Uferpredigten fast als ein sprachliches Bilderbuch des Volkes zu Schleiermachers *Reden über die Religion an die Gebildeten (unter ihren Verächtern)*. Eine gegenseitige Beeinflussung liegt nicht vor, auch wenn man annehmen kann, daß Kosegarten dann Schleiermachers Reden gelesen hat. Beide sind sich auch später hier auf Rügen begegnet. Wenn Schleiermacher in einem Brief vom 6.12.1804 an Charlotte Pistorius bemerkt, daß er "arg genug an Kosegartens hier noch schädlichen Maximen leide, der mehr für sich predigt als für seine Zuhörer"[8], lassen sich doch die geistigen Bezüge nicht übersehen. Kosegarten eigen war allerdings als "gottbegeisterter Lehrer" eine gewisse Eitelkeit, die ihn von Schleiermachers Wesen trennte.

Beide wollen Begeisterung für die Religion wecken. Beide verstehen sich als Mittler.

Wenn Kosegarten den Menschen dahin führen will, daß er überall Gottheit ahnt, so trifft sich das mit Schleiermachers Formel, Religion sei "Sinn und Geschmack fürs Unendliche."[9] Anschauung und Gefühl bedingen einander gegenseitig.

Schleiermachers Gedankengänge sind tiefgründiger. Er schließt nicht mehr unmittelbar von der direkten Anschauung der Naturschönheit auf Gott, sondern verweist auf das Wirken und ihre Gesetze.[10] Natur und Freiheit gehören für beide untrennbar zusammen. Hier enthebt sich Religion dem allein moralischen Bereich. Die Freude am Dasein zu wecken, zu einer Grundgestimmtheit im Leben werden zu lassen, bilden einen Zielpunkt in

Kosegartens Uferpredigten. "Den Weltgeist zu lieben und freudig seinem Wirken zuzuschauen, das ist das Ziel unserer Religion, und Furcht ist nicht in der Liebe."[11] Hier berühren sich beide auf das engste. Der Mensch soll einstimmen in den Lobpreis der Natur (Ps. 19, 2). "Alles, was Odem hat, lobe den Herrn" steht über dem Eingang zu der von Kosegarten gegründeten Kapelle Vitt.

Schon unbewußt birgt jeder Aufenthalt im Freien auch etwas befreiendes für den Menschen in sich. Erst in diesem Gefühl der Freiheit kann der Mensch seine Grenzen überschreiten und wird fähig zur Liebe – auch zur Feindesliebe.

Natur weist also immer über sich hinaus und wird zur "Schule des Menschengeschlechts", wie Kosegarten es in seiner Predigt "Hier ist gut sein" zu Mt. 17, 4 für die Bewohner Wittows zusammenfaßt.[12] Denn jeder Vorzug des Landes birgt seine Lehre an den Menschen. Die Stille und Abgeschiedenheit lehrt Frieden halten, die Güte des Klimas auf Gesundheit achten, die Ergiebigkeit des Bodens sollte Beschränkung (!) auferlegen, die Nähe zum Meer und die Schönheit des Landes Unendlichkeit und Allgegenwart Gottes wahrnehmen und diese Welt immer als Schwelle zur besseren betrachten helfen. Diese konkrete Predigtweise Kosegartens im Unterschied zu Schleiermacher brachte auch die spezielle Situation hier auf Rügen mit sich.

Kosegarten will dem Menschen, indem er sein Naturgefühl bestärkt und deutet, ihm seine religiöse Tiefe erschließt, Kraft zum Bleiben vermitteln und ihn in die Geborgenheit der von Gott erzählenden Natur einbinden.

Die Wiederbetonung der Welt als Gottes gute Schöpfung könnte den Menschen heute auf neue Weise wieder in lebendige Beziehung zur Natur treten lassen. Allerdings nicht ungebrochen. Gerade im Gegenüber zur Natur wird der Mensch bekennen müssen, daß er versagt hat. Es wird laut das Eingeständnis unserer Schuld, die wir vom Opfer leben. Bei Kosegarten wird die Natur idealisiert und ästhetisiert, alles Negative, Böse und Zerstörerische ausgegrenzt, bzw. sofort dem Guten untergeordnet und dienstbar gemacht.

Die Infragestellung der Welt und des Menschen von Gott her bleibt aus. Wenn die Kraft zum Leben aus der verklärten Sicht der Natur erwächst, dann ist allerdings die Gefahr des Verstummens dieser Kraft groß. Sie kann leicht mißbraucht werden, die Mißstände der Wirklichkeit zuzudecken, anstatt den Menschen zu aktivieren, sie zu verändern. Erst wenn die Wirklichkeit durch Jesus Christus gesehen wird, der für uns gestorben und auferstanden ist, erwächst die Kraft, die Wirklichkeit neu zu gestalten. Diese radikale Sicht des Umdenkens gab es für Kosegarten nicht. Auf diesem Weg ging Schleiermacher weiter. Zu viel setzte Kosegarten auf eigenes Erkennen, die Vernunft und die Weisheit des Menschen. So heilt für ihn auch die Idylle Wittows den realen Unruhen der Franzosenzeit nicht stand. Die geistigen Flügel sanken ihm. Er verließ Wittow. Der Sänger verstummte, er wandte sich der Mystik zu . . .

Und doch bleibt ihm zu danken, daß er weit über die Grenzen seines Landes den Menschen die Augen für die nordische Schönheit geöffnet hat.

Anmerkungen

1. G.L. Kosegarten, Reden und kleine prosaische Schriften, 3 Bände (Band 1: Uferpredigten), hrsg. von G. Mohnike, Stralsund 1831-1832.
2. Diese Schrift ist aufgenommen in: G.L. Kosegarten, Rhapsodien. Erster Teil, Leipzig 1790, S. 5-40.
3. G.L. Kosegarten, Hainings Briefe an Emma, Leipzig 1791, Band 2, S. 4. In diesen Briefen an seine spätere Frau Katharine Linde aus Kasnevitz auf Rügen finden wir eine lebendige Kommentar zu seiner Schrift über die Schönheit.
4. G.L. Kosegarten, Rhapsodien. Erster Teil, S. 39f.
5. G.L. Kosegarten, Geschichte des fünfzigsten Lebensjahres, Leipzig 1816, S. 15f. In diesem Buch beschreibt er sein Wirken in Altenkirchen und verteidigt seinen Weggang gegen seine Widersacher in Greifswald.
6. So ließ Clemens Brentano auf einer Ausstellung in Berlin eine Demoisell antworten bei seiner Darstellung verschiedener Empfindungen vor einer Seelandschaft von Friedrich, worauf ein Kapuziner. 1810, in: Caspar David Friedrich in Briefen und Bekenntnissen, hrsg. von S. Hinz, Berlin 1984, S. 223.
7. G.L. Kosegarten, Briefe eines Schiffbrüchigen, in: Rhapsodien. Zweiter Teil, S. 92f.
8. Schleiermacher als Mensch. Sein Wirken, Familien- und Freundesbriefe 1804 bis 1834, hrsg. von H. Meisner, Gotha 1923, S. 28.
9. F.D.E. Schleiermacher, Theologische Schriften, hrsg. von K. Nowak, Berlin 1983, S. 79.

10. A.a.O., S. 92ff.
11. A.a.O., S. 93.
12. Diese Uferpredigt ist abgedruckt bei Mohnike, a.a.O., S. 127-146.

SECTION FOUR

SCHLEIERMACHER IN CONTEXT

XVII

SCHLEIERMACHER'S VISION OF THE UNITY OF RELIGION AND CULTURE

J. Harold Ellens

When Friedrich Schleiermacher died on 12 February 1834, at the age of 65, he was celebrated as a theologian who had clearly seen the essential issues of the interface of religion and culture. A century later, under Barthian attack, he was accused of having deflected the proper theological quest away from the gospel, toward a religion based upon psychology and cultural idealism. This was no more or less an accident of history than was Jesus' reputation of being an eater and drinker and an enthusiastic companion of whores and thieves.

Undoubtedly, the most revolutionary and valuable thing about Jesus of Nazareth was precisely the fact that he obviously cared so much for those for whom others cared so little. The crucial corollary fact in his life was surely this: that in his revolutionary caring, he had the courage to carry his cause forward with such consistency as to risk a reputation of disrepute. This risk he apparently understood well and accepted readily as the inevitable consequence of living his style of life in our crass, conservative kind of world. His style and courage brought him disrepute and death, but then a history-shaping, inescapable, and irreducible presence and claim on everything everywhere – a claim that continues to arise in the twentieth century, precisely out of that human enigma Jesus confronted, namely, the universal human perplexity with the problems of need, insensitivity, and abuse that provoked his insistence upon caring much for those little cared for.

Friedrich Schleiermacher's most significant contribution to the Christian faith and life lies in his heroic endeavor to relate religion and culture. This is also his signal gift to the entire human community and to the understanding of life and meaning. His entire work implies or is overtly dedicated to this quest. His achievement in relating faith and work, religion and culture, theology and psycho-sociology is genuinely astonishing. Schleiermacher is generally credited with shaping Prussian church life and culture, is recognized as the founder of modern Protestant theology, and is surely the most significant theologian of the nineteenth century. That his achievement was also recognized in his lifetime can be seen in that some 30,000 people are said to have attended his funeral in Berlin. His achievement, also understandably, provoked much critical re-evaluation by the twentieth-century Word-of-God theologians, such as Barth and Brunner. Like Jesus of Nazareth before him, Schleiermacher was guilty of just what he was accused him of doing: he operated with the assumption and implied claim that the business of Christianity was larger in scope than the kerygmatic gospel and that the business of significant religion was larger in scope than the Christian faith. Fortunately, on this point, Barth was wrong and Schleiermacher right. Theology worthy of the name has as its mandate and proper province a comprehensive address to the whole of human nature and life, in the light of, and before the face of God.

I am pleased to offer this chapter as the initial, formal stage in what will undoubtedly be the work of my remaining years, namely, a studied public articulation of my understanding and appreciation of Friedrich Schleiermacher's profound vision of the unity of religion and culture and his wisely oriented address to the entire scope of issues involved in the question of that interface.

May I be permitted, at this juncture, to share some of the emotion in my appreciation of this great man of faith and thought. I feel a great deal in common with him. I began my education and professional life, as did he, by intensive work in Greek and Roman Classics, as the context for proper biblical studies. I came early to a sense of vocation in Christian Ministry in the North German Reformed (in my case, Oostfrisische) tradition of my father's faith and family, as did he. My personal sense of vocation, as his, was shaped by an intense awareness of the scope and profoundity of human suffering in my immediate existential world and in my own life. From this, I think, came my growing conviction that the locus of the main theological enterprise was not in historical theology or systematic theology or even in the formal machinery of biblical theology, but in the applied issues of *Die Praktische Theologie*. This led me at the outset of my professional life into the military chaplaincy, with which Schleiermacher was surely familiar in some formative way, through his father's experience as a chaplain. The course of my theological development was strongly shaped, as was his, by interaction with and ultimately reaction to the Pietism of the German Rhineland or Moravian type, which was my mother's spiritual heritage and style. This personal odyssey led me to a sustained awareness of the critical significance of the personal psychological dynamics in all religious experience. It led me to a conviction of the overriding importance of objective theological, psychological, anthropological, sociological, and philo-sophical critique and reconstruction of such personal experience, and of the experience of religious communities, as those experiences constitute the history of the human truth quest and of religious and cultural enterprise. It led me, further, to the realization that the essential issues of theology and culture are anthropological issues. It led me to a commitment to the pursuit of theology and psychology as equivalent scientific enterprises. It led me to conceive the urgent need to address all this in anthropological perspectives and models, shaped in a concern for handling human nature and culture wholistically. And it led me, finally, to spend the last twenty years of my work on understanding the interface of theology and psychology, faith and life, religion and culture, spirituality and vocation. All this led me to Friedrich Schleiermacher.

Culture and Religion

The Issue of the Interface

For Schleiermacher, the question of how religion and culture relate – how they illumine, form, and inform each other – was a question that functioned in all arenas of the human quest for meaning, understanding, and action. In this sense he stood solidly in the Reformed or Calvinist tradition, in which every calling (*Beruf*) is a divine vocation, every creative act is a reflection and function of the *Imago Dei*, and every human enterprise is carried out "before the face of God." So Schleiermacher was deeply and directly involved in all issues: from philosophical epistemology in which he remained Kantian; to ontology in which he was an idealist; to philosophical ethics; to theoretical and applied concerns in each area of the entire encyclopedia of theological sciences; to psychology and sociology, such as it was in the nineteenth-century days of faculty psychology; to ecclesiastical forms, strategies, programs, structures and politics; and to the nature and function of government, society, arts, and education. Schleiermacher saw all these matters as of great cultural and religious significance, at every level, from the practicalities of personal human experience to ethereal notions about divine claims and expectations.

Schleiermacher was, therefore, at once a man of remarkably comprehensive theological vision and a Renaissance Man in philosophical and applied wisdom, knowledge, and skill. The twentieth-century investigation of the interface between culture and religion has been less integrated and coherent, if not more "schizophrenic". At least in North America, specialization in all the disciplines of the cultural quest has led to rather technical and compartmentalized struggles with the question of this interface. My work, of necessity, has been more concentrated upon the interface of Christian theology and the social sciences than upon some of the other disciplines. Most of my colleagues are even more specialized than I, concentrating specifically upon issues in the relationship of Christian personal faith experience and psychological function.

Three Alternatives

The investigation of this matter has followed a three-channel course in North America during the last sixty years. After the definitive work of G. Stanley Hall and William James, both of whom stood mainly in the nineteenth-century philosophical tradition and would have felt very much at home with Schleiermacher's Renaissance-Man style, the quest shaped itself largely in terms of the following three streams. The secular stream rejected the notion that there was a significant relationship between culture and religion, largely taking Freud's suggestion in identifying religion as a pathology. This course of thought has modified itself more recently by adopting a "History of Religions" approach to the question of religion and culture. Since this is remote from Schleiermacher's central commitment to understand religion as authentic and meaningful personal experience with a genuine transcendent reality, it is of less direct interest in our present agenda than the other two streams of thought.

The second stream takes its cue from such antecedents as William James and is represented well in such scholars as Reinhold Niebuhr and H. Richard Niebuhr. This school of thought is represented mainly by the religious communities which stand in the historic Reformation tradition of the Reformed, Presbyterian, and Lutheran Faiths in the USA. Its treatment of the interface of religion and culture attempts to hold in tension an equivalent appreciation of the contributions of theology and of the social sciences to the understanding of anthropology, or more particularly, to the appreciation of how religious faith and experience and human psychological nature and function mutually illumine each other.

This school has largely taken form in and through the prolific Practical Theology and the Pastoral Theology and Counseling movement in the USA during the last sixty years. The work of Seward Hiltner, Don Browning, Don Capps, LeRoy Aden, James Dittes, John Patton, Rod Hunter, Howard Clinebell, myself and others epitomizes this school of thought in what were once referred to as the mainline or liberal Protestant Churches of America. The terms liberal and conservative no longer characterize very precisely the churches of the USA, but the distinctiveness of this second perspective in contrast to that of the third option persists. The perspective is distinctive for its assumption that religion and culture are both "books" in which the nature and intent of God, or the transcendent meaning of human experience, can be discerned in the same and in an equivalent way. Both arenas are objective phenomena which are tractable and potentially subject to scientific investigation. Each will yield insight and truth which is ultimately coherent with that of the other, when adequately understood. Religion and culture are not inherently aliens who stand over against each other but rather differing facets of the same genius of human spiritual and creative function.

The third way of approaching this interface issue in North America has been that of the scholars who derive from Fundamentalist-Evangelical roots. They tend to approach the question of religion and culture with the assumption that the two are inherently alien to each other. These scholars operate with a conscious or unconscious apocalyptic and Manichaean or Zoroastrian assumption that the reality of personal experience and of transcendent meaning is dualist. There is a world of God and good and a roughly equivalent world of devil and evil. These stand forever at odds. The world of God and good is the world of true faith and sound religious experience. The world of devil and evil is the world of secular science and daily cultural experience.

Because this school perceives this docetistic contrast between true religion and real culture, it speaks of the enterprise of relating faith and work, spirituality and daily life, theology and psychology or the other social sciences in terms of "integration." Two inherently alien entities must be brought near to each other and force-fitted in order to make life coherent and Christian. The net result of this integration effort always tends to be the reduction of the social sciences to a rather "Jerry-rigged" private theology, as in the work of Jay Adams and Larry Crabb, or the reduction of the theological sciences to a kind of Sunday-School religion pasted on the side of scientific psycho-social inquiry, as in the work of Gary Collins and others. The very term "integration" is a distortion of the quest to understand the interface and mutual illumination, the forming effect, and the informing dynamic that religion and culture share.

Furthermore, this model of the relationship of the sciences and disciplines is essentially a pre-Christian and pagan model. That is, it has the shape and structure of Hellenistic thought as manifested in Neoplatonism. In its center is an idolatrous triumphantism. It assumes that if we find a way to force religion and science, faith and philosophy, or theology and psychology to fit together, we will be able to nail down the human quest in a final solution. This will deliver us from and transcend the pilgrimage character of human life and from the anxiety about our existential predicament of continuing to pick our way through ambiguity day by day, before the face of God.

The historical difference between stream two and three arises out of a fundamental theological and philosophical difference between the faith communities deriving from the Reformation tradition, on the one hand, and those deriving from the peculiar American frontier tradition that generated Evangelicalism in the USA, on the other. The former has always operated with the assumption that the transcendent deity is congenially immanent within the world, imbues all of it with creative and redemptive presence, is revealed by all aspects of its nature and function, and can be discovered and understood through the natural and social sciences as well as through the theological and philosophical sciences. This school has sometimes distinguished between "special revelation" in scripture, accessible by theology, and "general revelation" in nature and culture, accessible by the other sciences. That distinction, however, has been and is of far less importance than the assumption of the inherent unity of truth and experience in religion and culture. It is interesting that at a time when the distinction between general and special revelation and the corollary distinction between special and common grace had largely been outgrown by this movement in America the European "Evangelicals," Barth and Brunner, should have resurrected the use of those categories.

In any case, this second stream of North American thought on religion and culture, theology and psychology, faith and life would not tend to conceive of its agenda as that of integretation, but of understanding the interface and dynamically interactive, mutually creative relationship of these aspects of the human process. In this sense, it is this mainstream of American thought that most closely approximates the vision of Schleiermacher. The reasons for the shape of this progressive perspective are theological, philosophical, and psycho-social reasons. The reasons for the congeniality of this perspective with that of Schleiermacher are theological, philosophical, and psycho-social reasons as well. The reasons for the contrast between this perspective and that of American Evangelicalism are also theological and psycho-social reasons.[1]

The American Evangelical perspective stands in contrast with Schleiermacher because it stands in H. Richard Niebuhr's category of the "Christ against Culture" perspective.[2] Thus it tends to speak of the relationship of religion and culture, for example, in the problem of the interface of theology and psychology, as though the relationship is that of theology absorbing or using psychology as a handmaiden, or psychology absorbing or using theology as a handmaiden. In extreme cases, such as those of Hunt and Kilpatrick, the contrast and alienation between the two is described as so radical that true theology or spirituality must always reject psychology, and scientific psychology must always reject proper theology and true faith.[3]

An Attempted Resolution

Some Evangelicals, such as Carter and Narramore, have attempted to enlighten and modify this radical Manichaean perspective by working with Niebuhr's other categories: Christ above Culture, and Christ in Culture.[4] The work of Charles H. Kraft and H. Newton Malony achieve similar salutory gains in overcoming the docetism of their American Fundamentalist-Evangelical roots.[5] These scholars have emphasized the unitary nature of all truth, the revelatory value of all scientific inquiry, and the equivalent scientific character of theological and other kinds of cultural scholarship. They have retained their commitment to the inherently transcendent nature of all genuine spiritual experience.

It is remarkably humorous, as one reflects upon this history of the issue in North America during the last 60 years, to note that the Progressives have consistently chided the Evangelicals for not knowing how to do theology and for neglecting the real religious issues in the enterprise of "integration." The Progressives have been for the most part theologians, like Schleiermacher, endeavoring to come to terms with the data of the social sciences such as psychology and of the humanities such as philosophy. The Evangelicals, on the other hand, have consistently denigrated the Progressives for not knowing how to do proper and responsible psychology in their attempt to discover the mutual illumination of the two scientific disciplines. The Evangelicals have been, mainly, doctoral level psychologists, trying to come to terms with the data of the Christian religion.

The Progressives have avowedly endeavored to avoid selling out their theological perspective to the science of psychology and are, therefore, incorrectly I think, accused of a superficial understanding of that social science. The Evangelicals who are concerned about these issues have been trained mainly in Clinical Psychology and are, correctly I think, accused of a superficial understanding of the science of theology, resorting for the most part to placing a veneer of trivialized and individualistic biblicism over their basically secular psychology. Since this latter is the case, it is not surprising that Fundamentalist-Evangelicals such as David Hunt who have no psychological understanding, but who wish to retain evangelical theology with some consistency, resort to denigrating and demonizing culture and the social sciences, as enterprises alien to the ambitions of God in the world.

Schleiermacher's Vision and Model

Friedrich Schleiermacher would have found this debate quite amusing, though not mystifying. Its contours were not so different from those of his own struggle with the biblicist personalism of the Moravian Pietists, on the one hand, and the historic objectivity which his Reformed theological science attempted to maintain, on the other. As a philosophical idealist, a Reformed theologian, a passionate pastor, an honest pragmatist in applied people-care issues; as a consummate scholar with a persistent conviction that preoccupation with theoretical issues is obscene if theories are not worked out in their cultural consequences; as a Christian of intense personal piety who eventually defined religion and spirituality more in terms of Moravian psychology than in terms of scholastic Reformed theology, Schleiermacher implies that whatever else one may achieve in one's vision of the interface of religion and culture, theology and psychology, preaching and pastoring, faith and work, spirituality and daily life, one must at least work out the following, and must work in terms of the following.

Human persons are whole and unitary creatures, in our natures and our work. All expressions of human nature and work are cultural. All human culture is, therefore, inherently unitary. Religion and science, faith and work, spirituality and daily experience, theology and psychology are all elements and disciplines in the many faceted but unitary cultural enterprise of being human and alive. In all of these cultural expressions, humans are creatively articulating the image of God that is in our persons and personalities. Each of these various endeavors, therefore, calls for a consciousness of its interface with all the others and requires from every human a comprehensive sense of cultural responsibility to create spiritually authentic and religiously civilized life in every arena.

Schleiermacher's definition of religion as the affective experience of absolute dependence is very significant at this juncture. That definition describes the common ground from which all religion springs. That common grounds lies in the field of psychology. His theology is built on and around the fact that this universal and constant aspect of human consciousness makes us necessarily religious and creative.[6] In this "feeling of absolute dependence" lies the "original unity" of knowledge and action, of religion and culture.[7]

In his book, *On Religion*, he expressed the cosmic and transcendent dimension of this perspective, speaking of religion as "the feeling and intuition of the universe," "the sense of the Infinite in the finite."[8] Thus all human thought and action, work or worship, are expressions of this perception of living life "before the face of God." Indeed, in his discussion of ethics he elaborates upon this notion in its relevance to culture. He views ethics as "the intuition and action of the self in its individuality," that individuality actually being seen as "a unique 'organ and symbol' of the Infinite itself."[9]

Ultimately, Schleiermacher refined his definition of religion even further. In his *Christmas Eve* of 1805 he adopted his Moravian-like psychological epitomization of religion, not as feeling and intuition, but simply as feeling: the "immediate feeling that God lives and works in us as finite human beings."[10] This is the final definition which he ultimately incorporated into his most notable and, perhaps, preeminent work, *The Christian Faith*.[11]

It is possible, therefore, to formulate Schleiermacher's model of the relationship, indeed, the unity of religion and culture, approximately as follows. He saw the human spiritual appetite and reach for God as the innate quest for meaning. This quest is irrepressible because it springs from the image of God in us. It is answered and fulfilled in the actual spiritual experience of intuiting, perceiving, and feeling the presence of God in ourselves and in the universe. The presence of God in his world calls forth the religious dynamism in human personality and addresses it to the task of creating culture and building the Kingdom of Grace. This kingdom is the rule of God's love, grace, justice, and beauty in all the disciplines of culture and in all experiences of human living. To be religious is to be culture creating and culturally responsible.

The central dynamic of culture creating, civilization building, Kingdom facilitating, worship celebrating, and faith expressing is the presence of God in human personality, on the one hand, and in the cosmos, on the other, calling out to each other and calling each other forth into life and liveliness.

It may readily be seen, therefore, how building a philosophical *Weltanschauung*, articulating the principles of ethics, doing responsible pastoring, preaching the gospel, organizing the church for worship and work, creating educational institutions and curricula, and fashioning accountable political and social institutions and strategies were seen by Schleiermacher as the spontaneous and inevitable expressions of the very nature of humanness, on the one hand, and of the divine dimension of the universe, on the other.

In practical application, therefore, it should be no surprise that at each turn of his thought, Schleiermacher worked with and out of a Christian anthropology. This leads me to suggest that if he were working in the last decade of the twentieth century, he would give his assent to the following general model of the interface of religion and culture. This model is an elaboration and generalization of one that I published in 1982 to describe the specific relationship between theology and psychology. In its form as presented here, it achieves two things, in my judgment. First, it expresses the dynamics of the interface not only of the science of theology and of one of the social sciences but of all the subdisciplines of religion and culture.

Second, it serves as a model to concretize and visualize in modern categories and contours what seems to me to be the essence of Schleiermacher's way of looking at these same things.

A Graphic Model for the Interface of Religion and Culture

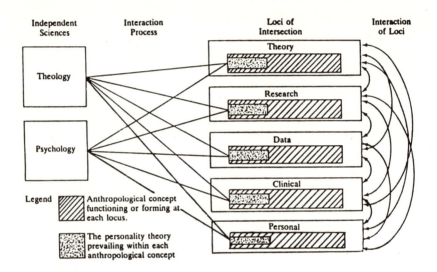

The disciplines of human culture all seem to me to interface with one another at five different levels of human function. This interaction is inevitable because of the unitary nature of reality in the universe, and in human nature and experience. Each discipline is illumined, formed, and informed to a significant degree, at each level of interface, by each of the other disciplines with which it interacts.

The five levels of cultural interface are, first, at the theoretical and theory building level, second, at the research models and methodology level, third, at the data selection and management level, fourth, at such implementation and application levels as parish pastoring, clinical practice, or university teaching, and, fifth, at the personal and personality level.[12] Schleiermacher seems to me to have operated with a clear sense of this structure, though he never formally articulated such a graphic model.

Moreover, for Schleiermacher, the primary disciplines in human culture and experience were those of theology and psychology, because those are the ones which he correctly saw as expressive of the generic role of human nature and personality in cultural process. He was aware, though he might not have said it in this way at his moment in the nineteenth century, that the mutually illuminating interface of the disciplines in human culture takes place at each level of interaction, precisely in the concept or model of *anthropology* which is forming or functioning in the interacting disciplines, at any level of interface, at any moment.

That is, in the interface of theology and psychology – for example, at the level of theory building – the conscious or unconscious concepts of anthropology which are forming or functioning in that process constitute the precise locus at which the two disciplines interact. One can go one step further in this case and suggest that within the anthropological concepts, it is the theory of personality that is the exact locus at which the main interaction takes place. Theology and psychology, as scientific disciplines and as human experiences, mutually illumine each other mainly at that locus and, therefore or thence, throughout the full range of both disciplines. What psychology can tell us about the nature of humans and the human enterprise informs us about essential truths for theology. What theology can tell us about the nature of humans and the human enterprise informs us about essential truths for psychology. Schleiermacher saw this clearly and consistently did his work in the light of this interface.

The same things can and must be said about the interaction of all the disciplines. Moreover, the interaction between the five different levels themselves also continues to illumine the work going on at each of the levels, for all the disciplines. When we compartmentalize our work in such a way that this interface is truncated, distorted, or eliminated we create a kind of "schizophrenic" science, life, and culture. Our technological age seems to have done this in many ways, thanks to the preoccupation with Positivist empirical priorities, affording little openness to the illumination that a proper interface between religion and these technical aspects of contemporary culture would bring. The resultant science and culture tends more toward an irresponsible scientism and schizoid culture. Schleiermacher had a better idea.

Whether he was dealing with political institutions and responsibility, social order and action, the form or content of the arts, the method or goals of philosophy, or the strategies and meaning of theological education, regardless of the cultural discipline, Schleiermacher pursued his course in terms of the claims of the theological anthropology to which he was committed, and with a sure confidence that all of culture was to be shaped by the claims of the essential nature of human personality as the reflector of God's nature and God's ambitions in this world.

Conclusion

Schleiermacher's vision of the unity of religion and culture is a vision in which religion is an inherent, inevitable, and universal expression of the irrepressible presence of the transcendent and infinite nature of God, immanent in human personality or persons and, in a corollary way, in the entire cosmos. It is a vision in which that creative spirituality and responsible morality, which is clearly necessary and appropriate to the full-fledged and healthy function of human persons in relationship to one another and in the cultural process, is the imperative for shaping every discipline of human endeavor. Culture building, therefore, in his view, is a religious imperative and a moral imperative. No aspect of human function or experience is outside this cultural and religious process. Moreover, the whole is a coherent and integrated dynamic system, because it moves out from and back to the infinite God who is immanent, finitely, in all persons and all created reality.

It is the proper province of another study to investigate the issue of authority in Schleiermacher's concept of truth and his concept of the relationship of religion and culture. That issue is of surmounting importance in the North American dialogue about the interface of religion and science. But that is another matter, for another occasion, and beyond the burden of this present work.

Notes

1. J. Harold Ellens, *God's Grace and Human Health* (Nashville: Abingdon, 1982). Cf. also J. Harold Ellens, *Psychotheology: Key Issues* (Pretoria: UNISA Press, 1987).

2. H. Richard Niebuhr, *Christ and Culture* (NY: Harper, 1951).

3. David Hunt, *The Seduction of Christianity* (Portland: Multnomah, 1985); William Kirk Kilpatrick, *Psychological Seduction, The Failure of Modern Psychology* (Nashville: Nelson, 1983).

4. John D. Carter and Bruce Narramore, *The Integration of Psychology and Theology* (Grand Rapids: Zondervans, 1979).

5. Charles H. Kraft, *Christianity and Culture* (Maryknoll: Orbis, 1979).

6. See note 1, above.

7. Friedrich Schleiermacher, *The Christian Faith*, ed. H.R. Mackintosh and J.S. Stewart, 2 vols. (NY: Harper-Torchbooks, 1963).

8. Friedrich Schleiermacher, *On Religion: Speeches to Its Cultured Despisers*, trans. by John Oman (NY: Harper-Torchbooks, 1958).

9. Robert P. Scharlemann, "Friedrich Schleiermacher," *Encyclopedia Britannica*, 15th Edition, *Macropedia*, Volume 16 (Chicago: Encyclopedia Britannica, Inc., 1974).

10. Ibid.

11. Cf. note 7, above.

12. See note 1, above.

XVIII

THE SEARCH FOR THE INFINITE GOD: UNITY AND FREEDOM IN SCHLEIERMACHER AND SPINOZA

Patrick D. Dinsmore

Friedrich Schleiermacher was charged with being a Spinozist by critics of his own day. It was a charge that meant pantheism at its best and atheism at its worst. It is a charge that rankled him and one which is still heard today.

Schleiermacher did not consider himself to be a Spinozist, at least of the kind he believed to be the distorted Spinozism of his time. He held a great admiration for Spinoza, calling him a man in whom the Holy Spirit dwelled.[1] Still Schleiermacher was also anxious to separate himself from Spinoza because Spinoza's pietism was not imbued with the Christian spirit.[2]

Baruch Spinoza (1632-1677) is often classified as a pure rationalist system builder, his *Ethics* (1677)[3] as a quintessential model of rationalist determinism. It is often charged that God, in Spinoza's use of the word, is no more than the sum total of the system of nature. Freedom was not only lacking in human beings, but also did not apply to God.

In this paper we will examine Schleiermacher's understanding of God as absolute infinite unity and of humankind's relation to God. It is asserted that Schleiermacher's God and Spinoza's God are essentially identical in these important respects. It is further claimed that this idea of God inevitably leads, as Spinoza demonstrated, to an understanding of the necessity of nature, human beings and ultimately God. Schleiermacher's concept of the feeling of utter dependence not withstanding, he too denies an absolutely "free will" even to God.

It is important, of course, to recognize that Schleiermacher was a developmental thinker. The first draft of the *Speeches* was completed in

April of 1799, a full thirty-one years before the April 1830 second edition of the *Christian Faith*. But it is equally significant that the 1831 edition of the *Speeches*, with its appended explanations, gave Schleiermacher ample opportunity to revise or retract his most "pantheistic" or "Spinozistic" statements. He did take the opportunity publically to distance himself from some of Spinoza's most fundamental concepts, especially concerning God in relation to substance with its attributes and modes. But he also stood by some other fundamental aspects of his view of God that, it is claimed here, are in accord with those of Spinoza. Specifically, he agreed with Spinoza on the infinite unity of God and its consequences for our understanding of freedom.

Schleiermacher himself encourages the reader to compare these speeches with, and refer to, his "Christliche Glaubenslehre" for many specific passages, and in general. He flatly denies that the two works are incompatible or contradictory while pointing out the difference in their respective purpose and audience.[4]

Therefore, although Schleiermacher denied the charges of Spinozism leveled against him, in examining God as infinite, eternal unity, the coherence of the God of Schleiermacher and the God of Spinoza becomes evident.

Spinoza and the Search For Certainty

Spinoza, reacting much as Descartes had done against the dogmatic metaphysics of the medieval period, was looking for certainty of knowledge, including, and especially, knowledge about God. He began his quest in *On the Improvement of the Understanding* (1660-61).[5] He wrote that

> after experience had taught me that all the usual surroundings of social life are vain and futile; seeing that none of the objects of my fears contained in themselves anything either good or bad, except in so far as the mind is affected by them, I finally resolved to inquire whether there might be some real good having power to communicate itself, which affects the mind singly, to the exclusion of all else: whether, in fact, there might

be anything of which the discovery and attainment would
enable me to enjoy continuous, supreme, and unending
happiness.[6]

So begins Spinoza's quest for that which would enable him to find the eternal
happiness that he considered entirely lacking in the normal pattern of social
life.

Spinoza was convinced that a new principle was needed, a principle of
which one could be certain, and which he identified with a good upon which
he could build. Such a good (or so reason dictated) must be eternal and
infinite. Thus the character of this highest good, writes Spinoza, is "the
knowledge of the union existing between the mind and the whole of nature."[7]

But how are we to arrive at such a knowledge? How are we to
perceive it? There are four common modes of perception, says Spinoza.
There is that arising from hearsay or sign. Secondly, there is that arising
from experience not yet classified by the intellect. Thirdly, there is that
arising when the essence of one thing is inferred from another thing,
although only inadequately. However it is the fourth one, that of perception
arising when a thing is present solely through its essence, or through
knowledge of its proximate cause, which is the mode by which we are able to
know things with certainty.[8] We will not go into Spinoza's discussion of the
various modes of perception but only remark that it is this fourth mode alone
that is adequate to the end of achieving the highest good with certainty.[9]
The truth itself possesses the subjective essence of things, "the mode in which
we perceive an actual reality is certainty."[10]

Spinoza concludes then that the idea of the most perfect thing (not
the idea of that idea only) must have the most perfect being for its object.[11]
But to arrive at a knowledge of this most perfect being is not an
instantaneous revelation. It is predicated on the accumulation or the
building up of true ideas. "For we may gather from what has been said,"
continues Spinoza, "that a true idea must necessarily first of all exist in us as a
natural instrument, and that when this idea is apprehended by the mind, it
enables us to understand the difference between itself and all other
perception."[12] Here we see the first glimmer of Spinoza's anthropology.
Clear and distinct ideas are natural and do exist in us. This is not a matter of

a demonstration but of experience, an experience of the mind, though ultimately of consciousness.[13]

Perfect knowledge is simply knowledge of the absolutely perfect being.[14] The mind gains strength, so to speak, the more things it knows and the better it understands the order of nature, which certainly includes its own nature. Thus it is then able to guide itself toward the absolute perfect knowledge.[15]

But this still leaves Spinoza with the burden of proving even a single idea upon which knowledge can be built. He rejects Descartes' "radical doubt" as a proof of anything, least of all knowledge. If one knows something it is impossible to doubt that one knows it.[16] The proof for Spinoza lies rather in those simple ideas which are "clear and distinct." A simple idea means, by definition, that it cannot be known in part, but only wholly, or not at all.[17] Consequently, a compound thing, if it can be known in its simple parts, can be known clearly and distinctly.[18] Spinoza writes:

> Thus falsity consists only in this, that something is affirmed of a thing, which is not contained in the conception we have formed of that thing . . . Whence it follows that simple ideas cannot be other than true - e.g. the simple idea of a semicircle, of motion, of rest, of quantity, etc.[19]

"The object aimed at," says Spinoza, "is the acquisition of clear and distinct ideas, such as are produced by the pure intellect. . . ."[20] We can observe here Spinoza's inclination always to look first to the mind for confirmation of the certainty of things. This initially seems to stand in clear and radical conflict with Schleiermacher's assertion of 'feeling.' But while Spinoza's ode to reason cannot be denied, it must also be pointed out that the mind for Spinoza (and this is especially clear in the *Ethics*) was much more than mere cognitive intelligence alone, but it included everything that went on inside.[21]

Spinoza believes that all things can be caused only in two ways. All things are either to be understood as self-caused or as caused by something outside of that thing.[22] That is, a thing is understood either through its essence, or through its proximate cause. And understanding things in either way is greatly facilitated as the thing is better defined."[23] A perfect definition must, naturally, explain the essence of a thing.[24] This definition of an uncreated thing must exclude an external cause, and cannot be explained in abstract terms. In such a definition there is no room for doubting the thing's existence. And finally, it should be possible, though not necessary, to deduce all the properties of the thing.[25] The goal, says Spinoza, is to determine if there is any such being that is the cause of all things, so that its essence, in thought, is the cause of all our ideas. In this way our mind will reflect "nature's essence, order and unity."[26] God becomes, for Spinoza, the 'cause' of all our ideas. But as we will understand shortly, Spinoza is not positing a first cause in any temporal (durational) sense. This is a crucial point and one which, we will see, brings Spinoza and Schleiermacher closer together.

Spinoza left the rest of this study of the understanding unfinished. He felt the need to turn instead to the subject of the *Ethics*. And it is here that Spinoza puts the ideas on the quest for certainty, happiness and immortality to work. The first part of the *Ethics* treats the nature and existence of God as absolute infinite unity. Our primary task here has been to show the founding principles and presuppositions of Spinoza in order to compare and contrast them with those of Schleiermacher.

Substance, or the Infinite God

It is important here to come to an understanding of Spinoza's conception of substance and of God as absolutely infinite and eternal substance. Spinoza concludes that God exists (Pr. 11, I) and in propositions 15 and 16 of Book I of the *Ethics* there is implicit the fact that God is not divisible, nor is there anything that is separable from God. In order to arrive at this proposition Spinoza first had to establish the unity of all that is. Therefore, he begins with certain common notions, clear and distinct ideas, whose truth is obvious to all who think clearly. Consequently, there are several important definitions in Book I. One of the most crucial is the third where substance is defined:

> By substance I mean that which is in itself and is conceived
> through itself; that is, that the conception of which does not

require the conception of another thing from which it is formed.[27]

Spinoza is establishing his definition of substance firstly in contradistinction to the notion of substance as solely corporeal and divisible and secondly, and especially, in opposition to the Cartesian notion of the two substances, mind and body.[28] God, as substance, is self-caused or that which is caused by nothing outside of itself. This is the basis of Spinoza's ontological argument:

God, or substance consisting of infinite attributes, each of which expresses eternal and infinite essence, necessarily exists.[29]

Definition 6 of Book I defines God as "an absolutely infinite being." One might argue that substance need not necessarily be defined as self-caused. Something, i.e., God, could have created or caused substance to come into being. This is a classical theological formulation. But Spinoza takes seriously the nature of God as "absolutely infinite Being." If God is absolutely infinite there cannot be, by the very definition of what it means to be God, anything outside of God, or else God would not be absolutely infinite.

Spinoza also introduces, as a definition, the concept of mode, or the affections of substance.[30] A mode is an expression of the affections of substance and thus does not proceed from itself, but from something else. Therefore, substance is prior to its affections.[31] A mode is, then, a derived, durational being; existence does not belong to its essence.[32]

The ontological argument is at the foundation of Spinoza's *Ethics*. But it is also God as absolute infinite essence that Spinoza intends to establish, and which he does in propositions 12 through 15 of Book I. In this demonstration Spinoza posits a thing's reality as a function of its power of being. This means that the more power of being a thing has, the more real it is. This is related to Spinoza's conclusion that the reality of a thing determines its consciousness and understanding of God as absolute infinite unity, and oneself as a part of all the finite expressions of the infinite substance. The outline of this demonstration is as follows: using Def. 4 and Def. 3 of Book I Spinoza proves that each attribute of substance that the intellect perceives as constituting its essence "must be conceived through itself."[33] Each entity must be conceived under some attribute. Therefore, the more being or reality the entity has, the more its attributes express "necessity, or eternity, and infinity."[34] That is, the more being or reality the entity has the more we must understand this entity as existing. Because an entity with infinite attributes expresses infinite being or reality, it necessarily exists. Therefore, "God, or substance of infinite attributes, each of which expresses eternal and infinite essence, necessarily exists."[35] Existence belongs to the essence of substance.[36] God, as infinite substance, *qua* God, is existence, and existence necessarily.[37]

We have seen here that for Spinoza all things must be regarded as possessing degrees of perfection or reality. The more perfection a thing has the more reality it has. Also the more reality a thing has the greater is its power of being.[38] Inseparable from the concept of the power of being and existence is the concept of *conatus*. The *conatus* of which Spinoza speaks, and which is fundamental to one's human nature, as well as to the nature of all things, is the drive to preserve oneself in one's being; it is the essence of one's being.[39] For human beings this means understanding oneself in relation to God. *Conatus* is the endeavor to increase one's power of existence, of reality, of being, and of perfection. The goal of this is exemplified by the ethical life depicted in Book V of the *Ethics*.

God is infinite, undivided Being. Human beings are modes or expressions of the infinite substance, of God. They are distinguished as durational, finite beings. They are only in and through God, the infinite substance. It is a mistake to equate substance with corporeal being. This puts a quantitative measure on God, even though it may be "infinite quantity." This, however, is the false infinite. Thus properly understood, Spinoza's God is not made up of merely all that exists. This puts the relationship backwards. Rather, nothing that is is outside God. This is a wholly different proposition. The infinite can be referred to, but not 'identified' in the way finite things can.

Schleiermacher's Existential Feeling

Schleiermacher's aim was somewhat different than Spinoza's. He was a committed Christian preacher and theologian, though hardly an orthodox one. In his 1799 *Speeches*, Schleiermacher's readers were those "cultured despisers" whose horizons he wished to broaden by expanding their understanding of what it meant to be religious. Religion was not something one believed in, but rather an expression of one's innermost being, an expression of one's existential relation with the Divine and the Infinite, that is, with God. The *Christian Faith*,[40] Schleiermacher's dogmatic statement of Christian piety, was not a philosophical tract, but a Christian apology. It sought to reinterpret Christian doctrine according to religious feeling and God-consciousness in the light of the historical Christ. It was directed not at despisers of religion but at Christians. Christ possessed the perfect God-consciousness and He communicated this to us. The true goal of all religion, and the task of the church, was to awaken and nurture the God-consciousness inherent in each human being. Consequently, Schleiermacher begins the *Christian Faith* with a discussion of the nature of religious piety and human consciousness. Our 'knowledge' of God needs only to be awakened and nurtured. To be sure, this work was not intended to perform this function itself, but rather it was aimed at the theologians, pastors, and professionals of the church to whom this task ultimately fell with the help of God's Spirit.

In some sense Schleiermacher began with a notion similar to Spinoza's "clear and distinct ideas." He, like Spinoza, believed in an original expression of our being, though for Schleiermacher it was definitely precognitive. This he identified as religious feeling or piety. Both thinkers, however, understood this existential nature of our being to be struggling to come to consciousness. For Spinoza the location was in intellectual intuition,[41] for Schleiermacher it was in the feeling of utter dependence (*das schlechthinnige Abhängigkeitsgefühl*).

Knowing and doing were the traditional concepts under which human beings were classified. That is, these were the two forms of expression of human beings and, therefore, the two ways by which we can know anything about being human. Schleiermacher maintained that there was a third mode of our being – feeling. Feeling was not merely a simple emotive response; feeling was an existential expression of our being. Piety is essentially, writes Schleiermacher, "a modification of Feeling, or . . . immediate self-consciousness."[42]

After having established Piety (a special modification of religious feeling) as a third element of human nature,[43] Schleiermacher turns next to the nature of piety itself. Piety, he says, is "the consciousness of being absolutely dependent, or which is the same thing, of being in relation with God."[44] He continues:

> In any actual state of consciousness, no matter whether it merely accompanies a thought or action or occupies a moment for itself, we are never simply conscious of our selves in their unchanging identity, but are always at the same time conscious of a changing determination of them.[45]

This means that all self-consciousness is a consciousness of a variable state of being. And this variable state of being cannot arise from the purely self-identical or it would in fact be the same. Schleiermacher is making the specific point that there is something decidedly distinct, in some sense, from ourselves. And this we apprehend in religious feeling or piety.

There are, then, two elements that we recognize for ourselves: a self-positing (*ein Sichselbstsetzen*) and a non-selfpositing (*ein Sichselbstnichtsogesetzthaben*). He also terms these elements Being (*ein Sein*) and Having-by-some-means-come-to-be (*ein Irgendwiegewordensein*).[46] Behind this factor is the source of the particular determination. Without this factor the self-consciousness could not know what it is.[47] Schleiermacher also refers to this factor as the "Other." But this Other is not objectively presented in immediate self-consciousness. These two elements of self-consciousness express the existence of the subject for itself and its co-existence with an Other.[48] Further, these two elements correspond to the subject's Receptivity (i.e., without the Other there is no receptivity as there is nothing to be receptive to), and the subject's Activity (i.e., without the Other our Activity would have no direction, but would only be an urge outward).[49]

We are never without an other. Therefore, in every outward tendency of self-consciousness the element of Receptivity is the primary one. Schleiermacher continues in the *Christian Faith*:

> . . . and even the self-consciousness which accompanies action (acts of knowing included), while it predominately expresses spontaneous movement and activity, is always related (though the relation is often a quite indefinite one) to a prior moment of affective receptivity, through which the original 'agility' received its direction.[50]

The Feeling of Dependence is the common element which expresses receptivity affected from an outside source. The Feeling of Freedom is the common element which expresses spontaneous movement and activity.[51] The Feeling of Dependence, then, is not just the influence of some Other in our arrival at such a state, for we could not have arrived as we have without the Other. Conversely, Freedom is the Other who is determined by us and could not have been so without us.[52] Schleiermacher is rejecting the more common notions of a free being as one who remains essentially self-identical, i.e., not influenced by an Other, as well as the notion of Dependence as being wholly determined from the outside without any action of our own.[53]

Reciprocity is the expression of the feeling of freedom and the feeling of dependence as the same for both. That is, the total self-consciousness of both together is one of reciprocity between a subject and a corresponding Other. The term expresses our connection with everything that appears to our receptivity or is subject to our activity.[54] It, therefore, pertains to our relation with a particular and with that which stands outside one, i.e., the World. "Accordingly," writes Schleiermacher, "our self-consciousness, as a consciousness of our existence in the world or of our co-existence with the world, is a series in which the feeling of freedom and feeling of dependence are divided."[55]

There is no feeling of utter dependence in the relationship described above. There is always some feeling of dependence but also always some feeling of freedom in relation to any particular Other or even group of Others. Schleiermacher writes: "For if the feeling of freedom expresses a forthgoing activity, this activity must have an object which has been somehow given to us, and this could not have taken place without an influence of the object upon our receptivity."[56] No feeling of utter dependence can arise from an object given to us. There is always a counterinfluence, at least as regards a single moment, "because such a moment is always determined, as regards its content, by what is given and, thus by objects towards which we have a feeling of freedom."[57] Schleiermacher continues:

> But the self-consciousness which accompanies all our activity, and therefore, since that is never zero, accompanies our whole existence, and negatives (sic) absolute freedom, is itself precisely a consciousness of absolute dependence; for it is the consciousness that the whole of our spontaneous activity comes from a source outside us in just the same sense in which anything towards which we should have a feeling of absolute freedom must have proceeded entirely from ourselves. But without any feeling of freedom a feeling of absolute dependence would not be possible.[58]

In religious consciousness, the particular experience (religious content) will be different according to the different data. But the essential element is the feeling of utter dependence, which is the same in all manifestations.[59]

Piety, as the expression of the feeling of utter dependence, is the essence of religion. This is why Schleiermacher could call Spinoza a man imbued with piety. Schleiermacher first called the feeling of utter dependence a feeling for a 'Whence,' writing:

> As regards the identification of absolute dependence with 'relation to God' in our proposition: this is to be understood in the sense that the 'Whence' of our receptive and active existence, as implied in this self-consciousness, is to be designated by the word 'God'....[60]

This Whence is implied in this immediate self-consciousness. Finally, Schleiermacher terms the Whence God. However, he is careful to distinguish the Whence, and hence God, from the mere totality of temporal existence (i.e., the World). In relation to the world we always maintain a feeling of freedom (albeit limited), because we are complementary parts of it. We always have the possibility of exercising influence on all its parts. A fundamental idea for Schleiermacher is that "God signifies for us simply that which is the co-determinant in this feeling and to which we trace our being in such a state; and any further content of the idea must be evolved out of this fundamental import assigned to it."[61] God is not just the world or creation. Schleiermacher does not understand himself as advocating a materialistic pantheism.[62]

Schleiermacher has also expressed this belief concerning the essence of piety in his *Speeches*. He wrote that "The contemplation of the pious is the immediate consciousness of the universal existence of all finite things in and through the infinite, and of all temporal things in and through the Eternal."[63] "Religion," continues Schleiermacher,

> is to seek this and find it in all that lives and moves, in all growth and change, in all doing and suffering. It is to have life and to know life in immediate feeling, only as such an existence in the Infinite and Eternal.[64]

How does Schleiermacher then characterize the life of the pious and religious? He writes: "Wherefore it is a life in the infinite nature of the whole, in the One and in the All, in God, having and possessing all things in God, and God in all."[65] But Schleiermacher is quick to add that this is not the same as knowledge or science of the world or of God. "Without being knowledge," he says, "it recognizes knowledge and science. In itself it is an affection, a revelation of the Infinite in the finite, God being seen in it and it in God.[66]

Schleiermacher, like Kant, was deeply critical of those who claimed a metaphysical knowledge in the same way one laid claim to a scientific knowledge. But he was equally critical of those "cultured despisers" who limited all knowledge to the dialectics of our cognitive experience. They have failed to distinguish its proper place in the intellect and thus deny any knowledge for religion different from that. This way of knowledge forever sees the world in division. Religion sees it in its wholeness and connectedness. Schleiermacher writes:

> Just because you do not acknowledge religion as the third, knowledge and action are so much apart that you can discover no unity, but believe that rightly knowing can be had without

right acting, and <u>vice versa</u>. I hold that it is only in contemplation that there is a division. There, where it is necessary, you despise it, and instead transfer it to life, as if in life itself objects could be found independent of one another . . . Because you do not deal with life in a living way, your conception bears the stamp of perishableness, and is altogether meagre. True science is complete vision; true practice is culture and art self-produced; true religion is sense and taste for the Infinite.[67]

I believe that it is this "sense and taste for the Infinite" which Schleiermacher found in Spinoza. And who could deny that Spinoza's science aimed for "complete vision" of the unity and connectedness of all things in the Whole, in God?

However, in one of the explanations in the 1831 edition referring to a passage in which Schleiermacher called God the "Highest Being," which seemed to some to be the world itself rather than the cause of the world, Schleiermacher answers that

I do not think that God can be placed in such a relation as cause, and I leave you to say whether the World can be conceived as a true All and Whole without God. Therefore I remained satisfied with that expression, that I might not decide on the various ways of conceiving God and the World as together or as outside of one another, which did not fall to be considered here, and could only have limited the horizon in a hurtful manner.[68]

How are we to view Schleiermacher's reluctance to address the relation of God and the World? Does his denial of God as cause distance him from Spinoza? Though Spinoza does refer to God as "first cause," Schleiermacher is not answering Spinoza here, but rather the system builders who posited God as the first cause in such a way that God is still considered as separated, in an absolute way, from the world and from all finite things. Rather, if the existence of all finite things is only properly conceived in the Infinite, then cause applied to God does not mean the same thing as when applied to any finite thing. In this respect, Schleiermacher and Spinoza are entirely in accord, especially when one considers Schleiermacher's numerous statements about the impossibility of being conscious of God without being conscious of all things in God. It is only in and through finite things that one becomes conscious of them in God and thus of all things in God, in the Infinite.

Spinoza and Schleiermacher both take the concept of the Infinite seriously. There is no 'cause' attached to the Infinite in the same way one finite thing can be the cause of another. True, Spinoza spoke of God as the cause of all things, but in the sense of the ground of all things. If one observes, in the *Ethics* the chain of cause and effect, if regressed, is infinite! There is no 'first cause' in this sense of an infinite regression of a series of finite things that leads to a beginning cause in the series. And Schleiermacher also rejects the notion of the merely connected:

> We do not feel ourselves dependent on the Whole in so far as it is an aggregate of mutually conditioned parts of which we ourselves are one, but only in so far as underneath this coherence there is a unity conditioning all things and conditioning our relations to the other parts of the Whole. Only on this condition can the single thing be, as it is here put, an exhibition of the Infinite, being so comprehended that its opposition to all else entirely vanishes.[69]

For Schleiermacher, however, it cannot be denied that the comprehension of the Whole, of the Unity, is first of all expressed in religious feeling (or this feeling which is therefore religious). As he writes in the *Speeches*:

> "The sense of the Whole must be first found chiefly within our own minds, and from thence transferred to corporeal nature ... The universe portrays itself in the inner life, and then the corporeal is comprehensible from the spiritual. If the mind is to produce and sustain religion it must operate upon us as a world and as in a world.[70]

The impetus for Spinoza's conclusions about God, at least formally, are found in his desire for certain knowledge. It would lead him to what one may know and thus of what one should know, and how one should live. It was certainly a rationalistic approach, nonetheless it led Spinoza to a concept of God as Infinite, Eternal Unity. This is the fundamental and crucial consciousness towards which, but ultimately by which, we, as human beings, must be directed.

It is only in this consciousness, in this understanding, that we can fully understand ourselves, can know ourselves and our world. The *conatus*, the impulse of our innermost being, pushes us towards this consciousness. But we must ourselves work to understand it so that we may be directed by it rather than by the "passions" which lead us away from it in their desire to satisfy themselves alone.

Friedrich Schleiermacher also perceived the notion of an existential relation with the Divine and the Infinite. There is a primal urge towards consciousness of this relation, but it is too often not recognized and thus fails to be nurtured. The feeling of utter dependence expresses for Schleiermacher our relation to the Infinite, Eternal God, which he also calls the Infinite Whole.

We have arrived at the preliminary understanding of God for both Spinoza and Schleiermacher. With this understanding we can proceed to examine particular expressions of Schleiermacher's writings in order to assess in what ways he may or may not properly be termed a Spinozist.

Schleiermacher the Spinozist (Or Not, as the Case May Be)

Spinoza, as we saw, begins with true (simple) ideas; Schleiermacher assumes an original pre-theoretical consciousness of reality. Robert B. Williams, in *Schleiermacher the Theologian*,[71] points out that God is also pre-theoretical. God is not a result of proofs and demonstrations, but rather is conditioned solely by the religious modification of feeling – that of utter dependence.[72] God is given in an original way, not as an abstraction. There is, in human beings, an apprehension (in some sense) of divine being and reality.[73] Feeling is an immediate presence of the highest unity. It is to feel, says Schleiermacher, "that our being and living is a being and living in and through God."[74]

But God is not an abstraction for Spinoza either; this, at least, is what he claims. We arrive at knowledge or consciousness of God, says Spinoza, by advancing from one real entity to another and finally we arrive at God – a real entity. Because of this method there is no room for abstractions or general ideas. Spinoza says that:

> Thus we can see that it is before all things necessary for us to deduce all our ideas from . . . real entities, proceeding, as far as may be, according to the series of causes . . . never passing to universals and abstractions.[75]

Williams wrote that Schleiermacher asserts that God is absolutely free.[76] Williams continues:

> But such freedom involves no arbitrariness or irrationality: unlimited self-actualization is ethically necessary. Thus Schleiermacher contends that nothing in God is free unless it is also morally necessary.[77]

Finally, concludes Williams, "this puts some distance between Schleiermacher and Spinoza."[78] It is not clear exactly what the nature of this distance is. If, however, Williams means here that Schleiermacher is positing an "ethical freedom" for God that then distances him from Spinoza, it seems difficult to conclude this from an examination of the relevant texts to which Williams refers in the *Christian Faith*, especially when they are compared with the relevant texts in Spinoza's *Ethics*.

Schleiermacher does say that God is absolutely free, but this is not in contrast to Spinoza. He continues on to explain that this does not mean God is able to choose among various options or that God can chose not to act according to God's own nature. He writes in the *Christian Faith*:

> But if we suppose that the free decision implies a prior deliberation followed by choice, or interpret freedom as meaning that God might equally well have not created the world (because we think that there must have been this possibility, otherwise God was compelled to create), we have then assumed an antithesis between freedom and necessity, and by attributing this kind of freedom to God, have placed Him within the realm of contradictions.[79]

Schleiermacher expressed the complimentarily of the free and necessary wills of God. In §54.4 of the *Christian Faith* he is very explicit. A free will applied to God that believes that God could have willed otherwise assumes, says Schleiermacher, that it "does not belong to His essence to reveal Himself."[80] This is clearly wrong for Schleiermacher. God wills necessarily because it is God's nature, and God could not act other than God's nature and be God. That is, it is God's nature to express God's self.

In the *Ethics* Spinoza also demonstrates that only God acts solely from the laws of God's own nature.[81] In the second corollary to Pr. 7 Spinoza asserts that:

> God alone is a free cause. For God exists solely from the
> *necessity* of His own nature and acts solely from the necessity of
> His own nature.[82]

In Br. 9, Bk. I of the *Ethics* Spinoza continues by claiming that nothing is contingent in nature, but all things are determined to act in a definite way from the necessity of the divine nature. But Spinoza does deny God a "free will."[83] The will for Spinoza is not a separate faculty but a "mode of thinking."[84] The will, therefore, always requires a cause. God "wills" in the sense that it is out of the necessity of God's own nature, but necessary by reason of God's "essence" and not some cause outside of God's essence, the way other things are termed necessary.[85] Thus Spinoza calls God the only "free cause."

But what of Spinoza's denial of an absolute will of God, which is affirmed by Schleiermacher?[86] Again, there is little if any distance between these positions. Schleiermacher's position is that God never wills conditionally, but always absolutely. Schleiermacher reasons that since God always wills to express God's nature God absolutely wills to do so.[87] While any individual thing is indeed conditioned, they are all conditioned ultimately, by the divine will, and therefore absolutely.[88] Now consider Spinoza on this subject when he says that:

> on God's decree and will alone does it depend that each thing
> is what it is. For otherwise God would not be the cause of all
> things. Further, there is the fact that all God's decrees have
> been sanctioned by God from eternity, for otherwise he could
> be accused of imperfection or inconsistency. But since the
> eternal does not admit of 'when' or 'before' or 'after,' it follows

merely from God's perfection that God can never decree otherwise nor ever could have decreed otherwise.[89]

Likewise, in the *Christian Faith*, Schleiermacher believes, as does Spinoza, that if God wills God's self,

> He wills Himself as Creator and Sustainer, so that in willing Himself, willing the world is already included; and if He wills the world, in it He wills His eternal and ever-present omnipotence, wherein willing Himself is included; that is to say, the *necessary will is included in the free, and the free in the necessary.*[90]

Spinoza had addressed the issue of the nature of the freedom of God outside of *The Ethics* as well. In a letter (1675?) to Oldenbergh, Spinoza restates his position while disclaiming that it leaves God subject to other forces:

> God is in no wise subject to fate: I conceive that all things follow with the *inevitable necessity from the nature of God* in the same way as everyone conceives that it follows from God's nature that God understands Himself. This latter consequence all admit to follow necessarily from the divine nature yet no one conceives God is under the compulsion of any fate, but that *He understands Himself quite freely, though necessarily.*[91]

We can clearly see here that Schleiermacher is not in disagreement with Spinoza on the issue of God's freedom. God's acts are both free and necessary – free because by the nature of God, God is not caused by anything outside of God, and necessary because God, as God, acts from that divine nature.

Freedom and Necessity

Albert Blackwell points out, in Schleiermacher's lectures on psychology (given four times between 1818 and 1834), that Schleiermacher makes a distinction between the various aspects of freedom. They are the impulse to self-preservation (*Selbsterhaltungstrieb*), self-acquisition (*Besizergreifen*) and self-manifestation (*Selbstmanifestation*).[92] In an address *Über den Unterschied zwischen Naturgesetz und Sittengesetz*, these three aspects of freedom were distinguished as appropriating (*aneignend*), cultivating (*bildend*), and manifesting (*offenbarend*).[93] And in his 1790-91 treatise, *On Human Freedom*, the ethical ideal is the fully cultivated personality. Blackwell summarizes Schleiermacher's viewpoint:

> The ethical ideal presented in Schleiermacher's treatise "On Human Freedom" is the personality whose cultivation is so complete, whose comprehension of the causal world order is so broad, that "he appears to act in accordance with circumstances but not to be altered by them."[94]

We can see in this distinction elements very much in harmony with Spinoza's idea of freedom, especially as understood under the impetus of one's *conatus*. *Conatus* is the drive to preserve one's being. This drive means a growing self-consciousness, a coming into one's full being. It is an acquiring of knowledge and control over one's environment, insofar as that control is in harmony with the environment, that is, with the whole of Nature. However, it is a freedom in which one is aware of one's ultimate connectedness to the all.

Passivity, for Spinoza, is being constrained to act by forces not in accordance with reason, causes that do not spring from one's own nature and being in harmony with reason.[95] Our freedom is freedom from the power of these forces that would determine us. It is freedom to act according to our nature, and this means according to reason, to the way things are.[96] For Schleiermacher, freedom is self-expression.[97] This does not mean that there is no determination in our actions, but our freedom consists in making this 'cause' our own. It is, writes Schleiermacher in the *Speeches*:

> to absorb it into one's innermost spirit and fuse it into a unity; to strip it of the temporal, so that it does not dwell in one as something discrete and disturbing, but as something eternal, pure, and calm. Then, from this inner unity, action springs of its own accord . . . Only when each [action] is in its own connection and its own place do they manifest in a free and characteristic way the whole inner unity of the spirit − not when they correspond in a dependent and slavish way to some particular stimulation.[98]

This view is in agreement with Spinoza as he wrote in the *Ethics*:

Therefore he who aims solely from love of freedom to control his emotions and appetites will strive his best to familiarize himself with virtues and their causes and to fill his mind with the joy that arises from the true knowledge of them.[99]

This understanding of one's emotions and oneself, to become conscious of oneself fully is equated with love of God for Spinoza.[100] This is the intellectual love of God.[101]

Williams points out that Schleiermacher makes a particular effort in the *Christian Faith* to express his agreement of the nature of feeling as the "immediate presence of whole undivided being" with his friend Heinrich Steffens, the Danish philosopher of nature. Williams notes that:

As such, feeling is essentially in correlation with the world at the prereflective level: "What we here call feeling is the immediate presence of whole undivided being, both spiritual and sensible, the unity of the person with his spiritual and sensible world."[102]

Schleiermacher was contrasting this view with another view present at the time.[103] This view is definitely in agreement with Spinoza's understanding of human being as individual but not as a part which is a separate "whole" together with other parts; it is a whole, as Schleiermacher concurs here with Steffens, of "undivided being."

Williams also examines Schleiermacher's notion of belief. Williams notes that for Schleiermacher belief is a "pretheoretical certitude concerning the codeterminant of self-consciousness."[104] This subjective certitude, different from objective certitude in kind, thus has its own standard of measure, continues Williams:

It is an intuitive certitude prior to and independent of representations, inference, and explicit judgment. It is a certitude generated by the direct concrete interaction with and apprehension of the things *as they give themselves*.[105]

This is similar to Spinoza's 'true ideas' of things, which is the essence of that thing as a thing is in itself, whether or not that thing is in itself or in another.

In the feeling of utter dependence, Schleiermacher has maintained
the distinction between God and the finite things of creation, between God
and humankind. In pantheism, at least materialistic pantheism, the charge is
that God is all things, and that all things are "parts" of God.[106] Neither
Schleiermacher nor Spinoza adhere to such a strict materialistic pantheism.
Schleiermacher expresses our relation to God existentially as given in the
feeling of utter dependence. It is perhaps less clear initially with Spinoza.
But if we examine his so-called pantheism, we will find it is not much
different from Schleiermacher's God-consciousness. In no way is the
existence of finite things equated with God in Spinoza. They are not simply
"parts" of a greater whole which make up a totality, even if one admits to an
infinite whole. This is simply a false infinity, one derived from the
"imagination."[107] Finite things exist as a natural and necessary expression of
God's nature. Only God receives existence as an essential attribute.
Existence does not pertain to the essence of any finite thing, including human
beings.[108] All finite things are dependent upon God for their existence
which is given, i.e., caused, by some proximate cause; ultimately this cause is
God. Schleiermacher writes in the *Christian Faith* that faith in God is
"nothing but the certainty concerning the feeling of utter dependence, as
such, i.e., as conditioned by a Being placed outside of us, and as expressing
our relation to that Being."[109] In this Schleiermacher seems to agree with
Spinoza concerning the nature of our self-consciousness, in so far as it is a
God-consciousness, which is an inner certainty. One knows its truth simply
because it is given one as true. But it is also at this exact point that
Schleiermacher again parts company with Spinoza. He continues:

> The faith of which we are now speaking, however, is a purely
> factual certainty, but a certainty of act which is entirely inward.
> That is to say, it cannot exist in an individual until, through an
> impression which he has received from Christ, there is found in
> him a beginning – perhaps quite infinitesimal, but yet a real
> premonition of the process which will put an end to the state of
> needing redemption.[110]

Christ is the historical cause; for Spinoza it is God. All other causes are
proximate causes. Schleiermacher would not deny that God is the ultimate

cause, but adds significantly that without Christ as fully human, fully developed God-consciousness, we would not have received the consciousness of the completion of our human nature, of our redemption.[111]

The aim of *The Ethics*, especially as its method is called "geometric," seems to suggest a goal of completeness of knowledge about God. This is not strictly correct. Blackwell seems to feel that Schleiermacher was convinced that no "geometrical" method could arrive at any completeness.[112] This is expressed by Schleiermacher's resignation to finiteness. In a letter to Charlotte Pistorius, Schleiermacher had written that "If there is in the *Soliloquies* no trace of any conflict with myself, then that is only because I am quite resigned to the fact that a person can only become progressively."[113] And in his 1792-93 essay "On the Worth of Life," he wrote that "In rules of the understanding, resignation is everywhere life's governing command."[114] Blackwell writes:

> It is Schleiermacher's conviction that despite the felt need of reason for unity and completeness, our knowledge in all spheres remains always partial. Philosophical wisdom therefore consists in learning to live with incompleteness, learning to accept it gracefully as an inevitable condition of human life.[115]

And by this argument, Blackwell is expressing exactly the conclusions of Spinoza.

Spinoza did strive for a kind of completeness, but it is a completeness not in the sense of infinite knowledge, but rather a knowledge <u>of</u> the infinite. Understanding is very much an understanding of one's own limitedness, of one's own finiteness. It is resignation. Nevertheless, understanding this, that is, the limit of one's nature, is to understand oneself as much as possible. And thus, it is freeing oneself from outside forces as much as possible. Therefore, Spinoza continues:

> If we clearly and distinctly understand this, that part of us which is defined by the understanding, that is the better part of us, will be fully resigned and will endeavor to persevere in that resignation . . . And so far as we rightly understand these matters, the endeavor of the better of us is in harmony with the order of the whole of Nature.[116]

Part of growing in understanding, of the development of self-consciousness, is recognition of, and resignation to, one's finite nature. This is true for both Schleiermacher and Spinoza.

'I Am Not a Spinozist'

Let us now examine Schleiermacher's own defense against the charges of Spinozism. While he clearly arrived at the same conclusions as Spinoza regarding the unity of the infinite God and the special freedom assigned to God according to God's essential and necessary nature, he just as clearly separated himself from Spinoza because Spinoza lacked a Christian Spirit. But upon examination of Schleiermacher's defense on this matter, it becomes less clear. We certainly will detect in them the sensitivity to the charge of Spinozism, as far as it relates to pantheism and atheism, but there is also an unmistakable sympathy for Spinoza's pietism, not an out and out defense to be sure, but at least a mild apology for his pantheism which is not so different from monotheism when properly understood.[117]

In the first edition of the *Speeches*, Schleiermacher gave what he latter admitted was the praise of youthful enthusiasm for Spinoza. In this speech, Schleiermacher had been addressing those who were looking for a pure 'scientific' formulation of the universe and of humankind's place in it, which Schleiermacher called "mechanical erections" rather than the "organic structure" of religion, and which result in dead science. It lacks the oneness "with the Eternal in the unity of intuition and feeling which is immediate."[118] The result? Schleiermacher continues by saying that "It annihilates the Universe, while it seems to aim at constructing it."[119] It is in this context that Schleiermacher offers his ode to Spinoza:

> Offer with me reverently a tribute to the manes of the holy, rejected Spinoza. The high World-Spirit pervaded him; the Infinite was his beginning and his end; the Universe was his only and his everlasting love. In holy innocence and in deep humility he beheld himself mirrored in the eternal world, and perceived how he also was the most worthy mirror. He was full of religion, full of the Holy Spirit. Wherefore, he stands there

alone and unequalled; master in his art, yet without disciples and without citizenship, sublime above the profane tribe.[120]

This passage was certainly one occasion for the charge of Spinozism against Schleiermacher. But interestingly, Schleiermacher is separating Spinoza's "system" from the merely mechanistic ones of the universe. In later editions of the *Speeches* Schleiermacher responded to this charge in notes added to the text. Spinoza was being attacked at the time as "godless by the literalists," writes Schleiermacher. In this 1831 edition he continues:

> It was incumbent upon me to protest against this view of Spinoza, seeing I would review the whole sphere of piety. Something essential would have been wanting in the exposition of my views if I had not in some way said that the mind and heart of this great man seemed deeply influence by piety, even though it were not Christian piety.[121]

Schleiermacher clearly recognized a deeply religious spirit in Spinoza. And he just as clearly did not view Spinoza's "universe" as mechanistic. He even goes on to suggest that Spinoza might have been Christian "had not the Christianity of that time been so distorted and obscured by dry formulas and vain subtleties that the divine form could not be expected to win the regard of a stranger."[122] Schleiermacher's sympathy lay much more with Spinoza than with the Christianity of Spinoza's time.

Again, in a letter to his friend Friedrich Lücke, first published in 1829, Schleiermacher defends his support for Spinoza:

> I have been condemned as a pantheist on the basis of my speeches solely because I wanted to show the despisers of piety that piety was everywhere, even where they sought it least. Therefore, I indicated its presence especially in a person whose speculation began at that time to be idolized in the most perverse manner, and to be condemned by others as severely as possible. Yet almost no one had noticed his genuinely human, inwardly gentle, and most attractive personality and his deep devotion to the supreme being.[123]

But Spinoza's piety was not Christian piety for Schleiermacher, as we noted above. Christian piety, for Schleiermacher, can only mean one's encounter with Christ's full God-consciousness. Full God-consciousness is the perfection of one's being, as it is with Spinoza. However, for Schleiermacher, it was because of Christ's full God-consciousness that we are able to appropriate it, or encounter it, for ourselves. And here we can clearly see that Schleiermacher parts paths with Spinoza. While we cannot discuss in detail Schleiermacher's Christology here, it is important to note that fellowship, as paramount to Christian community, is itself essentially fellowship with Christ and is a communication of His full God-consciousness.[124] This is the second significant departure, along with the nature of the origin of the "taste for the infinite," that Schleiermacher makes from Spinoza's consciousness of the absolutely infinite unity of God. Consequently, for Schleiermacher the Christian, we only come to full God-consciousness, which includes especially a consciousness of redemption, through Christ and through the Spirit of Christ which is the church.[125]

In his doctrine of creation, that is, in his distinction between the finite and the infinite, Schleiermacher explains it in very Spinozistic terms. Creation, that is all finite things, cannot be considered as other than totally dependent on God. Creation is *ex nihilo*, which simply "excludes the idea that before the origin of the world anything existed outside God, which as 'matter' could enter into the formation of the world."[126]

But Schleiermacher does not go as far as Spinoza explicitly to conclude that all finite things are modes of the attributes of thought and extension of God or substance. Yet there is nothing that is outside or separate in terms of independence from God. In fact Schleiermacher remarks that:

> the controversy over the temporal or eternal creation of the world (which can be restated into the question whether it is possible or necessary to conceive of God as existing apart from created things) has no bearing on the content of the feeling of absolute dependence, and therefore a matter of indifference how it is decided.[127]

The problem in this statement is Schleiermacher's conviction that it has no bearing on the feeling of utter dependence. For Spinoza, it would be important because the proper understanding of God is grounded in the very conception of the nature of the relation between the finite and the infinite. While this can be said of Schleiermacher as well, for Spinoza any idea of God as existing apart from creation, and thus of creation, as finite, as existing apart from God, is inimical to the proper understanding of the infinite unity of God. Schleiermacher here seems only to hold that as long as such a view does not conflict with the feeling of utter dependence the question is immaterial.

Spinoza would not condone a view that maintained that it is possible to understand God as truly infinite and yet maintain that there was an absolute and genuine separation of God and finite things. It remains unclear here if Schleiermacher, considering his emphasis on the feeling of utter dependence, is actually accepting the possibility of a God as something completely separate from us, but this seems unlikely. Elsewhere he has consistently maintained that God is not an object as other objects of our objective consciousness. There is no antithesis in God. Nor can there be such an antithesis in our consciousness of God. In any case, it is just such an abstract concept of God that Spinoza is decrying. Schleiermacher, however, goes on to say that if creation is a creation in time that is also the beginning of the divine activity, then God is rendered subject to time and change in the way finite things are.[128] This is unacceptable. The feeling of utter dependence would be lost. It is contended here that Schleiermacher's position on the creation of finite things, in so far as finite things can only be understood as utterly dependent on God for their existence and their being, is functionally equivalent of Spinoza's Pr. 15, I of the *Ethics*:

> Whatever is, is in God, and nothing can be, or be conceived without God.[129]

This certainly is the source of the charge of pantheism against Spinoza. And the degree to which Schleiermacher can be identified with this view he will be charged as being a Spinozist.

Schleiermacher, however, distanced himself from Spinoza in regard to the source of the unity of God which Spinoza found in substance. He defended himself in his notes to the *Speeches*. He wrote of Spinoza:

> Yet I had never defended his system and anything philosophic that was in my book was manifestly inconsistent with the

characteristics of his views and had quite a different basis than the unity of substance.[130]

And here Schleiermacher is correct. The unity of Substance which the mind finally arrives at through intellectual intuition based on original simple ideas and on the consequent compound ideas which followed from them, is a far cry from what Schleiermacher considered as original in religious piety, or the feeling of utter dependence. Schleiermacher begins with the experience of an existential relation, eschewing mere propositions and deduction. But, of course, Spinoza's system was not mere propositions and deduction. He did indeed build a 'system' using reason as the trusted guide toward an understanding of God and of the relation of human beings and the world to God. But he did not deny the role of feeling and experience of the mind. The intellect confirms what the mind senses and feels. The mind is not merely an instrument for abstractly constructing the universe. He began from his own experience, from the lack of satisfaction and happiness according to the usual way of conceiving things. There is an existential need (given expression in *conatus*) for intellectual certainty. Spinoza concluded, as we have seen, that such certainty was only possible in union with the infinite perfection, with God. These fundamental conclusions were the same in both of these "God-intoxicated" men, at least in their understanding of the nature of God as undivided unity, of God as both free and necessary in God's actions, of God's ceaseless activity, and of the need to come to understand, be resigned to one's finiteness, and to realize the nature of the infinite unity in consciousness.

It would be unfair to "brand" Schleiermacher a Spinozist in the full sense of the word. He publically distanced himself from some of Spinoza's fundamental concepts, like substance with its attributes and modes. But it is the conclusion here that Schleiermacher's God and Spinoza's God are the same in some equally important aspects. That is, God is infinite, undivided unity. Schleiermacher, as Spinoza did, saw the 'ethical life' in our developing God-consciousness. This meant consciousness of God as this infinite unity, of ourselves as a part of that unity, of the inclusion of everything "outside" of oneself as a part of that infinite whole, and of our relation to them and to God. Certainly many questions remain. The question of the nature of the historical connection of Spinoza and Schleiermacher is important for determining any influence, direct or indirect, of Spinoza on Schleiermacher. And a question important for any discussion of Schleiermacher's theology is whether, in the face of his view of the infinite unity of God, Schleiermacher's Christian God can be maintained consistently or if this God must succumb to the substance of Spinoza.

Notes

1. Friedrich Schleiermacher, *On Religion. Speeches to Its Cultured Despisers*, trans. John Oman, 1831 Edition (N.Y.: Harper and Row, Harper Torchbooks/The Cloister Library, 1958), p. 40.
2. Ibid., note, p. 104.
3. Baruch Spinoza, *The Ethics*. This work was not published until after his death in 1677, in *Opera Posthuma*. *The Ethics and Selected Letters*, translated by Samuel Shirley and edited by Seymour Feldman (Indiana: Hackett Publishing Company, 1982), will be used throughout this essay when referring to Spinoza's Ethics.
4. Schleiermacher, *Speeches*.
In explanation #5 of the Second Speech Schleiermacher:
For understanding my whole view I could desire nothing better than that my reader should compare these Speeches with my "Christliche Glaubenslehre." In form they are very different and their points of departure lie far apart, yet in matter they are quite parallel. But to provide the Speeches for this purpose with a complete commentary was impossible, and I must content myself with single reference to such passages as seem to me capable of appearing contrary or at least of lacking agreement. (p. 105.)
The 1831 edition will be used throughout for the reasons noted above.
5. There is a debate as to whether Spinoza ever finished this work. The entire manuscript, if it ever existed, has never been found. Spinoza never published this work during his lifetime and only a partially completed manuscript has been found. This was first published in 1677 after Spinoza's death in *Opera Posthuma*. A. Wolf, in *Spinoza's Short Treatise on God, Man And His Well-Being* (New York: Russell & Russell Inc., 1963) discusses the history of the Spinoza's writings. See especially pp. lvi-lxi.
6. Benedict de Spinoza, *On the Improvement of the Understanding, The Ethics, Correspondence*, trans. R.H.M. Elwes (N.Y.: Dover Publications, Inc., 1955), p. 3 (hereafter cited according to the specific work: either *I.U.* or *Correspondence*).
7. Ibid., p. 6.
8. Ibid., p. 8.
9. Ibid., p. 11.
10. Ibid., p. 13.
11. Ibid., p. 14.
12. Ibid., pp. 14-15. Emphasis added.
13. And, it might be said, of immediate experience or apprehension. While this is not as clearly shown as in Schleiermacher, Spinoza does allude to such a stance. In the Scholium

to Pr. 23, V of the *Ethics*, Spinoza speaks of the mind "sensing" what it conceives and of the "feeling and experience of our eternity."

    14. *I.U.*, p. 15.
    15. Ibid., p. 15.
    16. Ibid., pp. 19, 29f.
    17. Ibid., p. 23
    18. Ibid., pp. 23-24.
    19. Ibid., p.27.
    20. Ibid., p. 34.
    21. Spinoza, *The Ethics*. See the foreword by Samuel Shirley for an introduction to various terms used by Spinoza. Especially page 29 on the meaning of thought (*cogitatio*)
    22. *I.U.*, p. 34.
    23. Ibid., p. 35.
    24. Ibid.
    25. Ibid., p. 36.
    26. Ibid.
    27. Spinoza, *The Ethics*, Def. 3, I.
    28. Ibid., Preface, V.
    29. Ibid., pr. 11, I.
    30. Ibid., Def. 5, I.
    31. Ibid. Pr. 1, I
    32. Ibid., Pr. 24, I.
    33. Ibid. Pr. 10, I
    34. Ibid., Schol., Pr. 10, I.
    35. Ibid., Pr. 11, I.
    36. Ibid., Pr. 7, I.
    37. Spinoza offers a second proof as well. Everything has a cause, either a cause for a thing to exist, or for its not existing, because God, as absolute infinite substance, involves existence (Pr. 7; Axiom 7, II). There can be no reason or cause which prevents God from existing. So if there were such a cause, it is either in the nature of God, or it is not. To be external it must exist in another nature. But then it could have no effect on the other nature (Pr. 2; Pr. 3, I); it could not cause it to exist or not exist. If it is internal to God's nature, and thus of the same nature, then it must grant that God exists. "Therefore God necessarily exists," concludes Spinoza (Second Proof, Pr. 11, I).

    Spinoza also includes an a posteriori proof for the sake of clarity. To exist means the power to exist. If only finite entities existed, then finite entities would have more power to exist than God, an absolutely infinite entity. But this is absurd. Hence, if anything exists, God necessarily exists (Axiom 1, Pr. 7, I).

    38. In the Scholium to Pr. 11, I, Spinoza equates perfection and reality. The more perfection or reality a thing has, the more power of existence. Since substance has no external cause, it owes whatever degree of perfection it has to itself. And an absolutely infinite cause has infinite perfection and therefore infinite power of existence. Absolute perfection excludes all imperfection, or non-reality, non-being. Therefore, perfection posits an existence of an absolutely infinite, and hence perfect, substance.

    The power of existence to which Spinoza refers has a curious resonance. If existence is defined merely as that which i̲s̲, that is, as a "flat" existence, there is no level of power of existence than that which anything has to exist just as it is at each moment that it is. Therefore, it is obvious that Spinoza does not view existence as merely flat in this way. The perfection of being may have been a common notion to Spinoza which meant that an increase in the power of that being was therefore an increase in its reality. Shirley, in his foreword, understands Spinoza to equate perfection with completeness of being. (p. 27, see #18 on reality). And it seems clear, once one has read through *The Ethics*, that, for Spinoza, the power of being, reality and of existence refer directly to a thing's relation to God. The goal of the 'ethical life' is to understand God; it is understanding the unity of the absolute infinite God; it is being conscious of oneself and all other things as modes of the infinite unity of God. In ethical terms, this is the highest goal (Pr. 28, IV).

39. Ibid., Prs. 6&7, III.

40. Friedrich Schleiermacher, *The Christian Faith*, Edited by H.R. Mackintosh and J.S. Stewart (Edinburgh: T. & T. Clark, 1986). Hereafter cited as *C.F.*

41. Spinoza, *The Ethics*, Scholium 2, Pr. 40, II. Spinoza writes that "This kind of knowledge proceeds from an adequate idea of the formal essence of certain attributes of God to an adequate knowledge of the essence of things."

42. Schleiermacher, *C.F.*, §3.

43. Schleiermacher views life as an alternation between an abiding-in-self (*ein Insichbleiben*) and a passing-beyond-self (*ein Aussichheraustreten*) *C.F.*, §3.3). Knowing and feeling constitute an abiding-in-self as two forms of consciousness. Doing is a passing-beyond-self. This seems to suggest an antithesis between Knowing, Feeling, and Doing. But Knowing is a abiding-in-self in the sense of possessing knowledge. However, as an <u>act</u> of knowing, if it is to become real, it is a passing-beyond-self. In this sense then it is a Doing (*C.F.*, §3.3). Feeling, on the other hand, is entirely an abiding-in-self. This is a result of stimulation but also "even as the process of being stimulated it is not effected by the subject, but simply takes place in the subject and, thus, since it belongs altogether to the realm of receptivity, it is entirely an abiding-in-self (*C.F.*, §3.3)." And in this sense it is an antithesis to Knowing and Doing.

Piety, however, is in no way excluded from all connection with Knowing and Doing. As immediate self-consciousness it is always "the mediating link in the transition between moments in which Knowing predominates and those in which Doing predominates (*C.F.*, §3.4)." Piety stimulates Knowing and Doing. And when Piety predominates (in consciousness) it will always contain one or both in germ.

To look at it another way, if Piety consisted of knowing then it would have to have in its essence the entire knowledge of the Dogmatics of the Christian religion (dogmatics being the knowledge of faith) (*C.F.*, §3.4). And it will do no good to argue that it is not knowledge itself but the strength of the conviction of one's certainty that is the true measure of Piety (i.e., faith as fidelity to one's convictions). This is because all other knowledge is based on clarity measured by an amount, a completeness, of thinking. Rather the proper way to relate the knowledge which forms Dogmatics to Piety is to see that Piety is the object of this knowledge, and this knowledge is only explicated in virtue of a certainty "which inheres in the determination of self-consciousness (*C.F.*, §3.4).

What would be the consequence of Piety as Doing? The Doing that constitutes Piety could not be defined as its content, because both the most worthy and the completely unworthy things are done out of Piety. There <u>are</u> two *termini* of doing, says Schleiermacher – motive and goal. One cannot measure the Piety of an action merely by the completeness of the intended result. But if we include the motive of an action we are led back to a certain determination (i.e., as pleasure or pain) of the self-consciousness. So it is the feeling which has become affective and passed over into action which is the measure of Piety. Knowing and Doing "only pertain to it [Piety] inasmuch as the stirred-up Feeling sometimes comes to rest in a thinking which fixes it, sometimes discharges itself in an action which express it (*C.F.*, §3.4)."

Piety, then, is the state in which Knowing, Doing, and Feeling are combined. There is no subordination, but each remains essentially what it is. Though Feeling is subsequently caught up in thinking it is only so far as each one is inclined toward thinking. In the same way this inner piety emerges in a living moment – an action. Therefore, Feeling is not confused or inactive, but is at the root of every expression of our wills "and can be grasped by thought and conceived of in its own nature (*C.F.*, §3.5)."

44. Ibid., §4.
45. Ibid., §4.1.
46. Ibid.
47. Ibid.
48. Ibid.
49. Ibid.
50. Ibid.
51. Ibid., §4.2.
52. Ibid.
53. Ibid. Only God, as we shall see, is without influence from something outside. But this does not mean God is free to do anything. Even (and perhaps most especially) God acts as God must.
54. Ibid.
55. Ibid.
56. Ibid., §4.3.
57. Ibid.
58. Ibid. Schleiermacher's anthropology posits three levels of human consciousness. The first and lowest grade is the animal, in which there is no antithesis as consciousness remains confused. The middle grade is sensible self-consciousness which rests entirely upon the antithesis of consciousness. The highest grade is the feeling of sheer dependence in which again, as in the lowest grade, there is no antithesis, but here the subject unites and identifies itself with everything (C.F., §5.1). But is there perhaps another kind of self-consciousness which is not immediate but which overcomes the antithesis? If such a self-consciousness associated with Knowing existed it would be a highest knowledge, that is, objective consciousness. But objective consciousness is accompanied by a consciousness of conviction. Conviction, however, concerns a relationship of subject as knower and the object as known and therefore remains in the realm of antithesis. If it is associated with Doing it would be a highest kind of action, a resolve covering the whole field of spontaneous activity so that all subsequent resolves are born out of it. This self-consciousness also concerns the relation of the agent to the subject of its action, and thus the antithesis remains (C.F., §5.2).

What is the exact relation of these grades of consciousness to one another regarding religious feeling? The lowest animal grade gradually disappears as the sensible self-consciousness develops. And, in fact, the animal grade cannot remain at all when the feeling of utter dependence is present. But sensible self-consciousness must remain undiminished with the highest grade.

> It is impossible for anyone to be in some moments exclusively conscious of his relations within the realm of the antithesis, and in other moments of his absolute dependence in itself and in a general way; for it is as a person determined for this moment in a particular manner within the realm of the antithesis that he is conscious of his absolute dependence (C.F., §5.3).

The middle stage is necessary to provide the definiteness and clearness of the sensible self-consciousness. Schleiermacher writes:

> Described from above it is as follows: the tendency which we have described, as an original and innate tendency of the human soul, strives from the very beginning to break through into consciousness. But it is unable to do so as long as the antithesis remains dissolved in the animal confusion. Subsequently, however, it asserts itself. And the more it contributes to every moment of sensibly determined self-consciousness without the omission of any so that the man, while he always feels himself partially free and partially dependent in relation to other finite existence, feels himself at the same time

to be also (along with everything toward which he had that former feeling) absolutely dependent – the more religious is he (*C.F.*, §5.3).

59. Ibid., §5.4.

60. Ibid., §4.4.

61. Ibid.

62. In the explanations to the second speech in the 1831 edition of the *Speeches*, p. 115, Schleiermacher denies outright any materialist pantheism:
For myself I am supposed to prefer the impersonal form of thinking of the Highest Being, and this has been called now my atheism and again my Spinozism . . . But none who reflect on the little that is said about pantheism will suspect me of any materialistic pantheism. And if any one look at it rightly, he will find, on the one side, every one might recognize it as an absolute necessity for the highest stage of piety to acquire a concept of a personal God, and on the other he will recognize the essential imperfection in the conception of a personality of the Highest Being, nay how hazardous it is, if it is not most carefully kept pure . . . As it is so difficult to think of a personality as truly infinite and incapable of suffering, a great distinction should be drawn between a personal God and a living God. The latter idea alone distinguishes from materialistic pantheism and atheistic blind necessity. (pp. 115-116)

63. *Speeches*, p. 36.

64. Ibid.

65. Ibid.

66. Ibid.

67. Ibid., pp. 38-39.

68. Ibid., pp. 103-104, Second Speech, explanation #2.

69. Ibid., p. 106, explanation #5.

70. Ibid., p. 71.

71. Robert B. Williams, *Schleiermacher the Theologian* (Philadelphia: Fortress Press, 1978).

72. Ibid., p. 4.

73. Ibid., p. 4.

74. *Speeches*, p. 50. And in another explicit presentation, Schleiermacher writes: We do not feel ourselves dependent on the whole in so far as it is an aggregate of mutually conditioned parts of which we ourselves are one, but only in so far as underneath this coherence there is our relations to the other parts of the whole. Only on this condition can the single thing be as it is here put, as exhibition of the Infinite, being so comprehended that its opposition to all else entirely vanishes (*Speeches*, p. 106, Second Speech, explanation #5).

75. Spinoza, *I.U.*, pp. 36-37.

76. *C.F.*, §41, Postscript.

77. Williams, *Schleiermacher the Theologian*, p. 97, citings *C.F.*, §54.4.

78. Ibid., p. 97.

79. Schleiermacher, *C.F.*, §42, Postscript.

80. Ibid., §54.4.

81. Spinoza, *The Ethics*, Pr. 17, I.

82. Ibid., Cor. 2, Pr. 17. Emphasis added.

83. Ibid., Pr. 29, I.

84. Ibid., Proof, Pr. 32, I.

85. Ibid., Schol., Pr. 33, I.

86. Ibid., Schol. 2, Pr. 33, I.

87. Schleiermacher, *C.F.*, §54.4.

88. Ibid.

89. Spinoza, *The Ethics*, Schol. 2, Pr. 33, I. The indeterminate God is that which depends on nothing else for its own sufficiency. Determinateness and indeterminateness do not necessarily have the same connotation as dependence, of which Schleiermacher speaks. But dependence is implied here, and Spinoza speaks of our dependence on God when addressing the question of being and our actions as necessarily following from God:

> If by your Intellect only you had perceived what dependence on God means, you certainly would not think that things, in so far as they depend on God, are dead, corporeal, and Imperfect, . . . on the contrary, you would understand that for the very reason that they depend on God they are perfect, so that dependence and necessary operation may best be understood as God's decree, by considering, not sticks and plant, but the most reasonable and perfect creations [*Correspondence*, Letter to Blyenbergh, #XXXIV (XXI), Jan. 28, 1665, p. 342].

90. Schleiermacher, *C.F.*, §54.4. Emphasis added. Also in Schleiermacher's "Lectures on the Dialectics," 1811-1831 [*Dialektik*, ed. I. Halpern (Berlin: Mayer and Müller, 1903), pp. 197-98], Schleiermacher writes:

> Free and necessary are not mutually contradictory . . . Indeed, one can say that freedom and necessity are each the measure of the other. The freedom of something is that thing entire, and the necessity of something is also that thing entire, only regarded from another side. Everything is thus the image of the whole, only in various measures . . . Choice itself is in fact a product of the meeting of the person with all that is outward.

Cited in Albert Blackwell, *Schleiermacher's Early Philosophy of Life: Determinism, Freedom and Phantasy* (Chico, Calif.: Scholars Press, 1982), p. 74. See also *C.F.*, §164.3; §165.

91. Correspondence, Letter #XXIII (LXXV), p. 301. Emphasis added.

92. Friedrich Schleiermacher, *Psychologie*, ed. L. George, in *Sämmtliche Werke*, III/6 (Berlin: George Reimer, 1862.), pp. 243-61. Cited in Blackwell, *Schleiermacher's Early Philosophy of Life*, p. 84, note #14. And in the *Speeches* Schleiermacher writes:

> The human soul, as is shown by its passing action and its inward characteristics, has its existence chiefly in two opposing impulses. Following the one impulse, it strives to establish itself as an individual. For increase . . . it draws what surrounds it to itself, weaving it into its life, and absorbing it into its own being. The other impulse . . . is the longing to surrender oneself and be absorbed in a greater, to be taken hold of and determined (p. 4).

93. Friedrich Schleiermacher, *Über den Unterschied zwischen Naturgesetz und Sittengesetz*, in *Schleiermacher's Werke*, ed. Otto Braun and D. Joh. Bauer (Leipzig: Felix Meiner, 1910), p. 416. I have utilized the terms' english translation provided by Blackwell, p. 84.

94. Blackwell, *Schleiermacher's Early Philosophy of Life*, p. 85. Blackwell's citation from "Über die Freiheit des Menschen" 73; manuscript in *Schleiermacher Nachlaß #133*. Also abridged in Dilthey's *Leben Schleiermachers*, 1st edition (Berlin: Georg Reimer, 1870), "Denkmale," 19-46.

95. Spinoza, *The Ethics*, Pr. 6, V.

96. Ibid., Prs. 6&7, IV.

97. Schleiermacher, *The Speeches*, p. 48.

98. Ibid. P. 59

99. Spinoza, *The Ethics*, Schol. Pr. 10, V.

100. Ibid., Pr. 15, V.

101. Ibid., Cor., Prs. 32 & 33, V.

102. Williams, *Schleiermacher the Theologian*, p. 26. Citing Schleiermacher in *The Christian Faith*, §3.2, note. Schleiermacher was citing Steffens in *Von der falsche Theologie und den Wahren Glauben* (Breslau, 1823).

103. Schleiermacher wrote in a note at the end of §3.2 of *The Christian Faith*:
On the other hand, the account given by Baumgarten-Crusius (*Einleitung in das Studium der Dogmatik*, p. 56), apart from its antithesis between feeling and self-consciousness, (a) does not comprehend the whole, but only the higher regions, of feeling, and (b) seems to transfer feeling into the realm of the objective consciousness by using the word 'perception' (*Wahrnehmung*).

104. Williams, *Schleiermacher the Theologian*, p. 30.

105. Ibid.

106. The issue of pantheism per se is not central to this article. However, it is true that Spinoza and Schleiermacher adhered to a kind of rudimentary or basic pantheism, if this is defined as Alasdair MacIntyre does in his article on pantheism in *The Encyclopedia of Philosophy*. MacIntyre denotes two basic assertions of pantheism: that everything that exists constitutes a unity; and that this all-inclusive unity is divine. [Alasdair MacIntyre, "Pantheism," in *The Encyclopedia of Philosophy*, Vol. Six. Editor-in-chief, Paul Edwards. (New York: MacMillan Publishing Co. Inc. & The Free Press, 1972), pp. 31-35.] Both Spinoza and Schleiermacher professed this belief. The problem with such labels is that they do not do justice to the important subtleties in Spinoza's rationalist philosophy or Schleiermacher's Christian theology. Both men took the nature of that which is called infinite seriously and felt bound to conclude that there is nothing that can be absolutely outside that which is infinite. Pantheism, at least when applied to Spinoza and Schleiermacher, does not mean that everything is God, or is <u>identified</u> with God, or is "a piece" of God. Neither did they assert that something could not be distinguished from God. They did not believe, however, that anything could be separated, i.e., be alongside of God in the same sense as finite things were alongside one another.

Panentheism (the view that all reality is part of the being of God) as distinguished from pantheism (which identifies God with all of reality) can also be applied it seems. But it does little to help clarify how we might "classify" the God of Spinoza and the God of Schleiermacher. The fact that both of these terms may be applied only underscores the danger of such a classification. But again, that is not the purpose here. What is being attempted is to present some of the fundamental and essential concepts that form the respective understandings of God of these two great thinkers. And consequently, to consider the relation of this God to human beings and the universe in which we live. Certainly, the question of pantheism is important for any study of Schleiermacher's dogmatic statement on Christianity in the *Christian Faith*. But the judgment on the consequences of Schleiermacher's view of God, insofar as it is in accord with that of Spinoza's, must be left to others.

107. See *The Ethics*, Scholium, Pr. 15, I; and Spinoza's 1663 Letter #12, "On the Nature of the Infinite" to Ludwig Meyer, for a full discussion of the false and proper understandings of the nature of the infinite. "Imagination" for Spinoza means something quite different than it does for Schleiermacher. For Schleiermacher it is the tool by which reality is intuited. For Spinoza, however, the *imago* (image) is an affection of the body. It is knowledge of the 'first kind.' (Sch. 2, pr. 40, II) See also Samuel Shirley's foreword in *The Ethics*, page 27, definition #20.

108. *The Ethics*, Pr, 24, I.

109. Schleiermacher, *C.F.*, §14.1.

110. Ibid.

111. Ibid. §92.3. But Schleiermacher certainly does not deny the possibility of divinity to human beings. He writes:

For in the first place: as certainly as Christ was a man, there must reside in human nature the possibility of taking up the divine into itself, just as did happen in Christ. So that the Idea that the divine revelation in Christ must in this respect be something absolutely supernatural will simply not stand the test . . . But secondly: even if only the possibility of this resides in human nature, so that the actual implanting therein of the divine element must be purely a divine and therefore an eternal act, nevertheless the temporal appearance of this act in one particular Person must at the same time be regarded as an action of human nature, grounded in its original constitution and prepared for by all its past history, and accordingly as the highest development of its spiritual power. . . . (§13.1)

Can this be akin to Spinoza's causal nexus? Christ's divinity is a "supra-rational" but not a "supernatural" event (§13.2).

112. Blackwell, *Schleiermacher's Early Philosophy of Life*, p. 54.

113. Friedrich Schleiermacher, "Letter to Charlotte Pistorius, July 28, 1804," *Aus Schleiermachers Leben. In Briefen*, Vol. I (Berlin: Georg Reimer), p. 401. Cited in Blackwell, p. 256. Charlotte Pistorius and Schleiermacher had become friends shortly before this letter was written.

114. Friedrich Schleiermacher, "On the Worth of Life," in Dilthey, *Leben Schleiermachers*, 1st ed., "Denkmale," p. 63. Also in Friedrich Schleiermacher, "Über den Wert des Lebens," *Jugendschriften 1787-1796*, ed. Günter Meckenstock, Kritische Gesamtausgabe I/1, ed. Hans-Joachim Birkner et al. (Berlin/New York: Walter de Gruyter, 1984), pp. 391-471. Cited in Blackwell, p. 267.

115. Blackwell, *Schleiermacher's Early Philosophy of Life*, p. 53.

116. Spinoza, *The Ethics*, Appendix #32, IV.

117. Schleiermacher, *C.F.*, §8, Postscript 2.

118. Schleiermacher, *Speeches*, p. 40.

119. Ibid.

120. Ibid.

121. Ibid., p. 104.

122. Ibid.

123. Friedrich Daniel Ernst Schleiermacher, "Über seine *Glaubenslehre* an Herrn Dr. Lücke, zwei Sendschreiben," *Theologische Studien und Kritiken* 2 (1829): 255-84 (first letter) and 481-532 (second letter). Cited in *On the Glaubenslehre*, trans. James Duke and Francis Fiorenza (N.Y.: Scholars Press, 1981), "First Letter to Lücke," pp. 50-51.

124. Schleiermacher, *C.F.*, §§91ff. Still, the concept of fellowship is not foreign to Spinoza. At least this is the suggestion in a letter in January 1665 that he wrote to Blyenbergh:

So far as in me lies, I value, above all other things out of my own control, the joining of friendship with men who are sincere lovers of truth. I believe that nothing in the world, of things outside our own control, brings more peace than the possibility of affectionate intercourse with such men; it is just as impossible that the love we bear them can be disturbed (inasmuch as it is founded on the desire each feels for the knowledge of truth), as that truth once perceived should not be assented to. It is, moreover, the highest and most pleasing source of happiness derivable from things not under our control. Nothing save truth has power closely to unite different feelings and dispositions (*Correspondence*, Letter XXXII (XIX), p. 331).

This is quite a tribute to the value of friendship. Still, Spinoza obviously views friendship as something essentially out of our control. And control, and this means certainty, seems to remain the over-arching directive of the development of human consciousness, of the truth of the mind. See also *The Ethics*, 40, IV; Appendix, #9-12.

125. Ibid., §113.1.
126. Ibid., §41.1.
127. Ibid, §41.2.
128. Ibid.
129. Spinoza. *The Ethics*, Pr. 15, I.
130. *Speeches*, p. 104. James Duke and Francis Fiorenza, in *On the Glaubenslehre*, p. 49, note #85, point to the Appendix to *Über das Ansehen der heiligen Schrift und ihr Verhältnis zur Glaubensregel in der protestantischen und in der alten Kirche, Drei theologische Sendschreiben an Herrn Professor D. Delbruck in Beziehung auf dessen Streitschrift: "Philip Melanchthon, der Glauhenslehrer," von D. K. H. Sack, D. C. J. Nitsch, und D. Fr. Locke, Nebst einer brieflichen Zugabe des Herrn D. Schleiermacher über die ihn betreffen Stellen der Streitschrift* (Bonn: Eduard Weber, 1827) in which Schleiermacher offers several ideas which have no parallels in his own thought. Such ideas include the relation between mind and body, between object and motion, and the idea of the selfless love of God.

XIX

RESONANZ: DIE REAKTION EVANGELISCHER THEOLOGEN AUF DEN SPINOZASTREIT AM BEISPIEL JOHANN CHRISTOPH DÖDERLEINS UND CARL FRIEDRICH BAHRDTS

Rüdiger Otto

Unter den Vorwürfen, die Schleiermachers Gönner, der Hofprediger Friedrich Samuel Gottfried Sack, dem Verfasser der "Reden über die Religion" nicht ersparen zu können glaubte, kommt dem, seine Religionsschrift sei eine Apologie des Pantheismus und Spinozismus[1], das größte Gewicht zu. Schleiermacher bestritt das Recht der Behauptung Sacks[2] und eröffnete damit die andauernde Diskussion über die Stichhaltigkeit dieser Identifizierung. Verwunderlich an Sacks Worten ist aber zunächst einmal die Tatsache, daß Sack den Begriff des Spinozismus überhaupt pauschal und ohne jeden Vorbehalt als Synonym für Unchristlichkeit und Irreligiosität gebrauchen konnte. Dies entsprach zwar einer Tradition, die nach Spinozas Tod im Jahre 1677 mehr als ein Jahrhundert lang nahezu unbezweifelt im Gebrauch gewesen war, aber spätestens nachdem im Jahre 1785 Friedrich Heinrich Jacobi durch die Veröffentlichung seines Buches "Über die Lehre des Spinoza, in Briefen an den Herrn Moses Mendelssohn" mit Bezug auf Spinozas System einen Grundsatzstreit über die Begründung von Religion und Gotteserkenntnis angezettelt hatte, war die Einhelligkeit, mit der Spinoza als Prototyp des neuzeitlichen theoretischen Atheisten angesehen wurde, gestört. Für Jacobi und seinen Sekundanten Thomas Wizenmann blieb Spinozas "Ethik" freilich das atheistische System par excellence. Aber sie betrachteten dessen Atheismus als notwendige Folge des zugrundeliegenden Rationalismus und behaupteten, daß jeglicher Vernunftgebrauch in Religionsdingen unausweichlich auf einen als Atheismus apostrophierten Spinozismus führen muß[3]. Damit erstreckte sich die Beschuldigung des Atheismus auf Leibniz und Wolff genauso wie auf deren noch lebende Anhänger, d. h. auf nahezu alle zeitgenössischen Philosophen und Theologen, soweit sie sich als "denkende Gottesverehrer" begriffen. Die Ausweitung dieses Atheismusverdikts unter Jacobis Prämissen mußte mit der Frage nach seinem Recht auch das Nachdenken darüber provozieren, ob die geläufige Gleichsetzung von Atheismus und Spinozismus nicht einer Revision bedarf.

Im Verlauf des Streites mehrten sich die Stimmen, die von verschiedenen Ausgangspunkten aus Spinozismus und Religion, Spinozismus und Christentum für vereinbar hielten. Neben dem hannöverschen Geheimen Kanzleisekretär August Wilhelm Rehberg[4] und dem Leipziger Philosophen Karl Heinrich Heydenreich[5] sprach sich Moses Mendelssohn in diesem Sinne aus. In der Spinoza betreffenden Passage seines letzten großen Werks "Morgenstunden oder Vorlesungen über das Dasein Gottes" versuchte Mendelssohn, die Differenz zwischen Spinozas Gottesbegriff und dem der Wolffschen Schule zu überwinden und einen "geläuterten Spinozismus" zu gewinnen, der mit Religion und Moral vereinbar ist[6].

Weitaus entschiedener als alle anderen öffentlichen Beiträge zum Streit warb Johann Gottfried Herders 1787 erschienene Schrift "Gott" für die Rehabilitierung Spinozas. Herder trug kein Bedenken, den spinozischen Immanenzgedanken als angemessene zeitgenössische Ausdrucksweise der Idee, daß Gott Wurzel und Fülle des Daseins sei, zu empfehlen und Spinoza in eine Reihe mit Christus, Aposteln und Propheten zu stellen[7].

Soweit mir bekannt ist, gab es keine öffentliche Wortmeldung, die über Herders Adaption Spinozas das gleiche Anathema verhängt hätte, das bis zu diesem Zeitpunkt dem jüdischen Philosophen galt. Es lassen sich im Gegenteil Stimmen wie die des seinerzeit weit berühmten Leipziger Mediziners und Philosophen Ernst Platner ausmachen, der sich aufgrund der Darstellung Herders bewogen fühlte, sein langgehegtes Urteil über Spinozas Philosophie einer Revision zu unterziehen[8].

Vor diesem Hintergrund wirkt, zumal um 1800 Herders "Gott" erneut aufgelegt wurde, die Selbstverständlichkeit, mit der der Name Spinoza von

Sack als Abbreviatur für eine gegenchristliche Denkart verwendet wurde, zumindest erstaunlich.

Das Mißverhältnis zwischen der vorherrschenden Ansicht, die seit 1785 einen fundamentalen Wandel in der Einstellung der öffentlichen Meinung gegenüber Spinoza registriert, und der unbeirrten Ablehnung, die aus den Worten des naturwissenschaftlich und literarisch – ästhetisch interessierten[9] Oberhofpredigers Sack spricht, bedarf einer Erklärung. Sollte sie darin liegen, daß Sack die letzten anderthalb Jahrzehnte philosophisch-literarischer Entwicklung verschlafen hat? Wohl kaum. Ehe man ihn als Außenseiter betrachtet, müßte überprüft werden, ob die Position der die Umwertung Spinozas betreibenden Intellektuellen überhaupt repräsentativ ist. Das erfordert, den Blick auf den Prozeß um Spinoza von der Begrenzung auf die geistige Elite erster Ordnung zu lösen und die Breite und Vielgestaltigkeit möglicher Reaktionen zur Kenntnis zu nehmen. Es könnte sein, daß sich dann die Konturen einer Traditionslinie abzeichneten, die in der früheren Spinozainterpretation wurzelt und der auch Sack zugehörig wäre. In diesem Falle träte auch die Kühnheit, die trotz der Aktualisierung Spinozas in den achtziger Jahren Schleiermachers Einbeziehung Spinozas in den "Reden" innewohnte, deutlicher ins Licht.

Zu dahingehenden Vermutungen berechtigen jedenfalls die Reaktionen, die der Spinozastreit bei den beiden Theologen Döderlein und Bahrdt gefunden hat. Ob sie signifikant sind, läßt sich solange nicht entscheiden, wie eine Untersuchung auf breiter Materialbasis fehlt. Immerhin sprechen die Zeugnisse, die auf die Bedeutung der hier dargestellten Aufklärungstheologen hinweisen sollen, für eine gewisse Aufmerksamkeit für ihr Werk und vielleicht auch dafür, daß sie den Vorstellungen einer bestimmten Schicht des Lesepublikums Ausdruck verliehen haben.

Johann Christoph Döderlein, geboren 1746, war von 1782 bis zu seinem Tod 1792 Professor der Theologie in Jena. Daß er sich selbst als den bedeutendsten Theologen seiner Zeit ansah[10], spricht für sein Selbstgefühl, sagt aber wenig über seine tatsächliche Bedeutung aus. Auf diese weist dagegen der Titel eines "Melanchthon seiner Zeit"[11], der Döderlein angehängt wurde. Der renommierte Aufklärungs-Kirchenhistoriker Ludwig

Timotheus Spittler glaubte der christlichen Religion eine bessere Zukunft in Aussicht stellen zu dürfen, weil die künftige Theologengeneration von ausgezeichneten Lehrern und ihren Schriften ausgebildet werde. Neben Spalding und Herder nannte er Döderlein[12].

Döderleins Dogmatik "Institutio theologi christiani", 1780 zum erstenmal erschienen, erlebte bis 1797 6 Auflagen und wurde dadurch zu einem der verbreitetsten dogmatischen Lehrbücher der Zeit[13]. Für ihr Ansehen spricht auch die Notwendigkeit einer deutschen Ausgabe [14]. Diese wurde veranlaßt durch den "Wunsch mehrerer aufgeklärter Christen, auch außer der Klasse der Theologen, ein Buch näher kennen zu lernen, welches zwar nicht durch neue und sonderbare Behauptungen, aber doch durch den Beifall des Publikums Aufmerksamkeit erregt hat, und den Bedürfnissen unserer Zeiten angemessen zu sein schien"[15]. Döderleins deutsche Dogmatik basiert auf dem lateinischen Werk, ist aber wesentlich umfangreicher als dieses. Im Band 4 des "Christlichen Religionsunterrichtes nach den Bedürfnissen unserer Zeit" geht Döderlein im Rahmen der Gotteslehre auch auf die neueste Diskussion über den Spinozismus ein. Zur Hinführung sind einige Bemerkungen zum theologischen Standort und zur Heuristik Döderleins unumgänglich, zumal dadurch veranschaulicht werden kann, auf welche Voraussetzungen die Beiträge zum Spinozismus treffen. Der Neologe Döderlein entfaltet sein System in einer doppelten Frontstellung. Nach der einen Seite grenzt er sich gegen alle Gestaltungen dogmatischer Aussagen, die aufgeklärter Rationalität nicht standhalten können, ab, nach der anderen Seite distanziert er sich von jenem Vernunftgebrauch, der jede Form religiöser Wirklichkeitserklärung überhaupt ablehnt. Seiner Einschätzung nach bedingen sich Orthodoxie und Atheismus wechselweise, denn der Verzicht auf vernünftige Prüfung und die Forderung des Glaubensgehorsams bedeuten eine Ausgrenzung der Ansprüche der Vernunft, die die Vernunft geradezu dazu verurteilt, sich in Antithese zur Religion zu entwickeln[16]. Dem vernunftlosen Glauben hinwiederum bleibt vor den Attacken einer aggressiven Ratio nur der Rückzug in das unvermittelte Bekennen[17]. Gelegentlich kann Döderlein orthodoxe Systembildung und philosophischen Atheismus als die zwei Verirrungen der Vernunft in subtilen Scholastizismus und krankhafte Zweifelsucht bezeichnen[18], denen gegenüber er die

Orientierung an der gesunden Vernunft als goldenen Mittelweg in Erinnerung bringt[19].

Der durch ihren Gebrauch entwickelte Sinn für Mäßigung und Toleranz leitet Döderlein auch bei der Niederschrift des "Christlichen Religionsunterrichts". Er räumt der Explikation fremder Auffassungen viel Platz ein. Bisweilen ist hinter dogmengeschichtlichen Exkursen und der Schilderung möglicher Positionen seine eigene Auffassung nicht mehr erkennbar. Der Darstellung atheistischer Weltentstehungstheorien setzt er keine polemische Argumentation entgegen, sondern begnügt sich mit dem Hinweis, daß auch andere Erklärungen möglich sind[20]. Seine eigene Theorie entsteht nicht aus der argumentativen Überwindung alternativer Positionen, sondern empfiehlt sich vor anderen dadurch, daß sie Übereinstimmung mit der gesunden Vernunft, der Offenbarung und den Bedürfnissen des Herzens für sich reklamiert.

Karl Aner hat in seinem Buch über die "Theologie der Lessingzeit" zur Charakterisierung der Neologie die Faustformel Offenbarungsbegriff minus Offenbarungsinhalt zur Verfügung gestellt[21]. An Döderleins Werk ließe sich dies gut illustrieren. Döderlein sieht in der Vermittlung von Informationen Gottes über sich selbst den unbestreitbaren Vorzug der Offenbarungsreligion gegenüber jeder Form natürlicher Theologie[22]. Die Bestimmung darüber, was als Offenbarung gelten darf, obliegt freilich der Vernunft[23]. Auf diesem Wege wird von der Offenbarung Gottes ausgeschlossen und zum menschlichen Zusatz der Offenbarungsurkunden erklärt, was "mit den evidenten Lehren von Gottes Eigenschaften, mit der Natur des Menschen, mit seiner Bestimmung, und den unveränderlichen Gesetzen der Moralität nicht bestehen könnte"[24]. Dazu gehören u. a. Trinitätslehre, Zweinaturenlehre und die Vorstellung vom gekreuzigten Gott[25]. Die Rechte der Vernunft in Offenbarungsangelegenheiten werden theologisch mit der Einheit Gottes begründet, der als Urheber von Vernunft und Offenbarung einen Widerspruch zwischen beiden ausschließt[26].

Aus dieser Prioritätensetzung entsteht zunächst der Eindruck, daß der Offenbarungsbegriff innerhalb dieses Systems funktionslos und nichts als ein Überbleibsel der theologischen Tradition sei. Bei näherem Hinsehen erweist sich dieser Eindruck jedoch als falsch.

Döderlein hat ein eigenständiges Interesse daran, neben der Würde der Vernunft auch immer wieder ihre Schwäche, namentlich zur Erkenntnis metaphysischer Wahrheiten, zur Geltung zu bringen[27]. Daß selbst die höchsten Autoritäten des aufgeklärten Jahrhunderts: Rousseau und Voltaire, Bayle, Hume und Reimarus nicht übereinkommen können, wieweit die Zuständigkeit der Vernunft zur Erkenntnis der Wirklichkeit im allgemeinen und des höchsten Wesens im besonderen reicht, dient Döderlein als Beweis dafür, daß die Vernunft allein nicht imstande ist, auf diesem Felde eine Entscheidung herbeizuführen[28]. An diesem Punkt kommt der – durch Döderleins Vernunftbegriff gefilterten – Offenbarung wieder eine unverhoffte Entscheidungskompetenz zu. Sie wird, wo die in sich selbst uneinige Vernunft ihre Hilfe versagt, neben dem praktischen Interesse[29] und den Herzensbedürfnissen des Menschen[30] zur maßgeblichen Urteilsinstanz für die religiösen Angelegenheiten.

Mit dieser Verlagerung der Letztbegründung religiöser Wahrheit von der Vernunft zu Offenbarung und Praxis hat sich Döderlein das Recht zum Désengagement in bezug auf spekulative Erörterungen gesichert, und zugleich kann er insinuieren, wer hier mehr zu wissen vorgebe, verrate eher seinen intellektuellen Hochmut, als daß er zur Erkenntnis beitrage.

Das damit bereitstehende Instrumentarium – rational orientierter Offenbarungsbegriff, Gemeinverständlichkeit, praktische Ausrichtung, Nichtwissen in spekulativen Gedankenbewegungen, gestützt durch die Vielfalt möglicher Auffassungen – bietet Döderlein eine Handhabe auch zur Bewältigung der durch den Spinozastreit aufgeworfenen Fragen.

Döderlein kommt gleich zu Beginn der Gotteslehre im 4. Band des "Christlichen Religionsunterrichtes", der 1787 erschien, auf den spinozistischen Gottesbegriff zu sprechen[31]. Es ist augenscheinlich, daß er durch den aktuellen Streit um Spinoza zu dieser Auseinandersetzung veranlaßt worden ist, denn in der lateinischen Institutio von 1780 wird das Thema Spinoza nur beiläufig erwähnt[32]. Gleichwohl vermeidet er es, die Diskussion dort aufzunehmen, wohin sie durch die Argumentation der Kontrahenten geführt worden war.

In diesem Falle wäre er genötigt gewesen, seine Auffassung in einer Problemkonstellation zu entfalten, die eben erst aus dem Ungenügen an der von ihm festgehaltenen Denkweise entstanden war und zur Favorisierung des Spinozismus geführt hatte. Die Schwierigkeit des Unterfangens, auf eine aktuelle Debatte Bezug zu nehmen und sie dennoch zu unterlaufen, meistert Döderlein dadurch, daß er die Einwände, die im Laufe des gesamten Jahrhunderts gegen Spinoza vorgebracht wurden, Revue passieren läßt.

Zunächst greift er ins Arsenal der Argumente zurück, die Pierre Bayle an der Wende zum 18. Jahrhundert in seinem "Historischen und Kritischen Wörterbuch" gegen Spinoza vorgebracht hatte[33]. In dem Spinoza-Artikel dieses Wörterbuchs, der zur einflußreichsten Quelle der Kenntnis und der Widerlegung Spinozas im 18. Jahrhundert wurde, empört sich Bayle über die Absurdität des spinozischen immanenten Gottesbegriffes. Mit Bayle stößt sich auch Döderlein am Begriff einer Gottheit, die, da sie nicht extramundan konzipiert ist, in ganzem Umfang teilhat an der weltlich-vergänglichen, affektbeherrschten Wirklichkeitssphäre[34].

Auch die moralischen Einwände älterer Herkunft gegen den Spinozismus werden von ihm wiederholt. Sie entzünden sich am Immanentismus und Determinismus des Systems. Die Gleichung *Deus sive natura* impliziert in dieser Lesart eine Vergottung der Gesamtwirklichkeit. Damit aber läßt sich jedes Laster und jedes Verbrechen wegen seiner Teilhabe an der Gottnatur von vornherein entschuldigen[35].

Überdies ist der Mensch deswegen von jeder Verantwortlichkeit entbunden, weil er im spinozischen Kausalsystem die Freiheit der Wahl abgesprochen bekommt und sein Tun ohnehin nicht selbst steuern kann[36].

Auf der einen Seite übernimmt Döderlein Christian Wolffs auslegungsgeschichtliche wichtige Feststellung, daß Spinoza entgegen der landläufigen Auffassung Gott und Natur unterschieden habe[37]. Auf der anderen Seite fragt er, ob es nicht ein größeres Rätsel sei, das Denken als Resultat einer verstandeslosen Materie anzusehen, als eine durch einen Geist hervorgebrachte Materie anzunehmen, womit Spinoza die Identifizierung von Substanz und Materie unterstellt ist[38].

Nachdem Döderlein die Liste der Mängel des Systems vervollständigt und zu dem Eindruck verdichtet hat, diese Gedanken können keinem geordneten Kopf entsprungen sein, stellt er die erstaunte Frage, wie ein solcher Gottesbegriff dennoch Anhänger finden konnte. Er findet darin eine

Antwort, daß die "Losung der Pantheisten", "Eins ist alles", das "Gepräge des Tiefsinns" trägt und dadurch das Bedürfnis einer fragwürdigen Elite befriedigt, sich vom gemeinen Volk zu unterscheiden[39].

Die aufgezählten Widersprüche wertet Döderlein als Indiz für die Unverständlichkeit des Systems. Mit dieser Bilanz begibt er sich in die Arena, in der seine Zeitgenossen um das richtige Verständnis Spinozas ringen. Ohne sich auf die Intention der gegensätzlichen Interpretationen Spinozas einzulassen, nimmt er lediglich die Tatsache der Kontroverse selbst als schlagenden Beweis für die Richtigkeit seiner Behauptung über die Unverständlichkeit Spinozas. Daß die "berühmtesten Gelehrten" derart gegenteilige Auffassungen der spinozischen Philosophie bekunden, wird als beredtes Argument gegen deren Kommunikabilität angebracht[40].

Die Schwierigkeit eines angemessenen Verständnisses Spinozas widerspiegelt für Döderlein schließlich die Unmöglichkeit metaphysischer Gotteserkenntnis schlechthin. Der Streit der Gelehrten um den dunklen Denker wird zum warnenden Beispiel statuiert, dem eine programmatische Erklärung angehängt werden kann: "Der menschliche Geist fühlt, wenn ihm beim Blick in diese Tiefen der Dialektik und Grübeley alles finster vor Augen wird, in diesem Schwindel zu stark die Schwäche seiner Kraft und die peinliche Trostlosigkeit seiner Untersuchungen, als daß er nicht bald auf den Zurückzug auf eine ebnere und offnere Strasse denken sollte"[41]. Diese Worte bilden den Wegweiser im Labyrinth, mit dem Döderlein auf die idyllische Landschaft seiner eigenen Gotteslehre vorausweist[42]. Das letzte Wort über Spinoza hat sich Döderlein freilich noch vorbehalten. Da sein Urteil über die Unverständlichkeit des Pantheismus Spinozas den Verdacht zuläßt, es sage mehr über sein als über Spinozas Denken etwas aus, stellt er zuguterletzt seine Kompetenz durch eine Kurzinterpretation des Spinozismus unter Beweis.

In unausgesprochener Anlehnung an Herder sondert Döderlein Begrifflichkeit und Intention Spinozas voneinander ab. Als Intention hält er fest, daß Spinoza Gott und Welt unterschieden und die Wirklichkeit als Realisierung der unendlichen Gedanken Gottes verstanden habe. Die schöpferische Kraft der Natur rührt von Gott her, und insofern ist sie seine Kraft, weswegen jede Organisation zur Wahrnehmung und Bewunderung der

göttlichen Kraft Anlaß geben kann[43]. Mit dieser Auslegung wird Spinoza
zum physikotheologischen Normaldenker, und Döderlein kann resümieren:
"Wer dieß von der Gottheit denkt, entweihet sicherlich ihre Hoheit nicht;
wer so von ihr spricht, würde vielleicht nur den Vorwurf erhalten, daß er
nichts neues und unbekanntes lehre"[44].

Als Resultat der Ausführungen über Spinoza teilt sich die Botschaft
mit, Spinozas Philosophie ist entweder ethisch suspekt oder unverständlich
oder nicht originell oder das alles zusammen. Popularität jedenfalls, so kann
Döderlein versichern, wird diese Philosophie nie erreichen, und deswegen
muß man sie nicht als Bedrohung ansehen[45].

An Döderleins Ausführungen ist die gleiche Strategie der
Abwiegelung zu beobachten, mit der Mendelssohn in den "Morgenstunden"
den Behauptungen Jacobis, Spinozismus sei konsequenter Rationalismus und
jeder Vernunftgebrauch zur Begründung von Religion führe zu dem als
Atheismus deklarierten Spinozismus, die Spitze abbrechen wollte. Auch
Döderlein will Jacobis Versuch, die Vernunftreligion zu kompromittieren,
dadurch vereiteln, daß er ihm das Auslegungsmonopol für sein
Demonstrationsobjekt Spinoza bestreitet. Indem er Spinozas Philosophie als
Ansammlung von Widersprüchen vorstellt, konterminiert er Jacobis
Überzeugung von deren vorbildlicher Klarheit und Konsistenz mit einer
Gegenbehauptung. Fraglich ist bloß, ob der hinter der demonstrativen
Überzeugungsgewißheit versteckte Verzicht auf Argumentation nicht durch
sich selbst schon die Glaubwürdigkeit jener Gewißheit beeinträchtigte.

Würde man die Gotteslehre und die Christologie Döderleins und Carl
Friedrich Bahrdts einem systematischen Vergleich unterziehen, so wären die
Unterschiede vermutlich nicht gravierend. Gleichwohl führen Döderlein und
Bahrdt in Kompendien und Nachschlagewerken eine gesonderte Existenz.
Döderlein zählt zu den Neologen, Bahrdt gilt als Paradebeispiel des
Naturalisten[46].

Die Unterscheidung ist vermutlich gerechtfertigt. Nur ist sie weniger
in den Positionen begründet als in deren Einkleidung. Döderlin vermeidet
Konfrontationen, verdeckt Differenzen durch redundante Rhetorik und
bezieht zur Tradition trotz sachlicher Gegensätze eine vermittelnde
Stellung[47]. Bahrdt dagegen ist durch sein polemisch-satirisches Naturell

fortwährend in Auseinandersetzungen verwickelt, die selbst da, wo sachliche Übereinstimmung bestehen sollte, Trennungen provozieren.

In der Geschichtsschreibung der evangelischen Theologie stellt Carl Friedrich Bahrdt, sofern er überhaupt berücksichtigt wird, herkömmlicherweise ein Ärgernis dar. Die Geschäftstüchtigkeit und journalistische Versatilität, mit der dieser Mann das neueste aus dem Reich der Wissenschaft und der Religionspolitik samt seiner eigenen Lebensgeschichte zu vermarkten wußte, die lebhafte Empfänglichkeit für die verschiedenen Reize des Lebens, die abrupten Wechsel in seiner Biographie, die beim besten Willen nicht nur den finsteren Mächten der Zeit angelastet werden können, seine Unempfindlichkeit schließlich gegen den Unterschied von Wahrheit und Erfindung bei der Darstellung seiner vita und der darein verflochtenen Personen und Umstände – diese Züge passen nicht recht in das Bild des deutschen Aufklärers, das gemeinhin holzschnittartig mit Zügen von Geradheit, Wahrheitsernst und Ehrerbietung gegen das Herkommen ausgestattet ist. Die Tatsache, daß der ehemalige Theologieprofessor und Generalsuperintendent in den letzten Lebensjahren eine Gastwirtschaft betrieb und darüber seine gute Laune nicht verlor, brachten ihn vollends in den Ruf der Unseriosität. Die theologischen Sympathisanten der deutschen Aufklärung waren bemüht, Bahrdt als illegitimen Seitentrieb der Bewegung darzustellen, während ihre Kritiker in Bahrdts intellektueller und moralischer Physiognomie mit Vorliebe typische Züge des Aufklärers, wenn auch in überspitzter Ausprägung, registrierten[48].

Neuerdings erfährt Bahrdt als Gesellschaftstheoretiker und philanthropistischer Pädagoge, als Geheimbundorganisator und satirischer Literat im Dienst der Aufklärung zunehmende Beachtung[49]. Die Wiederentdeckung des revolutionären Potentials der deutschen Spätaufklärung befreit auch Bahrdt von der Rolle des zügellosen Libertins und notorischen Projektemachers, die ihm in psychologisierend-moralistischer Betrachtungsweise zuerkannt wurde. Ob Bahrdt allerdings als Radikaldemokrat mit jakobinischen Tendenzen richtig klassifiziert ist, ist ebenso umstritten wie die begriffliche Zuordnung der unterschiedlichen Repräsentanten der deutschen Spätaufklärung überhaupt[50].

Inzwischen wird auch Bahrdts theologiegeschichtliche Bedeutung, wenngleich sie weniger in Innovationen als im Festhalten und Popularisieren der neuesten exegetischen Einsichten und in konsequenter Abklärung der durch philosophische Forderungen und mehr noch durch den Stand der Exegese dringend gemachten Frage nach der Gestalt einer zeitgemäßen Dogmatik bestand, wieder in Erinnerung gerufen[51].

Wie auch immer die Bewertung ausfällt, Übereinstimmung besteht darin, daß Bahrdt dank der Konsequenz seiner Theologie- und Institutionskritik zur kleinen Schar der Radikalaufklärer in Deutschland zu rechnen ist. Bahrdt steht folglich am äußersten Rand des Meinungsspektrums der literarischen Öffentlichkeit seiner Zeit, ohne jedoch eine Randfigur zu sein. Im Gegenteil, er war "probably the most widely read German theologian except for Luther"[52], ganz abgesehen von der persönlichen Ausstrahlung, die seine rhetorische Befähigung ihm verlieh.

Bahrdts exponierte Stellung im Ensemble der geistigen Größen seiner Zeit lädt geradezu ein, nach einem Widerhall der durch den Spinozastreit verursachten "Explosion, welche die geheimsten Verhältnisse würdiger Männer aufdeckte und zur Sprache brachte"[53], im Werke Bahrdts zu suchen. Zwei Veröffentlichungen Bahrdts geben Aufschluß über die Wirkung des epochalen Ereignisses auf einen Mann, der zu dieser Zeit sein viertes Lebensjahrzehnt vollendet und nach mancherlei Gärungen seine Gedankenwelt zu einem durchsichtigen System geordnet hatte.

Im Jahre 1787, als die Wogen der Aufregung über das Gedankenduell zwischen Jacobi und Mendelssohn kaum verebbt waren, erschien anonym die zweite Ausgabe des "Kirchen und Ketzer-Almanachs"[54], einer Art "Who's Who", in dem der Autor Carl Friedrich Bahrdt die zeitgenössischen theologischen Schriftsteller Revue passieren ließ.

Die zuweilen maliziösen, aber treffsicheren[55] Urteile sind bemessen nach dem Grad an Aufgeklärtheit, die sein Verfasser bei den einzelnen Personen feststellen zu können meint. Was er allerdings über die Protagonisten des Spinozastreites notiert, ist so gut wie nichtssagend. Jacobi habe einen "schätzbaren Beytrag"[56] geliefert, Mendelssohn durch den Streit "ein wenig verloren"[57], Lessing werde "drüben" über die ganze Affaire "lächeln"[58] – das ist alles. Aussagen über sein Verhältnis zur Intention des jeweiligen Autors fehlen. Das könnte mit der Anlage des Almanachs zusammenhängen, die zu den einzelnen Personalartikeln nur jeweils knappe Bemerkungen gestattet. An anderen Stellen versteht es Bahrdt aber sehr wohl, sein Urteil über Gesinnung und Standort der betreffenden Person in eine pointierte Wendung zu fassen.

Auffälligerweise bezieht sich Bahrdt an allen drei Stellen auf "Asmus", d. h. auf die Rezensionen, die Matthias Claudius anläßlich der Streitigkeiten zwischen Jacobi und Mendelssohn veröffentlicht hatte[59]. Der Leser gewinnt den Eindruck, daß Bahrdt den gesamten Disput nur im Spiegel dieser Rezensionen zur Kenntnis genommen hat. Dieser Eindruck wird durch die Lektüre von Bahrdts "System der moralischen Religion", das 1787 bei Vieweg in Berlin erschien[60], nicht korrigiert. Bahrdts Biograph Gustav Frank nennt das "System" Bahrdts "bestes und gemeinnützigstes Buch"[61], und er wiederholt damit nur Bahrdts eigene Einschätzung dieses Werkes[62]. Spinozas Denken wird hier, ohne irgendeine Bezugnahme auf den Streit um die rechte Interpretation, im Zusammenhang der Problematik der Entstehung der Welt als eine von den Auffassungen vorgeführt, deren augenfällige Unmöglichkeit die Richtigkeit der Version Bahrdts bestätigen soll.

Eine weiter ausgreifende Präsentation des grundlegenden Gedankengangs des Buches, in dem Bahrdt die "Resultate" seines "vieljährigen Prüfens und Nachdenkens"[63] aufbewahren wollte, vermag mit der erkenntnistheoretischen Basis und der Funktion des Gottesgedankens im System Bahrdts zugleich auch schon die Motive sichtbar zu machen, die sein Verhältnis zu Spinoza und zu den neuesten Streitern um dessen Hinterlassenschaft bestimmen.

Bahrdt tritt mit dem Anspruch an, "dem Leser die ganze Summe derjenigen Kenntnisse deutlich, zusammenhängend und überzeugend vorzulegen, welche er zu seiner Glükseligkeit nöthig hat"[64]. Zwei der wichtigsten Stichworte dieses Kompendiums bürgerlichen Wissens sind damit gleich auf den ersten Seiten genannt: Glückseligkeit und Kenntnis. Beide sind unlöslich miteinander verbunden, denn wahre Glückseligkeit ist nicht möglich ohne Wissen, das vorab den Schein vermeintlichen Glücks zerstreut.

Aus diesem Grunde leitet Bahrdt sein Werk mit einer Darstellung der Grundlagen des Wissens ein. Im Zusammenhang dieser erkenntnistheoretischen Erörterungen, die sicheres Wissen allein in bezug auf Wirklichkeit, die durch Sinneswahrnehmung erfaßbar ist, einräumen, versäumt Bahrdt nicht, Immanuel Kant, über den er andernorts notiert "Unter den Europäischen Philosophen der Erste"[65], seine Reverenz zu erweisen. Die Einbeziehung transzendentalphilosophischer Einsichten beschränkt sich indes auf einen faktisch irrelevanten Hinweis. Bahrdt schlägt zwar das Thema kräftig an – "Und so kennen wir von allen Dingen nichts als ihre Erscheinungen, . . . aber die . . . Dinge an sich, kennen wir nicht"[66] – , er läßt es jedoch nicht nur abrupt und folgenlos wieder fallen, sondern ist im Gegenteil daran interessiert, eventuell daraus entstehenden Zweifeln an der menschlichen Erkenntnisfähigkeit a limine zu wehren. In der Tat würde es einem System, das kraft der Kompetenz der Vernunft für alle Bereiche des bürgerlichen Lebens Handlungsanweisungen erteilen will[67], schlecht anstehen, wenn ausgerechnet bei der Festlegung der Grundlagen seines Anspruchs auf Vollmacht die Anzeige der Problematik sicheren Wissens den Begleittext bildete. Der Vorzug vernünftiger Erkenntnis gegenüber aller bloß autoritativ tradierten und von der Vernunft nicht verifizierbaren Wahrheit soll eben darin bestehen, daß sie von Unsicherheit frei bleibt, womit der Gesinnung diejenige Dauerhaftigkeit verbürgt ist, die allein verbindliche Lebensführung und damit Glückseligkeit ermöglicht. Bahrdts am eklektizistischen Begriff von Philosophie orientierte Einschätzung des Vermögens der Vernunft resultiert aus seiner lebensgeschichtlichen Prägung.

Sein Lebensweg ist charakterisiert durch die sukzessive Ablösung aus dem orthodoxen Milieu seiner Herkunft, die ihm zu einem reinen Naturalismus führt, in dem jedoch, im Unterschied etwa zu Reimarus[68], Jesus nicht disqualifiziert, sondern selbst zum vorbildlichen Naturalisten stilisiert wird[69]. Durch verschiedene Repressionen wurde Bahrdt in Entscheidungszwänge gebracht, die seine Distanzierung von der orthodoxen Tradition beschleunigten. Der Verlauf der Auseinandersetzungen kristallisierte sich in seiner Sicht zu einer Polarisierung von hergebrachtem Glauben, der ein Gemisch aus Irrtum und Betrug ist, und Vernunft, die als Organon zur Ermittlung der ewigen Wahrheiten von Gott, Tugend und

Unsterblichkeit fungiert. Diese Frontstellung bestimmt sein Vernunft-verständnis so ausschließlich, daß ihn die durch Kant ausgelöste Revolution der Denkart ebensowenig erreicht, wie der Atheismus für ihn eine ernsthafte Gefährdung darstellt. Gelassen kann er den Atheismus als übermäßigen Gebrauch der Vernunft diagnostizieren. Die Atheisten "sind zu weit in die Sonne gegangen und haben mehr Licht verlangt, als das Auge ertragen konnte"[70]. Zwischen Vernunftlosigkeit und Vernunftübermaß, zwischen Aberglauben und Zweifelsucht[71], zwischen Fehlorientierung der Vernunft und ihrer starren Fixierung auf einen Punkt, die ihrer Funktionstüchtigkeit auch Abbruch tut[72], steuert Bahrdt die recta ratio sicher hindurch.

Bahrdts Auffassung von der Leistungsfähigkeit der gesunden Vernunft, von der er sagen kann, sie sei "unter gewissen Bedingungen infallibel"[73], ist getragen von einem Grundvertrauen in die sinnvolle Einrichtung der Natur. Aus der Analogie zu anderen Naturkräften, z. B. zum Instinkt der Tierwelt, der exakt den Bedingungen der entsprechenden Lebenswelt angepaßt ist, schließt Bahrdt, daß es eine Entsprechung von Anlage und Vermögen gibt, denn "die Natur irt sich nie"[74]. Da die Vernunft auf Erkenntnis der Wahrheit hin angelegt ist, kann sie nicht ewig dem Zweifel anheimgegeben sein, sondern muß bei normalem Gebrauch die Erfüllung ihrer Bestimmung finden können.

Es ist augenfällig und bedürfte des zusätzlichen Verweises auf die Weisheit des Schöpfers gar nicht[75], daß dieser Forderung ein teleologisch ausgerichtetes Wirklichkeitsverständnis zugrunde liegt, das schon immer und vor jedem Beweis ein sinnvolles Prinzip des Ganzen voraussetzt.

Die Vernunft als natürliches Vermögen ist wie auch das Wahrheits-bedürfnis bei allen Menschen angelegt[76]. Dies impliziert die Verpflichtung zu ihrem Gebrauch und schlägt bei der Bestimmung der Wahrheitskriterien zu Buche. Die Wahrheit allerdings, die jedermann sich selbständig zuzueignen verpflichtet ist, wird von Bahrdt gemäß seinem auf Eigenerwerb und nicht auf eine Vielzahl von Kenntnissen ausgerichteten Begriff von Aufklärung, qualitativ eingegrenzt. "Sie muß algemeinnützig seyn, d. h. sie muß wirklich deine Tugend oder deine Gemüthsruhe befördern"[77]. Der Aufklärungsbegriff enthält mithin eine doppelte Bestimmung. Auf der einen Seite soll Aufklärung sein, damit der Mensch in "Gemüthsruhe" und durch die Souveränität des zur Herrschaft gebrachten Verstandes frei von den Unwägbarkeiten des (Aber-) Glaubens und der Leidenschaft seinen Interessen nachkommen kann[78]. Auf der anderen Seite soll Aufklärung aus ebendem Grunde nicht in Gelehrsamkeit ausarten, die den Bürger auch nur von seinen Geschäften abziehen würde. Unterscheidung von wichtigen und unwichtigen Wahrheiten ist also unerläßlich, "damit du deine kostbare Zeit nicht unnüz verschwendest"[79]. Wichtig in diesem Sinne sind Wahrheiten der Moral und der natürlichen Religion, deren Erkenntnis die nötige Stabilität der Lebensführung vermittelt. Da alle Menschen zur vernünftigen Prüfung verpflichtet sind, muß die religiös-moralische Wahrheit auch allen Menschen zugänglich sein. Sie darf "kein Genie, keinen Tiefsinn erfordern"[80]. Das zur Autoritätsstruktur führende religiöse Spezialistentum soll ja gerade durch das Prinzip der Zustimmung aller durch Einsicht, die ihrerseits Leichtfaßlichkeit erfordert, ersetzt werden. Indem Bahrdt neben den inneren Kriterien die "Zusammenstimmung der Weisen"[81] als äußerliches Kennzeichen der Wahrheit namhaft macht, bringt er zwar die "Kategorie der Öffentlichkeit"[82] ins Spiel, die einen kritischen Maßstab gegenüber allem Denken und Handeln darstellt, das sich allgemeiner Billigung entziehen will. Aber dieses Kriterium birgt auch die Möglichkeit, Infragestellungen der communis opinio unter dem Gesichtspunkt ihrer Nichtübereinstimmung mit der Allgemeinheit zu übergehen. Bahrdts Katalog der Kriterien zur Wahrheitsfindung – Leichtverständlichkeit, Nützlichkeit, Allgemeinheit – schützt die allgemeinen religiösen Wahrheiten vor unnötiger Problematisierung und bietet, wenn man sich ihnen anvertrauen kann, einen festen Schild dar, an dem die zersetzenden Pfeile der Skepsis oder religiöser Skrupulosität wirkungslos abprallen.

Bahrdt hatte einleitend als Ziel seines "Systems" die Vermittlung der Kenntnisse angegeben, die zur Glückseligkeit nötig sind. Im Hinblick darauf entsteht durch die Kennzeichnung der moralischen und religiösen als wichtigste, jedermann angehende Wahrheiten die Frage nach der Beziehung von Religion und Glückseligkeit. Gerade hier aber zeigt sich eine gewisse Unausgewogenheit seiner Beweisführung. Das liegt darin begründet, daß Bahrdt die ganze Skala menschlichen Wohlbefindens als Glückseligkeit gelten lassen will. Er verzichtet darauf, sinnliche Vergnügungen durch die

Beschwörung ihrer Vergänglichkeit zu diskreditieren und den Begriff der Glückseligkeit allein für den spirituellen Bereich zu reservieren. Das bringt einen erheblichen Realitätsgewinn, stellt aber die Notwendigkeit der Religiosität für die Erlangung der Glückseligkeit in Frage. Selbst die Einführung von Wertparametern, die als höchste Form der Glückseligkeit die "Zufriedenheit"[83] ausweisen, die sich dem Vermögen der Vernunft verdankt, das Gute als Quelle dauerhaften, von äußeren Wechselfällen unabhängigen Vergnügens vom bloß sinnlich Angenehmen zu unterscheiden, selbst diese Einfügung stellt noch immer keinen Anknüpfungspunkt zur Verfügung, durch den sich das Thema Glückseligkeit mit dem der Religion ungezwungen verklammern ließe. Die Notwendigkeit der Religion begründet Bahrdt schließlich mit dem nach seinen Voraussetzungen eher blamablen Argument, daß das zuvor benannte Gute von den meisten, im Vernunftgebrauch ungeübten Menschen nicht sicher erkannt werden könne und des richtig gefaßten Gottesbegriffes zu seiner Stütze bedürfe[84]. Der Kontext verweist die Religion in die Funktion, moralische Kenntnis bei den Unbelehrten solange zu vertreten, bis sie sich durch deren vernünftige Einsicht erübrigt. Zwar wird die Bedeutung der Religion, für ihn identisch mit "Gottkentniß"[85], nachträglich aufgewertet, indem die Fähigkeit zur Unterscheidung zwischen gut und angenehm ihr zugerechnet und der mit dem Gottesbegriff verbundene Lohn- und Vergeltungsgedanke als unersetzlicher Garant für eine stabile Tugend angesehen wird. Aber auch das gelingt insofern nur mittels eines immanenten Widerspruchs, als diese Aufwertung auf Kosten der zuvor geltend gemachten Vernunftautonomie geht.

Religion als Ort, wo der Mensch sich seines Wertes dadurch versichern kann, daß er sich von einem wohlmeinenden, absichtsvoll handelnden Urheber her begreift, der auch "die täglichen Geschäfte, die ich als Bürger und Hausvater – zum Wol meiner Mitmenschen verrichte, als eine Verehrung ansieht, die ich ihm selbst leiste, als Erfüllung seines Willens"[86], setzt einen entsprechendem Gottesbegriff voraus. Bahrdts Definition: "Wenn wir sagen, es giebt einen Gott, so wollen wir damit anzeigen, es gebe ein Wesen, das von der Welt unterschieden und von ihr selbst der zureichende Grund ist"[87]. Bahrdt reproduziert den

kosmologischen, der ihm die Faktizität Gottes, und den physikotheologischen Gottesbeweis, der ihm die Modalität, d.h. die Weisheit und
Güte des Schöpfers veranschaulicht[88], vermittels des Satzes vom
zureichenden Grunde. Die auf diese Weise erreichte Gewißheit der Existenz
eines weisen Schöpfers will Bahrdt durch den Nachweis der Unzulänglichkeit
der drei anderen möglichen Weltentstehungstheorien befestigen. In diesem
Zusammenhang wird nach Verwerfung der Theorie eines regressus in
infinitum und der epikuräischen Weltentstehungslehre auch die Philosophie
Spinozas, soweit sie darauf Bezug nimmt, einer Sichtung unterzogen.

Die voranstehenden Ausführungen dürften hinreichend verdeutlicht
haben: Die Problemanzeige des Spinozastreites hat in Bahrdts Denken keine
Spuren hinterlassen. Deshalb kann es kaum wundernehmen, daß die
aktuellen Debatten um die angemessene Interpretation Spinozas mit den
dazugehörigen Implikationen von ihm stillschweigend übergangen werden.
Hätte er sich darauf eingelassen, dann hätte ihm seine Denkart zum
Verteidiger Mendelssohns bestimmt, dessen Auffassung von der Suffizienz
der gesunden Vernunft in metaphysicis ohne Zweifel seiner eigenen
entsprach. Eine solche Auseinandersetzung, ernsthaft geführt, hätte Bahrdt
schwerlich die Einsicht in das Unzeitgemäße seines Vernunftbegriffs und der
ihm entspringenden Folgerungen erspart. Bahrdt kam die Eigentümlichkeit
im Bereich philosophischer Differenzen zugute, daß Standpunkte sich nicht
durch die Überwindung des ihnen Entgegenstehenden rechtfertigen müssen,
sondern solange gültig sind, wie ihnen Zustimmung nicht gänzlich entzogen
wird. Man braucht im übrigen keine umständlichen Erklärungen zu
bemühen, um Bahrdts Schweigen plausibel zu machen. Sieht man davon ab,
daß Bahrdts Interesse am Kennenlernen fremder Gedanken nicht sehr
ausgeprägt war[89], so bot ihm sein Vernunftbegriff selbst eine Handhabe, von
vornherein jede Überlegung zu übersehen, die für sein harmonistisches
Konzept eine Irritation hätte darstellen können.

In Bahrdts Koordinatensystem zur Bestimmung des Wahren ist für
das Raisonnement der neuen Spinozisten und Antispinozisten kein Platz:
Die Forderungen der Allgemeinverständlichkeit erfüllen die betreffenden
Schriften nicht, wie schon rein äußerlich am Gelehrtenzank um ihre richtige
Interpretation ersichtlich ist. Die Behauptung, daß konsequenter

Vernunftgebrauch zum Spinozismus führe, muß Bahrdt nicht mehr beunruhigen als die verschiedenen Atheismen selbst, die durch übermäßigen Vernunftgebrauch zustandegekommen waren. Die Neuheit schließlich und das sektiererische Auftreten der sonderbaren Anwälte Spinozas steht Bahrdts Forderung nach Übereinstimmung der Weisen gänzlich entgegen. In bezug auf Spinoza hält sich Bahrdt an das ihm unmittelbar einsichtige alte Wahre. Er faßt Spinozas Grundgedanken mit den Worten zusammen, "daß die Welt selbst das ewige und nothwendige Wesen ist, daß man außer ihr sucht"[90]. Präzisierend schreibt Bahrdt, Spinoza habe sich die "Summe der thätigen Kräfte" als eine die Materie belebende, Regelmäßigkeit hervorbringende Weltseele vorgestellt. "Und man könte diese Weltseele Gott nennen"[91]. Aller Wahrscheinlichkeit nach greift Bahrdt hier auf die Argumentation Bayles zurück, der im Zusammenhang der Herleitung der spinozischen Lehre in derselben die stoische Auffassung von der Weltseele wiedererkennen wollte[92]. Die Vermutung über den Anteil Bayles an Bahrdts Spinozaverständnis wird daran bestätigt, daß Bahrdt auch Bayles Auffassung von den grotesken Konsequenzen des Spinozismus kolportiert und mit eigenem Bildwerk ausziert: "Alles – die tükische Katze und der freundliche, getreue Hund, der blutdürstige Tiger und der großmüthige Löwe, --- Luther und Lojola, . . . Christus und Belial alles wäre nichts als verschiedne Modifikation eines Wesens? – Der Straßenräuber, der Richter, der Henker, der Galgen, alles ein Wesen?" usw.[93] Die aus diesen Folgerungen offenkundige Verirrung der Vernunft wird aber am Ende nicht Spinoza selbst, sondern den orthodoxen Theologen angelastet, wodurch sich erhärtet, daß Bahrdts polemischer Eifer in diesem Gegenüber sein Angriffsziel sucht: "Gewiß, nur jene scheuslichsten Begriffe von einem in Zorn und Liebe sich selbst widersprechenden Gott, die Priester erfanden, um als Vermittler der Gottheit Gut und Herrschaft an sich zu ziehn, – konten die Weltweisheit verscheuchen und die Menschen geneigt machen, zu solchen Ungereimtheiten ihre Zuflucht zu nehmen, um jene noch größern nicht zur Schande der Menschheit dulden zu müssen"[94]. Die Wahngebilde Spinozas dienen dazu, – einmal mehr – die Monstrosität der Orthodoxie zu demonstrieren. In einem weiteren Zusammenhang bezieht sich Bahrdt noch einmal auf Spinoza. Sein Verständnis von Religion als Grundlegung von

Glückseligkeit findet am bloßen Prädikat der Existenz Gottes mit den Merkmalen der Außerweltlichkeit, Vollkommenheit, Immaterialität u. ä. kein Genüge. Es verlangt nach einem Gottesbegriff, der Garantien für das menschliche Glücksbedürfnis vorzuweisen hat, sonst wäre er überflüssig. Gottes Wesen wird von Bahrdt mit dem Begriff der altruistisch verstandenen Liebe bestimmt, der gegenteilige Prädikate ausschließt und andere dominiert[95]. Aus dieser Bestimmung folgt, daß Gott seine Seligkeit anderen Wesen mitteilen will. Gott erschafft die Welt nicht zur Demonstration seiner Macht oder seiner Weisheit, "Gott will die Glükseligkeit seiner Geschöpfe – sie ist sein Zwek"[96]. Dieser Anthropozentrismus ist strikt auf das Glück des einzelnen orientiert und verhält sich zu Leibniz' Hypothese der besten Welt, in der zum Bestand des Ganzen Nachteile für dessen Glieder einkalkuliert sind, ablehnend[97]. Ebenso wird das Theoriefundament der Funktionstüchtigkeit der besten Welt verworfen: Bahrdt wendet sich gegen die Vorstellung eines Uhrmachergottes[98] und betont die Notwendigkeit einer fortgesetzten aktiven Erhaltung der Schöpfung durch Gott, denn wenn Gott lediglich am Anfang Gesetze installiert hätte, um dann die Welt dem Selbstlauf zu überlassen, "so wäre ich eben so verlassen, als wenn ich keinen Gott kente: so sähe ich mich im Strome der Nothwendigkeit ... : so wäre ich nicht das Kind eines Vaters, sondern das Glied einer Maschine: so wäre für das Ganze, aber nicht für mein Individuum gesorgt"[99]. Eben diesen Gedanken der aktiven Omnipräsenz Gottes, die Vorstellung, "daß Gott kein müßiger Zuschauer seiner durch ewige Geseze fortdaurenden und reifenden Werke sey, sondern daß er vielmehr selbst fortgesezt thätig sey in der ganzen Schöpfung und allen Theilen" konzediert Bahrdt nun auch Spinoza, "der sich nur minder bequem ausdrukte und eben dadurch sich den Verdacht jener Ungereimtheit zuzog, die wir oben widerlegt haben"[100]. Erstaunlich ist, daß Bahrdt in diesem Zusammenhang den Namen Spinozas nicht mit der Vision einer maschinellen Notwendigkeit verkoppelt, obwohl gerade dieser Topos zu den Standards der antispinozistischen Polemik gehört. Bahrdt betrachtet offenbar nicht den Determinismus, sondern den Immanenzgedanken als das Spezifikum des Spinozismus, und er kann demselben einen religiösen Sinn abgewinnen, indem er ihn als Oppositionsmodell zu einem religiös sterilen Uhrmachergott begreift. Aber diese Aufwertung Spinozas geschieht um den

Preis seiner Vereinnahmung. Das tertium comparationis zwischen Spinozas Immanenzgedanken und Bahrdts liebenden Vatergott besteht im Sachverhalt der Nähe Gottes, dem freilich in den wechselnden Bezugsfeldern eine ganz unterschiedliche Bedeutung innewohnt: während sich für Spinoza damit ein Wechsel der Perspektive von anthropozentristischen Verkürzungen auf die einheitliche Totalität des Seins verbindet, verwendet Bahrdt im diametralen Gegensatz zu Spinoza den Gedanken gerade zu einer letzten Steigerung der anthropozentrischen Fassung des Gottesbegriffs. Wie im Falle Döderleins beruht auch Bahrdts Bereitschaft zur Anerkennung Spinozas auf der Voraussetzung seiner Verharmlosung. Damit bestätigt sich, was – am Gesamtumfang gemessen – die Beiläufigkeit der Erwähnung Spinozas ohnehin schon dokumentiert, daß von irgendeinem Einfluß der Positionen des Spinozastreits auf Bahrdts Denken nicht gesprochen werden kann.

Im Jahre 1797 erschien bei Vieweg in Berlin die vierte Auflage des "Systems" unter dem Titel "Moral für Alle Stände". Daß der Verleger sich zu einer neuen Auflage entschließen konnte, deutet auf einen guten Absatz und anhaltende Nachfrage hin – mitten im großen Jahrzehnt der klassisch-romantischen Literatur. Als Herausgeber dieser posthumen Auflage fungierte Wilhelm Abraham Teller, einer der namhaften Berliner Aufklärungstheologen. Mit kritischen Anmerkungen distanziert sich Teller von einigen Auffassungen Bahrdts. Sie betreffen das Verhältnis vom Pflichtgefühl und Glückseligkeitstrieb am Zustandekommen moralischer Handlungen, nicht aber die Gotteslehre und schon gar nicht die Passagen über Spinoza[101]. Es ist gewiß zuviel gesagt, aufgrund der Herausgeberschaft Tellers Bahrdts Ausführungen zum Gottesbegriff als autorisierte Zusammenfassung der Gedankenwelt der Berliner Aufklärung anzusehen, als deren bedeutendste theologische Repräsentanten neben Teller Johann Joachim Spalding und eben Friedrich Samuel Gottfried Sack anzusehen sind[102]. Höchstwahrscheinlich aber signalisiert die personelle Verbindung eine sachliche Übereinstimmung im Grundsätzlichen, d. h. in der Ablehnung supranaturalistischer, irrationalistischer und atheistischer Theoriegebilde. Im Hinblick auf unsere Fragestellung sprechen die Indizen für eine Kontinuität der restriktiven Behandlung der im Spinozastreit artikulierten Probleme.

In einigen Thesen soll abschließend versucht werden, die vorangegangenen Überlegungen zusammenzufassen.

Döderlein, Bahrdt, Sack u. a. repräsentieren eine Gestalt von Aufklärung, die es als ihr Verdienst ansah, gegen den vereinten Widerstand der Sachwalter überlebter Tradition Christentum und Religion von allen unvernünftigen Bestandteilen gereinigt und auf die Höhe der Zeit geführt zu haben.

Der Spinozastreit ist ein Krisensymptom dieser moralischen Vernunftreligion. Seine Protagonisten signalisieren ihr religiöses und intellektuelles Ungenügen gegenüber solchem aufgeklärten Christentum, und dies keineswegs aus Bedenklichkeiten orthodoxer Provenienz. Im Medium der Philosophie Spinozas tragen sie Konzepte vor, die jenseits der rationalen Theologie der deutschen Aufklärung die religiöse Dimension des Menschen adäquater erfassen sollen.

Am Beispiel Döderleins und Bahrdts wird deutlich, daß es nicht gelungen ist, die im Spinozastreit artikulierte Problemkonstellation ins allgemeine Bewußtsein einzusenken. Döderlein und Bahrdt nehmen die Herausforderung nicht an. Sie sind nicht bereit, die gegenüber der theologischen Tradition ausgeübte zersetzende Kraft der Vernunft in einem Akt kritischer Selbstreflexion auf diese selbst anzuwenden. Statt dessen entwickeln sie Strategien, die die provokatorischen Fragestellungen als irrelevant ausgrenzen sollen.

Der Verzicht auf theoretische Konsequenz und spekulativen Enthusiasmus wird durch praktisches Engagement ausgeglichen. Die unlösliche Zuordnung von Wahrheit und Praxis, von Religion und Moral, von Gottesglaube und Lebensgewißheit und von individuellem und allgemeinem Denken bildet das selbstauferlegte Maß, von dem aus jede Abweichung der Vernunft als bedrohlich diffamiert oder als exzentrisch marginalisiert wird. Diese konservative, auf Integration und Selbstbejahung ausgerichtete Religionstheorie stellte vermutlich für einen breiten Rezipientenkreis die Möglichkeit zur Identifikation bereit. Der Preis: sie klammert freiwillig eine geistige Avantgarde als Adressaten aus.

Es ist Schleiermachers Verdienst, eine Religionstheorie im Anschluß an den fortgeschrittensten Stand des Bewußtseins konzipiert zu haben. Die

Bestimmung seiner Religionsschrift "an die Gebildeten unter ihren Verächtern" ist wörtlich zu nehmen. Durch die gelungene Einbeziehung des Kritizismus und verschiedener Elemente des Neuspinozismus konnte er in diesem Empfängerkreis darauf aufmerksam machen, daß die Fähigkeit des Christentums zur Regeneration sich nicht in der Gestalt der Aufklärungstheologie erschöpft hat.

Anmerkungen

1. Aus Schleiermacher's Leben: in Briefen. 3. Bd./hrsg. von Ludwig Jonas und Wilhelm Dilthey. Berlin 1861, 276f.
2. Ebd. 282ff.
3. Friedrich Heinrich Jacobi: Über die Lehre des Spinoza in Briefen an den Herrn Moses Mendelssohn. Breslau 1785. Neue vermehrte Ausgabe: Breslau 1789. Ausgabe letzter Hand: Friedrich Heinrich Jacobi: Werke. Bd. 4,1 u. 4,2. Leipzig 1819: reprograf. Nachdr. Darmstadt 1968. Kritische Ausgabe in: Die Hauptschriften zum Pantheismusstreit zwischen Jacobi und Mendelssohn/ hrsg. von Heinrich Scholz. Berlin 1916, 45-282. (Neudrucke seltener philosophischer Werke; 6). (Thomas Wizenmann:) Die Resultate der Jacobischen und Mendelssohnschen Philosophie; kritisch untersucht von einem Freywilligen. Leipzig 1786.
4. August Wilhelm Rehberg: Ueber das Verhältniß der Metaphysik zu der Religion. Berlin 1787.
5. Karl Heinrich Heydenreich: Natur und Gott nach Spinoza. Bd. 1 (mehr nicht erschienen). Leipzig 1789.
6. Moses Mendelssohn: Morgenstunden oder Vorlesungen über das Daseyn Gottes. Berlin 1785. Wiederabdruck: Moses Mendelssohn: Gesammelte Schriften: Jubiläumsausgabe Bd. 3,2/bearb. von Leo Strauss. Stuttgart-Bad Cannstadt 1974, 1-175; vgl. hierzu 121-124.
7. Johann Gottfried Herder: Gott: einige Gespräche. Gotha 1787. 2., verkürzte und vermehrte Ausgabe 1800. Kritische Ausgabe: Johann Gottfried Herder: Sämmtliche Werke/ hrsg. von Bernhard Suphan. Bd. 16. Berlin 1887, 400-580. Vgl. Johann Gottfried Herder: Briefe. Bd. 5/bearb. von Wilhelm Dobbek und Günter Arnold. Weimar 1979, 90.
8. Ernst Platner: Philosophische Aphorismus nebst einigen Anleitungen zur philosophischen Geschichte. Ganz neue Ausarbeitung. Bd. l. Leipzig 1793, 565f. Vgl. die vorangegangene Auflage der Aphorismen, in der Spinoza ohne Einschränkung als Atheist rubriziert ist: Neue durchaus umgearbeitete Ausgabe, Bd. l. Leipzig 1784, 430f.
9. Vgl. Annelies Roseeu: Zur Theologie und Kirchenpolitik am preußischen Hof (1786-1850): dargestellt an den preußischen Hofpredigern Sack, Eylert, Strauß. Göttingen 1957, 11-13. (maschinenschriftlich) Göttingen, Univ., Philos. Fak., Diss., 1957.
10. Gustav Frank: Geschichte der Protestantischen Theologie. Bd. 3 Leipzig 1875, 113.
11. Ebd.
12. Ludwig Timotheus Spittler: Grundriß der Geschichte der christlichen Kirche. 2., verb. Aufl. Göttingen 1785, 522. Weitere Literatur über Döderlein, in der auch seine Bedeutung als Herausgeber der "Auserlesenen Theologischen Bibliothek" (1780-1792) und als Teilnehmer am Fragmentenstreit gewürdigt wird, ist angegeben bei Eberhard H. Pältz: Art.:

Döderlein, Johann Christoph. In: Religion in Geschichte und Gegenwart. 3. Aufl. Bd. 2 (1958), 217.

13. Johann Christoph Döderlein: Institutio theologi christiani in capitibus religionis theoreticis nostris temporibus accomodata. 2 Teile. Nürnberg; Altdorf 1780; 6., verb. u. verm. Aufl./hrsg. von Christian Gottfried Junge. 1797. Über ihre Vorbildwirkung für spätere dogmatische Kompendien vgl.: Heinrich Döring: Art.: Döderlein (Johann Christoph). In: Allgemeine Encyklopädie der Wissenschaften und Künste/hrsg. von Johann Samuel Ersch und Johann Gottfried Gruber. Bd. 25 (1834), 251-255, 255.

14. Johann Christoph Döderlein: Christlicher Religionsunterricht nach den Bedürfnissen unserer Zeit: nach dem Lateinischen von dem Verfasser selbst ausgearbeitet. 5 Bände. Leipzig; Frankfurt 1785-1791.

15. Ebd. Bd. 1, 3.

16. Ebd. Bd. 3, 16f.

17. Ebd. 73f.

18. Ebd. 23. 52. 76ff.

19. Ebd. 82.

20. Vgl. z. B. ebd. Bd. 4, 122-125.

21. Karl Aner: Die Theologie der Lessingzeit. Halle 1929 (reprograf. Nachdr.: Hildesheim 1964), 4.

22. Döderlein: Christlicher Religionsunterricht. AaO. Bd. 1, 93ff. 110. Wodurch sich Offenbarung im Sinne Döderleins auszeichnet, bedürfte allerdings einer Untersuchung. Wenn er sie als "Zusammentreffen von Vorstellungen in der Seele, welche einzeln und zerstreut schon vorhanden waren" (ebd. 95) beschreibt, so erscheint die Offenbarung als eine Art Intuition, deren Abgrenzung von der Eingebung des Genies durch den Hinweis auf ihre göttliche Herkunft (ebd. 95) gezwungen wirkt. Andernorts, bei der Verifizierung der Offenbarungsqualität des Christentums, listet er Kennzeichen der Offenbarung wie Sendungsbewußtsein (ebd. 173ff), Inhalt und Wirkung der Lehre (ebd. 193ff), Wunderwerke (ebd. 238ff) u. a. auf, die auf Geltung jedoch nicht isoliert, sondern nur in gegenseitiger Verschränkung und nach angemessener Prüfung durch die Vernunft Anspruch erheben dürfen. Als Gesamttendenz ist die Zurückbiegung der Offenbarung in den Bereich der natürlich erfahrbaren Wirklichkeit erkennbar, die sich in dem Diktum "alle Natur ist Offenbarung und alle Offenbarung ist Natur" (ebd. 37) bündelt. In dem Zusammenhang ist auch Döderleins Bezug auf Lessing aufschlußreich. Sieht man von Auffassungen wie denen ab, daß Wahrheit in allen Religionen zu finden (ebd. 19) und an ihren Früchten, d. h. den Taten ihrer Bekenner, zu erkennen ist (ebd. 111), die zwar in der Ringparabel ihren klassischen Ausdruck gefunden haben, im übrigen aber zum Allgemeingut der Aufklärung gehören, ist dieser Bezug auf Lessing in der z. T. durch Zitat gekennzeichneten (ebd.51f. 166) Übernahme von Konstruktionselementen der "Erziehung des Menschengeschlechts" bemerkbar. Dazu gehören die Gleichsetzung von Offenbarung und Erziehung (ebd. 48f. 109), die Funktion der Offenbarung zur Beschleunigung der Entwicklung der Vernunft (ebd. 37. 166), die stufenweise Ordnung der Offenbarung (ebd. 166. Bd. 3, 41), die Notwendigkeit der Überführung der Offenbarung in Vernunftwahrheiten (ebd. Bd. 1, 5lf. Bd. 3, 35) und die Einsicht in den langsamen und mit Umwegen verbundenen Gang der Vernunft (ebd. Bd. 1, 92). Selbst gewisse Rätsel der Erziehungsschrift Lessings sind in Döderleins Text eingegangen, so die Ungewißheit, ob der Verfasser meint, daß die Offenbarung nur Wahrheiten enthält, die die Vernunft, wenngleich später, auch selbständig gefunden hätte, oder Wahrheiten, auf die sie von selbst nie gekommen wäre (vgl. ebd. 35-37).

23. Ebd. Bd. 3, 38. 50. 56.

24. Ebd. 56.

25. Ebd. 50.

26. Ebd. 8. 35f.

27. Ebd. 50. 75-85. Ein Kernsatz seiner Gotteslehre lautet: "Über Gott werde ich nie speculieren" (ebd. Bd. 4, 200; vgl. ebd. 25-28).

28. Ebd. Bd. 1, 91f.

29. Ebd. 14f. Bd. 3, 65f.

30. Ebd. Bd. 1, 215. Bd. 3, 44. Bd. 4, 129.

31. Ebd. Bd. 4, 37-55.

32. Döderlein: Institutio. 6. Aufl. AaO. (Anm. 14), 268. In dem von Döderlein besorgten Rezensionsorgan wird von den Schriften zum Pantheismusstreit nur Mendelssohns Werk "Morgenstunden" referiert. Vgl. Johann Christoph Döderlein: Auserlesene Theologische Bibliothek. 3. Bd., 9. Stück (1786), 639-662. Woran dieses Defizit liegt, ist schwer zu beurteilen. Das Programm der Zeitschrift rechtfertigt es nicht. Danach sollen Schriften vorgestellt werden, die "für die Religion und die Theologie wichtig", "neu" und "zur Beförderung der reinen und wahren theologischen Gelehrsamkeit" dienlich sind. Ebd. I. Bd., 1. Stück (1780), 6f.

33. Bayles Wörterbuch erschien in seiner ersten Auflage 1695-97 in zwei Foliobänden. Die zweite Auflage von 1702 umfaßte vier Bände. Nach Bayles Tod (1706) wurde es teils in dieser Form, teils gekürzt wieder aufgelegt und in verschiedene Sprachen übersetzt. Über Bayles Wirkung in Deutschland vgl.: Gerhard Sauder: Bayle-Rezeption in der deutschen Aufklärung (Mit einem Anhang: In Deutschland verlegte französische Bayle-Ausgaben und deutsche Übersetzungen Baylescher Werke). In: Deutsche Vierteljahresschrift für Literatur- und Geistesgeschichte 49 (1975), Sonderheft, 83-104.

34. Über Bayles Verwerfung des Substanzmonismus vgl.: Pierre Bayle: Dictionaire historique et critique. 5. éd. Amsterdam; Leiden; La Haye; Utrecht 1740. T. 4, 259-262, Anm. N. In Entsprechung dazu heißt es bei Döderlein über die Konsequenzen der All-Eins-Lehre Spinozas: "So verzehrte die Gottheit sich selbst. In der Blume erscheint sie prachtvoll und nahrhaft; im Käfer zerstört sie die Blume, im Vogel verzehrt sie den Käfer, im Menschen frißt sie den Vogel, im Tyrannen tödtet sie den Menschen; in jedem ihrer Theile wüthet sie gegen einen anderen, der eben so gut zu ihr gehört" usw. Döderlein: Christlicher Religionsunterricht. AaO. Bd. 4, 40. In vergleichbarer Weise haben im Gefolge Bayles etliche Bestreiter Spinozas bei der Schilderung der destruktiven Folgen des Monismus ihre Phantasie spielen lassen, wie auch das Beispiel Bahrdts zeigt (s. u.).

35. Ebd. 45.

36. Ebd. 45f.

37. Ebd. 41f. Vgl. Christian Wolff: Natürliche Gottesgelahrtheit. Bd. 2. Halle 1745, 36f.

38. Döderlein: Christlicher Religionsunterricht. AaO. Bd. 4, 46.

39. Ebd. 48.

40. Ebd. 51.

41. Ebd. 51f.

42. Döderlein gibt gelegentlich zu erkennen, daß ihm die Problematik der Gottesbeweise bewußt ist. (Ebd. 73. 129f) Aber ihn berührt das nicht, da er davon ausgeht, daß die demonstrative Beweisart ohnehin nur die Verstandeskräfte zum Nachteil der Herzensfrömmigkeit strapaziert, daß seine antispekulative, praktisch-vernünftige Ausrichtung mit Kants Kritik der Gottesbeweise übereinstimmt und daß trotz dieser Kritik den Gottesbeweisen hinreichend Überzeugungskraft eignet, um durch sie religiöse Gewißheit zu begründen. (Ebd. 73ff. 129f) Die ausführlichen, mit suggestiven Pathos vorgetragenen Passagen über Gottes Dasein, Geistigkeit, Allwissenheit, Allmacht etc. (vgl. ebd. 200-362; Bd. 5, 1-206) beziehen ihre Wahrheit außer aus Bibelzitaten vornehmlich aus der Geltung dieser Beweise.

43. Ebd. Bd. 4, 53f.

44. Ebd. 54.

45. Ebd. 51. 55.
46.   Vgl. z. B. Heinrich Hoffmann: Art.: Rationalismus: II. Rationalismus und
Supranaturalismus. In: Religion in Geschichte und Gegenwart. 2. Aufl. Bd. 4 (1930), 1715f.
Bengt Hägglund: Geschichte der Theologie: ein Abriß. Berlin 1983, 272.
47.   Karl Aner hebt Döderleins Aufgeschlossenheit für die orthodoxe Tradition
ausdrücklich hervor. Aner: AaO. (wie Anm. 21), 308.
48.   Vgl. als Repräsentanten der jeweiligen Position Emanuel Hirsch: Geschichte der
neuern evangelischen Theologie im Zusammenhang mit den allgemeinen Bewegungen des
europäischen Denkens. Bd. 4. 3. Aufl. Gütersloh 1964, 116 und Karl Barth: Die
protestantische Theologie im 19. Jahrhundert. 3. Aufl. Berlin 1961, 147f.
49.   Vgl. Jörn Garber; Hanno Schmitt: Utilitarismus als Jakobinismus?: Anmerkungen zur neueren Bahrdt-Forschung. In: Jahrbuch des Instituts für Deutsche Geschichte XII
(1983), 437-449. Ulrich Herrmann: Die Kodifizierung bürgerlichen Bewußtseins in der
deutschen Spätaufklärung: Carl Friedrich Bahrdts "Handbuch der Moral für den Bürgerstand"
aus dem Jahre 1789. In: "Die Bildung des Bürgers": die Formierung der bürgerlichen
Gesellschaft und die Gebildeten im 18. Jahrhundert/ hrsg. von Ulrich Herrmann. Weinheim;
Basel 1982, 153-162 (dort weitere Lit.). (Geschichte der Erziehungs und Bildungswesens in
Deutschland; 2). Günter Mühlpfordt: Ein radikaler Geheimbund vor der Französischen
Revolution: die Union K. F. Bahrdts. In: Jahrbuch für Geschichte des Feudalismus 5 (1981),
379-413. Ebd. 382, Anm. 13 Hinweise auf frühere Aufsätze Mühlpfordts zu Bahrdt. Ludger
Lütkehaus: Karl Friedrich Bahrdt, Immanuel Kant und die Gegenaufklärung in Preußen
(1788-1798). In: Jahrbuch des Instituts für Deutsche Geschichte IX (1980), 83-106. Lütkehaus
würdigt hier Bahrdts Lustspiel "Das Religions-Edikt", das unterdessen auch in seiner
editorischen Betreuung veröffentlicht wurde: Karl Friedrich Bahrdt: Das Religions-Edikt ein
Lustspiel. Faks. der Ausgabe von 1789/mit e. Nachwort hrsg. von Ludger Lütkehaus.
Heidelberg 1985. Bahrdts Satire gegen Wöllners Religionsedikt erschien anonym, aber die auf
königlichen Befehl angestellten Nachforschungen ermittelten Bahrdt als Verfasser, der
daraufhin mit Festungshaft bestraft wurde. Vgl. dazu: Hans-Ulrich Delius: Der Prozeß gegen
Dr. Karl Friedrich Bahrdt: aus einem bisher unbekannten Aktenstück. In: Jahrbuch für Berlin-
Brandenburgische Kirchengeschichte 55 (1985), 181-198.
50.   Als Präjakobiner bzw. revolutionärer Demokrat rangiert Bahrdt in den Aufsätzen
Günter Mühlpfordts. Vgl. außer der in Anm. 49 genannten Literatur noch: Günter
Mühlpfordt: Bahrdts Weg zum revolutionären Demokraten: das Werden seiner Lehre vom
Staat des Volkswohls. In: Zeitschrift für Geschichtswissenschaft 29 (1981), 996-1017. In enger
Anlehnung an Mühlpfordt wurde diese Auffassung publizistisch verwertet von Bernt
Engelmann: Trotz alledem: deutsche Radikale 1777-1977. Reinbek bei Hamburg 1979, 45-48.
(rororo 7194) Kritische Vorbehalte gegen Mühlpfordts Begriffskatalog und Textinterpretation
äußern Jörn Garber und Hanno Schmitt: AaO. (wie Anm. 49). Zur Problematik der
Definition deutscher Aufklärer als Jakobiner vgl. Volker Mehnert: Protestantismus und
radikale Spätaufklärung: die Beurteilung Luthers und der Reformation durch aufgeklärte
deutsche Schriftsteller zur Zeit der Französischen Revolution. München 1982, bes. 18-59.
Über Bahrdt vgl. ebd. 157-160.
51.   Vgl. Gert Röwenstrunk: Art.: Bahrdt, Carl Friedrich. In: Theologische Real-
enzyklopädie 5 (1980), 132f.
52.   Sten G. Flygt: Art: Bahrdt, Carl Friedrich. In: The Encyclopedia of Philosophy 1
(1967), 242.
53.   Johann Wolfgang Goethe: Aus meinem Leben: Dichtung und Wahrheit/hrsg. von
Siegfried Seidel. Leipzig 1977. Bd. 1, 690.
54.   (Carl Friedrich Bahrdt:) Kirchen- und Ketzer- Almanach. Zweites Quinquennium
ausgefertigt im Jahre 1787. Gibeon (Berlin) bey Kasimir Lauge.
55.   Aner: AaO. (wie Anm. 21), 202, Anm. l.

56. Bahrdt: Kirchen- und Ketzer- Almanach 1787. AaO. (wie Anm. 54), 95.
57. Ebd. 134.
58. Ebd. 121.
59. Matthias Claudius: Zwey Recensionen etc. in Sachen der Herren Leßing, M. Mendelssohn, und Jacobi. Hamburg 1786. Abgedruckt in: Matthias Claudius: Sämtliche Werke. München 1968, 348-360. Im Anmerkungsteil dieser Ausgabe wird die in der Claudiusforschung gängige Behauptung wiederholt, Wieland habe die Aufnahme von Claudius' Rezension der Spinozabriefe Jacobis in den "Teutschen Merkur" abgelehnt (ebd. 1028). Diese Behauptung fußt auf Bemerkungen in einem Brief Goethes an Jacobi vom Januar 1786, die jedoch keineswegs eindeutig diesen Bescheid enthalten. Vgl. Wolfgang Stammler: Matthias Claudius der Wandsbecker Bothe: ein Beitrag zur deutschen Literatur- und Geistesgeschichte. Halle 1915, 155. In der jüngsten Monographie zum Thema wird der Sachverhalt weiter verunklart: Burghard König: Matthias Claudius: die literarischen Beziehungen in Leben und Werk. Bonn 1976, 110f. In Wirklichkeit ist die Renzension abgedruckt: Anzeiger des Teutschen Merkur. Jänner 1786, I-III.
60. Carl Friedrich Bahrdt: System der moralischen Religion zur endlichen Beruhigung für Zweifler und Denker: allen Christen und Nichtchristen lesbar. 2 Bände. Berlin 1787. Bahrdt hatte, bevor das Werk unter seinem Namen und mit dem genannten Titel erschien, denselben Text bereits unter dem Titel "Ausführliches Lehrgebäude der Religion: erbaut auf der reinen und unvermischten Lehre Jesu . . . " anonym ausgehen lassen, um eine durch die Nennung seines – in der Öffentlichkeit belasteten – Namens mögliche Präokkupation der Rezensenten zu verhindern. Vgl.: Carl Friedrich Bahrdt: Geschichte seines Lebens, seiner Meinungen und Schicksale: von ihm selbst geschrieben, Bd. 4. Berlin 1791, 243. Über die verschiedenen Titel und Auflagen des "Systems" und die in engem zeitlichen und ideellen Bezug dazu stehenden Werke vgl.: Gustav Frank: Dr. Karl Friedrich Bahrdt: ein Beitrag zur Geschichte der deutschen Aufklärung. In: Historisches Taschenbuch/hrsg. von Friedrich von Raumer. 4. Folge. 7. Jg. Leipzig 1866, 203-370, 359, Anm. 77.
61. Frank: Dr. Karl Friedrich Bahrdt, AaO. (wie Anm. 60), 272.
62. Carl Friedrich Bahrdt: Moral für alle Stände. 4. Aufl. Mit e. Vorrede, Verbesserungen und Zusätzen von W. A. Teller. Berlin 1797, Bd. 1, IV.
63. Bahrdt: Geschichte seines Lebens. AaO. (wie Anm. 60), 242.
64. Bahrdt: System. AaO. (wie Anm. 60) Bd. 1, IX.
65. Bahrdt: Kirchen- und Ketzer- Almanach 1787. AaO. (wie Anm. 54), 100.
66. Bahrdt: System: AaO. (wie Anm. 6o) Bd. 1, 31.
67. Nachdem Bahrdt im ersten, grundlegenden Teil Erkenntnistheorie, natürliche Religion und verschiedene Bereiche der Ethik allgemein bestimmt hat, trägt er im zweiten, umfangreicheren Teil Entfaltungen und Konkretionen vor. 1791 erschien in Riga als dritter Teil des "Systems": "Rechte und Obliegenheiten des Regenten und Unterthanen in Beziehung auf Staat und Religion", Bahrdts politische Ethik. Vgl. dazu Mühlpfordt: Bahrdts Weg. AaO. (wie Anm. 50). Mühlpfordt zeigt, daß die Jahresangabe auf dem Impressum, 1792, eine Vordatierung ist (ebd. 1017).
68. Vgl. Bahrdts Einspruch gegen die Mißachtung der Person Jesu unter den neueren Theologen in der 1. Auflage des "Kirchen und Ketzeralmanach". (Carl Friedrich Bahrdt :) Kirchen- und Ketzeralmanach auf das Jahr 1781. Häresiopel (Züllichau). Im Verlag der Ekklesia pressa, 243-245. Vgl. auch Bahrdts Bemerkungen im Reimarus-Artikel des Almanachs, daß Reimarus nun, nach seinem Eingang in die Ewigkeit, erfahren haben werde, daß Jesus nicht nach einer irdischen Krone gestrebt habe (ebd. 142); ebenso in der 2. Ausgabe: Bahrdt: Kirchen- und Ketzer-Almanach 1787 (wie Anm. 54), 153.
69. Vgl. Bahrdt: System. AaO. (wie Anm. 60) Bd. 1, 50-71. Jesus wird die größte Autorität unter allen Menschen zuerkannt.
70. Ebd. 119.

71. Vgl. ebd. 98ff.
72. Vgl. ebd. 29f.
73. Ebd. 90.
74. Ebd. 91.
75. Vgl. ebd. 91f.
76. Ebd. 91.
77. Ebd. 40.
78. Ebd. 77. 81f.
79. Ebd. 40.
80. Ebd. 40.
81. Ebd. 41.
82. Gernot Koneffke: Einleitung. In: Carl Friedrich Bahrdt: Handbuch der Moral für den Bürgerstand. Unveränderter Neudruck der Ausgabe Halle 1789. Mit e. Einl. von Gernot Koneffke. Vaduz/Liechtenstein 1979, V-LXI, XLVI.
83. Bahrdt: System. AaO. (wie Anm. 60) Bd. 1, 112f.
84. Ebd. 115.
85. Ebd. 115.
86. Ebd. 117.
87. Ebd. 119.
88. Vgl. ebd. 119-131.
89. In dem in seinen Urteilen sehr ausgewogenen Nekrolog auf Bahrdt heißt es: "Er kannte und las die besten Schriftsteller nicht". Nekrolog auf das Jahr 1792: enthaltend Nachrichten von dem Leben merkwürdiger in diesem Jahr verstorbener Personen/gesammelt von Friedrich Schlichtegroll. 3. Jg. l. Bd. Gotha 1793, 119-255, 226.
90. Bahrdt: System. AaO. (wie Anm. 60) Bd. 1,134.
91. Ebd. 134.
92. Bayle: Dictionaire. AaO. (wie Anm. 34), 253.
93. Bahrdt: System. AaO. (wie Anm. 60) Bd. 1, 135.
94. Ebd. 136.
95. Ebd. 140-149.
96. Ebd. 142.
97. Ebd. 144.
98. Ebd. 152.
99. Ebd. 154.
100. Ebd. 151.
101. Bahrdt: Moral. AaO. (wie Anm. 62) Bd. 1, 109-112. 126f.
102. Vgl. Walter Wendland: Siebenhundert Jahre Kirchengeschichte Berlins. Berlin; Leipzig 1930, 147-171, 147. 165.

XX

DIE URSPRÜNGLICHE EINHEIT VON DENKEN UND SEIN. ZUR PHILOSOPHISCH- THEOLOGISCHEN BEGRÜNDUNG DER VERNUNFT BEI HAMANN UND SCHLEIERMACHER

Michael Eckert

"*Seyn, Glaube, Vernunft* sind lauter Verhältnisse, die sich nicht absolut behandeln lassen, sind keine Dinge, sondern reine Schulbegriffe, *Zeichen* zum Verstehen und Bewundern, Hülfsmittel, unsere Aufmerksamkeit zu erwecken und zu feßeln, (sie sind) wie die Natur *Offenbarung*, nicht ihrer selbst, sondern eines höheren Gegenstandes"[1]. Ganz offensichtlich bringt sich in diesem Text Hamanns eine Tendenz zum Ausdruck, die im 18. Jahrhundert Kritiker der Aufklärung, trotz aller Unterschiede und aller Originalität ihres Denkens, vereint. Im Versuch, den subjekt-philosophischen Ansatz der Transzendentalphilosophie Kants zu überwinden, intendiert diese Gegenbewegung eine weithin theologisch motivierte Kritik der Vernunft-kritik Kants. Den gemeinsamen Ausgangspunkt in dieser Ausein-andersetzung bildet die *Frage nach der ursprünglichen Einheit der Wirklichkeit*, die als Erfahrungshorizont ihre Eigenständigkeit gegenüber jenem Denken zu behaupten hat, das Wirklichkeit nur unter den Bedingungen reflexiver Differenz zu erfassen vermag.

In der Forschungsliteratur finden sich, soweit ich sehe, kaum Hinweise auf geistige Verwandtschaft Hamanns zu Schleiermacher. Die folgenden Überlegungen versuchen schlaglichtartig, ohne den Anspruch einer systematischen Kohärenz, einige Aspekte im Grundanliegen beider theologischer Kritiker der Aufklärung zu erörtern. Zu Schleiermacher selbst habe ich mich an anderer Stelle eingehend geäußert[2].

Die auffälligste Übereinstimmung Schleiermachers mit Hamann findet sich wohl in der 1799 erschienenen Schrift "Über die Religion. Reden an die Gebildeten unter ihren Verächtern". Nicht nur der eigentümliche Stil des Werkes selbst, der die Sprache der Romantik in ihrem bildhaft-phantasiereichen Gestus übernimmt und weniger der Anstrengung des Begriffs verpflichtet ist, erinnert unmittelbar an Hamanns genial assoziativen Denk- und Sprachduktus. Es ist vor allem eine bis in analoge Sprachbildungen reichende Ähnlichkeit, die die zugrundeliegende gemeinsame Überzeugung beider theologischer Denker unübersehbar macht. In einem ersten Schritt werde ich im folgenden unter Rekurs auf Hamann den Kernpunkt der behaupteten Übereinstimmung in der *Frage nach der ursprünglichen Einheit von Denken und Sein* deutlich machen. In knappen Zügen werde ich anschließend die *ontologische Dimension des religiösen Grundgefühls* darlegen, *in dem die Selbstdarstellung des Unendlichen im endlichen Individuum* bei Schleiermacher expliziert werden kann. Diesem Ansatz Schleiermachers stelle ich schließlich in einem dritten Schritt, ohne einen ausdrücklichen Vergleich zwischen Schleiermacher und Hamann zu intendieren, das Verständnis der *Einheit von Unendlichem und Endlichem* bei Hamann gegenüber. Die in der *Religion* begründete Einheit menschlicher Wirklichkeit konzentriert Hamann auf das Phänomen der Sprache.

I.

Der Kernpunkt von Hamanns sprachtheoretischer Kritik an der transzendentalphilosophischen Lösung der Subjekt-Objektfrage konzentriert sich auf die Vermittlungsproblematik zwischen der Allgemeinheit der Begriffe und der Mannigfaltigkeit der Erfahrung. Allgemeinheit der Vernunft und konkrete Wirklichkeit der Erfahrung werden von Kant methodisch grundsätzlich getrennt; Hamann jedoch sieht demgegenüber die verschiedenen Pole immer schon im Erfahrungszusammenhang verbunden. Dieser bildet das ursprüngliche, der Trennung durch die Reflexion vorausliegende Ganze der Wirklichkeit. Die geschichtliche Wirklichkeit der Sprache wird zum Ausgangspunkt der Kritik der Vernunft und ihrer Begriffe. So stellt Hamann vom Phänomen der Sprache her die Frage, ob überhaupt die methodische Trennung von Geistigem und Sinnlichem bzw. von Anschauung und Denken möglich ist und welche Bedeutung schließlich der

Sprache für den Zusammenhang und die Einheit von Denken und Sein zukommt. Hamann tendiert letztlich dazu, sich von jener durch die methodischen Voraussetzungen der Vernunftkritik Kants gegebenen Bedingungen abzugrenzen, die Vernunft und Sprache aus ihrer ursprünglichen metaphysischen Einbindung lösen. Die Kerngedanken hierzu entfaltet Hamann in der "Metakritik über den Purismum der Vernunft" als der kritischen Auseinandersetzung mit Kants "Kritik der reinen Vernunft". Kants restringierter Begriff der Erfahrung bildet dabei die Grundlage einer "Metakritik" der transzendentalen Vernunft, die das, man könnte sagen, "Andere der Vernunft" gegen die Vernunft selbst einklagt. In seiner "Kritik" hatte Kant zwar von einer "gemeinsamen Wurzel"[3] gesprochen, die der Unterscheidung von Sinnlichkeit und Verstand als Bedingung ihrer Möglichkeit vorausliegt. Kant hatte diesen Zusammenhang aber nur notiert. Hamann stellt nun seinerseits die Frage nach der ursprünglichen Einheit des von der Reflexion Getrennten in die Mitte einer kritischen Selbstreflexion der Vernunft. "Entspringen . . . *Sinnlichkeit und Verstand* als zwey Stämme der menschlichen Erkenntnis, aus Einer *gemeinschaftlichen Wurzel*, so daß . . . durch jene Gegenstände gegeben und durch diesen gedacht werden; zu welchem Behuf nun eine solche gewaltthätige unbefugte, eigensinnige Scheidung desjenigen, was die Natur zusammengefügt hat! Werden nicht alle beyden Stämme durch eine Dichotomie oder Zwiespalt ihrer gemeinschaftlichen Wurzel ausgehen und verdorren? Sollte sich nicht zum Ebenbilde unserer Erkenntnis *ein einziger Stamm* besser schicken, mit zwei Wurzeln, einer obern in der Luft und einer untern in der Erde? Die Erste ist unserer Sinnlichkeit preisgegeben; die Letzte hingegen unsichtbar und muß durch den Verstand gedacht werden, welches mit der Priorität des Gedachten und der Posteriorität des Gegebenen oder Genommenen, wie auch mit der beliebten Inversion der reinen Vernunft in ihren Theorien mehr übereinstimmt"[4]. Hamann zufolge gibt uns die "gemeine Volkssprache", die von Individuen gebrauchte Alltagssprache, "das schönste Gleichnis für die hypostatische Vereinigung der sinnlichen und verständlichen Naturen"[5]. Erfahrung und Geschichte, Wort und Wirklichkeit bilden nach Hamann in der Sprache *eine untrennbare, von der Natur selbst gestiftete Einheit.* Wie das Bild des einzigen Stammes zeigt, sollen sich die von Kant genannten beiden

Stämme der Erkenntnis allein aus dem Medium der Sprache und aus dem sich in ihm abspielenden Ineinander von Sinnlichem und Geistigem erklären. Im Gegensatz zu Kant bedarf es für Hamann angesichts der "Hauptfrage: Wie das Vermögen zu denken selbst möglich sey? . . . keiner Deduktion, die genealogische Priorität der Sprache vor den . . . Functionen logischer Sätze und Schlüsse"[6] zu beweisen. Die geschichtliche Einheit der Sprache liegt den Trennungen durch das Bewußtsein immer schon voraus. Die Sprache schließt den Verstand in das Gebiet des Sinnlichen wieder mit ein, von dem er sich, um seine Apriorität zu sichern, abzugrenzen suchte. Im Rekurs auf das der Vernunft ursprüngliche Verhältnis zu den Bereichen des Natürlichen, der Geschichte, der Erfahrung und Tradition gelingt es Hamann vom Phänomen der Sprache her die Transzendentalität der Vernunft in Frage zu stellen. *Die Sprache wird so zur Kritik der Vernunft*, denn "nicht nur das ganze Vermögen zu denken beruht auf Sprache, . . . sondern Sprache ist auch der Mittelpunct des Mißverstandes der Vernunft mit ihr selbst"[7]. Wenn daher Vernunft, wie Hamann sagt, ohne Sprache unsichtbar bleibt, dann wird damit zum Ausdruck gebracht, daß die Sprache das Material der Erfahrung an das Denken immer schon vermittelt hat. Die Erfahrungseinheit sprachlicher Wirklichkeit liegt der transzendentalen Reflexion immer schon voraus und vermag durch sie allein nachträglich methodischen Differenzierungen zu unterliegen.

Man wird ganz unmittelbar an Schleiermacher, so läßt sich vorgreifend sagen, erinnert, wenn Hamann das Medium der Sprache mit all jenen Attributen ausstattet, die die apriorische Vernunft von ihrem Selbstverständnis her, das Allgemeinheit intendiert, ausgeschlossen hatte. Von einer "erbärmlichen Allgemeinheit" und "leeren Nüchternheit" sei, wie es in den "Reden" heißt, das Apriori der Vernunft Kants; ja alle metaphysischen Vorstellungen bleiben im Verständnis Schleiermachers "dürftig und armeselig", "mager und dünn"[8] gegenüber aller positiven Vielfalt der Wirklichkeit. Von genau dieser Einsicht her insistiert Hamann auf dem untrennbaren Zusammenhang von Spontaneität und Rezeptivität der Vernunft, weshalb er unter Rückgriff auf das bisher Dargelegte, die Vernunft als Vermögen der Sprache interpretiert. Die "genealogische Priorität" der Sprache vor der logischen Funktion des Denkens[9] soll ontologisch verstanden werden. Sprache ist die Einheit des von Kant formal-apriorisch gefaßten Verstandesbegriffs und dessen empirischer Entsprechung; Sprache ist die Einheit von Denken, Handeln, Sich-Mitteilen (Spontaneität) und Sich-Einlassen auf das Sinnliche (Rezeptivität). "Sensus und vita sind das principium intellectus"[10], diesen Text kommentiert Hamann mit dem Hinweis, daß "sich unsere Denkungsart auf sinnliche Eindrücke und die damit verknüpften Empfindungen gründet, . . . (was) eine *Übereinstimmung der Werke des Gefühls mit den Springfedern der menschlichen Rede* vermuten" läßt[11]. Ohne diese Stelle überinterpretieren zu wollen und ohne eine offensichtlich gegebene Übereinstimmung zwischen Hamann und Schleiermacher im Begriff des "Gefühls" hier falsch zu gewichten, läßt sich aus dem Zusammenhang, in dem Hamann die "Werke des Gefühls" mit der Dimension der Sprache in Verbindung bringt, die mit beiden Begriffen jeweils identische sachliche Intention formulieren.

Die Reflexion auf das Phänomen der Sprache dient Hamann dazu, auf *das Ursprüngliche, der Trennung durch die Reflexion vorausliegende Ganze menschlicher Wirklichkeit* abheben zu können. Das Problem der Sprache formuliert demnach die Frage nach der ursprünglichen Einheit, nach der gemeinsamen Wurzel von Sinnlichkeit und Verstand, von Denken und Sein. Im Problem der Sprache spiegelt sich für Hamann in gleicher Weise wie im Problem des "Gefühls" bei Schleiermacher das sinnlich-geistige Wesen des Menschen. Diese Einheit menschlicher Wirklichkeit kennt in ihrer ursprünglichen, von der Natur vorgegebenen präreflexiven Einheit noch nicht jene erst dem Bewußtsein entstammende Trennung von Sinnlichem und Geistigem. Die ontologische Bedeutung des Problems der Sprache darf nicht übersehen werden, sonst entstünde der Eindruck, Hamann intendiere lediglich eine Reflexion auf sprachliche Vollzüge der Subjektivität. Es ist die Ebene der Existenz und des Lebens, auf die Hamann vom Phänomen der Sprache her verweist, jene Ebene, die das Ganze des Daseins in allen ihren individuellen Lebensvollzügen meint.

Der von Kant vollzogene Übergang von der Metaphysik zur Erkenntnistheorie zeigt sich, blickt man von Hamann und Schleiermacher auf Kant zurück, als überaus aufschlußreich: während Kant das Problem einer gemeinsamen Wurzel der Erkenntnisstämme nur notiert, die Einheit der Gegensätze selbst aber nicht mehr zum Gegenstand der Reflexion macht, suchen seine theologischen Kritiker dieses Defizit aufzuheben. Im Problem der Sprache bzw. im Problem des "Gefühls" suchen sie den Grund der Einheit menschlich-individuellen Seins zu erschließen. Die Wirklichkeit des Subjekts soll als jener Grund wieder sichtbar gemacht werden, in dem von Natur aus ursprünglich vereint ist, was Reflexion nachträglich trennt. Während Kant von den transzendentalen Bedingungen der Vernunft her das Sein der Wirklichkeit zu konstituieren sucht, will Hamann in der Sprache jene ursprüngliche Einheit von Denken und Sein zur Geltung bringen, die aller Transzendentalität vorausliegt. In genau dieser Intention trifft sich Hamann mit Schleiermacher. *Das Problem der Sprache ist ebenso wie das Problem des "Gefühls" letztlich von einer ontologischen Reflexion her zutreffend zu verstehen.* Diesen Zusammenhang von Schleiermacher her deutlich zu machen, ist die Absicht der folgenden Ausführungen.

II.

Was bedeutet das Prinzip des "Ein und Alles" für Schleiermachers Begriff der Religion?

Im Prinzip des "Ein und Alles" ist enthalten der Übergang vom "Ein" zu dem, was der Einheit widerspricht, nämlich Vielheit. Beide werden durch das Bindeglied des "und" verstanden als Einheit von "Allem", d.h. als Einheit von Einheit und Vielheit. Schon dieser Hinweis macht deutlich, daß das anfängliche "Ein" nicht in sich verbleiben kann, sondern notwendig unter die Bedingung seiner Entäußerung gerät und darin Teilung der Einheit impliziert: *Das Ganze kann nicht vermittelt werden, ohne sich selbst zu teilen.*

Dieses innere Wesensgesetz des "Ein und Alles" bildet für Schleiermacher sowohl die ontologische Dimension des "Grundgefühls" der Religion als auch die Grundstruktur des Göttlichen: "Ihr wißt, daß die Gottheit durch ein *unabänderliches Gesetz* sich selbst genötigt hat, ihr großes Werk bis ins Unendliche hin zu entzweien, jedes bestimmte Dasein nur aus zwei entgegengesetzten Kräften zusammenzuschmelzen, und jeden ihrer ewigen Gedanken in zwei einander feindseligen und doch nur durch einander bestehenden und unzertrennlichen Zwillingsgestalten zur

Wirklichkeit zu bringen. Diese ganze körperliche Welt ... ist ... ein ewig fortgesetztes Spiel entgegengesetzter Kräfte"[12]. Die unmittelbare Identität des Unendlichen "muß ein Prinzip sich zu individualisieren in sich haben, weil es sonst gar nicht dasein und wahrgenommen werden könnte"[13], d.h. die Vermittlung des Unendlichen, des Göttlichen bedingt notwendig dessen Entäußerung.

Die Selbstdarstellung des Unendlichen im Endlichen bringt sich als Identität und Differenz der Grundbeziehung von Gott und Mensch in der *Religion* zum Vorschein. Dieser Zusammenhang soll im folgenden nun eingehend dargestellt und interpretiert werden.

Die anfängliche Einheit des "Ein und Alles" steht für das umfassende "Grundgefühl" des Religiösen im Individuum, d.h. für die präreflexive Antizipation aller noch reflexiv-möglichen Interpretationen des "Ganzen", dessen, "in dem wir leben, weben und sind"[14]. Schleiermacher führt den Begriff des "Grundgefühls" des unendlichen Seins ein, womit er den Begriff von etwas, das vorgängig alles Spätere in sich enthält, faßt. Dieses "Grundgefühl" meint die inbegriffliche Ganzheit einer Erfahrung, vor deren Aufgliederung in einzelne Vorstellungselemente.

Die Ganzheits-Dimension der Unmittelbarkeit benennt Schleiermacher in seiner "Dialektik" (1822) genauer: "Wir haben also die Identität des Denkens und Wollens im unmittelbaren Selbstbewußtsein. Dieses unmittelbare Selbstbewußtsein, als wirklich erfüllte Zeit gesetzt, wollen wir durch den Ausdruck 'Gefühl' bezeichnen. Wir haben in unserer Sprache keinen anderen Ausdruck hierfür, und es ist nur Mangel an Distinktion, wenn man glaubt, daß dieser Ausdruck noch etwas anderes bedeuten könnte. Es ist dies keine subjektive Passivität, diese heißt vielmehr 'Empfindung'. Der Gegensatz Subjekt-Objekt bleibt hier gänzlich ausgeschlossen als ein nicht anwendbarer. Inwiefern von einem Zustand die Rede ist, so ist es freilich etwas Subjektives; aber jedes Denken ist auch ein Subjektives"[15]. Der Begriff des Gefühls darf also nicht verstanden werden als Begriff eines bloß subjektiven Empfindungszustandes; als umgreifender Begriff schließt er gerade die objektive Erscheinungswelt mit ein. Das *"Grundgefühl"* meint demnach eine *ontologische Dimension*, die aller einzelnen Wahrnehmungsmöglichkeit bestimmend vorausliegt, insofern in ihr das Wirklichkeitsganze, das Unendliche früher ist als die Teilwirklichkeit des Subjektiven und des Objektiven, des Endlichen also. Der Bewußtseinszwiespalt von Ich und Welt gründet immer schon in einem ursprünglicheren Zusammenhalt, jenem "höheren Realismus" "innerer Harmonie"[16]. Der Bezug zum ontologischen Verständnis von Sprache bei Hamann ist inhaltlich und sachlich evident.

Um das präreflexive Grundgefühl religiöser Totalitätserfahrung, in der sich das Unendliche im endlichen Individuum selbst zur Darstellung bringt, zur Sprache zu bringen, ist es notwendig – entsprechend dem unabänderlichen Wesensgesetz des "Ein und Alles"-Prinzips –, *die ursprüngliche Identitätserfahrung in die Differenzbestimmung des Subjektiven und Objektiven zu bringen.* Schleiermacher weist daher darauf hin, daß die "Religion nie rein erscheint"[17], d.h. daß sie nie nur in ihrer Unmittelbarkeit in sich verschlossen bleiben kann, aus dieser Unmittelbarkeit in Vermittlung tritt.

Der Versuch der Interpretation der unmittelbaren Totalitätserfahrung der Religion läßt sich demnach beschreiben als eine Bewußtmachung eines vorgängig unmittelbaren Bewußtseins, in dem, wie es in den "Monologen" (1800) heißt, "Vorstellung" und "Empfindung" bzw., wie es in den Reden heißt, "Anschauung" und "Gefühl", noch nicht getrennt sind, wo das Grundgefühl und sein Gegenstand, das unendliche Sein, noch verwoben und eins sind. Schleiermacher formuliert sehr genau in den Reden, wenn es heißt: "Ehe ich Euch aber in das Einzelne dieser Anschauung und Gefühle hineinführe, welches allerdings mein nächstes Geschäft an Euch sein muß, so vergönnt mir zuvor einen Augenblick darüber zu trauern, *daß ich von beiden nicht anders als getrennt reden kann*; der feinste Geist der Religion geht dadurch verloren für meine Rede, und ich kann ihr innerstes Geheimnis (die unmittelbare religiöse Totalitätserfahrung, M.E.) nur schwankend und unsicher enthüllen. Aber *eine notwendige Reflexion trennt beide*, und wer kann über irgend etwas, das zum Bewußtsein gehört, reden, ohne erst durch dieses Medium hindurch zu gehen? Nicht nur wenn wir eine innere Handlung des Gemüts mitteilen, auch wenn wir sie nur zum Stoff der Betrachtung machen, und zum deutlichen Bewußtsein erhöhen wollen, geht gleich *die unvermeidliche Scheidung* vor sich: das Faktum vermischt sich mit dem ursprünglichen Bewußtsein unserer doppelten Tätigkeit, der herrschenden und nach außen wirkenden, und der bloß zeichnenden und nachbildenden, welche den Dingen vielmehr zu dienen scheint, und sogleich bei dieser Berührung zerlegt sich der einfachste Stoff in zwei entgegengesetzte Elemente: die einen treten zusammen zum Bilde eines Objekts, die anderen dringen durch zum Mittelpunkt unseres Wesens, brausen dort auf mit unsern ursprünglichen Trieben und entwickeln ein flüchtiges Gefühl. Auch mit dem innersten Schaffen des religiösen Sinnes können wir diesem Schicksal nicht entgehen; nicht anders als in dieser getrennten Gestalt können wir seine Produkte wieder zur Oberfläche herauffördern und mitteilen. Nur denkt nicht – dies ist eben einer von den gefährlichsten Irrtümern – daß religiöse Anschauungen und Gefühle auch ursprünglich in der ersten Handlung des Gemüts so abgesondert sein dürfen, wie wir sie leider hier betrachten müssen"[18].

Schleiermachers Grundbestimmung von Religion als "Anschauung und Gefühl des Universums", die vom "Geist der Religion"[19] reden will, nimmt in dieser Begrifflichkeit die transzendentalphilosophische Unterscheidung der "zwei Stämme der menschlichen Erkenntnis" wieder auf, freilich in abgeänderter Terminologie. Die nach außen gerichteten Bewußtseinsakte nennt Schleiermacher "Anschauungen", die nach innen gerichteten Bewußtseinsakte "Gefühl". In den Monologen, darauf habe ich hingewiesen, hießen die entsprechenden Begriffe Vorstellungen und Empfindungen.

Mit diesem Ansatz sollte der von Kant aufgestellte Primat des Verstandes über die Sinnlichkeit überwunden werden. "Anschauung ohne Gefühl ist nichts und kann weder den rechten Ursprung noch die rechte Kraft haben; Gefühl ohne Anschauung ist auch nichts: beide sind nur dann und deswegen etwas, wenn und *weil sie ursprünglich eins und ungetrennt sind*"[20], d.h. sie sind eins in der Unmittelbarkeit der religiösen Totalitätserfahrung, die vorgängig alles in sich faßt, was die reflexive Dualität notwendig in Anschauung und Gefühl zerlegt.

Das Grundproblem der Reden besteht demnach darin, das präreflexiv-religiöse Grundgefühl (1) mit den notwendigen Differenzbestimmungen der Reflexion (2) in einer Einheit der Gegensätze (3) zu vermitteln. Anders formuliert: etwas auf den Begriff bringen, was dem, was

im Begriff nachträglich gefaßt wird, immer schon vorausliegt, heißt, im
vorliegenden Zusammenhang, die Frage nach der Einheit der Religion als
Identität und Differenz von Erfahrung der Totalität und begrifflicher
Individuation aufzuwerfen.

Schleiermacher hat – im Anschluß an die Romantik – die Einheit
der Gegensätze in der religiösen Betonung des Lebensbegriffs gefunden.
"Ein und Alles", dieses Prinzip der Religion meint für Schleiermacher eben
"Leben". Das Leben aber vollzieht sich im ständigen Wechsel von Aneignung
und Entäußerung. Entsprechend dem schon von mir angeführten
unabänderlichen Lebensgesetz als dem Spiel entgegengesetzter Kräfte, sagt
Schleiermacher an der eben zitierten Stelle: "Jedes *Leben* ist nur Resultat
eines beständigen Aneignens und Abstoßens, jedes Ding hat nur dadurch
sein bestimmtes Dasein, daß es die beiden Urkräfte der Natur, das durstige
Ansichziehen und das rege und lebendige Sichverbreiten, auf eine
eigentümliche Art *vereinigt und festhält*"[21]. Dieses Lebensprinzip, das in
gleicher Weise für "jede menschliche Seele"[22] gilt, übernimmt Schleiermacher aus dem Denken der Romantik. Und mit ihr erklärt er *Religion zum
Lebensprinzip* als gegensätzlich-gleichgewichtiges Zusammen von Totalitätserfahrung und Individualität.

Die Selbstdarstellung des Unendlichen als Totalität im Endlichen
vollzieht sich im Individuum in einem Prozeß von drei verschiedenen
Stadien. Die Unmittelbarkeit des Grundgefühls schließt in sich das
schlechthin Ganze des Seins (1). Das, was schon immer, ohne artikuliert zu
sein, präsent ist, gilt es zu äußern, begrifflich zu fassen. Denn allererst diese
sprachliche Formulierung des sprachlos erfahrenen Inhalts bringt diesen
selbst hervor in dem, was mit ihm gemeint war (2). Dieses In-Worte-Fassen
des Erfahrungsinhalts erzeugt ein Wissen über das Bewußtsein des Ganzen.
Wenngleich, wie Schleiermacher ausdrücklich betont, das Innere zur
Äußerung zwingt, "die notwendige Reflexion trennt beide", so bleibt dennoch
eine grundlegende *Spannung von In-sich-Verbleiben* und *Mitteilung der
religiösen Innerlichkeit*. Ein Sichäußern und sprachliches Offenbaren des
Innern, das seinen Inhalt gänzlich und vorbehaltlos mitgeteilt hätte, hätte
sich in der Mitteilung selbst schon erübrigt, wäre restlos aufgegangen und
ausgestanden. Daher bleibt notwendig, durch diese Spannung bedingt, ein

Rest, d.h. ein Überschuß des Inhalts über seine Artikulation. Die qualitative Unerschöpflichkeit des religiösen Grundgefühls, das vom Ganzen des Seins getroffen wird (Schleiermacher nennt dies die Einwirkung des Unendlichen aufs Endliche), impliziert, daß das Wissen um die religiöse Innerlichkeit die Grenzen des Sagbaren erreicht, wenn es versucht, das unaussprechlich immer schon vorgängig Ganze in notwendig trennender Begrifflichkeit zu fassen (3).

Diese komplexe Grundstruktur liegt dem Phänomen der Religion, das Schleiermacher in den Reden darzustellen versucht, zugrunde. Das Sprachproblem selbst ist offensichtlich geworden, es erklärt auch in weiten Bereichen die oszillierende Sprachgebärde der Reden "Über die Religion".

Gegenüber einem transzendentalphilosophisch geprägten Begriff von Religion sucht Schleiermacher in der Öffnung des Menschen auf das Unendliche, das den Menschen aus seiner Verstrickung in die Endlichkeit befreit, Religion als das vollkommene Gleichgewicht der entgegengesetzten Bewegungen der menschlichen Seele zu fassen. "Alle Begebenheiten in der Welt als Handlungen eines Gottes vorstellen, das ist Religion, es drückt ihre Beziehung auf ein unendliches Ganzes aus"[23] und: "So setzt der Mensch dem Endlichen, wozu seine Willkür ihn hintreibt, ein Unendliches, dem zusammenziehenden Streben nach etwas Bestimmtem und Vollendetem das erweiternde Schweben im Unbestimmten und Unerschöpflichen an die Seite; so schafft er seiner überflüssigen Kraft einen unendlichen Ausweg und stellt das Gleichgewicht und die Harmonie seines Wesens wieder her, welche unwiederbringlich verlorengeht, wenn er sich, ohne zugleich Religion zu haben, einer einzelnen Direktion überläßt"[24].

Religion nimmt daher eine versöhnende Rolle ein. So vermeidet Religion sich in egoistischer Vereinzelung zu verlieren, d.h. wie einsichtig ist, im einseitigen endlichen Subjektivismus theoretischer Vernunftautonomie; sie vermeidet gleichfalls, sich in die Mannigfaltigkeit des Handelns zu verlieren, d.h. im einseitigen endlichen Subjektivismus praktischer Vernunftautonomie. So bildet für Schleiermacher, deutlich kantkritisch gewendet, Religion das "*notwendige und unentbehrliche Dritte*"[25]. Und die Identität des Denkens und Wollens, die Schleiermacher in seiner "Dialektik" benannt hatte, ist in den Reden so formuliert: "Jenseits des Spiels seiner besonderen Kräfte und seiner Personalität faßt sie den Menschen und sieht ihn aus dem Gesichtspunkte, wo er das sein muß, was er *ist*, er wolle oder wolle nicht"[26].

III.

Die Überlegungen zu Schleiermacher haben unsere Perspektive erweitert: die an Hamann orientierte Frage nach der ursprünglichen Einheit von Denken und Sein hatte sich auf philosophisch-ontologische Aspekte beschränkt. Die religionsphilosophischen Erörterungen der "Reden über die Religion" haben nun *die theologische Dimension der ursprünglichen Einheit von Denken und Sein sichtbar gemacht. Die Vermittlung von Unendlichem und Endlichem im "religiösen Gefühl"* kann aber von einer religions-philosophischen Reflexion her auch *für das Problem der Sprache im Denken Hamanns* nachgewiesen werden. Dies gilt es im folgenden zu zeigen.

Hamanns Rekurs auf die sprachliche Bedingtheit der Vernunft ist immer schon eingebunden in die religiösen Voraussetzungen seines Denkens. Es ist letztlich die religiöse Option, die nach Hamann die Vernunft veranlaßt, den Grund ihrer selbst nicht in sich selbst zu suchen. Die schon genannte Frage, wie das Vermögen zu denken selbst möglich sei bzw. was die Vernunft in ihrem Wesen sei, enthält in sich die *Frage nach der Bedingung der Möglichkeit von Vernunft selbst*. Daß das Sprachdenken Hamanns keineswegs im Widerspruch zu einer Selbstreflexion der Vernunft steht, hat Hegel mit wünschenswerter Deutlichkeit für Hamann behauptet: "In Hamanns Werk ist Vernunft, in der Einsicht ihrer sprachlichen Bedingtheit . . . sich selbst zum Problem und zum Problem der Sprache geworden. Hamanns zeitgebundene Schriften verweisen damit zugleich auf den systematisch-philosophischen Gedanken der Selbstreflexion der Vernunft"[27]. Die Reflexion auf den unverfügbaren Bestimmungsgrund der Vernunft, der durch Reflexion selbst nicht eingeholt zu werden vermag, sucht Hamann in der vorgegebenen Einheit sprachlicher Wirklichkeit sichtbar zu machen. Kant hatte sehr wohl diese Problemstellung gesehen, konnte jedoch von seiner transzendentalen Fragestellung her jene der Vernunft vorausliegende Identität von Denken und Sein nicht mehr zum Gegenstand der Reflexion machen. Die transzendentale Reflexion bricht mit der Voraussetzung der "transzendentalen Apperzeption" – im Sinne Kants methodisch konsequent – ab.

Ich habe an anderer Stelle die Auseinandersetzung Schleiermachers mit dem Denkansatz der Transzendentalphilosophie Kants eingehend erörtert als die Einsicht in die Unmöglichkeit reflexiver Selbstbegründung des Selbstbewußtseins. Indem Hamann die von der Vernunft postulierte Autonomie auf ihre Voraussetzung und Legitimation hin befragt, führt er die Vernunft auf die Frage nach dem, was sie in ihrem eigentlichen Wesen *ist*, d.h. Hamann verknüpft in der Frage nach der Legitimation der Vernunft die ontologische Reflexion mit einer religionsphilosophischen Reflexion auf das Phänomen der Sprache. Der Grundsatz von Hamanns Sprachdenken – "Vernunft ist Sprache, Logos"[28] – impliziert bei Hamann dabei ein Verständnis von Vernunft im traditionellen Sinne, d.h. als vernehmende Vernunft, als Vermögen zur Einsicht in das Wesen der Dinge. Vernunft ist in diesem traditionellen Sinne als jenes geistige Vermögen bestimmt, das, wie eingangs formuliert ist, Offenbarung "eines höheren Gegenstandes" ermöglicht. Von daher ist verständlich, wenn Hamann knapp formuliert: "Vernunft (ist) . . . im Grunde . . . Sprache Gottes"[29]. Wenn darüberhinaus vom "göttlichen Ebenbilde in unserer Vernunft"[30] die Rede ist, dann zeigt sich die *Frage nach dem Wesen der Vernunft* letztlich beantwortbar aus dem Zusammenhang von endlicher Wirklichkeit der Sprache und göttlicher Transzendenz. Wie ist dies näherhin zu verstehen?

Die Unmöglichkeit reflexiver Selbstbegründung der Vernunft ist für Hamann – ebenso wie für Schleiermacher – keine als isoliert zu betrachtende Einsicht. Vielmehr bringt sich in ihr in negativer Weise die Bestimmung der Vernunft zum Ausdruck. Vernunft vernimmt sich als begrenzt und in eben dieser Bestimmung ist sie in positiver Hinsicht zu verstehen als Relation zwischen Göttlichem und Menschlichem. In der präreflexiven Einheit sprachlicher Wirklichkeit der Vernunft ist das vernehmende Vermögen der Vernunft immer schon mitangelegt, wie Hamann sagt, als "*communicatio göttlicher und menschlicher idiomatum*"[31]. So wird die Begegnung mit der erfahrbaren Wirklichkeit für die Vernunft zu einer Begegnung mit dem Göttlichen, die erfahrbare Wirklichkeit wird selbst

zur "Sprache Gottes". Das Ziel der Vernunftkritik ist erreicht, insofern die
Vernunft in der Kommunikation mit dem Göttlichen ihre Bestimmung aus
der ihr vorgegebenen Wirklichkeit vernimmt, die auf die Transzendenz ihres
Urgrundes verweist.

Mit Blick auf die grundlegende Übereinstimmung von Hamann und
Schleiermacher läßt sich für Hamann vom Problem der Sprache her, für
Schleiermacher vom Problem des "Gefühls" her jenes ursprüngliche Anliegen
formulieren, aus dem ihr ganzes Denken lebt. Beide sind durchdrungen von
der religiös-theologischen Option, alles Endliche aus seinem Bezug zur
Transzendenz zu verstehen. In der Aufwertung einer allem Anspruch
subjektiver Vernunft vorausliegenden erfahrbaren Wirklichkeit sehen beide
eine *immer schon gegebene Vermittlung von Endlichem und Unendlichem*, von
Göttlichem und naturhaft Menschlichem. Für Schleiermacher wie Hamann
bildet die Transzendentalphilosophie Kants die Manifestation eines
Mißverstandes der Vernunft mit sich selbst. Dem Nachweis der Begrenztheit
endlicher Vernunft und der Verwiesenheit der Vernunft auf das nicht ihren
Möglichkeiten entspringende Vernehmen ihrer Bestimmung gilt ihr
gemeinsames Interesse.

Es ist in dem hier gesteckten Rahmen nicht meine Absicht, die
Unterschiede zwischen Hamann und Schleiermacher hervorzuheben und zu
betonen. Ein solches Interesse hätte sich eingehend mit Schleiermachers
Hermeneutik auseinanderzusetzen und sicherlich das in späteren Jahren
Schleiermachers sehr stark ausgeprägte systematische Erkenntnisinteresse in
philosophischer wie theologischer Hinsicht abzuheben von Hamanns stärker
philologisch und literarisch geprägten Interessen, worauf Hegel schon
hingewiesen hatte.

In den bisherigen Ausführungen zu Hamanns Reflexion des
Phänomens der Sprache war einerseits eine gewisse Ambivalenz im
Verständnis dessen, was mit Sprache gemeint ist, unüberhörbar; andererseits
war mit der Einbindung der Vernunft in die ihr vorgegebene sprachliche
Wirklichkeit diese zugleich ausgezeichnet als Medium und Vermittlungsort
von Unendlichem und Endlichem. Mit diesem Anspruch verbindet sich aber,
ohne daß dies ausdrücklich bisher formuliert wurde, die *Verbindung des*
Vernunftbegriffs mit dem Offenbarungsbegriff über den Begriff der Sprache bei

Hamann. Dieser Zusammenhang wird unmittelbar deutlich, wenn man sieht, daß Hamanns "Sprachprincipium der Vernunft"[32] in *schöpfungstheologischen Voraussetzungen* begründet liegt. Gemäß christlicher Offenbarungs- vorstellungen manifestiert sich der göttliche Logos im Akt der Schöpfung als Wort. Alle Wirklichkeit als geschaffene Wirklichkeit ist von daher begründet im Wort Gottes, durch das die Welt ist. In metaphorischer Rede kann Hamann deshalb die Wirklichkeit selbst als Sprache, als "Natursprache"[33] bezeichnen. Von daher erschließt sich die geschaffene Wirklichkeit nicht nur als ein sich sprachlich offenbarendes Sein, das in vielfältiger Form auf seinen Urgrund verweist; vielmehr erklärt sich auch allein von den schöpfungstheologischen Voraussetzungen her der Zusammenhang zwischen der Rezeptivität der Vernunft und der sprachlichen Offenbarung ihres Urgrundes. Insofern nämlich endliche Vernunft selbst geschaffene Wirklichkeit ist, wird sie selbst Medium der Offenbarung, von der her Vernunft sich zu verstehen und zu bestimmen hat. Im Gegensatz zu Kant wird bei Hamann die Vernunft selbst das Auge, das in ihrem vernehmenden Vollzug das Wesen der Dinge, d.h. letztlich ihr Begründetsein im Schöpfungsakt Gottes erkennt. "Das Licht der Wahrheit liegt also im anschauenden Auge, und die Offenbarung der Gegenstände geschieht durch einen unmittelbaren Actum gesunder Empfänglichkeit"[34].

Wenn Hamann "Sprache, die Mutter der Vernunft und Offenbarung, ihr Alpha und Omega"[35] nennt, dann wird man nach dem bisher Gesagten eine Übertragung des von Hamann Gemeinten in den Kontext Schleiermacher'schen Denkens vornehmen dürfen. Der Gedanke des "Gefühls" hat für Schleiermacher eine ähnlich vermittelnde Funktion wie das mit Sprache bei Hamann Gemeinte, wobei zugleich die oszillierende Bedeutung der Begriffe nicht übersehen werden kann. Zugleich muß die kritische Wendung gegenüber der Transzendentalphilosophie Kants immer als Hintergrund mitgedacht werden. Von daher versteht sich dann auch der Versuch, Sprache bzw. "Gefühl" als ontologisch-präreflexive Dimension der Vermittlung von Endlichem und Unendlichem einzuführen und zugleich in subjektiver Hinsicht als vernehmendes Vermögen zu behaupten. In seiner Dogmatik (1830) stellt Schleiermacher die vernunftkritische Wendung klar, wenn er seinen Begriff des "schlechthinnigen Abhängigkeitsgefühls" davon abgrenzt, "als ob dieses Abhängigkeitsgefühl selbst durch irgendein vorheriges Wissen um Gott bedingt sei. Und dies mag umso nötiger sein, da viele, welche sich eines vollkommenen *begriffenen* ursprünglichen, d.h. von allem Gefühl unabhängigen *Begriffs von Gott* sicher *wissen* in diesem höheren Selbstbewußtsein, . . . eben das Gefühl, welches uns für die Grundform aller Frömmigkeit gilt, als etwas fast Untermenschliches weit von sich weisen"[36]. Wenn Schleiermacher, wie unsere Ausführungen (Teil II) zu den "Reden" deutlich zu machen versuchten, das religiöse Grundgefühl als umfassendes Lebensprinzip verstehen will, in dem sich das Unendliche im Endlichen selbst zur Darstellung bringt, dann zeigt sich: die sprachliche Wirklichkeit bzw. die Wirklichkeit des "Gefühls" soll jene präreflexive, nicht vom Bewußtsein bestimmte ursprüngliche Einheit, in der Denken und Sein zur Identität gebracht sind, bezeichnen. Das Bewußtsein unserer Abhängigkeit bzw. das Vernehmen der "Sprache Gottes" erschließt die eigentliche Bestimmung der Vernunft, wie Hamann sagt: "Ohne Wort keine Vernunft – keine Welt"[37].

Mit diesen Überlegungen sind die Voraussetzungen zum Verständnis des Phänomens der *Religion* in der Sicht Hamanns und Schleiermachers vorbereitet. Die These unserer Überlegungen, daß im Ausgang von der ursprünglichen Einheit von Denken und Sein für Hamann wie für Schleiermacher die Legitimationsbasis einer theologischen Begründung der Vernunft gegeben ist, erfährt vom Verständnis der Religion her seine letzte Bestätigung. Aus eben diesem Grund wurde auch auf Schleiermachers Schrift "Über die Religion. Reden an die Gebildeten unter ihren Verächtern" (1799) verwiesen. Für Hamann wie für Schleiermacher handelt es sich letztlich um eine Reflexion der religiösen Grundoption ihrer eigenen Lebensgeschichte, die ihr gesamtes Denken und Handeln bestimmt und prägt. Die Grundproblematik, die sich in der Erörterung der Frage nach dem Wesen der Religion stellt, ist das Verhältnis von Unendlichem und Endlichem, für dessen religiösen Vermittlungspunkt die Tradition schon immer sehr verschiedene Benennungen kannte.

"So wie alle Arten der Unvernunft das Daseyn der Vernunft und ihren Mißbrauch voraussetzen: so müssen alle Religionen eine Beziehung auf den Glauben einer einzigen, selbständigen und lebendigen *Wahrheit* haben, die, *gleich unserer Existenz, älter als unsere Vernunft* seyn muß und daher nicht durch die Genesin der letzten, sondern *durch eine unmittelbare Offenbarung der ersteren erkannt werden kann.* Weil unsere Vernunft bloß aus den äußeren Verhältnissen sichtbarer, sinnlicher, unstätiger Dinge den Stoff ihrer Begriffe schöpft, um selbige nach der Form ihrer inneren Natur selbst zu bilden, und zu ihrem Genuß oder Gebrauch anzuwenden: so liegt der *Grund der Religion in unserer ganzen Existenz und außer der Sphäre unserer Erkenntniskräfte*, welche alle zusammengenommen, den zufälligsten und abstractesten Modum unserer Existenz ausmachen. Daher jene *mythische und poetische Ader aller Religionen*, ihre Thorheit und ärgerliche Gestalt in den Augen einer heterogenen, incompetenten . . . Philosophie, die ihrer Erziehungskraft die höhere Bestimmung unserer Herrschaft über die Erde unverschämt andichtet"[38]. Es bedarf wohl der Kenntnis von Schleiermachers gesamten Schrift "Über die Religion", um Hamanns Nähe zum Denken Schleiermachers zutreffend einschätzen zu können. Auch Schleiermacher beschwört einen "höheren Realismus" der Religion, eine "eigene Provinz"[39] der Religion, die ihre Bestimmung sich selbst verdankt, und nicht fremder Indienstnahme unterliegt: "Nachdem ihr Euch selbst ein Universum geschaffen habt, seid ihr überhoben, an dasjenige zu denken, welches Euch schuf"[40]. Religion ist für Hamann wie für Schleiermacher aus dem Zusammenhang menschlicher Existenz gesehen immer der Ausdruck einer Verbindung und eines Bandes zwischen Gott und Mensch, das die Grundsätze menschlicher Vernunft umkehrt und die Ausrichtung des menschlichen Daseins auf seinen Ursprung in Gott lenkt. Diese Umkehrung des Verstandes wird auch mit dem Hinweis auf die Geschichtlichkeit, das Poetische und Mythische aller Religionen betont, da diese sich nicht nur auf die Erkenntnismöglichkeiten des Menschen, sondern auf die Inanspruchnahme der ganzen Existenz des Menschen beziehen. Es ist ganz offensichtlich, daß beide Denker auch eine Abgrenzung gegenüber der natürlichen Vernunftreligion der Aufklärung beabsichtigen, wenn sie Mythos und Poesie als zur Religion gehörig behaupten.

Wichtig zu sehen ist, daß Mythos und Poesie in je eigener Weise ebenso wie die Religion Formen der Vermittlung von Unendlichem und Endlichem darstellen. Gegenüber der Philosophie, die das Unendliche

durch Reflexion zu begreifen versucht, sucht die Poesie, und in ähnlicher
Form der Mythos, in der Sprache metaphorischer Bilder symbolisch das
Göttliche zu vergegenwärtigen. Religion ist darüberhinaus die existentielle
Form der Vermittlung von Göttlichem und Menschlichem. Für Hamann
wird die Wirklichkeit der Sprache als "Sprache Gottes" jenes Medium, in
dem ahnungsvoll das Ganze in der Einheit von Denken und Sein und damit
die Wahrheit des Ursprungs menschlicher Existenz berührt zu werden
vermag. Wenn Schleiermacher in seiner späteren Zeit vom "Mitgesetztsein
Gottes im Menschen" spricht, dann ist dies die den Menschen in der Religion
eingeschaffene, unergründliche Fähigkeit sich seiner transzendenten
Bestimmung bewußt werden zu können. Diese Ahnung der höchsten Einheit
und Wahrheit, die alles Endliche und Einzelne von dieser Wahrheit her
begreifen läßt, ist bis in sprachlich identische Formulierungen bei Hamann
und Schleiermacher zu finden.

Hamanns auf Kierkegaard verweisende Rede vom "paradoxalen"
Zusammenhang von Unendlichem und Endlichem, der letztlich eine
existentielle Entscheidung des Menschen für eine transzendente, von der
Vernunft nicht faßbare Wahrheit verlangt, hat Schleiermacher so nicht
formuliert. Wenn ich richtig sehe, läge der schärfste Gegensatz zwischen
Schleiermacher und Hamann wohl letztlich auch darin, daß Schleiermacher
an einer *Vermittlung von Glauben und Wissen* festhält, die auch der Vernunft
ihr Recht zubilligt. Dieser fundamentaltheologisch interessante Aspekt im
Denken Schleiermachers ist schon in den "Reden", trotz aller Differenzen
ihrer Interpretation, die Legende sind, zu finden: Religion "muß doch etwas
Eigenes sein, was in der Menschen Herz hat kommen können, etwas
*Denkbares, wovon sich ein Begriff aufstellen läßt, über den man reden und
streiten kann*"[41]. Das Problem der Kritik der Rationalisierung religiöser
Erfahrung einerseits und der gleichzeitigen Unentbehrlichkeit philosophischer Reflexion andererseits wird sich in der Spätzeit Schleiermachers
immer deutlicher ausprägen. Wenngleich meine Kenntnis Hamanns nur in
einer ersten Annäherung besteht, konnte ich nicht den Eindruck gewinnen,
Hamann habe eine ähnliche Vermittlung von Glauben und Wissen
intendiert.

Der enge *Zusammenhang von Religion, Sprache und Geschichte*, der sich von Hamanns Offenbarungsverständnis her ergibt, zeigt aber schließlich, und darauf muß in bezug auf Schleiermacher ebenfalls hingewiesen werden, ein Verständnis der *Religion als positiver Religion* im Unterschied zu einer natürlichen Vernunftreligion. Ebenso wie Schleiermacher betont Hamann, daß es immer nur geschichtlich verfaßte Gemeinschaften gab, in denen sich ganz bestimmte, geschichtlich tradierte Religionsformen artikulieren. Hamanns Verständnis der Religion als der in der "Sprache Gottes" begründeten ursprünglichen Einheit menschlichen Lebens, von Schleiermacher "schlechthinniges Abhängigkeitsgefühl" genannt, ist mit der geschichtlichen Einbindung menschlichen Lebens immer schon historisch mitgeformt von den Bedingungen jeweiliger Lebenswelt. Ein "Purismum der Vernunft", damit auch die Möglichkeit einer aus den Bedingungen der Vernunft konstruierten Religion, ist von den schöpfungstheologischen Voraussetzungen eines Verständnisses der Wirklichkeit her ausgeschlossen. In der Religion, als dem in der Existenz des Menschen zum Bewußtsein kommenden Vermittlungsort von Unendlichem und Endlichem, ist die "Wahrheit . . . gleich unserer Existenz, älter als unsere Vernunft"[42].

Gegen Descartes formuliert Hamann jenen Zusammenhang der ursprünglichen Einheit von Denken und Sein, dessen transzendente Bedingtheit menschlich-religiöses Bewußtsein nachträglich erschließt, stellvertretend für Schleiermacher, aber in gleicher Weise für dessen Denken gültig: "Nicht cogito, ergo sum, sondern umgekehrt, oder noch hebräischer *Est, ergo cogito*, und mit der Inversion eines so einfachen Principii bekommt vielleicht das ganze System eine andere Sprache und Richtung"[43]. Hamann und Schleiermacher stehen damit in der Linie der Argumentation der Spätphilosophie Schellings, dessen ontologische Fundierung der Vernunft im Horizont des ontologischen Gottesbeweises der Tradition formuliert wird. Indem Schelling die begriffliche Bestimmung des Wesens der Dinge durch die Vernunft abhängig macht von der vorgängigen Existenz der Dinge, spricht er der Vernunft zugleich die Möglichkeit ab, aus sich selbst die Existenz der Dinge begründen zu können. Das "Was", d.h. das Wesen der Dinge kann die Vernunft nach Schelling nur erkennen, "wenn" die Dinge sind. Die Vernunft kann das "Daß" der Dinge nur als "unvordenkliches Sein" der Dinge einsehen, das der Vernunft in ihrem "unendlichen Mangel an Sein"[44] selbst vorausliegt.

Anmerkungen

1. ZH VII 172,36 (zitiert nach: Briefwechsel, hrsg. v.W. Ziesemer und A. Hentel, 1955 ff; abg. ZH). Als Forschungsbericht vgl. E. Büchsel, Geschärfte Aufmerksamkeit – Hamannliteratur seit 1972, in: DVjS 60 (1986), 375-425.
2. Vgl. M. Eckert, Gott – Glauben und Wissen. Schleiermachers Philosophische Theologie, 1987 (Schleiermacher-Archiv 3).
3. Kant, KrV, B 30.
4. N III 286,29; Herv. v. mir (zitiert nach: Hist.-krit. Ausg. sämtlicher Werke in 6 Bdn von J. Nadler, 1949ff; abg. N).
5. N III 287,14.
6. ZH VII 173,3.
7. N III 286,9; vgl. zum Problem der Sprache bei Hamann W. Benjamin, Über Sprache überhaupt und über die Sprache des Menschen, in: GS, hrsg. v. R. Tiedemann u. H. Schweppenhäuser, 1980, 140-157.
8. R, 277; 248; 275 (zitiert nach: Über die Religion. Reden an die Gebildeten unter ihren Verächtern, hrsg. v. R. Otto. 6. Aufl. 1967; abg. R). Hierzu vgl. M. Eckert, Das Verhältnis von Unendlichem und Endlichem in F. Schleiermachers Reden "Über die Religion", in: Archiv für Religionspsychologie 16 (1983), 22-56.
9. N III 286,4f.
10. N III 39,10.
11. N II 123,22; Herv. v. mir.
12. R, 6.
13. R, 241.
14. Apg 17, 28; vgl. R, 295.
15. F. Schleiermacher, Dialektik, hrsg. v. R. Odebrecht, 1976, 287.
16. R, 54.
17. R, 47.
18. R, 71 ff; Herv.v. mir.
19. R, 72.
20. R, 73.
21. R, 6.
22. R, 6.
23. R, 57.
24. R, 115.
25. R, 52; Herv. v. mir.
26. R, 51f; Herv. v. mir.
27. G. W. Hegel, Hamanns Schriften, in: Werke 11, hrsg. v. E. Moldenhauer u. K. M. Michel, 1970, 248.
28. ZH V 177,17.
29. ZH VI 296,6.
30. N I 305,19.
31. N III 27,7.
32. ZH VII 169,22.

33. N III 287,13.
34. N IV 423,52.
35. ZH VII 108,20.
36. F. Schleiermacher, Der christliche Glaube, 2. Aufl. 1830, hrsg. v. M. Redeker, Bd 1, 1960, 23; Herv. v. mir.
37. ZH VII 172, 27.
38. N III 191,22; Herv. v. mir.
39. R, 37.
40. R, 2.
41. R, 47; Herv. v. mir.
42. N III 191,22.
43. ZH V 448, 26; Herv. v. mir.
44. Vgl. M. Frank, Der unendliche Mangel an Sein, 1975, sowie ders., Das individuelle Allgemeine, 1985 (zu Hamann 135, 150f).

XXI

SCHLEIERMACHER IM URTEIL WILHELM HERRMANNS UND DES JUNGEN KARL BARTH

Hans-Jürgen Gabriel

50 Jahre nach Schleiermachers Sendschreiben an Lücke hat Wilhelm Herrmann (1846-1922) in seiner ersten großen Schrift zur Grundlegung der Theologie *Die Religion im Verhältnis zum Welterkennen und zur Sittlichkeit* (1879) dessen Anliegen aufgegriffen, "einen ewigen Vertrag zu stiften zwischen dem lebendigen christlichen Glauben und der nach allen Seiten freigelassenen, unabhängig für sich arbeitenden wissenschaftlichen Forschung, so daß jener nicht diese hindert und diese nicht jenen ausschließt". Diese Anknüpfung im Prinzipiellen verbindet Herrmann jedoch sofort mit einer Kritik im Detail: Es genüge nicht, wie Schleiermacher um die Demonstration bemüht zu sein, "daß jedes Dogma ... auch so gefaßt werden kann, daß es uns unverwickelt läßt mit der Wissenschaft", vielmehr müßten die Grenzen, die hier dem christlichen Glauben gezogen werden sollen, "von ihm selbst aus als durch sein eigenes Wesen gesetzt begriffen werden können". Eine Grenze, die den Glauben "von außen her durch das Welterkennen gezogen wird", würde "seine Aussagen auf die Überzeugungskraft einer wahrscheinlichen Annahme" reduzieren. Herrmann sucht eine solche Grundlegung der Theologie, die es nicht nötig hat, zur Erhaltung ihrer Glaubhaftigkeit mit der sich entwickelnden Wissenschaft einen zeitlich begrenzten Kompromiß einzugehen, sondern von vornherein deren Weg nicht kreuzt, da sie "aus dem Welterkennen nicht hervorgeht".[1]

Um Herrmanns Intention und die aus ihr hervorgehende Kritik an Schleiermacher zu verdeutlichen, ist es erforderlich, zunächst die Position, von der her sie vorgetragen wird, zu umschreiben. Die von Herrmann

unternommene Grundlegung der Theologie, die Überlegungen Albrecht
Ritschls aufnimmt und mit subjektivierender Tendenz weiterführt, muß im
Zusammenhang mit dem Aufkommen des Neukantianismus und der
Lebensphilosophie gesehen werden. Namentlich zu letzterer in ihrer von
Wilhelm Dilthey vertretenen Form kann sie als theologiegeschichtliche
Parallele betrachtet werden. Herrmanns Beschäftigung und Auseinander-
setzung mit Schleiermacher kann insofern besonderes Interesse
beanspruchen, als seine theologische Konzeption – historisch betrachtet –
Übergangscharakter aufweist. Einerseits ist sie der auf Schleiermacher
fußenden und von ihm inspirierten liberalen Theologie in Deutschland
zuzurechnen, andererseits legen es die genannten Charakteristika nahe, sie
als Vorstufe für den von Kierkegaard beeinflußten theologischen
Neuaufbruch nach dem I. Weltkrieg, die frühe dialektische Theologie, zu
sehen. Signifikativ hierfür ist die Tatsache, daß Herrmann der theologische
Lehrer von Karl Barth und Rudolf Bultmann ist, die diesem bei aller
Unterschiedlichkeit ihrer Auffassunge und in Verbindung damit auch ihres
Schleiermacher – Verständnisses wesentliche Impulse verdanken.

Herrmann ist bestrebt, den erreichten Fortschritten sowohl in den
Naturwissenschaften als auch in der Erforschung der Geschichte des
Christentums Rechnung zu tragen, und versucht vorrangig, die angesichts des
schwindenden Einflusses des Spätidealimus im Banne des natur-
wissenschaftlichen Materialismus oder der Philosophie Kants bzw. des
Neukantianismus stehenden Gebildeten anzusprechen. Neben der
Respektierung der errungenen Erkenntnisse und des möglichen
Erkenntnisfortschritts in Naturwissenschaften und Geschichte (besonders in
den kritischen Bibelwissenschaften) bestimmen des weiteren das Bestreben,
auf ethische Probleme – besonders im Anschluß an Kants praktische
Philosophie – einzugehen, und die Kritik an dem Unvermögen des natur-
wissenschaftlichen Materialismus, gesellschaftlichen Fragen gerecht zu
werden, Herrmanns theologische Neukonzeption.[2] Seine Theologie basiert
ebenso wie die Lebensphilosophie von Dilthey auf der in Anknüpfung an
Kants Gegenüberstellung von theoretischer und praktischer Vernunft
vorgenommenen Unterscheidung zwischen Erkennen und Erleben.[3] Wie
Dilthey macht Herrmann geltend, daß Kants philosophisches Grundgerüst in

Bezug auf das wollende und fühlende menschliche Individuum anzuwenden sei, nicht – im Sinne des Neukantianismus – auf ein abstraktes Denksubjekt.[4] Über Dilthey hinausgehend prätendiert Herrmann darauf, Kant als christlichen Denker zu interpretieren und von dieser Voraussetzung her auch zu kritisieren. Kant sei sich zwar seiner Übereinstimmung mit dem Christentum bewußt, jedoch trage er in der konkreten Ausführung seiner Philosophie, insbesondere der praktischen, diesem ihn verpflichtenden Hintergrund seines Denkens nicht genügend Rechnung. Er vernachlässige die Probleme des Übels, der Schuld und der Sünde sowie die Bedeutung des Glaubens. Gemeinsam mit Schleiermacher lehnt Herrmann den rationalistischen Grundansatz der kantischen Religionsphilosophie ab.[5] Deutlich wird jedoch an Herrmanns Kant-Kritik der Einfluß der nach 1815 einsetzenden Erweckungsbewegung, zu der sich Schleiermacher im Widerspruch befand. Herrmann versteht seine eigene theologische Grundlegung als eine sachliche Richtigstellung der Philosophie Kants, die es auf den lebendigen Menschen zu beziehen gelte und deren Herkunft aus der christlichen Offenbarung voll zum Tragen zu bringen sei.

Fundamental wirkt in Herrmanns Überlegungen das Anliegen, christlicherseits die Persönlichkeit des Menschen zu begründen und zu sichern. Angesichts der industriellen Entwicklung und des Aufschwungs von Naturwissenschaft und Technik erhebt er den Vorwurf, daß "der Mensch ein Sklave seiner Arbeit geworden" sei. Gegen die innere Leere und die Verkümmerung der Persönlichkeit, von der sowohl die Intelligenz wie die Arbeiter bedroht seien, bilde nur der christliche Glaube einen wirksamen Schutz. Durch Förderung sittlichen Verhaltens bewahre dieser zugleich die moderne Gesellschaft davor, "in Unfrieden (zu) vorkommen."[6] Die durch die Gottesreichsverkündigung Jesu ermöglichte Konstituierung der Persönlichkeit stelle dem Menschen die mit unerbittlicher Logik Anerkennung fordernde Aufgabe, sich über die Natur zu erheben. Von dieser Voraussetzung her kann Herrmann behaupten, daß das Christentum "der wahre geistige Fortschritt der Menschheit" sei – ein Gedanke, der ihn in die Nähe Schleiermachers führt. Herrmann vertritt die Auffassung, daß die moderne Naturwissenschaft ihre Entstehung dem Schoße des Christentums verdanke, in dem auch der natürliche Selbstbehauptungswille des Menschen gegenüber seiner Umwelt zu seiner Vollendung komme.[7]

Herrmann geht aus von der in Kants Philosophie vertretenen Einheit der theoretischen und praktischen Vernunft. Mit ihrer Anwendung auf den konkreten Menschen, der mit dem Erkennen zugleich ein Gefühl für Werte und den Willen zum Handeln verbindet, geht bei Hermann nun freilich eine Akzentuierung der bei Kant vorliegenden agnostizistischen und subjektivistischen Momente einher. Herrmann leugnet die Möglichkeit einer objektiven Erkenntnis der Naturzusammenhänge. Da das Erkennen dem Handlungszweck untergeordnet sei, präge dieser das Ergebnis der Erkenntnis. Die Voraussetzung für die "Hypothese von der Begreiflichkeit der Natur" sei ausschließlich der Wille des Menschen, die Natur zu beherrschen. Nach Hermanns Auffassung denken wir uns nur die "als Objekt unseres Handelns, als Naturboden unserer Zwecke" aufgefaßte Natur als "notwendig zusammenhängend erklärbar". Für ihn ist das Weltganze eine Vorstellung, die der erkennende, Werte fühlende und handeln wollende Mensch aus sich herausprojiziert. Herrmann Denkansatz läuft darauf hinaus, dem Wollen und Werten, d.h. der menschlichen Praxis, ein Übergewicht gegenüber dem theoretischen Erkennen beizulegen. Indem er Kant folgend davon ausgeht, daß menschliches Wollen und Werten geleitet wird von dem "unerklärbare(n) Sittliche(n), das Anerkennung gebietet", rangiert dies für ihn als diejenige Instanz, die das Streben nach einer einheitlichen und zusammenhängenden Anschauung der Welt letztlich motiviert.[8]

Von seinen Voraussetzungen her bestreitet Hermann die Möglichkeit, durch Verallgemeinerung wissenschaftlicher Forschungsergebnisse zu einem zwar der ständigen Überprüfung bedürftigen, aber dennoch wirkliche Zusammenhänge erfassenden Weltbild zu gelangen. Jeder in dieser Richtung unternommene Versuch – Herrmann verwendet hierfür angesichts der ihm bekannten Entwürfe (von Hegel, Schelling und Vertretern des Spätidealismus wie des Materialismus) die Bezeichnung "Metaphysik" – sei subjektiv und habe nichts mit theoretischer Welterklärung zu tun, sondern sei lediglich Ausdruck praktischen Verhaltens zur Welt. Derartige "Metaphysik", "die der weitergleitende Strom der wissenschaftlichen

Bewegung unwiderstehlich zusammenbrechen läßt", bezeichnet Herrmann als ungeeignet, das menschliche Bedürfnis, "eine einheitliche Welt anzuschauen", zu befriedigen. Metaphysik, und d.h. für Herrmann in der Konsequenz Philosophie überhaupt, habe zwar ihren Stellenwert als Erkenntnistheorie der Naturwissenschaften, dürfe aber nicht auf die eigentlichen Belange des Menschen übergreifen, die der Ethik und Religion vorbehalten sind.[9] Herrmann kritisiert an der von ihm als "Metaphysik" abgetanen weltanschaulichen Verallgemeinerung ihren kontemplativen Charakter, der dem praktischen Bedürfnis des Menschen und der von hier ausgehenden Motivation, die Welt als Einheit aufzufassen, nicht Rechnung trage. Folgt man seinen Darlegungen, die bestrebt sind, eine Disproportion zwischen theoretischem und praktischem Verhältnis des Menschen zur Welt aufzuweisen, so wird damit die Grundvoraussetzung aller menschlichen Einwirkung auf die Natur, nämlich daß diese den menschlichen Handlungszwecken unterworfen werden kann, fraglich, weil sie aus der Praxis keine Bestätigung erfährt. Ihre Verifizierung kann nach Herrmanns Ausführungen nur aus der mit der Ethik in Korrelation stehenden christlichen Religion erfolgen.[10] Letzterer fällt insofern anstelle der Metaphysik die Aufgabe zu, eine einheitliche Weltanschauung zuwege zu bringen.

Wenden wir uns nunmehr der Funktion von Moral und Religion sowie dem Verhältnis zwischen beiden in Herrmanns Überlegungen zu. Er folgt Kant mit der Auffassung, daß der an Werten orientierte und auf Handeln angelegte Mensch nicht denkbar ist ohne eine intentionale Bezugnahme auf ein "unbedingtes Gesetz des Wollens, welches sich durch sich selbst eine Geltung verschafft, die aus keiner Reflexion auf irgendeine Lusterfahrung gewonnen werden kann". In der Unterwerfung unter dieses für alle Menschen verbindliche Gesetz, das dem Menschen im Gegensatz zu seinem empirischen Selbst das Bewußtsein der Freiheit ermögliche und die Autonomie seines Willens begründe, werde es ihm möglich, sich als Endzweck zu denken.[11]

Ist Herrmann bis hierher Kants Begründung des kategorischen Imperativs gefolgt, so weicht er nunmehr in der Näherbestimmung des Verhältnisses von Moral und Religion von ihm ab, Im Gegensatz zu Kant, der die Religion faktisch als Bestandteil der praktischen Philosophie in den von der Ethik bestimmten Rahmen integriert, kehrt Hermann dieses Verhältnis um in dem Sinne, daß das Bewußtsein des Sittengesetzes als Prädisposition für die christliche Religion fungiert. Mit Kant hält Herrmann zwar daran fest, daß das Moralgesetz keiner religiösen Begründung bedarf, aber er verbindet damit die Feststellung, daß "die persönliche Aneignung des Sittlichen oder die Sittlichkeit sich notwendig (Unterstreichung vom Vf.) vollzieht in der Form einer religiösen Welterklärung" und "der Mensch zum Verständnis und zur wirktlichen Aneignung derselben durch die geistige Freiheit, die ihm der Glaube verschafft, aufgeschlossen wird".[12] Nach Herrmanns Auffassung qualifiziert erst das Sittengesetz den Menschen zum Subjekt der Religion, und für das Christentum soll hiernach eine "solidarische Verbindung von Religion und Sittlichkeit" charakteristisch sein.[13] Herrmann, dem der Fortschrittsoptimismus Kants und der Evolutionsgedanke Schleiermachers zweifelhaft geworden sind, muß damit auf die Voraussetzung verzichten, daß Natur und Gesellschaft dem dem Sittengesetz verpflichtet handelnden Menschen zum Endzweck seiner und aller Menschen Glückseligkeit dienstbar sind.[14] Diese Voraussetzung sucht Herrmann jedoch mittels der Religion aufrecht zu erhalten. Die Religion bewirke – das Leistungsvermögen theoretischer Welterkenntnis überbietend – eine dahingehende Änderung des menschlichen Bewußtseins, daß ihm Natur und Gesellschaft als dem Endzweck, der Glückseligkeit aller Menschen, dienstbar erscheinen. "Der christliche Glaube an Gott schließt das Urteil ein, daß die natürlichen Bedingungen, an welche gebunden der Mensch sich zum höchsten sittlichen Gute emporstreckt, trotz des Widerspruches, den die menschliche Erkenntnis dagegen einlegt, keine Schranken für den sittlichen Geist sind, sondern die seinem eigenen innersten Wesen entsprechenden Formen für die Verwirklichung seines Zwecks."[15] Daraus resultiere die Gewißheit, "daß die Seligkeit des Menschen der Sinn alles Tatsächlichen ist".[16]

Ist die Religion somit wieder enger mit der Moral verflochten, so ist Herrmann nunmehr auch bestrebt, ihr nicht nur ihren Ort im subjektiven Erleben anzuweisen, sondern sie dank ihrer notwendigen Bezogenheit auf die Moral auch an deren Allgemeingültigkeit partizipieren zu lassen.[17]

Zusammen mit Schleiermacher lehnt Herrmann zwar den rationalistischen Grundansatz der Religionsphilosophie Kants ab,[18] aber die von ihm angestrebte Überwindung ist fragwürdig. Unterstrichen wird dies, wenn Herrmann erklärt: "Alles, was als religiöse Erkenntnis oder religiöses Gefühl genannt wird, muß sich dadurch legitimieren können, daß es dazu dient, die sittliche Persönlichkeit in sich zu vollenden und als Endzweck über die Welt zu erheben. Es wird als ein Moment wirklicher Religion erst verstanden, indem diese Beziehung an ihm aufgefaßt wird. Die Religion wird zum Aberglauben, wenn es unmöglich ist, in ihr die göttliche Offenbarung zu erkennen, welche die Seligkeit des Menschen als einer sittlichen Person verbürgt."[19] Damit ist die Position bezeichnet, von der her Herrmanns Verhältnis zu Schleiermachers Kritik an Kants Religionsphilosophie zu beleuchten ist. Er greift die Abgrenzung der Religion gegenüber Metaphysik und Moral auf, die Schleiermacher 1799 in seinen *Reden über die Religion* getroffen hatte,[20] jedoch verfehlt er auf Grund seiner selbständigen Auseinandersetzung mit Kant die Intention des jungen Schleiermacher, Religion als "das notwendige und unentbehrliche Dritte"[21] gegenüber Spekulation und Praxis zu konstituieren. Herrmann behauptet zwar, daß "sich weder das sittliche Bewußtsein aus der Religion noch diese aus jenem ableiten" lasse,[22] aber das hindert ihn nicht an dem Vorwurf gegenüber Schleiermacher, den Rahmen der notwendigen Korrektur, die in der Betonung der Selbständigkeit und Unabhängigkeit der Religion bestehen mußte, überschritten zu haben. Schleiermacher vernachlässige die Bindung der Religion an die sittliche Person.[23] Nach seiner Definition wäre die Religion "als eine notwendige Funktion des persönlichen Geistes als solchen" nicht zu erweisen. Vielmehr widerspreche Schleiermachers Voraussetzung einer "transzendenten Einheit des Geistigen und Dinglichen" dem sittlichen Bewußtsein; denn in ihr verschwinde die "Differenz des geistigen Lebens von der Naturwelt".[24] Im Zusammenhang mit einer Gottesvorstellung, in der "der Unterschied des Sittlichen und Natürlichen prinzipiell aufgehoben ist", gebe es keine "religiöse Erhebung des Menschen über die Welt". Nach Herrmanns Auffassung kennt jedoch das Christentum "keinen identischen Grund der sittlichen Welt und der Natur,"[25] und insofern sei Schleiermachers Religionsbegriff, der "den Kosmos als die unbedingt übergeordnete Größe geltend" mache, nicht christlich, sondern stehe in "direkter Analogie zum Heidentum". Schleiermacher vertrete eine in die Form der Religion gekleidete Metaphysik. Herrmann wirft ihm vor, sich damit lediglich an den Bedürfnissen der Gebildeten zu orientieren, anstatt die "Erkenntnis des Wesens der wahren Religion . . . in dem fruchtbaren Bathos des Menschenlebens" zu suchen.[26] Demgegenüber ist freilich an Herrmann die kritische Frage zu richten, ob nicht bei seiner Verhältnisbestimmung – entgegen seiner Absicht – die Moral die Basis der Religion und die Religion ein im Dienst der Moral stehender Metaphysikersatz wird.[27]

Einzugehen ist nunmehr auf die von Herrmann praktizierte Dialektik von Freiheit und Abhängigkeit. Sein Denkansatz geht aus von der Sicherung der Freiheit des sittlich bestimmten Individuums, und zu diesem Zweck tritt der Dienst, den die Religion mit dem Ziel einer "religiösen Welterklärung" leistet, hinzu. Herrmann begreift Religion in Anlehnung an Schleiermacher primär als "Bewußtsein der Abhängigkeit", aber es kommt ihm darauf an, daß "dieses Bewußtsein der Abhängigkeit . . . nun aber an derselben Stelle" auftritt, "an welcher das Bewußtsein der Freiheit entspringt" und somit dieses nicht ausschließt. "Indem wir als bedürftige Wesen dem Gott vertrauen, dessen Wille die Macht des Guten über die Welt ist, so ist dieses Verhältnis der Abhängigkeit doch so beschaffen, daß es durch die Forderung sittlicher Selbständigkeit nicht durchbrochen wird . . .". Und deshalb seien für den, dem es um die Aneignung des Sittengesetzes gehe, das Bewußtsein der Abhängigkeit und das der Freiheit keine einander ausschließenden Gegensätze.[28] "Die religiöse Abhängigkeit des Menschen ist der notwendige Hintergrund des Faktums, daß er in seiner natürlichen Bedingtheit die Stimme des Sittengesetzes vernimmt und versteht."[29] Herrmanns auch in späteren Schriften mehrfach wiederholter Vorwurf gegen Schleiermacher besteht nun darin, daß er die Zusammengehörigkeit und Dialektik von Abhängigkeits- und Freiheitsbewußtsein zu ungunsten des letzteren nicht richtig zum Ausdruck bringe.[30]

Ein weiterer Vorwurf Herrmanns gegen Schleiermacher lautet, daß er trotz aller Abgrenzung gegenüber der von Kant vollzogenen rationalistischen Entleerung der Religion selbst dem theologischen Rationalismus nicht entgangen sei.[31] Trotz der Beteuerung, auf jeden Beweis für die Wahrheit und Notwendigkeit des Christentums verzichten zu wollen,[32] bemühe sich Schleiermacher um einen solchen, indem er im Rahmen eines allgemeinen Religionsbegriffes das Christentum als höchste Stufe der Frömmigkeit darzutun suche.[33] Rationalistisch sei es, daß Schleiermacher in der *Glaubenslehre* das Christentum als Modifikation des Abhängigkeitsgefühls entwickele.[34] "Das, was die Tatsache der Religion im Selbstbewußtsein dem Metaphysiker Schleiermacher leistet, bleibt der höchste Gesichtspunkt, unter welchen die einzelnen Aussagen des Glaubens genommen werden."[35] Indem die "Indifferenz der Weltgegensätze" der "eigentliche Gehalt der Gottesidee" Schleiermachers sei, lebe bei ihm der neuplatonische Gottesbegriff ("das farblose Jenseits zu der lebendigen Fülle des Daseins") wieder auf.[36] Glücklicherweise habe Schleiermachers persönliches Glaubenszeugnis den Wirkungen der fragwürdigen Voraussetzungen seiner Theologie entgegengestanden.[37]

Pointiert wird das bisher Ausgeführte von Herrmann resümiert in einer Einschätzung von Schleiermacher, die er fast 20 Jahre später äußerte.[38] Gewürdigt wird Schleiermacher als derjenige, der die Überwindung von Orthodoxie und Rationalismus eingeleitet hat, kritisiert werden die von ihm verursachte "Lähmung der Gedanken des Glaubens durch ihre Zusammenfassung mit den Gedanken der Metaphysik oder des wissenschaftlichen Welterkennens" sowie ihre willkürliche Anpassung an eine Metaphysik, "die kein Jenseits kennt". Hinzukommt der implizit geäußerte Vorwurf, daß Schleiermacher der Religionskritik von Feuerbach Vorschub geleistet habe.

Die Auseinandersetzung mit Schleiermacher in Herrmanns späteren Schriften läßt eine gewisse Akzentverschiebung gegenüber seinen früheren Äußerungen deutlich werden, indem er nunmehr das Zu-sich-selbst-Kommen des Menschen hervorhebt. Das sittliche Gebot, dessen Unabhängigkeit von der Religion Herrmann nach wie vor betont, habe seinen Kern in der Forderung, innerlich selbständig und unabhängig zu sein und nur der eigenen Überzeugung zu folgen.[39]

In der Arbeit "Die Lage und Aufgabe der evangelischen Dogmatik in der Gegenwart" (1907) wird Schleiermacher im Zusammenhang mit

Erörterungen über das Schriftverständnis als derjenige gewürdigt, der gegenüber Orthodoxie und Rationalismus Luthers fundamentale Einsicht erneuert habe, "daß einem Christen nur das helfen kann, was er als zu seiner eigenen Wirklichkeit gehörig erfaßt", und daß dieses Erfassen nur in Bindung an die Bibel und "die aus ihr hervorgehende Verkündigung" erfolgen kann.[40]

Noch massiver zeichnet die Arbeit "Christlich-protestantische Dogmatik" (2. Aufl. 1909) Schleiermacher als Nachfolger Luthers. Bei aller Anerkennung der Größe von Schleiermacher heißt es: "Das Neue, das er gebracht hat, ordnet sich dem Werke Luthers ein. Er ist der Befreier einer zuerst in dem Reformator hervorgebrochenen Tendenz."[41] Herrmann bestreitet auch hier, daß es Schleiermachers Verdienst sei, "die Religion als ein besonderes Gebiet des geistigen Lebens" gegen Erkennen und Wollen abgegrenzt zu haben. Entscheidend für ihn ist aber, daß Schleiermacher in der Nachfolge Luthers die Erlangung wahrhaftigen Lebens als Grund- anliegen der Religion bestimmt habe, daß der Glaube, aus dem nach Schleiermacher die religiösen Gedanken überhaupt erst entstehen, "die zu ihrer Wahrheit kommende Existenz des Menschen selbst" sei.[42] Diese Feststellung ist insofern interessant, als sie Herrmann als das entscheidende Kettenglied eines theologiegeschichlichen Wandels von Schleiermacher zu Bultmann ausweist. Fraglich ist jedoch, ob die Intention von Schleier- machers *Glaubenslehre* getroffen ist, wenn Herrmann erklärend beifügt, daß Offenbarung, die im individuellen Menschen die Religion begründet, sich dadurch ereignet, "daß sich ihm die Tiefen seines eigenen Daseins öffnen".[43] Schleiermachers Satz, man könne auch sagen, "Gott sei uns gegeben im Gefühl auf eine ursprüngliche Weise",[44] meint etwas anderes. Als ein wesentliches Verdienst Schleiermachers betont Herrmann, daß er dadurch, daß er die Bezogenheit der Religion auf das Individuum herausstellte, Orthodoxie und Rationalismus überwand. Damit gehöre er "in die erste Reihe der religiösen Denker aller Zeiten". Jedoch habe Schleiermacher in der *Glaubenslehre* diesen Gedanken nicht entfaltet, vor allem komme hier – Herrmann nimmt damit einen wichtigen Punkt seiner früheren Schleiermacher-Kritik wieder auf – die Relation von Abhängigkeitsgefühl und Freiheitsgefühl zu kurz.[45] Auch trotz der oben angedeuteten Akzentverschiebung in der Theologie des späteren Herrmann bleibt der

Grundvorwurf gegen Schleiermacher der alte, die Bindung der Religion an die sittliche Person vernachlässigt zu haben. Er habe damit einen schädigenden Einfluß auf die Theologie des 19. Jahrhunderts ausgeübt.[46] Im Zusammenhang damit steht nun auch ein prinzipieller methodischer Einwand Herrmanns gegen Schleiermachers *Glaubenslehre*. Von seiner eigenen Orientierung aus, die darauf gerichtet ist, in immer neuen Anläufen und Varianten darzutun, wie im sittlich bestimmten Individuum der christliche Glaube keimt und sich entfaltet, kritisiert Herrmann den statischen Charakter der *Glaubenslehre*. Indem Schleiermacher es unternommen habe, nicht anzunehmende Lehren, sondern den Glauben als lebendige Religion darzustellen, und nur Aussagen zu treffen suche, die eigene Erkenntnisse des Glaubenden sind, habe er damit begonnen, die alte Dogmatik durch eine dem evangelischen Christentum entsprechende Theologie zu ersetzen. Aber es genüge nicht, die *Glaubenslehre* als Ausdruck der christlich frommen Gemütszustände darzustellen und dabei letztlich gegenüber der Religion als einer erfahrungsmäßig vorliegenden Tatsache deskriptiv vorzugehen. Denn damit werde lediglich ein allgemeinmenschlicher Gefühlszustand oder eine bestimmte Denkweise beschrieben, nicht aber der im Individuum als persönliche Überzeugung erwachsende Glaube zum Ausdruck gebracht. Nach Herrmanns Sicht faßt Schleiermacher den christlichen Glaube "nicht als eine fortwährend aus ihrem Grunde sich erhebende Gewißheit, sondern als einen tatsächlich gegebenen Gemütszustand, zu dessen Eigenart bestimmte Vorstellungen gehören".[47]

Mit dieser Kritik an Schleiermacher hängt nun auch eine weitere Abgrenzung zusammen. Fragt man nach Herrmanns christologischen Auffassungen, so ist hervorzuheben, daß er Jesu Leben und Wirken als den "geschichtlichen Grund des Glaubens" darzulegen bestrebt ist.[48] Während Schleiermacher die Urbildlichkeit des Erlösers und die ihn auszeichnende "stetige Kräftigkeit seines Gottesbewußtseins" betont,[49] ist Herrmann unter ethischer Fragestellung an der Person Jesu interessiert. Die "unmittelbar religiöse und persönliche Bedeutung Christi" bestehe darin, daß man "allein durch ihn", den "Grund unserer religiösen Gewißheit", eine seiner selbst gewisse Person sein könne.[50] Jedoch liegt Herrmann nicht daran, Jesus lediglich auf eine historische Persönlichkeit, mit der "die christliche

Weltanschauung erstmals in Erscheinung getreten wäre", zu beschränken, sondern er akzentuiert das Zutrauen zu dieser Person, das der sittlich bestimmte Menschn zu fassen vermag.[51] Durch die Wirkung des Eindrucks von der Person Jesu und seines inneren Lebens, den das Neue Testament vermittele, komme der sittlich bestimmte Mensch zum Glauben, werde christliche Gemeinde konstituiert.[52] Von dieser Position her erhebt Herrmann gegenüber Schleiermacher den Vorwurf, in der *Glaubenslehre* die nach Herrmanns Auffassung veraltete altkirchliche Zweinaturenproblematik wieder aufzugreifen. "Für Christen dagegen, die in der Tatsache, daß sie selbst mit der Person Jesu zusammentreffen, eine Erlösung finden, die sie selbst erleben, muß jenes Problem widerwärtig werden." Mit diesem wie mit anderen Rückfällen in scholastische Theologie verstoße Schleiermacher gegen den von ihm selbst anerkannten Grundsatz, daß im Protestantismus die geltende Lehre immer erneut kritisch zu befragen ist, ob sie dem Glauben gemäß ist.[53]

Läßt sich Schleiermachers Ethik begreifen als eine umfassende Kulturtheorie, die auch die historische Perspektive mitbedenkt, und ist ihr eine prinzipielle Bejahung des Fortschritts und der Entwicklung der menschlichen Kultur zueigen, wobei dem Christentum die treibende und letztlich leitende Rolle zufällt und als Ziel seine zunehmende Dominanz in allen Bereichen der menschlichen Kultur formuliert werden kann,[54] so wird dieser historische Optimismus von Herrmann nicht mehr in gleichem Maße aufrechterhalten. Zwar bietet auch seine Ethik den Entwurf für eine vom Christentum geleitete und korrigierte Entwicklung der Kultur, doch sind daneben gewisse resignative Töne unüberhörbar. Herrmann folgt Schleiermacher, wenn er formuliert, "mit seiner gesamten Existenz ein Zeugnis und ein Werkzeug der erlösenden Wirksamkeit Gottes zu werden", sei "die einzige Aufgabe des Christen in der Welt".[55] Auch in Bezug auf die Zielstellung des Handelns befindet sich Herrmann auf der von Schleiermacher vorgezeichneten Linie, wenn er akzentuiert, durch selbständiges ethisches Tun in der irdischen Arbeit beizutragen zum Reich Gottes, zur jeweiligen Verwirklichung des von Christus gestifteten, in der Geschichte weiterwirkenden Lebenszusammenhanges, zur Schaffung "universelle(r) sittliche(r) Gemeinschaft", die "alle natürlich bedingten sittlichen Gemeinschaften" in sich aufhebt, "ohne sie zu vernichten, aber auch ohne von ihnen abhängig zu sein".[56] Andererseits ist als resignativer Grundzug die Betonung der Gesinnung hervorzuheben. "Das innere Leben des Menschen in einer befestigten Gesinnung ist wichtiger als alle Sachen." "Die Folgen unseres Wirkens in der Welt stehen nicht in unserer Hand."[57] Die Überzeugung, daß sittliches Handeln der Realisierung seiner Zielsetzung dient, resultiert für Herrmann, wie bereits angedeutet, aus der christlichen Religion.[58] Er kann dazu tendieren, resignierend Staat und Gesellschaft ihrer Eigengesetzlichkeit zu überlassen, wobei es dem Christen, sofern er sich aus dem Getriebe der Gesellschaft zurückzieht, zufällt, innerhalb seines durch den Beruf bezeichneten Wirkungskreises soviel wie möglich an den Zuständen zu bessern.[59] Herrmanns Ethik oszilliert zwischen Teilnahme und Abwendung gegenüber Kultur und Gesellschaft, wobei erstere zwar die Oberhand behält, letzterer aber ein unübersehbarer Stellenwert eingeräumt wird. Herrmann möchte das im Urchristentum vorhandene Moment der Weltflucht als ein das Verhalten des Christen zwar nicht regulierendes, aber doch mitbestimmendes festgehalten wissen.[60] Verhindere es doch ein Aufgehen des Menschen in reiner Diesseitigkeit und bahne dadurch einem ethisch bestimmten Verhalten den Weg. Der Christ dürfe nicht vergessen, "daß die Erfolge seiner Arbeit in der Industrie, der Wissenschaft, der Kunst dem Staat den Abgrund öffnen, der seine Zukunft zu begraben droht". Rettung gebe es nur, "wenn ihn die Gewalt der sittlichen Erkenntnis über alle diese Herrlichkeit hinwegträgt".[61]

Auf Grund seiner von Schleiermacher abweichenden Verhältnisbestimmung von Sittengesetz und christlicher Religion, wonach jenes als Prädisposition für diese fungiert, kritisiert Herrmann den nichtimperativischen Charakter von Schleiermachers Ethik, seine Methodik, die christliche Sittenlehre als Handlungsweisen, die aus dem christlich-frommen Selbstbewußtsein hervorgehen, anzulegen.[62] Herrmann macht geltend, "daß eine Ethik, die sich christlich nennen will, ebenso im Namen der Religion wie im Namen der Wissenschaft die Selbständigkeit der sittlichen Erkenntnis fordern und vertreten" müsse.[63] Theologiegeschichtlich sei es zwar ein Fortschritt gewesen, daß Schleiermacher "einer christlichen Ethik die Aufgabe stellte, das Verhalten zu beschreiben, zu dem sich der Mensch gedrängt sieht, wenn christlicher Glaube in ihm entsteht". Doch habe sich Schleiermacher im Zusammenhang mit dem statischen Charakter seiner *Glaubenslehre*, wonach der Glaube als etwas Gegebenes und nicht in seinem Werden erfaßt werde, darauf beschränkt, "zu zeigen, welche Impulse zur Tätigkeit aus dem christlichen Bewußtsein hervorgehen".[64] Werde aber die Bedeutung des Sittengesetzes vernachlässigt, so drohe der Ethik mit ihrer Erweiterung zu einer Theorie der Kultur die Verflachung, eine Gefahr, der Schleiermacher nicht völlig entgangen sei.[65]

In Herrmanns Spätwerk (ab 1911) verändert sich seine Haltung gegenüber Schleiermacher scheinbar. Der junge Schleiermacher der *Reden* von 1799, der die Unabhängigkeit der Religion von Welterkennen und Moral betont, erfährt jetzt verbal erhöhte Wertschätzung, ja wird von Herrmann sogar als Hauptquelle für seine eigene Konzeption in Anspruch zu nehmen gesucht.[66] Verfolgt man indes Herrmanns Ausführungen genau, so ergibt sich keine wesentliche Änderung seiner Haltung gegenüber Schleiermacher, sondern lediglich eine Verschiebung der Akzente. Im Zuge einer Auseinandersetzung mit Bestrebungen, von Schleiermacher eine Gefühls-religion herzuleiten, möchte Herrmann das Erbe Schleiermachers nicht seinen Gegnern überlassen und geht deshalb dazu über, die aus seiner Sicht starken Seiten des jungen Schleiermacher hervorzuheben und demgegenüber seine Kritik vorsichtiger und nachsichtiger vorzutragen. Herrmanns Kritik an Schleiermachers *Reden* beschränkt sich jetzt darauf, "manches anders sagen" zu wollen. Auf Grund seines Gegensatzes zu den Kantianern sei Schleiermacher "allzu ausschließlich darauf gerichtet" gewesen, "die selbständige Würde der Religion zu betonen", und habe deshalb nicht ausreichend "die Zusammengehörigkeit von Religion und Sittlichkeit", d.h. "die Notwendigkeit, daß in der Religion der sittliche Wille mitwirken muß", hervorgehoben, geschweige denn "die Art, wie diese Mitwirkung sich vollzieht, genauer" ermittelt. Herrmann bestreitet, daß sein Unternehmen, diese Lücke zu ergänzen, ein Abweichen von Schleiermacher bedeutet, es handele sich vielmehr um die Fortsetzung seines Werkes.[67]

Läßt sich, wie dargestellt, Herrmanns Bezug zu Schleiermacher als ein spannungsvolles Verhältnis von Anknüpfung und Widerspruch, von Rezeption und Kritik beschreiben, so hat auch Herrmann dies aus seiner

Sicht zum Ausdruck gebracht, wenn er äußerte, daß bei Schleiermacher häufig "die glänzendsten Einsichten mit seinen Irrtümern verbunden sind",[68] oder indem er schrieb: "In dem, was bei Schleiermacher groß und ursprünglich war, weiß ich mich ganz als sein Nachfolger. Allerdings stehe ich an einem bestimmten Punkte auch in Gegensatz zu der Darstellung der *Reden*. Und mein Widerspruch wächst, wenn ich sehe, wie der spätere Schleiermacher immer mehr sich selbst entfremdet wird . . ."[69]

Von Herrmanns Beschäftigung mit Schleiermacher zeigt sich der junge Karl Barth, der 1908 in Marburg sein Schüler wurde, wesentlich bestimmt. Barth, der mit dem selbständigen Studium von Schriften Schleiermachers bereits begonnen hatte, bevor er sich intensiv Herrmanns theologischen Auffassungen anschloß, folgte seinem Lehrer freilich nicht in dem Bestreben, den jungen Schleiermacher der *Reden* gegenüber dem späteren besonders positiv abzuheben.[70] Gemeinsam ist indes beiden das Bestreben, Schleiermacher als Nachfolger Luthers zu sehen, und d.h. im weiteren Sinne, die theologischen Konzeptionen von Schleiermacher und den Reformatoren zu vereinigen. Signifikant hierfür ist Barths während seines Genfer Vikariats 1910 verfaßter Vortrag "Der christliche Glaube und die Geschichte". Mit dem Bestreben, in Herrmanns theologischen Grundansatz, der vom inneren Leben Jesu ausgeht, die von Paulus und den Reformatoren betonte zentrale Stellung von Kreuz und Auferstehung Christi sowie die paulinische wie reformatorische Rechtfertigungslehre zu integrieren, verbindet Barth eine über Herrmann hinausgehende positive Bezugnahme auf Schleiermacher. Einerseits ist seine Absicht unverkennbar, auch diesen für Herrmanns theologische Konzeption zu vereinnahmen, andererseits ist aber auch die Schleiermacher zugedachte Schlüsselfunktion von Bedeutung, wenn Barth ihn als den Mann bezeichnet, "der uns gelehrt hat oder lehren sollte, auf dem Boden des modernen Denkens das wahre Erbe der Reformation zu erwerben, um es zu besitzen".[71] Mit seinen in der 2. Rede über die Religion vorgetragenen Ausführungen über Unterscheidung und Zusammengehörigkeit von Anschauung und Gefühl gebe Schleiermacher dem, was die Reformation unter *fides* und *iustificatio* verstanden habe, in der Terminologie der Romantik Ausdruck.[72] Angesichts dieser hohen Wertschätzung, die Barth Schleiermacher zuteil werden läßt, ist nun aber doch die Frage zu erheben, ob nicht bereits hier Barths spätere Ablehnung ihm gegenüber, die sich mit seiner nach 1914 vollzogenen theologischen Neuorientierung verbindet, ihre Schatten vorauswirft. In seiner Schleiermacher-Vorlesung von 1923/24 geht Barth kritisch auf die damalige Schleiermacher-Rezeption ein, als deren "markanteste(n) Erscheinung" er "W. Herrmann auf dem einen und E. Troeltsch auf dem anderen Flügel" bezeichnet.[73] Gegenüber Troeltsch, der sich als Fortsetzer des Gesamtwerkes von Schleiermacher verstand,[74] macht Barth jedoch schon 1910 massive Vorbehalte geltend. Anstößig ist ihm Troeltschs religionsgeschichtlicher Standpunkt, sein Unternehmen, von der allgemeinen Religionsgeschichte her durch geschichtsphilosophische Überlegungen den christlichen Glauben zu rechtfertigen. Barths diesbezüglicher Vorwurf, der sich später auch gegen Schleiermacher richtet, lautet, daß in diesen Überlegungen nicht von Gottes Offenbarung in Christus die Rede sei, bzw. daß sie sich "außerhalb des eigentümlich theologischen Problemkreises" befänden.[75] Trotz dieser Kritik an Troeltsch blieb Barth bis zum I. Weltkrieg seiner Hochschätzung für Schleiermacher treu. In einer Predigt von 1913 charakterisierte er ihn als einen "der tiefsten christlichen Denker aller Zeiten . . . , voll Ehrfurcht und Verständnis Jesus gegenüber".[76] Der spätere Barth ist zwar nicht zu diesem Urteil über Schleiermacher zurückgekehrt, aber fraglich wurde ihm die Selbstverständlichkeit der Ablehnung, die er in seiner SchleiermacherVorlesung 1923/24 ausgesprochen hatte.[77]

Anmerkungen

1. Friedrich Schleiermacher – Auswahl mit einem Nachwort von Karl Barth, München und Hamburg 1968, S. 149; Wilhelm Herrmann, Die Religion im Verhältnis zum Welterkennen und zur Sittlichkeit, Halle 1879, S. 448-450.
2. Wilhelm Herrmann, Die Gewißheit des Glaubens und die Freiheit der Theologie, 2. Aufl. Freiburg 1889, S. 7-13; Wilhelm Herrmann, Die Metaphysik in der Theologie, abgedruckt in: W. Herrmann, Schriften zur Grundlegung der Theologie, hrsg. von P. Fischer-Appelt, Band I, München 1966, S. 5-16.
3. W. Herrmann, Die Religion . . . , S. 103-109, 441.
4. aaO, S. 35, 39 f., 46-49, 63.
5. aaO, S. 283-289, 293 f., 297-299.

6. W. Herrmann, Gesammelte Aufsätze, hrsg. von F.W. Schmidt, Tübingen 1923, S. 447-451.

7. Herrmann, Die Religion ..., S. 318, 401, 348; ders.Aufsätze ..., S. 445 und 447.

8. Herrmann, Die Religion ..., S. 34-47, 51, 62 f.

9. aaO, S. 75-79, 360.

10. aaO, S. 80, 320.

11. aaO, S. 158 f., 274 f., 185, 166 f., 156 f.; Wilhelm Herrmann, Ethik, 4. Aufl., Tübingen 1909, S. 81 f.

12. Herrmann, Die Religion ..., S. 166 und 298.

13. aaO, S. 205 und 217.

14. W. Herrmann, Kants Bedeutung für das Christentum, in: Schriften zur Grundlegung der Theologie, Band I, S. 119.

15. Herrmann, Die Religion ..., S. 322.

16. aaO, S. 326.

17. aaO, S. 251-254, 256f., 275, 280.

18. aaO, S. 283-289, 293 f., 297-299.

19. aaO, S. 268.

20. F. Schleiermacher, Über die Religion, Reden an die Gebildeten unter ihren Verächtern, hrsg. von Martin Rade, Berlin O.J., S. 27, 30, 36-38, 95.

21. aaO, S. 38.

22. Herrmann, Die Religion ..., S. 223.

23. "Für bloß erkennende Wesen ist die Wahrheit der Religion nicht vorhanden; ihr Geltungsbereich liegt in der praktisch bedingten Gemeinschaft von Personen. Wer diese und sein eigenes von ihr unablösbares Innenleben als eine Wirklichkeit eigener Art nicht anerkennen und beachten mag, darf weder für noch wider die Religion gehört werden." (aaO, S. 253) Schleiermacher sei auf die "abstruse Konsequenz" geraten, "daß das Gefühl selbst in seinem Unterschied von Wissen und Wollen die Wirklichkeit der Religion sei". (Wilhelm Herrmann, Schriften zur Grundlegung der Theologie, hrsg. von P. Fischer-Appelt, Band II, München 1967, S. 55.)

24. Herrmann, Die Religion ..., S. 260-263, vgl. S. 171 und 174.

25. aaO, S. 355.

26. aaO, S. 265-267.

27. vgl. hierzu aaO, S. 265.

28. aaO, S. 257 f., 259 f.

29. aaO, S. 269.

30. aaO, S. 261, 263, 264; vgl. Herrmann, Schriften ..., Band I, S. 314f.; Band II, S. 55-57, 246, 248.

31. Herrmann, Die Religion ..., S. 300.

32. F. Schleiermacher, Der christliche Glaube, hrsg. von M. Redeker, Berlin 1960, Band I, S. 83.

33. Herrmann, Die Religion ..., S. 300 f.

34. aaO, S. 306.

35. aaO, S. 309.

36. aaO, S. 208.

37. aaO, S. 310.

38. Herrmann, Aufsätze, S. 87-89.

39. Herrmann, Schriften ..., Band I, S. 272, 289.

40. Herrmann, Schriften ..., Band II, S. 73.

41. Herrmann, Schriften ..., Band I, S. 310.

42. aaO, S. 311.

43. aaO, S. 312.

44. Schleiermacher, Der christliche Glaube, Band I, S. 30.
45. Herrmann, Schriften . . . , Band I, S. 312-314, 317.
46. aaO, S. 315.
47. aaO, S. 322-326.
48. Herrmann, Die Religion . . . , S. 312.
49. Schleiermacher, Der christliche Glaube, Leitsätze §§ 93 und 94.
50. Herrmann, Die Religion . . . , S. 373.
51. aaO, S. 312.
52. aaO, S. 390, 380, 398 f., 401; Herrmann, Schriften . . . , Band I, S. 171, 173, 176 f., 168, 205, 170, 196; Herrmann, Aufsätze, S. 341.
53. Herrmann, Schriften . . . , Band I, S. 324.
54. vgl. H.-J. Birkner, Schleiermachers christliche Sittenlehre, Berlin 1964, S. 37 f., 88-93.
55. Herrmann, Ethik, 4. Aufl., S. 163 f.
56. Herrmann, Die Religion . . . , S. 401 f., 351, 339; Ethik, 4. Aufl., S. 50 f., 57, 157.
57. Ethik, 4. Aufl., S. 215.
58. aaO, S. 138.
59. W. Herrmann, Ethik, 1. Aufl., Tübingen und Leipzig 1901, S. 181, 166, 172 f., 186 f.
60. Herrmann, Ethik, 4. Aufl., S. 170 f.; Schriften . . . , Band I, S. 236.
61. aaO, S. 235.
62. Birkner, aaO, S. 48 und 68; Herrmann, Ethik, 4. Aufl., S. V (Vorrede zur 1. Aufl.).
63. Herrmann, Ethik, 4. Aufl., S. 2.
64. aaO, S. 6-8.
65. aaO, S. 17 f.
66. Herrmann, Schriften . . . , Band II, S. 266-268; vgl. S. 243 und 285 sowie bereits S. 56.
67. aaO, S. 267 f., 269, 271.
68. aaO, S. 174.
69. aaO, S. 265.
70. Schleiermacher-Auswahl, S. 291.
71. Karl Barth, Der christliche Glaube und die Geschichte, in: Schweizerische Theologische Zeitschrift, Jg. 1912, S. 64.
72. aaO, S. 51 f.
73. Karl Barth, Die Theologie Schleiermachers. Vorlesung Göttingen Wintersemester 1923/24, hrsg. von Dietrich Ritschl, Zürich 1978, S. 2.
74. Ernst Troeltsch, Schleiermacher und die Kirche, in: Schleiermacher, der Philosoph des Glaubens, hrsg. von F. Naumann, Berlin 1910, S. 35.
75. Barth, Der christliche Glaube . . . , aaO, S. 3 f.; vgl. hierzu: Die Theologie Schleiermachers, S. 461 f., wo gegenüber Schleiermacher der Vorwurf der "Entartung der protestantischen Theologie" erhoben bzw. ein grundsätzliches Nein "zu der ganzen Schleiermacherschen Religions- und Christentumslehre" vorgetragen wird.
76. Karl Barth, Predigten 1913, hrsg. von N. Barth und G. Sauter, Zürich 1976, S. 26.
77. vgl. Schleiermacher- Auswahl, S. 307 ff.

SCHLEIERMACHER: STUDIES-AND-TRANSLATIONS

1. Friedrich Schleiermacher, **Brief Outline of Theology as a Field of Study,** Terrence N. Tice (trans.)

2. Friedrich Schleiermacher, **On the Academy,** Terrence N. Tice and Edwina Lawler (trans.)

3. Friedrich Schleiermacher, **Sermons on The Christian Household,** Dietrich Seidel and Terrence N. Tice (trans.)

4. Friedrich Schleiermacher, **On Music,** Albert L. Blackwell (trans. and introduction)

5. Herbert W. Richardson (ed.), **Friedrich Schleiermacher and the Founding of the University Of Berlin: The Study of Religion as a Scientific Discipline**

6. Ruth Drucilla Richardson (ed.), **Schleiermacher in Context: Papers from the 1988 International Symposium on Schleiermacher at Herrnhut, the German Democratic Republic**

7. Ruth Drucilla Richardson, **The Role of Women in the Life and Thought of the Early Schleiermacher (1768-1806): An Historical Overview**

8. Friedrich Schleiermacher, **Occasional Thoughts on Universities in the German Sense, With an Appendix Regarding a University Soon to Be Established (1808),** Terrence N. Tice and Edwina Lawler (trans.)

9. Friedrich Schleiermacher, **On Freedom,** Albert L. Blackwell (trans., annotation and introduction)

10. Friedrich Schleiermacher, **On the Highest Good,** H. Victor Froese (trans., annotation and postscript)

11. Sergio Sorrentino (ed.), **Schleiermacher's Philosophy and the Philosophical Tradition**

12. Iain G. Nicol, **Schleiermacher and Feminism: Sources, Evaluations, and Responses**

13. Friedrich Schleiermacher, **Luke: A Critical Study,** Connop Thirlwall (trans., with introduction); Terrence N. Tice (ed.)

DATE DUE

			Printed in USA